ORGANIZATION ANALYSIS

DRYDEN SERIES IN MANAGEMENT

WILLIAM F. GLUECK
CONSULTING EDITOR

ORGANIZATION ANALYSIS
THEORY AND APPLICATIONS

ELMER H. BURACK

Professor of Management

Harold Leonard Stuart School
of Management and Finance

Illinois Institute of Technology

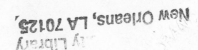

THE DRYDEN PRESS
HINSDALE, ILLINOIS

Acknowledgments

1. Exhibit 3–5   Joan Woodward, *Problems of Progress in Industry No. 3—Management and Technology.* Used with permission of the Controller of Her Britannic Majesty's Stationery Office.
2. Exhibit 3–6   Elmer H. Burack, "Industrial Management in Advanced Production Systems: Some Theoretical Concepts and Preliminary Findings," *Administrative Science Quarterly,* Volume 12, #3 (December 1967) pp. 479–500.
3. Exhibit 3–8   *Automation and Management,* James R. Bright (Boston, Mass.: Division of Research, Harvard Graduate School of Business Administration, 1958).
4. Exhibit 4–12   Carzo and Yanouzas' adaptation from Donald J. Clough, *Concepts in Management Science,* © 1963. Reprinted by permission of Prentice-Hall, Inc., Englewood Cliffs, New Jersey.
5. Exhibit 4–13   Carzo and Yanouzas' adaptation from Donald J. Clough, *Concepts in Management Science,* © 1963. Reprinted by permission of Prentice-Hall, Inc., Englewood Cliffs, New Jersey.
6. Exhibit 4–14   Carzo and Yanouzas' adaptation from Donald J. Clough, *Concepts in Management Science,* © 1963. Reprinted by permission of Prentice-Hall, Inc., Englewood Cliffs, New Jersey.
7. Exhibit 4–15   Carzo and Yanouzas' adaptation from Donald J. Clough, *Concepts in Management Science,* © 1963. Reprinted by permission of Prentice-Hall, Inc., Englewood Cliffs, New Jersey.
8. Exhibit 6–4   Based on concepts proposed by Arlyn Melcher, working papers, Kent State University.
9. Exhibit 8–4   James V. Clark, "Motivation in Work Groups: A Tentative View." Reproduced by permission of the Society for Applied Anthropology from *Human Organization,* Volume 19, #4 (Winter 1960–1961).
10. Exhibit 10–3   This Table summarizes some of the key points from the analyses of George Homans, *The Human Group,* copyright, 1950, by Harcourt Brave Jovanovich, Inc. and abstracted pp. 13–18, with their permission.
11. Exhibit 10–4   This Table summarizes some of the key points from the analyses of George Homans, *The Human Group,* copyright, 1950, by Harcourt Brace Jovanovich, Inc. and abstracted pp. 13–18, with their permission.
12. Chapter 7, footnote 14   J. A. Vaughan and A. M. Perat, "Managerial Reactions to Computers," April 1967; "How Management Views Computer Operations," June 1967; and "Management Views on The Importance of Computers to Staff Promotions," July 1967; *Banking,* The Journal of the American Bankers Association.

This one is for Ruth, Chuck,
Bob, and Al.

PREFACE

The really important challenges to the new hiree or seasoned practitioner are to view and structure their problems, situations, or environments in a creative, insightful way.

Several years ago, toward the end of the semester, one of my students (let his name be Bob Franks) stopped by the office to review his job plans. As so often happens, we got on the subject of classes and teaching. One of his major concerns—one echoed by many other students—was a lack of confidence in his ability to usefully relate his many courses in organization, personnel, management principles, and behavioral sciences to the "world of work." His concern was not unfounded, for many of my acquaintances and associates in business and government continue to decry the inability of the new hiree or seasoned manager to confront the myriad of organizational problems in a creative, viable way.

The student of organizations, as well as the organization member, must be able to connect "learning to living." And as Bob the student, and many of his contemporaries have noted, "The theories are great, but what can we do with them?" Bob's counterpart in the organization will often ask me: "What have you academic guys been cooking up that might be useful to me in running my department or organization or coping with such-and-such kinds of problems?" Now each in his own way was "giving me the needle," but I think the need is real.

There needs to be a crossroad of theory, research, and application. For a considerable time, I have felt that the student of organization, as well as the enlightened practitioner, was in need of course development and supportive material to lessen the gap between academic exposition and the complexity of the challenges and problems embedded in organization life. Consequently, the general approach assumed in this book is that of putting theory and findings to work within real situations. The book is laced with end-of-chapter application questions and situations, and Part III is given over almost entirely to applied issues.

As a practical matter, the proliferation of theories and research findings makes it difficult (if not impossible) for any but advanced students to assimilate all this information. In addition, singular theories cannot encompass the widely varying specifics and great diversity of particular organizational situations. Thus, while appropriate areas of theoretical and research studies are referenced, a flexible posture in using this literature and focusing it to meet particular situations is indicated. No attempt is made to exhaust the literature, but important, representative studies are employed in the discussions and an up-to-date bibliography can be utilized for more comprehensive study.

I've had the good fortune to work with undergraduate and graduate students at four quite different universities (Illinois Institute of Technology, Northwestern University, San Diego State University, and the University of Illinois at Chicago Circle) in developing these approaches. The interplay of these academic experiences with research and consulting assignments led to some new constructs and to modifications of others.

To meet the needs of the student and interested practitioner, the objectives of this book are to

1. Develop the ability to model complex organizational situations, using a selected group of conceptual tools that facilitate organizational analysis and presenting special material on model development and systems diagramming.

2. Integrate important areas of the research findings, using model and systems approaches. These syntheses are also meant to serve as a vehicle for building competency in modeling.

3. Promote flexibility in problem definition and solution.

4. Provide a contemporary but selective body of research findings.

The concerns in this book involve people (either individually or collectively), work, formal organization, and the environments where these are to be found. Often, the thrust of these concerns will deal with performance in both qualitative and quantitative terms, but the individual is central and foremost in each approach. Thus a question concerning the generation of new ideas or increasing the level of production performance, aside from technological improvements, very quickly turns to behavioral matters, involving such things as motivation (inclination and ability to move in a given direction), leadership (actions of individual A influencing B, whether a person or a group, in a particular direction), and communication (information flow between people/points).

Readership and Level

In general, readers of this book should have had some background in the behavioral sciences, a course or two in psychology or sociology, and a course such as introduction to business/management, personnel, or organization theory. Organization theory is viewed as dealing with tentative explanations of human behavior in formal organizations, based on research from the social-physical sciences or, occasionally, wisdom based on individual insight and experience. For graduate students, where some time has elapsed since their undergraduate preparation, a review of the most recent introductory literature of the field has proved helpful. The same would apply to the practitioner who has been out of school for some years.

School Differences

Positioning of this material in terms of academic level may vary because of the great differences and continuing changes in various school programs. Some schools currently place great stress on developing an extensive behavioral science, systems, and general management background in the early years of undergraduate preparation. Also, they may have students with strong college preparatory backgrounds. For these situations, the use of this material at the junior level would likely be congenial with program development. In other undergraduate situations, where programming is given over to "bringing students up" and then strengthening areas in the behavioral and management sciences, the use of this book in the senior year would be a realistic consideration.

The material may also be quite suitable for graduate programs. Where graduate work builds on general educational preparation at the baccalaureate level, the use of this book as a first- or second-level course in organization theory/behavior may present interesting possibilities for opening up an exciting area of analysis in complex organizational problems, issues, and challenges.

Student Learning Experiences—Frustration and Excitement

My experiences with teaching this material may prove of assistance to students seeking to employ the proposed approaches to organization analysis. Frequently the first few weeks of development lead to highly mixed reactions ranging from confidence to frustration. Some responses were "I've seen this before." "Skipping the exhibits shortens the reading time," or "What's this leading up to?" Since the discussions and analyses often build on previously described material and increasingly deal with the vast and complex contingencies affecting organizational actions, conceptual complexities tend to grow. Some may experience a sense of frustration in seeking to deal simultaneously with multiple factors. For those who experience difficulty in understanding the initial chapters, feelings of uncertainty are frequently replaced by growing confidence after several more weeks, as expertise in the use of the various tools, perspectives, and concepts grows.

Many students find that the application examples assist in putting chapter ideas to work and thereby extend their skills in the use of these ideas. Discussion and application situations are drawn from a "real world" context—and it is difficult to match the richness, challenge, and fascination of matters lifted from our organizations and institutions.

Framework for Organization Analysis

Individual behavior and organizational performance depends on human, work task/technological, *and* environmental factors. Thus organizational analysis commonly deals with situations containing these elements under a particular set of conditions. Because of the infinite combinations of variables and associative conditions, generalization is deemphasized in favor of constructing models to fit specific circumstances.

In Part I we take environmental, structural, and systems factors as the causal variables and suggest their impact on organizations, temporarily setting aside the behavioral influences. In Part II, behavioral variables, such as motivation and leadership, are analyzed as major determinants of organizational activity and performance—yet an attempt is made to reckon with the variables of Part I. Finally, in Part III, environmental and individual factors are jointly brought to bear on important applications and problems in manpower planning and managing organizational change.

The characteristic mode of development in each chapter is to

1. Establish the specific subject matter for analyzing organizations.

2. Develop subject matter based largely on the use of propositional or schematic models and citing relevant research.

3. Seek to impart specific areas of structured knowledge to the reader while building his competence to model organizational situations.

Key Perspectives and Tools

A comparatively small set of tools and perspectives can prove helpful in organizational analyses. They straddle various research, teaching, and application approaches, and are as follows:

a. *Systems perspective.* Organizational phenomena such as leadership, control, or work are viewed as interrelated internal (*contextual*) elements. The systems perspective employed here visualizes the connection and impact of events in the external environment on members of the organization, including officials and managers, emphasizing flows, connections, and sequence.

b. *Contingency.* The various approaches described in the book build largely around a technique of analysis increasingly described as "contingency." The central aim is to stipulate the set of critical situational or personal variables under which particular theory or research appear related to the problem or situation being considered.

For example, the desired style of leadership for good performance and satisfaction of work group members is more readily asserted if the contingencies of work, leader-member relationships, and leader's influence in the organization are stipulated. The structure of authority, span of command (supervisory-subordinate ratio), and use of support personnel for high performance can be more readily stated for production organizations if we can identify the contingencies regarding the level of technological achievement and aspects of change. The span of command of top managers is more readily understood in the light of the contingencies concerning the adequacy of subordinate training, the number of subordinates, and the relative stability or turbulence of the organization's environment.

c. *Modeling.* Two types of models have been found highly useful for analysis, and numerous examples of them are found throughout the book—schematic models that depict key variables and suggest important relationships and/or system flow, and propositional models that are logical statements of the "If . . . , then . . ." form. These models have proved useful in crystallizing ideas, creating testable assertions, converting "facts" into broader ideas, and providing an initial step in formulating comprehensive explanations for complex problems or situations.

Both schematic and propositional models are useful to the extent that they provide insight into complex relationships through crystallizing relationships, relevant variables, and possible cause-result connections. Either approach requires careful specification of the assumptions under which the schematic or propositional model is thought to hold.

d. *Micro-macro perspectives.* Three basic viewpoints represent the elementary forms for virtually all of the models and approaches discussed in the book. One emerges from the broad outlook of economists, which visualizes the interactions (and exchanges) of the firm and its external environment. For example, competition, legislation, and the availability of material resources, and how these shape the general features of the organization, would emerge from this vantage point.

The second is the sociological, which views more selective features of the external environment (social mores, values, culture) and the manner in which these shape the roles (outlook and performance) of organization members, affect the relationship of the individual to work group members, and so forth.

The third perspective is the psychological, centered on the individual, his outlooks (perception), the factors shaping these, and his response to particular actions.

Where appropriate, these perspectives may be used singly; however, complex problems or situations may necessitate a "holistic" approach, which may require their simultaneous usage.

e. *Substantive ideas and findings.* These are drawn selectively from the journal literature of the behavioral and managerial sciences, plus applied management publications such as *California Management Review, Harvard Business Review,* Indiana's *Business Horizons,* and the *M.S.U. Business Topics.*

To briefly sum up, I feel that the key challenge to the school of management and to the student of management is to bridge theory and practice. The fast-growing complexity of organizations and the organizational field involving theory and behavior demands a highly flexible approach to accommodate change and a diversity of situations. Flexibility in analysis or problem solving can be gained from a modest number of concepts, perspectives, and learned abilities. A useful framework for behavioral analysis can be gained from the systems perspective; the contingency concept; ability to model; multiple perspectives for analysis, including those of the economist, sociologist, and psychologist; and a body of selected findings from these areas.

This book has benefited substantially from a number of useful suggestions made at various points in its development. Professors J. G. Hunt (Southern Illinois University), James P. McNaul and Robert C. Miljus (Ohio State University), Robert Roe (University of Wyoming), John Slocum (Pennsylvania State University), Edward T. P. Watson (Northwestern University), and Richard J. Whiting (California State University) were most helpful in raising questions and providing constructive ideas in this undertaking. A special note of thanks is extended to the advisory editor for this series, Professor William Glueck of the University of Missouri (Columbia), for his many helpful ideas.
Yet, despite these acknowledged contributions, the responsibility for the final product must ultimately rest with the author. I have sought to incorporate various suggestions in shaping the viewpoints and ideas expressed here. However, one's own human frailties in understanding, interpretation, and expression can result in a product somewhat afield from one's intent. Nevertheless, I assume responsibility for the final effort.

CONTENTS

ORGANIZATION ANALYSIS

Learning Objectives

Develop Systems Perspective
   Role of Environment
   Concept of Open Systems
   Concept of a Socio-Technical System
   Understand Mutual Interaction: Environment/System
   Understand Organization as an Open Social System
   Notion of System Objectives
Basics of Model Development
   Indicators of Performance
   Technology Variables
   Behavioral Variables
Theory and Research in Analysis
   Formulating Propositions
   Use of Research-Theory in Modeling
Overview of Book

Chapter **1**

INTRODUCTION

APPROACH

This chapter includes an overview of the book, substantive information for analysis and a case example, and general guidelines in the use of theory and research. Important relationships may be seen when the three areas of analysis (aside from the overview) are viewed jointly. Theory and research provide an indispensable underpinning to systems ideas and modeling, suggesting connections between variables and a basis for speculation concerning problems or existing organizational arrangements. Also, systems are frequently the subject of modeling efforts. In addition, modeling approaches may spark research, or even theory building. These discussions are intended to give the reader a familiarity with fundamentals of systems and modeling as well as with the use of theory-research, which will enable him—or her—to more readily get to the core of the book's discussions.

This book on organization analysis proposes a set of approaches deemed necessary for application. Structure, technology, systems, *and* behavioral factors all receive attention in order to develop one's abilities in application to organizational situations. In the past, behavioral or other singular approaches have been pursued. Yet, over time, organizations continue to grow in complexity in response to accelerating change, the growing influence of environmental forces, and the shifting roles of people and institutions. No single approach can hope to deal effectively with this complexity. Structure is the framework within and about which people interact and support the central work mission of the organization. Technology is a vehicle for the conduct of work, as in production or the processing of information. Structure and technology establish work activities and needed accomplishments to maintain continuity and achieve institutional goals.

A systems perspective is also critical in this approach. It provides an explanation for existing relationships or an approach for reforming them so as to improve performance or secure goals. It sensitizes one to the interplay and potential outgrowth of the structure, technology, and people mix.

3

Modeling is stressed throughout the book as a key tool for analysis, and models assist in the identification of important variables in particular situations. Second, they assist in "trying out" relationships among the variables, so as to find one that seems to best fit the circumstances or serves to suggest possible interactions based on theory or research. In the hands of the analyst, models can serve to lessen risks in problem solutions by permitting the prior working out of "traps," inconsistencies, or improved alternatives.

Thus the dynamics and complexity of emergent organizations signal a multiprong approach in order to dissect problems or prescribe remedial strategies. One must move beyond the clearly apparent similarities of organizations to the dissimilarities, which are of equal or greater importance.

With the systems perspective, the book takes into account the basic economic resources of a firm's operations (man, machine, capital, and entrepreneurship) and views them in an environmental and behavioral context.

Structure constitutes the framework within which the relationships among these resources are explored. Structure also provides a viewpoint for examining the interface of company resources with forces in the environment outside the firm.

Technological systems for production and for the transmission of information connect structural functions with flows or movements for work accomplishment, the transmission of data to meet accounting-financial needs, and intelligence for planning and control.

Behavioral systems, guided by the entrepreneur, are intertwined with structure and technological systems, and give rise to motivation, social work groups, and leadership.

Finally, decision systems tie together the human and impersonal elements of the organization for the accomplishment of its goals.

A composite representation of the organizational components and processes described above is shown in Exhibit 1–1. Its outermost frame represents the external environment, within which the firm or institution carries out goal-directed activity. Various environmental forces shape the interactions of the firm with unions, labor markets, and competition, thereby setting in motion forces that affect the firm's internal technological and behavioral structures and activities.

CONCEPTUAL APPROACHES TO MANAGEMENT: MODELING

The problem solving, strategies, and innovative approaches required of managers demand a disciplined approach to the development, structuring, and application of knowledge.[1] Thus inductive reasoning, built on a taxonomic approach in differentiating, classifying, and organizing concepts and information, is indicated as one major area of future development for managers.

EXHIBIT 1–1. Conceptual Overview

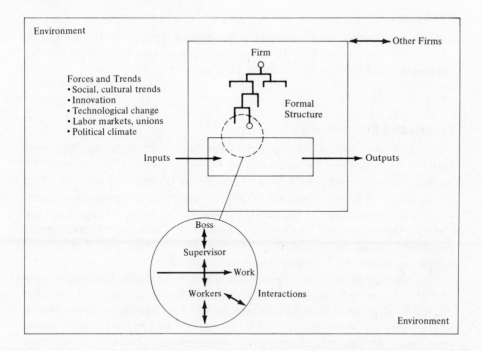

The ability to conceptualize the issues that confront management is one important means of developing general management skill. The formulation and interpretation of schematic models (diagrams), which depict the principal variables and relationships within a situation, and the order of decision-outputs-ideas that arises from them provide useful insights into complex administrative and operating systems. Such models, however, require:

1. A clear statement of the problem or activity to be analyzed

2. Identification of the goals toward which the activity is directed

3. Isolation of key components and subsystems that are pertinent to the analysis, but that may not include all variables

4. Presentation of logical relationships

5. Organizing all factors into an interrelated whole

Conceptual models can be used to organize a variety of complex situations, problems, and goals into an intelligible whole. Because they abstract the essence of a complex situation, models can be useful in a myriad of managerial functions and processes.

SYSTEMS

These approaches are central to the discussions throughout the book. This section will serve to identify the important assumptions underlying systems approaches and the key perspectives that are employed.

System and Environment

Although the analyses developed in the book will typically distinguish between a system and its environment, the term "system" can be used for anything one wishes to study as an entity.[2] The diversity of systems in our discussions will range from individuals or groups as components of social systems or *sub*systems, to technological (work) systems, to organizational systems. "Environment" lies outside the system. Thus, for a worker group positioned within an organization, we may refer to this aspect of a social system as within the "organizational environment."

Also, we may describe an organizational system as within the broader context of the external (outside) environment. When organizational activities are the focal point, different environments can be identified—those external to (outside) the organization and those internal to (inside) organizational boundaries. At times the designation "organizational boundary" is arbitrary, but for our purposes, and unless otherwise stated, it will encompass all the systems, structures, and personnel directly controlled and typically compensated by the institution. Thus physically decentralized facilities, and even sales representatives deriving their primary compensation from the organization, would be included within "organizational boundaries."

Thus three levels of analysis emerge that will be of interest in subsequent discussions:[3] (a) environment and system, (b) system and system, and (c) subsystem and subsystem or intrasystem.[4]

Open Systems

The concept of a "closed" system (one with hypothetically impermeable boundaries) has considerable theoretical and scientific significance, but the systems of most interest in this book, involving living entities, people, and organizations, are more aptly described in terms of *open system* concepts.[5] "Open systems," as employed here, are those in which continuing exchanges or interactions occur between the organizational system and (a) the environment or (b) other systems (see Exhibit 1–2).

In this regard, a view of particular interest is that in which a continuing flow of resources and inputs from the environment (e.g., materials, supplies, information, human resources, patients) enters the system. These are pro-

EXHIBIT 1–2. Environmental and Organizational Systems Interactions

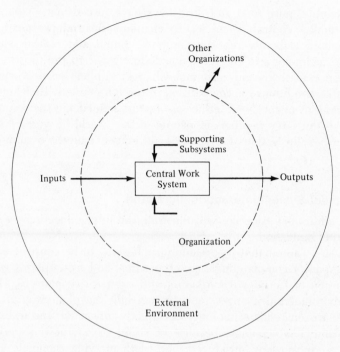

cessed or transformed to output products (cars, industrial goods) or services (a "well patient"). The outputs possess economic utility—they are valuable or useful. They become the basis for economic exchanges (dollars received for product or service provided) that support the procurement or attraction of additional inputs. The input-transformation-output cycle forms the basis for the notion of a "socio-technical" system,[6] which receives considerable attention in Chapters 3 and 4 and constitutes a basic reference concept throughout the book.

Role of Environment

The concept of an open system (as expressed here) visualizes various types of interactions, exchanges, and influence patterns. The interaction notion of environment-system extends the view of the dynamic interdependencies linking the two. The environment itself contains vital forces that influence and shape organizational system activities and performances. F. E. Emery and E. L. Trist describe this situation as the "causal texture" of organizational environments.[7] Economic, social, legislative, political, and ideological trends, along with scientific innovation and technological change, are among the environmental forces affecting the organization and its systems.

For example, pure food and drug laws have forced many companies to acquire quality control personnel, to change industrial processes, and to institute more elaborate reporting systems. Rapid and radical changes in electronic technology in the television industry led to the drastic revision of production methods and personnel. Changes in plant location contributed to favorable conditions for competition in foreign markets. Redefinition and shifting notions of the "work ethic" are factors influencing the response and productivity of large numbers of people in the "world of work," [8] and provide a further illustration of environmental influence on the organization.

Environment-System Interaction Illustrated

A few additional examples will illustrate the interconnections of environment and organization.

(a) A new, automated food canning plant was to be constructed, based on a company's commanding market position and assumptions regarding the extension of traditional marketing and competitive patterns. However, major environmental changes took place while the plant was under construction: frozen food technology was greatly advanced; the utilization of cans became less economic because of rising prices; new, superior competitive products were introduced; and, with growing economic affluence, market demand evidenced further shifts toward frozen products.

The company's failure to recognize the changing character of the environment resulted in a severe financial strain. The completion of a multimillion dollar plant, virtually outmoded from the start, severely penalized this company's designs for the future and required major adjustments in its other operations.[9]

(b) For many years a savings and loan association in a large metropolitan center maintained a stable organization and relationship with its clientele. However, with urban decay and the movement of affluent economic classes to the suburbs, the association's neighborhood and surrounding area changed rapidly. Institutional survival in this changing environment dictated considerable flexibility. The change in the character of commerce and clientele to lower economic classes, racial minorities, and smaller businesses indicated radical redevelopment of the association's mode of doing business.

A few examples of these were: (1) New social mannerisms had to be understood in order to communicate effectively, to seek out opportunities and define client needs. (2) New procedures and bases for financial transactions had to be developed because of changing loan needs, available cash, collateral, and risk assessment. (3) The character of the work force and key managerial positions shifted as turnover increased and new personnel were integrated into the organization.

MUTUAL INTERACTION

To round out this discussion of interaction and influence, we wish to take note of (a) the organization's (system's) potential to influence the environment or other organizational systems and (b) intra-system interactions. In economic competition one organization's tactics and strategies have varying degrees of influence on the actions and responses of other organizational systems; the economist uses theories of pure competition, oligopoly, and monopoly to more precisely describe these interorganizational interactions. Aside from economic considerations, influence may be viewed along other lines. Some organizations may influence developments in the environment through lobbying (e.g., getting favorable legislation passed); coopting officials, individuals, or enterprises to further support their own purposes; and influencing community, professional, or governmental bodies through the use of economic power.

Thus the "open system approach" (described here) seeks to convey a dynamic picture of environment-system or system-system interactions. Subsequent discussions will frequently refer to the environment-system interaction with particular emphasis on the environment's influence on the organizational system.

Subsystems—An Initial View

The other point to be clarified concerns intra-system effects. System hierarchies exist, so that a given organizational arrangement is simply one of a number competing, for example, in a particular industry. A particular organizational system, in turn, is comprised of various component subsystems. A work system for accomplishing the main mission of the organization is the key system about which various supportive subsystems (materials, supplies, personnel) are erected.[10] The dominant input-conversion-output system for a university, for example, involves the transformation from student to graduate (or flunk-out or drop-out), utilizing educational technology, facilities, and teachers.[11]

The managerial subsystem, which overlays the principal work system and various supportive systems, accomplishes coordination and control. Forces influencing the central organization system for mission accomplishment additionally work their way into established systems, setting further waves of change in motion.

The managerial subsystem, consisting of various managers and supervisors, acts to coordinate, control, and service the primary organizational task system. It has its own technology for problem analysis and decision making, built on experience, structured knowledge, and analytical techniques. The managerial subsystem guides overall system operations, including the service and support subsystems.[12] The care with which the various subsystems are integrated (e.g., collaboration and understudy) and provide support of the central work system directly affects organizational (system) output and performance.[13]

ENVIRONMENTAL DYNAMICS AND SYSTEMS

As already suggested, the environment encompasses diverse forces and trends which influence organization system character and functioning. The character of the environment shapes the degree of pressure for change, the immediacy for change, and uncertainties confronting the organizational system.[14] Environments that are relatively "placid" are more predictable and permit varying organizational strategies. For example, manufacturers of glass containers incurred few changes until the competition from plastic items. In contrast, "turbulent" environments are dynamic and are characterized by complex and rapidly changing conditions which impinge upon organizational systems. With turbulent conditions, uncertainty increases, control lessens, and prediction becomes more difficult.[15] Under turbulent conditions, differing patterns of system behavior and modified organization structures (relative to those found under placid conditions) are required or indicated.

Systems and structures are "tailored" to the contingencies of particular situations.[16] For example, a series of significant changes in electronic circuitry led to a prolonged period of upset and shake-out in the production and marketing of TVs and radios. The matter of situational contingencies is developed at various points in the book, including Chapters 3, 4, 9, 12, 13, and 14. The next discussion delves into the workings of organizational systems and provides some of the detail only briefly referenced in preceding discussions.

SYSTEM WORKINGS

Objectives

Work systems seek specific accomplishments. The manufacturing system seeks to provide a product reflecting various *quality* elements, with a given output potential (*quantity*) per unit of time. Thus the level of system accomplishment is tied to system elements (materials, machines, and labor resources) and their manner of work accomplishment (efficiency, motivation) relative to the raw materials committed to the system.

Subsystems

Systems are dynamic in concept, emphasizing flows (often related) and relationships directed toward achieving specific objectives. "Flow" implies movement and "relationship" involves ordering or sequence, and thus direction, as well as specification of particular elements.

A system, in one of its simplest forms, may describe a manufacturing activity having particular resource inputs and a production capability that leads to marketable outputs (see Exhibit 1–3A). Here three systems com-

EXHIBIT 1–3A

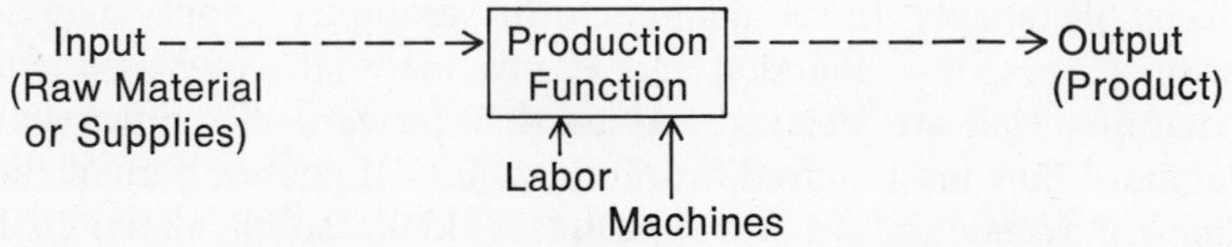

Input — — — — — — —→ Production — — — — — — —→ Output
(Raw Material   Function   (Product)
or Supplies)
                                   ↑   ↑
                              Labor |
                                    Machines

ponents are identified (input, production function, and output), with the flow of activity suggested by the arrows. At this level of development, the interpretation of "flow" would suggest that the movement (or commitment) of various materials to the production function, which contains machines and labor resources, permits the processing of the input materials into a modified or wholly new form. For example, crude oil (input) may be transformed by refinery equipment and personnel into a wide variety of oils, chemicals, and gasolines (outputs).

If we wish to move beyond this simple production analogy, we could visualize system flow in a service context, such as a hospital (Exhibit 1–3B),

EXHIBIT 1–3B

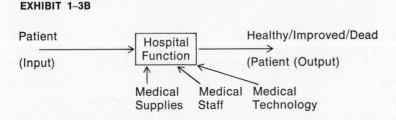

where the flow emphasis is based upon the entry of the patient (input), his interaction with the hospital service capability (consisting of medical people, supplies, and technology), and the outcome of the process: the "healthy" patient (output).

Relationships

Several important relationships were defined in the simple examples above. For the manufacturing example, *sequence* or *direction of movement* designates inputs of raw materials and supplies, *to* the production function, *to* achievement of the product. "Relationship" also designates the three main system components as *input, production function,* and *output,* with labor and machines constituting the main elements of the production function.

As already noted, systems are comprised of combinations of subunits (subsystems) that bear a logical relationship to successively larger system arrangements. Thus systems are hierarchical in construction, or subdivided (specialized) into subsystems that are committed to particular processes and accomplishments. In the manufacturing example, "input" may actually comprise a "receiving" function and a "raw material warehouse" function, such that materials are received and are then forwarded to a warehouse for holding until they are required for production. (Of course, both of the input functions of receiving and warehousing could be subdivided into further subsystem functions.)

The hierarchical arrangement of subsystems is suggested in Exhibit 1–3C.

EXHIBIT 1–3C

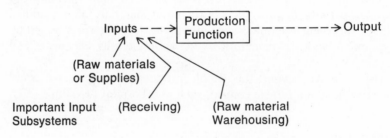

We could, of course, carry out subsystem development for the other two system components (production function and output), as well as for the hospital service example. In the hospital, the subsystems of the input (patients) would consist of office procedures, securing patient information, room assignment, etc. In an insurance company, the subsystems of the input (information concerning policyholders) might consist of analyses by actuaries, medical examinations, office procedures, and the like.

For some purposes, such as transportation studies or market analysis, the internal system could be moved backward to suppliers or extended forward to identify key functions in product distribution and marketing (see Exhibit 1–3D).

Organizations as Open Social Systems

The social (sub)system functions to provide "the psychological cement that holds the organizational structure together."[17] In contrast to the main

EXHIBIT 1–3D

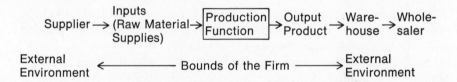

work system focus on resource transformation, the social (sub)system focuses on people-related processes to help assure continuity in the social structure and the roles people carry out. People must be attracted to the organization, people must be retained in it, and people must function in certain roles which are critical to organizational purposes and goal accomplishments. This system involves individual rewards and sanctions, but also the social values and norms (standards, expectancies) of behavior that support the role activities for organizational continuity. This is established through task interdependencies, and sustained through their rewards and social-psychological returns. The social subsystem serves to integrate the individual into the broader organizational structures and systems; organization structure seeks to rationalize the collective effort of the social system members for reliability and efficiency.

The social subsystem is tied to the organization through various other subsystems. It is embedded within the productive subsystem. And it intersects with the managerial subsystem, which helps to integrate subsystem functioning by providing coordination, control, and a decision-making capability.[18]

The analyses in Part II will bring out some of the critical dimensions of these behavioral (sub)systems. While structure and technology assist in providing form and direction to organizational actions, there are real limits to the degree they alone can assure performance through impersonal mechanisms, coercion, or threat. These limitations have been underscored by major societal changes involving the pace of change, economic growth, and shifts in individual need and bases for motivation. For example, the limitations of traditional authority seem likely to become more pronounced, and this in turn will place additional emphasis on the efficient functioning of the social (sub)system to meet organizational and personal need.

MODEL DEVELOPMENT: A CASE EXAMPLE

Modeling, the ability to represent complex situations or to develop insightful characterization of relationships, is one of the most important tools available to the researcher and practitioner. Of equal importance is the proposition. This section develops and elaborates a modeling approach to personnel-manpower in which behavioral science approaches may be usefully applied.

The personnel manager of Supreme Foods Company, Fred Jenks, has been asked to help with a performance problem at one of Supreme's packing plants. Before going out to the plant, Fred decided to do some "homework" so that he could be more responsive at the meeting with the plant manager. Although the problem at the plant was described initially over the phone as a performance problem, Jenks realized that performance might readily assume a number of different forms (Exhibit 1–4A).

EXHIBIT 1–4A

Cost Production
Quality } Specific Production Indicators

Turnover
Absenteeism } Production-Manpower Indicators

Also, based on his previous experiences and education, he recognized the relationship of performance with such behavioral matters as morale and motivation. Thus the initial model he established suggested Exhibit 1–4B:

EXHIBIT 1–4B

Morale
Motivation ———> Performance

He recalled from a special course he had taken in organizational analysis that a common representation for describing behavioral models is patterned along the lines of the psychologist's model (Exhibit 1–4C):

EXHIBIT 1–4C

S (Stimulus) ———> Individual ———> R (Response)

Combining the S–R model with some of the specifics of the problem led to Exhibit 1–4D:

EXHIBIT 1–4D

Plant Activity ———> Plant ———> Performance
(or Program)   Worker

Adding Exhibit 4B to Exhibit 4D led to Exhibit 1–4E:

EXHIBIT 1–4E

Plant ——→ Plant ——→ Morale ——→ Performance
Activity   Worker   Motivation

Jenks's preliminary work was still not done, for he realized that various packing-plant equipment and procedures played an important part in the output of this plant, although it was not nearly as automated as some industrial plants (Exhibit 1–4F).

EXHIBIT 1–4F

Plant Technology
Work Procedures ————→ Performance
Work Design

As Jenks thought about his model, he recognized that technology, work design, and the like are bifunctional, in the sense that they directly affect output (e.g., machine speed) yet could also affect the attitude of the worker at the work station (e.g., employee groupings, physical dimensions, energy consumed, work variety, and diversity of situations) (Exhibit 1–4G).

EXHIBIT 1–4G

Technology
Work Procedures ——→ X ——→ Performance
Work Design   ↑
                      Morale
                      Motivation
                           ↑
                      Worker
                           ↑
                      Plant Activity

Combining 4E, 4F, and 4G led to a composite representation of the man-machine complex at the packing plant, with both man and machine instrumental in performance (Exhibit 1–4H).

EXHIBIT 1–4H

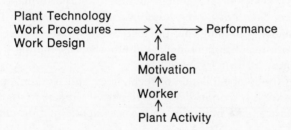

Plant Technology
Work Procedures ——→ X ——→ Performance
Work Design   ↑
                      Morale
                      Motivation
                           ↑
                      Worker
                           ↑
                      Plant Activity

Work performance is a dynamic phenomenon that may prove to be only partially responsive to behavioral modifications or designs. The influence of the work group, the type of remedial approaches taken, and the performance measures being employed all affect the interpretations to be attached to behavioral and design changes. These dynamic phenomena change over time, and possibly bring about effects that move in different directions. For example, seeking to improve absenteeism might not improve quality, might perhaps even worsen it, if workers are sullen or uncooperative. These points suggest 1–4I,

EXHIBIT 1–4I

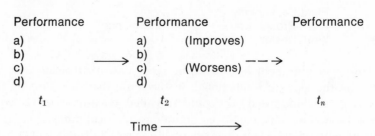

Performance	Performance		Performance
a)	a)	(Improves)	
b)	b)		
c)	c)	(Worsens)	
d)	d)		
t_1	t_2		t_n

Time ⟶

where t_n could extend into many months or even years.

Clearly, the choice of directions for any remedial program must take account of a wide variety of behavioral phenomena. In order to gain some perspective on these possibilities, Jenks elected to set down some propositions that he felt would suggest possible courses of action if they seemed appropriate in his discussion with the plant manager. The closer these propositional statements could be tailored to the circumstances of the packing plant, the more likely they would prove beneficial in treating plant-performance problems.

Propositions

Jenks knew that the basic form of the proposition was a type of conditional statement that assumed the form, "*If* _____, *then* _____ _____." An initial proposition that occurred to Jenks was one interrelating worker (job satisfaction) morale[19] and performance: *If worker morale is raised, then output/performance will be improved.* This seemed initially reasonable, providing that the increase in worker morale was closely tied in with work-related phenomena—in other words, morale that emerged from job features.

Recognizing the joint influence of technology and worker inputs on performance suggested: *If work is designed to permit workers to use their talents more fully, morale will improve, and consequently performance.* In this instance, an important assumption is the priority or importance a particular worker assigns to the opportunity to use the full range of his abilities.

ANALYSIS AND USE OF RESEARCH

The growing sophistication of management approaches to strengthening organizational performance increasingly depends upon the contributions of a variety of disciplines, which include the behavioral, mathematical, and engineering sciences. It is necessary for management to explore these sciences because the rich insights they yield are virtually indispensable to understanding the increasingly complex organizations of today and tomorrow.

The use of research as a basis for analysis of organizational problems requires a firm grasp of the criteria by which research can be appraised and its relevance determined.[20] First, the objectives of the research must be established: What was the objective; what was the researcher seeking to learn or determine? What preliminary hypotheses, assumptions, and postulates offered a point of departure for the research? What conclusions were reached in the study? Can the results be fruitfully applied to a particular organizational situation?

Once the preliminary step of identifying objectives has been completed, analysis of the research can become more detailed: What means (survey, questionnaire, interview, or mathematical analysis) were used as a basis for exploring the problem? How suitable were they to the objectives of the study? For instance, were survey instruments or other broad types of research used for situations that call for much more precise definition and refinement of the data? What means were used to measure the variables? Could they be replicated?

Did the researcher attempt to employ precise scales for problem solution in what was a highly unstructured situation? How realistic was the weight given to the findings within the broader perspective of business or society? Finally, were the conclusions compatible with the scope of the research— do they fall within the framework of the research itself, or do they go beyond the scope of the study? To what extent can the findings be generalized? These are the questions by which any piece of research can be critically reviewed and possibly applied to an administrative problem.

SEQUENCE OF TOPICS IN THE BOOK

Part I undertakes to elaborate a systems view of the *structure* and *technology* of the organization, beginning with basic concepts of structure in Chapter 2. "*Structure*" means the formal distribution of authority, individual responsibilities, and the physical aspects of relationships within the organization, that is, relationships between (a) headquarters and plant, (b) plant and department, (c) middle and top managers, and (d) managers and workers. The discussion of production systems (Chapters 3 and 4) emphasizes the flow of materials, product, and information between individuals or functional units in carrying out the objectives of the organization. Control systems are discussed in Chapter 5. Communication and information systems (including the impact of the computer on the latter) are discussed in Chapters 6 and 7.

Part II treats *behavioral* systems: *motivating* individual performance (Chapter 8), *leadership* (Chapter 9), *social systems* (Chapter 10), and *decision making* (Chapter 11), the keystone chapter, bringing together the technical and behavioral components in analysis of the organization.

Part III examines selected areas of *organization development, manpower planning*, and *change management*. Manpower planning (forecasting needs and programming for the use of human resources) is discussed in Chapter 12. The problem of obsolescence (within the framework of managing change) is an example of the issues examined within the perspectives of the business firm, from the standpoint of both the individual and the job/function (Chapter 13). Finally, managerial performance in the face of environmental trends and technological innovation is the task of *managing organizational change* (Chapter 14). Change management brings together the topics of Parts I and II. Chapter 15 offers some speculations on the future.

Once we have established a basic perspective on the socio-technical system, attention can be directed to ancillary issues that emerge from it. In manpower development, they are such things as hiring, training and development, recruitment, and testing and evaluation. For general management, planning for and managing change are critical factors. Manpower planning seeks to conserve scarce human resources already in the firm, ensure an adequate supply for the future, move people to points in the organization where they can make the most effective contribution, and help develop a high level of organizational performance.

The foregoing conceptual approach to organizational analysis may be summarized as follows:

    A. Factors for establishing functions, interrelating them into a meaningful whole, and making the interconnections for accomplishment of work or movement of data or intelligence

       1. Structure

       2. Technological systems

          a) Production

          b) Control

          c) Communication-information

   B. Interrelationships of human resources (bringing them to high levels of performance)

     1. Work-social groups

     2. Motivation

     3. Leadership

     4. Decision making

   C. Ancillary issues: manpower planning and managing change; organization development

NOTES

1. See Frederick G. Lippert, "Toward Flexibility in Application of Behavioral Science Research," *Academy of Management Journal,* 14, no. 2 (June 1971): 195–201.

2. H. M. Blalock Jr. and Ann B. Blalock, "Toward a Clarification of System Analysis in the Social Sciences," *Philosophy of Science,* 26 (1959): 84–92.

3. Ibid.

4. Frank Baker, "Introduction: Organizations as Open Systems," in Frank Baker (ed.), *Organizational Systems: General Systems Approaches to Complex Organizations* (Homewood, Ill.: Richard D. Irwin, 1973).

5. Ibid. Also A. K. Rice, "Individual, Group, and Intergroup Processes," *Human Relations,* 22 (1969): 565–584.

6. Central ideas for the socio-technical approach are based on F. E. Emery and E. L. Trist, "The Causal Texture of Organizational Environments," *Human Relations,* 18 (1965): 21–32; A. K. Rice, *The Enterprise and Its Environment* (London: Tavistock Publications, 1963); Louis E. Davis and E. L. Trist, "Improving the Quality of Work Life," in Harold L. Sheppard (ed.), *Work in America* (Cambridge, Mass.: M.I.T. Press, 1973); Daniel Katz and Basil S. Georgopoulos, "Organizations in a Changing World," *Journal of Applied Behavioral Science,* 7 (1971): 342–370, and reprinted in Baker (ed.), *Organizational Systems,* pp. 120–140.

7. Emery and Trist, "The Causal Texture."

8. Harold L. Sheppard, "Some Selected Issues Surrounding the Subject of the Quality of Working Life," in Gerald G. Somers (ed.), *Proceedings of the Twenty-fifth Anniversary Meeting,* Industrial Relations Research Association (Madison: University of Wisconsin Press, 1973).

9. Elmer H. Burack and Thomas J. McNichols, *Human Resource Planning: Technology, Policy, Change* (Kent, O.: Kent State University, Bureau of Business and Economics Research, 1973).

10. Emery and Trist, "The Causal Texture"; Rice, *The Enterprise and Its Environment;* Davis and Trist, "Improving the Quality of Work Life."

11. A. K. Rice, "Individual, Group and Intergroup Processes," *Human Relations,* 22 (1969): 565–584.

12. Ibid.

13. Baker, "Introduction: Organization," p. 18.

14. Shirley Terreberry, "The Evolution of Organizational Environments," *Administrative Science Quarterly,* 12, no. 4 (March 1968): 590–613.

15. Ibid. Also see Baker, "Introduction: Organization," pp. 12–15. John J. Cabarro, "Organizational Adaption to Technological Changes," in Baker (ed.), *Organizational Systems,* pp. 196–215.

16. Paul R. Lawrence and Jay W. Lorsch, *Organization and Environment* (Homewood, Ill.: Richard D. Irwin, 1969).

17. Katz and Georgopoulos, "Organizations in a Changing World," pp. 342–370; and reprinted in Baker, *Organizational Systems.*

18. Ibid.

19. The specification of the source of morale is a point to be emphasized. In earlier studies of morale, the lack of specification of, for example, "job related morale" led to seemingly conflicting results. More on this point may be found in Edward F. Lawler and Lyman Porter, "Effects of Performance on Satisfaction," *Industrial Relations,* 7, no. 1 (October 1967): 20–29.

20. A similar point can also be raised regarding the reader's ability to critically examine the wide body of research underlying many of the discussions in this book. To an important extent, the author frequently assumes the initial burden and responsibilities of providing a balanced perspective, the introduction of alternate (opposing) viewpoints and findings, or developing a critical analysis of a particular theory or research findings. However, with the enlargement of individual understanding and knowledge and in pursuit of intellectual independence, more and more of the responsibility can shift toward the reader.

REFERENCES

Aldrich, Howard. "Organizational Boundaries and Interorganizational Conflict." *Human Relations,* 24 (1971): 279–293.

Baker, Frank (ed.). *Organizational Systems.* Homewood, Ill.: Richard D. Irwin, 1973.

Bertalanffy, L. von. *General Systems Theory.* New York: George Brogilleo, 1968.

Burack, Elmer H., and Thomas J. McNichols. *Human Resource Planning: Technology, Policy, Change.* Kent, O.: Bureau of Business and Economic Research, 1973.

Burns, T., and G. M. Stalker. *The Management of Innovation.* London: Tavistock Publications, 1961.

Dill, William. "The Impact of Environment on Organizational Development," in Sidney Marlick and E. H. Van Ness, *Concepts and Issues in Administrative Behavior.* Englewood Cliffs, N.J.: Prentice-Hall, 1962.

———. "Environment as an Influence on Managerial Autonomy." *Administrative Science Quarterly,* 2, no. 3 (December 1958): 409–443.

Drucker, Peter F. "New Templates for Today's Organizations." *Harvard Business Review,* 52, no. 1 (January–February 1974): 45–53.

Duncan, Robert B. "Characteristics of Organizational Environments and Perceived Environmental Uncertainty." *Administrative Science Quarterly,* 17, no. 2 (September 1972): 313–327.

Emery, Frederick E. "The Next Thirty Years: Concepts, Methods and Applications." *Human Relations,* 20 (1967): 199–238.

Garner, Wendell R. *Uncertainty and Structure as Psychological Concepts.* New York: John Wiley & Sons, 1962.

Groggins, William C. "How the Multidimensional Structure Works at Dow Corning." *Harvard Business Review,* 51, no. 1 (January–February 1974): 54–65.

Hilton, Gordon. "Causal Inference Analysis: A Seductive Process." *Administrative Science Quarterly,* 17, no. 1 (June 1972): 44–54.

Lawrence, Paul R., and Jay W. Lorsch. *Organization and Environment.* Homewood, Ill.: Richard D. Irwin, 1969.

———. "Differentiation and Integration in Complex Organizations." *Administrative Science Quarterly,* 12, no. 1 (June 1967): 1–47.

Litterer, Joseph A. *Organizations: Systems, Control and Adaptation.* New York: John Wiley & Sons, 1971.

McMahon, J. Timothy, and G. W. Perritt. "Toward a Contingency Theory of Organization Context." *Academy of Management Journal,* 16, no. 4 (December 1973): 624–636.

Miller, James G. "The Nature of Living Systems." *Behavioral Science,* 16 (July 1971): 278–301.

———. "Living Systems: "The Organization." *Behavioral Science,* 17 (1972): 1–182.

Perrow, Charles. "A Framework for the Comparative Analysis of Complex Organizations." *American Sociological Review,* 32, no. 2 (April 1967).

Rice, A. K. *The Enterprise and Its Environment.* London: Tavistock Publications, 1963.

———. *Productivity and Social Organization: The Ahmedabad Experiment.* London: Tavistock Publications, 1958.

Sayles, Leonard R., and M. K. Chandler. *Managing Large Systems.* New York: Harper & Row, 1971.

Seiler, J. A. *Systems Analysis in Organizational Behavior.* Homewood, Ill.: Richard D. Irwin, 1967.

Shannon, C., and W. Weaver. *The Mathematical Theory of Communications.* Urbana: University of Illinois Press, 1949.

Thompson, James D., and Victor R. Vroom (eds.). *Organizational Design and Research.* Pittsburgh: University of Pittsburgh Press, 1971.

Trist, E. L., and K. W. Bamforth. "Some Social and Psychological Consequences of the Long-Wall Method of Goal-Getting." *Human Relations,* 4 (1951): 3–38.

Wierner, Norbert. *Cybernetics.* New York: John Wiley & Sons, 1948.

Part I
STRUCTURE, TECHNOLOGY, AND SYSTEMS

Part I embraces the structural and systems discussions in this book. The foundation for this development is established in Chapters 2 (Structure), 3 (Technological Systems, Part 1), and 4 (Technological Systems, Part 2). Subsequent discussions both extend and apply these concepts within control systems (Chapter 5), communications (Chapter 6), and computers, management, and organization (Chapter 7). Control and communications impart, respectively, assurance in direction and the channels for information flow to meet organizational purposes.

The descriptions of Chapters 2–4 provide a view of structure and work system to convey their dynamic character as they are shaped by environmental forces, internal (organizational) circumstances, and people. Prescription and "what should be" are set beside the realities of people and change to emphasize the need for flexibility in analysis, design and constructions centered on specifics of situation rather than generalities. No neat answers exist, as resolutions must be made of forces pressuring for independence versus the need for integration and coordinated activity. This general approach is then extended into the remaining chapters of Part I.

Learning Objectives

Key Features of Weberian Model
   Notion of Ideal Type
   Design Variables, Including Specialization and Division of
     Labor
Span of Management as a Design Variable
   Influence of Organization Variables on Span
Factors Shaping Organization Structure
   Environmental
   Organizational
   Relation to Managerial Strategy
   Resolving Need to Differentiate, Integrate Activity
   Influence of Size versus Work Technology
Bases for Systematic Characterization of Structure
   Possibilities
   Limitations

Chapter 2

STRUCTURE

APPROACH

A convenient point of departure for introducing a whole range of structural matters, managerial challenges, and behavioral problems is the concept of bureaucracy proposed by Max Weber. This is followed by a discussion of several basic topics that continue to occupy the attention of analysts interested in dealing with structural matters: specialization and the division of labor, span of supervisory control, and size. An application example, based on the insurance industry, amplifies these concepts.

The emergence of structure is not capricious but rather is responsive to various environmental conditions, possibilities, and pressures—Alfred Chandler's research and analyses provide excellent insight into the connections between "strategy and structure."

With basic definitions and concepts of structure in hand, the discussion of somewhat more complex but important topics becomes feasible. First, the notions of "differentiation and integration." These concepts, related to work undertaken by Paul Lawrence and Jay Lorsch, have been prominent in structural discussions (and criticisms). Similarly, studies undertaken by the Aston group in England (Derek Pugh and his associates) have received a good deal of attention from theoreticians and organizational analysts, and a few notions from their extensive work are included in the discussions as well as in the appendix to this chapter.

A structural view of the business organization is helpful in understanding the "skeletal" features upon which the flesh of organizational processes, groupings, and activities resides. An operating definition of the word *structure* would include the overall distribution of the functions, offices, departments, and other units vital to the organization and the responsibilities and authority they carry within the organization. As a rule, the groupings within the organizational structure do not occur in a random fashion, although doubtless there are notable exceptions. They reflect a systematic arrangement that exists for the purpose of achieving the goals of individual departments, as well as the goals of the organization as a whole. However, it does not always follow that bettering individual unit performance betters that of the whole.

THE WEBERIAN MODEL: THE IDEAL TYPE [1]

Historically, the Weberian model has been used as a standard for judging administrative efficiency. To the extent that the Weberian model captures the essence of structure in organizations, especially complex ones, its study is of interest.

Organizations are complex, goal-seeking social units that must achieve at least two tasks for survival. They must be able to adapt to the external environment while maintaining their internal systems, which include coordination of human undertakings. "Adaptability" is a term for the organization's transactions and exchanges with the external environment. "Reciprocity" is the process of internal compliance and accommodation between organization officials and employees. "Bureaucracy," conceptualized by the German sociologist Max Weber, became the social arrangement for accomplishing the joint tasks of "adaptability" and "reciprocity" in highly efficient fashion. Man's needs, through bureaucracy, were linked to organization goals. Employees obeyed because of the rights of office and the technical competence of superiors. Employees in turn were to be freed from subjective judgments or even the personal subjugation characterizing early-day organizations. Internally, the division of labor was based on functional specialization. Briefly, an organization is characterized by the Weberian construct in the following ways:

1. *Functional differentiation:* the degree to which labor is divided into separable, functional units.

2. *Support specialization:* the degree of specialization of labor by individuals or groups who possess specialized knowledge and who support operational activities.

3. *Centralization of coordination and control:* reflects the degree of complexity in communication problems and the organization of diverse resources.

4. *Hierarchical authority:* the number of supervisory levels and the extent to which supervision is centralized. The greater the number of subordinate levels, the more bureaucratic the organization.

5. *Personnel administration:* the degree to which job/office specifications are rationalized, indicating the classification of tasks and presenting a basis for objective comparisons of performance.

6. *Continuity:* employment and institutional stability and the degree of institutionalization within a given business organization.

7. *Stature:* the mastery and use of bureaucratic approaches and procedures and the extent to which the members of the organization take pride in its accomplishments.

8. *Information restriction:* the degree to which information is withheld from the public, reflecting the organization's ability to maintain the confidentiality and integrity of its activities and regulate the external dissemination of information.

The concept of hierarchy sets the tone for the rationalization of responsibilities within the organization. Hierarchy is a gradient of authority areas, moving downward from the general to the highly specific, in such a way that subordinate activities are completely encompassed by the authority of the superior. Rules, regulations, and procedures provide a basis for clearly allocating responsibilities and work procedures; they are tailored to the specific organization, and training assists in their accomplishment. Finally, with appropriately trained personnel assigned to their proper places within the bureaucratic structure and carrying out their prescribed assignments, some type of high-level or optimal performance should emerge.

The Weberian model contains useful notions about formal organization that serve as good points of departure in structural analysis, especially division of labor and specialization. In a real sense, the Weberian model is the epitome of these concepts, and they pervade the entire model.

CHARACTERIZING STRUCTURE

The Weberian model of what organization structures looked like ideally has been described. But more recent organization theorists have stressed that differences between organizations structures are as important, if not more important, than the similarities.

One of the most significant bodies of work with this emphasis is that of the University of Aston (England), led by Derek Pugh.[2] Over a ten-year period, the Aston group developed research instruments to measure organization structure more precisely than Weber or others had done. The details of this research are given in the appendix to this chapter. (The appendix includes the research schedules, as well as a critique of the Aston work by Howard Aldrich.) [3]

Once the Aston group had devised its approach to measuring organization structure, it used the instruments to study fifty-two widely different organizations in Birmingham, England. These organizations varied in ownership and purpose. Once the field studies were completed, they were able to compare and contrast the organizations along significant structural dimensions such as specialization and centralization. Exhibit 2–1 is typical of the profiles.

EXHIBIT 2–1. Structural Profiles of Five Organizations

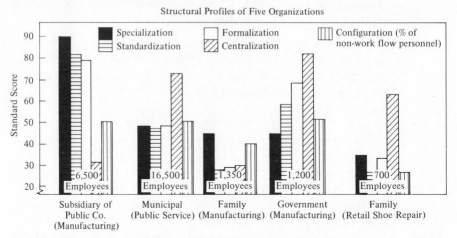

Structural Profiles of Five Organizations

From D.S. Pugh et al., "Dimensions of Organization Structure," *Administration Science Quarterly,* 13, 1:80.

Some of the more important conclusions they drew from their data about these organization structure dimensions include:

1. Specialization is highest in large manufacturing companies, lowest in family businesses, and average in municipal and government organizations. This is understandable in light of the highly competitive milieu in which the manufacturing firm operates.

2. Centralization was highest in manufacturing. This was also to be expected, since high specialization would by definition mean high division of labor and thus high centralization of authority.

3. The most formalized organizations were the large government and public manufacturing companies; the least formalized were the family businesses.

4. The most standardized organizations were the large government and public manufacturing companies; the least standardized were the family businesses.

5. Configuration (the percentage of non–work flow personnel) was lowest in the family businesses and about equal in the other organizations.

The work of the Aston group contributed significantly to the methodology of studying organizations. Many of the conclusions of their studies are being analyzed in current research activity.

These brief discussions of the early Weberian model and the contemporary work of the Pugh team suggest the wide range of structural notions considered by theoreticians and empiricists. At this juncture we return to some of the concepts that have displayed continuing relevance over time and further develop them. Two of the basic notions, which are referenced in the Weberian work, are "division of labor" and "specialization."

Division of Labor

Division of labor is most commonly thought of in terms of task subdivision—that is, the successive subdivision of a whole task by breaking it up into smaller and smaller elements in order to facilitate its execution. The concept of subdividing a task in the interest of increasing the efficiency of its individual elements has become most popularly associated with the Frederick W. Taylor approaches to man-machine engineering. The activities of Taylor and his followers in the late 1800s and early 1900s culminated in the automotive assembly lines of Detroit, the "personification" of mass production. Consequently, mass production activities that enfold a number of repetitive, short-cycle work functions are frequently viewed as an outstanding example of the application of this concept. However, a number of subtle points underlie the notion of division of labor.

The division of labor concept provides a fundamental guiding principle for structuring relationships, organizing resources, and allocating organizational responsibilities and authority. The specific composition of the organizational system under study varies widely with the goals of the unit. In a utility, the engineering division constitutes a critical supporting element; in an engineering firm, the engineer's activities are the essence of the organization. Scientific research may be viewed as an important staff service in an industrial concern, but as an all-important mission for a research organization. The number of different roles within a system is sometimes viewed as a measure of division of labor.

More formally, division of labor is viewed as the extent to which system tasks are subdivided. It may be viewed as *fragmentation* of responsibilities into simple activities (frequently accompanied by routinization and deskilling), stemming from economic notions of efficiency.

Some of the factors complicating the effective use of the concept involve both institutional and personal considerations. For example, what company and organization features restrain or dictate specific features? Will fragmentation lead to routinization and the lessening of morale and motivation? Does *fragmentation* work against job interest?

Specialization

Specialization is the application of systematic bodies of knowledge for the purposes of analysis, study, and the improvement of work performance. The specialist works in such areas as product development, engineering, and statistical quality control. Industrial psychology is an example of specialization in terms of the systematic application of concepts related to a particular discipline, which are often applied to the improvement of work performance.

The concept of specialization focuses on emergent roles in the organization, based on disciplined approaches to functional activities, a codified body of knowledge, and frequently requiring formal education as opposed to experience. Thus the terms "specialist" and "technical support group" are used interchangeably to refer to such occupations as quality control, plant engineering, and systems.

Functionality of the Bureaucratic Model

Though the bureaucratic model evidences important shortcomings regarding behavioral matters, nonetheless it has been able to achieve notable advances in management organization and practice. The use of bureaucracy concepts in complex organizations and various units of government, such as the National Aeronautics and Space Administration, has decreased the emotional or subjective treatment of organization members and has witnessed the introduction of rules for impartial treatment. Definition of authority structure, systems of procedures, and the support of policy and rules has materially eased the tensions and conflicts of complex organizations where the lack of these definitions led to uncertainties in a variety of decision situations, inconsistencies in action, and general unreliability in meeting time/money commitments. Selection and promotion of people based on technical competence rather than whim or fancy bolsters confidence in the rationality of organization actions and clarifies personal approaches to upward mobility.

Thus where environments in the past have been characterized by highly unpredictable individual actions, where uneconomical actions emerge for lack of procedures and rules, where organizations' environments are complex yet are not changing rapidly (more in Chapter 4), the bureaucratic model approach has registered some important gains. However, this model has some notable shortcomings, which are discussed next.

Dysfunction

Although the Weberian model represents the epitome of structural rationalization in organizational design, it is nevertheless subject to the dysfunctional consequences of failing to take into account the individual or behavioral aspects of the people who work within the organization system. Consequently, a changing and unpredictable environment strains the internal organization. Thus, in the very process of erecting a highly rationalized structure for carrying out the business of the organization, various kinds of

EXHIBIT 2–2. Dysfunction

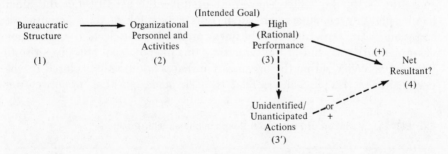

dysfunction typically emerge. These problems are evident in the areas of human behavior, especially if jobs are devoid of innovation, creativity, or the opportunity to put to work other individual abilities (e.g., problem solving), the exercise of which is most rewarding to employees in terms of achievement and personal satisfaction.

Dysfunction may also be observed in an emphasis on rules that leads to conformity versus creative behavior and in the locating of decision-making authority at the top of the hierarchy. For example, the latter fails to deal fully with issues of centralization versus decentralization and recourse to information.

The analytical concept of dysfunction in the Weberian model is illustrated in Exhibit 2–2. This model suggests that the intended goal (3) of rational performance is compromised (3′), at times seriously, by adverse forces such as the failure to satisfy behavioral needs or by environmental developments such as innovation by competitors. Thus one can realistically refer to a *net resultant* of structural bureaucratic design (4), which may oppose, unexpectedly, the initial design intent.

However, as previously pointed out, the Weberian model can serve some highly useful purposes. It represents a model of formal structure that must be considered jointly with the behavioral system in the formulation of an organizational system of interdependent activities.

Some of the typical problems encountered with the Weberian prescriptive model relate to "span of command." The following discussions bring out some of the important organizational or contextual variables affecting the number of people assigned to, or supervised by, a given individual. Although many of the points may appear obvious, they are brought together in order to underscore the discussion on dysfunction and to support the situational or contingency approach.

STRUCTURE AND FUNCTION

Every activity within the structure of the business organization has multidimensional characteristics. Robert Dubin conceptualizes them as tasks, duties, and responsibilities (see Exhibit 2–3). For the administrative or consulting staff, the "office" may best describe the activity. On the other hand, operating managers and supervisors may think of their activities as "positions." The structure of a business organization reflects the allocation of formal authority, but at the same time this phenomenon also gives rise to informal behavior within the organization that is additionally colored by the personality of the job holder. That is, each office, position, or job carries

EXHIBIT 2–3. Variation of Functional Responsibilities with Position

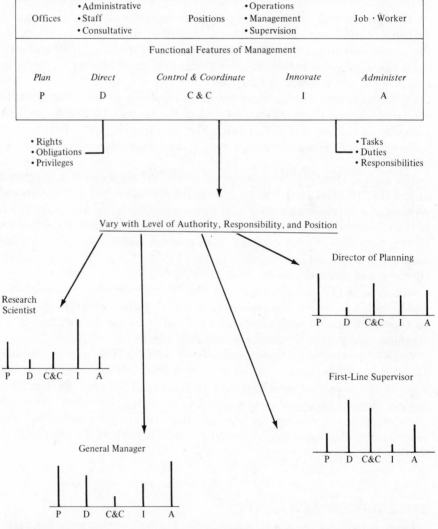

Based on some concepts in Robert Dubin, *World of Work* (Englewood Cliffs, N.J.: Prentice-Hall, 1958).

with it a task specifically related to the organization's technology, duties and responsibilities with their attendant ranges or limits, and certain obligations, privileges, and rights. Emergent behavior reflects the influence of work technology, as well as such factors as the worker's peer group and education and experience—expected and actual behavior (discussed under "Dysfunction") are not one and the same.

Structure also implies the distribution of functions. When all of the functions within an organization are seen within the perspective of the whole, they reflect an allocation of responsibilities or duties in the functional areas of planning, direction, control, organization, innovation, or administration. As suggested in Exhibit 2–3, the structure of an organization may be viewed as complex building blocks that represent a configuration or distribution of activities for each major area of organizational effort.

It follows that the level of activity in one function (e.g., planning or direction) differs from other functions in such features as time horizon for planning, scope, and ability to make dollar commitments. These observations on the distribution of activities and functional responsibilities reflect the fundamental concepts of structural design, specialization, and divison of labor.

REAPPRAISING THE SPAN-OF-COMMAND CONCEPT [4]

A long-standing area of controversy in the literature of organization theorists concerns the number of subordinates who can be controlled by a single superior. The arguments that support a limited number of people, say six to ten, often fail to reckon with parameters such as (a) level of authority (general manager versus first-line supervisor), (b) differences in individual capability, (c) job differences, despite the fact that several people may carry the same title, (d) differences in supporting technologies or staff groups, and (e) individual differences among subordinates that may call forth different leadership patterns.

Company size obviously plays an important part in defining the types and numbers of managerial personnel who are to be found in a given organization. The conglomerates and corporate units of the Fortune 500 list typically represent complex organizations where the president and executive officers assume major responsibilities for charting the course of their companies' future and spend a major amount of time and energy in this activity. A particular officer will often "supervise" a number of highly talented senior managers, so that the "span" figures could easily equal twenty.

However, the higher management levels of smaller corporate units take on a wider cross-section of problems, many of which are importantly related to guiding or coaching subordinates—an important personal leadership function. Thus factors limiting the span in these smaller units include the personality of the top man, the personalities and capabilities of his subordinates, and certain practical business realities such as the complexity of the product line, the number of key locations, and the like.[5] This point is borne out in some company studies undertaken by Harold Steiglitz,[6] which demonstrated that spans exceeding ten appear to bear a rough association with size as measured by either sales or the number of employees. Undoubtedly, this rough correlation suggests the increasing diversification possibilities realized by larger firms, as well as the newer control possibilities from the automation of information (EDP).

Middle management groups present a more complex problem in rationalizing the span of management; their activities dovetail into a diversity of specialized services and support functions. On the one hand, middle line managers direct functionalized activities that must integrate into the parties and services surrounding the function, yet the middle line manager is also one who is directed. Thus this area is a complex overlay of personnel, communications, and coordinating systems. The complexities encountered at the middle management level are further extended at the first-line supervisory level, where the foreman interfaces with the worker group.

CORPORATE STRUCTURE AND SPAN

The organization structure of several large United States companies illustrates some of the complexities cited above. Gerald Fisch makes the point that diversification possibilities increase with size, and, consequently, the larger the size, the larger the span of management.[7] To demonstrate this point, Fisch proposed viewing the structures of four companies: DuPont, General Motors, Johns-Manville, and Koppers. Key descriptive factors of these companies, along with the presidents' span, are summarized in Exhibit 2–4 (from Fisch's paper). It seems reasonably clear that a narrow, centralized span strengthens control, but a well-established policy framework or a policy committee (DuPont) may serve the same purpose.

In the General Motors organization, the span ranges from five to nine at the executive vice president level. Undoubtedly this narrow span results from the rather specialized character of the GM focus on automotive production. Another point is that the managers reporting to a particular executive are typically a mixed group of supporting (staff) and action (line) managers, and the numbers of each may vary considerably.

In conclusion, managerial span is a complex aspect of structure where broad prescriptions are likely to have little utility. A contingency approach, based on points brought out in this section, would signal the inclusion of the following types of factors:

a. Authority level being considered

b. Variations in individual capability

c. Differing leadership requirements, dependent on task need and group member ability

EXHIBIT 2–4. Structural Features of Some Large Organizations

Company	Diversity of product line	Organization approach	President's span
DuPont	Wide: 12 industrial departments and 11 supporting departments	Powerful policy committee to counter complexity	23
General Motors	Narrower: 8 automotive, 6 operating, 9 direct support, plus committees, offices, and staff	Groups, divisions; Separate strategic and tactical groups; Multidivisional product groupings	17
Johns-Manville	8 action divisions plus functional officers	Highly diversified; General managers with high degree of autonomy	8 action plus 9 support
Koppers	8 product plus 8 support	Group management president plus 3 vice presidents	3 vice presidents plus 8 staff departments plus 8 operating divisions

Derived from Gerald G. Fisch, "Stretching the Span of Management," *Harvard Business Review*, 41, no. 5 (September–October 1963).

    d. Differences in company need that arise from economic size and internal complexity (product, product families, process)

    e. Talent and availability of support staff

    f. Company philosophy and approaches to control

INDUSTRY STRUCTURE AND SIZE

Specialization and division of labor also become more complex concepts when they are considered within the framework of interindustry comparison. It should come as no surprise that the relative proportions of managerial support and clerical personnel differ widely among industries. For example, the Census of Manufacturers indicates a ratio of managerial, professional, and clerical personnel to production personnel that varies from about 0.140 in apparel and accessories to about 0.740 in office computing and accounting machinery, with corresponding variations in the other industry segments. Furthermore, industry differences indicate a four times variation within the managerial category, a twenty times variation in the professional category, and a four times variation in the clerical group. Clearly, managerial, professional, and clerical groups undertake decidedly different work roles within these industries. However, it is still meaningful to ask whether systematic patterns of variations are detectable among these apparent differences.

One analysis suggests a relationship of division of labor and the number of administrative personnel.[8] Considering division of labor as the comparative complexity of industrial configuration (number of structural parts, departments, levels, occupations, and distribution of personnel among jobs), we can say that the greater the division of labor, the greater the number of administrative personnel. Yet there are some notable qualifications:

a. In smaller firms, with production personnel numbering less than 1,000, the proportion of clerical, professional, and managerial groups increases directly as the organization grows more complex.

b. In larger firms, with production personnel numbering more than 10,000, the proportion of professional groups clearly grows with the growing complexity (division of labor). The proportion is less marked with clerical groups and is not evident in managerial groups.

A number of interpretations may be made of these data. Growth in organization size (number of production personnel) brings about new production roles and new needs for coordinating a diversity of processes and activities. The professional groups (e.g., engineers and production planning personnel) represent the seat of technical expertise, and are also increasingly charged with general direction, control, and coordination of production. Thus the use of these groups represents an effective alternative to a continued growth in the number of managers and the proportionate growth of the managerial structure.

The number of production personnel (size) bears an inverse relationship to the number of administrative personnel (professional, clerical, and managerial). Units of greater size (number of production personnel) are associated with a smaller *proportion* of administrative people. Have those industries, typified by large concentrations of production personnel such as meat processing and older steel operations, been able as yet to make widespread use of advanced managerial or production technology? Undoubtedly, the problems of coordination that arise with greater size—say more production people—differ qualitatively from those associated with an increasing division of labor. Also, growth in scale of operation may mean more of essentially the same types of activities for administrative personnel.

These points may help account for the inverse relationship between the *relative* number of administrative and production personnel. Not so in the case of division of labor, where *new* rather than simply expanded roles start to dominate with increasing size.[9]

In short, the size of the production assignment and the division of labor apparently are associated with forces and industry factors that move counter to each other, at least insofar as the relative number of administrative personnel is concerned.

In Chapters 3 and 4 the discussion of the level (state) of production technology introduces another variable, and it is at this point that we can present a fuller explanation for these relationships and clarify some of the questions that remain to be analyzed.

A theme that has not received much attention thus far pertains to the influence of various external environmental features on structure. This idea ties back to one of the central notions described in Chapter 1, and also sets forth a perspective largely ignored in the Weberian approach.

STRUCTURE AND MANAGERIAL STRATEGY [10]

Each stage of organizational growth is accompanied by different types of organization structures that reflect a combination of environmental trends, marketing requirements, entrepreneurial needs, product, and confrontation of organizational problems. Some key stages in organizational development are characterized in Exhibit 2–5 and compared across four structural forms.

In type A organizations, the personality of the chief executive (entrepreneur) colors the entire organization, and he or she is often the focal point of the decision-making process. This initial stage of organizational development is characterized by a narrow or single product line, and expertise is limited to a particular function, such as marketing or production. The eventual rationalization of resources and emphasis on efficiency leads to the development of the vertically integrated, functionally coordinated business shown as type B.

Typically, a B type of organization continues to provide limited product line. The inherent weakness of the type B structure is rooted in the relatively narrow executive base for decision making, limited managerial training opportunities, and an inability to efficiently incorporate a diversity of production and marketing activities within functional assignments. Expansion of the product line, analysis of profit and performance, and greater needs for product control frequently lead to coordination of needs and activities. This is especially true at lower authority levels, where substantial numbers and types of resources (men, material, and equipment) are involved (logistics system).

The type C structure reflects a movement of organizations into multidivisional lines in order to absorb diversification in product lines. Here functional responsibilities are assigned to divisional management. The relatively autonomous divisions permit better profit control and easier communication, and provide a fertile training ground for managers, thus permitting additional expansion. With a wide range of expertise in general management,

EXHIBIT 2-5. Emergence of Structure in Organizational Development

	Types of Organization Structure			
Stage of organizational development	Type A organization Single line, functional specialization	Type B organization Vertically integrated, functionally coordinated	Type C organization Multidivisional product structure	Type D organization Conglomerate
1. Resource accumulation and initial expansion	XXX			
2. Rationalization of resources: • Marketing opportunities • Technological changes • Innovation in material and process • Trends—economic, social, political	XXX	XX		
3. Expansion into new markets: • Diversification strategies • Problems of administration and organization • Multinational	X	XXX	XX	XXX
4. New/modified corporate structures and functional activities			XXX	XXX

Key: X = Nominal importance
XX = Increasing importance
XXX = Characteristic development

For added detail, see Alfred D. Chandler Jr., *Strategy and Structure* (Cambridge, Mass.: M.I.T. Press, 1962), and Lawrence E. Fouraker and John M. Stopford, "Organizational Structure and the Multinational Strategy," *Administrative Science Quarterly*, 13, no. 1 (June 1968): 47–64.

technology, staff, and product support, the type C structure appears to be adaptable to a heterogeneous group of products and activities, and is typical of many major companies that emerged in the 1920s (for instance, DuPont, Sears, General Motors, and Standard Oil of New Jersey). More details of this study are provided in a subsequent section.

Following the thrust of the Chandler work, we might well add the type D structural forms. The conglomerate-type organization often assembles a diversity of business activities while using the financial leverage of a core business(es) to acquire new businesses. ("Core businesses" represent the central undertakings where capital was accumulated.) The availability of smaller businesses, opportunities to "shield" current profits, lack of growth opportunity in core business undertakings, and desires for diversification are some of the factors in the conglomerate's growth. Structurally, business members of the conglomerate family may maintain a high degree of autonomy in administration and management, retaining the president and other key officers of the acquired firm. Control and coordination are exerted through boards of directors (with each company represented), liaison officials and specialists, and budgets and capital expenditure procedures.

The responsiveness of structural design to emerging business needs is a dynamic process that occurs over an extended period of time, and within which structural features are subjected to continuous modification. The diversification strategies represent a response to environmental opportunities and challenges. However, diversification of product lines does not occur without considerable complication for the organization. There is an increasing need for structural formats that will permit the consolidation of existing positions and subsequent expansion into diverse areas of activity.

OVERALL CHARACTERISTICS AND DETERMINANTS OF STRUCTURE

Organization structure is a product not only of managerial strategy but of diverse social, political, and economic forces as well. Thus structural features of the business organization are produced by the dynamic interaction of the environment and the principal managerial groups, particularly top management. Exhibit 2–6 represents a simplified overview of this interaction and points to the consequent emergence of structure. This model illustrates how the structure of a business organization emerges from the environment (1), which includes the major social forces and consumer and personal needs, represented by product or service demands that must be satisfied.

Top management's philosophy on business operations is an important intervening force. Finally, behavioral factors, including the personality of important managers and executives, reflect the influence of the human element.

Organization niche (2) is another important dimension—it reflects the products, services, and processes dominating a firm's activities. For instance,

EXHIBIT 2–6. Environment and the Emergence of Organization Structure

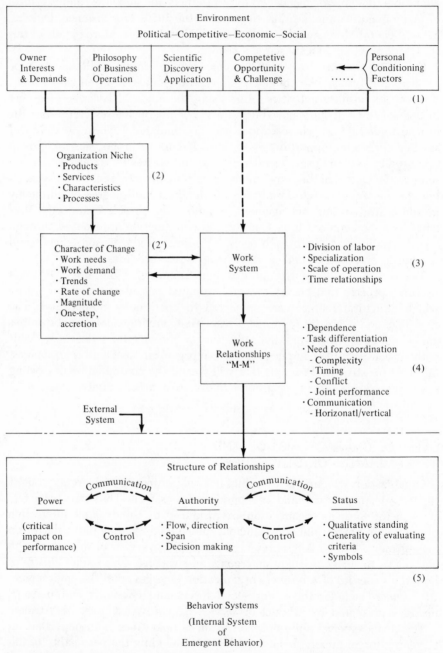

The terminology, "internal system" and "external system" is associated with the work of George C. Homans.

a top-management decision to service a particular market unleashes a stream of organizational activity, which in turn may bring about a new distribution system, field sales force, or regional sales center.

The determination of organization niche has an important influence on the functions of groups within the company. Scientific innovation (Exhibit 2–6) can dictate conditions or present opportunities that the organization must satisfy, particularly in the sense of modifying structural arrangements to accommodate these needs. For example, the advent of solid-state circuitry forced the electronics industry to revise many existing products, and at the same time provided the opportunity to develop new products. Many organizational rearrangements took place, with the introduction or reshaping of product development departments and the modification of plant and personnel departments (engineering, quality control, and methods).

For members of the utility industry, particularly the large ones, atomic energy has meant the growth of new organizational units, both at the power-generating plant level and within the corporate-level staff engineering groups that back up plant operations. At the plant level, the use of atomic fuel has given rise to the formation of groups responsible for the engineering and servicing of special control gear. At the headquarters level, engineering functions have been modified. In a fossil fuel (coal or oil) plant, material handling is an important subsystem, whereas the movement of atomic fuels is a comparatively minor consideration and disposal is a more substantial problem.

The selection of organization niche—the configuration of the product, services, or processes to be undertaken by a company—establishes the basic fabric of a work system. This work system (3) reflects the needs of the organization, and places specific demands upon the *personnel* assigned to its operations. It is in this area that man-to-man and man-to-system types of relationship emerge. Structure establishes a basis for task dependencies as well as task differentiation. It is "around" and "through" structure that the communication network is rationalized to reinforce organization processes.

As depicted in Exhibit 2–6, environmental factors, niche, and the work system comprise key elements of the external system. Authority lines (5) evolve within the organization, having powerful behavioral implications that include both a structure of power and factors involving the relative status of individuals within the organization (social elements of the internal system).

Features of the operating or work system (2, 3, and 4) emerge for the furnishing of product or service, but they also display a sensitivity to innovative forces in the external environment that set in motion internal change processes. Exhibit 2–6 portrays important emergent structures (5) in the organization as a strategy of management, but also as accommodations or adjustments among individuals, groups, and particular jobs.

Work systems, which tend to be oriented horizontally, must be integrated with authority structures, which often have a vertical orientation. Thus the elementary production system depicted in Chapter 1, with the imposition of various authority relationships, would be as shown in Exhibit 2–7. The question marks indicate areas where the character of authority relationships can enhance communications, minimize conflict, support coordination, and facilitate work accomplishment. The interfaces between production systems and authority structures have given rise to numerous behavioral studies, many of which are cited in Parts I and II of this book.

EXHIBIT 2–7. Work Systems and Authority Orientation

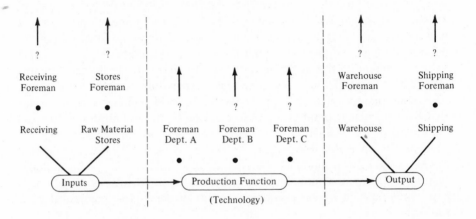

CASE APPLICATION 1: EMERGENCE OF STRUCTURE IN INSURANCE UNITS

In the course of these general discussions, one may lose sight of the interrelationships among the variables or dimensions of organization because of the sheer size or complexity of the units involved. Consequently, the following discussion portrays the emergence of structure from a much more modest base—that of a small company, often individually owned, and in one particular industry (insurance). This example should clarify points which have been raised and impart direction to this discussion.

Early insurance companies reflected a simple structure that was typical of industrial units in the early stage of development, as shown in Exhibit 2–8. The development of commercial centers around seaports was among the important factors contributing to specialized insurance needs, which were met by a small number of simple business organizations (panels I and II). With the early use of agents, relationships were modified to the extent that a second party (the agents) was inserted between owner and client (frequently shipping ventures or shipping lines).

The major factor permitting the rapid growth of the insurance industry was the introduction of industrial insurance.[11] The rapidly growing movement from farm to city and the expansion of industrial and commercial

EXHIBIT 2–8. Early Insurance Structures

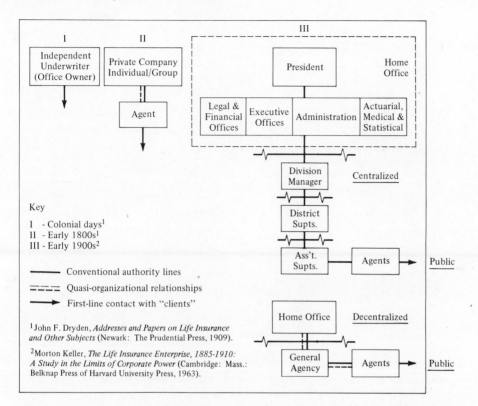

centers brought together large groups of people who shared common needs and risks, permitting low-cost coverage. These two factors established accessibility and need. The "industrial insurance" package of standard coverages, exclusions, and benefits permitted mass merchandising approaches.

Two characteristic organization structures emerged in this era, which reflected two essentially different philosophies of business organization:

a. *Centralized organization* typified the Metropolitan Life model, which concentrated authority, control, policy, and coordination in a central location and led to the formation of decentralized offices for channeling information and money flow to the central facility while maintaining routine client relationships.

b. *Decentralized organization,* where comparatively simple home offices were maintained and the bulk of the business was conducted through a field agency structure. Here field operations emerged within the general policy guidelines established at headquarters.

EXHIBIT 2–9. Contemporary Insurance Organization

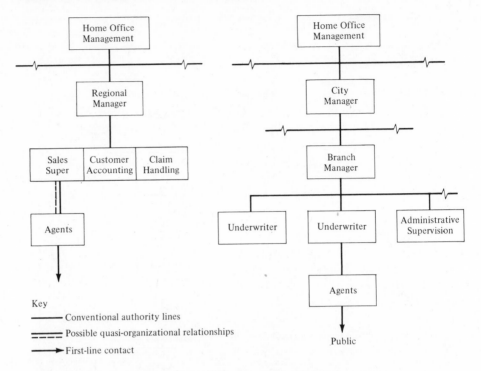

Key
———— Conventional authority lines
===== Possible quasi-organizational relationships
——▶ First-line contact

Source: John Bainbridge, *Biography of an Idea: The Story of Mutual Fire and Casualty Insurance* (Garden City, N.Y.: Doubleday, 1952).

In Exhibit 2–9 some typical models of contemporary insurance structure represent an extension of the forms noted previously. With the advent of the standardized insurance package, new possibilities emerged for the widespread and large-volume use of information (a point pursued in Chapter 7).

In sum, this treatment of structural development in insurance organizations had the purpose of depicting

a. The responsiveness of structure to important environmental variables, including population, industrial, and marketing trends

b. The influence of the managerial philosophy variable in shaping structural modes of organization

CHANDLER'S PERSPECTIVE ON STRUCTURAL DEVELOPMENT

Chandler examined fifty of the largest industrial enterprises of 1901 and seventy of the largest industrials in 1948, and carried out intensive case studies of four of the largest United States concerns: Sears Roebuck, General Motors, Standard Oil (New Jersey), and DuPont.[12] These analyses concentrated on administration practice, structural change, and the decentralized mode of organization. In the decentralized model, a central facility establishes general plans and objectives and allocates needed resources to branches or divisions possessing their own administrative heads and supportive staffs.

Typically, the central facility monitors the activities of the branches or divisions, which themselves monitor profit responsibility and direction over product lines, geographic areas, client groups, or facilities.

The general model of organization viewed in these analyses is hierarchical in form, with policy and strategic planning focused at the top and planning activities and functions specializing at successively lower levels. Additional characteristics of the model, based on the Chandler analysis, are as follows.

a. Hierarchical organization:

1. *General office* at the top, including executives and staff specialists, responsible for broad-range planning, policy development, establishing goals, controls, and resource allocation for semi-autonomous divisions

2. *Divisions* and their *central offices,* which administer a sizable number of functional departments and assume responsibilities for product lines, geographic areas, or clientele

3. *Departmental headquarters,* which administer, coordinate, and monitor the activities of various field units, which are characterized by production plants, sales units, warehouses, and the like

b. Large company enterprises, typified by administration as full-time undertakings. In a small firm, the top executives tend to be generalists and carry out a variety of tasks. In larger firms, administration is often a specialty, dealing with longer-range planning problems yet also dealing with short-run developments and contingencies.

A Model of Strategy and Structure

Key ideas from Chandler's analysis are presented in Exhibit 2–10. Important environmental trends (*1*) in such things as population shifts, competitive pressures, and innovation set in motion new needs, pressures, and opportunities for the firm (*2*). The executive's "reading" of these trends and developments (*3*) leads to the formulation of new or modified goals (*4*) for the enterprise, and thereby establishes the base for emergent strategies

EXHIBIT 2–10. Structural Development as a Strategy

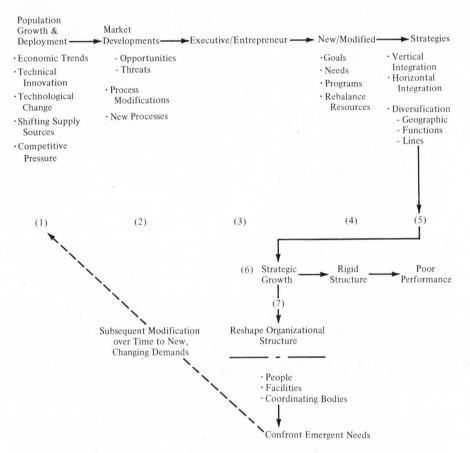

For a detailed treatment see A. D. Chandler Jr., *Strategy and Structure* (Cambridge, Mass.: M.I.T. Press, 1962), 13–16.

(5), with individual circumstances dictating feasible directions or combinations of these elements. Strategic growth (6) creates internal strains or demands on existing organization structures, and thus sets into motion necessary structural adjustments to avoid ineffective organization. The confrontation of emergent needs completes the cycle, and further illustrates the dynamic change characteristics of these processes over time.

Departmentalization, a basic concept in structure, defines the method of work allocation among divisions. The degree of interdependence among divisions directly affects allocation of authority, responsibility, and necessary working relationships. Four types of departmentalization constitute common forms of organization development: *product, territorial,* and *client* allocation frequently have low levels of interdependence; *process* or *functional* allocation often has a high level of interdependence and need for cooperative effort (coordination).

EXHIBIT 2–11. Company Complexity and Departmentalization

Phase of corporate development	Type of departmental-ization	Focus	Complexity of products (technology and markets)	Profit effect
1	Specialized	Resource accumulation (plant, equipment, people)	Modest	High
2	Functional departments	Rationalization (established functional departments for administration)	Growing	High
3	Highly specialized	Continual growth (diversification)	Complex	Declining
4 ↓	Multidivision (departmental-ization less specialized)	Rationalization of expanded resources	Very complex	High
Future ?				

A high degree of company complexity may present demands such that highly specialized departmentalization may be inappropriate. Chandler's study illustrates this point, which is summarized in Exhibit 2–11.[13]

Multidivisional structure, which hardly existed in 1920, was by 1960 a dominant form of management for diverse and complex American enterprises; it reflected population growth and technological and market complexity. DuPont is a case in point. Highly specialized departmentalization had been developed to manage a single line of products, with specialists in charge of various departments. Yet as product lines grew, organizational problems arose, and a highly centralized, functionally departmentalized structure was unable to meet a postwar strategy of product diversification.

As organizations grow in complexity, one is forced to speculate about the structural modifications or innovations that will have to be introduced to maintain company vitality and effectiveness. A more advanced perspective for crystallizing some of these complex structural issues is set forth in the following discussion.

DIFFERENTIATION AND INTEGRATION

Competitive forces and the continuous drive for increased efficiency in production have brought about an ever-increasing division of labor and specialization for workers and managers. This is known as *differentiation* in organizational functions, since it requires specialization in goals and skills and more formalized interpersonal relationships.[14]

Greater specialization has, by its very nature, narrowed the field of knowledge of the technician. Thorstein Veblen said that the specialist is characterized by "trained incapacity" [15]—he is an expert in one field, but by virtue of this very expertise he is inept in other fields. Two other characteristics are identified in specialists: (1) regularizing or institutionalizing the distinctions between the expert and the nonexpert[16] and (2) development of a myopic view of his function within the organization and a sense of limited responsibility.[17]

The specialist's sense of limited responsibility and his "trained incapacity" have created an urgent need for a unifying, coordinating, and controlling element that would direct the efforts of specialists toward achieving the goals of the larger organization. This is the *integrating* function, and the person who performs it is known as the "integrator."

In a study by Lawrence and Lorsch,[18] various aspects of the integrator's function and preferred organizational and personal characteristics were investigated, and new light was shed on this very important managerial function. The following are some of the highlights of their findings.

1. It is preferable to make the role of the integrator legitimate by using a formal title (and job description) rather than leave him in an informal status.

2. The behavorial characteristics of the successful integrator are:

   a. Competence and knowledge: he does not rely on his contacts or the authority of his position.

   b. Balanced orientations and behavior patterns.

   c. He feels rewarded by his total product/area responsibility, not for his performance as an individual.

   d. He is able to resolve interdepartmental conflicts and mediate disputes.

3. The personality traits of the good integrator are:

   a. A very high need for affiliation with other persons.

   b. A lower than average need for managerial achievement.

   c. An average need for organizational power.

4. The preferred style for the integrator includes:

   a. High initiative.

    b. Seeking of status.

    c. A significant degree of social poise.

    d. Preference for flexible ways of acting.

It is also found that the structural solution to the organizational integration problem varies with the stability and the homogeneity of the environment. Thus where the environment is both stable and homogeneous a general manager can act as the integrator. In a semidynamic and heterogeneous environment, separate staff integrators are needed; and in highly dynamic and heterogeneous situations, a formal integrating department is necessary.

A final point on the integrating function concerns alternative modes of its accomplishment. Although this section has stressed human or functional approaches, procedures and mechanically linked equipment can also provide a coordinating capability. A procedure that stipulates timing, sequence, and provision for contingency serves to achieve coordination, as does the linking of one machine to another to assure flow. More on these matters will be found in Chapters 3 and 4.

DIFFERENTIATION VERSUS INTEGRATION

There are substantial variations in the Weberian model that require an understanding of both type and structural geometry as applied to the business organization. "Type" applies to the bureaucratic and rationalized business structure; "geometry" applies to the organization that is functionally and hierarchically differentiated. As organization size grows, functional differentiation or horizontal division of labor increases, the number of organizational subunits grows larger, and decision-making authority tends to become more centralized. Yet differences at lower organization levels require a generalized authority approach. Here regulations permit wide discretion to supervisors, and relatively little importance is attached to rules that set criteria for decisions; consequently, the authority of higher-level managers is neither delegated nor preempted.

On the other hand, as the number of hierarchical levels grows, authority for making decisions is decentralized, but managerial decision making is tempered by a rapid burgeoning of rules that specify criteria for decision making. Here the elongation of the authority structure frequently inserts additional hierarchical levels in functionally related areas, so that provision must be made to assure an integration of related activities and responses. Thus in the growth of "tall" structures, organizational controls are effectively complemented by a comprehensive set of impersonal rules. So far, comparatively little attention has been directed to the inherent conflicts that require resolution within high levels of performance. Consistently high profit, regular introduction of new products, high levels of customer service, and technological leadership frequently point toward essentially different, often conflicting missions in organization subsystems. Specialization, division of effort, product diversity, and functional differentiation typically support (a) technical competence and high performance in functional units and (b) decentralization of authority and decision making; but integration is frequently seen as a necessary outgrowth of efforts to coordinate subsystems.

Despite all this, the need for coordination of resources may argue for formalization of rules and procedures and the centralization of decision functions (particularly for logistics management). One might reasonably ask "What is the relative weight of the determinants in tendencies toward centralization or decentralization of authority? What is the need for standardization versus flexibility?"

Scientific advances and new materials and products are among the factors supporting change and structural *flexibility;* here uncertainty or lack of predictability is common. Conversely, the need for stability and systematic problem solving argues for regularity and standardization; environments are more certain and formalization is desirable. Marketing activities and research-development functions are typical of organizational units spearheading change; financial and production functions are characterized by greater predictability and a desire for stability.

These functional groups may thus differ significantly in terms of such structural factors as supervisory span of control, review periods, specificity of performance, and evaluation and formalization of rules. Also, they may differ in orientation (time span, either short run or long run; goals and manner of servicing other functions or clientele; and relative focus on task or human elements).

A high degree of successful coordinative effort is called for if organizational subunits with differing structural features are to be integrated. However, preserving the differences of selected subsystems in order to achieve high levels of performance is also necessary.

DIVISION OF LABOR AND SPECIALIZATION— OPPOSING TRENDS?

The modern divisional type organization and the rapidly emerging conglomerate pose significant problems for the design and rationalization of organization structure. Greater "horizontal" separation of functional activities into corporate divisions, for example, or the acquisition of essentially independent operating companies (conglomeration) raises problems of coordination that become more compelling as the size or diversity of activities increases. Review, for example, the problem of differentiation versus integration. If we treat this problem at the plant, division, or company level, we necessarily turn to the needs for coordination as a determinant of the dominance of differentiating or integrating forces.

Three of these needs have been identified by Paul Lawrence and Jay Lorsch and include financial, managerial, and operational dependencies (synergism).[19] Any organization may present varying degrees of needs or problems in each of these areas at a particular point in time. For example, the corporate acquisition of firms that are essentially independent in operations may result in preoccupation with financial or manpower needs, the former being concentrated in such areas as financial management and capital expenditure, the latter in manpower planning or moves of personnel across organizational lines. Operational integration poses relatively familiar problems associated with product/process integration, both forward and backward.

Under one scheme of company development, financial coordination problems may initially dominate, allowing for a high level of decentralized managerial decision making at the division or group level. Over time, needs may arise for such steps as (a) interchanging managerial manpower to compensate for a manpower shortage, (b) consolidating company-wide hiring requirements, or (c) consolidating development programs. These considerations would direct attention to manpower planning. Similarly, the greater the degree of product/process relationship among operating units, the greater the need for coordination.

In short, the greater the common dependence of the various functions (financial, manpower, and operational) on common task processes, activities, or markets, the greater the need for coordination and the greater the tendency to (re)centralize decision making in the areas affected. What at first may have appeared to be opposing viewpoints in Lawrence and Lorsch versus Pugh et al. can be reconciled within this larger perspective. The key dimensions of this model, based on the Lawrence-Lorsch arguments, are summarized in Exhibit 2–12. In this tabulation each organizational consideration (coordination, communications, and managerial) is seen within organizations where time/space dependencies may be viewed in terms of (a) financial, (b) manpower, or (c) operational characteristics.

In general, the tabulation suggests that (1) standardization supports higher-level coordination; (2) interdependence dictates the use of the integrative function, which might be located at a high management level (group general manager) or at the level of a staff support function (planning); (3) the narrower the scope of functions affected by organizational dependencies, the greater the opportunity for decentralization of management responsibility and differentiation of activity; (4) the greater the differentiation of activity, the broader the scope of communications media needed; and (5) the greater the technical dependencies or complexities, (a) the greater the need for coordination, (b) the more critical the communication, and (c) the greater the use of planning or integrative groups.

EXHIBIT 2–12. Resolution of Processes Tending toward Differentiation and Integration

Organizational factors	Area of organizational dependence		
	Financial	Manpower	Operational
Coordination	• Financial management	• Typically involves personnel and manpower functions	• The greater the technical dependency, the greater the need.
	• Financial coordination	• Horizontal transference, development, or hiring programs require centralization of responsibilities in these areas where managers interchange at operating levels	• The greater the economic consequences, the stronger the factor
			• The greater the dependency, the higher the locus of activity
Communication	• Confined to largely impersonal facts or considerations	• Becomes more critical	• The greater the technological dependency, the more critical the communication
	• Encourages use of written communiques or computer-information system for financial analysis	• Requires establishment of a data base	• The more technologically advanced the process, the greater the reliance on empirical criteria
	• Verbal interchanges on objectives		

Organizational factors	Area of Organizational Dependence		
	Financial	Manpower	Operational
			• The more complex the process, the greater the reliance on verbal and written media
Managerial	• Narrowly confined to financial considerations • Operating managers can exercise a high degree of discretion within financial plan	• Operating management increasingly relies on higher levels for policy and integration • Operational levels increasingly share responsibilities with higher levels	• Operating groups increasingly give way to integrating groups on planning, logistical, and control functions • Maintaining the system becomes an area of responsibilities

Added details may be found in Paul Lawrence and Jay Lorsch, "Organization Structure and Design," a paper presented at the 28th Annual Conference of the Academy of Management, Chicago, December 1968.

SOME PROBLEMS OF ENVIRONMENTAL MEASUREMENT

To an important extent, the notions of differentiation and integration described here have built on research studies undertaken by Lawrence and Lorsch, which have probed the environments of various concerns (and their functional units). These analyses have followed contingency approaches in which an attempt is made to identify or specify moderator variables that, when present to the prescribed degree, bring about (for example) appropriate structures (Chapters 3 and 4) or motivational (Chapter 8) or leadership patterns (Chapter 9). In this environmental research, functional units (marketing, manufacturing, R&D) were analyzed in conjunction with top executives; various characteristics of the uncertainty of these environments (more in Chapters 4 and 13) were identified. These environmental determina provided a basis for identifying the differentiation-integration needs and structural arrangements described in this section.[20]

The environmental research referenced here, though perhaps conceptually clear, is difficult to carry out. Methodology and accuracy of measurement, by themselves, are commanding problems. Even more fundamental problems may exist if one considers the underlying meaning of the variables being measured or their sufficiency ("Have all relevant environmental factors been identified?") for contingency purposes. Not surprisingly, various criticisms have been lodged against this particular research. For example, in one replication study, conducted by Henry Tosi et al., measurement, accuracy, and meaningful criticisms have been leveled at the underlying Lawrence and Lorsch research.[21] Their research findings suggest that the L&L studies exhibit significant problems in both methodology and concept (although the L&L findings may also make good intuitive sense) but may require clinical rather than the broad-scale approaches employed.[22] However, the type of study carried out by Tosi and his associates is not without its own problems, one of which is the measure they have employed ("volatility") for uncertainty. As the authors say,

> To equate uncertainty with volatility may differ to some extent from the intent of Lawrence and Lorsch. Stability may, for instance, indicate the ability to cope with uncertainty, rather than the lack of uncertainty. It seems reasonable, however, that volatility and uncertainty should be highly correlated.[23]

On balance, it appears that Lawrence and Lorsch have identified a major contingency factor in organization-structural designs (environmental uncertainty), but much more attention must be directed to the theoretical and methodological issues if the notions are to be fully exploited.

SUMMARY

It seems clear that a number of different forces and approaches are gathering momentum in an effort to bring more light on the intricacies of organization structure. Classical approaches based on different functional features of organization life long ago proved inadequate to describe the complex business units and operating plants that have emerged in recent years. The conceptual approaches described in his book, along with analytical and statistical models supported by the computer, promise substantially greater progress for future analysis. Nevertheless, it is worth emphasizing that the factor retarding development of suitable analysis thus far has *not* been the lack of "computational horsepower." We have seriously lagged in conceptualizing organization relationships and processes, and until they are better understood, more systematic approaches will make little headway. However, it should be clear that contemporary approaches are starting to take hold, and we can view the future optimistically.

The Weberian model described in this chapter represents a point of departure for discussion and a comparative model for the alternative approaches introduced in subsequent developments. Although it was presented as a highly rational model of specialization and division of labor, the failure to fully reckon with the human dimensions of organization frequently lead to serious dysfunctional results in attempting to employ the highly structured Weberian approach. Another source of organizational dysfunction is the inability to jointly resolve those forces and needs indicating differentiated activity, yet meeting overall requirements for coordination. It was suggested that under these types of conditions, coping mechanisms such as linking agents must be sought in structural approaches if these joint requirements are to be satisfied.

A second major theme concerned the traditionally important matter of span of authority or control. Clearly, generalization proves to be of little help as the organizational analyst must cope with variability in span due to such matters as level in the structure and character of the institution. This discussion on span set the stage for a still broader analysis and view of structural issues, especially the overall structural features and the factors shaping these.

Size, management strategy, technology, and marketing niche were among the factors interacting within a complex matrix leading to specific structural features. Chandler's perspective on this dynamic, interacting system of variables provided an enlightening base of concepts for rationalizing contemporary or emergent structures. It is with an understanding of the dynamics of structural development that it becomes easier to understand the challenges confronting organizational analysts who seek to develop mathematical or biological models that provide considerable insight to the patterns of institutional life. However, this book assumes the position that more systematic approaches will become additionally feasible as conceptual approaches are advanced.

Structure serves to support, administer, and direct organizational systems that are the mechanisms for work accomplishment, communications, control, and information transmittal. The next two chapters focus on technological systems for work accomplishments. To a large extent, these systems are the "world of work" to vast numbers of workers, supervisors, and specialists.

Appendix

DIMENSIONS OF ORGANIZATION STRUCTURE
OPERATIONAL CONCEPTS AND SOME KEY FEATURES

A need persists for the characterization of structural features of organization to facilitate analysis. Thus these features should facilitate intercomparison of disparate organization forms (e.g., production and service units) on structural dimensions which serve to highlight important similarities and differences. Pugh et al. have addressed themselves to this area for a number of years and have finally arrived at six structural measures which appear to serve these needs well: specialization, standardization, formalization, centralization, configuration, and traditionalism. The Pugh et al. exhibit displayed in this chapter (2–1) is the product of this approach.

The purpose of this appendix is to present to the reader the highlights of the Pugh et al. taxonomy and sufficient information to convey the manner in which the characterizations were arrived at. Consequently, each structural characterization is followed by examples of the organizational features used to operationalize (measure) this concept.

Although this work is still developmental, the major time commitment to these analyses has resulted in an approach worthy of note by the student of organization.

This study was based on a field research study of fifty-two different English organizations. It centered on five major dimensions of organization structure: specialization, standardization, formalization, centralization, and configuration; also, a composite measure, traditionalism, was incorporated in the study. These structural variables were operationalized and interpreted in terms of sixty-four individual factors. Relying heavily on an analytical technique termed "principal components analysis," the study of intercorrelations (factor analysis) among the sixty-four factors led to the identification of four independent characteristics of structure:

1. The structuring of activities, heavily loaded on standardization, specialization, and formalization

2. The concentration of authority: centralization versus autonomy (decentralization)

3. Line control of work flow

4. Size of the supportive component: indirect personnel and vertical span

Thus the structure of a given organization (this selection of companies produced four) may display varying combinations or degrees of these factors. The next section summarizes some of the interesting implications of this research, and Part II presents the major dimensions of organization structure and illustrations of factors and examples that underlie them, including some of the bases for measurement.*

Specialization[1]

(a) Functional: Exclude work flow; not in line chain of command
                   Performed full time (one or more people)
                   Employed by organization

    Examples: "Public relations," "sales/service," "maintenance," "production control," "market research"—for a total of sixteen possible titles.

(b) Role: Distribution of subtasks within functions or titles. The function of "production control" provides an example of this analysis.

    Examples: For production control; progressing, planning and scheduling, progressing specialized by process, machine loading for accounts; auditing, budgeting, cost follow-up, wages clerk, cost clerk, ledger clerk, cashier, financial accounting, product/factory costing, financial data processing, and salaries payment.

This type of analysis was carried out for all sixteen functional titles (jobs).

Standardization[2]   Regularity of occurrence and legitimized by organization rules/definitions which purport to cover all circumstances invariably
                        Doesn't take into account actual use
                        Procedures defining task

Formalization[3]   Extent to which rules, procedures, instructions, and communications are written
                      Considers (a) range of documents and (b) range of personnel to whom documents applied

---

* Summarizes key structural features derived from D. S. Pugh, D. Hickson, C. Hinnings, and C. Turner, "Dimensions of Organization Structure," *Administrative Science Quarterly,* 13, no. 1 (June 1968), pp. 65–105.

[1] Sixteen items; principal components analysis accounts for 65 percent of variance.

[2] One hundred fifty-seven items: two factors account for 40 percent of variance.

[3] Thirty-eight documents and usage range generates fifty-five items.

Examples: (a) Role definition (organization charts, number of handbooks, proportion of employees with handbooks, written operating instructions, manual of job descriptions)
   (b) Information flow (suggestion scheme, memo form, minutes, conference reports, house journal)
   (c) Recording of role performance (record of inspection performed [certificate, card], work study record, record of maintenance performed, record of direct workers' time, employee requisitions)

Centralization[4]   Locus of authority in decision making, that is, the last or highest person before action can be taken on common batch of decisions

Examples: (a) Labor force requirements, (b) Representing the organization in labor disputes, (c) Number of supervisors, (d) Salaries of supervisory staff, (e) Selection of new equipment type, (f) New product, (g) Training methods, (h) Allocation of work among available workers, (i) Altering staff responsibilities for thirty-seven factors

Comparative: Above chief executive to whole organization to all work flow levels. Activities to work flow subunit to supervision to operating level. This level of analysis provides for six possible decision levels regardless of organization.

Configuration   Shape of the total structure, viz., a comprehensive and detailed organization chart based on
   (a) Vertical span of control (line of command) equivalent to number of job positions between chief executive and worker
   (b) Lateral widths which include chief executive's span of control, ratio of supervisors to subordinates, and percent of direct workers (cashiers, drivers, etc.)

This analysis covered twelve basic procedures, including control (of stock, operations, finance, people), inspection, communications, ideas for recruiting, materials, training, publications, sales, and miscellaneous.

Examples: 1. Inspection
   (a) Frequency—none, haphazard, random sample, 100 percent
   (b) Method—none, visual, attributes, measurement-range
   (c) Type—none, one of raw material, process

[4] Thirty-seven decisions generated 148 biserial items; develop scale in degree of autonomy on twenty-three most discriminating items.

type or final inspection; process and final
inspection; raw material, process, and final
inspection
   (d) Special
   (e) Statistical quality control—special

2. Stock control: stock taking (never, yearly, semi-
   annually, quarterly, monthly, weekly, daily)

3. Financial control
   (a) Type—historical, job costing, budgeting, standard
       cost, marginal cost
   (b) Range—whole firm, one product, some
       products, all activities
   (c) Budget comparison—none, yearly, half
       yearly, quarterly, monthly, weekly, con-
       tinually

4. People (control)
   (a) Definition of task (custom, work study, and
       description)
   (b) Job evaluation: discipline (offensive)
   (c) Discipline (penalties)
   (d) Salary and wage review
   (e) Personal supervisory reports
   (f) Staff establishment
   (g) Labor budgets

Traditionalism[5]   Standardization through custom or rules (influence of both
                custom and bureaucratic procedure)
Examples: (a) Overall standardization (inspection frequency, work flow
                scheduling, maintenance, work study, central recruiting)
            (b) Overall formalization: record of inspection performed, work
                flow schedules, management approval in writing

Exhibit 2–1, which is reproduced from the Pugh et al. article in *Administrative Science Quarterly,* displays the profiles for five companies interpreted in terms of five dimensions of organization structure. The differences
in individual dimensions (let alone the overall profile) are substantial.

The research reported in this paper raises a number of interesting problems and questions concerning the structural analysis of organizations.
Would institutions from the same industry display similar profiles? What
factors might bring about significant differences? For a given class of industries, such as manufacturing firms, what would be the effects of the degree
of technical sophistication? Of size of plant?

---

[5] Ten standardization items and ten formalization items.

Note: (1) Comparability is obtained between organizations by converting raw scores
into standard scores with a common mean of 50 and standard deviation of 15 in profile analysis. (2) Measures *do* provide comparisons between organizations on a particular scale.

Implications

1. Since the Weberian model is typically characterized in terms of dimensions such as specialization, standardization, etc., this study indicates that the bureaucratic stereotype is *not* a unitary concept. Organizations may be bureaucratic in a number of different ways; consequently, the Weberian "ideal" model may be severely limited as a useful construct.

2. Components underlying such dimensions of structure as "structuring of activities" and "concentration of authority" provide a multivariate (analytical) approach for ascertaining causality and undertaking systematic comparisons of different organization features, such as performance.

3. A means is provided of analyzing the influence on particular dimensions of structure of such variables as size and technology.

4. As specialists increase in numbers, they introduce procedures to regulate the activities for which they are responsible.

> Tall hierarchies result to encompass specialists and the large number of non-work flow jobs.
> The greater the specialization, the greater the distribution of authority to specialists.

5. It is *not apparent* that bureaucracies pass decisions to upper levels; that is, specialization, formalization, and centralization are not highly correlated.

6. The higher the complexity, the lower the centralization (complexity = task specialization + length of training). High scores on specialization, standardization, and formalization provide for high levels of employee control (range and structuring of activities).

7. The greater the percentage of line hierarchy, the more concentrated the authority and the more centralized the decisions down the line.

A Critical View of the Aston Group's Findings on Structure

Though only a brief summary description of the Aston research has been provided here, the reader may sense some of the research difficulties embedded in these structural characterizations and in the "size" theme. The research undertaken by Pugh and his associates (the Aston group) has suggested that size is a major consideration in organization structure—and of much greater importance than a factor such as technology (more on this in Chapters 3 and 4). The prominence accorded this research suggests some added commentary.

Without attempting to initiate an extended discussion, it is well to recognize that the "size" theme and related matters have *not* been established on a wholly solid foundation. Howard E. Aldrich has advanced some telling arguments:

1. The arguments have not been codified in order to clarify the hypothesized relationships, despite the fact that the Aston research has been part of a long-term project.

2. Though denying attempts to establish a causal model, statements are nevertheless made that retain a strong flavor of causality.

3. The Aston work was initially derived from cross-sectional data, yet a more thorough examination of this work would suggest the inclusion of longitudinal data in order to incorporate effects of change over time.

4. Some of the data analyses obscure important relationships; also, the multivariate analyses may fall short in clarifying important theoretical considerations.

5. The operationalizing (for measurement) of some important study variables (including technology) falls short.

6. The thrust of their organizational-structural measures is (largely) to create a dichotomous population of manufacturing and non-manufacturing concerns. To the extent that this has taken place, a certain degree of artificiality is introduced, and thereby clustering emerges.

QUESTIONS AND DISCUSSION ISSUES

1. Based on the discussions concerning span of command, develop functional statements (models) relating "span" to various characteristics and features of organizational processes, activities, and resources. For example, "The better workers are trained, the wider the possible span of control."

   Relate this model to the following situation by providing a preliminary assessment of span-of-command requirements for the field sales manager.

   Company: ethical drugs
   Subordinates: salesmen
   Field sales responsibilities:
   Technical service
   "Missionary" work
   Commercial sales

   Make and state whether assumptions you feel are necessary to re-respond to the question.

2. The research by Alfred D. Chandler Jr. (for which James L. Price has developed propositions) on structure and strategy comments on the phenomenon of departmentalization, that is, work allocation among divisions. Departmentalization is then related to interdependence among divisions.

   Develop some propositions concerning some of the common types of departmentalization. What relation does interdependence, which is referenced here, have for cooperative effort (coordination) when company complexity is also considered?

3. Consider the portrayal of institutional structures in the insurance industry:

What are some of the key interactions and institutional responses demonstrated by this portrayal?

Speculate on contemporary trends and developments that may serve to further modify or define these structures.

4. Why do businesses view stability and predictability as highly desired objectives? (Hint: Use the bureaucratic model as a reference point.)

What are the likely behavioral implications of relatively stable and predictable conditions? Of unstable conditions?

5. Considering the discussions based on the Chandler investigation and the portrayal of emergent structure in the insurance industry, discuss the merits and shortcomings of centralized versus decentralized modes of organization.

Given the computer's information capabilities, how would the additional consideration of information (computer) technology or relative economic size influence the arguments advanced in this discussion?

6. Based on the portrayal of factors shaping the structure of insurance companies ("reading abstract"), discuss the relative influence of the philosophy variable as compared to the requirements to satisfy economic bases for operation.

7. Can highly specialized departmentalization be maintained in the face of growing company complexity?

8. With the continuing growth of firms, including those described as conglomerates, what new structural modifications or innovations are indicated in order to maintain organizational vitality and human and economic performance?

9. A well-known behavioral scientist maintains that department or functional size is dependent largely on the effectiveness of leadership and the demands imposed on (or need for) communications.
   a) Assuming the structural viewpoint, counter this argument.
   b) Describe a situation you are familiar with, where you feel this assertion would be valid, and state what you feel are the reasons for this situation to exist.
   c) Develop a more general model for unit size, using functional notation, that is, unit size $(U) = f$ (?).

10. One of the larger savings and loan associations in the United States operates with a highly informal organization characterized by minimum rules, regulations, procedures (other than those for processing transactions), and authority lines. This institution has consistently demonstrated above-average performance in the usual economic indicators.

What structural factors or considerations would help account for this situation?

11. An oft heard complaint in public service institutions is leveled by both practitioners and organizational analysts concerning structural rigidities. It is asserted that change is most difficult to bring about because of such things as Civil Service regulations, complex procedures or techniques

for work accomplishment that tend to be pervasive, political influence, and the constantly changing leadership scene brought about by election cycles.

As an organizational consultant, speculate on structural approaches you would propose to improve this situation.

12. Debate the proposition: "Company complexity and highly specialized departmentalization are congenial."

13. Debate the proposition: "Although subject to considerable criticism in recent years, the Weberian model still constitutes a highly useful tool for structural analysis."

NOTES

1. References here would include the basic work of Max Weber, *The Theory of Social and Economic Organization* (Glencoe, Ill.: Free Press, 1947), plus related materials such as Richard H. Hall, "The Concept of Bureaucracy: An Empirical Assessment," *American Journal of Sociology,* 69, no. 1 (July 1963): 32–40, and Chris Argyris, *Integrating the Individual and the Organization* (New York: John Wiley & Sons, 1964).

2. D. S. Pugh, D. J. Hickson, C. R. Hinnings, and C. Turner, "Dimensions of Organization Structure," *Administrative Science Quarterly,* 13, no. 2 (June 1968): 91–114.

3. Howard E. Aldrich, "Technology and Organization Structure: A Re-examination of the Findings of the Aston Group," *Administrative Science Quarterly,* 17, no. 1 (March 1972): 26–44.
   Some preliminary research results suggest that the level of specification of variables, which ultimately account for behavior, must cut more deeply beyond structure into organizational matters. Organization status, interactions, and relationships, which to some extent emerge from structure or technology, may be the level of specification needed for making meaningful behavioral inferences. See Linda E. Rice and Terence R. Mitchell, "Structural Determinants of Individual Behavior in Organizations," *Administrative Science Quarterly,* 18, no. 1 (March 1973): 56–71.

4. Developed in considerable detail by Gerald G. Fisch in "Stretching the Span of Management," *Harvard Business Review,* 41, no. 5 (September–October 1963): 74–85.

5. Ibid., p. 76.

6. "Corporate Organization Structures: Studies in Personnel Policy," no. 183 for the National Industrial Conference Board (1961).

7. Ibid.

8. William A. Rushing, "The Effects of Industry Size and Division of Labor on Administration, *Administrative Science Quarterly,* 12, no. 2 (September 1967): 273–295.

9. Size has also been found to relate to behavioral measures such as satisfaction; see Harrell H. Carpenter, "Formal Organizational Structural Factors and Perceived

Job Satisfaction of Classroom Teachers," *Administrative Science Quarterly,* 16, no. 4 (December 1971): 460–465.

10. For added detail, see Alfred D. Chandler Jr., *Strategy and Structure* (Cambridge, Mass.: M.I.T. Press, 1962). Additional references are cited in the body of this material.

11. Events of this era are graphically portrayed in John Bainbridge, *Biography of an Idea: The Story of Mutual Fire and Casualty Insurance* (Garden City, N.Y.: Doubleday, 1952); John F. Dryden, *Addresses and Papers on Life Insurance and Other Subjects* (Newark, the Prudential Press, 1909); Morton Keller, *The Life Insurance Enterprise, 1885–1910: A Study of the Limits of Corporate Power* (Cambridge, Mass.: Belknap Press of Harvard University Press, 1963).

12. Chandler, *Strategy and Structure.*

13. For added details on this approach, see James L. Price, *Organizational Effectiveness* (Homewood, Ill.: Irwin, 1968), pp. 15–47, and Chandler, *Strategy and Structure.*

14. Paul Lawrence and Jay Lorsch, "Differentiation and Integration in Complex Organization," *Administrative Science Quarterly,* 12, no. 1 (June 1967): 1–47.

15. Robert Dubin, *Human Relations in Administration* (3d ed.; Englewood Cliffs, N.J.: Prentice-Hall, 1968).

16. Wilbert E. Moore and Melvin M. Tumin, "Some Social Functions of Ignorance," *American Sociological Review,* 14 (December 1949): 788–789.

17. Robert K. Merton, "The Machine, the Workman, and the Engineer," *Science,* January 24, 1947, pp. 79–81.

18. Paul R. Lawrence & Jay W. Lorsch, "New Management Job: The Integrator," *Harvard Business Review,* 45, no. 6 (November–December 1967): 142–151.

19. Paul Lawrence and Jay Lorsch, "Organization Structure and Design," paper presented at the 11th Annual Conference, Academy of Management, Chicago, December 1968.

20. Paul R. Lawrence and Jay W. Lorsch, *Organization and Environment* (Homewood, Ill.: Irwin, 1969).

21. Henry Tosi, Ramon Aldag, and Ronald Storey, "On the Measurement of the Environment: An Assessment of the Lawrence and Lorsch Environmental Uncertainty Subscale," *Administrative Science Quarterly,* 18, no. 1 (March 1973): 27–37.

22. Ibid., p. 35.

23. Ibid., p. 31.

REFERENCES

Structure

Barnard, Chester. *The Functions of the Executive.* Cambridge, Mass.: Harvard University Press, 1938.

Blankenship, L. Vaughn. "Organizational Structure and Managerial Decision Behavior." *Administrative Science Quarterly,* 13, no. 1 (June 1968): 106–120.

Blau, Peter M., Wolf V. Heydebrand, and Robert E. Stauffer. "The Structure of Small Bureaucracies." *American Sociological Review,* 31, no. 2 (April 1966): 186.

Carzo, R., and J. Yanouzas. "Effect on Flat and Tall Organizational Structure." *Administrative Science Quarterly,* 14, no. 2 (June 1969): 178.

Galbraith, Jay R. "Matrix Organization Designs (How to Combine Functional and Project Forms)." *Business Horizons,* 14, no. 1 (February 1971): 29–40.

Gouldner, A. W. *Patterns of Industrial Bureaucracy.* Glencoe, Ill.: Free Press, 1954.

Gruber, William H., and John S. Niles. "Put Innovation in the Organization Structure." *California Management Review,* 14, no. 4 (Summer 1972): 29–35.

Hollander, Edwin P. "Style, Structure and Setting in Organizational Structure." *Administrative Science Quarterly,* 16, no. 1 (March 1971): 1–9.

Inkson, J., Derek S. Pugh, and David J. Hickson. "Organization Context and Structure, an Abbreviated Replication." *Administrative Science Quarterly,* 15, no. 3 (September 1970): 318–329.

Lawrence, Paul R., and Jay Lorsch. "New Management Job: The Integrator." *Harvard Business Review,* 45, no. 6 (November–December 1967): 142.

Pugh, Derek S., David J. Hickson, C. R. Hinnings, and C. Turner. "Dimensions of Organization Structure." *Administrative Science Quarterly,* 13, no. 1 (June 1968): 65–105.

————. "The Context of Organizational Structures." *Administrative Science Quarterly,* 13, no. 4 (March 1969): 91–114.

Pugh, Derek S., D. J. Hickson, C. R. Hinnings, K. M. MacDonald, C. Turner, and T. Lupton. "A Conceptual Scheme for Organizational Analysis." *Administrative Science Quarterly,* 8, no. 1 (June 1963): 289–315.

Rice, A. K. *The Enterprise and Its Environment.* London: Tavistock, 1963.

Robinson, E. A. G. *The Structure of Competitive Industry.* Chicago: University of Chicago Press, 1958.

Scott, W. Richard. "Theory of Organizations," in Robert E. L. Fairs (ed.), *Handbook of Modern Sociology.* Chicago: Rand McNally, 1964.

Simon, Herbert A. *Administrative Behavior.* New York: Macmillan, 1957.

Weber, Max. *The Theory of Social and Economic Organization.* Glencoe, Ill.: Free Press, 1947.

Structural Analysis: Analytical Approaches

Brogden, H. E. "A New Coefficient: Applications to Biserial Correlation and to Estimation of Selective Efficiency." *Psychometrika,* 14, no. 3 (September 1949): 169–182.

Harmon, H. H. *Modern Factor Analysis.* Chicago: University of Chicago Press, 1960.

Lord, F. M. "Biserial Estimation of Correlation." Psychometrika, 28, no. 4 (December 1963): 81–85.

Structural Analysis: Comparative Analysis and Structural Approaches

Evans, W. M. "Indices of the Hierarchical Structure of Industrial Organizations." *Management Science,* 9, no. 3 (April 1963): 468–477.

Hage, J., "An Axiomatic Theory of Organizations." *Administrative Science Quarterly,* 10, no. 3 (December 1965): 289–320.

Hall, Richard H. "The Concept of Bureaucracy: An Empirical Assessment." *American Journal of Sociology,* 69, no. 1 (July 1963): 32–40.

———. "Inter-Organizational Structural Variation." *Administrative Science Quarterly,* 7, no. 3 (December 1962): 295–308.

Hinnings, C. R., D. S. Pugh, D. J. Hickson, and C. Turner. "An Approach to the Study of Bureaucracy." *Sociology,* 1, no. 1 (January 1967): 61–72.

Pugh, D. S., et al. "A Conceptual Scheme for Organizational Analysis." *Administrative Science Quarterly,* 8, no. 3 (December 1963): 289–315.

Udy, S. H., Jr. "The Comparative Analysis of Organizations," in James G. March (ed.), *Handbook of Organizations.* Chicago: Rand McNally, 1965.

Learning Objectives

Interworking of Environmental Variables, Technology, and
Structure
Joan Woodward's Research on Technology and Structure
   Bases for Describing Technology
   Technology Continuum
   Limitations
Systematic Bases for Describing Technological Systems
   Technology Scales and Typologies
Reckoning with Technological Change
   Influence of Organization Size
   Change and Structural Impact
Technology-Size Controversy
Formulating Propositions on Technology, Organization,
and Change

Chapter **3**

INTRODUCTION TO
TECHNOLOGICAL SYSTEMS
(PART 1)

This chapter is one of two that are focused on technological systems as part of the factors affecting structure and organizational activities. The environment-organizational system theme described in Chapter 1 receives considerable attention here. The initial discussion is a portrayal of a meat processing organization confronted with major environmental changes, the technological responses to these forces, and the subsequent adjustments of organizational structure and processes. The technological system and environment for change found in the meat processing unit are then contrasted with a service-based (insurance) organization.

These illustrations of various organizational factors and technological systems establish a basis for the first central discussion of the chapter concerning the research, findings, and implications of the industrial studies undertaken by Joan Woodward. The Woodward findings suggest some systematic linkages between technology and structure; and these notions are both extended and reshaped (in selected areas), based on the introduction, for example, of the change dynamic and institutional size. Also, note is taken of some of the debates that have swirled about the technology-structure thesis, and elements of this controversy are introduced.

The final chapter discussions deal with systematic means of portraying technological systems as a basis for organizational analysis. The notion of a technological continuum is expanded upon in the work of James R. Bright, and the "Bright profile" of technological systems is illustrated.

At this point we still do not have a perfectly clear picture of the major variables that influence structural development and the allocation of responsibilities and activities within the organization. Additional factors must be identified in order to clarify the processes by which an organization develops a given structure and set of activities. One of these factors is the character of the technological system.

The usual definition of technology as "industrial arts" or "industrial science" appears overly restrictive. Over time, technology has functioned as a central factor in societal improvements and gains in performance and output. It embodies the total of machines, tools, procedures, knowledge, and experience for bringing about societal improvements. Technology, for our purpose, is defined as the human employment of an aid, physical or intellectual, in generating structures, products, or services that can increase man's productivity through better understanding, adaptation to, and control of his environment.

Information derived from a research investigation in a processed-meat firm will provide some of the preliminary information necessary for understanding structural adjustments brought about by technological change. The transformation of authority structure, depicted in Exhibit 3–1, reveals several characteristics peculiar to the processed-meat organization.

The following points (deduced from Exhibit 3–1) constitute observations at different levels of analysis.

FIRST-LEVEL ANALYSIS

1. Structural complexity has increased—that is, functional offices have been added, a new committee has been formed, and an additional authority level has emerged. Presumably, there has been growth in volume. Clearly, the organization of the 1960s appears more complicated.

2. There is evidence that changes in environmental demands on the organization have taken place. Functional differentiation (more departments) or increased specialization is evident on the chart. In addition, the product itself has been modified in appearance and quality.

3. Several new positions have been added, including "packaging," which did not appear in the earlier version of the organization.

4. The presence of a planning committee suggests attempts to incorporate new management techniques.

SECOND-LEVEL ANALYSIS

1. A new type of interrelated behavior is apparent. The interactions between people or between man and machine have drawn closer.

2. Changes in cultural values and managerial approaches can be seen in the increased emphasis on group activities.

3. Different types of production activities have appeared.

4. The appearance of purchasing and planning positions reveals that the focus of the organization has shifted from production to marketing and distribution.

EXHIBIT 3–1. Transformation in the Production Organization of a Processed-Meat Plant from the Early 1950s to 1964

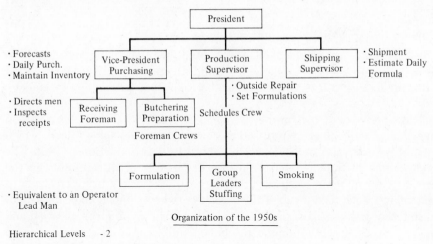

· Forecasts
· Daily Purch.
· Maintain Inventory

· Shipment
· Estimate Daily Formula

· Outside Repair
· Set Formulations

· Directs men
· Inspects receipts

Schedules Crew

Foreman Crews

· Equivalent to an Operator Lead Man

Organization of the 1950s

Hierarchical Levels   - 2

Span of Control
(First-Line Level)   - 1/2 (Shipping)
                        1/6 (Production)
                       - 1/8 (Butchering)

Organization of the 1960s

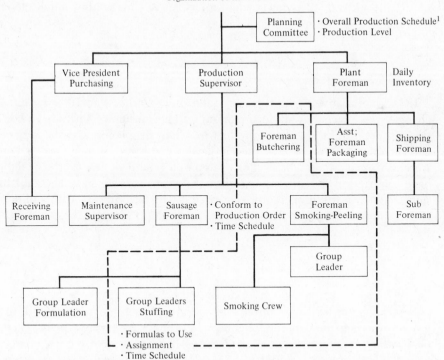

· Overall Production Schedule[1]
· Production Level

Daily Inventory

· Conform to Production Order
· Time Schedule

· Formulas to Use
· Assignment
· Time Schedule

Hierarchical Levels - 4
Span of Control - 1/4 (Formulation)
(First Line)   - 1/8 (Packaging)

[1] (.) Designates major activities.
Source: Plant record and IIT Project, C. Meyer and R. A. Mann, research assistants, Jan. 1965.

Environment, Technology, and Structure

What are the technological changes behind the organization developments in this company, and what emerging trends in the environment contributed to them? Exhibit 3–2 clarifies some of the changes in production technology that took place.

The number of arrows in the left panel of Exhibit 3–2 indicates a system in which a good deal of interaction among personnel takes place, which existed primarily for movement and control in the production process. The high degree of human intervention, several points of discontinuity in the process, and minimum mechanization reveal a relatively primitive level of technology. The center panel illustrates the types of technological changes introduced within a short period of time, including more mechanization and higher speeds, more automatic machines, and compound (multifunction) equipment, which integrated what had been essentially independent or semi-independent work activities. Finally, the right panel illustrates further refinements, as equipment was selected and consolidated.

Why did the meat processing industry automate? One reason was a change in consumer demand, requiring uniformity of product within much closer tolerances.

Environmental Changes

In a comparatively short period following World War II, substantial changes took place in retail food marketing. The consumer demanded a convenient, uniform, high-quality product in which size, color, and shape were not variable. Before the war, products were highly variable in quality and were sold on a weight basis. For example, a pound of frankfurters might have consisted of five, seven, or eight hot dogs of varying size. The shift to supermarket distribution required a package of frankfurters with uniform count, color, and weight. This led, for one thing, to plant packaging operations for retail packs.[1]

Planning

New channels of distribution and growth of volume necessitated the formalization of the planning function. The ad hoc day-to-day type of scheduling, which frequently characterized the earlier meat processing technology, proved wholly unsatisfactory for the needs of the large-scale merchandisers. Consequently, the planning committee—which brought together managers from production, marketing, and purchasing—became a coordinative necessity. We see here how changes in the outside environment of a firm can have

EXHIBIT 3–2. Technological Updating of Processed-Meat Production, 1950–1964

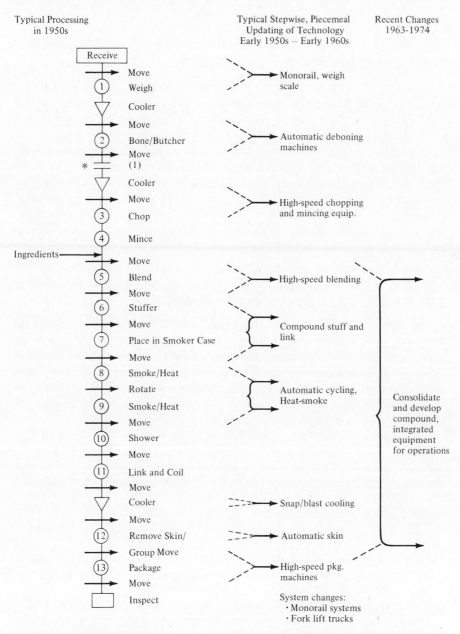

Typical Processing
in 1950s

Typical Stepwise, Piecemeal
Updating of Technology
Early 1950s — Early 1960s

Recent Changes
1963-1974

Receive

Move
1 Weigh

Cooler

Move
2 Bone/Butcher
Move
* (1)

Cooler

Move
3 Chop
4 Mince

Ingredients—— Move
5 Blend
Move
6 Stuffer
Move
7 Place in Smoker Case
Move
8 Smoke/Heat
Rotate
9 Smoke/Heat
Move
10 Shower
Move
11 Link and Coil
Move

Cooler

Move
12 Remove Skin/
Group Move
13 Package
Move

Inspect

Monorail, weigh
scale

Automatic deboning
machines

High-speed chopping
and mincing equip.

High-speed blending

Compound stuff and
link

Automatic cycling,
Heat-smoke

Snap/blast cooling

Automatic skin

High-speed pkg.
machines

System changes:
· Monorail systems
· Fork lift trucks

Consolidate
and develop
compound,
integrated
equipment
for operations

* In the preparation of kosher products, a ritualistic sequence was performed at this point.
Source: IIT Project, C. Meyer and R. A. Mann, research assistants, Jan. 1965.

extensive change effects on that industry's technology, structure and organization.

Staff Support and Production Supervision

In achieving such systems-type operation the costs of disruption become very high. The longer a system disruption lasts, the greater the cost and production loss. This imposes burdens on planning, staff support, and production supervisory functions very different from those in the past.

Specialization became the dominant theme in staff support services with the rationalization and refinement of the production system. The high level of self-determination exercised by production supervisors in the past assumed secondary importance to the demands of new marketing channels. Consequently, the largely independent prerogatives of the foreman in determining schedules gave way to conformity based on generalized schedules that were developed outside the production function.

STRUCTURE: PHILOSOPHY AND TECHNOLOGY

The models of Exhibit 3–3 emphasize the additional complications in structural analysis introduced by the technological factor. It has already been suggested (in Chapter 2) that managerial or owner philosophy may influence structural development.[2] However, an advanced production technology may substantially modify the prerogatives that can be exercised at higher managerial levels. In the case of insurance companies, the philosophy variable had a direct impact on the structure of the organization.

For example, in the 1880s and 1890s (Chapter 2) the Metropolitan Life

EXHIBIT 3–3. Contrasting Structural Adjustments in Meat and Insurance Organizations

Model 1: Insurance Organization:

```
                                          Philosophy
                                              |
                                              v
Market developments      Needs,                         Insurance
Social trends        ──> possibilities,  ──────────>    structure
Urban development        and demands
```

Model 2: Meat Processing Organization:

```
                                       Philosophy
                                           |
                                           v
Market developments    Needs,
                  ──>  possibilities, ──> ⊗ ──> ΔT ──> Structure
Social trends          and demands         |
                                           v
                                       Administrative
                                       adjustments
```

mode of organization leaned toward a highly centralized structure in contrast to other members of the insurance industry who were inclined toward a highly decentralized mode of organization. Centralized decision making permitted tight control by headquarters of field organizations. For those companies electing the decentralized mode of organization growth, the delegation of decision making represented in some cases a counterthrust to growing complexity and a desire to stay close to particular field problems or situations. Thus in the decentralized organizations, relatively complex structures emerged in field operations that in many cases persist to the present day.

In the meat processing industry, however, the new merchandizing channels and consumer demand caused substantial modifications in technology. These were mediated by managerial philosophy in the choice of particular production systems, the volume of activities, and the markets to be served. At the same time, philosophy of operation was an important factor in the creation of planning committees and other specialized administrative functions. Thus structural modifications in the meat processing industry were determined by both technological change and administrative adjustments.

At the same time the breadth of managerial decisions in the meat processing firms was often constrained by clear-cut economic considerations, which reduced the number of options. In the matter of centralization or decentralization of decision making in the insurance firms, the economic costs of the alternatives were certainly not as clear cut, and even today represent substantial controversy.

Business philosophy and technological change play key roles in shaping the structure of the organization, and will be major areas of concern in this book in rationalizing the forces behind the emergence of business and institutional structures.

WOODWARD'S TECHNOLOGY RESEARCH

The meat packing case broadly indicated how technology in general and technological change in particular had an impact on organization structure. This theme is pursued and supplemented in subsequent discussions dealing with the interaction between technology, structure, and organization size.

A study that has had a major influence on the course of organizational analysis, particularly as it relates to technology, was the one conducted by Joan Woodward in the mid-1950s on a group of one hundred English manufacturing firms. Results from this study suggested the possibilities of a systematic relationship existing between the level of technology and important structural features of organization.[3]

The Woodward research on technology suggested that structural features of industrial organization might be related to the level of technical achievement of a manufacturing unit. The results from this research provided information on important structural features such as levels of authority, span of control, and ratio of indirect to direct personnel. The idea of a level of technical achievement is embodied in the Woodward technological scale. The nine stages of Woodward's model emphasize the gradual transformation from man-oriented, unit product activities to flow-type process production. The stages are shown in Exhibit 3–4.

EXHIBIT 3–4. Woodward's Technology Scale

Unit	Small batch			Large batch	Mass production	Small batch process	Semi-process	Process
1	2	3	4	5	6	7	8	9

Although these nine stages emphasize the changing character of manufacturing systems through the use of refined technological categories the measurement problems are in no way resolved. Criteria are still needed that would permit the analyst to distinguish between such items as "unit" and "small batch" production, "large batch" and mass production.

The results from the Woodward study are reported under three principal, technological categories—unit production, mass production, and process production—highlighting the median values found within each category, but one cannot disregard the ranges of value in each category. A summary of some of the Woodward results are included at this point (Exhibit 3–5) to suggest the possibilities for organizational design that emerge from this elemental but systematic approach.

In this exhibit it can be seen that the median values of organizational variables, such as the first-line span of control and number of authority levels, *may be importantly* influenced by the level of technical sophistication achieved within an industry. It was from the research based on this typology of technological systems and classifications of structural features that the technological force and the concepts of socio-technical systems became powerful factors in the analysis of organizations and change. Yet the Woodward research was "cross-sectional"; that is, across a group of industrial units as of a "point" in time. Little provision was made to incorporate some important notions of change, which are indispensable to interpreting these results more fully.

STRUCTURE AND TECHNOLOGY CHANGE

Thus far we have been comparing approaches to structure and observing how it affects organizational activity, centering our attention on the Chandler, Fisch, and Woodward studies. But it is important to keep in mind the static model of the organization underlying the Woodward analyses. The characterization of industrial units on the basis of structural features, such

EXHIBIT 3–5. Woodward's Typology of Technology and Structural Features of Organizations

The Number of Levels of Authority in Management Hierarchy

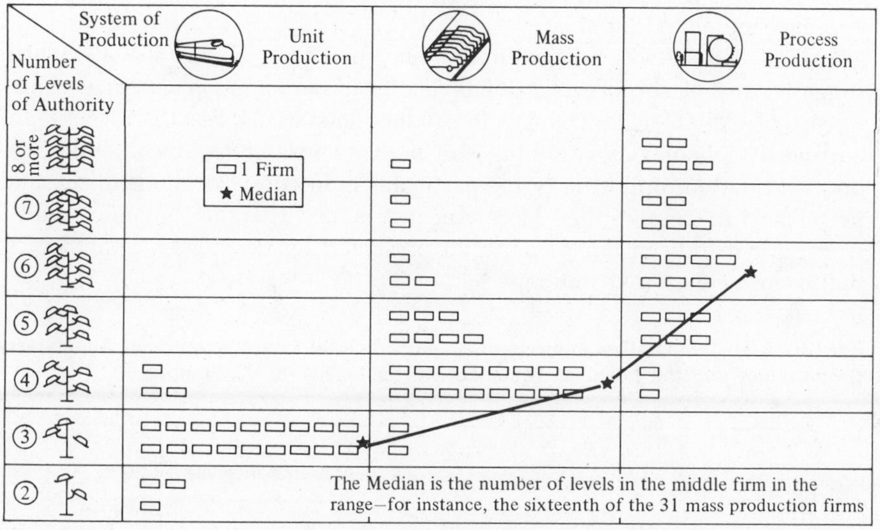

System of Production / Number of Levels of Authority	Unit Production	Mass Production	Process Production
8 or more	□ 1 Firm ★ Median	□	□ □ / □ □ □
7		□ / □	□ □ / □ □ □
6		□ / □ □	□ □ □ □ / □ □ □ ★
5		□ □ □ / □ □ □ □	□ □ / □ □ □
4	□ / □ □	□ □ □ □ □ □ □ □ / □ □ □ □ □ □ □ □ ★	□ / □
3	□ □ □ □ □ □ □ □ □ / □ □ □ □ □ □ □ □ □ ★	□	
2	□ □ / □		

The Median is the number of levels in the middle firm in the range—for instance, the sixteenth of the 31 mass production firms

Span of Control of First-Line Supervision

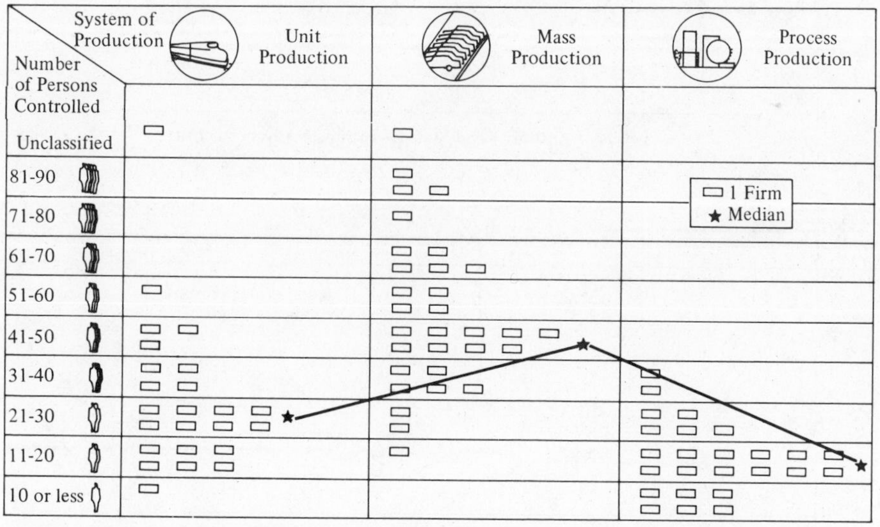

System of Production / Number of Persons Controlled	Unit Production	Mass Production	Process Production
Unclassified	□	□	
81-90		□ / □ □	
71-80		□	□ 1 Firm ★ Median
61-70		□ □ / □ □ □	
51-60	□	□ □ / □ □	
41-50	□ □ / □	□ □ □ □ / □ □ □ □ ★	
31-40	□ □ / □	□ □ / □ □ □	□ / □
21-30	□ □ □ □ / □ □ □ □ ★	□ / □	□ □ / □ □ □
11-20	□ □ □ / □ □ □	□	□ □ □ □ □ □ / □ □ □ □ □ ★
10 or less	□		□ □ □ / □ □ □

From J. Woodward, *Management and Technology* (London: Her Majesty's Stationery Office, 1958.)

as number of authority levels and the span of first-line supervisors, falls short of revealing shifts that have been taking place in these structural components as technologies have advanced. In short, the dynamics of *change* is a new force with which we must contend.

It is with this realization that Burack undertook studies that included the effects of technological change on organizational structure.[4] In these studies, only a portion of the type of units treated by the Woodward analyses was included, namely, advanced production units including refined mass production and automated types.

Exhibit 3–6 shows changes in company units 18, 22, 17, and 13, which suggest some of the organizational modifications taking place as a consequence of technological changes in production systems. For this selection of advanced technologies, attaining still higher levels of technical sophistication provided an opportunity for particular industries (steel, chemical, and petroleum) to simplify their hierarchical structure. It is this dynamic quality, seen most readily in the possibilities presented by the newer technologies, that is not evident in a static model.

EXHIBIT 3–6. Comparative Analysis of Some Structural Characteristics of Supervisory Organization and the Level of Technical Advancement for 13 Companies.

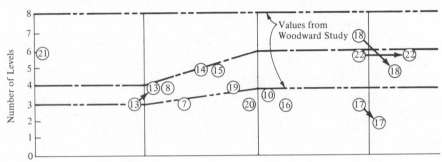

Levels of Authority and State of Technical Advancement

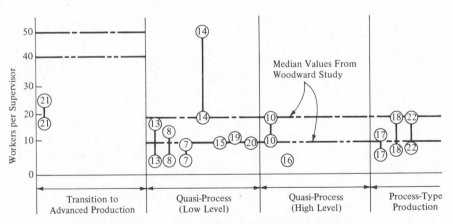

Span of Control and State of Technical Advancement

Reproduced with permission of the editor, *Administrative Science Quarterly;* Elmer H. Burack, "Technology and Supervisory Functions: Some Theoretical Concepts and Preliminary Findings," *Administrative Science Quarterly,* 12, No. 2 (December 1967), p. 476.

Woodward and Dynamic Change Processes

As just noted, the Woodward findings for advanced systems are at variance with those reported by Burack (illustrated in Exhibit 3–6). Here the introduction of change suggests several different structural possibilities that might be influenced by technological level. The more advanced states of technology in some cases provide new possibilities for the simplification of authority structure, as in the case of petroleum refinery (number 18) illustrated in Exhibit 3–6. On the other hand, in the case of the meat processing firm described earlier, the more complex structure represented the sum of two divergent forces: *simplification* of structure through the technical integration of meat processing lines as opposed to the increased *complexity* of structure through the accommodations necessary for meeting new marketing needs. It was the combined effects of size and marketing necessity that led to a net increase in authority levels in this firm.

The industrial case study of the meat processing firm provided a view of the various organizational effects of numerous technological changes over time. Viewed historically, the modification and improvement of technical procedures has been a continuing process since the time of the Industrial Revolution.

The need to compare different technological units for organizational and change studies has led to the search for scales or descriptive means of facilitating these comparisons—the technological scale or continuum is one of these.

CONCEPT OF A SCALE OF TECHNOLOGICAL SOPHISTICATION

Studies by Joan Woodward and others suggest that a relationship exists between the technology of a firm and the control system employed by the firm.[5] Careful analysis and in-depth research concerning this relationship will reveal the kinds of control systems that can be adaptable to given sets of technological changes. A more detailed explanation of control systems, technology, and behavior will be presented in Chapter 5.

In Exhibit 3–7 the technological continuum reflects a scale of successively higher levels of technological refinement as production units incorporate some of the latest scientific innovations. For example, in the early 1800s, as represented in the lower portion of panel A, textile factories that were able to organize their work for a high level of division of labor had the potential to attain more advanced levels of operation than those that did not employ this concept. Although the other plants may have produced similar products, the *whole* task was not accomplished with the efficiency derived from the division of labor and specialization concepts identified with Adam Smith, Charles Babbage, and others.

EXHIBIT 3–7. The Concept of a Technological Continuum

A. General Industrial Representation

As of Points in Time

View No. 1		View No. 2		View No. 3	
Low	High	Low	High	Low	High
Manual Nonspecialized	Specialization Division of Labor	Craft	Mass Production	Craft	Auto
Technology Continuum (Early 1800s) Craft Operations		Technology Continuum (Early 1900s)		Mass Production Technology Continuum (Late 1950s)	

B. An Industry Representation

General Industrial Continuum

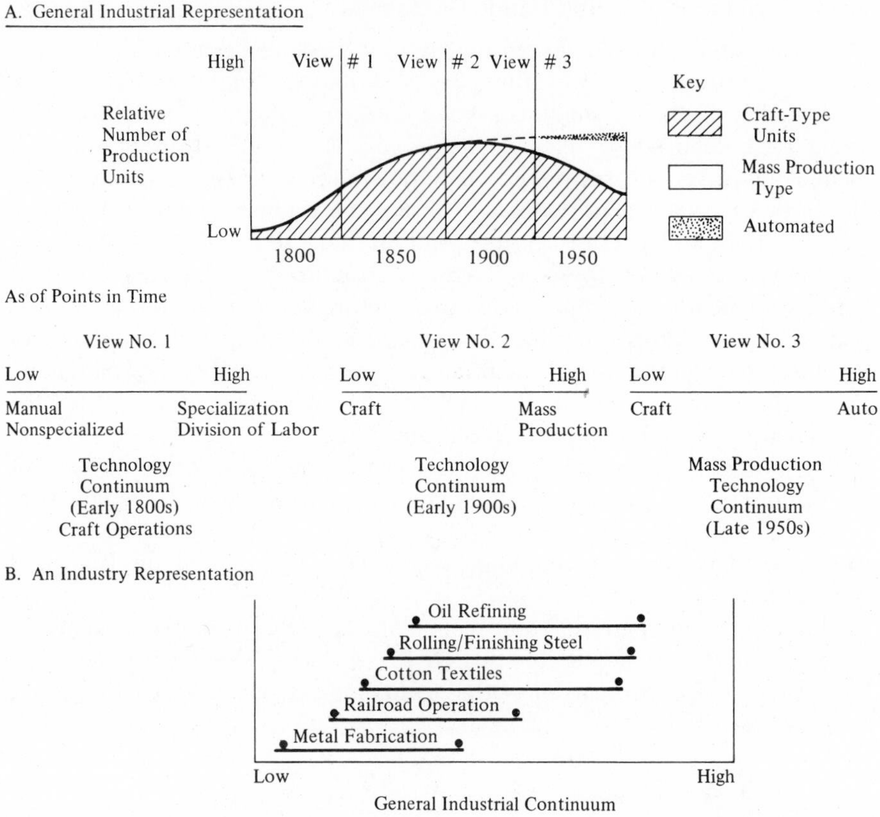

In the late 1800s and early 1900s the most advanced technical sophistication was to be found in the "mass production" industries. The organization of industrial units on a mass production basis brought together the most advanced form of mechanical accomplishment. In the automotive assembly lines (e.g., the Model-T Ford) this meant quality control, personnel management, measurement techniques, and a managerial support group consisting of specialists and operating supervisors who worked in close proximity and coordinated their efforts with the mechanical engineering system. In panel A the emergence of systems now known as "automation" can also be seen. Also note the relative number of given forms of production systems. The conceptual model suggests the growth in number of units organized on a mass production basis, but contemporary trends indicate that automated units have been growing in importance.

In short, the technological continuum may be viewed either as a representation of technical advancement over time or as a cross-sectional characterization of technical advancement at any given point in time.

Another perspective of the technological continuum utilizes *industry activities* as a point of reference. In panel B of Exhibit 3–7 some of the industry relationships that emerge from the technological continuum notion can be seen. One would correctly surmise that certain industries, because of volume and uniformity of product, have been able to incorporate some of the most advanced features of our industrial society. In this sense, oil refining, chemical processing, and electric power generation and distribution systems represent the most advanced forms of contemporary technology. The basic steel production plants, suggested in Exhibit 3–7, span a wide range of technical accomplishment in basic oxygen processes, continuous casting, and computer direction of rolling operations. The metal fabrication industries are in another sense characterized by unit production or batch-oriented production, and from this perspective remain at a low point of technological development. On the other hand, those elements of the metal fabrication industry that have utilized numerical control techniques based on the computer, plus automotive-type transfer line operations, are examples of a new technical capability. These technical innovations permit high-volume operation, closer control, or the lowering of requisite skill levels.

Finally, it should be noted that the preoccupation here is not simply with the technological or engineering aspects of these industries but rather with describing possible crossover relationships between industries, and with suggesting the possibilities for organizational change. Industry similarities exist on the basis of system properties that go beyond the technical specifics of each industry. In this sense, the *oil refining system*, as compared with the *cotton textile system*, bears certain mutual relationships in terms of system properties that are independent of technical specifics. We are seeking to develop concepts—taxonomies for analysis—of technological systems, which permits broader analytical approaches and goes beyond the specifics of empirical observation. Herein lies the advantage in assuming the organizational systems approach to the analysis of socio-technical systems.

OTHER TYPOLOGIES OF TECHNOLOGICAL SYSTEMS

The conceptual approaches to organizational analysis presented in this book have emphasized the fundamental importance of taxonomy (or typology) as a device for organizing information and formulating intelligible concepts. Three typologies, each with its own advantages and limitations, were applied to production systems in this section. One, introduced earlier in this chapter, was based on the conceptual notion of a "technological continuum," and stressed the relationships among industrial units, utilizing technical, managerial/economic, and system features, which include:

1. Technical factors: level of mechanization and the degree of process control

2. Managerial/economic features: the division of labor and specialization of professional manpower

3. System features: degree of time interdependence and the sophistication of production, materials handling, and resource flow

The approach based on the concept of the continuum portrays broad
relationships but poses significant problems of measurement in comparing
specific systems among different industries.[6] The model does not permit
highly detailed comparisons, nor was it designed for that purpose. In this
regard, the nine-state characterization developed by Woodward [7] provides
a more detailed continuum than the three-stage model just discussed. As already indicated, this continuum emphasizes the technical updating of production units proceeding from the man-oriented work system of "unit production," through the stages previously discussed, and terminating in
"process production."

The typologies of technological systems already described attempted to
depict *entire* production units within particular descriptive classes. A newer
approach (Bright's) [8] sidesteps this problem of classification and concentrates on an operation-by-operation characterization built on *systems* concepts. Each operation of a production sequence is classified, according to
its automaticity, on a seventeen-point scale. As noted in Exhibit 3–8, the
Bright scale spans a range from manual operation to a self-regulating, feedback operation. When this scale is applied to each step in a production
sequence, a profile emerges that depicts a *composite* level of technical refinement. This profile has important implications for organization design and
analysis: two systems may be compared on a step-by-step basis to identify
points for improvement (e.g., consolidating otherwise low-level steps, or
technical updating). The following are some of the possibilities for application of the Bright formulation.

1. System comparisons, as noted in Exhibit 3–8

2. Organization/job analysis operation by operation, which suggests

   a) The extent to which process controls regulate performance
      and/or the need for supervisory surveillance

   b) The level of overall system control and coordination required
      to successfully bring human and technical elements together

   c) The level of technical advancement used as a basis for iden-
      tifying the requisite problem-solving skills and general need
      to rationalize technical procedures.

EXHIBIT 3–8. Systems Analysis: Bright Formulation

A. System Comparisons

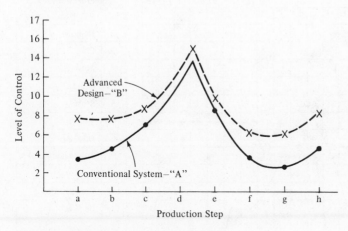

Production Step

B. Organizational Analysis (Conventional System)
   Steps
   a. Manual steps indicate supervisor surveillance
   b. —
   c. High level of procedural regulation—standby operation
   d. Highly advanced operations indicating close attention to advanced planning and coordination
   e. —
   f. —
      Opportunities for consolidating production steps and new organizational functions
   g. —
   h. —

For a detailed treatment see, J. R. Bright, *Management and Automation* (Cambridge, Mass.: Harvard Graduate School of Business, 1958).

It is evident from these observations that a typology of technical systems bears importantly on the usefulness of organizational analyses. More advanced systems generally elevate control, coordination, and problem-solving needs, but to the extent that surveillance (or direction) needs are considered, one must also reckon with such factors as subordinates' level of training and availability of ancillary services.[9]

APPLICATION OF BRIGHT-TYPE PROFILE

The power and versatility of the Bright-type profile is illustrated by a recent industrial research study in the meat processing (hot dog) plant of a large corporate organization. Prior to World War II, the production processes were highly dependent on skilled hand labor. Motorized equipment provided an assist, but only as an adjunct to human effort.

Continued innovations in production procedures, machines, smoking equipment, and other procedures led to substantial changes in meat pro-

EXHIBIT 3–9. Automation Profile: Production of Hot Dogs

Level of Development		Process Stages 1 2 3 4 5 6 7 8 9 10 11 12 13
Self-correcting	H	
	M	
	L	
Pre-programmed	H	
	M	
	L	"B"
Automatic	H	Integrated O–O
	M	"A"
	L	O x—x—x O
Power Assist	H	x
	M	x
	L	O x—x x x
Hand Operation	H	
	M	x x
	L	x x

	Key To Process Stages
1.	Weigh-Store
2.	De-bone
3.	Chop
4.	Mince
5.	Blend
6.	Stuff
7.	Smoke A
8.	Smoke B
9.	Rotate and Smoke
10.	Shower
11.	Link and Coil
12.	De-Skin
13.	Package

Key

X——X = Existing Process
O – – – O = Advanced System

H = High
M = Medium
L = Low

Initially proposed by J. R. Bright in *Automation and Management*.

cessing. Although most material movement was still manual, individual activities were substantially changed through technical innovations. (A typical installation of the 1950s is represented in Exhibit 3–9 by the solid line.) Even with the extensive installation of motorized equipment and controls, the low level of technological development of the system is apparent. The dominance of power-assisted equipment and the essential lack of activity integration attest to the low state. The advent of the supermarket signaled profound changes in the character of these systems as volume opportunities stimulated the search for newer technological procedures. Technical advances in a number of related and unrelated industries were available for transfer to meat processing. Also, new legal demands required a level of quality assurance and surveillance not previously encountered. Finally, self-service packaging necessitated individual wrapping and packaging capabilities within meat processing firms.

The net result of these dynamic, interacting forces was a further and substantial advance of meat processing technology. On the one hand, individual unit operations were mechanically and electrically linked (integrated) into high-performance sections. Additionally, major sections were joined, so that some of the systems began to assume truly advanced characteristics.

The dotted line in Exhibit 3–9 is a Bright-type profile of the advanced meat processing system—the differences are immediately apparent in almost all unit activities.

PERSPECTIVE: TECHNOLOGY AND STRUCTURE

Exhibit 3–10 provides an overview of some of the important organizational variables that have been introduced in our discussions of structural changes in production systems. As has been suggested, external forces (such as changes in consumer demand) give rise to increases in volume and improvements in equipment and systems. Typically, low-order combinations of mechanization, process controls, or division of labor emerge as systems are updated. These changes would correspond to the situation in the left-hand portion of Exhibit 3–10, where some of the technical possibilities are illustrated. For purposes of reference, the Woodward scale of technical refinement (complexity) is provided at the bottom of the model. The box titled "Supervisory Structure" indicates findings from the Woodward study, which noted growth in the number of authority levels and reductions in span of control for first-level supervisors as more advanced systems bring increased mechanization, rationalization of work organization, and growth in time interdependencies.

Another point is that workers are intimately involved in the production technology, especially in assembly and fabricating plants. This is much less the case in plants where more advanced systems have been approximated (e.g., manufacturing engine blocks for automobiles). Growing operational complexity and the logistics of material movement within and between plants lead to significant problems in planning, coordination, and control.

The typical response to these systems needs is clarification of the authority structure, the introduction and addition of technical specialists, and a greater number of *impersonal controls* (e.g., job specifications and position descriptions). The impersonal controls are the rules, system procedures, cost controls, and more broadly conceived policy declarations used to achieve coordination and control in various operational functions. The rhythm or pace of mass production lines additionally supports formalization.

The right-hand portion of Exhibit 3–10 suggests some of the broad technical changes that signal further, sometimes sweeping changes in organization structure (e.g., the number of authority levels). Process changes that may occur as a result of technological advancement (toward automation) include changes in the means of work accomplishment, changes in social relationships, and shifts in the importance of particular specialties. The results of the Woodward research point toward more authority levels, decreasing supervisory span of control, and a greater proportion of staff specialists. Note that it is in this area of change, in contrast to Woodward's findings, that organizational simplification appears to be a distinct possibility.

EXHIBIT 3–10. Technology and Supervisory Structure

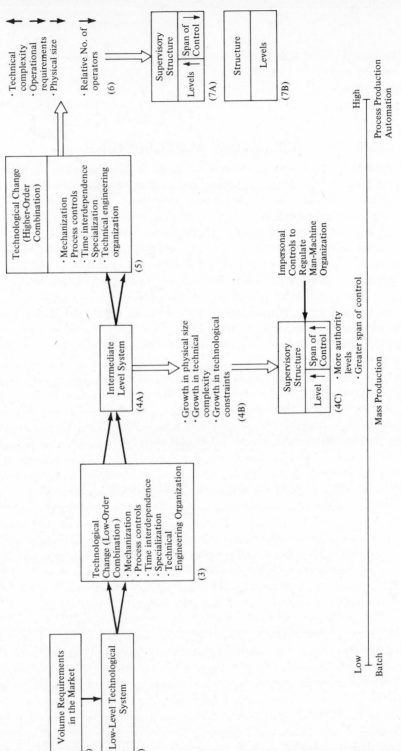

Plants built around the A-type model (Exhibit 3–9) retained appreciable levels of handcraft elements, and were labor-intensive operations. The B model represented systems with a substantial mechanical-electrical base, where support specialties played an important role. A step-by-step comparison of model's A and B indicates the technological changes.

Underlying these changes were vast shifts in supportive functions and structure. Maintenance, engineering, and quality control are essential factors in high-paced operations. Workers are mostly "operators" with machines, and assume a standby status. Maintaining higher-level operations also necessitated shifts in organization structure—planning functions were formalized to work closely with the high-volume supermarkets and to provide the internal work necessary for mass purchasing and the launching of production programs. Also, a production and an inventory control function had to be added to support production and inventory procedures.

In summary, market demands, legal developments, and the achievement of a more advanced technological state in these systems necessitated a major redefinition of organization structure in meat units. Planning, production/ inventory control, quality control, and packaging functions were incorporated. The relative number of indirect personnel increased substantially, with professional-level personnel assuming a new and major role.

INFLUENCE OF TECHNOLOGY AND SIZE FACTORS

Size vis-à-vis technology has received considerable attention in the literature and thus warrants this note on the controversy. The Aston studies[10] indicate that

> Given information about how many employees an organization has, and an outline of its technology in terms of how integrated and automated the work process is, its structuring of activities can be estimated within fairly close limits. Likewise, knowing the dependence of an organization on other organizations and its geographical dispersion over sites tells a great deal about the likely concentration of authority in its structure.[11]

The influence of "size" is increasingly pervasive in large organizations (say, over several thousand employees) and especially strong beyond the area of the production function. Similarly, the Aston studies conclude that the "variables of operations technology will be related only to those structural variables that are centered on the work flow." The smaller the organization, the greater the structural effects of technology; the larger the organization, the more the technological effects are confined to particular work-related variables, with size having a greater overall impact: In large organizations, such factors as support specialists and standardized procedures buffer the direct impact of work technology on structure.

A different position is taken by Howard Aldrich,[12] who maintains that the size variable described in the Aston work, since it reflects numbers of workers and not output, is not akin to the economist's notion of scale of operation, and thus casts a cloud over the Aston propositions.

> It should be noted that many theorists who consider size an important variable have in mind things related to the magnitude of an organization's output, not the size of the labor force ... economies of scale seem to indicate an important role that size plays in industrial organizations. In this case, however, size refers to the scale of an organization's operation and not necessarily to the size of the labor force. The Aston group has no measure of the magnitude of output and so unfortunately many key propositions about the effects of size cannot be dealt with in this article.[13]

Aldrich also questions the causal impact of size on the structure of organizational technology. He suggests that it might be more plausible to assume that the definition of desired employee behavior, degree of role specialization, extent of rule formalization, etc., are planned for and at least partially determined *before* work-force size increases.[14]

· What, then, are we to conclude concerning technology and structure? Simply that the rejection by the Aston group of technology as a key variable affecting structure is ill advised. Longitudinal studies support this position, and future research will likely seek to define more precisely the concept of size and fit it into the complex picture. At this stage of development, the analyses of size and technology developed in this chapter appear congenial with emerging information—that is:

1. For smaller firms (measured on scale of output) or firms heavily oriented to a particular production technology, as in chemicals and steel, production technology assumes a primary role in organizational structure.

2. For firms with less orientation to production because of such factors as product diversity, multi-processing operational and distribution stages, and major specialist/support structures (for development or control, for example), the technology effect is mitigated considerably by size.

3. Non-production firms (e.g., insurance, banks) often relegate the work processing (of information) to a lesser role. Thus internal structuring is due to environmental (e.g., client) needs, work function, logistics, and specialist needs. Size is a dependent variable.

ORGANIZATION SIZE AND CHANGES IN STRUCTURE

Unlike very large corporations, small organizations can accommodate (and indeed may be forced to make) rapid changes in structure or personnel in order to keep up with new possibilities in the marketplace. Small organizations are more "fluid" in their ability to accommodate change. Less complex organization structures and shorter lines of authority and communication are among the structural factors facilitating change in small organizations, yet the lack of staff support specialties (rationalized planning or analysis units) or nonstructural factors (economic resources) may move counter to the introduction of change.

Conglomerates,[15] however, are essentially collections of largely independent operating units, whose parent corporate structures provide general guidance and approve high-level capital expenditure requests. Conglomerates, having reached a certain critical mass, place basic operational responsibilities in the hands of subunit general managers, vice presidents, or presidents. In such cases, one must ask: "What are some of the factors that prevent uncontrolled growth in the organization?"

Some of the more common and obvious means are (1) greater efficiency in work techniques, (2) development of the profit-center notion, (3) the gathering together of essentially sovereign groups of operating organizations, and (4) computer technology. Yet the growing complexity of organizations and the attendant control/coordination needs may overly limit the ability of an organization to effectively respond to rapid change. Will the thrust of current changes be to further complicate activities and relationships within the organization? Can the gap between organizational need and the ability of the organization to respond to that need be closed by certain technological advances that hold new possibilities for control? For analysis? For coordination?

CHANGE AND THE RESTRUCTURING OF PRODUCTION UNITS

The types of technological changes described in this chapter have an impact on organization, activity, and manpower that should be more evident at this point. The research citations represent only a small portion of a rapidly growing literature in this area, but one research thrust that has looked particularly promising is E. R. F. W. Crossman's in England, and the more recent work of a research group at the University of California.[16]

Crossman identifies several factors that are needed in order to predict changes in the manpower and skill requirements for a particular industry. They include:

a. The method of production used for each distinct product of the industry and its manpower and skill requirements

b. The new methods that are technologically feasible alternatives

c. The rate at which each new method will spread, and hence to what extent each present process will have been replaced at the time for which predictions are required

d. The manpower and skill requirements of each new process when it has reached a steady state:
   1) Per unit of production (the elastic component) and
   2) Per plant installed (the inelastic component)

Several conclusions that can be drawn from Crossman's research are summarized as follows.

1. Automation is the replacement of brainpower by versatile machine information processors.

2. When its first phase (viz., automation) is complete in a given industry, it abolishes direct production work, leaving an essentially constant labor force independent of demand; that is, marginal labor requirements tends to zero.

3. The classical economic chain of dependence from demand to production to man-hours worked to incomes, and back to demand, will be broken and a new model will apply. This will have important consequences for the business cycle, and, in the long run, the level of employment seems likely to be determined solely by installed productive capacity and not at all by demand.

4. In the still longer run (probably several decades from now), a second phase of automation will substantially reduce the remaining, constant labor force.

5. Most industries are not even nearing completion of phase one of automation. Manpower predictions for them must be based on a detailed study of technological progress as it affects each distinct product, in particular the probable rate of diffusion of each distinct new method and the comparative labor requirements of old and new processes.

6. The "skill-input profile"—the direct and indirect man-hour inputs required for a given product at each of several skill levels—is a useful tool. Skill levels may be assessed by analyzing the information processes required to be performed in the work.

7. Further industry-by-industry analytical studies of technology and manpower should be undertaken as a routine procedure by a government agency such as the Bureau of Labor Statistics.[17]

The Crossman analyses have important implications for organizational analyses as they relate to structure, work processes, and the use of human resources. However, the preceding summary does not make clear what industrial segments will "resist" technological innovations and thus this source of change. Economic considerations (great variety, low demand) are among those factors limiting technological interventions. Yet these same industrial units, resistant to technical change, may be highly vulnerable to social change or other sources of environmental turbulence (see Chapters 1, 4, 12, and 15).

Cost Features

The Crossman analyses and earlier discussions cite the characteristics of emergent production systems that modify cost and performance features, thus influencing the work-related activities of key manpower groups. Exhibit 3–11 clarifies some of the production economics (cost characteristics) of technological systems that dictate the functions of support and supervisory groups.[18]

In Exhibit 3–11A, some general relationships between labor and capital are shown. Generally, the capital base dominates in the advanced systems. Exhibit 3–11B depicts the typical cost functions that attend *time-interdependent* units. The advanced units favor high volume, and display obvious advantages at high production levels. Finally, in Exhibit 3–11C we note the costs of disrupting comprehensive production units. The justification for extensive process controls in these units—the channeling of supervisory and support functions to minimize breakdowns and quickly resolve malfunctions —becomes more evident here.

At this point we seek to bring together various elements of the change theme, introduced in this chapter, through a series of propositions.

PROPOSITIONS ON ORGANIZATIONAL VARIABLES RELATED TO CHANGE

It is clear that the variables that shape organization features are related in a complex manner and, furthermore, importantly moderate the forces of change. Some of these relationships are crystallized in the following propositions.[19]

1. *The ease of modifying structure generally has an inverse relationship to the size of the organization.* The greater the size or the more complex the structure, the less the propensity or the ability to make structural modifications that significantly affect the character of the organization.[20] By the same token, the greater the size, the less influence any individual will have in organizational matters, and the willingness of the organization to accommodate individual idiosyncrasies will be less.

EXHIBIT 3–11. Cost Characteristics of Technological Systems

A. System Composition: Labor-Capital

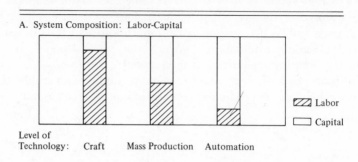

Level of
Technology: Craft   Mass Production   Automation

• Responsiveness of Labor Component to Production Level Changes:

Craft	Mass Production	Automation
High	Irregular	Low

B. Typical Cost Functions

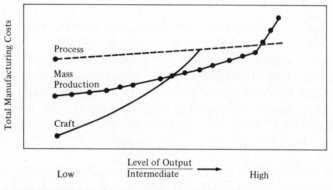

C. Costs of Disruption

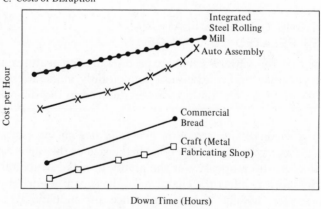

This view emphasizes the increasing difficulty of launching change as the organization grows in size or structural complexity, or where little job change has taken place in the past.

2. *The propensity of an individual to accommodate changes is related to his length of time in a particular position and his past pattern of job change.* The longer a supervisor has been in grade or in a given position, the less his inclination to take on new work patterns, relationships, or methods. Yet the greater the need to accommodate changes in the past, the more has change constituted an acceptable mode of work life, and the greater the willingness to accept impending change.

For this reason, better superior/subordinate relationships and good communication support change.

3. *The older the organization, the less it is inclined to accommodate change.* The age of the organization is a limiting factor, to the extent to which relationships and structure have become frozen. The degree of formalization is an important factor in the willingness to accommodate structural modifications.[21]

4. *The production function is an independent factor limiting change.* A manufacturing company finds it more difficult to change than, say, an information-oriented service firm, because of the added problems of changing the production functions and the influence of capital investment.

SUMMARY

Exhibit 3–12, which enlarges the concepts set forth in Exhibit 3–10, brings together many of the characterizations of socio-technical systems presented in this chapter. Trends in the general enviromnment create company needs and opportunities, and shape the technological strategies that emerge in response to these developments. Management's philosophy regarding structure and rate of change is one of the most important considerations shaping an industry's technology.

Exhibit 3–10 depicts the transformation of general technological change into the technical specifics of given industries. However, Exhibit 3–12 adds at least one new dimension to the picture, which has not been drawn out in previous discussions: the transformation of technical specifics to more general system analyses. For example, the incorporation of automatic machinery or the mechanization of materials handling equipment or the installation of a new type of chemical process is translated from specific changes into broader system concepts based on the analyst's insights.

It is this transformation that provides the power to build on the fractional theories or the empirical findings of given research studies. It also provides the student of management with the opportunity to generalize on research experiences and undertake organizational analysis, often for the purpose of elevating the performance of administrative units.

EXHIBIT 3–12. Technological Change and Management Function

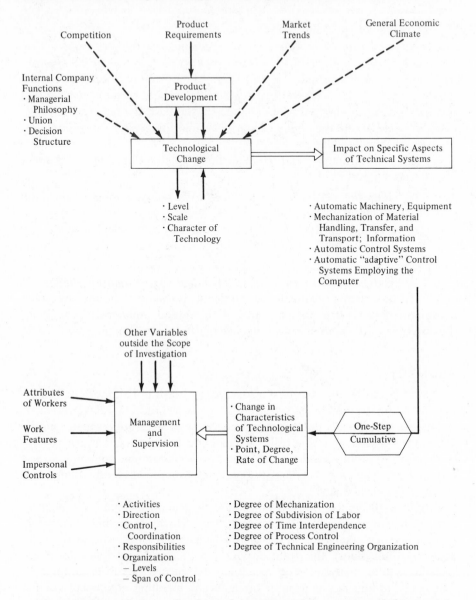

The coupling of the technological system and its structural features is suggested by the "Management and Supervision" box in Exhibit 3–12. The translation of system needs into the formal work-related functions of coordination, direction, and supervision constitute the work-related repertoire of the various supervisory and support groups. However, these approaches do not provide a basis for fully anticipating the behavior that is a consequence of the tension, stresses, or built-in social relationships of the plant, or the broader environmental-organizational system.

In short, a theme, characterized as "technological determinism" by the behaviorists or technologists, is employed here. There has been a tendency to overstate the impact of "technological determinism," but this is no more serious than an overemphasis on size or purely behavioral factors.

What has been described in this chapter constitutes the technological base for the social relationships and individual behavioral patterns that emerge from these systems. Also, these discussions have included the changing character of the authority structure in production operations, work demands for operating and support groups, and approaches to socio-technical analysis.

Work provides a major source of status in our society. The specialization and subdivision of work that has accompanied mechanization has largely removed the status associated with crafts and specialized skills. This trend has been compounded by automation, which threatens to substitute electronic circuitry, controls, and processing equipment for human judgment and involvement in work. People are becoming alienated from work. Since status, use of human abilities, worker satisfaction, performance, and meaning in life have been inexorably bound up with work, we will have to reappraise such things as the concept of work for those remaining within organizational work bodies. In addition, new insights for organizational analysis are indicated as the composition of work units shifts and increasingly favors technical, support (staff), and administrative functions.

QUESTIONS

1. It has been said that recognizing the growing interdependencies and cost-performance features of advanced systems helps to account for important areas of accommodation in organizational support groups. What groups are vitally affected by these developments, and what types of adjustment take place?

2. The dynamic factor, technology, is portrayed over time in terms of the technological scales of Exhibit 3–7. Utilizing this historical portrayal as a reference point, speculate on the future course of technological transformation in production units.

3. To what extent are the Woodward results consistent with the meat processing application case described in this chapter? What are the differences? How would you account for these differences?

4. In what way would the thrust of technological change and structural accommodations in the meat processing application example be similar to that in oil refineries? In what way would it be different?

5. Compare and contrast the character of change and structural accommodations relating to the insurance industry application example (Chapter 2) and the processed-meat firm described in this chapter. You may wish

to consider such things as *type* of change, factors bringing changes about, and speed and scope of change. Other matters of interest might include the character of organizations, philosophy, and work methods.

6. The application case concerning companies in the meat processing industry describes a complex series of organizational and technological changes that affected many companies in this industry. To what extent are the organizational-structural accommodations technologically related? Related to environmental forces? Ownership philosophy of business operation?

7. For the types of technical changes described in Exihibit 3–3 (panels A and B), how would line supervisors be affected in terms of skills, training, educational needs, etc. What is the impact of these changes on the maintenance of organization?

8. What effect does size, as opposed to technology, have on structural features?

9. To what extent do the Woodward results carry beyond the plant or production organization? In the same vein, how would one account for possible differences that might be attributed to the English industrial culture as compared to that in the United States?

10. What are some of the indicators of important types of innovation or change in the offing? What system might be erected to connect these environmental "readings" with human resource planning and programming?

11. Compare and contrast the typologies of technology discussed in this chapter. Propose a way in which one of these classification schemes can be combined with important organizational variables pertaining to structure or behavior. Thus:

Your Classification Scheme of Technology Typologies

Organization or behavioral variables	a	b	- - - - - - - - - - -	j
		Fill in the cells		

12. In a manner similar to the step-by-step portrayal of structural and technological developments in the meat processing units, propose a likely sequence of events as the technology depicted in the center of Exhibit 3–2 shifts toward a still more highly automated system (right side). Assume an increasing tempo of technological change and further growth in size and number of supermarket establishments with product quality ever more important and reduced costs still more urgent. State additional assumptions.

13. As one familiar with the Woodward research, how would you seek to account for the following structural characteristics in your electric motor, mass production facility: three authority levels, a production department with sixty workers (one supervisor), and a second department with thirty workers and one supervisor? Make and state the necessary assumptions.

14. For the technology depicted in Exihibit 3–9, speculate on the structural consequences of automating the linking, dispensing, and packaging operations (steps 11, 12, and 13). Make and state necessary assumptions.

15. How do considerations of age or level of education complicate the proposition on technological change and organizational matters (no. 2) related to individual ability to accommodate change?

16. Much of Dr. Crossman's analysis has developed from consideration of industries with homogeneous products. How would you extrapolate his conclusions to heterogeneous industries, that is, machinery and appliances?

NOTES

1. For more on the environmental theme, see John J. Gabarro, "Organizational Adoption to Environmental Change," in Frank Baker (ed.), *Organizational Systems* (Homewood, Ill.: Richard D. Irwin, 1973).

2. This question may also be viewed in terms of alternate *executive* structures and their behavioral consequences. See Alonzo McDonald, "Conflict at the Summit: A Deadly Game," *Harvard Business Review,* 50, no. 2 (March–April 1972): 59–68.

3. Joan Woodward, *Industrial Organization: Behavior and Control* (London: Oxford University Press, 1970).

4. Elmer H. Burack, "Technological Change and Advanced Process Units: Some Theoretical Notions and Some Preliminary Findings," *Administrative Science Quarterly,* 12, no. 2 (December 1967): 479–500.

5. Woodward, *Industrial Organization.*

6. For some applications of this type of concept, see Elmer H. Burack, "Technology and Industrial Supervision: A Model Building Approach," *Academy of Management Journal,* 9, no. 1 (March 1966); idem, "Technology and Supervisory Practice: A Preliminary View," *Human Organizations,* 26, no. 4 (Winter 1967): 256–264;

and idem and Frank H. Cassell, "Technological Change and Manpower Development in Advanced Production Systems," *Academy of Management Journal,* 10, no. 3 (September 1967).

7. Joan Woodward, *Industrial Administration: Theory and Approaches* (London: Oxford University Press, 1965).

8. James R. Bright, *Management and Automation* (Cambridge, Mass.: Harvard Graduate School of Business, Division of Research, 1958).

9. Additional points are summarized in Elmer H. Burack and Thomas J. McNichols, *Human Resource Planning: Technology, Policy and Change* (Kent, O.: Kent State University Bureau of Business Research, 1973).

10. D. S. Pugh, D. J. Hickson, and C. R. Hinnings, "The Context of Organization Structures," *Administrative Science Quarterly,* 14, no. 1 (March 1969): 65–105.

11. David J. Hickson, Derek S. Pugh, and Diana C. Pheysey, "Operations Technology and Organization Structure: An Empirical Reappraisal," *Administrative Science Quarterly,* 14, no. 3 (September 1969): 378–397.

12. Howard E. Aldrich, "Technology and Organization Structure: A Re-examination of the Findings of the Aston Group," *Administrative Science Quarterly,* 17, no. 1 (March 1972): 26–43. Also see Andrew J. Grimes and Stuart M. Klein, "The Technology Imperative: The Relative Impact of Task Unit, Modal Equity, and Expectancy," *Academy of Management Journal,* 16, no. 4 (December 1973): 583–598. The description of Aldrich's position is presented here to sharpen the issues in the size-technology discussions and to establish, subsequently, points of compatibility.

13. Aldrich, "Technology and Organization Structure," pp. 33.

14. Ibid., p. 32.

15. For an interesting discussion of the organization and problems of some of these units, see Louis M. Stern, "Merging under Scrutiny," *Harvard Business Review,* 47, no. 4 (July–August 1969).

16. E. R. F. W. Crossman, "Automation, Skill and Manpower Predictions," in *Seminar on Manpower Policy and Program* (Washington, D.C.: U.S. Government Printing Office, 1966).

17. Crossman, "Automation."

18. The cost functions in panel B suggest the benefits of mass production versus batch systems with volume increases. In turn, to the extent that intermediate-level systems can be transformed to full flow, advanced, process-type systems, further economies are realizable. The cost functions in panel C emerged from the Management and Automation Study (see note 11).

19. Based on Burack and McNichols, *Human Resource Planning.*

20. Other aspects are treated in J. Inkson, Derek S. Pugh, and David J. Hickson, "Organization Context and Structure: An Abbreviated Replication," *Administrative Science Quarterly,* 15, no. 3 (September 1970): 318–329.

21. The age of the firm as it relates to certain activities associated with change, adaptation, and R&D has been investigated by Anthony Akel in "Age of Firm, Change and Adaptations by R&D," in process.

REFERENCES

Technology: Production

Aldrich, Howard E. "Technology and Organizational Structure: Re-Examination of the Findings of the Aston Group." *Administrative Science Quarterly,* 17, no. 1 (March 1972): 26–43.

Beaumont, R., and R. Halfgott. *Management, Automation, and People.* New York: Industrial Relations Counselors, 1964.

Blauner, R. *Alienation and Freedom.* Chicago: University of Chicago Press, 1964.

Bright, J. R. *Automation and Management.* Cambridge, Mass.: Harvard University Graduate School of Business Administration, Division of Research, 1958.

Burack, Elmer H. "Technology and Industrial Supervision: A Model Building Approach." *Academy of Management Journal,* 9, no. 1 (March 1966).

––––––. "Technology and Supervisory Practice: A Preliminary View." *Human Organization,* 26, no. 4 (Winter 1967): 256–264.

–––––– and Frank H. Cassell. "Technological Change and Manpower Development in Advanced Production Systems." *Academy of Management Journal,* 10, no. 3 (September 1967).

Woodward, Joan. *Industrial Organization: Theory and Practice.* London: Oxford University Press, 1965.

Technology: Forecasts, Diffusion

Baram, Michael S. "Law and the Social Control of Corporate Technology." *Technology Assessment,* 1, no. 4 (1973): 225–237.

Bright, James R. *Technological Forecasting for Industry and Government.* Englewood Cliffs, N.J.: Prentice-Hall, 1968.

Cetron, Marvin J., and Don H. Overly. "Disagreeing with the Future." *Technology Assessment,* 1, no. 4 (1973): 245–255.

Coates, Joseph F. "Technology Assessment: The Benefits . . . the Costs . . . the Consequences." *Futurist* (December 1971), p. 225.

Faunce, W. "Automation in the Automobile Industry: Some Consequences for In-Plant Social Structure." *American Sociological Review,* 23, no. 4 (August 1958): 401–407.

Harvey, Edward. "Technology and Structure of Organizations." *American Sociological Review,* 33, no. 2 (April 1968): 247–259.

Hattery, Lowell H. "Corporate Technology Assessment." *Technology Assessment,* 1, no. 4 (1973): 219–225.

Huddle, F. P. "The Social Management of Technological Consequences." *Futurist* (February 1972).

National Academy of Sciences. *Technology: Process of Assessment and Choice.* Washington, D.C.: U.S. Government Printing Office, 1969.

Springer, M., "Social Indicatory, Reports and Accounts: Toward the Management of Society." *Annals of the American Academy of Political Social Science,* 388 (March 1970).

Thrall, C. A., and J. M. Starr (eds.). *Technology, Power and Social Change.* Boston: D. C. Heath, 1972.

Turoff, M. "Communication Procedures in Technological Forecasting." Annual meeting paper, I.E.E.E., March 1973.

————. "An Alternative Approach to Cross-Impact Analysis." *Technological Forecasting and Social Change,* 3 (1972): 309–339.

————. "Delphi Conferencing: Computer-based Conferencing with Anonymity." *Technological Forecasting and Social Change,* 3 (1972): 199–204.

Utterback, James, and Elmer H. Burack. "Technological Innovation and Organizational Processes." Paper presented at the international meeting of the Institute of Management Sciences, Boston, 1974.

————. "The Process of Technological Innovation within the Firm." *Academy of Management Journal,* 14, no. 1 (March 1971): 75–88.

Technology and Environment

Burack, Elmer H., and Thomas J. McNichols. *Human Resource Planning: Technology, Policy, Change.* Kent, O.: Bureau of Business and Economic Research, Kent State University, 1973.

Emery, F. E., and E. L. Trist. "The Causal Texture of Organizational Environments." *Human Relations,* 18 (1965): 21–31.

————. "Socio-Technical Systems" in C. W. Churchman and M. Verhulst (eds.), *Management Sciences: Models and Techniques,* vol. 11. London: Pergamon Press, 1960.

Hunt, Raymond G. "Technology and Organization." *Academy of Management Journal,* 13, no. 3 (September 1970): 236–252.

Lipstreau, O., and K. Reed. "A New Look at the Organizational Implications of Automation." *Academy of Management Journal,* 8, no. 1 (March 1965): 24–31.

Mann, Floyd C., and R. L. Hoffman. *Automation and the Worker: A Study of Social Change in Power Plants.* New York: Holt, Rinehart and Winston, 1960.

Meyer, M. W. "Automation and Bureaucratic Structure." *American Journal of Sociology,* 74, no. 3 (November 1968): 256–264.

Mohr, Lawrence B. "Organizational Technology and Organizational Structure." *Administrative Science Quarterly,* 16, no. 4 (December 1971): 444–459.

Pugh, Derek S., David J. Hickson, and Diana C. Pheysey. "Operation Technology and Organization Structure: An Empirical Reappraisal." *Administrative Science Quarterly,* 14, no. 3 (September 1969): 378–397.

Rice, A. K. *The Enterprise and Its Environment.* London: Tavistock, 1963.

Sayles, L. *Behavior of Industrial Work Groups.* New York: John Wiley & Sons, 1958.

Technology and the American Economy. Washington, D.C.: U.S. Government Printing Office, 1966.

Trist, E. L., and K. W. Bamforth. "Some Social and Psychological Consequences of the Long-Wall Method of Goal-Getting." *Human Relations,* 4, no. 1 (February, 1951): 3–38.

Trist, E. L., G. W. Higgins, H. Murray, and A. B. Pollock. *Organizational Choice.* London: Tavistock, 1963.

Terreberry, Shirley. "The Evolution of Organizational Environments." *Administrative Science Quarterly,* 12, no. 4 (March 1968): 590–613.

Walker, Charles. *Toward the Automatic Factory: A Case Study of Men and Machines.* New Haven, Conn.: Yale University Press, 1957.

————— and R. H. Guest. *The Man on the Assembly Line.* Cambridge, Mass.: Harvard University Press, 1952.

————— and Arthur N. Turner. *The Foreman on the Assembly Line.* Cambridge, Mass.: Harvard University Press, 1956.

Woodward, Joan (ed.). *Industrial Organization: Behavior and Control.* London: Oxford University Press, 1970.

Learning Objectives

Elaborating Features of the Socio-Technical System
    Role Participants' Relationships
    Supervisory Support System
    Other Support Systems
    System Boundaries
Performance
    Alternate Models: Technological vs. Behavioral
    Influence of Technological and Supervisory Factors
Change and the Socio-Technical System
    Redefinition of Worker Skill
    Shifting Organizational Functions
    Level of Technological Advancement and Supervisory
        Functions
Recap and Alternate Approaches to Analyzing Socio-Technical
        Systems
    Use of Environmental Descriptors, "Uncertainty" and
        "Complexity"
    Simulation
    Summary of Technology and Structure Approaches

Chapter 4

TECHNOLOGICAL SYSTEMS (PART 2): THE SOCIO-TECHNICAL COMPLEX

OVERVIEW

This chapter extends the analyses of Chapter 3 by providing an elaboration of concepts useful in dealing with complex socio-technical systems. Technical change in the high-volume production units of the baking industry is used as an initial point of departure to develop various system-to-system comparisons, pose questions, and suggest characterizations that may be useful in socio-technical analyses.

The first series of analyses focuses on system features, participant roles, and relationships. Some of the key subsystems that support central work processes are described along with the manner in which work establishes worker roles and relationships. Next, performance is considered, including alternate approaches, technological and behavioral, in bringing about accomplishments and variations.

Change is a central force reshaping jobs, relationships, organization, and attendant worker skill. In these discussions, improvements in technology are translated in terms of their likely consequences on organization features, responsibilities, and systems.

In the concluding discussion, descriptive bases for characterizing socio-technical systems are summarized, along with the introduction of two alternate approaches. In one of the newly introduced procedures, "uncertainty-complexity analysis," approaches are described for portraying features of both external and internal environments that shape organizations, systems, and job roles. These approaches are attracting a great deal of attention from theoreticians and empiricists in design. Construction of models depicting complex systems, and especially models that are amenable to computer approaches, characterizes simulation procedures. An example of this approach is provided, along with some useful inferences emerging from this type of model.

HIGH-VOLUME BAKERIES

High-volume bread-baking firms are of special interest because they represent a bridge between mechanically based unit and mass production systems, and process or automated systems.[1] Also, the comparative simplicity of these production units assists in relating technological features to organization and job characteristics, and ultimately to individual behavior.

Exhibit 4-1 shows three plants (A, B, C), each of which illustrates a technology at a point on a continuum of progressive technical refinement. As more highly mechanized production is achieved, the work structure changes. The seventeen workers required to operate plant A become only six workers in plant C. The job-related movements of workers also change considerably. In plant A, worker dispersion reflects highly subdivided, routinized tasks. Plant C is characterized by a high level of movement, but the movement does not mean that the workers have more to do. It really reflects a major change in the composition of the workers' tasks: doing in plant A, monitoring and patrolling in plant C.

From these observations we can see how the general properties of technological systems are translated into the specifics of change, including the kinds of equipment that must be added. The technological systems in this industry have been engineered to the point that level-to-level changes have been codified in great detail, including cost economies and returns. Exhibit 4-2 summarizes the impact of change on the worker groups in terms of craft skills and important job functions and roles.

Unfortunately, the behavioral aspects of job demands are given little attention in decisions to update productive facilities. For example, perhaps the work demands on the foreman with six workers actually exceed those on the foreman with seventeen workers. It is important, then, to consider the following qualifying conditions in attempting to determine a so-called optimum ratio of supervisors to subordinates:

1. Relative expertise of the workers
2. Number of problems emerging from the system
3. Frequency with which these problems occur

Changes in skill (level and type) are characteristic of shifts from low-level technologies toward advanced technologies for high-volume production.[2] Supervision assumes a greater role in maintaining system output, supported by broader, more impersonal controls. These developments illustrate some of the behavioral and interpersonal implications of technological change. The wide dispersion of workers to relatively isolated positions, "watch and wait" activities, and the responsibility of the supervisor for process flow maintenance rather than worker direction suggest new types of relationships among workers and supervisors.

EXHIBIT 4–1. Changes in Technology and Dispersion of Operating Personnel in High-Volume Bread Plants

Plant A Basic production unit	Plant B Mechanized material handling	Plant C Continuous production
Manpower: 1 foreman 17 workers	Manpower: 1 foreman 12 workers	Manpower: 1 foreman 6 workers
Production features: Manual material handling Minimal automatic control Basic production equipment	Production features: Mechanized material handling partially accomplished Extend automatic controls Higher productivity equipment	Production features: Complete mechanization of material handling Automatic control and direction of most production steps Integrated production equipment
Worker features: Material handling (manual) Equipment assignments Small groups—bridge production units; assignments to critical points	Worker features: Modest manual material handling Equipment assignments Clusters—bridge some production units; assignments to critical points	Worker features: Monitoring Widely dispersed—mostly solitary patrol assignments

EXHIBIT 4–2. Organizational Implications of Technological Change in a Group of Commercial Bakeries

Technological changes

Mechanization
Process controls
Equipment integration
Division of labor

Organizational shifts

Workers	Supervisors	Systems
Craft skills *down*	Direction *down*	Disruption cost *up*
Task involvement *down*	Flow maintenance *up*	Impersonal controls *up*
Schedule adherence *up*	Craft background *down*	Use of specialists *up*
Monitoring *up*	Standby time *up*	Emphasis on:
Mobility *down*	Number of subordinates *down*	Long-range plans
Work pace control *up*	Responsibility for execution *up*	Quality control
Experience factor *down*	Short-run planning *up*	Industrial engineers
Isolation *up*		Logistics

THE TECHNOLOGICAL CONTINUUM: INDUSTRIAL APPLICATIONS

The notion of the technological continuum may be applied to a distribution of production units in the baking industry in terms of their relative technical sophistication.[3] The profile of baking industry units in Exhibit 4–3 indicates a shift during a comparatively short period (ten to fifteen years), beginning in the late 1940s and early 1950s. Note that the distribution of

EXHIBIT 4–3. Technological Distribution of Commercial Bread Units: 1940s–1960s

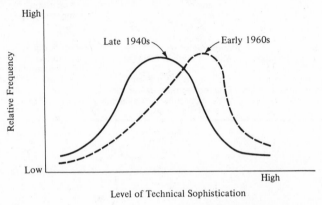

Given: 1 State of baking art
2 State of art in equipment manufacture

From E. H. Burack research studies, "Technology Working Papers" (1965–1969).

technology in this industry has shifted toward more advanced mechanized production, materials transfer equipment, and process controls. However, not all of these shifts occurred within the framework of the baking art and its equipment *as it was then known*. The discovery of new techniques, new approaches to production, or the installation of new designs in equipment destroys the underlying assumptions of a given state of the industrial arts for a theoretical distribution of production units. The actual distribution reflects the emergence of new technological concepts that constitute the leading edge of technical innovation. At any point in time, as a matter of fact, a distribution of technical sophistication reflects, at its upper limits, elements of new industrial arts.

One might well question whether there is some lower-level state of technology wherein production is uneconomical. From the data provided in Exhibit 4–3, the answer would be a qualified no. Production units can operate at what appear to be less than profitable levels of productivity (in manufacturing) because of certain other factors in the industry. Such factors in the commercial bread industry include economies of scale, geographical location, and individual market taste, as well as the basis of ownership—individual or corporate—where ownership is willing to assume different profits or risks. There is also a possibility that the marginal cost difference between the most advanced baking firms and those that are less advanced is such that lower operating costs (and hence profit contribution) may not be sufficient to upset the overall financial balance of the organization. Some firms also employ other economies, such as managerial efficiencies or leverage in advertising, which may make up for what would otherwise be excessive production costs.

Aside from the technological implications of these industry distributions, a series of key questions arises regarding the socio-technical systems in these different states of technological refinement. Alterations in the activities of the supervisors, managers, and workers who staff the firms are of special interest. One must confront such organizational questions as "How do organizations' functions and the activities of their manpower compare with their counterparts in less advanced firms?" "Can the same type of foreman direct the activities of a seventeen-man crew in a lower-level technology as well as a group of five or six in an advanced production unit?"

FEATURES OF THE SOCIO-TECHNICAL SYSTEM

Technical and Social Subsystems

> The concept of a socio-technical system arose from the consideration that any production system requires both a technological organization—equipment and process layout—and a work organization relating to each other those who carry out the necessary tasks. The technological demands place limits on the type of work organization possible, but a work organization has social and psychological properties of its own that are independent of technology.[4]

Rice's research (of Indian Textile Mills) enforced the contention that a productive organization is a socio-technical system where the subsystems are articulated in order to achieve effective performance. Specifically, Rice's research dealt with determining why the introduction of new automatic loom machines in an Indian manufacturing plant did not increase worker productivity. It appeared that the worker morale was good and the supervisor-worker relationships were also good. What, then, was the problem? The researchers found that ambiguities existed in the relationships among the workers; that is, twelve different occupational roles were assigned to individual workers to assure continuous operation of the looms.

The solution that was proposed was to hold a group of workers responsible for a group of looms and to have a leader responsible for each group. The different groups also shared the previous fractionalized job assignments. The results obtained by adoption of the proposed solution were increases in worker productivity.

The following adjustments were also made to (hopefully) continue the increase in productivity:

> Allow adequate time for the training of new workers
>
> Provide spare workers for increased stoppage rates with increased speed of production
>
> Keep a group on the same type of yarn as long as possible.
>
> Confine experimental types of yarn to whole groups rather than spreading them over all groups

Trist's studies of British coal mines[5] investigated how certain technological changes—the introduction of the longwall system—affected the reorganization of jobs, work relationships, and productivity. His conclusions were similar to Rice's in that both noted the importance of the socio-psychological system that was associated with the new technical system or technology that had been adapted by the firms studied. (Some detailed results of Trist's and Rice's studies are outlined at the end of this chapter.)

SYSTEM BOUNDARIES

Organization boundaries and boundary interfaces have direct effects on job satisfaction and worker productivity. They delineate systems or subsystems subject to various environmental influences and change.

Katz and Kahn noted:

> In general, positions contained deep within the organizational structure were relatively conflict-free; positions located near the skin or boundary of the organization were likely to be conflict-ridden. Thus jobs involving labor negotiations, purchasing, selling, or otherwise representing the organization to the public were subjected to greater stress. Living near an intraorganization boundary—for example, serving as liaison between two or more departments—revealed many of the same effects but to a lesser degree.[6]

Kahn's research shows that system boundaries affect the degree of role conflict within the organization. Boundary interfaces, as noted, also affect worker productivity. Katz and Kahn identify three types of boundary systems that emphasize the input-transformation-output process:

1. The procurement operation

2. The disposal function

3. The institutional (organizational) system

The procurement system concerns the input of materials to be converted and the input of personnel to get the job done, that is, procurement of materials and recruiting of personnel. The disposal function deals with marketing the product, and the purpose of this function is to induce the public to purchase the product of the organization. The institutional system involves the interaction of the firm with society, its central mission.

Rice and Trist have shown that job boundaries must be clearly defined. In the British coal mine study the artificial distinctions between the jobs failed to recognize the common underlying ability required of all miners. Because work boundaries were not clearly defined and because the new technical system was not coordinated with the needed social system, or with the work system that was appropriate for the utilization of the workers' experience and ability, the productive performance of the workers declined.[7]

Socio-technical systems, as noted in this and the preceding discussion, establish a "plane" of jobs and job relationships and present an important initiating point for behavioral analyses. The next discussion brings out more aspects of these interrelationships.

ROLES AND RELATIONSHIPS

Exhibit 4–4 brings together several important elements in model form that constitute the relationships found in the socio-technical complex, including the following:

1. Formal work roles, including workers, foremen, managers, and technical (staff) support groups

2. Formally prescribed relationships (discussed further in Chapter 8)

3. The links between communication and information systems that provide the basis for the conduct of both formal and informal relationships and functions. These links are crucial in determining the effectiveness of the system.

4. The range of behavioral demands within work systems, from the purely "technical" to the "informal"

The man on the production line is constrained in his work-related activity by the discipline of the technology, supervisory surveillance, and organizational controls. In addition, the function and performance of the individual

EXHIBIT 4–4. Groups and Relationships in Socio-Technical Systems

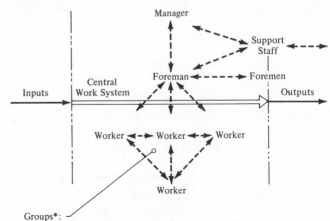

Groups*:
    Technological: specific to job, job relations; confers authority status,
    Formal: organization requirements to maintain affiliation
    Informal: voluntary interaction
    Non-formal: allowable deviation in "formal"

* Concepts clarified in R. Dubin, *The World of Work* (Englewood Cliffs, N.J.: Prentice-Hall, 1958).

are mediated by motivational processes that reflect his perception of his environment and his colleagues. The worker, manager, or professional exhibits a variety of behavioral patterns, including the "technological," which pertain specifically to the job, and the "formal," which typically are prescribed by rules and regulations.[8] The combination of "technological" and "formal" behavioral patterns constitutes an *external system*, within which are "non-formal" and "informal" patterns, designated the *internal system*. Where organizational systems lack the structuring of a work technology, proportionally greater weight is placed on other constraints or guidelines.

In the internal system, values governing behavior may be internalized, and an opportunity provided for individuals to work out meaningful relationships in terms of life goals. However, stresses may be "locked in," and therefore preclude the working out of meaningful relationships, either within a work situation or in terms of life goals. The *internal system* is not typically the result of singular actions by the organization but rather a bilateral interaction between organizational personnel and authority levels. Its actions, in turn, feed back on and affect the *external system*. Consequently, production procedures or rules, for example, may be moderated from pressures exerted by the *internal system*. (This point is expanded in Chapter 8.)

TAXONOMY OF SUPPORT GROUPS

Exhibit 4–4 defines a number of work roles that are crucial to organizational performance. Among these roles is one in particular that has received inadequate attention from organization theorists: that of the technical (staff) support groups. Support groups fall into three categories:

1. *Technological process support groups,* which include maintenance, production, electrical, and mechanical, and pertain primarily to process maintenance and performance

2. *Supervisory-process support groups,* which include control groups (production and quality) and industrial engineers. These personnel interact with supervisors, managers, workers, and work process and staff groups that have more general missions (personnel, research, etc.).

3. *Administrative support groups,* which include personnel, systems, and general administrative functions. These groups provide vital links between organization functions and possess the administrative capacity needed for maintaining the organization.

What is the significance of such a taxonomy? The three types above suggest essentially different preparation, needs, and functions. For example, organizational changes have different effects on these three types of groups. That is, responsibilities, skills, and educational needs for each are affected by change but *not* uniformly. If technological changes are introduced that shift the bases of work processes from mechanical to electronic systems, *process support groups* will be forced to master a significantly different industrial art. The use of linear programming models, sophisticated continuous-quality monitoring equipment, and job-shop scheduling models are among the newer tools for supervisory-support groups under modified process conditions. Finally, technological changes of the type described affect the general administrative groups. Increased process interdependencies necessitate the revision of procedures and the basis for interconnecting work-related units. The personnel function is now confronted with a new set of manpower needs.

In short, a support group taxonomy directs the attention of the analyst away from the amorphous classification "support" to one where duties, modified functions, education and training needs, and work relationships can be logically prescribed or anticipated. This predictive capability is attainable, in one way, through simulation approaches. The simulation model is a highly effective technique for formulating the "what if?" kind of management question and then providing information that will guide decisions. More on this approach shortly.

In extending these discussions of socio-technical systems, another relationship to be developed is that between the form or sophistication of the system and attendant worker skill requirements. The latter notion is a key term in virtually any discussion of work.

The discussions thus far in the chapter have stressed general attributes of socio-technical systems; performance or productivity has received little attention. Yet the supervisory subsystem may play an important role in performance, the technical features notwithstanding. The following discussion introduces and develops the role and impact of supervision on performance.

TECHNOLOGY, SUPERVISION, AND PERFORMANCE

Of particular interest in assessing output and productivity are the factors of production technology and supervision and the influences of work associates ("friends" and "informal groups").[9] The contribution of the worker himself is set aside temporarily. Functionally, this focus is reflected in the expression Productivity $=f$ (Technology, leadership, and group influences).

The role of technology in performance may be viewed as an increasingly pervasive force as one scans the technological continuum, ranging from a modest force in "craft level" systems to a major determinant in advanced process systems.

In "man-machine" systems the worker may have an important influence on quality, and perhaps even quantity of output, depending on the type of production system.

The Crossman work noted in Chapter 3 dramatically highlights the performance designed into advanced process systems; thus quality and quantity are largely engineering decisions made at the planning stage of a project. In low-level unit or small-batch production, the frequent dominance of general-purpose equipment (or mechanical information processes) often permits a high degree of worker influence. We can conclude that *non*technical influences on performance are more important considerations in less advanced technologies and of lesser importance in more advanced technologies. What is the character of these nontechnical influences on productivity? Traditionally, supervision has played an important role because of its impact on the performance of organizational units.

Supervision influences output through both directive authority and leadership. The efficacy of the three major functions of managerial personnel—technical, administrative, and human relations—may be affected by some of the structural considerations (specialization, division of labor, allocation of responsibilities) developed in Chapter 2. Particularly in the decentralized unit, more reliance may be placed on individual supervisory capabilities, thus permitting the supervisor to better develop the best qualities of his subordinates. In proposition form, this suggests that the fewer the authority layers and formal controls, the better the communications, the more opportunities to improve human relations, and the greater the reliance on leadership.[10]

The idea that size alone tends to influence morale is closely related to this point. Small organizations are thought to be better able to establish high morale than large units.[11] However, some research has reported more favorable situations in medium-size organizations.[12]

From the standpoint of leadership, significant areas of functional responsibility have been taken away from the foreman. He no longer "hires, pays, promotes, demotes, or fires his men." [13] Thus his inability to provide direct rewards and punishment detracts from his role as a leader. On the other hand, leadership performance may be improved to the extent that a supervisor can

1. Counterbalance the social isolation resulting from the impersonal effects of size and centralized decision making

2. Act as a buffer between workers and the effects of higher management decisions

3. Mediate conflict between staff or line supervision and worker groups

Informal groups can also influence output to the extent that they affect the standards of output through group action. From the standpoint of technological change, how can group behavior be used in a positive way to gain acceptance for changes in production methods, processes, or techniques? [14] Some answers will be implicit in subsequent sections.

THE FIRST-LINE SUPERVISORY ROLE AND PRODUCTIVITY

Fritz Roethlisberger's apt characterization of the foreman as the "man in the middle" [15] suggests a good perspective for understanding the pressures and changes in the foreman's role with respect to such issues as

1. The potential effectiveness of first-line supervision in small, as opposed to large, organizations, and the implications for training personnel and staff support groups

2. The effects of supervisory pressure and whether, under certain conditions, the lessening of pressure might have negative effects on productivity

3. The conflicts that emerge from the responsibilities assigned to supervision and the type of dependence shown by subordinates, and how these potential conflicts and dependencies might be affected by the character and level of technology

TECHNOLOGICAL AND BEHAVIORAL MODELS

The behavioral scientist and the technologist often use basically different models and perspectives in their approaches to organizational analysis (these approaches are illustrated in Exhibit 4–5). The technologist may use as his point of departure the technological system; from this he deduces the extent to which formal role demands affect the allocation of responsibility, the character of analytical and control problems, and the levels of productivity.

The behavioral model of the firm might include such variables as supervisory attitudes, leadership qualities, or informal group processes that influence the worker and affect creativity, motivation, morale, job satisfaction, and productivity. Note that in the case of productivity, both the behavioral and the technological models may lead to the same output variable. The

EXHIBIT 4–5. Technological and Behavioral Models for Organizational Analysis

A behavioral approach

Inputs:	→ Worker →	Outputs
• Supervisory attitudes, interpersonal relationships, or quality of leadership • Informal group processes		• Level of creativity • Motivation • Morale/job satisfaction • Level of productivity, quality

Given: A State of Technology

A technological approach

Inputs:	→ Prod. System →	Outputs:
• Change • State of technology • Features of the production system		• Formal role demands (external system) • Level of productivity/quality • Character of analytical, planning, and control problems • Informal organization (internal system)

Given: Supervisor-Worker Relationships

behavioral model assumes a given technological condition; that is, it specifies the level of technology at which the variables affecting worker motivation are relevant. A similar discipline might be applied to the technological model by presenting this question: *Given* a certain supervisory-worker relationship, what might be the impact of technological changes in a particular production system on various output features of the system?

Change is a central force in organizational life, occasioning the continuing analysis, design, or redrafting of structural and work arrangements. It forms the basis for the next series of discussions.

Change and Socio-Technical Systems

SKILL AND THE LEVEL OF TECHNOLOGY

One link between behavior and technology is the manpower-skill requirements that accompany technological changes in system operation.

Exhibit 4–6, which shows the need for skills in relation to the state of the technology, suggests that the required job skills vary widely in low-level (unit or small batch) production systems, ranging from purely physical exertion in a road gang (nominal skill) to such occupations as tool-room polisher, which demands a low level of mechanization but a high level of craft art. As intermediate states of technology are reached (as in mass production, automotive assembly, or appliance lines), the range of worker aptitudes required by the system narrows—skill requirements decrease for the lower-level craft arts but increase for the manual work groups. This phenomenon has caused a great deal of confusion in reporting changes in the level of skill required by changes in production technology, and the confusion is due to differing bases for comparison. For automated systems, some uncertainty exists as to the levels of skill required. In this case the confusion results from the fact that the definition of "skill" for automated systems varies widely.

Modification of skill requirements reflects the joint interaction of needed worker attributes and job requirements. Worker abilities are based on education, experience, and personal traits; on job duties, decision making, and influence on productivity; and on seniority (tenure), location, and work

EXHIBIT 4–6. Variations in Skill Requirements According to Level of Technology

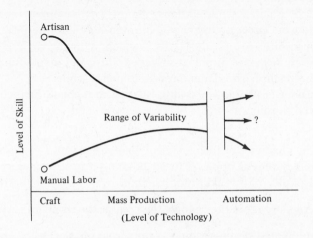

conditions. When these worker attributes and job factors are jointly viewed over varying levels of mechanization and automation, seemingly contrary skill trends can be rationalized.

With replacement of machine operators for automated operations, equipment adjustment is more complex and requires a wider range of technical knowledge and competence. The relative changes in requisite skills depend on the degree of sophistication of predecessor systems. At some point, however, the automation of equipment and processes begins to reduce skill demands on the workers. New process components require new job functions, such as an "electronic maintenance man," but these developments are counterbalanced by a reduced need for many traditional, craft-oriented skills (less downtime). Consequently, a wide variety of quantitative changes takes place in maintenance groups, ranging from reductions to expansions. Finally, little need is visualized for engineers and technicians to design and operate the highly automatic units.

Occasionally, engineering graduates may be hired as line or maintenance supervisors in response to missing ingredients of alertness, perception, and judgment in equipment operation and the implications of downtime. Extensive retraining and major skill shortages in automated plants do not appear to describe the situation realistically. However, important compensation issues may emerge that necessitate careful analysis of proper bases for compensating automated jobs and developing pay systems where automated and nonautomated jobs exist side by side.

There seem to be at least two different definitions of "skill." In one, skill is interpreted in terms of the traditional motor skills, such as dexterity and coordination. These are associated with older production systems, including both craft and mass production operations. As newer, more advanced systems appear, skill has had to be redefined.

In successive steps from the intermediate-level (mass production) technologies, worker and superior are dispersed over wider production areas: concentrated in isolated work stations, removed from direct interpersonal contact in the work process, and engaged in more monitoring positions. The emphasis thus shifts to "mental skills," which demand such abilities as prompt, accurate response, problem-solving ability, and mental dexterity. In short, the shift in emphasis is from physical to mental skills.

The dimensions of manpower skill in relation to technological change can be summarized as follows.

1. The character of technological change (updating a mass production system as opposed to introducing a process-flow system, for example) affects skill requirements.

2. The more rapid the change, the greater the strain on current skills.

3. Automated systems require a shift from physical to mental skills.[16]

TRANSITIONAL PRODUCTION SYSTEMS: MASS PRODUCTION TOWARD AUTOMATION

Exhibit 4–7 illustrates the shifts in technology from a lower base toward more advanced systems in which the supervisor-worker relationships and the functional aspects of supervision undergo modification. This exhibit provides a quantitative comparison of those features of supervision that involve direction, control, and administration. In the highly automated systems, the supervisory span becomes much smaller in view of the total set of supervisory activities. Similarly, direct interaction with subordinates or others for purposes of coordination takes up a much smaller portion of the supervisor's time, so more time appears to be available for the standby and administrative activities characteristic of the supervisor's function. Again, the tran-

EXHIBIT 4–7. Some Principal Functions of Supervision and the State of Technology

	State of technology[1]			
	Low A	B	C	High
	(Job shop	Auto assy.	High vol.)	High vol.
		Line	Bread #1	Bread #2
Supervisory direction of subordinates[2]	33.7%[5]	18.3%[5]	1.6%	0.8%
Supervisory control and coordination activities[3]	25.1	23.9	26.7	9.5
Supervisory standby and administrative functions[4]	41.2	57.8	71.7	90.5

1. Figures are rounded to facilitate comparison.
2. Direct supervisory interaction with *subordinates* (operator, utility, or repair) to correct/aid their activity.
3. Direct supervisory contact with colleagues, superiors, and operation specialists (maintenance, quality control, standards, scheduling, production control, material handling, etc.) in order to check or regulate current operations.
4. Includes the servicing of operator needs (wages, hours, absenteeism, etc.), casual observation, standby, and idle time.
5. These two studies were carried out in essentially identical manner. Figures were consolidated to facilitate comparison, as indicated in notes 2, 3, 4.

Sources: John N. Yanouzas, "A Comparative Study of Work Organization and Supervisory Behavior," *Human Organization*, 23, no. 3 (Fall 1964), 245–253. Charles R. Walker, Robert H. Guest, and Arthur N. Turner, *The Foreman on the Assembly Line* (Cambridge, Mass.: Harvard University Press, 1956), p. 86. Elmer H. Burack, "Technology and Supervisory Practices: A Comparative Analysis," *Human Organizations*, 26, no. 4 (Winter 1967).

sition from physical activities to mental processes places a premium on quick, accurate response, problem solving, and a temperament suited to "watch and wait."

TECHNOLOGICAL CHANGE, FUNCTION, AND ORGANIZATION

The organizational implications of shifts toward mass production systems are summarized in Exhibits 4–8A and 4–8B. In the less advanced technologies we note that additional specialization, mechanization, and the introduction of process controls affect the needs of the work system. The routinization of tasks or subdivision of activities makes it necessary for the worker to adhere to schedules. Change has an impact on the supervisor's directive functions, control activities, and both the technical and nontechnical aspects of his administrative responsibilities. However, these changes are not uniform in the sense of requiring more or less directive effort. Increased dependence upon machines, for example, might require more supervisory direction because of an absence of worker skills. From the broader point of view of organizational systems, planning may assume additional importance, impersonal controls may increase, and the technical staff support groups may become more important.

EXHIBIT 4–8. A. Supervision and Technological Change: Toward Mass Production

Technological change		
Single items or low-order combinations of		
Division of labor	System logistics	
Mechanization	Specialization	
Process control	Time dependencies	

Effects on work system needs and problems		
Workers	*Supervisors*	*System*
Job knowledge *down*	Need for knowledge *up*	Impersonal controls *up*
Routinization *up*	Retraining *up*	Use of technical specialists *up*
Subdivided tasks *up*	Machine responsibility *up*	Broader planning for production and quality *up*
Mobility *down*	Maintenance flow *up*	Authority levels *up*
Work pace control *down*	Short-run planning *up*	First-line span *up*
Monetary incentives (?)	Work with colleagues *up*	
Dependency on machines *up*	Work with technical specialists *up*	
Craft lore *down*	Responsibility to develop *down;* to carry out *up*	
	Service worker needs *up*	

EXHIBIT 4–8. B. Organization Changes in More Advanced Process Systems

Technological changes

Mechanization
Process controls/computers
Equipment improvements

Involve

System	Worker requirements	Managerial–support
Cost of disruption *up* More delicately *balanced* Operating efficiencies *critical*	Motor skills *decreased* Mental skills *increased* Monitoring, interpretation, problem solving *up*	Use of system specialists *up* Need for coordination *up* System orientation *up* Greater need to work with colleagues

Leading to

Modified Organizational

Functions	and	Focus
Scheduling at higher levels Upward shift of power and responsibility Emphasis shifts from production to perfecting information system		Short-run outlook to long-run planning Greater reliance on impersonal controls Growing sensitivity to importance of manpower resources Heightened importance of managing change

These shifts in organizational structure have additional consequences for the role of supervision. For example, the increasing participation of technical specialists in areas traditionally controlled by line supervisors suggests that the short-run planning responsibilities of supervisors become relatively more important than long-run planning responsibilities, which are reassigned to higher organization levels. Exhibits 4–8A and 4–8B highlight some of these factors. This type of summary (or model) may be applied to a wide variety of technical changes by utilizing some of the general categories of system effects, supervisory effects, job effects, and other areas subject to the impact of technical change.

In Exhibit 4–9 a similar type of model is used for changes in "automated" systems. System changes in specialization, mechanization, process control, and the like may modify the degrees of integration in the system. Note the manner in which some of the activities move in opposite directions. This affects the worker when his job takes on new features, such as monitoring functions, increased mental attention, and adaptation or acquisition of new skills. At the same time, system changes have a substantial impact on super-

EXHIBIT 4–9. Supervision and Technological Change: Toward Automation

Technological change as combinations of

Division of labor	System logistics
Mechanization	Specialization
Process controls	Time dependencies

Effects on work system needs and problems

Workers	Supervision	System
Task specialization *up*	Proximity to unit *up*	Progressive, sequential, and integrated cost of breakdown *up*
Social isolation *up*	Needed education *up*	
Concept of skill *changed*	System maintenance responsibility *up*	Forward planning *up*
Monitoring *up*	Direction *down*	Ability to anticipate system *up*
Worker mobility (?)	Work with colleagues *up*	Impersonal controls *up*
Adherence to schedule *up*	Responsibility to develop *down;* to carry out *up*	Use of technical specialists *up*
Control of pace *down*		First-line span *down*
Need for quick and accurate response *up*	Work with specialists *up*	Authority levels *down*

visory performance and job demands. The cost of breakdowns rises, and technical specialists are added. These are the types of changes that affect the supervisor in a complex socio-technical system.

TECHNOLOGY: UNDERLYING DIMENSIONS, ALTERNATIVE APPROACHES

It is clear that technology (type or level) is an important variable affecting structural arrangement, but both alternative variables and more deeply rooted technical-organizational dimensions have been proposed. Aside from the Aston arguments (Pugh et al.) concerning size, "technical diffuseness" or specificity has been proposed by Edward Harvey as a more relevant descriptor than the technology measure.[17] This measure deals with technology form and the amount of change within the form.

Raymond Hunt goes beyond the general technology descriptor and provides an explanation and approach to clarifying the organizational similarities of "unit" and "process" production described in Woodward's studies.[18] His notion suggests that structuring is more specifically identified with the character of activities focused on (a) performance versus (b) problem solving. In "unit" production, there are a number of exceptions in processing orders and specifications requiring high problem-solving activity.

In process production, high rates of manufacturing place a premium on maintaining continuity—when exceptions occur (disruption, breakdown, off-specification), problem-solving activity is of major importance in reestablishing smooth-running, stable conditions. As an appendage to Hunt's observations, we should also note that Woodward herself has sought the underlying dimensions of the technology constructs. One aspect of these dimensions may be the presence of personal or mechanistic controls and the degree of layering (single versus multilevel) in the use of controls.[19] Thus new advances in research involving contingency approaches continue to refine and/or reshape the theories and methodologies employed in conjunction with them.

ANALYSIS OF SOCIO-TECHNICAL SYSTEMS

It is clear that organizational analysis may capitalize on a diverse group of conceptual approaches to meet differing needs. These approaches provide different perspectives on the organization, manpower, and systems in a socio-technical structure. The models that have been used in the first four chapters of this book are summarized in Exhibit 4–10, which highlights the areas in which they can be applied.

EXHIBIT 4–10. Conceptual Models in the Analysis of Technological Systems and Related Variables

Model	Focus	Derived organizational information
Woodward	Structure (static)	Levels of authority, first-line supervisory ratio, relative use of professional and technical personnel, control systems
Burack	Structure (change) with some emphasis on advanced systems	Authority levels, allocation of responsibilities, emergent problems (obsolescence), manpower planning and the management of change
Chandler	Structure	Centralization/decentralization, departmentalization, policy strategies and their relation to structure
Lawrence and Lorsch	Process of organization	Differentiation of functional specialties and department activities and integration of work and function. Role of coordinative functions
Pugh et al.	Structure, size, and character of business	Relative importance of organizational variables
Bright	Organizational systems	Properties of technical systems (profiles). Modification of work structures
Simulation	Organizational system	System properties, work necessities, role of ancillary systems in primary system performance

Although we have placed them within the category of "models for organizational analysis," the information disclosed and the perspectives differ substantially among the models. For example, both Woodward and Burack focus on technology, but Woodward probes structural variables and Burack emphasizes change, functional activities, and manpower issues. Chandler, like Woodward, concentrates on structure, but in response to management strategies rather than technology. His emphasis is on the emergence of various structural forms and configurations, with an eye to capitalizing on business opportunities and constraining internal forces.

In this context, the Pugh research team (Chapter 2 appendix) sheds light on organizational variables similar to those examined by Chandler. However, in the Pugh et al. approach an attempt is made to isolate organizational variables (e.g., size and character of the business) and to determine the relative contribution of each to structural development, using a quantitative approach.

In yet another attack on structural features, Lawrence and Lorsch examine the purpose and function of key units in the organization and set out the role demands of the coordinative functions.

The model proposed by Bright, or the systems simulation described in this chapter, provides bases for analyzing the properties of organizational systems as an initial step in analysis of relationships, flows, and attendant supporting activities.

Consequently, both the quantitative and the qualitative models described above reveal organizational features, but serve widely different purposes in a conceptual approach to organizational analysis.

UNCERTAINTY–COMPLEXITY ANALYSIS

What is sure to be a major activity among organizational analysts is the systematic study of structural-system problems using concepts of uncertainty and complexity. *Uncertainty* defines factors of which we lack full knowledge because they lie in the future, or are subject to forces outside our control. *Complexity* refers to situations involving many and varied elements or interdependencies. Early work by Burns and Stalker and more recent analysis by Lawrence and Lorsch, Jay Galbraith, Reeves and Turner, Robert Duncan, and Burack have established a fund of concepts and perspectives in this area.[20]

The central idea in the uncertainty–complexity (U–C) approach is the identification of those factors in a firm's external and internal environment that shape organizational needs for specialization, coordination, division of labor, and information features (quality, quantity, and feedback). When focused on a structural unit (e.g., division, department) or system (production, control, order processing), U–C analysis involves linking agents, span of control, number of authority levels, and such dimensions of decision making as problem identification and selection of alternatives.

To summarize, the U–C model seeks to identify important elements in both the external and internal environments of a company by degree of uncertainty or complexity and relate them to design requirements of the functions or systems being considered. Thus results of U–C analysis can be depicted as profile scales or bar charts, and a simplified example will assist in clarifying the U–C approach. Although this example is built largely around developments in the external environment, a similar approach would be indicated for issues emerging in internal environments, or for a combination of both.

EXAMPLE OF U–C ANALYSIS

The field sales division of a large manufacturer reflected progressively poorer performance in both sales and the servicing of client requests and complaints.

Analysis disclosed a pronounced shift in markets and competitive conditions. First, the entry of a number of new manufacturers vastly increased market uncertainties regarding competitive price strategies, product features, promotion plans, and services. Second, demographic and area analysis disclosed that market complexities had increased as a consequence of population shifts, indicating a need to deal with fractionated or decentralized markets rather than concentrated markets centered on major cities.

Further analysis disclosed (1) additional uncertainties about the competence of field personnel whose backgrounds were largely experience rather than training and education and (2) added complexities encountered by the manufacturer's salesmen because of greater technical complexity in the product and the availability of added product configurations.

The U–C analyses were represented in bar-chart form (Exhibit 4–11), depicting judgments of past levels of "U" and "C" compared (on a five-point scale) with emergent trends. "Values" were derived by seasoned managers making judgments based on general criteria supplied by the analysts.

For example, the uncertainty analyses regarding competitive trends indicated poor information feedback on emergent conditions. This discovery led eventually to a market research capability in the field sales division. Uncertainties regarding salesman competence led to a new training program for encumbents and a shift in recruiting policies toward men with formal education rather than simply field experience.

By the same token, complexity analysis revealing fractionation of markets indicated a more difficult job of coordination, information exchange, and need for specialization. The response to these needs led to the reorganization of the division into city and suburban sales departments (specialization), a "sales coordinator" to assure good use of personnel in the expanded sales territories, and careful meshing of promotional programs, field efforts, and after-sales service of accounts.

EXHIBIT 4–11. U–C Analysis

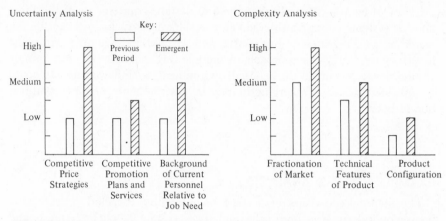

E. H. Burack, "Uncertainty–Complexity Approaches in the Planning for Health Care Systems," *Proceedings, Annual Meeting, Amer. Inst. of Decision Sciences,* Nov. 1972; and E. H. Burack and H. Zia Hassan, "A Newer Tool for Managerial Analysis," IIT Working Papers, 1973.

U–C ANALYSES AND PREVIOUS MODELS

Although these U–C discussions have advanced a newer tool for analysis, uncertainty and complexity features are embedded in the structures and systems already discussed. For example, low-level production technologies (unit or batch production) frequently contain uncertainty and complexity— processing jobs to customer order, job diversity, and multiple processing routes ("job-shop scheduling" options). Under these conditions, a first-level supervisor often assumes important job-related responsibilities for quality assurance, work flow, and the like. Such support systems as production control, although important, are limited in the assistance they can provide.

In intermediate-level systems (e.g., mass production of automobiles) the obvious complexities of size, multiple processes, and widely varying technologies—for example—are met through fixed-path materials travel, detailed procedures, extensive support assistance, production and engineering coordination, and specialization. Order-release programs and job de-skilling are further examples of how potential uncertainty is confronted. The high-volume characteristics of the market dictate a comprehensive economic system of production. Although the trim and style combinations are many (great diversity, as in batch production), all are concerned with one product, the automobile.

This same type of analysis can be extended to process or advanced production companies. The point is simply that U–C approaches relate to previous discussions, and represent a technique for arriving at specific recommendations once conceptual models for analysis have been developed.

MEASUREMENT IN U–C ANALYSIS

Uncertainty–complexity (U–C) analyses pose considerable measurement problems. The previous application or example of U–C analysis described a situation in which various management judgments were employed to derive elements comprising "U" and "C" and, subsequently, their ratings. This on-site, exploratory application sought to ascertain the utility to top management of isolating factors in their environment that influenced planning and decision making.[21] The opportunity for executives to view their assessments in a comparative manner proved of importance in reconciling previously unspoken assumptions and differences. Yet, to go beyond this type of tool application and develop measurements suitable for cross-comparisons and more precise approaches poses significant problems. Previously, for example, Lawrence and Lorsch attempted to set out more systematic approaches to environmental assessment (uncertainty), for which Henry Tosi et al. posed significant questions. Yet even in this critique of the Lawrence and Lorsch measurement approach, Tosi's group employed a "volatility" factor for uncertainty that Lawrence and Lorsch found unacceptable.[22]

SIMULATION EXAMPLE: SYSTEMS ANALYSIS

This simulation model[23] encompasses the total production system of a manufacturing firm and includes raw material (work-in-process) inventory, the production function, finished goods inventory, and shipping. The "intelligence" effort for coordinating production, procurement, sales, and shipping is vested in the support groups represented by decision centers I and II in Exhibit 4–12.

The relationships and operations in this model are characterized as follows:

1. *Operations.* Suppliers provide material inputs, which are temporarily stored in inventory (WIP). Raw materials are released to production, and the output of finished items is put into finished-goods inventory for subsequent shipment to customers.

2. *Decision centers.* These centers govern the inflow of raw materials and the shipment of finished items, based on receipt of orders from customers and prior management decisions regarding service policy, inventory investment, and production policy—as well as the physical limitations of suppliers, production equipment, warehouse space, and shipping capacity. This control is exercised on the basis of decision rules (impersonal controls) that guide the actions of the decision centers.

EXHIBIT 4–12. Simulated Production System with Information Control Support Functions

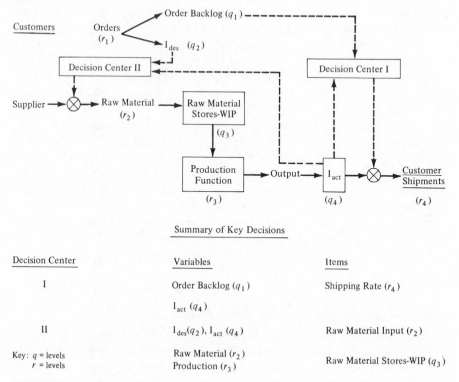

Summary of Key Decisions

Decision Center	Variables	Items
I	Order Backlog (q_1)	Shipping Rate (r_4)
	I_{act} (q_4)	
II	I_{des}(q_2), I_{act} (q_4)	Raw Material Input (r_2)
	Raw Material (r_2)	
	Production (r_3)	Raw Material Stores-WIP (q_3)

Key: q = levels
     r = levels

Based on D. J. Clough, Concepts in Management Science (Englewood Cliffs, N.J.: Prentice-Hall, 1963).

The specific responsibilities of each control center are:

a. Decision center I: Joint view of the order backlog (q_1) and actual inventory level (q_4), which helps to determine the appropriate shipping rate (r_4).

b. Decision center II: Joint consideration of the desired (q_2) and actual (q_4) levels of inventory, which govern the rate at which raw material will be ordered (r_2). Note the rate at which material is removed for production (r_3).

   The production rate (r_3), which goes into finished inventory (q_4), as opposed to the rate at which items are shipped (r_4), determines the actual level of inventory (I_{act}), q_4.

These points are summarized in the lower panel of Exhibit 4–12.

EXHIBIT 4–13. Mathematical Functions and Decisions Underlying the Simulated System

Level Equations (q)

Function	Symbol	Relationship
Order Backlog	$q_{1(t)} = q_{1(t-1)} + (r_{1(t)} - r_{4(t)})\,\Delta t$	
Desired Inventory	$q_{2(t)} = 5\,\dfrac{(r_{1(t)} + r_{1(t-1)}) + \cdots + r_{1(t-9)}\cdot\Delta t}{10}$	
Work-in-Process (Raw Material Stores)	$q_{3(t)} = q_{3(t-1)} + (r_{2(t)} - r_{3(t)})\,\Delta t$	
Actual Warehouse Inventory	$q_{4(t)} = q_{4(t-1)} + (r_{3(t)} - r_{4(t)})\,\Delta t$	

Flow Rate Equations (r)

	Symbol	Relationships
Orders	r_1	
Raw Material Inputs	$r_{2(t)} = 20\,\dfrac{q_{2(t-1)}}{q_{4(t-1)}}$; if $\leqslant 50$	
	$= 50$; if $20\,(\quad) \geqslant 50$	
Production Output	$r_{3(t)} = (q_{3(t-1)}/4)\,\Delta t$	
Shipping Rate	$r_{4(t)} = $ a) $\dfrac{q_{1(t-1)}}{\Delta t}$; if $\dfrac{(q_{1(t-1)})}{\Delta t} \leqslant \dfrac{q_{4(t-1)}}{\Delta t} \leqslant 35$	
	b) $\dfrac{q_{4(t-1)}}{\Delta t}$; if $\dfrac{q_{4(t-1)}}{\Delta t} \leqslant \dfrac{q_{1(t-1)}}{\Delta t} \leqslant 35$	
	c) 35; if $\dfrac{q_{1(t-1)}}{\Delta t}$ or $\dfrac{q_{4(t-1)}}{\Delta t} \geqslant 35$	

From Clough, Concepts in Management Science.

The mathematical expressions that characterize the relationship of the technology to the logistics of movement are summarized in Exhibit 4–13. These expressions combine both mathematical relationships and decisions made by managers based on such items as service policy, investment dollars available (for inventory), the character of past business (especially fluctuations), and physical or technological limitations. Consider, for example, the expression for "desired inventory level" (q_2), where the quotient $[r_1(t) + r_1(t-1) +$

EXHIBIT 4-14. Simulation A

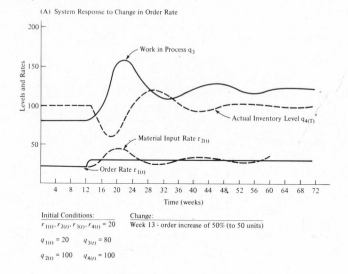

(A) System Response to Change in Order Rate

Initial Conditions:
$r_{1(t)}, r_{2(t)}, r_{3(t)}, r_{4(t)} = 20$

$q_{1(t)} = 20$ $q_{3(t)} = 80$

$q_{2(t)} = 100$ $q_{4(t)} = 100$

Change:
Week 13 - order increase of 50% (to 50 units)

(B.) Simulation of System Behavior

Week t	Rate $r_{1(t)}$ Exoge-nous	Rate $r_{2(t)}$	Rate $r_{3(t)}$	Rate $r_{4(t)}$	Level $q_{1(t)}$	Level $q_{2(t)}$	Level $q_{3(t)}$	Level $q_{4(t)}$
11	20	20	20	20	20	100	80	100
12	20	20	20	20	20	100	80	100
13	30	20	20	20	30	105	80	100
14	30	21	20	30	30	110	81	90
15	30	24	20	30	30	115	85	80
16	30	29	21	30	30	120	93	71
17	30	34	23	30	30	125	104	64
18	30	39	26	30	30	130	117	60
19	30	43	29	30	30	135	131	59
20	30	46	33	30	30	140	144	62
21	30	45	36	30	30	145	153	68
22	30	43	38	30	30	150	158	76
23	30	39	40	30	30	150	157	86
24	30	35	39	30	30	150	153	95
25	30	32	38	30	30	150	147	103
26	30	29	37	30	30	150	139	110
27	30	27	35	30	30	150	131	115
28	30	26	33	30	30	150	124	118
29	30	25	31	30	30	150	118	119
30	30	25	30	30	30	150	113	119
31	30	25	28	30	30	150	110	117
32	30	26	28	30	30	150	108	115
33	30	26	27	30	30	150	107	112
34	30	27	27	30	30	150	107	109
35	30	27	27	30	30	150	107	106
36	30	28	27	30	30	150	108	103
37	30	29	27	30	30	150	110	100
38	30	30	28	30	30	150	112	98
39	30	30	28	30	30	150	114	96
40	30	31	29	30	30	150	116	95
41	30	32	29	30	30	150	119	94
42	30	32	30	30	30	150	121	94
43	30	32	30	30	30	150	123	94
44	30	32	31	30	30	150	124	95
45	30	32	31	30	30	150	125	96

Source: Donald J. Clough, **Concepts in Management Science** (Englewood Cliffs, N.J.: Prentice-Hall, Inc., © 1963), pp. 379, 380.

$r_1(t-9)\Delta t] \div 10$ constitutes a ten-week (acceptable to management) moving average. The multiplier (5) represents management's judgment of the desired relationship between order rate (r_1) and the desired inventory level (q_2).

Several additional examples of managerial analysis and decision are represented by the rate equations. Raw material input from suppliers (r_2) is governed by the relationship between desired (q_2) and actual (q_4) levels of inventory and a fixed coefficient (20), which jointly constitute the bases for raw material orders. The conditions imposed on the relationships (less, equal to, or greater than) reflect permissible raw material order patterns and possible supplier limitations. Similar observations could be made concerning the production output (r_3) or shipping rate (r_4). In short, the production system is defined by a coherent set of expressions that reflect policy and management decisions for production control.

The first major step in analysis is to probe system characteristics as revealed through simulation. The symbol t, used in these functions, brings about dimensional agreement, so that rate expressions (number of items per unit of time) may be converted into "level" expressions (units) in multiplying by the time interval considered. (For the functions in Exhibit 4–13, the time period is one week.) In system simulations, the initial conditions usually constitute stable conditions for system behavior and a starting point for subsequent disturbance of equilibrium.

SIMULATION A—ORDER RATE CHANGE

A change in order rate takes place at week 13, and the resulting changes in rate and level variables are depicted in Exhibit 4–14, which also depicts the initial conditions. It is apparent from the graph that the rate and level variables react violently at first, but at about the forty-ninth week, system characteristics stabilize (recall the impersonal managerial controls incorporated in the functions) and fluctuation is lowered considerably. The following are sample calculations for period 20.

  a. Work in Process (q_3):

$$\text{WIP}_{20} = \text{WIP}_{19} + (1) \times (\text{Matl. Input}_{20} = \text{Prod. Output}_{20})$$
$$q_{3(20)} = q_{3(19)} + (\Delta T)(r_{2(20)} - r_{3(20)})$$
$$= 131 + (1)(46 - 33)$$
$$= 144$$

  b. Shipping Rate (r_4):

  Decision rule based on values of

        1. $q_{1(t-1)}$; $q_{4(t-1)}$; 35

        2.   30;   59; 35 or

        3. $q_{1(19)} \lesseqqgtr q_{4(19)} \lesseqqgtr 35$

          $\therefore r_4 = 30$

c. Actual Inventory Level (I_{act}):

$$q_{4(20)} = q_{4(19)} \qquad\qquad t(r_{3(20)} - \qquad \bullet \quad r_{4(20)})$$

$$= I_{act} \text{ of} \qquad\qquad \text{Production} \qquad \text{Shipping}$$

$$\text{Last Period} \qquad\qquad \text{Output} \qquad\qquad \text{Rate}$$

$$= 59 + (1)\ (33 - 30)$$

$$= 62$$

The simulation suggests that the decision system and rules for the technological and logistics system are able to reassert system balance at a permanent increase in customer order rate. However, the thirty weeks or so required to regain control seem rather long. Futhermore, ad hoc efforts to compensate for the order increase could have significantly strained internal procedures, manpower training buildup, and procurement function, for example.

Thus system performance could be interpreted in terms of ability to stabilize, the time required, and the level of values attained. It could also be interpreted in terms of inconsistencies in decision rules. This simulation model defines organization structure in the sense that specific relationships and interactions can be anticipated. This is more generally viewed as a system design for *interdependent* functions, which limits the range of behavior and activity of its members.

SIMULATION B—IMPACT OF COMMUNICATIONS DELAY

The material input factor (r_2) represents supplier limitations (not to exceed fifty items per week), rules regarding the ratio of desired and actual inventory, and a judgment of the speed of response (immediate past period) both possible and desired. Now *what if* communication delays materialize, or supplier difficulties emerge, so that it is necessary to plan this period's supply of material ($r_{2(t)}$) $q_{2(t-4)}/q_{4(t-4)}$ instead of the rapid one-week response currently employed, $q_{2(t-1)}/q_{4(t-1)}$? Consequently, an additional three weeks pass before the supplier's raw material shipments are adjusted.

The impact of this change is illustrated in Exhibit 4–15. We see that the system is unable to moderate the internal forces set in motion by the attempt to cope with the order increase. Although only one decision rule was changed, it is clear that, for the 1.5-year cycle depicted, there was no stability in time and level. Here the decision system proves unable to cope with the demands of the customer or with serious restrictions in the material supply.

To the extent that this simulation model mirrors actual conditions within an organization, the inadequacies of impersonal controls become glaringly apparent.[24]

SUMMARY

In keeping with the conceptual orientation of this book, Exhibit 4–16 summarizes some of the key points introduced in this and the preceding chapters.

EXHIBIT 4–15. Simulation B: Communication Delay: System Change and Adjustment of Material Input Rate

A. System Responses to a Change in Order Rate

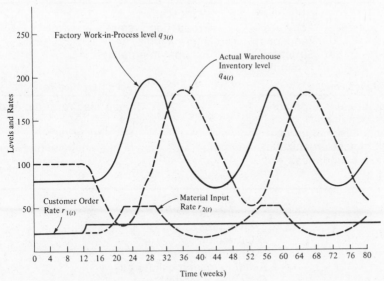

Communication Delay in Material Input Rate, i.e.

$$\left(\frac{q_{2(t-1)}}{q_{4(t-1)}} \right) \longrightarrow \frac{q_{2(t-4)}}{q_{4(t-4)}}$$

(B.) Simulation of System Behavior

Week t	Rate $r_{1(t)}$	Rate $r_{2(t)}$	Rate $r_{3(t)}$	Rate $r_{4(t)}$	Level $q_{1(t)}$	Level $q_{2(t)}$	Level $q_{3(t)}$	Level $q_{4(t)}$
11	20	20	20	20	20	100	80	100
12	20	20	20	20	20	100	80	100
13	30	20	20	20	30	105	80	100
14	30	20	20	30	30	110	80	90
15	30	20	20	30	30	115	80	80
16	30	20	20	30	30	120	80	70
17	30	21	20	30	30	125	81	60
18	30	24	20	30	30	130	85	50
19	30	29	21	30	30	135	93	41
20	30	34	23	30	30	140	102	34
21	30	42	26	30	30	145	118	26
22	30	50	30	26	34	150	138	32
23	30	50	35	30	34	150	153	35
24	30	50	38	34	30	150	165	39
25	30	50	41	30	30	150	174	50
26	30	50	44	30	30	150	180	64
27	30	50	45	30	30	150	185	79
28	30	50	46	30	30	150	189	85
29	30	50	47	30	30	150	192	102
30	30	47	48	30	30	150	192	120
31	30	38	48	30	30	150	181	138
32	30	35	45	30	30	150	171	153
33	30	29	43	30	30	150	157	166
34	30	25	39	30	30	150	143	175
35	30	22	36	30	30	150	129	181
36	30	20	32	30	30	150	117	183
37	30	18	29	30	30	150	106	182
38	30	17	27	30	30	150	96	179
39	30	17	24	30	30	150	89	173
40	30	16	22	30	30	150	83	165
41	30	16	21	30	30	150	78	156
42	30	17	20	30	30	150	75	146
43	30	17	19	30	30	150	73	135
44	30	18	18	30	30	150	73	123
45	30	19	18	30	30	150	74	111

Source: Donald J. Clough, **Concepts in Management Science** (Englewood Cliffs, N.J.: Prentice-Hall, Inc., 1963), pp. 282, 381.

EXHIBIT 4–16. Structure, Technology, and Organization

Building blocks	Systems
Objectives	Work system
Activities	Production system
Functions	Information system
Structure	External/internal systems
Technology	

Socio-technical	Production function as:
Structure of interpersonal relationships	Unique feature of the systems view
Formal/informal groups	Support groups
Environment-organization interaction	Line management
System boundaries	

Illustrations
Case applications
Insurance
Meat processing
Oil refining
Commercial baking
Reading resource material
Conceptual models

Organizations were examined in terms of some of their key substructures and functions, which can be viewed realistically as building blocks. Systems in combination with structure are the primary notions upon which the discussions in Chapters 2, 3, and 4 developed. Structure was reviewed in terms of such common features as specialization, authority levels, and allocation of responsibility.

These analyses were then extended to the added complexities of size, managerial philosophy (strategy), and the concepts of differentiation and integration. The systems notion was explored in terms of both technological and manpower features, with analyses focused on providing a perspective on interactions, both formal and informal. Alternative approaches were proposed for characterizing complex systems.

The production function, because of its unique contribution to general systems approaches, became the central topic of Chapters 3 and 4. Here, special emphasis was placed on perspectives for analyzing a variety of organizational questions dealing with the formal and, to some extent, informal aspects of these systems.

Alternative models, including an "uncertainty–complexity" approach, were summarized. For formal systems, the simulation approach discussed in this chapter is especially promising.

Finally, a series of case applications and resource materials were offered as illustrations of real-world situations.

Appendix

TRIST'S RESEARCH IN LONG-WALL METHODS OF COAL MINING

Comparison of Two Work Groups*

Measure	Conventional	Team composite
Rate of absenteeism		
Total	2 1/2x	1x
Voluntary	10x	1x
Productivity	80%	95%

Organization of conventional system:
1. Competitive; pay differences, questions of equity
2. Distrust but supportive relations among workers
3. Greater stresses: can fall back on work associate
4. Status distribution (psychological separation)
5. Preferential treatments in assignment—job picking order
6. Fractionation (vs. variety in previous setting)

Organization of composite groups:
1. Shift team among tasks, avoid specialization
2. Evidence range of needed skills in each team
3. Cohesion secured through
    a. Selecting own members (multi-skilled; same level of interchangeability)
    b. Assuming responsibility for overall task
    c. Allocating task among members (job and shift rotation)
    d. Tying compensation to group productivity

*(a) Composite team accomplishes performance beyond role requirements *and yet,* at the same time, advances organization toward its goals. (b) Composite required less supervision. (c) In another industrial study, developed by Rice in Indian textile mills, productivity in team areas was 95 percent of potential versus 80 percent for conventional, and quality showed steady improvement from a high of 25 to a low of 15 percent after the same two years.

Based on E. L. Trist and K. W. Bamforth, "Some Social and Psychological Consequences of the Long-Wall Method of Goal-Getting." *Human Relations,* 4 (1951): 3–38.

THE FIT BETWEEN TECHNICAL AND SOCIAL SYSTEMS IN CHANGE

Concept of socio-technical system: Work system requires

a. *Technological elements* and organizations (process layout, procedures, and equipment)

b. Work (people) organization (to carry out); latitude limited by technological elements; has own social and psychological properties

In change (or ongoing activity), what is the best fit of the social and technological? Need to balance technical priorities with social (re: Rice) necessities:

a. Closure or sense of completion

b. Some level of task control

c. Satisfactory relationships with those performing related tasks

Group can provide format (if accorded legitimacy and sufficient degrees of freedom) to work one out.

1. Closure may be by a small group.

2. Need for autonomy (self-determination through task control) can be gained by simple participation in group decision making.

Cohesion of group, plus its stability, depends on prestige; status differences within group; range of skills it enfolds (Rice, pp. 37–38).

References: Louis E. Davis, "Quality of Working Life: National and International Developments," in Gerald G. Somers (ed.), *Proceedings of the Twenty-fifth Anniversary Meeting, Industrial Relations Research Association* (Madison: University of Wisconsin, 1973); A. K. Rice, *Productivity and Social Organization: The Ahmedabad Experiment* (London: Tavistock Publications, 1958); E. L. Trist et al., *Organizational Choice* (London: Tavistock Publications, 1963).

QUESTIONS

1. Based on the material of Chapter 4, discuss your ideas on the performance effects of technology versus supervisory effort.

2. Compare and relate the simulation approach to the Bright model and to those discussed in Chapter 3 in terms of
   (a) Usefulness in characterizing organizations
   (b) Possibilities and limitations

3. What factors guide performance in those organizations that lack the constraints of technological systems?

4. Offer propositions concerning organization size, surveillance, and formal rules under the following sets of circumstances:
   (a) Advanced production systems and unit production systems
   (b) Advanced computer information systems
   (c) Stable-unstable business and operational developments
   (d) Highly trained/poorly trained subordinates
   (e) Span of control

5. What hypotheses or propositions would you offer for administration approaches and size under the following circumstances?
   (a) Varying levels of technological sophistication
   (b) Varying institutional circumstances, such as insurance, banks, chemical manufacturers
   (c) In the plant component as opposed to the headquarters component
   (d) Absolute numbers and percentages

6. For an organization you are familiar with, develop an "uncertainty–complexity" analysis. State the necessary assumptions.

7. The works of Adam Smith and others suggest a number of approaches to improvement of task performance, largely built around the benefits of division of labor, wherein more finely divided tasks permitted shorter learning time, higher performance, less scrap, shortened setup times, fewer job changes, less task innovation, and the development of specialized equipment. Based on these observations, one could develop a proposition suggesting

   > The greater the subdivision of labor and task, the more opportunity for technical improvements and individual efficiency gains, and the better the performance.

   Yet, in more recent times, a behavioral scientist would demand a recasting of this proposition:

   > The greater the wholeness of the task, and the greater the opportunity for individual self-realization, the better the performance.

   Discuss and reconcile these viewpoints.

8. In the final assembly plants of many automobile manufacturers the characteristic mode of organization is a six- to eight-level authority structure, from first-line supervisor to plant manager. Although automotive assembly work involves a high level of human interaction, substantial improvements have been made in productivity through the introduction of new technologies and methods. In a plant of one of the "big three," the impact of continuing improvements over a long period has resulted in a 10 percent reduction in the number of plant employees, and a 15 percent decrease in the number of professional and managerial personnel, while output has been maintained at about the same level.

   State initial assumptions and speculate on the organizational outcomes of continuing technological changes and improvements in these plants. Clearly set out the thinking underlying your assertions.

NOTES

1. Some of the research underlying this approach is reported by Elmer H. Burack, "Some Aspects of Industrial Supervision in Advanced Production Units," *Human Organizations,* 26, no. 4 (Winter 1967).

2. Some observations on these changes may be found in Elmer H. Burack, "Industrial Management in Advanced Production Systems: Some Theoretical Concepts and Preliminary Findings," *Administrative Science Quarterly*, 12, no. 4 (December 1967); Thomas J. McNichols and Elmer H. Burack, "Management and the New Technologies," in Elmer H. Burack and James R. Walker, *Manpower Planning and Programming* (Boston: Allyn & Bacon, 1972); and Burack and McNichols, *Manpower, Policy and Change* (Kent, O.: Kent State University Bureau of Business Research, 1973).

3. Elmer H. Burack, "Industrial Management and Technology," technology working papers, Illinois Institute of Technology, 1970.

4. A. K. Rice, *Productivity and Social Organization: The Ahmedabad Experiment* (London: Tavistock Publications, 1958). Also see his more recent works in the socio-technical concept: *The Enterprise and Its Environment* (London: Tavistock Publications, 1963), and "Individual, Group, and Intergroup Processes," *Human Relations*, 22 (1969): 565–584.

   Many other members of the Tavistock group have addressed themselves to socio-technical concepts and applications, including F. E. Emery and E. L. Trist; for example, see their "Causal Texture of Organizational Environments," *Human Relations*, 18 (1965): 21–32, and Louis E. Davis, "Quality of Working Life: National and International Developments," in Gerald G. Somers (ed.), *Proceedings of the Twenty-fifth Anniversary Meeting, Industrial Relations Research Association* (Madison: University of Wisconsin Press, 1973).

5. E. L. Trist and K. W. Bamforth, "Some Social and Psychological Consequences of the Long-Wall Method of Goal-Getting," *Human Relations*, 4 (1951): 3–38.

6. David Katz and Robert L. Kahn, *The Social Psychology of Organizations* (Englewood Cliffs, N.J.: Prentice-Hall, 1966), p. 81.

7. Katz and Kahn, *Social Psychology of Organizations*, pp. 81, 192.

8. Dubin provides excellent insights into work, jobs, and behavioral systems in Robert Dubin (ed.), *Handbook of Work, Organization and Society* (Chicago: Rand McNally, 1973).

9. Important approaches to this perspective are Delbert C. Miller, "Supervisors: Evolution of an Organizational Role," pp. 104–132, and George C. Homans, "Effort, Supervision and Productivity," pp. 51–67, in *Leadership and Productivity* (San Francisco: Chandler Publishing Co., 1966), and Elmer H. Burack and Thomas J. McNichols, *Manpower, Policy and Change* (Kent, O.: Kent State University Bureau of Business Research, 1973), esp. chap. 4.

10. Miller, "Supervisors," p. 212.

11. A classical study in this area is James C. Worthy's observations in "Organizational Structure and Employee Morale," *American Sociological Review*, 15, no. 170 (April 1950).

12. Stuart Klein in a paper presented at the 13th annual meeting of the Midwest Division of the Academy of Management, Washington University, St. Louis, April 1967.

13. Homans, "Effort, Supervision and Productivity," p. 62.

14. Leonard R. Sayles, "Work Group Behavior and the Larger Organization," in Robert T. Golembiewski (ed.), *Managerial Behavior and Organization Demands* (Chicago: Rand McNally, 1966), pp. 168–169.

15. *Management and Morale* (Cambridge, Mass.: Harvard University Press, 1941).

16. See James R. Bright, "Does Automation Raise Skill Levels?" *Harvard Business Review,* 36, no. 4 (July–August 1958), pp. 85–98, and Richard A. Beaumont and Roy B. Helfgott, *Management, Automation, and People* (New York: Industrial Relations Counselors, Inc., 1964), esp. pp. 43, 44, and 136.

17. Edward Harvey, "Technology and Structure of Organizations," *American Sociological Review,* 33 (1968): 247–259.

18. Raymond G. Hunt, "Technology and Organization," *Academy of Management Journal,* 13 (1970): 235–252. For an alternate approach, using uncertainty–complexity characterizations of the environment, see Tom Kynaston Reeves and Barry A. Turner, "A Theory of Organization and Behavior in Batch Production Factories," *Administrative Science Quarterly,* 17, no. 1 (March 1972): 81–98.

19. Joan Woodward, "Technology, Material Control, and Organizational Behavior," in A. R. Negandhi and J. P. Schwitter (eds.), *Organization Behavior Models* (Kent, O.: Comparative Administration Research Institute, Bureau of Economic and Business Research, Kent State University, 1970), pp. 21–31.

20. Tom Burns and G. Stalker, *The Management of Innovation* (London: Tavistock Publications, 1961); Jay W. Lorsch and Paul R. Lawrence, "Organizing for Product Innovation," *Harvard Business Review,* 43, no. 1 (January–February 1965): 109–122; Jay Galbraith and M. L. Lavin, "Information Processing as a Function of Task Predictability and Interdependence," *Annual Proceedings, American Institute of Decision Sciences* (1970), pp. 117–121; Reeves and Turner, "A Theory of Organization and Behavior in Batch Production Factories," pp. 81–98; and Elmer H. Burack, *Structural Strategies,* in process; and Burack and Dennis Waller, *A Newer Management Tool: Uncertainty–Complexity Analysis,* in process. Also see the work of Robert Duncan reported in *Administrative Science Quarterly* (Fall 1972) and *Annual Proceedings American Institute of Decision Sciences,* New Orleans, 1972.

21. Further applications of U–C analyses and measurement approaches are described in Robert B. Duncan, "Characteristics of Organizational Environments and Perceived Environmental Uncertainty," *Administrative Science Quarterly,* 17, no. 3 (September 1972): 313–328, and Peter Pekar, "Uncertainty–Complexity Determinants in Managerial Planning and Control of Major Projects," unpublished Ph.D. thesis, Illinois Institute of Technology, 1974.

22. See Paul R. Lawrence and Jay W. Lorsch, *The Organization and Its Environment* (Homewood, Ill.: Richard D. Irwin, 1969), and Henry Tosi, Ramon Aldag, and Ronald Storey, "On the Measurement of the Environment: An Assessment of the Lawrence and Lorsch Environmental Uncertainty Questionnaire," *Administrative Science Quarterly,* 18, no. 1 (March 1973): 27–37. For the Lawrence and Lorsch response, see "Letters—A Reply to Tosi, Aldag, and Storey," *Administrative Science Quarterly,* 18, no. 3 (September 1973): 397–398.

23. Taken from Donald J. Clough, *Concepts in Management Science* (Englewood Cliffs, N.J.: Prentice-Hall, 1963).

24. For an excellent description of a simulation model, see George W. Gershefski, "Building a Corporate Financial Model," *Harvard Business Review,* 47, no. 11 (July–August 1969): 61–73.

REFERENCES

Socio-Technical Approaches: Organizations, Jobs, Roles

Davis, Louis E. "Quality of Working Life: National and International Developments" in Gerald G. Somers (ed.), *Proceedings of the Twenty-fifth Anniversary Meeting.* Industrial Relations Research Association, Madison: University of Wisconsin, 1973.

——— and E. L. Trist. "Improving the Quality of Work Life" in Harold Sheppard (ed.), *Work in America.* Cambridge, Mass.: M.I.T. Press, 1973.

Davis, Louis E., and J. C. Taylor (eds.). *The Design of Jobs.* London: Penguin Books, 1972.

Emery, F. E. (ed.). *Systems Thinking.* London: Penguin Books, 1969.

——— and E. L. Trist. "The Causal Texture of Organizational Environments." *Human Relations,* 18 (1965) pp. 21–32.

———. "Socio-Technical Systems" in C. W. Churchman (ed.), *Management Sciences: Models and Techniques,* Vol. II. London: Pergamon Press, 1960.

Lawler, E. E. III. "Job Design and Employee Motivation." *Personal Psychology,* 22, No. 4 (1969) pp. 426–435.

Price, Charles (ed.). *New Directions in the World of Work.* Kalamazoo, Mich.: W. E. Upjohn Institute for Employment Research, March 1972.

Rice, A. K. "Individual, Group, and Intergroup Processes." *Human Relations,* 22 (1969): 565–584.

———. *The Enterprise and Its Environment.* London: Tavistock Publications, 1963.

———. *Productivity and Social Organization: The Ahmedabad Experiment.* London: Tavistock Publications, 1958.

Trist, E. L., et al. *Organizational Choice.* London: Tavistock Publications, 1963.

Trist, E. L., and K. W. Bamforth. "Some Social and Psychological Consequences of the Long-Wall Method of Goal-Getting." *Human Relations,* 4 (1951): 3–38.

Technology, Environment, Organization

Bright, James R. "Evaluating Signals of Technological Change." *Harvard Business Review,* 48, no. 1 (January–February 1970): 62.

Foster, Richard N. "Organize for Technology Transfer." *Harvard Business Review,* 49, no. 6 (November–December 1971): 110–120.

Gilman, Glen. "Technological Innovation and Public Policy." *California Management Review,* 13, no. 3 (Spring 1971): 13–23.

Greiner, Larry E. "Evolution and Revolution as Organizations Grow." *Harvard Business Review,* 50, no. 4 (July–August 1972): 37–47.

Slevin, Dennis P. "The Innovation Boundary: A Specific Model and Some Empirical Results." *Administrative Science Quarterly,* 16, no. 4 (December 1971): 515–531.

Terryberry, Shirley. "The Evolution of Organizational Environments." *Administrative Science Quarterly,* 12, no. 4 (March 1968): 590–613.

Woodward, Joan. *Industrial Organization Theory and Practice.* London: Oxford University Press, 1965.

Utterback, James. "The Process of Technological Innovation within the Firm." *Academy of Management Journal,* 14, no. 1 (March 1971): 75–88.

———— and Elmer H. Burack. "Identification of Technical Opportunities and Threats by Firms." Paper delivered at international meeting of the Institute of Management Sciences, Boston, April 1974.

Organizational Analyses

Dubin, Robert. *Human Relations in Administration,* 3d ed. Englewood Cliffs, N.J.: Prentice-Hall, 1968.

Gabarre, John J. "Organizational Adaptation to Environmental Change," in Frank Baker (ed.), *Organizational Systems.* Homewood, Ill.: Richard D. Irwin, 1973, pp. 196–215.

Grimes, Andrew J., and Stuart M. Klein. "The Technological Imperative: The Relative Impact of Task Unit, Modal Equity, and Expectancy." *Academy of Management Journal,* 16, no. 4 (December 1973): 583–598.

Lawrence, Paul R., and Jay W. Lorsch. *Organization and Environment.* Homewood, Ill.: Richard D. Irwin, 1969.

————. "New Management Job: Integrator." *Harvard Business Review,* 45, no. 6 (November–December 1967): 142–151.

Litterer, Joseph A. *The Analysis of Organizations.* New York: John Wiley & Sons, 1965.

McClelland, David. *The Achieving Society.* Princeton, N.J.: Van Nostrand, 1961.

Merton, Robert K. "The Machine, the Worker, and the Engineer." *Science,* January 24, 1947, pp. 79–84.

Moore, Wilbert E., and Melvin M. Tumin. "Some Social Functions of Ignorance." *American Sociological Review,* 14, no. 6 (December 1949): 788–789.

Pugh, D. S., D. J. Hickson, C. R. Hinnings, and C. Turner. "Dimensions of Organization Structure." *Administrative Science Quarterly,* 13, no. 2 (June 1968): 65–105.

Learning Objectives

Concept of Multiple Criteria in Organizational Performance
Components of a Control System
   Key Role of Feedback
Options in Designing Control Systems
   Vast Range of Alternatives, Overlaps, and Latitude of Choice
   Organizational Factors Affecting Choice
   Behavioral Implications of Control Approaches
Distinction between Control and Evaluation of Past Action

Chapter 5

ORGANIZATIONAL CONTROL SYSTEMS

OVERVIEW

With some basic understandings of structure and systems established (Chapters 1–4), attention is directed in this and the remaining chapters of Part I to dealing with the processes that serve to tie them together. Control of organizational undertakings, processes, and participants (Chapter 5), communications (Chapter 6), and a selected subset of communications and information systems (Chapter 7) are the concluding topics of Part I.

The first discussion in this chapter establishes an understanding of performance criteria that serve as standards for comparison and control. Next, various types of control strategies are explored, encompassing those that are essentially mechanistic to the highly personal that are dependent on human interactions.

The other discussions in this chapter cover a wide range of control applications: profit centers and budgetary processes, socio-technical systems and organizations in continuous process systems, and research and development procedures. These discussions also embrace dysfunction for organizational processes and members where control is poorly devised or applied.

PERFORMANCE CRITERIA

Control systems regulate organizations' activities toward predetermined objectives. "Performance criteria" convey to management the conformity of oganizational performance to time schedules, predetermined objectives, and measures of output.

Exhibit 5–1(*1*) is the typical input/output model from which a control and evaluation system is built. The model uses direct and indirect measures of performance. The former may be quantified; the latter are inferential, and are taken as *relative*. Direct evaluation criteria may include such impersonal items as records, budgets, and standards; inferential measures rely on such

EXHIBIT 5-1. Performance Criteria and Control: A Systems View

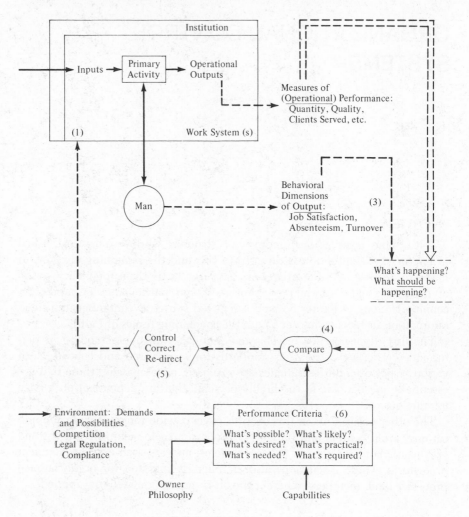

Key:
---- Elements of control system
==== Control on operational outputs

behavioral variables as satisfaction, morale, and attitudes. The selection of performance criteria is determined in part by the broader objectives and plans of the organization; thus the performance of a particular subsystem is blended in with the goals of the larger system.

Several features of the systems representation in Exhibit 5-1 serve to tie together the notion of performance criteria in their relation to control of organizational activities and work processes. Perhaps the most direct observation to be made concerning performance criteria and control is that the two are inexorably woven together and that control (regulation, capability to re-direct) incorporates a comparison step (4) that implies a standard (standards) of comparison: the more complex the phenomena to be controlled, the more likely that multiple criteria rather than single measures of performance (6) will be needed.

The second point concerns the role of performance criteria and control in their relation to system functioning. The socio-technical perspective set forth in the previous chapters has emphasized the linkage of a firm to the external environment (inputs, changes, demands, possibilities), as well as the internal linkages for transformation of input to output. Information must be secured from these environments, which on the one hand, and most generally stated, assure organizational survival; here control is very broadly conceived and deals with the very destiny of the organization. However, information must also be secured from these environments that assists in bringing about and guiding the necessary short-run actions that meet long-run requirements for survival.[1]

The third point to be made is that operational outputs (pieces, number of policies, or dollar volume transacted) are products of various institutional work activities. Direct measures of these outputs can be secured. Yet at the same time the organizational systems of most interest to us bring together man and work components within a socio-technical framework. The human dimension of these systems is both affected by (influenced or controlled) and affects work functioning. Behavioral dimensions of a work system (3), reflecting the adequacy of human arrangements (detailed extensively in Part II), may include such measures as job satisfaction and turnover. The latter are *indirect* measures of system performance in that they are not the central outcomes sought in work design. Yet the behavioral dimensions are of major importance in organizational functioning and are slowly gaining prominence in all manner of institutions. More on this in Part II.

The performance criteria (6) in Exhibit 5–1 respond to such questions as "What's possible?" or "What's required?" Except for some rather obvious situations where mechanical or electronic design provides a given performance level with a high degree of assurance, the "answers" to performance criteria questions frequently come only with considerable analysis. On the one hand, competition may establish a performance target that we would *like to achieve* or one that we *must achieve* for cost purposes.[2] But do we have the needed managerial, technical, and administrative skills?

Many important performance criteria–control system questions involve broad institutional issues, beyond the specifics of an operational system. They may deal with total institutional performance. For example, the need for legal compliance may establish targets for work force composition in terms of racial minorities or females, which then serve as performance criteria (regarding hiring practices). Of course, the ownership's (or top management's or government's) philosophy of operation or general policy may also govern what's to be viewed as the acceptable criteria of performance. The latter, for example, could range from the level of participation of organizational members in community affairs to next year's sales targets to the rate of improvement of work practices.

Single and Multiple Performance Criteria

The engineer or the analyst can frequently formulate problems so that *single* measures of success may be applied, for instance, optimality, single-point solutions, or units of production. Yet single measures of performance may be inappropriate for complex situations. Consider, for example, the automobile. What constitutes acceptable automotive performance—gas mileage, ride, cornering, gas mileage adjusted for weight? From what perspective are we interested in automotive performance—that of the automotive engineer, or Mrs. or Mr. Consumer? Even if we designate one party—say the automotive engineer—as analyst, we would be hard pressed to name any single item that would adequately express automobile efficiency. Therefore *multiple* rather than single measures are best.

Performance Criteria in a Variety of Institutional Settings

It is important to observe the development of performance criteria in a variety of institutions to see how they are modified for particular circumstances. For example, how might an initial set of hospital performance measures be modified if the hospital is linked with an educational institution, a research unit, or a large outpatient clinic? How might the measures be modified by public or private ownership of the hospital? If performance is to be rated in terms of patient care, one might consider the number of deaths, the recovery period for certain kinds of illness, the number of oral or written complaints, attitude surveys among patients, or the judgments of a panel of experts. The economic performance of the hospital might be measured in terms of loss, breakeven, or profit. Once a particular institutional format has been established, the diverse functions of the organization can be translated into meaningful measures for judging its performance. However, until detailed performance measures are agreed upon, there can be no realistic basis for assuring conformity of performance to institutional objectives.

It is even more difficult to arrive at the right set of evaluation criteria when the goal of an organization's activity is ambiguous, or when concepts of performance differ widely. One might question, for instance, how the efficacy of a research and development effort could be measured realistically. An R&D effort might be considered from the point of view of the client, the parent company, product patentability, or output per researcher. Work in industrial research and development units reveals a variety of performance measures, which include effect on sales volume, savings on economic resources, profits, time and cost of solution, feasibility of solutions, customer satisfaction, information intelligence, and contribution to patent position. At the same time, objective criteria, some quite diffused, have been employed by management to gauge R&D performance: level of internally purchased services, royalties, return on investment, payoff on researched and nonresearched products, number of valuable ideas submitted, and the number of problems successfully solved.[3]

Data Feedback

One aspect of control focuses on the accumulation of performance data for comparison purposes and to signal control adjustments. The feedback (i.e., reporting back on a timely basis) of performance data (cost and various quantitative measures of performance) is a support system in its own right, typically built around accounting and budgetary control functions. This support system operates at two levels of controls. First, daily activities are monitored against predetermined standards and appropriate adjustments are made. Second, costs and performance, summarized over extended time periods, are evaluated against budget. Thus budgets are a vehicle for translating the broader plans of an organization into operationally meaningful control measures. The translation of corporate planning procedures to operationally meaningful controls procedures constitutes a process central to carrying out institutional controls. This process also creates the information and measures that are necessary inputs to the other control undertakings discussed in this chapter.

THE CONTROL PROCESS

A control system has the following key components: a sensing element to capture information, a basis on which to compare behavior against predetermined objectives or performance criteria, and a means of corrective action. Control options include such factors as style of leadership, impersonal controls (budgets, procedures, and the like), the structural features of the organization (number of hierarchical levels, the centralization or decentralization of authority), the role of support groups, and the technology itself. All of these factors together affect the nature of the control system, the distribution or locus of control in the organization, and supervision's control of subordinates. (The term "options" is employed to suggest that organizational planners have some degree of latitude in seeking to fashion a control *system.*)

The criteria and need for control may vary among different organizations, depending, for example, on production technology. The supervisory aspect of control provides a good example. Supervision might play only a minor role in a craft-oriented and highly skilled low-level technology; in the rhythm of the mass production line, supervision may be crucial to work system performance. On the other hand, supervision is less crucial to control in the automated system, where the supervisor provides surveillance but has little direct contact with operators. The same kind of analysis might be applied to impersonal controls. As we have seen in the Woodward study, the elaborate hierarchy and complexity of the mass production system bring about a greater number of impersonal controls. In Exhibit 5–2 the various control options are summarized; also, control approaches are arranged in matrix form, with "rows" representing levels of technology.

EXHIBIT 5–2. Organizational Control Systems: Models with Behavioral Implications

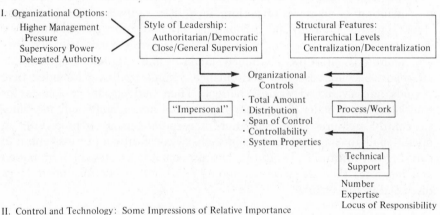

I. Organizational Options:

II. Control and Technology: Some Impressions of Relative Importance

Types of Control

Level of Technology	Technical Support Groups	Supervisory	Impersonal	Process
Craft	X	X	X	X
Mass Production	XX	XXX	XXX	XX
Automation	XXX	XX	XXX	XXX

The upper portion of Exhibit 5–2 establishes four areas that contribute jointly to organizational controls, but with varying degrees of emphasis or relative importance.[4] The five major groupings depicted here include

> 1. *Style of leadership,* which centers on interpersonal actions. The degree of influence (dealt with in detail in Chapter 9) reflects

personal characteristics, character of the work situation, the leader's ability to secure valued items (services for the group), and the quality of leader-group relationships.

2. *Impersonal controls.* In contrast to leadership approaches, these controls build on rules, procedures, and policies. Not surprisingly, degree of conformity varies widely, depending on organizational norms of conduct—what's been acceptable, co-worker actions, and degree of concern expressed for these controls by authority figures.

3. *Structural features.* Control is embedded in structural characteristics such as number of authority levels and the locus (level or point in the structure) where control responsibility is delegated. "Tall" structures (many levels) tend to reduce span of control and thereby permit finer division of responsibilities, greater division of organization members, and closer personal scrutiny by supervisors of group member efforts.[5]

   The relative positioning (locus) of control responsibilities is another dimension of control approaches. For example, proximity to relevant information and contacts may dictate that the control of field salesmen be positioned at the lower end of the hierarchy and within field sales organization. Conversely, the control of major budget expenditures is typically a major organizational commitment, such as that of a parliament with an executive committee for "centralization" of control.

4. *Process, work systems.* Socio-technical systems often contain technologies that establish pace, work station position, sequence of activity, and permissible movement. As developed in Chapters 3 and 4, mass production systems greatly constrain (control) workers in the manner described here. Advanced process systems, where process controls are consolidated within control rooms, establish the work area for operators and supervisors. In technological systems of low technical attainment, technology tends to be nonconstraining and control generally depends on leaders' abilities and impersonal approaches. If the individuals are craftsmen, the values of work conduct among these artisans may suffice in itself to bring about needed conformity to specification or timing.

5. *Technical support groups.* Groups such as quality control, market research, and production control are instrumental in bringing about and supporting control functions. Technical support groups receive information and data describing operational variables and transform them into useful measures for regulatory purposes.

However, this activity is typically an intermediate one, with the product of these efforts passed along to various officials, managers, and supervisors as a basis for action, correction, or direction.

What are the options within these generalized control requirements? In any of these technologies there can be some interchange of control systems. Thus it is possible that in a craft-level technology, low employee skills may be counterbalanced by strong supervision or more extensive use of technical support groups.

Standing back, as it were, from these five elements of control, we can see that many control configurations (combinations) are possible. The perceptions and interpretations of control needs by each firm, even if they are members of the same industry, vary—as do the size of firm, deployment of facilities, and access to resources of men and technology to support control. Finally, these parameters notwithstanding, owner philosophy or the personalities of various key organizational members may further shape these combinations of control elements.

Uncertainty and Control

The control and technical variables relate to organization behavior in that together they affect the degree of uncertainty in an organization. Case studies cited by Woodward [6] have shown that the amount of uncertainty in an organization task is a major determinant of the way that the task can be controlled. A high degree of precision and explicitness in the objective-setting process is associated with mechanical and unitary control procedures. Unit production is linked with personal single-system control and continuous flow production with single-system mechanical (or electronic) control. Technology itself is dependent on a number of factors that can be viewed as sources of uncertainty. These factors include

Product uniformity

The markets that are being served

The techniques that are available to process raw materials and components (e.g., stability)

The hardware available to process raw materials and components (i.e., routine operation versus experimentation)

The design of control systems that reduce the uncertainty arising from technology is the concern of the industrial engineer. Woodward's research suggests that the degree of uncertainty with which an organization has to contend determines the amount of overlap between the system that designs and programs the production task and the system concerned with its execution. The inability to comprehend the production system in its entirety is the defining characteristic of batch production. In conditions of high uncertainty, it is impractical or uneconomic to collect enough information to know exactly what is happening at any given moment in time. The result is that people who work at different points in the system have access to only limited amounts of information and therefore form different conceptions of what the total system is like.

The field work done by Woodward proposes that control may be plotted on a scale ranging from completely personal hierarchical control at one extreme to completely mechanical control at the other. Between these two extremes come the administrative, but impersonal, control processes.

The classification of both technology and control systems depends upon a fairly detailed examination of the manufacturing process. The nature of the task, and also the way in which it is controlled, are the determinants of organizational behavior.

Linking what has been said about control variables and technical variables in the firms studied, we note that their significance for organizational behavior seems to be related to the fact that together they determine the degree of uncertainty with which an organization has to contend.

Technology is itself dependent on a number of factors: the nature of the product, the range of products, the market served, and the techniques and hardware available to process the appropriate raw materials and components, all of which can be sources of uncertainty.

As these case studies have shown, the amount of uncertainty in an organizational task is a major determinant of the way that the task can be controlled. A high degree of precision and explicitness in the objective-setting process is associated with mechanical and unitary control procedures. Referring to Exhibit 3–4, we see that unit production is linked with personal single-system control, batch production with fragmented control, and continuous flow production with single-system mechanical control.

But the case studies also show that the control system can reduce or increase the amount of uncertainty in the technology.

The design of control systems that reduce uncertainty arising from technology is the concern of the production engineer rather than the social scientist. The social scientist is more interested in the way that technology and control systems and the uncertainty they generate influence patterns of structure and behavior inside organizations. As far as structure is concerned, the case studies suggest that it is the degree of uncertainty with which an organization has to contend that determines the amount of overlap between the system that designs and programs the production task and the system concerned with its execution.

The lower portion of Exhibit 5–2 depicts some possible combinations of control options employed within various technological systems. The representations of control emphasis reflect general trends observed in our industrial studies:[7] the more advanced the state of technology, the greater the employment of technical support groups and the incorporation of process control devices directly within the system. Supervisory control is depicted as relatively high in the intermediate level, mass production-type system, where great emphasis is placed on continuity of production and supervisory intervention or surveillance has a measurable effect.[8] In low-level technologies ("crafts"), to the extent that control is internalized within craftsmen, personal control is deemphasized. (Other details and features of control in industrial operations are taken up in a subsequent section of this chapter. The following discussion clarifies the orientation of control designs in the industrial systems just described.)

Exhibit 5–3 presents four different views of process control at successive levels of refinement. In the first panel, a simplified representation, man is central in governing the control system. Input information is provided to the operator, who decides whether or not corrective action should be taken.

Panel 2 depicts human surveillance of control procedures. In some sales departments, panel 2 can apply as follows: strategic information (sales performance data) is brought to the attention of a decision maker (the sales manager) for possible action (communication with a salesman concerning individual performance). In this case, the operator is outside the control loop and observes system performance, making adjustments when they are indicated—as when the sales manager sends out correspondence on a routine basis when sales fall below a certain point.

EXHIBIT 5–3. Options in Process Control

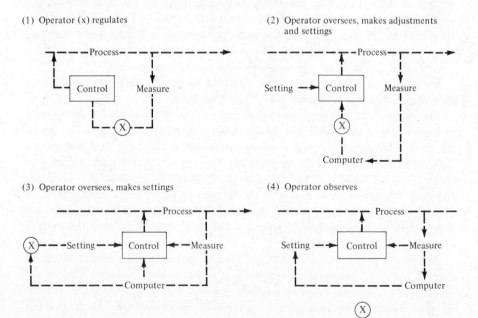

(1) Operator (x) regulates

(2) Operator oversees, makes adjustments and settings

(3) Operator oversees, makes settings

(4) Operator observes

Panel 3 depicts a much more sophisticated control system, one that uses a computer and complex programming parameters to govern a particular set of operating conditions. The parameters may be adjusted at the operator's discretion. Finally, in panel 4, the control loop is completely closed, and adjustments or settings may be made automatically, "on line."

Control Continuum and Structure

Exhibit 5–3 can be placed along a continuum (see Exhibit 5–4) from direct manual control to a closed loop with on-line, real-time control. In between the two extremes we can see the emergence of the closed loop-type of design through the successive steps of (1) data logging and the accumulation of managerial intelligence, (2) model development, and (3) the development of some type of open-loop design.

For situations corresponding to the extreme left of Exhibit 5–4, mechanical

EXHIBIT 5–4. Control Continuum and Structure

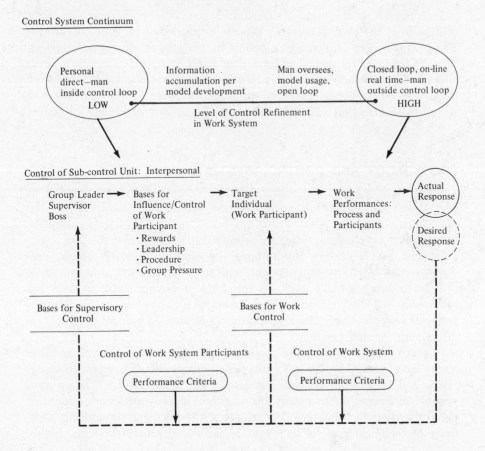

feedback is absent, and regulation is achieved wholly through human effort. The balance of the continuum reflects the gathering of intelligence/information and its synthesis into model form. Additional insight into the data leads to the formalizing of control design, and ultimately the achievement of an advanced, on-line, closed-loop arrangement.

Another feature of Exhibit 5–4 requires some elaboration. The discussions of control/performance criteria have centered on general approaches to designing and rationalizing these support systems, and at this point we wish to make the point that control processes reflect a structure of interrelated procedures. Exhibit 5–3 largely depicted the direct influence of an operator on work activity—but he in turn is also subject to control, and this is emphasized in Exhibit 5–4. For example, the work group supervisor secures information on performance outputs of both man and process (socio-technical complex), which affords the basis for his control posture and relationship to work group members. Deviations between actual response and desired response are signaled through direct supervisory observation or report data. Comparisons are made by the supervisor against preestablished performance criteria and/or his subjective notions as to what constitutes acceptable performance.

Thus two levels of control are illustrated here: In one, the operator exerts control over his own actions or process adjustments to gain conformity. These range from direct participation to adjustment of control devices. Second, supervisory control is leveled at work group members to redirect human activity or actions in order to gain coincidence of actual and desired performances. And of course there is the need to control supervisory actions. A subsequent section will advance these discussions of control structure.

TECHNOLOGY AND CONTROL SYSTEMS

The technology of an organization helps determine the character of its control system. As controls move up from subordinate to superior in the operational hierarchy, they are often based on impersonal performance criteria such as schedules, budgets, productivity indexes, and the like.

In craft-level operation, the authority structure tends to be simple, production work modestly independent, and order volume low, but employee skill levels are relatively high. In this kind of environment, workers are reasonably self-directed and require nominal supervision and impersonal controls. Comparatively simple procedures minimize logistical planning requirements for staff personnel.

In sharp contrast is the mass production situation, where control requirements are generally higher in all categories, especially with regard to supervisory and impersonal controls because of the relatively high labor component. Of course, to the extent that workers are assigned simple repetitive tasks, the need for direction decreases, but the need for supervising assistance or technical counsel increases. In advanced process systems, highly interdependent processes require a level of control beyond that possible under manual direction; hence process controls are extended as far as the development of control instruments permits. The following oil refining case example illustrates the extreme of automated, impersonal process control.

The changes pictured in Exhibit 5–5 support several points that were made in Chapters 3 and 4:

a. The gradual buildup in the direct labor component with the expansion of output, leveling out and then declining in absolute numbers despite the continued growth in plant capacity

b. Growth of the *maintenance* component of the work force, even after the direct labor has started to decline, to a point where it surpasses direct labor and ultimately starts to decline as the technology is perfected

EXHIBIT 5–5. Changing Composition of Refinery Manpower, 1920–1968

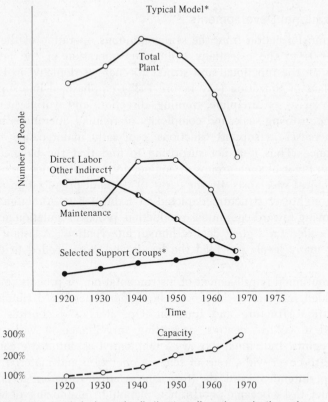

* Includes "technical service," "systems," and production planning.
† Clerical, administrative, supervising, and managerial.
Based on the records of two large petroleum refineries.

c. Growth of selected support groups, especially technical service, systems, and production planning

d. Decline of historically important support functions, such as quality control, as both process and control technologies improve (see Exhibit 5–3)

The experiences in the two refineries (upon which the figures in Exhibit 5–5 are based) merit additional comment. Trends in manpower composition and numbers were directly related to the character of the technologies that typified refinery operation. Continued improvement in petroleum processes and equipment permitted the benefits of large-scale operation, while overall plant employment declined. Perfection of process equipment reached a point where the previous trend toward increasing numbers of maintenance help was reversed, and ultimately it became possible to shift some maintenance work to outside (contract) services.

Organizational Developments

The transformation from the semicontinuous operation of the 1940s and early 1950s to the essentially continuous operation of the late 1950s is mirrored in the functional and structural changes depicted in Exhibit 5–6. Early plant organization (say before 1935) emphasized line supervision in such key areas as discipline, training, direction, and working time. By the 1940s the growing scale and complexity of refining operations necessitated large increases in support functions, especially maintenance and quality surveillance. Thus it is not surprising to find that the balance of power shifted in favor of such groups as engineering, maintenance, administrative, and technical specialists. By the early 1950s plant organization reached the massive eight-tier structure depicted in Exhibit 5–6. Although operations were moving toward continuous production, process regulation and monitoring still called for a great deal of human intervention. "Assistant" classifications at many levels provided the hands and eyes needed to control this complex.

The continued improvement of instrumentation for process control, along with added refinements in process equipment, permitted simplification of organization structure and function. Operators and controls were consolidated in control centers, permitting surveillance of wide areas from central points. Individual jobs were eliminated as automatic controls were installed to cover wide areas of refinery operation and material movement. The superintendent and the foreman assumed broader responsibilities: their chief tasks became short-range planning, minimizing downtime, improving performance, and monitoring worker activities to help ensure economic objectives. Concepts of supervision and skill changed materially

EXHIBIT 5–6. Evolution and Rationalization of Plant Organization in Some Oil Refineries, 1900–1967

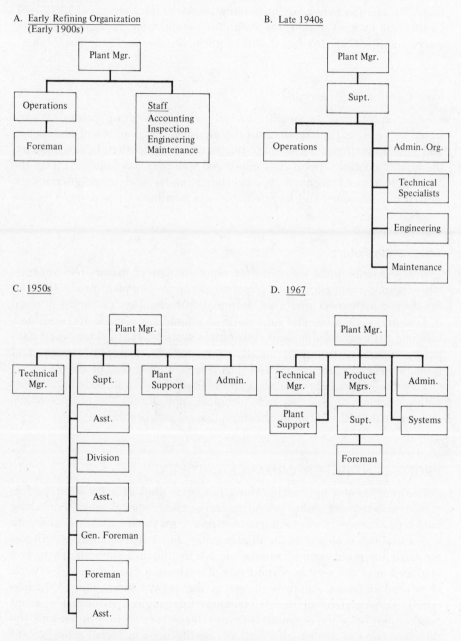

A. <u>Early Refining Organization</u>
   (Early 1900s)

B. <u>Late 1940s</u>

C. <u>1950s</u>

D. <u>1967</u>

R. W. Hidy and M. E. Hidy, *Pioneering in Big Business* (New York: Harper & Row, 1955); U.S. Dept. of Labor, *Studies in Automatic Technology,* Reprint No. 120 (Washington, D.C.: U.S. GPO, 1967; and IIT Technology Studies, 1965–1969.

with the introduction of advanced production systems. The responsibilities of first-line supervision expanded substantially to encompass multiple-process units. Today's foreman bears little resemblance to the foreman of 1930–1957. In the case of worker skill, the emphasis swung from physical skills (e.g., motor coordination) to mental skills (quick response and problem solving).

New Control Technologies

Older approaches to quality control in manufacturing processes were based on "wet" chemistry, or test-tube methods. The number of technicians and laboratory personnel in these plants was considerable. In one refinery, the quality-control support staff numbered well over one hundred. With the advent of electronic technology, solid-state circuitry, and computer control, it shifted to continuous and largely automatic monitoring equipment.

Toward the Future

Developments in the refineries are representative of mature technologies, where management efforts concentrate upon improving plant production and developing manpower resources. Information technology (a theme pursued in Chapter 7) has become important as attempts are made to coordinate far-flung drilling, refining, and distribution systems. It is evident that manpower resources, expecially in planning, systems, technical service, and economic analysis, are crucial and thus receive a great deal of attention.

These notes conclude our discussions of control and evaluation approaches with particular emphasis on socio-technical applications. The balance of the chapter deals with control applications, issues, and problems.

PROFIT-CENTER PERFORMANCE CRITERIA

The profit-center approach, which has been used as a basis for performance measurement, delineates structural or technological subsystems along lines representing self-containment or expressing a profit capability; and with responsibilities centered on an administrative head, it frequently constitutes the basis for profit-center formulation. As Exhibit 5–7 suggests, there is a clarification of the very important role of evaluation (performance) criteria at several different authority levels in the organization. The evaluation criteria employed by divisional managers for gauging performance is but another portion of the organization's overall control system. Futhermore, the the channeling of diverse information (intelligence) to higher management permits broader and more refined types of analyses, which pertains as well to other divisions.

Exhibit 5–7 expresses the emergence of an organizational control system as

EXHIBIT 5–7. Profit-Center Performance Criteria

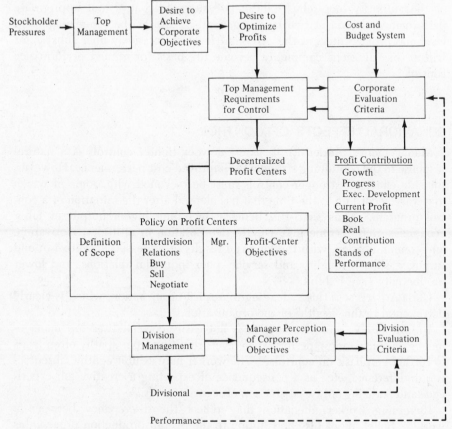

Based on concepts formulated by Joel Dean.

a response to top management's desire to gain confidence in the attainment of corporate objectives. The creation of functional substructures along product, geographic, or regional lines (for example) increases the "visibilities" of the boundaries for a profit center. Delegation of administrative and operating responsibilities to profit-center heads increases their opportunities to directly affect the destinies and welfare of profit-center functions. To the extent that profit-center heads largely control resource allocations and performances within their areas, the more they can be held accountable for the total product of center efforts. Presumably, this decentralization of responsibility to a center head positions him for better performance control than a highly centralized model with detailed controls at the top of the structure with top management.

This same principle of decentralizing performance responsibilities (and attendant needs for control) can be "layerly" extended within profit centers to substructures or to functions of them. Thus a complex structure of "control systems within control systems" starts to emerge within and at various levels of the authority hierarchy. Exhibit 5–7 suggests control and appropriate performance criteria at two levels: general control at the top-management level and profit centers at the "division" level. Successively finer subsystems within the "division" commonly become the basis for refined performance control.

BEHAVIORAL EFFECTS OF CONTROL

Management's propensity to assert new or tighter controls is a natural response to the continuing struggle for improved cost performance. However, the side effects of stronger controls must be reckoned with, some of which may vary according to the time that has elapsed after the initiation of a control program.[9] Thus short-run benefits, including higher output or labor economies, may in time give way to deterioration in attitudes, motivation, and communication, with the long-run results of increased absenteeism and turnover, slips in quality and service, poor industrial relations, and lower productivity (see Exhibit 5–8).

Chris Argyris sees this as leading to a spirit of alienation, which is clearly detrimental to the "health" of the organization.[10]

Unfortunately, such dysfunction is not easily corrected, as top management's response to low performance levels resulting from apathy often leads to further emphasis on controls.[11] The worker may exhibit apathy, absenteeism, indifference, etc., as a consequence of expecting a creative job experience and realizing only a satisfaction of security needs.[12]

Increasing worker alienation may reflect the discrepancy between a worker's belief about his contribution to the overall production process, his desired contribution or expectations, and his compensation. That is, increased management control eliminates some of the worker's ability to control his own activities and typically increases the routinization of the job. Short-term production efficiency and cost reductions are secured, and the worker's compensation may even increase, yet expectations regarding involvement of self beyond the use of nominal physical skills may be even more remote. Also, the worker is perhaps less able to justify (to himself) receiving the same or more pay for "less" work. Unfortunately, this new attitude may lead to undesirable behavior: apathy, absenteeism, indifference, etc. For example, the highly paid automobile assembly line worker may express job dissatisfaction, contribute to high absenteeism, perform sloppy work, and reflect a general hostility toward management.[13]

Difficulty in recognizing or correcting behavioral dysfunction in control systems may arise from (a) apparently unconventional behavior that is difficult to detail, (b) a time lapse between initiation of controls and the sur-

EXHIBIT 5-8. Dysfunctional Consequences of Control

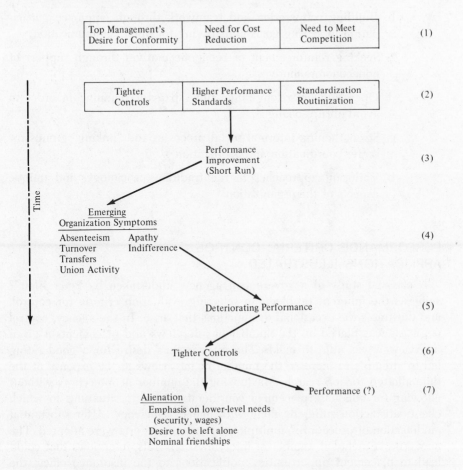

facing of negative results,[14] (c) organizational procedures or information systems that cannot sense or isolate causal factors, and (d) the nature of change, whereby deterioration of organizational tone, health, relationships, and performance typically develops slowly. Research in this area reveals that adverse side effects frequently accompany *departures* from past performance patterns, and are not necessarily concomitants of change per se.[15]

A natural question at this point is "Which control approaches may prove superior in the long run, particularly in preventing dysfunction?" Likert and Seashore propose an approach to meet this need, and their key to improved controls is a selective approach to cost-control programs and elicitation of cooperative rather than hostile attitudes from organization members. Research conducted by Likert at the University of Michigan suggests several points that management might include in control programs:

a. Avoidance of direct hierarchical pressure

b. Building cooperation and teamwork through employee participation in setting goals and striving for open communication

c. Seeking reinforcement of economic motives through support of noneconomic motives

d. Operating on a long-range time span for planning in order to avoid abrupt change

e. Strengthening informal social processes and "linking" groups for better coordination and cooperation

f. Tailoring approaches to the traditions, sociology, and unique aspects of the organization[16]

PERFORMANCE CRITERIA: CONTROL APPLICATIONS ILLUSTRATED

A classical study of a government agency, undertaken by Peter Blau,[17] suggests the inherent problems in selecting evaluation criteria for control, and illustrates the occasional dysfunctions that arise. In the agency, control emphasis was placed on the number of interviews and placements a given interviewer was able to make. The interviewer's desire for a good rating led to attempts to increase the number of interviews at the expense of the time allotted for job search. Maximizing the number of interviews without allowing for adequate placement considerations led to situations in which client satisfaction suffered, along with agency efficiency. After substantial modification of procedures, multiple performance criteria were adopted. The new criteria included number of interviews, referrals, interviews that could lead to placement opportunities, notifications to the insurance office, the number of application forms made out, and so forth. Two months after the new system was implemented, placements had risen from 2,159 to 2,286, although job openings had decreased from 3,944 to 3,425 within an overlapping period of four months.

R&D CONTROL

Exhibit 5–9 shows an organizational control system for research and development. The flow of the exhibit describes the initiation at the corporate level of objectives for the research and development effort, which are often dictated by economics, and the translation of these objectives into project missions. Note the development of evaluation criteria (4 and 5), which form a basis for examining the product of the research effort. An important technical distinction is that control tends to be oriented toward the short term or the current time period, whereas evaluation (through step 6) is typically retrospective, dealing with past performance. In the R&D process, as depicted in the exhibit, the evaluation of *past* performance, objectives, character of products, and quality of effort becomes a basis for evaluating *current* research and development outputs. The exhibit distinguishes between control (step 7 and beyond) and evaluation stages. Note that, in the upper left-hand portion of the exhibit, the decision-making subsystem is depicted, where evaluation of past performance combines with top management's interpretation of competitive demands and customer needs, and provides the basis for the decisions that affect the R&D system. Top management's desires for research and development combine with current information from the R&D effort to influence the activities that comprise input to the organization. The heart of control for the R&D effort, then, centers around the performance criteria (4), which are selected to guide R&D efforts within policy objectives.[18]

Saxberg and Slocum note four approaches to the managerial control of scientific manpower. These include traditional control, bureaucratic control, cybernetic control, and behavioral control.

Traditional control involves management's operating rules, for example,

EXHIBIT 5–9. Control and Evaluation in R&D

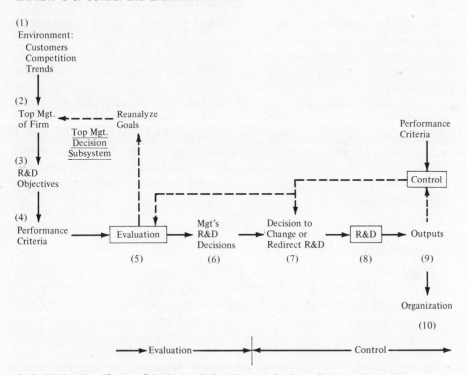

A. D. Rubinstein, "Setting Criteria for R&D," Harvard Business Review, 35, 1, 1957.

performance standards, budgets, definitions of job tasks. The authors conceptualize this control process as the choice of operating rules and methods for the employees and the enforcement of these rules by management. Traditional control also involves management communication, motivation approaches, and leadership styles. These types of control relate to management's ability to influence the exchange transaction between the company and its employees.

Bureaucratic control, the type developed by Max Weber, emphasizes the formality of control. Formality involves clearly defining certain patterns of activity. Control is achieved through directives coming from the top of the pyramid and being transmitted through formal lines of communication down the hierarchy. The power to enforce control thus derives from the status of the office.

"Cybernetic system" control is essentially a system of feedback control. The concept of feedback involves a premise that "in a goal seeking system relationship, a circular flow of information has a reciprocal effect on behavior and action. This circular pattern involves an information flow to the point of action, a flow back to the point of decision with information on action, and then a return to the point of action with new information . . . . Decisions are events which enter the network that constitutes the communications system."[19]

The above three methods of control involve monitoring the subordinates' work and activities vis-à-vis the required behavior of the job. The behavioral approach emphasizes the external as well as the internal pressures and forces influencing individual behavior in the work environment. This type of control deals with influencing the individual's perceptions, learning, and motivation.

In the industrial scientist's setting, the behavior control approach seems to be the most appropriate. Saxberg and Slocum note that in their account of the dimensions of management control of industrial scientists, professional values have occupied the center of the stage; values, sentiments, and norms shape the individual's performance and motivate him. Yet varying combinations of these control approaches are the reality with which analysts most likely will contend.

QUALITY CONTROL

Simulations provide the means by which management can rationalize complex systems and identify alternatives by which performance can be improved. In the appendix to Chapter 4, simulation was discussed in terms of production and inventory control systems. Here we shall emphasize another important subsystem—quality control—and focus more specifically on the underlying model in order to achieve a more viable simulation.

In thinking of a quality control system, we frequently tend to visualize a rather simple input-output model, as depicted in panel A of Exhibit 5–10.

Note that quality control scrutinizes the production subsystem, removes unacceptable products, and maintains a specified level of good items Presumably it also alerts production to off-standard products. However, this simplified representation is a long way from the realities of a working system in terms of functions, additional subsystems, and the complexity of human relationships.

Panel B provides for the main work activity (in this case fabrication), storage, in-process holding of partly finished items for assembly, finished goods, and final inspection. A second important component is the realistic

EXHIBIT 5–10. Quality Control System: Modeling Bases for Simulation

A. Initial Conception

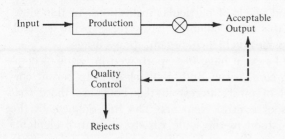

B. Closer Approximation of Ongoing System

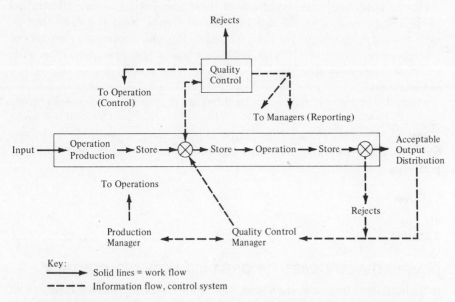

Key:
→ Solid lines = work flow
---- Information flow, control system

For a detailed explanation, see E. B. Roberts, "Industrial Dynamics and the Design of Management Control Systems," in Bodini et al. (eds.), *Management Controls* (New York: Mc-Graw-Hill, 1964), 102–126.

addition of time delays in the processing of reject information. Third, the field performance of the completed product cannot be ignored, particularly where customers or field representatives channel information back to the production manager and then to the manager of quality control.

SUMMARY

This chapter focused on rationalizing the control system, which, with communications (Chapter 6) and technology (Chapters 3 and 4), constitutes the principal organizational systems when interlaced with structure.

The central feature of the control system is that of performance criteria, multiple means by which the quality and quantity of activities in complex organizations can be judged. Performance criteria are formulated to meet the strategic plans, goals, and needs of particular institutions. In this view, budgets constitute one of the more common bases for evoking control, and they serve as a central business vehicle in organizational usage.

Key features of the control system have been portrayed in terms of components that permit sensing, comparison, and feedback so as to permit corrective action. The systems of most interest in this book are those that possess mixed combinations of control elements. The full richness of the control system is best understood in the wide variety of control elements that evidence some level of interchangeability; these elements range from the behavioral to the impersonal mechanistic.

Chapters 3 and 4 suggested some of the technological considerations that prescribe appropriate combinations of these elements. The case illustration of the refinery indicated the shifts in control organization and configuration over time as technology was updated. Also, the philosophy of management and client requirements (Chapter 2), to name a few examples, represents additional elements that serve to determine the control profile of a given organization.

Control systems evidence considerable potential to impart desired (or undesired) behavioral outcomes to organizational members. Thoughtful combinations of control elements can assist in minimizing undesirable outcomes; they can also encourage individual contribution and growth, and thus support long-run institutional objectives.

Appendix

DEMONSTRATION CASE OF ORGANIZATION AND CONTROL

A metropolitan transit system was confronted with increasing numbers of customer complaints regarding schedules, driver attitude, and passenger comfort. With encouragement from the mayor of the city, a systems analyst and a route supervisor were asked to study the situation and propose a control model to aid in alleviating the situation.

At first, the problem appeared relatively simple, and the systems analyst sketched a crude control model that included driver, bus, and shop maintenance personnel—all considered crucial variables for control (see Exhibit 5A–1). Through regular inspection of equipment, close checking of time schedules, and random observance of drivers under operating conditions (among other measures), it was felt that service could be significantly improved.

EXHIBIT 5A–1. Preliminary Control Model

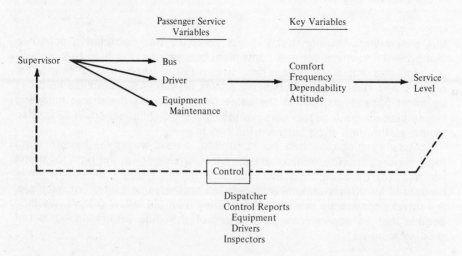

But to whom should the inspectors and dispatchers report? Should supervisors assume general responsibility and have the drivers and controllers report to them? Clearly, some type of overall control was desirable that would permit independence of judgment, promote good working relationships, and raise the level of customer service.

It should be top management, through public relations, and *not* supervisors, who receive the reports from the inspectors, for the following reasons.

    a. The objective of quality control (to increase customer satisfaction) has effects on the total company image.

    b. Route supervisors generally do not have a broad enough perspective to exercise discretion in public relations matters.

    c. If supervision constituted the decision-making center, the resulting low-level closed control loop would be difficult for top management to control, and might permit tactics that would negate the entire control system if the supervisors as a group decided to thwart the objectives of top management.

d. The advantages of an overall control system could still exist if top management used supervision as an instrument for initiating corrective action, provided the supervisors could be motivated.

Let us examine the situation more closely.

Physical condition of buses. Buses are to be cleaned by maintenance personnel at the garages before they go out. The drivers are expected to remove large trash items at the end of each run, including newspapers, pop cans, etc. Thus the degree of cleanliness in the buses is controlled both in the garages and on the road.

Bus scheduling. Assume that the bus company has designed a schedule that provides for frequent and convenient bus service. If this is true, schedule problems would arise from drivers who fail to observe their schedules. A driver who runs ahead of schedule makes his job easier because he picks up fewer passengers, but at the same time he forces the driver following him to pick up more passengers, so that he falls behind schedule. This also increases the time span between the two buses.

Scheduling problems can be controlled in two ways: (a) by providing route supervisors who would make sure that drivers are at the right locations on time; (b) by comparing the total fare money brought in with what is brought in by drivers on similar schedules on the same route. For example, if a driver consistently brings in less money than his fellow drivers, we may deduce that he consistently runs ahead of schedule (assuming he is not stealing money).

Driver attitude. This is a difficult variable to control. It depends to a large extent on the drivers' social and economic backgrounds, as well as many other variables that are beyond the control of the company. The company should attempt to develop favorable attitudes among the drivers during their training periods and to create working conditions that encourage good driver attitudes.

Poor attitudes could be detected by "passenger" inspectors, who would board the buses and observe the drivers' attitudes without their knowledge. For greater efficiency, control efforts should be concentrated in areas with the greatest number of complaints.

A system model. As a system, the transportation company can be visualized as an aggregate of subsystems, each model as shown in Exhibit 5A–2, assuming decentralized garage locations.

Similar systems could be instituted in the other garages. The only difference would be the number of inspectors in each garage, in proportion to the level of passenger complaints. If the number of complaints in a certain

EXHIBIT 5A–2. Control System for One Garage

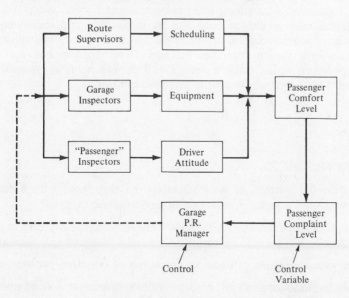

area were too low to justify an independent control department, the departments that control two or more garages could be incorporated into one. This could be best decided by using a city map to identify locations.

The organizational structure of the control system would be as shown in Exhibit 5A–3. Public relations would be instrumental in scrutinizing the operation of the garage, as well as assessing route and passenger variables; also, competition among garages could be encouraged. Control would be

EXHIBIT 5A–3. Organizational Structure of the Control System

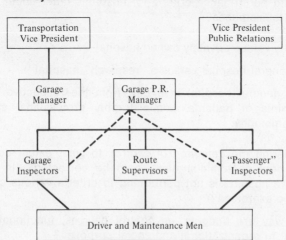

built around the physically decentralized units, rather than around functions, in order to minimize intradepartmental control and coordination. Drivers and maintenance men would be observed by inspectors and supervisors, who would report any conditions not consistent with company objectives to the public relations manager of their garage. The manager, being a second-level supervisor, would issue warnings and initiate punitive measures when indicated. This setup would ensure effective control.

QUESTIONS

1. How do the outputs of an R&D effort, as compared with a service or product unit, affect the selection of performance criteria?

2. How would you maintain a balance between supervisory and impersonal controls?

3. What criteria would you use as measures of effective decision making?

4. What dysfunctions might emerge within divisional management of a profit-center decentralized organization?

5. How can management recognize behavorial dysfunctions of control, pinpoint them, and correct them?

6. Compare and contrast performance criteria for the following situations:

    a. Housewares manufacturer

    b. General hospital

    c. "Park district" of a large city

7. How would performance criteria for hospitals differ under the following sets of circumstances?

    a. City versus privately owned hospital

    b. General hospital versus a "research" hospital

    c. A general hospital in a city, from the respective viewpoints of patients, administration, professional staff, and the community.

    Considering the definition of control, to what extent do you feel inefficient practice/administration could be corrected? (In other words, what if the hospital is not performing to criteria various citizens would like to see exercised?)

8. In what way are budgets, as control devices, functional and/or dysfunctional to organizational and social purposes?

9. Do the roles played by finance personnel and factory supervisory personnel contain inherent conflicts?

10. In what manner are budgets and their associated activities functional and/or dysfunctional to organizational purposes? To social purposes?

11. Contrast the perceptions of financial and supervisory personnel concerning budgets as

    a. Control devices

    b. Bases for motivating personnel

    c. Channelers of activity

    d. Influences on innovation

    e. Sources of conflict

12. What approaches to budgeting can be proposed to make them more functional to management and organization members?

13. Suggest some propositions concerning needed closeness of supervision and predictability of subordinate tasks under the following circumstances:

    a. Varying institutional situations

    b. Supervisors disposed to laissez-faire approaches

    c. Impressions of closeness of supervision (employee perception) and objective time measurements made by an industrial engineer

14. In what manner do the varying types of "professional" training influence individual expectations for discretion in the discharge of individual duties?

15. Comment on the strong trend of many businesses to use profit centers as a means of furthering control, from the standpoint of

    a. Differentiation versus integration

    b. Dysfunction

16. What are the implications of the control options displayed in Exhibit 5–3 in conjunction with the information of case 9 (refineries) for

    a. Selection of personnel to man these systems?

    b. Expected behavioral outcomes?

17. Consider Exhibit 5–2, which summarizes organizational control systems.

 a. What are the implications for a plant modernization program?

 b. What are the behavioral implications for the various possibilities you are considering?

 c. State all necessary assumptions.

DISCUSSION QUESTION

Recently a major metropolitan newspaper endorsed a particular political. candidate, yet:

 a. A staff writer openly attacked the politician in his column.

 b. A group of reporters signed a petition indicating their endorsement of the politician's opponent.

Discuss this situation from the standpoint of organization control.

Group role-playing exercise. The material for the demonstration case of organization and control which follows focuses on the organizational and behavioral problems of a large metropolitan transportation system. After reading the material assume the following roles in discussing these matters:

 a. Systems analyst

 b. Supervisor

 c. Driver

 d. Customer

 e. Panel of experts who must recommend a course of action at conclusion of dialogue

NOTES

1. This broad perspective of control for socio-technical systems is developed in A. K. Rice and E. J. Miller, *Systems of Organization: The Control of Task and Sentient Boundaries* (London: Tavistock Publications, 1967).

2. For much greater elaboration on the influence of competition on control, see, for example, Pradik N. Khandwalla, "Effect of Competition in the Structure of Top Management Control," *Academy of Management Journal,* 16, no. 2 (June 1973): 285–296.

3. Borje O. Saxberg and John Slocum, "The Management of Scientific Manpower," *Management Science,* 14, no. 8 (April 1968): B478–B489.

4. For a good general discussion of the positioning of controls and control systems within organizations, see Joan Woodward, *Industrial Organization, Behavior and Control* (London: Oxford University Press, 1970).

5. For some analyses bringing together structure and control strategies, see John Child, "Organization Structure and Strategies of Control: A Replication of the Aston Study," *Academy of Management Journal,* 17, no. 2 (June 1972): 163–178.

6. Woodward, *Industrial Organization.*

7. Many of these are summarized in Elmer H. Burack and Thomas J. McNichols, *Human Resource Planning: Technology, Planning, Change* (Kent, O.: Kent State University, Bureau of Business and Economics Research, 1973).

8. Elmer H. Burack, "Some Aspects of Supervisory Control in Advanced Production Systems," *Human Organization,* 26, no. 4 (Fall 1966): 256–264, and "Some Aspects of Industrial Supervision," *Academy of Management Journal,* 9, no. 1 (March 1966): 43–67.

9. This section draws on a number of useful insights developed by Rensis Likert and Stanley E. Seashore in "Making Cost Control Work," *Harvard Business Review,* 41, no. 6 (November–December 1963): 96–108.

10. Chris Argyris, "The Organization: What Makes It Healthy?" *Harvard Business Review,* 36, no. 6 (November–December 1958): 107–156.

11. For a discussion of reinforcement conditioning to gain quality/quantity control, see Everett E. Adam Jr. and William E. Scott Jr., "The Application of Behavioral Conditioning Procedures to the Problems of Quality Control," *Academy of Management Journal,* 14, no. 2 (June 1971): 175–193.

12. For a description of alienation in a highly controlled, unitized environment, see Richard E. Walton, "How to Counter Alienation in the Plant," *Harvard Business Review,* 50, no. 6 (November–December 1972): 70–82.

13. See, for example, Harold L. Sheppard, some abstracts of his observations on quality of work life" issues, in Gerald G. Somers (ed.), *Proceedings of the Twenty-fifth Anniversary Meeting, Industrial Relations Research Association* (Madison: University of Wisconsin Press, 1973), and Elmer H. Burack, "The Quality of Work Life: An Important and Complex Issue," *Technology and Human Affairs,* 5, no. 2 (Spring 1973).

14. For a description of the long time lags often incurred due to three types of changes, see Rensis Likert, *The Human Organization* (New York: McGraw-Hill, 1967).

15. Likert and Seashore, "Making Cost Control Work," p. 96.

16. Likert, *The Human Organization.*

17. Peter F. Blau, *Dynamics of Bureaucracy* (Chicago: University of Chicago Press, 1955).

18. For related research in R&D organizations, see Saxberg and Slocum, "The Management of Scientific Manpower."

19. Ibid.

REFERENCES

Bowers, Donald G. "Organizational Control in an Insurance Company." *Sociometry,* 27, no. 2 (June 1964): 230–244.

———— and S. E. Seashore. "Predicting Organizational Effectiveness with a Four-Factor Theory of Leadership." *Administrative Science Quarterly,* 11, no. 2 (September 1966): 238–263.

Child, John. "Organization Structure and Strategies of Control: A Replication of Aston Studies." *Administrative Science Quarterly,* 17, no. 2 (June 1972): 163–177.

Coch, L., and J. R. P. French. "Overcoming Resistance to Change." *Human Relations,* 1, no. 3 (August 1948): 512–532.

French, J. R. P., J. Israel, and D. As. "An Experiment on Participation in a Norwegian Factory." *Human Relations,* 13, no. 1 (February 1960): 3–20.

Guetzkow, Harold. "Communications in Organizations," in J. G. March (ed.), *Handbook of Organizations* (Chicago: Rand McNally, 1965).

Koontz, Herold, and Robert W. Bradspies. "Managing through Feed-Forward Control—A Future Directed View." *Business Horizons,* 15, no. 3 (June 1972): 25–36.

Likert, Rensis. *The Human Organization* (New York: McGraw-Hill, 1967).

McMahon, J. Timothy, and G. W. Perritt. "The Control Structures of Organizations." *Academy of Management Journal,* 14, no. 3 (September 1971): 327–339.

Patchen, M. "Alternative Questionnaire Approaches to the Measurement of Influence in Organizations." *American Journal of Sociology,* 69, no. 1 (July 1963): 41–52.

Shepard, H. "Changing Interpersonal and Intergroup Relationships in Organizations," in J. G. March (ed.), *Handbook of Organizations* (Chicago: Rand McNally, 1965).

Smith, C. G., and M. E. Brown. "Communication Structure and Control Structure in a Voluntary Organization." *Sociometry,* 27, no. 4 (December 1964): 449–468.

Smith, C. G., and A. S. Tannenbaum. "Organizational Control Structure: A Comparative Analysis." *Human Relations,* 16, no. 4 (November 1963): 299–316.

Tannenbaum, Arnold S. "Control and Effectiveness in a Voluntary Organization." *American Journal of Sociology,* 67, no. 1 (July 1961): 33–46.

————. *Control in Organizations* (New York: McGraw-Hill, 1968).

Learning Objectives

Rationalizing a General Model of a Communication System
Institutional and Environmental Features Shaping the
  Communication System
Internal Factors Shaping Communication System Characteristics
Influence of Communications on Role Formation and
  Development
Interplay of Communications and Work Technology
Communications and Group Processes
Bases for Systematic Study of Communication Systems

Chapter 6

COMMUNICATIONS

OVERVIEW

Communications are inexorably tied to the functions and processes of organization. Systems for communications that are formally designed, as well as the informal linkages that arise to meet business and social purposes, are the concerns of this chapter. The initial discussions seek to establish the definition of terms and concepts employed throughout the chapter, and which are further related to a systems-oriented model that underlies subsequent discussions.

The first major discussions take up three perspectives on the emergence, form, and utilization of communications, reflecting (a) external environmental factors, (b) internal environmental factors, reflecting behavioral and technological matters, and (c) a phenomenon emerging (and changing in character) over time.

Next, a comprehensive model, proposed by Arlyn Melcher, assists in positioning the role and function of communications in the broader sweep of organizational processes. The results and implications of various research studies are the focus of the subsequent studies in the chapter.

Technological processes (Chapters 3 and 4) bear an important influence on the character, direction, and frequency of communications—research in various work systems assists in enlarging the understanding of this manner of interaction and influence. Also, considerable work has been undertaken on the effects of structure and property of communications within and between work groups. Group processes, roles, decision making, and social relationships are some of the many factors involved in these discussions.

Communication systems provide the fabric that connects administrative and operating functions for purposes of transmitting and processing information, leveling influence, and conducting much of the affairs of organization. More specifically, *communication* represents the transmittal of symbols, data, or information for purposes of influence, analysis, understanding, and/ or control. Communication processes may emerge between individuals, groups, or combinations of these; underlying exchanges between people are important psychological and sociological phenomena.

The *communications system* consists of a network of relationships generally dedicated to a specific purpose or task function, frequently comprising humanistic and impersonal elements, possessing encoding (input) and decoding (output) elements, and delineated in scope for the convenience of usage or analysis. Computer-based systems are viewed as a particular subset of communication systems largely dedicated to information encoding, processing, transmittal, and decoding (Chapter 7).

The *properties* of a communication system are those features of the system that portray its functional characteristics, for example, response rate, distortion/screening of information, and frequency of response.

Many of the key ideas set forth in this section have benefited from a perspective initially proposed by Robert L. Kahn and Daniel Katz.[1]

GENERAL COMMUNICATIONS MODEL

Exhibit 6–1 is a systems view of a communication network, with emphasis on its design and behavioral implications. Subsystems A and B of the exhibit constitute the mainstream and feedback control loops. Section C presents some of the points to consider in designing the structure of a system, along with some possible dysfunctional consequences inherent in system operations.

In subsystem A the encoding of information constitutes the initial inputs into the communication system. Encoded information is exchanged between individuals, between individual and group, or between department and department. Information can be data or ideas to complete cause-result statements that contain both premises and implications.[2] Fragmentary information is obscure and requires clarification. For instance, a simple presentation of sales figures does not convey such important ideas as trends, new market potential, or possible loss in sales effectiveness, which are important concomitants of these figures.

Encoded information may also be characterized by its relevance over time. Important information can serve its purpose in the short run. Methods, orders, mathematical and statistical analyses, priority lists, and selected studies are typical of such project-oriented, temporarily useful information. Other types of information guide organization activities over an extended time period, and include policy and planning programs. The time frame for information is important for design features and system functions.

Another useful classification for information is "factual" versus "subjective." This involves the potential distortions that can occur in attempting to take encoded information from one part of the system and use it in another. "Factual" connotes that which conveys a largely universal meaning

EXHIBIT 6–1. General Organization Model of a Communications System

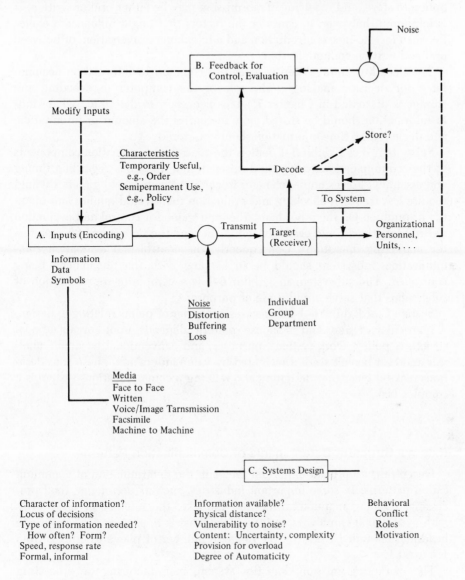

Noise

B. Feedback for
    Control, Evaluation

Modify Inputs

Store?

Characteristics
Temporarily Useful,
  e.g., Order
Semipermanent Use,
  e.g., Policy

Decode

To System

A. Inputs (Encoding)

Transmit

Target
(Receiver)

Organizational
Personnel,
Units, . . .

Information
Data
Symbols

Noise
Distortion
Buffering
Loss

Individual
Group
Department

Media
Face to Face
Written
Voice/Image Tarnsmission
Facsimile
Machine to Machine

C. Systems Design

Character of information?	Information available?	Behavioral
Locus of decisions	Physical distance?	Conflict
Type of information needed?	Vulnerability to noise?	Roles
How often? Form?	Content: Uncertainty, complexity	Motivation
Speed, response rate	Provision for overload	
Formal, informal	Degree of Automaticity	

and is subject to minimum interpretation. "Subjective" applies to the kind
of information that can lead to a wide variety of interpretations.

Another element of communications illustrated in subsystem A of Exhibit
6–1 is "buffering," or distortion potential. Distortion may be related to either
the system or the personnel. Information that is withheld or incomplete poses
as serious a problem in decision making as that which is intentionally dis-

torted. Subsystem A also presents the elements of transmission, decoding, option to store, and receiving. Transmission may be either oral or written. It is important, however, to consider the factors that might influence a choice between face-to-face confrontation and a telephone conversation, or between oral and written communication.

The decoding-storage step is a feature common to information accumulated for decision making. (The role of the computer in decoding and storage is discussed in Chapter 7.) It is necessary to determine what kinds of information should be stored, how to control the amount of information, and the length of time information should be stored.

Subsystem B of Exhibit 6–1 depicts the control and evaluation components of the communication system, and raises design questions regarding timing and accuracy. For example, changes in competitive marketing tactics would require less frequent checking and evaluation than would quality and quantity of product. On the other hand, the time frame for control and evaluation of R&D functions could easily extend far beyond the time frame for monitoring marketing operations. Consequently, the control and evaluation communication subsystem should be in keeping with the phenomena being controlled. The subsystem in Exhibit 6–1 is a composite representation of subsystems that serve a multitude of purposes.

Section C of Exhibit 6–1 summarizes a number of points relating to design. A particular design and response pattern depends upon organizational structure, policy, work systems, purposes, and conventional economic analysis and cost-benefit studies weighted by value judgments. These considerations make it clear that designing and refining a communications system is a complex task.

External Structure Determinants of Communication Patterns

Decentralization is an important factor in the determination of communication patterns. In some important industries, such as petroleum, food processing, clothing manufacturing, and the like, the number of large firms with over 10,000 employees varies widely. That is to say, for each corporate headquarters unit (a "firm"), the range in number of plants to firms is from 1:1 to 50:1.

The marketing mission, logistics system, manufacturing or processing technology, and related technical functions are other determinants of the communications system.

The interplay of these factors is illustrated in Exhibit 6–2, which presents several prototypes. For example, the regional production units of the commercial bakery in panel A are largely independent of one another. The physically decentralized units serve regional areas and their communications with corporate headquarters staff are largely concerned with quality control, cost auditing, and new product development. The very large corporate chains

EXHIBIT 6–2. Communication Patterns and Industry Structure

A. Semi-autonomous Divisions (Baking Industry)

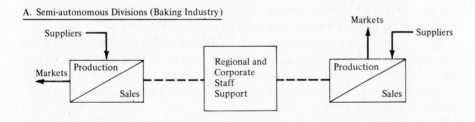

B. Integrated Operations (Steel, Petroleum, Railroads)

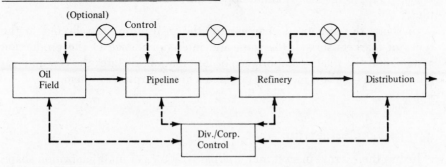

C. Functional Departments (Printing)   D. Service Organizations (Insurance)

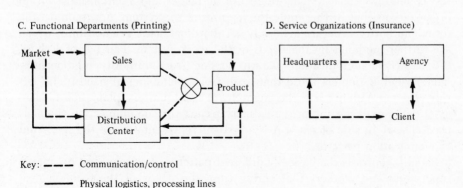

Key: – – – – Communication/control

——— Physical logistics, processing lines

may have thirty, forty, or fifty field units, each semi-independent, to serve
different markets. This independence is modified if the regional centers specialize in production and interchange products to serve multiproduct markets. For example, one regional unit might specialize in bread and another
in cake products. Where the market of each unit requires both types of
products, they exchange. Thus the character of communication between
plants changes: new interdependencies arise, which require closer coordination of production, sales, and shipping.

The integrated steel or petroleum system in panel B represents another structural pattern among physically decentralized units, and calls for another type of communications pattern that is highly interrelated. Highly interdependent technologies require tight coordination and planning to assure balance at all points on the production/continuum distribution.

Panel C portrays a marketing (sales)-distribution-production complex. In this type of system (a type of "all channels") there is interrelated effort between all major components relative to order flows, production flows, purchasing operations, replenishment of orders at distribution centers, and complaints and orders from the field.

In panel D, a service organization (insurance) is largely concerned with information flows. The greater significance of communication in this type of business represents a substantial opportunity for the automation of information.[3]

In short, the structural character of the institution, as reflected in the types of markets served, the form and interdependence of the production system, and the relative importance of information, dictates the communications pattern that best meets the needs of a given corporate system.

INTERNAL STRUCTURE

Just as the exernal market and internal structure of an organization shape the communications system, there are activities and relationships within organizations that further mold the features of the system. For example, the formal authority structure defines boss-subordinate-staff relationships, which are further modified by the needs of the work system. Panel A of Exhibit 6–3 depicts communication patterns arising from authority relationships, while panel B depicts those that arise from technological needs. The left side of panel A shows how the hierarchy of headquarters, plant, and department determines the authority relationships and the communication channels used. The right side of panel A is a systems representation of the work and communication patterns.

Panel B contrasts the basically different patterns of communication among supervisors and workers that spring from the needs of the technological system. In low-level technology production systems, the work stations (departments) have a low time dependency, so that the flow of information between workers and supervisor parallels departmental lines and concerns work functions. Interchanges of information may also reflect the application of supervisory authority or problem-solving activities. Interactions among supervisors would involve coordination in the movement of materials between departments, as well as quality control and order expediting. In the absence of features in the technological system that assure a fixed path of movement, coordination depends upon supervisory groups and support personnel.

This contrasts with mass production systems, where continuous work flow

EXHIBIT 6–3. Communication Patterns Shaped by Authority Structure and Technology

A. Authority Structure

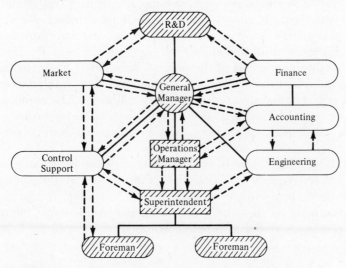

█████ Direct line-of-authority relationship

B. Technology and Communications

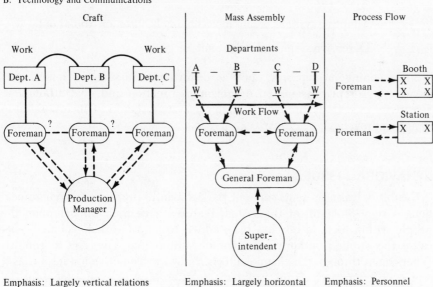

Craft

Emphasis: Largely vertical relations

Mass Assembly

Emphasis: Largely horizontal relations

W = Worker

Process Flow

Emphasis: Personnel monitoring system

is usually an inherent part of the work system design. In the intermediate mass production technologies, time dependencies are substantial, but the coordination of flow between work stations is built in. (This should not be confused with the development, prior to operations, of overall plans for coordination of resources. Support systems require an intensive effort by specialists—production control and industrial engineers to meet the time-place-quantity-quality dimensions of the production system.) The interchange of communication between worker and foreman on the assembly line typically *does not* reflect the exercise of supervisory authority. The technology has already accounted for material flow: highly detailed impersonal controls in the form of methods, procedures, and specifications guide the worker's activity.

What, then, is the nature of communication on the line? Frequently, exchanges involve requests for materials or the help of the foreman to ensure line movements. In a sense, then, the worker is "directing" the foreman. The cost of disruption on these lines is so high that considerable informal authority (power) is vested in communcations *from subordinate to superior*.

COMMUNICATION OVERLOAD

The response of the system to overload stress is viewed as either "adaptive" or "defensive," [4] and can be described briefly as follows:

   a. Adaptive systems create more channels, filter, or "round out."

   b. Defensive systems distort, omit, or guess.

Some coping mechanisms, such as distortion, omission, or delays, may have serious repercussions on organization function and goal attainment. Sensitivity to such dysfunctions within the system should be incorporated in design approaches.

BEHAVIORAL ISSUES

Exhibit 6–1 also presents some of the behavioral problems in communications design. Since all of the system features have their impact upon the people within them, a box has been added to loop C titled "conflict"—because the implied authority of communications may give rise to conflict. What comes through the channel affects the worker's motivation insofar as it represents company policies, problems, relationships, or even esteem for the recipient himself.

The behavioral implications of superior-subordinate relationships may be seen in the qualitative characteristics of information flow, which may be direction, orientation, feedback, or indoctrination.[5] These types of exchange may be viewed as an outgrowth of leadership, but training or indoctrination influences the subordinate on a longer-term basis. Note that the information communicated serves a variety of purposes. Thus leadership is not only directive in nature, flowing from superior to subordinate, but supportive, in that it bolsters social relationships among isolated worker groups—here, the flow of information is *to the superior* rather than to the subordinate. Consequently, the various needs served by communication are not all immediately apparent.

The motivational aspects of a communication system involve the perceptual processes of the receiver, and are colored by his social and educational background, values and norms of behavior, and his self-concept. Special notice is given to "training" in order to suggest both the opportunities and the potential dangers involved in transmitting ideas in the training effort. The materials, coaching, and classroom technique in training should anticipate or help to relieve stress within the socio-technical system. Training in communications, deepening the understanding of socio-technical systems, and work with task groups are common approaches to improving matters in this area.

Communication and Role Conflict

Role relationships can be a potent model for clarifying sources of tension, misunderstanding, or conflict in communications. Recent research suggests that most *mis*communication occurs in simple role exchanges (dyad).[6] Instead of an "I–thou" relationship expressing empathy and human understanding, role relations may be "I–it," or even "it–it." Thus the communication challenge might be viewed as converting the "I–t" type to the "I–thou," and it has been posited that empathy for others plays a key part in this conversion.[7]

Three factors are related to empathy: (a) the inclination or motivation to empathize, (b) the information base, or knowledge about the other person, and (c) methods of adaptation or role adjustment (e.g., training). All of these factors would be instrumental in securing empathy and affecting the flow of understanding between a "giver" and "receiver," supervisor and subordinate, or potential antagonists.

A prescriptive approach to establishing a sound behavioral relationship between two roles would encompass, for example, role playing to facilitate adaptation, information analysis to strengthen the knowledge base, and/or formal learning or direct situational exposure to modify attitudes. But two cautions: attempts to develop empathy are frequently blocked, so selection of a strategy must contend with this phenomenon. Second, the three factors identified as relating to empathy are not likely to be of equal importance; experience suggests that the "inclination to empathize" is the most critical factor in the set, and is difficult to bring about if it is not present to begin with.

COMMUNICATION AND ROLE DEVELOPMENT

The human dimension of the communication system has many facets that are related to both the formal and the social aspects of organization life. In this way, communication and structure help set the base from which individuals assume their roles in the organization.[8] The formal features of the organization, including its structure, dictate the allocation of responsibilities, and consequently determine roles, relationships, functions, direction, and to some degree cooperation and even the level of conflict and tension. The formal roles to be taken are prescribed by official responsibilities, but the time allocated to communication and the selection of the media for communication may be partially determined by the individual. For example, formal rules may dictate a "write it, don't say it" approach. The individual, however, may opt to supplement these written messages with an occasional phone call or visit.

Communication systems are the vehicle for conveying likes and dislikes, esteem, sanctions, or censures. These overtones are achieved by the various gestures used to supplement verbal communication and by the element of tone and timing in written communication.

The communication system also constitutes the vehicle for the emergence of leadership in the organization. Communicated ideas may spring from the formal assignments of responsibilities to leaders. A more broadly conceived theory of leadership is predicated on acceptance or demonstrated performance. The establishment of this type of leadership depends largely on communicated ideas and insights for the demonstration of leadership qualities. For example, persuading an individual to follow a given course of action, based on superior insights or knowledge, would constitute one instance of a vital activity discharged through communication.

Training is another key function for which communication is an indispensable vehicle (see Chapter 13). Training manuals and the directions of the trainer for the use of information, symbols, and approaches are the essence of communication in this area. Both leadership and training are major factors in individual motivation. The communication system builds on the information, symbols, data, and ideas directed at the individuals in the organization in the hope of "turning them on" to high levels of performance.

CHANGING ROLE OF COMMUNICATION
VIEWED HISTORICALLY

In the days of "industrial concentration" (the late 1800s) communication between superior and subordinate was often based on formal authority and close direction. Domination, or even physical threat, was important for maintaining the role of the superior in relation to his subordinate. The flow of communications was predominantly downward. As social institutions grew larger, business assumed bureaucratic characteristics, and the roles of both superior and subordinate were modified when the structure of social institutions became more complex. Some roles were institutionalized, and thereby the character of communication was prescribed to an important degree.

It is important to realize that these changes in the character of communication in business took place within broader social changes and along with a growing acknowledgment of the intrinsic worth of people and the necessity to treat an individual as a person. The idea of manipulating individuals, at least from the point of view of communication, was replaced by attitudes in which positive incentives became a force in the relationship between superiors and subordinates.[9]

One approach—by Professor Arlyn Melcher—to modeling organizational variables is especially interesting because it attempts to reconcile a diverse group of phenomena while remaining easily comprehensible.[10] Although not strictly a communications model, it assists in establishing a perspective on the part played by communications in organizational processes. The effects on behavior of primary variables, which include size, technology, physical features, and relative stability or organization processes, are influenced by mediating variables such as leadership and personality (see Exhibit 6–4).

The primary variables, such as work flow and size of the formal organization, are taken as key determinants of human behavior and performance in organizations. These variables reflect a multitude of historical developments in organization growth, and establish the substructure from which formal authority, control, and communication emerge for the guidance of organizational effort. The system of mediating variables counterbalances the requirements of the primary variables. In order to understand how this compensation mechanism operates, consider the following example.

A company grows in *economic size* because of increased business volume, new products, and the like. At the same time, new work technologies are introduced for more economical and higher-volume production, but they modify the work structure and relationships between supervisors and workers, imposing new oganizational demands for conformity and coordination. Unless balancing forces are introduced, increased size and complexity will complicate the predictability of outcomes; thus the maintenance of balance calls for compensating mechanisms. Formal authority and structure introduce "official" relationships and the allocation of responsibilities, and further define functional boundaries, suggesting a basis for work direction. The information and communication systems represent the vehicle by which data are conveyed, intelligence is formulated, and the myriad organization activities are carried out and controlled.

Thus the various possible combinations of the primary variables in a given organization establish the substructure and "space" within which company life materializes. It is justifiably contended that both middle and lower managerial levels have little effect on these primary and mediating

EXHIBIT 6–4. Global Model of Organizational Processes

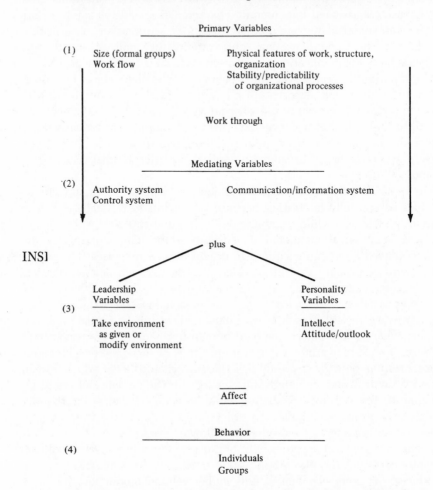

Based on concepts in A. Melcher's working papers, Kent State University.

factors, especially in the short run.[11] In the long run, however, influence processes that have been set in motion by organizational personnel can restructure the primary variables substantially. Consequently, the role of formal leadership becomes one of supporting (not undermining) the efforts of subordinates within a framework that is largely "given" (more on this in Chapters 8, 9, and 10).

On the other hand, top-management leadership can have a significant impact in both the short run and the long run. The challenge to top-management leadership is to "structure the organizational environment and work climate so as to secure company goals and permit individual growth among employees." Thus the leadership problems that confront top managers differ considerably from those facing lower-level managers. (These topics are discussed further in Chapter 9.)

The model (Exhibit 6–4) is completed by factoring in the personality variable. Considering the personality characteristics of supervisors, professionals, and workers provides an additional basis for anticipating organizational behavior and performance patterns. Thus taking into account individual traits such as aggressiveness, empathy for people, intelligence, and physical size permits a more refined approximation of outcomes.

MEASUREMENT AND PREDICTION

Melcher's approach to behavioral analysis goes beyond the conceptual model presented here to one that attempts to portray environmental and human variables in quantitative terms. A large group of scales and sets of questions are employed to measure the variables. Although this model is still in the experimental stage, and provides a basis for a group of field studies, it is probably more taxonomic than predictive. Considering the interplay of variables in this system and the curvilinear relationships, the possibility of using this model for prediction is questionable. Furthermore, when the dynamics of change are introduced into the organizational situation, the need arises for perspectives that go beyond this largely static model.

RESEARCH ON COMMUNICATION

A number of communication studies have concentrated on the direction of the flow of communication,[12] and on those factors that might help to account for the qualitative character and direction of the flow. The traditional communications model is built along hierarchical lines, with the flow of information following authority lines. Consequently, the flow of communication has been seen as following a vertical direction, for the most part. However, research has been done that challenges the traditional vertical characterization flow. When the features of the work system are taken into account, a redefinition and more precise statement of the character and direction of communication flow are indicated (see Exhibit 6–5).

COMMUNICATIONS AND TECHNOLOGY

One study in a textile factory revealed that the vertical flow of communication in a highly mechanized mill was greater than the horizontal flow (between departments).[13] Presumably, the advanced level of technology placed a premium on superior-subordinate relationships *within* departments. The horizontal flow of communication between foremen in those departments was largely concerned with the allocation of work.

EXHIBIT 6–5. Communications and Level of Technology

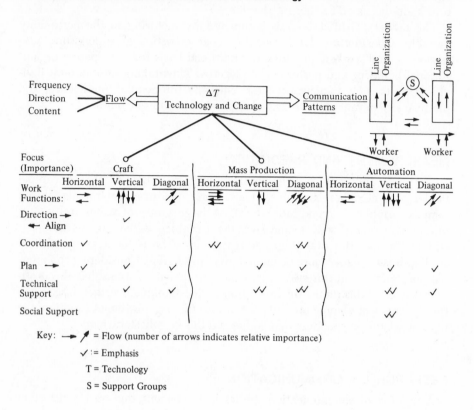

Key: → ✦ = Flow (number of arrows indicates relative importance)

✓ := Emphasis

T = Technology

S = Support Groups

In craft (unit) production systems, a high level of vertical communication would be expected because the character of the technology minimizes the coordinative needs of material logistics (horizontal communications), and supervisory activity is oriented to departmental needs. In mass production units, coordination of the production flow in a time-dependent system of man-machine components results in a decrease in vertical communication.[14]

However, vertical communication along hierarchical lines would reflect monitoring (control) of subordinate performance by supervisors. Communication in the planning function would precede monitoring, and would establish the base of resources and priorities from which operations would emerge.

Finally, at the "automated" level, vertical interaction among supervisors and subordinates would be encouraged in order to sustain problem solving and timely, accurate response to emergencies. In advanced systems, minute-to-minute operation is typically outside the control of the operator. Greater dependence is placed on such activities as problem solving, alertness, and creativity.

It should be clear that the direction of flow, the intensity of interaction, and the content of communication are all-important dimensions of analysis.

WORK STUDY APPROACHES TO
COMMUNICATION ANALYSIS

Other research on technological systems provides objective data on communication interactions among role members and thus indicates the magnitude of time commitments and establishes a basis for more systematic designs. Some research results disclose, in a quantitative fashion, the overall needs of a particular work system as reflected in the time allocated to certain functional activities. For example, some features of communication are described in numerical terms.[15] Fifty-five foremen on an automotive assembly line observed that almost 57 percent of their total time was allocated to communication. Of this time, 14 percent (about one-fourth of the total time) was spent outside the foremen's work section, and 43 percent was spent within it. However, the character of information transferred from foreman to worker was not determined; thus, whether communications involved *direction* or *support* of worker activity remained an unanswered question.

The Walker, Turner, and Guest studies suggest that some 50 percent of the total communication activity involves superior and subordinate, higher levels of authority, or colleagues. The superior-subordinate relationship accounts for more than two-thirds of this time, higher echelons or staff departments 9 percent, and only 7 percent paralleled the line of technological flow. In contrast with the findings of previous studies, the need for coordination, although regarded as an important activity in assembly lines, received little actual time. In other words, the amount of time allocated is not a reliable index of importance. It would be profitable to reexamine Exhibit 6–5 in light of these findings, noting the distinction between importance and time allocated.

Later studies provide additional information on the character of communication in low-level and intermediate (batch or mass production) units, including a footwear manufacturer, a packaging operation, and a brewery.[16] The results are summarized in Exhibit 6–6.

The factors have been organized under three general categories: direction, control, and administration. Quantitatively, the communication dimension ranges from 9.5 percent in the bread operation to 55 percent in the footwear operation—a notable spread.

Thurley and Hamblin, who attempted to correlate leadership roles and reject rates (an objective measure), found the following time allocations to communication in percentages (for each supervisor) and the average rejects in relation to each type of supervisory role[71]:

EXHIBIT 6–6. Some Principal Functions of Supervision in Low-, Intermediate-, and High-Level Technologies

Supervisory activity	State of technology									
	Low 8		8	Medium 8		8		High 9		9
	Packaging [4]		Footwear [5]		Electronics [6]		Brewery [7]		High volume bread, No. 1	High volume bread, No. 2
Supervisory direction of subordinates[1]	4%	3%	1%	1%	2%	1%	1%		1.6%	0.8%
Supervisory control and coordination activities[2]	39	22	55	27	49	53	33	30%	26.7	9.5
Supervisory standby and administrative functions[3]	57	75	44	72	49	46	66	70	71.7	90.5

1. Direct supervisory interaction with subordinates (operator, utility, or repair) to correct/aid his activity. Based on the Thurley and Hamblin study, this was considered as "stand and supervise."

2. Direct supervisory contact with colleagues, superiors, and operation specialists (maintenance, quality control, standards, scheduling, production control, material handling, etc.) in order to check or regulate current operations. In the results from the Thurley and Hamblin study, "inspection," "responsible manual" work, and "communication" were considered as roughly corresponding to this category of activities.

3. Includes the servicing of operator needs (wages, hours, absenteeism, etc.), casual observation, standby, and idle time. Based on the Thurley and Hamblin study, this was considered as "ordinary manual" operation, "walking," "personal and no apparent activity," "break time," "not seen," and miscellaneous.

4. Preparation and packing departments, respectively, of a "small batch" firm.

5. Large and small departments, respectively, of a "large batch" firm.

6. Departments X and Y, respectively, of a "mass production" firm.

7. Process and production department of a "process production" firm.

8. Based on the Thurley and Hamblin study.

9. Based on the Burack study.

Sources: K. E. Thurley and A. C. Hamblin, *The Supervisor and His Job* (London: Her Majesty's Stationery Office, 1963), pp. 18–23; Elmer H. Burack, "Technology and Supervisory Practices: A Comparative Analysis," *Human Organizations*, 26, no. 4 (Winter 1967).

1. "Autocratic" supervisor—17%, 25%, 15%, 8%; reject average (—) 1.0%.

2. "Consultive" supervisor—23%, 23%, 8%, 12%; reject average (+) 1.0%.

3. "Permissive" supervisor—3%, 13%, 12%, 11%; reject average, "average."

The autocratic supervisor actually had a lower reject rate than the consultive or the permissive supervisor, and a higher commitment to communications interaction. One might speculate that the autocratic supervisor had his subordinates under close direction, with a correspondingly high commitment to communication to assure performance.

A final note on Exhibit 6–6. In advanced processing systems, such as those found in the commercial bread companies, both direction and control diminish materially as these functions become more a part of the technology itself and as the role of supervision becomes one of standby alertness.[18] Unit 2 in the exhibit was more advanced than unit 1, indicating the further decline of time requirements for direction and control. An important prescription is involved here: *What amount of time should be allocated* by a supervisor to communicating with a subordinate in order to *achieve acceptable behavioral results?* There may be a considerable difference between the time requirements dictated by the technology and the same requirements as understood in light of the training and experience of the supervisor and his subordinates.

COMMUNICATION NETWORKS

At the base of the experimental study of communication networks[19] is the notion that these systems influence the ability of participants to organize information and reach timely decisions. The "spoked-wheel" type of communication network, with one person at the center, is best for rapid exchange of information. The "circle" or "all-channel" type of network is not as efficient. (Note that the design can be visualized as paralleling the structure of plant departments and information systems described earlier in the chapter.) A much greater "warm up" time is required to achieve an efficient level of system performance for the all-channel configuration, but once such a system is organized, it operates with an efficiency essentially equal to other types.

The foregoing differences have important implications for administrative design. Where it is necessary to organize personnel with dispatch, a spoked-wheel net operating through one individual promotes immediate coordination and diffusion of information for directing the activities of the group. This type of communication configuration should be given serious consideration in project missions and any other kinds of activity where severe time restraints exist. However, in other cases, coordinative communication may be secondary to interchange of ideas, and the spoked-wheel configuration is not as effective. While one person is the focal point of activity, playing a coordinative role and enjoying the "power" of that role, the creative efforts of other group members may be thwarted. If the individual at the hub of the information flow is ill equipped for his task because of personal limitations, a significant time delay in organizing information can result, and eventually the efficient operation of the system may be impaired. It is easy to see how such limitations can even reach a point where, for practical purposes, the system is inoperative, so that one "can't get an answer."

COMMUNICATION AND GROUP PROCESSES

Other research on communication involves groups such as committees and project teams. Exhibit 6–7 illustrates the conference type of project group. The character of group communication reflects leader-group relationships and the dynamics of the climate created by the leader. The research behind this conceptual model [20] is helpful in organizing teams or committees for "brainstorming," problem solving, new product development, or the like.

The research suggests that the ability to participate in the group decision process is importantly influenced by the leader, his attitude, and his ability and desire to involve the members of the group in group processes. The participation of members, the communication of ideas, and the means of arriving at solutions depend upon the background of the individuals, "felt" independence, encouragement to participate, and the relative "felt" differences of individuals' credentials. The ability of the leader to deal with individual differences that inhibit desire and group processes and to encourage active participation by members of the group is essential to effective group performance.

It should not be inferred that group processes are uniformly superior to individual effort. There are conditions under which individual effort can be equally successful, or even superior—for example, where such a person is an expert and others possess only contact knowledge.

COMMUNICATION AND SOCIAL RELATIONSHIPS

The systems perspective may also be used to describe those communications networks through which formal, professional, and social roles are sustained within the structure of the organization.[21] Exhibit 6–8A translates the conventional organization chart into a systems chart; Exhibit 6–8B illustrates some typical communications patterns.[22] The systems chart facilitates analysis of interpersonal relationships by schematizing the flow of information between decision-making points. The upper panel of Exhibit 6–8B

EXHIBIT 6-7. Communications, Group Relationships, and Decision Making

Chairman/
Project Leader

(1)

→ Conduct of
  Meeting—Team →
  Leadership

(2)

Background
Permanence in Group
Other Factors
  →
Individual

(3)

→ "Felt" Status
  Differences and
  Individual
  Independence

(4)

→ Expression of
  Member's Opinion

(5)

→ "Felt" Participation
  in Group Decision
  Making (6)
    →
  Individual
  Performance in
  Groups (7)

  Quality of Solution
  Decision Making (8)
  Is Affected by
  Amount of allowable errors
  Judgments
  Group adaptation
  Risk taking

EXHIBIT 6–8A. Communication Nets for Organizational Analysis

Conventional Organization Structure

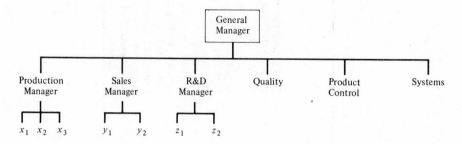

Systems Representation

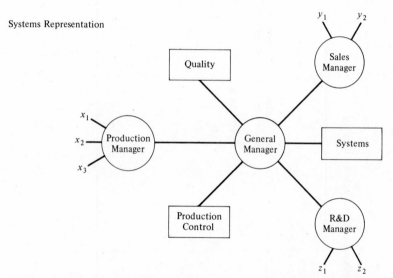

depicts a social group that includes staff members of the production and the R&D departments, along with the key production-control man. Observation of informal social groups can provide insights into such important behavioral aspects of organizational life as potential patterns of influence among organization members, social isolation and its implications for affiliation and identification, and informal leadership.

The lower panel of Exhibit 6–8B shows a communications network that is based on the affiliation of technical personnel with a professional group. This communication pattern suggests that the principle in these systems may be the acknowledged leader of this technically oriented network. If that judgment is correct, then a formal communication system might be developed to parallel the informal one. For example, professional relationships could help to establish viable working relationships for the introduction or extension of a computer-based information system.

EXHIBIT 6–8B. Interaction Patterns for Communications Analysis

Social Grouping

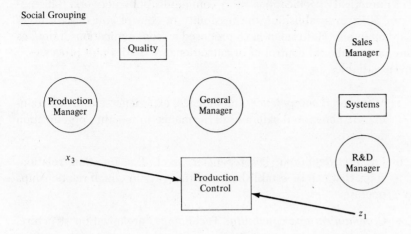

Professional Affiliation

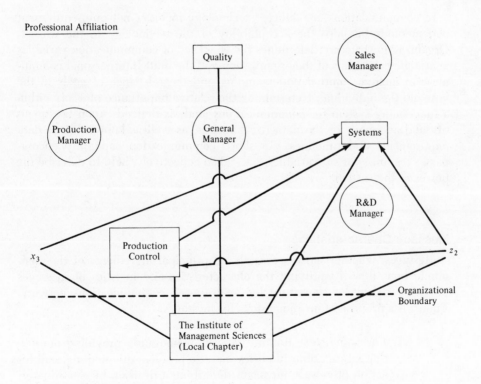

In addition to qualitative characteristics there are some interesting possibilities in numerical specifications for a communications network. This approach can assist in establishing the feasibility of control and design directions. Vardaman and Halterman have proposed a "communications index" as a measure of managerial control of organizational activities and processes.[23] The crucial variables are

 a. *Managerial competence:* Intelligence, experience-education-training, demonstrated skill and performance in meeting organization demands.

 b. *Problem definition:* Discrepancies, level of recognition, relationships that can be established, and the ways in which relationships operate.

 c. *Communications capability:* Technology, organization structure, interpersonal communications, and the relevance of job data.

In communications capability,[24] technology includes not only equipment and methods but also the acceptability of the technology to the worker. Organization structure determines the efficiency of communication variables in attaining the goals of the organization and the unit. Interpersonal communication includes mutual understanding and the relevance of goals to the firm and the individual. Determining the relative importance of a job within a functioning system for communications analysis depends upon the quantity and adequacy of the data it commands, as well as knowledge of data requirements and timeliness. In short, communication capability encompasses a number of subvariables that, taken collectively, help to describe the power of the system.

Message Characteristics

Messages, whether written or oral, are principal ingredients of the communications flow. Identifying the characteristics and logistics of messages provides a point of departure for analyzing a communications network. Eilon[25] has proposed four dimensions for messages:

 1. *Form—written:* Routine reports; memoranda providing nonroutine information; inquiries that are problem oriented and call for action proposals; messages describing a decision by the initiator; messages giving a decision and indicating the action to be taken. *Oral:* Meetings that seek to effect problem solving, time commitments, or quality of solution; face-to-face or telephone exchanges.

2. *Functional area of activity:* May vary from the traditional marketing, production, and finance classifications to organization procedures and performance evaluation.

3. *Importance and priority:* Distinguishes the trivial from the important, where "importance" may hinge on time priority, commitment of resources, impact on the business, and similar factors.

4. *Intent and impact:* May be psychological in nature: for instance, a call for immediate action. Dysfunction may arise because of perceptual distortions or misunderstanding.

Typically, more detail is sought in describing the character of communications, so that subcodes are used, as in (a) describing a routine procedure or (b) conceiving a novel situation. The data derived from a communication study may be recorded in several different forms, each of which serves a somewhat different purpose for the analyst. For written messages, a study that traces out communication patterns among managers of functional departments and also employs a continuous time scale is quite useful for tracing job-oriented work. Exhibit 6–9 offers an example of this type of development.

Message categories provide, for example, added insights into message media, content, method of gathering information for problem solving, and techniques of arriving at decisions. Beyond this, specialized analysis may

EXHIBIT 6–9. Systems Analysis: Communications

Time Period	Managers						Committees and Project Groups		
0	1	2	3	4	5	6	f_1	f_2	f_3
0	A	.							
1			.	. B .					
2	.	C	.	.					
3	.			.		. G			.
4	.	C .		. B	⌐ .				
5		.	.		.		D	.	
6		.	. E .						

Key: A, B, C, D, E, F are message categories (routine, memorandum, etc.).

A broader demonstration of this technique is developed in Samuel Eilon, "Taxonomy of Communications," *Administrative Science Quarterly,* 13, no. 2 (September 1968).

include combinations of functions or managers' work activities and time. In Exhibit 6–10 the role of a particular manager is seen from the perspectives of the media he has used and the time period the message required.

EXHIBIT 6–10. Specialized Communication Analyses

A. Work Assignment and Managers

Work Functions	Managers					
	1	2	3	4	5	6
10	A	F		D		A
11	B		C	C	F	B
12	—	D	E	—	F	—
13		—	R	B	E	
14		D	E	—	C	A
15		C	B	R	—	C

B. Time Frame and Managers

Time Period	1	2	3	4	5	6
a	A	C	B		B	A
b	—	E	E	E	C	C
c	B	—	F	D	—	—
d	—	F	—	F		C
e	D	C	D	C	D	—

Note: A, B, C . . . are message categories.

For a discussion and detailed representation of this approach, see a development by Eilon, "Taxonomy of Communications," pp. 285–286.

SUMMARY

This chapter has focused on defining communications and communications systems with the express purpose of establishing their central role in undertaking and facilitating organizational processes, whether human or impersonal. The systems approach emphasized structural features of information encoding, processing, and decoding, along with design and information system properties. Thus, converting fragmentary to useful information, information needs for particular functions, and distortion and selection of communication vehicles were emphasized in this approach. Also, the systems approach provided a vehicle to identify some of the behaviorally related phenomena likely to arise within communications channels.

The skeletal outline of the communication system does not arise capriciously—it frequently reflects the basic physical logistics of organizational enterprise, with priorities and flow directions and relations often generally governed by such factors as physical dispersion, markets, raw material, location, clientele, distance, technological relationships, and size. Similarly, a firm's commitment to a particular niche or product form is often accompanied by a particular technological form, and thus a characteristic mode of communications may be established.

Communications was also described as a central factor in behavioral processes, became embedded within it are the bases for influencing personal courses of action (leadership), training, formulating social groupings, direction of influence, and the creation or resolution of conflict. Communications was also described as a central vehicle for defining the character of role relationships or providing the means of establishing behaviorally satisfying relationships. Finally, communication functions that serve to convey such behaviorally related factors as esteem, sanctions, and likes or dislikes were also developed. Thus, with their potential to affect behavior, communications constitute a central matter in training and at the same time serve as a central vehicle to facilitate training.

Communications research supports the influence of technology on direction of flow and the intensity and character of interactions. However, quantitative studies of communications have emphasized the need to carefully distinguish the priority or importance ascribed to particular communications and the actual time involved—these may not correspond closely at all, yet they have been a great source of confusion in the literature. For those situations where workers can mutually influence quality or quantity of output, leadership style in communications can be seen as having a pronounced effect on output variables. However, more advanced systems, which have achieved a stable state, notably lessen personal influences and thus may greatly diminish leadership's communications influence.

Finally, this chapter described various representations for communications systems and several approaches to analysis of flows, importance of participants, and priority.

Appendix Case

DATATRONICS INC.

Introduction of a New System

In October 1974 the manager of Product Engineering, Mr. T. L. Farnsworth, sent bulletins to all division managers and certain staff specialists con-

Case prepared by Elmer H. Burack and Thomas M. Calero, Stuart School of Management and Finance, Illinois Institute of Technology. All names have been changed to maintain anonymity.

concerning a "New Idea" communication system (see Exhibit 6A-1 for the memo). The issuance of this memo represented the culmination of many months of preparatory work before the project reached a point at which the vice president for research and development, Mr. K. C. Binyon, felt the procedures were operational and could be implemented.

Immediately prior to the installation of the New Idea system, K. C. Binyon had authorized the issuance of several informational bulletins in order to fully describe the

a. Purpose of the New Idea system (see Exhibit 6A-2)

b. Procedure for preparing New Idea memos

Perspective

Datatronics was a leader in research into and development of information systems. Through the efforts of a large force of advanced degree scientists and engineers, Datatronics had established a reputation as one of the country's outstanding companies in information equipment and applications. Often the basic scientific research had combined with creative engineering efforts to produce procedures, transmission, and computation equipment

EXHIBIT 6A–1. Memorandum from Product Engineering Division

Datatronics Inc.
Corporate Offices
1000 Harbor
Carver, Ohio

October 2, 1974

MEMORANDUM:

To: Division Managers and Staff Coordinators

Subject: Procedure for "New Idea" Memos

Since Product Engineering has been established as the New Idea Memo Processing Center, all Memos originating in this corporation should be submitted in duplicate to Product Engineering. Ordinarily the originator's manager will countersign and forward the Memos, but if the originator's manager is not available, Memos may be transmitted directly to Product Engineering. If a patent recommendation is to be submitted to the Legal Department, it should be accompanied by a 100-word New Idea Memo. It need not be approved by the manager.

T. L. FARNSWORTH

Division Manager
Product Engineering

TLF/we

EXHIBIT 6A–2. Memorandum from R&D Division

Datatronics Inc.
Corporate Offices
Carver, Ohio

September 20, 1974

MEMORANDUM

To: All Division Managers

Subject: New Idea Memo System and Processing Center

As this corporation grows, develops new technologies, products, and markets, and becomes more widely dispersed geographically, we place an increasingly heavy burden on our conventional means of communication. Yet in Datatronics we have always recognized that good communication has been an important factor in our continued success.

One of the major problems which faces us today, in a rapidly changing technological environment, is the prompt identification and dissemination of technical achievements to those who might use them to further their own efforts. In order to meet the challenge this problem presents, we must take a new approach to communicating this information to our technical personnel. Product Engineering has been assigned responsibility for establishing and operating, on a pilot basis, a "New Idea Processing Center."

The communications vehicle in the system will be a "New Idea Memo" of 100 words or less. The "New Idea Memo" will provide:

A. A means for alerting our professional and managerial people to unique developments, new ideas, solutions, techniques, and problems at the time such knowledge becomes known;

B. A method for disseminating information which does not lend itself to formalized reporting media but is of value to others engaged in similar work; and

C. Recognition for a greater number of our professionals who contribute to Datatronics technical advances than are now acknowledged by existing programs.

I believe the new system can be effective in minimizing unknown duplication of work areas of technical exploration, development, and testing. The system can be of real value as a key to the great wealth of "unpublished" technical know-how and knowledge which is being generated every day.

The overriding purpose of this system is to place professionals engaged in similar work in contact with one another. It does not substitute for regular reporting and publication requirements. It is not to be used as a management audit or general evaluation of project progress.

K. C. BINYON

Vice President
Research and Development

KCB/aj

that represented the very best efforts of manufacturers in this field. The patent position that the company had achieved through a regular succession of "firsts" had greatly extended its competitive strength.

Management had become increasingly aware of the importance of capitalizing upon the creative ideas generated in the organization. The most significant element in the company's systems leadership was the ability of its scientists and engineers to produce ideas, develop patents, and then exploit these patents in terms of advanced equipment designs. The New Idea memo was visualized as an internal device that would help further management's objectives of stimulating, even more, coordinated development work by rapidly channeling and interchanging current thinking to a wide audience of potential users within Datatronics.

"New Idea" Memo: Preparation Instructions

The "New Idea" Memo is an instrument for the prompt dissemination of information within this corporation. New Idea Memos will make available to personnel in related or similar activities information of potential value arising from current efforts. The type of information which should be included is that which is at present exchanged in personal conversations (and never recorded) and that which is accumulated for eventual inclusion in formal reports.

New Idea Memos can be likened to headlines in a newspaper. They alert interested people of activity at the reporting locations. They should not contain manpower or funding information. They may contain quantitive and qualitative information, providing this is essential for intelligent, meaningful communication.

It is recognized that every condition which would warrant submission of a New Idea Memo cannot be predicted; however, the following actions are considered to be the minimum events to be reported for effective system operation:

A. At the start of a new project or task.

B. Where significant results, positive or negative, are identified as work progresses.

C. At the completion of a project or task.

D. When reports on accomplishments enter the process of publication.

In general, all current information which will assist others in similar or related efforts should be included. Most authors are inclined to report ingenious solutions, but negative information is of particular value in alerting others of hazards to be avoided.

No rigid format is established for preparing New Idea Memos, and no special form is required for their submission. Normal divisional letterheads or memoranda stationery are suggested. In order to ensure some uniformity of input and obtaining the necessary information for system operation, certain essential elements must be included. The suggested format closely parallels the normal intracorporate memoranda style. Each New Idea Memo should include the following:

a. Originating location address and division

b. Date

c. Subject:
   The subject is the title or caption of the message. It is suggested that it be prepared after the message portion is written so that it accurately reflects the informational content of the Memo.

d. Reference:
   Each Memo should contain two references to related Datatronics efforts previously reported in Memos, patent papers, or journals.

e. Message:
   Should be restricted to 100 words and be stated in concise form.

f. Author:
   Include the name(s) of the person who (1) performed the work and (2) the person transmitting it.

g. Contract or project number

h. Suggested distribution:
   Persons or groups who should receive copies of the Memo.

Upon receipt of a New Idea Memo at the Product Engineering Processing Center, it will be registered and handled as follows:

1. It will be converted to EDP equipment use.

2. Reproduced on a card facsimile.

3. Distributed to both individuals and groups specified by the author.

4. A copy will be sent to the author.

5. Copies will be held for central file at the Processing Center.

The distribution of information in this form will provide a constant source of valuable guidance and stimulation. Also, secondary channels of distribution will be facilitated by virtue of this new vehicle for internal technical information flow.

EXHIBIT 6A–3. "New Idea" Memo Sample

Headquarters
Information Systems Development Division
4400 Rindell Boulevard
St. Louis, Missouri

New Idea Memo to: New Idea Processing Center

Subject: Message Exchange Monitoring

Reference:
a) New Idea Memo of D. K. Johnson, number 621
b) H. M. Lobin, "Higher Order Business Systems," *Journal of Applied Science,* V. 5, Number 1, Jan. 1966. pp. 10–14

(100-word message dealing with the principal ideas or preliminary results, using crisp, news-headline-type of writing)

                                        HARPER T. MARKS

                                        Dept. number 23

Recommended distribution:

　Mr. John Banks, GBG, Atlanta
　Mr. Gerald Franks, Lang. Anal., Carver
　Dr. Drigsby Manners, GBG, Cleveland
　All LaSalle Lab. Adv. Engrng. Grp.

It was hoped that the New Idea-system woud function as a self-propelling exchange device, once installed, understood, and its benefits experienced by scientists and engineers. The memos were to be limited to 100 words so that the essential ingredients of new ideas could be readily grasped by recipients.

Implementation of the New Idea Memo System

From the very beginning, the New Idea system was met with mixed reactions. Some of the response was quite enthusiastic. For example, one project supervisor said:

> In the beginning we were asked to write New Idea Memos.
> They sounded like a good idea and we tried to cooperate.
> In the first two or three months the memos were scanned by
> quite a large group in our installation.

And scientists or engineers were easily found who favored the system for one specific reason or another:

I like to read them. They take such a short time to learn what's going on.

The Memos are useful in that we can tell pretty quickly whether one has what you're interested in or not.

I feel they're helpful to prevent the duplication that can happen if you don't have an internal system.

I use them to find the author's names in particular fields that I need to stay up on.

Because these Memos give the author's name, it gives you quicker access to someone to talk to.

I'm going to write one as an advertisement for people to work on a new technology we're getting into. Sort of a "help wanted" ad.

I like to browse through these Memos because it triggers new ideas for me.

However, other men felt that the initial briefing had been inadequate to fully convey the working of the new system:

We should have had more education on a proposal like the New Idea Memo system, not just the circulating of a memorandum. Before long many people started to react as if it was just another boondoggle.

There are a lot of different versions on the New Idea System. Unfortunately, it was put out to the managers—seemed more or less secret. It was not generally understood that they could pass them on to others.

Some managers even claimed that they had never seen the instructions that were initially circulated and that described the intentions behind the procedures to be used for the system. They believed that the new plan had received insufficient publicity and support at the level of section and project groups. For example:

I think that there are a lot of people here who don't know what the New Idea Memo system is all about yet.

Another manager observed:

Without some kind of push behind it or immediate return from the system, there is not a self-sustaining drive in it.

These feelings indicated that at least some people who worked with New Idea Memos lacked enthusiasm for them. They believed that either motivation was lacking or that it was of the wrong kind. One high-level staff man observed:

The only reason a majority of New Idea Memos got written
was that managers would tell their men "Write one." Otherwise few got written.

And further down the line, an engineer was heard to say:

I have written Memos when I was told to. There is no reward
for this extra effort on my part.

Even the authors of memos did not necessarily consider them as intrinsically
worthwhile. As one said:

That Memo that I wrote should never have been written. It
was far too general and really said nothing—but my manager
asked me to put something together.

There were, furthermore, different views about the type of information that
should be committed to the New Idea system. For instance, one manager
suggested that

All patent recommendations coming from my department
should automatically go out as New Idea Memos; otherwise
they wait a long time to get publicized.

By contrast, another manager felt that this was an improper use of the
system:

The Memo system was designed for the task of announcing
new work—not completed results ready for patenting. It
should not be used to announce routinely the completion of
a project but only when something unexpected comes out.

Other problems came to light as implementation of the New Idea system
was pressed forward. Some of the men who were interested in capitalizing
upon the information circulated in the system experienced difficulty with the
requirement that the author of a memo identify people or project groups
who should receive it:

When you write a new Idea Memo, you're supposed to list
people who might be interested. This is impossible for me to
know and serves no purpose. Those who I do know who are
interested are already in phone contact with me. The people
who run this system should know this and find those interested. I can't possibly know all the people in the company
who might care about what I'm doing.

Additional facets of the system were criticized by larger or smaller numbers of men in various company locations. Some of these criticisms are summarized below.

1. Physical aspects of the system—distribution, format, and filing procedures—tended to restrict use on the receiving end. For example:

> The file of Memos is not right here, it's down the hall.

> It's difficult to use because Memos are kept in the manager's office.

> I looked for the Memos once. Finally discovered the manager's secretary had locked them in her desk. She was out at coffee. I haven't remembered to look for them since.

> These Memos are treated as "confidential" for some reason. This presents annoying problems in terms of storage, use, and disposal. And almost nothing in them justifies all these security precautions.

2. The system jarred with ways the men usually worked:

> If I know of information that is of importance to another group, it is better, faster, and cheaper for me to just get on the phone and call them.

> The Memo system started out assuming a need that might not exist. Engineers basically don't like to write; so if they don't feel the need for it, they just won't go along with the system.

> The really creative guys get their satisfaction just out of creating the idea. They don't feel the need to publish their ideas as such.

> My job is to finish the project I'm on. That's what I get credit for, not for writing a Memo.

> This constricted, short-hand kind of writing [asked for by memo procedures] is not normal practice for technical people.

3. Some felt they might be giving away a promising idea through premature publication:

> Why give someone else advance notice of what I'm working on? They might try to beat me to it or preempt it.

> The engineer is thinking about internal status, not outside competition. He wants to hang on to anything that will make him look good.

4. Other people don't want to chance having their ideas "shot down" by their peers:

> No one wants to publish and then feel like a damn fool when his idea doesn't work out.

> There is a reluctance to go out on a limb. A man wants to have all the facts and figures neatly tied up before he lets it see daylight outside the project group.

5. Competition between groups was cited as another inhibiting factor:

> You may just plain not want another group to know what you are doing. Stealing ideas *does* happen.

> There is a lot of empire building going on in the company. One division will compete with another to see who gets to work on new projects.

6. Several people said it is unrealistic for professional people to be expected to broadcast their failures. An example is the man who said:

> Getting men to put their failures on record would be so important. But no system like the New Idea Memos can do this because it goes against the human grain to do so.

7. Also, quite a few men, in a rather surprised tone, reported that the New Idea system worked rather slowly, and thus was out of line with a basic element of the original conception:

> It's supposed to only take a day or two from input to output, but it's a lot more like two or three weeks.

> The big problem is the reproduction time, apparently. At any rate the Memos get hung up for days and days. So the thing doesn't operate on the "real time" it was ballyhooed to do.

8. Finally, again by way of direct quotation from people who had watched the system from its inception, it is useful to add one more from an experienced line manager, in which he summarized his impressions:

> New Idea Memos are more concerned with glorious solutions than in understanding the problems.

Management of Datatronics Troubled

The difficulties experienced by the New Idea system perplexed the management at Datatronics. There was general agreement that critical needs existed for the rapid dissemination and exchange of technical information. The management and scientific personnel were largely in accord on these scores, but indications with the New Idea system were that it was not fulfilling the original hopes and expectations.

Heightened competition and the wide dispersion of Datatronics personnel and operations made it quite vulnerable to the inroads of other companies. Increased dependence upon new, productive ideas compounded the serious situation with which Datatronics management felt itself confronted.

QUESTIONS

1. Exhibit 6–3 summarizes, in symbolic form, communications patterns and the focus of various functional activities. What conflicts or dysfunctions are an inherent part of these systems? Be sure to state reference points and assumptions.

2. What inherent conflicts exist between functional organization and work flow?

3. Do you feel that Simpson has demonstrated the case for horizontal versus vertical communications?

4. What communication patterns would you expect to find for various technological systems? What similarities and what differences?

5. Develop some functional statements that suggest
   The frequency of communications $= f\,(?)$
   The direction of communications $= f\,(?)$

6. Compare and analyze the character of communications in a highly centralized insurance company that operates nationally yet maintains tight at-the-top controls versus one largely decentralized in decision making and operation.

7. Are all numerical data factual information—that is, not subject to varying interpretations? Explain.

8. Under what conditions would information be transmitted from remote locations, given the following options: computer terminal, wire service, phone line, and written message?

CLASS EXERCISE

Compare and contrast the communication structure (directions, lines, and intensity) for the functional organization shown in Exhibit 6–11. State any necessary assumptions.

Develop a communications structure for

    a. An electronics manufacturer supplying components to several large producers of radios, television sets, and electronics equipment.

    b. A large food retailing firm (150 outlets) that manufactures some of its own high-volume bakery and dairy products.

EXHIBIT 6–11. Organization Chart

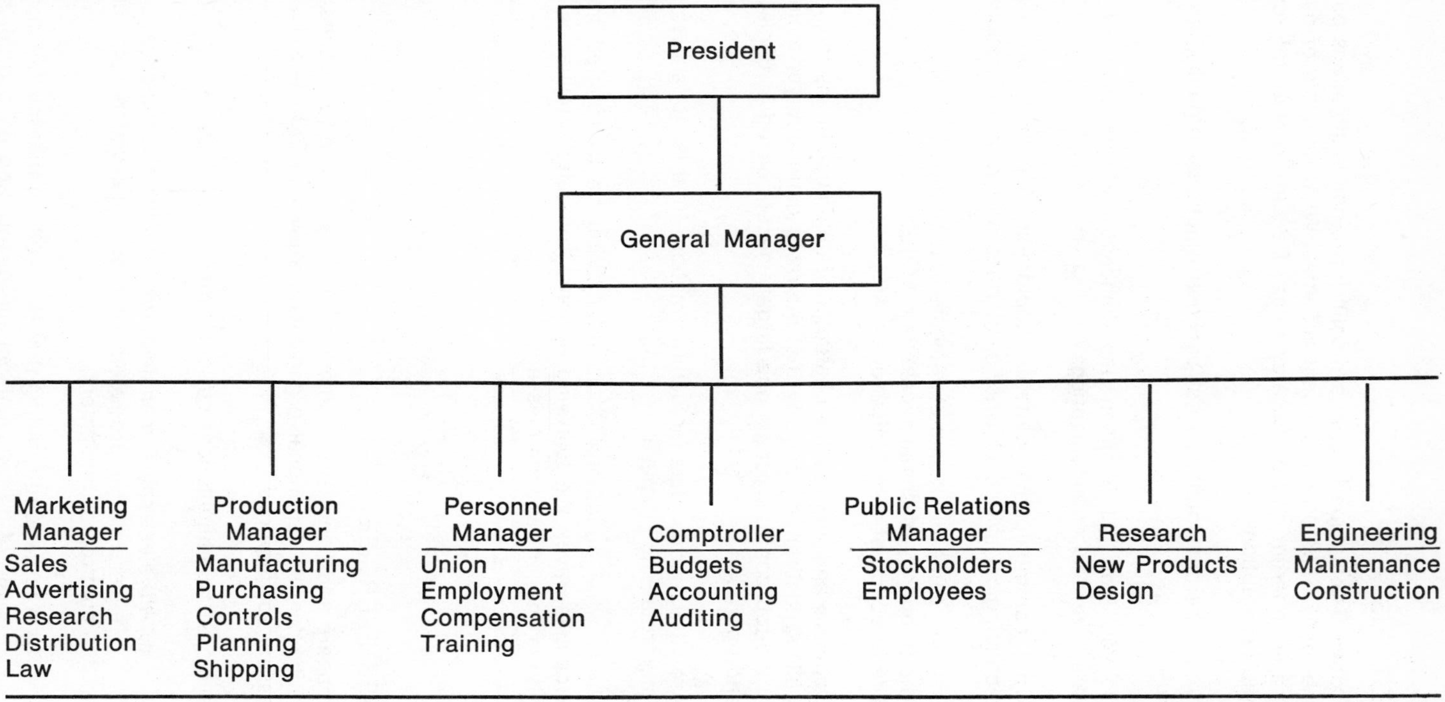

```
                    ┌─────────────┐
                    │  President  │
                    └─────────────┘
                           │
                    ┌─────────────┐
                    │General Manager│
                    └─────────────┘
                           │
 ┌──────────┬──────────┬──────────┬──────────┬──────────┬──────────┐
```

Marketing
Manager
_____
Sales
Advertising
Research
Distribution
Law

Production
Manager
_____
Manufacturing
Purchasing
Controls
Planning
Shipping

Personnel
Manager
_____
Union
Employment
Compensation
Training

Comptroller
_____
Budgets
Accounting
Auditing

Public Relations
Manager
_____
Stockholders
Employees

Research
_____
New Products
Design

Engineering
_____
Maintenance
Construction

NOTES

1. *The Social Psychology of Organizations* (New York: John Wiley & Sons, 1966).

2. The importance of completeness in communicated information is developed in Manley H. Jones, *Executive Decision Making* (rev. ed.; Homewood, Ill.: Richard D. Irwin, 1962).

3. This topic is treated in greater detail in Chapter 7.

4. Daniel Katz and Robert Kahn, *The Social Psychology of Organizations* (New York: Wiley, 1966), chap. 9.

5. For some comments on new multimedia modes of employee communications, see Dan H. Fenn, Jr. and Daniel Yankelovich, "Responding to the Employee Voice," *Harvard Business Review*, 50, no. 3 (May–June 1972): 83–91.

6. Roy Wood, "Communication and Human Relations," Northwestern University Alumni-Faculty Seminar, May 1972.

7. Ibid.

8. This topic is discussed at length in Chapter 10.

9. Some interesting insights into characteristic organizational activity and emergent communication needs and patterns are provided by Morris Janowitz, "Challenging Organizational Patterns of Organization Activity," *Administrative Science Quarterly*, vol. 3 (1959).

10. Arlyn Melcher, "A System Model," presented at the Conference on Organizational Behavioral Models, College of Business Administration, Kent State University, May 16, 1969. Papers were analyzed by the author in the *Conference Proceedings*.

11. Ibid.

12. Peter Blau, "Formal Organizations: Dimensions of Analysis," *American Journal of Sociology*, 62 (July 1957): 58–59; Frank J. Jasinski, "Adapting Organization to New Technology," *Harvard Business Review*, 37, no. 1 (January–February 1959): 77–86; and William A. Faunce, "Automation in the Automobile Industry," *American Sociological Review*, 23, no. 4 (August 1958): 405–407. For a review of other research on communications and information, see Joe Kelly, *Organizational Behavior* (Homewood, Ill.: Dorsey Press, 1974), pp. 421–424, 448–498.

13. Richard Simpson, "Vertical and Horizontal Communications in Formal Organizations," *Administrative Science Quarterly*, 4 (1959): 188–196.

14. Blau, "Formal Organizations," pp. 58–59.

15. Richard Guest, "Of Time and the Foreman," *Personnel Magazine* (May 1956), pp. 478–486; Charles R. Walker and Richard H. Guest, *The Man on the Assembly Line* (Boston: Harvard University Press, 1952); Franklin Jasinski, "Technological Delimitation of Reciprocal Relationships," *Human Organization* (Summer 1956); Charles R. Walker, Richard H. Guest, and Arthur N. Turner, *The Foreman on the Assembly Line* (Boston: Harvard University Press, 1956), pp. 86–87.

16. K. E. Thurley and A. C. Hamblin, *The Superior and His Job* (London: Her Majesty's Stationery Office, 1963), pp. 16–21; Elmer H. Burack, "Technology and Supervisory

Practices: A Comparative Analysis," *Human Organizations,* 26, no. 4 (Winter 1967).

17. Thurley and Hamblin, *The Superior and His Job,* pp. 16–21.

18. Added details of these studies are discussed in Elmer H. Burack, "Technology and Industrial Management," Technology working papers, Illinois Institute of Technology, 1965–1969.

19. Harold Guetzkow and Herbert A. Simon, "The Impact of Certain Communication Nets upon Organization and Performance in Task-oriented Groups," *Management Science* 1 (1955): 233–250; Alex Bavelas, "Communication Patterns in Tech-oriented Groups," *Journal of Accoustical Society of America,* 22 (1950): 725–730; Harold J. Leavitt, "Some Effects of Certain Communication Patterns on Group Performance," *Journal of Abnormal and Social Psychology,* 46 (1951): 38–50.

20. Early research in this area, which provided a basis for this analysis, includes Solomon E. Asch, "Opinions and Social Pressure," *Scientific American,* 196, no. 5 (November 1959): 31–35, and E. Paul Torrance, "Function of Expressed Disagreement in Small Group Processes," *Social Forces,* 35, no. 4 (1957).

21. George T. Vardaman and Carroll C. Halterman, *Managerial Control through Communication: Systems for Organizational Diagnosis and Design* (New York: John Wiley & Sons, 1968).

22. Similar charts are presented and described in greater detail in Vardaman and Halterman, *Managerial Control,* pp. 46–59.

23. Ibid.

24. Ibid., pp. 85–91.

25. Samuel Eilon, "Taxonomy of Communications," *Administrative Science Quarterly,* 13, no. 2 (September 1968): 267–288.

REFERENCES

Albaum, Gerald. "Horizontal Information Flow: An Exploratory Study." *Academy of Management Journal,* 7, no. 1 (March 1964): 21–33.

Allen, Thomas J., and Stephen I. Cohen. "Information Flow in Research and Development Laboratories." *Administrative Science Quarterly,* 14, no. 1 (March 1969): 19–20.

Bavelas, Alex, and Dermot Barrett. "An Experimental Approach to Organizational Communication." *Personnel,* 44, no. 2 (March 1951): 336–371.

Becker, Selwyn. "Personality and Effective Communications in Organization." *Personnel Administration,* 27, no. 4 (July–August 1964): 28–30.

Bradford, B. Boyd, and J. Michael Jensen. "Perceptions of the First Line Supervisor's Authority: A Study in Superior-Subordinate Communication." *Academy of Management Journal,* 15, no. 3 (September 1972): 331–342.

Burgess, Robert L. "Communication Networks and Behavioral Consequences." *Human Relations*, 22, no. 3 (April 1969): 137–160.

Burns, Tom. "The Directions of Activity and Communication in a Departmental Executive Group." *Human Relations*, 7, no. 1 (February 1954): 73–97.

Carzo, Rocco, Jr. "Some Effects of Organization Structure on Group Effectiveness." *Administrative Science Quarterly*, 7, no. 4 (March 1963): 393–424.

Cohen, Arthur M. "Changes in Small Group Communication Network." *Administrative Science Quarterly*, 6, no. 4 (March 1962): 443–462.

———. "Communication Networks: In Research and Training." *Personnel Administration*, 27, no. 3 (May–June 1964): 18–24, 43.

——— and W. G. Bemis. "Predicting Organization in Changed Communication Networks." *Journal of Psychology*, 54, no. 2 (October 1962): 391–416.

Davis, Keith. "Grapevine Communication among Lower and Middle Managers." *Personnel Journal*, 48, no. 4 (April 1969): 269–272.

———. "Success of Chain of Command Oral Communication in a Manufacturing Management Group." *Academy of Management*, 11, no. 4 (December 1968): 379–387.

Etzioni, Amitai. *A Comparative Analysis of Complex Organization*. New York: Free Press of Glencoe, 1961.

Fenn, Margaret, and George Head. "Upward Communication: The Subordinates' Viewpoint." *California Management Review*, 7, no. 4 (Summer 1965): 75–80.

Flesch, Rudolf. *The Art of Plain Talk*. New York: Harper & Row, 1946.

Guetzkow, Harold. "Communications in Organizations," in James March (ed.), *Handbook of Organizations*. Chicago: Rand McNally, 1965, pp. 534–573.

——— and William R. Dill. "Factors in the Organizational Development of Task-oriented Groups." *Sociometry*, 20, no. 3 (September 1957): 175–204.

Guetzkow, Harold, and Herbert A. Simon. "The Impact of Certain Communication Nets upon Organization and Performance in Task-oriented Groups." *Management Science*, 1, no. 3–4 (April–July 1955): 233–250.

Hall, Edward T., and William F. Whyte. "Intercultural Communication: A Guide to Men of Action." *Human Organization*, 19, no. 1 (Spring 1960): 5–12.

Hall, Edward. *The Silent Language*. Garden City, N.Y.: Doubleday, 1959.

Haney, William V. "A Comparative Study of Unilateral and Bilateral Communication." *Academy of Management Journal*, 7, no. 2 (June 1964): 128–136.

Hertz, David B., and Albert H. Rubenstein. "The Role of Communications in Research," in Robert T. Livingston and Stanley H. Milberg (eds.), *Human Relations in Industrial Research Management*. New York: Columbia University Press, 1957, pp. 197–207.

Indik, Bernard P., Basil S. Georgopoulos, and Stanley E. Seashore. "Superior-Subordinate Relationship and Performance." *Personnel Psychology*, 14, no. 4 (Winter 1961): 357–374.

Jones, John Paul. "Leadership, Motivation and Communication." *Personnel Administration,* 33, no. 4 (September–October 1970): 4–7, 13–14.

Kelley, Charles M. "The Myth of the Key Communicator." *Personnel Journal,* 45, no. 1 (January 1966): 39–42.

Kelley, Harold. "Communication in Experimentally Created Hierarchies." *Human Relations,* 4, no. 1 (February 1951): 39–56.

Lawson, Edwin D. "Change in Communication Nets, Performance and Morale." *Human Relations,* 18, no. 2 (May 1965): 139–147.

Leavitt, Harold J. "Some Effects of Certain Communication Patterns on Group Performance." *Journal of Abnormal and Social Psychology,* 46, no. 1 (January 1951): 38–50.

Likert, Rensis. *New Patterns in Management.* New York: McGraw-Hill, 1961.

McMurray, R. N. "Clear Communications for Chief Executives." *Harvard Business Review,* 43, no. 2 (March–April 1965): 131–147.

Maier, Norman, L. Richard Hoffman, John J. Hoovan, and William H. Read. *Supervisor-Subordinate Communication in Management,* American Management Association Study No. 52. New York: American Management Association, 1961.

Massie, Joseph L. "Automatic Horizontal Communication in Management." *Academy of Management Journal,* 3, no. 2 (August 1960): 87–92.

Meier, R. L. "Communications Overload: Proposals from the Study of a University Library." *Administrative Science Quarterly,* 7, no. 4 (March 1963): 521–544.

Miller, J. G., "Information Input, Overload, and Psychopathology." *American Journal of Psychiatry,* 116, no. 8 (February 1960): 695–704.

Mulder, M. "Communication Structure, Decision Structure and Group Performance." *Sociometry,* 23, no. 1 (March 1960): 1–4.

Pfeffer, Jeffrey. "Interorganizational Influence and Managerial Attitudes." *Academy of Management Journal,* 15, no. 3 (September 1972): 317–330.

Piersol, D. T. "Communication Practices of Supervisors in a Mid-Western Corporation." *Advanced Management,* 23, no. 2 (February 1958): 20–21.

Read, W. H. "Upward Communication in Industrial Hierarchies." *Human Relations,* 15, no. 1 (1962): 3–15.

Rogers, Carl R., and F. J. Roethlisberger. "Barriers and Gateways to Communication." *Harvard Business Review,* 30, no. 4 (July–August 1952): 46–52.

Safford, E. S. "After the Communication Revolution—Then What?" *Conference Board Record,* 7, no. 11 (November 1970): 35–39.

Sanborn, George A. "An Analytical Study of Oral Communication Practices in a Nationwide Retail Sales Organization." Unpublished doctoral dissertation, Purdue University (1961), pp. 312–316.

Shaw, Marvin E. "Some Effects of Problem Complexity upon Problem Solution Efficiency in Different Communication Nets." *Journal of Experimental Psychology,* 48, no. 3 (July 1954): 211–217.

———— and Wallace T. Penrod Jr. "Does More Information Available to a Group Always Improve Group Performance?" *Sociometry*, 25, no. 4 (December 1962): 377–390.

Simpson, R. L. "Vertical and Horizontal Communication in Formal Organizations." *Administrative Science Quarterly*, 4, no. 2 (September 1959): 188–196.

Wickesberg, A. K. "Communication Networks in the Business Organization Structure." *Academy of Management Journal*, 11, no. 3 (September 1968): 253–262.

Ziller, Robert C. "Communication Restraints, Group Flexibility, and Group Confidence." *Journal of Applied Psychology*, 42, no. 5 (October 1958): 346–352.

Learning Objectives

Perspective on Shifting Roles and Organizational Functions
Emerging from Computer-based Change
Model for Rationalizing Stages of Computer-based Change
Impact of Computers on Management Decision Making
Computers in Management Control Systems
Organizational-Structural Changes Emerging with Introduction
or Advancement of Computer Systems
Controversy Regarding Future Directions of Computer-based
Change

Chapter 7

COMPUTERS, MANAGEMENT, AND ORGANIZATION

OVERVIEW

This chapter places the basic concepts of communication-information systems developed in Chapter 6 into the context of computer technology to establish a perspective for understanding the effects the computer has had on organizations. At the same time, it seeks to provide a basis for anticipating its impact on management and organizations in the future.

The initial discussion portrays the vast changes under way in management systems under the impact of computer introductions. These changes, in turn, suggest important role modifications for key organizational groups, including staff support groups, managers, officials, and workers. Organizational implications are sharpened in a series of questions and statements that seek to crystallize important thrusts of computer-based developments.

The next series of discussion introduces various systems perspectives, classification schemes, and models to suggest systematic approaches in analyzing the organizational aspects of computer introductions and diffusion into supportive subsystems. The implications of computer-based information systems for control, decision making, and planning are among the topics developed here. Synopses of case studies in manufacturing and service-oriented firms portray the diverse aspects of these changes.

The final discussion in this chapter provides some speculations for the future, based on some of our research studies as well as those reported in the literature.

This chapter also assumes an important bridging function to the behavioral discussions of Part II and the application discussions, including the management of change in Part III. Computer-based change frequently modifies the roles of managerial, support, and worker groups (Chapter 10). The role changes, in turn, reflect shifts in decision-making functions (Chapter 11) and leadership (Chapter 9) and pose significant motivational problems (Chapter 8) for incumbents who may be challenged by change. Finally, the thoughtful management of change and the preparation of organizations to absorb, and capitalize on, this type of change is a central concern in the concluding chapters (12–15).

INTRODUCTION

There has been rapid growth in computer use since 1950 and in its effects on organizational life. Exhibit 7–1 shows how the use of digital and analog computers has rapidly accelerated, from approximately 35,000 in 1965 to 65,000 in 1970, with further substantial growth anticipated for the remainder of the decade. Nearly half of the machine tools built in 1970 were con-

EXHIBIT 7–1. Total Number of Computers in Use (Growth of Computer Use, 1950–1970)

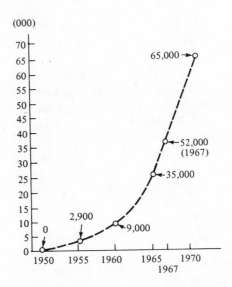

structed to permit numerical control.[1] Hence the importance and pervasiveness of computers in process applications, in managerial technology, in simulation (the use of mathematical models for decision making), and in the formation and growth of operations research.

The introduction of computers into an organization is often accompanied by the formation of new types of information services. New opportunities arise for scrutinizing organizational functions and supporting coordination and control. There are also new possibilities for industrial engineering, production, quality control, and accounting, all of which enjoy the use of more powerful tools for executing their jobs and monitoring a firm's activities. Physically decentralized divisions and plants are drawn more tightly into the organization, and new information strategies are sought for using data that have been regarded as largely routine.[2]

The computer era brought with it a notion of machine performance that emphasized operational sequence, the utilization of stored information, a predetermined data base, and high speed. This computer capability provided the opportunity to incorporate higher-order decision rules, to undertake heuristic approaches to complex administrative problems, to develop new roles for existing personnel, and to conceive a new use for information as an integral part of the organization.

SOCIOLOGICAL IMPLICATIONS OF EDP [3]

The professional staffers associated with EDP have become "fair-haired boys," but they are in an ambivalent position because of the tug of war in labor displacement versus new information possibilities. Also, they may possess a major degree of "trained incapacity" for any important managerial function that is beyond the immediate control of "synthetic intelligence." Officials and managers who view organizational changes are frequently ignorant of information developments and assume a "watch and wait" attitude.

New promise is brought to advocates of centralization, rather than continued diffusion of function and responsibility. Top-management control potential has been extended. In addition, functional separation (marketing and production) is threatened, as the economics and "controllability" of central operations assume added attractiveness.

Computer-based introductions signal complex shifts in the role performance and relationships of diverse organizational groups. As already noted, those personnel directly associated with the computer operation may assume new status in the organization and open new promotional routes to higher management positions. However, important contingencies may exist here, depending on the criticality of the EDP function to the basic work system, performance, and profit. Also, the importance of these computer-related roles may reflect the newness of this function in the organization's routine performance and the function's representation (visibility) in the upper reaches of management.

The roles of non-computer supervision may also shift dramatically as work content and relationships change. The codification of experience within a computer's memory and its support in problem analysis, work performance, and decision making suggest important content changes in role. Viewing the relationships of the supervisor to colleague, computer personnel, and worker suggests new functional relationships and bases for work interactions. The potential reduction of routine work activities may well make considerably greater time available for the more challenging aspects of one's job, as well as behaviorally supportive interactions with subordinates.

Also, one can't ignore the possibilities for increased tension and stress as power loci shift. Incumbents can be expected to resist the potential or real loss of authority and possible shifts in decision responsibility. New promotion paths may suddenly alter individual perceptions and possibilities for upward movement and the "fairness" of these situations.

Separation of supervisory and managerial strata becomes vague under the aforementioned developments, and "milestone" rungs in the promotional ladder disappear. Capitalizing on EDP and its synthesis with organizational policy represents a potent combination for the new manager and executive. Finally, the "ideal" conception for information flow, as viewed by EDP personnel (direct lines), frequently runs counter to a hierarchical structure which seeks to maintain flow in channels.

ORGANIZATION ISSUES [4]

Nevertheless, compelling reasons exist for automated information systems, which include reversing the trends in past years that threatened to swamp organizations with information, red tape, and unmanageable support groups.

Office automation can assume clerical functions and provide information or approaches not feasible with standard techniques. Organizational restraints notwithstanding (lethargy, traditional thinking, and lack of information), important planning implications for higher management can be suggested:

1. The organization should be tailored more closely to the needs and capabilities of the system.

2. The equipment base of the organization is increased, and management problems in work force adjustments are lessened.

3. Functions such as long-range planning, coordination, and control are elevated to new importance.

4. Effectiveness of management control can be extended.

5. A broader knowledge base of system function for higher-level managers may be necessary.

6. Better human performance is available.

7. Existing skill requirements must be changed in diverse directions (increase some, decrease others).

8. Reexamination is required of needed supervisory skills in work performance and handling subordinates, particularly where they are technically trained or under substantial job pressure.

9. Job tension may be elevated and individual worker dependencies increased.

ORGANIZATION QUESTIONS [5]

Crucial to the successful introduction of a computer-based information system is anticipation of answers to certain questions about organizational changes and circumstances:

1. What is top management's posture vis-à-vis innovation and change? What has been the company's position in the past regarding change?

2. To what extent do the natural logistics of information processing lend themselves to computer adaptation? What is the firm's current state of information development? To what extent do future need and current feasibility—enough profit to pay for it—correspond?

3. What is the effect on clerical personnel? On middle-management activities? On the locus of decision making? On routine versus nonroutine decisions?

4. Organizationally, where is the locus of responsibility for computer planning and application? What is the stature and prestige of this office or individual?

5. In what manner does the introduction of computer-based systems or the installation of more advanced systems affect organizational systems (subsystems) supporting the primary work function (system)? How are planning, coordination, and control affected? In what manner does the supervisory support system (and functions) change?

6. How important is top-management recognition and support for fostering computer-based change?

7. What role is played by staff support groups, including computer personnel, in promoting the diffusion of change? What is the role of "users" as participants in the change process?

8. To what extent has management formalized its approaches to developing computer and systems knowledge among its manpower sources? Are these programs oriented toward application or are they more broadly conceived?

Some insights into the answers to these questions will be found as this chapter progresses.

THREE STAGES OF DEVELOPMENT

Initially, computer installations usually focused on "transaction" applications, on displacing clerical personnel (the most common initial justification for computer installation), or on elementary computational applications, as in engineering. Exhibit 7–2 shows that the disruption of organization func-

EXHIBIT 7–2. Computer System Development and Organization Implications

Stage	I	II	III	
	Operational	Functional	Managerial	Organizational Developments

Time

1950
- Mechanization, labor displacement; high volume, standardization of information
- Economic justification
- Discernible patterns of activity
- Minimize disruption of organization functions
- Emphasis on personnel with technical expertise

1960
- External organizational procedures
- Interchange information between functions
- Organization changes
- Reanalysis of organization functions
- Creation of some new groups
- Build data file
- "New" functional applications
- External organization and process controls

1970
- Higher-level management usage
- Reanalysis of organization structure, function, purposes, new organizational modes
- Creation of information function or agencies
- New management "hardware" to support decision making

For a more detailed treatment, see E. H. Burack, "Impact of the Computer on Business Management," *Business Quarterly,* 30, 1 (Spring, 1966).

tions is minimized when changes are largely confined to specific departments and system modifications are nominal.

Second-state changes usually extend functional applications to other departments. At this point changes become more pervasive, and manpower displacement no longer dominates the scene, but managerial and organizational changes are more frequent. Third, movement toward advanced systems or organizational functions requires reanalysis along the lines suggested in the discussion of systems that follows.

Application of Systems Concepts

Systems notions allow a greater sensitivity to the interaction between men and machines and, consequently, a greater awareness of the effects of change upon manpower. The use of mathematical models and systematic routines in problem solving or cost analysis is facilitated. Also, the systems approach leads to the ready development of a checklist of related activities necessary for the accomplishment or modification of a total project mission. At the same time, systems concepts establish a base for coherent controls of cost, inventory, production, and allocation of resources. Finally, the systems concept helps to ensure a comprehensive, logical approach to planning and programming for economic, service, and operational goals. Given these considerations, it is not difficult to visualize a total systems approach in which all resources are marshaled to provide the right information for the right people at the right time and at the right cost.

When businesses were smaller, an owner had complete knowledge of transactions since he was at the crossroad of information. This capability has largely disappeared with the advent of today's large, complex organizations in which there is great volume of information and a high level of communication among diverse areas. "Patchwork" approaches to information processing have resulted in curious combinations of manual writing, forms control, accounting methods, and the partial mechanization of procedures.

A more rigorous approach to information and communication is shown in Exhibit 7–3. Such an approach interrelates decision making, forecasting, policy, design of programs, implementation, feedback, and evaluation so as to cross-link all components, so that a total system can be realized, with the

EXHIBIT 7–3. Total Systems Approaches to Organizations: Computer-based Management Information Systems

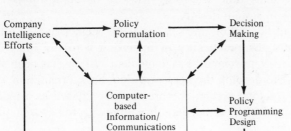

For a detailed treatment, see A. T. Spaulding, Jr., "Is the Total System Concept Practical?" in *Systems and Procedures Journal* (Jan.-Feb. 1964).

computer as the hub for controlling and communicating the various functions of the process. In this case, a theoretical information concept can be transformed into a practical arrangement if management wants one and states what it desires from the system. These requirements are translated into a coherent network of related activities and objectives of the organization.

The practicality of the systems approach has been demonstrated under a variety of circumstances, but a particularly interesting case concerns the rapid expansion of commercial aviation. Joseph D. Blatt, of the FAA, noted that the mission of air traffic control is

> the safe and expeditious handling of air traffic. The system must therefore have two objectives: . . . the safe separation of aircraft in order to prevent midair collisions, and . . . *most effective* use of the airspace, thus insuring a smooth and expeditious traffic flow.

Consequently, from the systems perspective, the objectives—safety and performance—are clearly set out. In addition, a justification for the systems approach is given:

> The problem must be approached from the overall system standpoint. For too many years we have attempted to resolve the airway/airport system problem by first dividing it into its subsystems—airports, terminal navigation . . . and then doing what was economically feasible to better the sub-system. This produced piecemeal solutions which resulted in imbalances and tended to shift the bottlenecks from one part of the system to another.[6]

It is clear that closely allied functions or units, be they operational or administrative, require a broad approach that encompasses all crucial elements. At the same time, a strong case can be made for centralizing the responsibilities in system design.

An important distinction must be made between assuming a total systems perspective and the practicality of operating a totally integrated system. Progress toward comprehensive management systems has been slow, as companies attempt to develop the necessary data base, orientation, organization, and hardware. A total system is more usefully viewed as a model of possibilities so as to highlight needed developments for system planning and implementation.

SYSTEM DESIGN INFORMATION FOR DECISION MAKING

The purpose of an information system is to take data input and produce information output for decision making, and the systems concept is useful for visualizing this function. The central idea in systems approaches to decision making[7] is to differentiate among decision levels by means of

a. *Institutional decisions,* typically concerning strategic planning and the formulation of company policy, objectives, and organization structure. (Here, decisions must also reckon with environmental developments.)

b. *Managerial decisions,* pertaining to functional planning, goal implementation, and the broader allocation of resources to attain objectives.

c. *Technical and operational procedures,* or the control and planning that go into the detailed acquisition, allocation, and use of resources.

Exhibit 7–4 depicts the decision hierarchy and the relationships among dependent systems. These system characterizations and the rapid advance

EXHIBIT 7–4. Systems Perspective—Decision Making

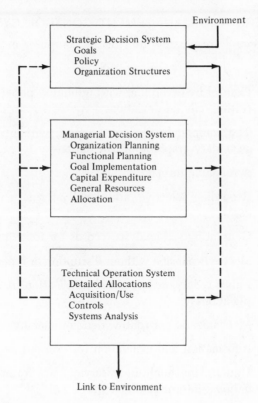

— — — Information flow

For a more detailed treatment, see R. A. Johnson et al., *The Theory and Management of Systems* (New York: McGraw-Hill, 1968).

of computer equipment and supporting hardware have led many management experts[8] to speculate on the possibilities of supplying real-time information for top management (general managers and executives). Appropriate hardware (e.g., remote terminals) would permit the capture, analysis, and feedback of information rapidly enough to affect ongoing activities. (Real-time applications also appear to have substantial possibilities for logistics, where speed and volume of information are critical and often require response with minimum delay.)

Potential top-management use of real-time information may be evaluated in light of the traditional organization functions: planning (short and long range, manpower, finance, and innovation); control and coordination; direction and administration; establishing objectives; identifying, evaluating, and selecting alternatives; and launching programs.

COMPUTERS AND MANAGEMENT CONTROL SYSTEMS

The following are possible uses of the computer in management control systems.

1. Control by exception, with minimum paper output and concentrating only on deviations

2. The completely processed report, without carrying out added secondary graphing or calculations

3. A readable format

4. Recording selective, additional information for possible future use

5. Generating self-analysis records for items processed

6. System expansion without disruption or repetition

7. Labor reduction (an initial justification for many computer applications)

8. Mechanization of routine decision making

9. Information and evaluation for nonroutine decisions

10. Undertaking analysis or services not formerly feasible (e.g., a national information system)

Items 1 through 5 govern the important areas of management information and stress the selective accumulation of information, as well as maintaining the relevance of data. Item 6 presents the notion of expandability without disruption in order to permit the continuity of managerial controls. Item 7 is the traditional labor displacement idea in cost control, which is less prominent as new computer capabilities emerge.

Item 8 and 9 move into the area of decisions, where both routine ("transaction") and nonroutine decisions provide potent areas for computer-based controls. Nonroutine decisions present difficulties because of complexity *and* lack of volume.[9] In inventory management, the development of computer applications taxes management's ability to assimilate the results. Forecasting, replenishment, age analysis, and investment studies are some of the many types of decisions based on computer technology.

One of the new types of information service, presented in item 10, permits almost instantaneous feedback on credit applications. Moreover, national information networks facilitate the monitoring of physically decentralized production units and services.

The level in the organization at which the authority of computer operations is lodged has obvious effects upon the creativity, scope, and depth with which control applications are developed. The results of a 1963 study by McKinsey & Company, which included twenty-seven companies and 130 computers, suggested that the businesses that demonstrated above-average profit performance typically lodged the information functions high in the organization and in close proximity to the chief executive.[10] The distribution is shown in Exhibit 7–5.

EXHIBIT 7–5. Positioning of Computer Head in Authority Structure

Authority level	Above-average companies (n = 9)	Average companies (n = 18)
One level below chief	5	3
Two levels down	4	9
Lower	—	6

Source: McKinsey & Co., New York; in-house study, 1963.

The locus of computer operations may shift upward as more sophisticated applications are attempted and the use of information spreads. Thus the differences cited for "above average" companies may also describe the direction of movement for companies not yet advanced in the use of information.

Work functions in primarily service-oriented organizations are largely built around information processing. The use of computers and information in manufacturing organizations has its own features. Exhibit 7–6, abstracted from a forty-four-company study[11] of the organization and manpower problems that accompany technological change, describes important organiza-

EXHIBIT 7-6. Projected Organizational Effects of Computer Use in Advanced Production Units

| Company | Job attributes and functions | | | | | | | | Formal training |
| | Decision process | | | Work with support groups | | Major groups involved | | | |
	Problem identi- fication	Analysis	Problem solving	Reliance on support groups	Communi- cation with support	Oper- ations, first line	Higher management	Support	
A† Medium- size steel*	XX	X	X	XXX	XXX	XX	XX	XXX	XX
B†† Medium- size utility	XXX	XXX	XXX	XX	XXX	X	X	XXX	X
C† Large petroleum	XX	XX	XX	XX	XXX	XX	XX	XX	XX
D†† Large petroleum	XXX	XXX	XXX	XXX	XXX	XXX	XXX	XXX	XXX
E†† Large food	XX	X	X	XX	XX	XX	X	XX	X

X: Modest emphasis

XX: Of some importance

XXX: Major importance

X: Area of anticipated change: short to intermediate range.

* Based on plant size, where "medium" is 400 to 1,000 and "large" is over 1,000 plant personnel

† Based on corporate affiliation and share of industry: ranks medium size

†† Based on corporate affiliation and share of industry; ranks large in size

Source: Elmer H. Burack and Thomas J. McNichols, *Human Resource Planning: Technology, Policy, and Change* (Kent, O.: Kent State University Division of Business and Economics Research, 1973).

tional effects of computer use, and highlights transformations in work roles, relationships, and functions. In general, the tabulation suggests that

1. Problem identification is important.

2. Analysis and problem solving vary widely in firms where computers are used extensively.

3. Many problems are technical, and can be defined in the symbols necessary for computer processing.

4. Involvement of organizational groups varies. First-line supervision is affected only when proven managerial or process applications are installed that require their attention. First-line supervisors evidenced disinterest in computer information use (and systems) except where they were engaged in the operation and carefully oriented, or where higher managerial levels encouraged computer use. Reaction was similar among higher managerial levels. The support groups working extensively with line functions (maintenance, production control, and inspection) showed a growing interest in computer outputs—but active encouragement by superiors and direct involvement of line personnel were important considerations in application accomplishments. Where interdependencies were growing between operational units, planning and production control made extensive use of computer analysis to support both planning and coordination.

5. Formal training reflects widely different degrees of company commitment. In training, much more is typically discussed than is realized.

To the extent that managerial development activities in computer usage took place in the companies of the study, the focus was on application rather than theory, approaches, or systems concepts, even in the large firms. Although rather extensive programs were planned for the future, such training plans proved to be quite fragile and vulnerable to economic shifts.

TRANSITION TO EDP IN A LARGE
SERVICE-ORIENTED FIRM [12]

A large information-oriented concern (such as those found in insurance, mail order, credit, or financial institutions), which had maintained routine data processing operations for a number of years, set out to update and enlarge its information system. The punched card ("EAM") system gave way to a computer-based (EDP) system in 1965. The following tabulation describes the "before" and "after" effects on the organization.

Before 1965	1965 and after
Accounting oriented	Increase EDP staff (40 to 100)
Routine management information	Raise status of computer-related
Under financial officer	people (programmers, systems)
Little outside expertise brought in	through promotions
Acquired EDP because it was	Create new V.P. for information
fashionable	Consolidate market research
Use of in-house talent	under credit billing under new
	position
	Extend application area to two
	major departments heavily com-
	mitted to clerks (400)
	Add terminal operations,
	60 employees (1967)
	Reduce clerks (350)

As the information system was extended, the varying combinations of human-system interfaces necessitated an examination of system controls in order to more fully realize the potential of the system. This attempt to exert control raised questions concerning the accuracy of information inputs, timely performance, selective report distribution, and close scrutiny of possible applications. Yet, although the proposed system was a radical departure from older operations, little orientation preceded its installation—and many top and middle line managers were confused.

In June 1967 a series of extensive organization and procedural changes was launched (Exhibit 7–7) that involved the extension of EDP to several major administrative (information processing) departments, coinciding with preparation for installing a new generation of EDP equipment (the organi-

EXHIBIT 7–7. System Developments

Computers: Step I, 1965–1967	Computers: Step II, Developing data base, 1968n	
System installation based on economic justification	Demographic information	
System change confined to well-defined areas	Customer activity (4 years)	
Most of organization not affected	Customer buying patterns	
Acquire outside talent	Account classification	
High volume of routine procedures characterized applications	Systems training	
Extend existing procedures	**Subject**	**Time**
Integrate some subsystems where information is interrelated	Fundamentals I,	$1^{1}/_{2}$–$2^{1}/_{2}$ days
Little procedural or support changes in the conversion (mechanization) of the customer, credit billing group	II, III	1 day
	Visual display	4 days
	Computer system	5 days
	System design	2 days
	Seminar	

zational changes are depicted in Exhibit 7–8). The subdivision of section
functions in the organization prior to June 1967 was extensively revamped
in favor of computer terminal operations and supporting work groups; the

EXHIBIT 7–8A. Data Processing Organization

Before 1967 (1965)

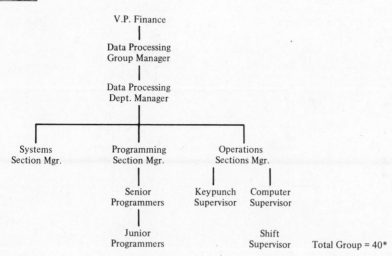

Total Group = 40*

After 1967 (1968)

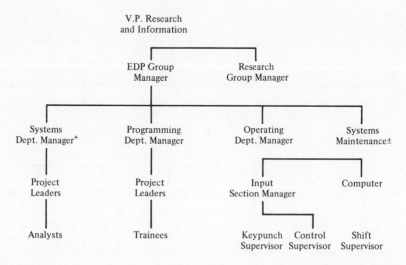

Total Group = 100*

* Charges include staff additions: 4 programmers, 4 computer operators, 18 keypunch operators,
15 control clerks, systems people.
‡ To be formed.
† Includes credit system team (moved from "credit").

EXHIBIT 7–8B. Changes in Major Administrative Functions

Before June 1967

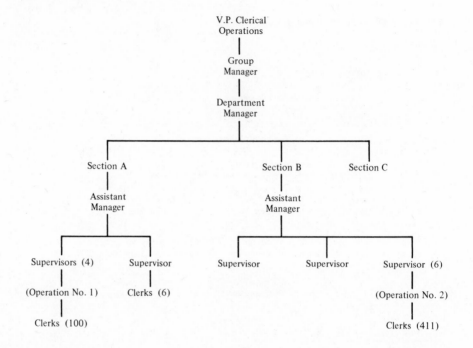

After June 1967

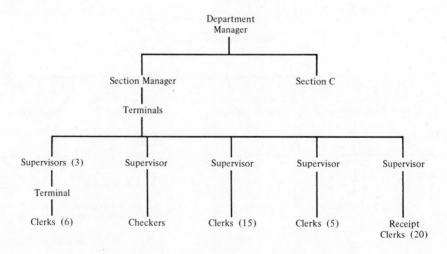

EXHIBIT 7-9. Service and Production Functions Contrasted

Organizational variable	Service orientation	Production orientation
I. Technical interpretation and evaluation (decision to accept or reject consumer's order)		
A. Background of the decision maker	Generalized knowledge of business and company practices	Technical and specialized product knowledge
B. Vulnerability of decision maker to displacement	High—particularly where there is the ability to systematize basis of decisions (large volume of standardized information)	Low—singularity of cases requires high level of personal attention
II. Characteristics of the work function		
A. Orientation	Informational	Technical
B. Flexibility of work function	High, due to absence of constraints other than that which reflects the level of information attainment	Low, due to technological constraint of "state of the art" (e.g., chemicals and mechanically based products)
C. Diversity of jobs performed	Relatively low, due to absence of requirement for specializing the information process to the "product"	High, due to extensive specialization and division of labor, as well as variety of input factors requiring major organizational functions of coordination and control
D. Role of information technology in the work function	Information is the essence of the "product" as well as the work function	Abridging the production function of physically separated units
III. Planning (translation of demand into operational requirements)	Relatively simple, due to ready availability of data and analytical techniques. Two significant variables to be considered: manpower and information capabilities	Complex, due to many combinations of manpower, material, machines, money, and information capabilities
IV. Interpersonal relationships (includes physical mobility and creativity in information innovation)	Mobile, with few constraints	Relatively constrained

Source: Elmer H. Burack and Bernard H. Baum, "Information Technology in Product and Service Firms," I.I.T. working paper (Spring 1969).

elimination of clerical personnel was extensive. Also, the data processing systems group was moved from the vice president of finance to a newly created position, vice president of research and information.

Information Technology and Organizational Function

The use of information systems in manufacturing units differs from their use in service units. For organizational subunits involved in computational activities, such as actuarial (insurance), production control, systems, and industrial engineering and design departments, information processing is a central concern. At the level of the firm, insurance companies, banks, and credit organizations are largely information oriented. Information systems are also crucial to railroads and airlines for scheduling purposes. The use of the computer as an integral part of manufacturing systems is limited to the extent that the production function can be rationalized; however, information processes are important as support systems for production. Some of the distinctions between service-oriented and product-oriented functions are listed in Exhibit 7–9.

Within the broader concept of an organizational system, the performance of the information system depends upon the extent to which the production function can be described in symbolic form. Exhibit 7–10 is a systems model

EXHIBIT 7–10. Contrasting Systems Model—Production and Information Technology

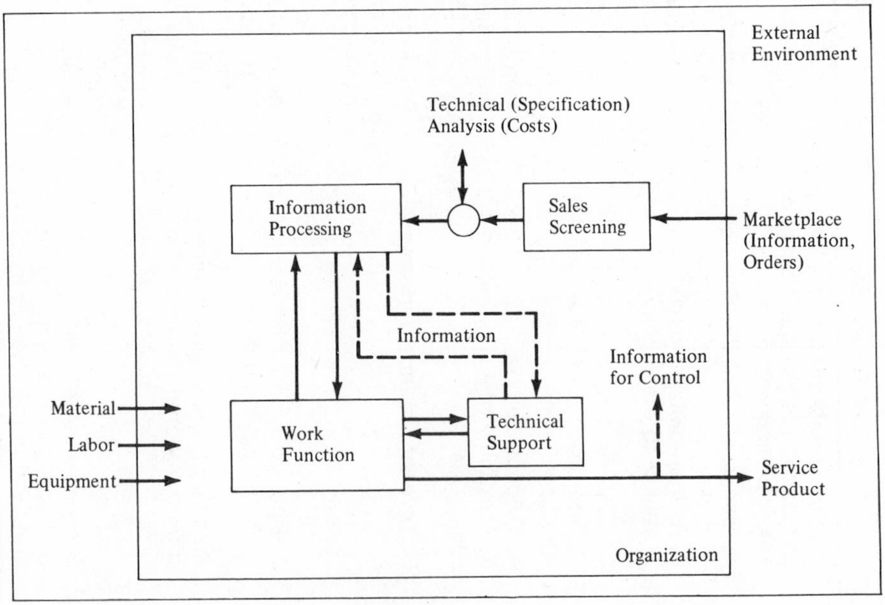

that highlights the supportive or functional aspects of production and information technologies as they might coexist. Supporting *sub*systems that are information oriented may absorb a high level of information outputs and techniques, but overall *system* development is limited by the "weakest links."

Manufacturing organizations must overcome additional complications (as compared to service units) in attempting to rationalize an information-communication system. These complications emerge largely from the problems of integrating the production function. Within institutions, this distinction can be further refined as we look at specific functions or departments and pose the question "Which functional units or services in a company (production control, quality control, market research, actuarial, science, and so on) are most adaptable to information technology?" In other words, "Which decisions can be most readily translated into the language of information?"

Institutions may be classified for their overall ability to absorb information in terms of (1) their structural features, (2) the presence or absence of the work function or the manufacturing arm of the total organization, and (3) the adaptability of particular functional units to the utilization of information. Consequently, whatever gains may be made in developing a comprehensive information system will be limited by the ability to incorporate and utilize information inputs and outputs within, to, and from the production function. As a result, the more advanced the manufacturing or production function and the greater the ability to apply information technology, the more closely one would expect the communication system to approximate those of other institutions whose activities are based on information.

This point is illustrated in Exhibit 7–11, where information-oriented systems and work-oriented systems may be viewed along continua as they move toward advanced technologies. In the case of the information-oriented system, the degree of system advancement largely reflects (a) information volume and diversity and (b) the ability to bring together the various functional activities of the organization. For the information-oriented system, movement along a continuum represents an extension of information applications in both depth and breadth. Furthermore, such movement reflects the use of successive generations of powerful computer-based systems.

In the production system built around the worker, depicted in the lower portion of this panel, movement along the scale represents successive levels of improved technical achievement. The outgrowth of continuing improvements more closely approximates these kinds of systems that *share* information problems (manufacturing) with those that are information oriented (service). Note, however, that in attempting to characterize total system development there are important exceptions where portions of a system may be adaptable to information outputs, whereas the system as a whole may not. A case in point is the utilization of numerical control tapes produced

EXHIBIT 7–11. System Development and Information

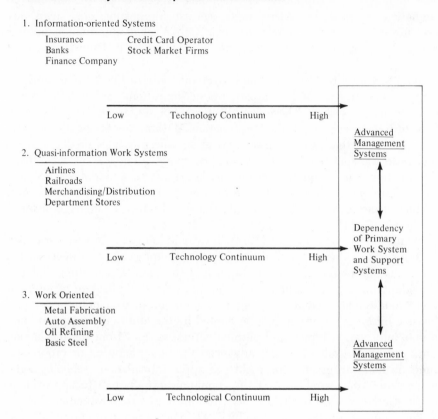

1. Information-oriented Systems

Insurance	Credit Card Operator
Banks	Stock Market Firms
Finance Company	

Low   Technology Continuum   High

Advanced Management Systems

2. Quasi-information Work Systems

Airlines
Railroads
Merchandising/Distribution
Department Stores

Low   Technology Continuum   High

Dependency of Primary Work System and Support Systems

3. Work Oriented

Metal Fabrication
Auto Assembly
Oil Refining
Basic Steel

Advanced Management Systems

Low   Technological Continuum   High

by computer-based programs. These permit a very advanced level of automatic machine-tool use, even in somewhat backward industries such as the metal cutting trade.

Another example is the application by IBM of some of its own computer developments within its manufacturing organization. By 1968 IBM had constructed and placed in operation several plants where computers permitted numerical control of equipment, process controls, and monitoring quality. The day of the automatic factory was one step closer.

Some important segments of the machine-tool industry have been able to make great strides along the continuum of production technology, to a point that the systematic treatment of production variables has permitted the direct use of computer-based information systems within their operations. In fact, advancements have reached the point where integration of factory applications with other organizational subsystems (accounting and production control, for example) has become possible. Around the mid 1960s, several large companies installed computer-oriented production lines (assembly, quality control) in mass production plants, including the showcase installations by IBM.

ORGANIZATIONAL EXPERIENCES WITH A NEW TECHNOLOGY

A number of research studies are instructive in analyzing the organizational effects of incorporating computer-based information systems. Particular attention should be given to distinctions between changes in service organizations versus changes in manufacturing firms.

A Pioneering Study

A study of considerable importance took place in an electric utility that serviced over one million customers and retained some 800 accounting employees.[13] The system was originally based on manual bookkeeping methods, until, early in the 1940s, a conversion was made to an IBM punched card system. Then, in 1953, another conversion program was launched, and finally terminated in 1957 with the installation of a computer-based system.

Through this conversion, the function of the entire accounting section changed, together with its relationship to sales and marketing, production, and other functions of the utility. Customer records were consolidated and procedures were improved, but some notable problems emerged:

a. Restraints in promotional policy. There was also a necessity to reclassify employees as some jobs changed, disappeared, or were created. The fast pace of change had important implications for morale, needed work, and requisite skills.

b. A high level of distrust of the information provided. Frequently the men associated with the information system became the targets for blame when errors occurred.

c. Change of status for people *within* the information system, as well as for those at the interface *with* the system. Greater formalization of work procedures and lines of communication modified both the status and power of individuals and groups within the system.

d. Time interdependencies increased within the functions comprising the information system. Consequently, *down time* assumed new importance, whereas it had been relatively unimportant in the past.

e. Real complexities emerged in organization and social problems, but new possibilities for promotion and more effective organizational procedures to some extent counterbalanced the manpower problems.

An increasingly widespread problem is that many larger organizations have overcome the problems of *installation* of computer-based information systems but are having difficulties because the era of cost savings has passed and they are not making effective use of their computer capacities. This represents not only a loss of profit potential but an opportunity cost in terms of future undertakings to improve organizational performance.

An Information-oriented Organization

Some findings have been reported that fit in with the model of a complex, administratively oriented organization whose programming focus is on the processing of information.[14] In this context fall banks, insurance companies, credit groups, hospitals, and other service-oriented, information-based institutions. One may contrast the characteristics of information-oriented concerns with institutions that have complex work technologies comprised of both information and manufacturing elements. The emphasis and dependency on information in the indicated service units are quite pronounced.

The Vaughan and Perat banking study, which included 354 officers, is especially interesting because it involved branch operations and thus provided some information on decentralized activities—the Mann-Williams study (previously referenced) concentrated largely on a centralized organization. The results of the first part of the banking study were as follows.

1. Scope of Decision Making. In departments that were highly dependent on computer output, such as marketing, economic analysis, and the operating department, the computer is visualized as increasing the range of decision making. However, the strength of this view diminishes substantially with the age of the responding group, so that the younger groups see a greater effect on the scope of decision making than the older groups (under 30 years, 65 percent; 50–59 years, 49 percent). The younger groups also see a greater effect on themselves (identify with change) than on the older group. In another analysis, the under-40 group saw a greater effect on *themselves* than on their bosses, but the older group saw more effect *on their bosses* but *less* effect on subordinates (including younger elements).

In many cases there was an increase in the dollar amount of loans approved by loan officers (broadening of decision making) but a decrease in the number of cases requiring their personal evaluation, because routine acceptance criteria were invoked for handling ordinary applications. Consequently, many decisions were handled more or less automatically, but an overall judgment on the range of decision making involving individual time and talent was difficult to make.

2. Rationality of Decision Making. The departments that have had the least direct experience with the computer feel that the computer is likely to make their decisions more rational. Thus it would appear that knowledge of computers brings with it a more realistic view of their capabilities.

3. Visibility of Decision Makers. Greater visibility ("high profile") to organizational participants, which is ascribed to the personnel dealing with computer operations, seemed to parallel heavy user departments and significantly color the response of the branch managers in decentralized operations. The ease with which computer outputs are distributed and monitored and the systems' demand for conformity and reporting from branch managers would surely help account for the feelings of increased visibility.

4. Computer Potential. The respondents who felt the computer would have considerable potential for the future tended to be young. Those who felt the computer is good for data processing but not for decision making were distributed as follows:

Age 20–29—27%

30–39—47

40–49—51

50–59—63

These figures show the effect of age on attitudes toward computer potential, but it must also be recognized that the types of decisions confronting the senior personnel are substantially different from those facing the younger members of the organization. Reactions to the future of computer use in decision making were mixed, but the younger groups again tended to ascribe greater importance to computer capability.

5. Computer Education. One of the key questions in the Vaughan and Perat series concerned educational programs for bank personnel involving material on computer operations. Many of the respondents (50–60 percent) were of the opinion that it is *not* easier to give computer people an understanding of banking than to give bankers an understanding of the computer. Development would more strongly favor computer education for bankers, rather than banking education for computer men.

6. Computers and Job Promotion. An important finding of the study confirms other studies: promotion is seen as easier in departments that have been strengthened or created by computer availability. The same results were found for the heavy users of computers (seven out of ten officers). Conversely, departments that carried out routine assignments or were only very recently affected by the computer ascribed little promotional effect to it.

Branch managers also ascribed little promotional power to the computer. This viewpoint was rationalized on the basis of the large amount of work that had already been removed from the branch offices and incorporated in the *centralized* computer. Because the branch managers were completely isolated from the headquarters, where the computer facility was housed, they viewed their performance as more directly related to activities in their own branch.

Members of the younger group, 20 to 29 years of age, were hired *after* the computer was in use; therefore they had little basis for judging relative changes in promotional opportunities. On the other hand, 63 percent of the 30–39 age group, which had witnessed developments before and after installation of the computer, foresaw promotion effects. Again, the older groups saw substantially fewer such effects, perhaps because they had already achieved advanced positions.

TOWARD THE FUTURE

The computer is slated to play an ever-increasing role in the panorama of company activities, and this development points to an important impact on management and organizational systems. Research studies on the impact of the computer[15] suggest some of the major shifts in organizational processes, reporting relationships, and bases for decision making that are currently emerging. The concepts set forth in this chapter provide a basis for rationalizing the variables underlying these changes and for formulating a structured approach to anticipating and capitalizing on them.

In the early years of computer usage, organizational direction or the computer department was frequently lodged within the accounting or financial departments. Recently, in a group of 108 highly successful firms surveyed by Dean, some 40 percent of the applications lay outside the accounting-financial area. Furthermore, the prognosis for this group of firms indicates a distinct, *relative* decrease in accounting-financial applications and a strong surge in the use of computer-based information systems in operation, distribution, planning, and information.

Thus the shift in computer usage visualized for the future bears out the concepts expressed earlier in this chapter: a relative decrease in "transaction" (operational) applications; more "computational" (functional) applications; and gradual progress toward integrated systems, especially for the more sophisticated users and those systems where information is crucial. The system-oriented changes described suggest only the outward signs of deeper organizational changes affecting authority structures, decision making, work, and work content. However, these organizational changes should not be viewed as universal trends; they apply differently to various institutional structures (production versus service, support group versus operations, computational groups versus administrative groups).

Research suggests widespread changes in large administrative units that are characterized by large numbers of clerical help, staff (technical) specialists, and functional administration.[16] This model for change features corporate headquarters and divisional units, and includes such institutions as insurance companies, banks, department stores, and airlines, many of which have satellite plants and distribution and service centers. Recent research on these institutions points to a modification of authority structure wherein the relative clerical content stabilizes or decreases, and levels of authority and the supervisory span of control decrease. The work content of the residual group of jobs may display a narrower focus or more routine components, but skills may be higher if *current* trends persist.

Another trend noted in this research are selective but distinct moves toward centralization of authority and surveillance of personnel. The rationalization and quantification of the bases for decisions appear to be persistent trends, which run the risk of destroying the flexibility required for quick maneuvering in changing situations. Participation in the decision process also appears to be changing considerably. Note the following five steps of the decision process and the patterns of participation in each by middle management or staff groups vis-à-vis top management:

1. *Identification*—equal involvement

2. *Analysis*—largely assigned to middle management

3. *Identification of alternatives*—frequently provided by middle management, but top management plays an important role

4. *Evaluation*—largely a mixed area with a high level of involvement by both groups

5. *Selection*—essentially a top-management function

Organizational changes concomitant with computer usage bring with them a gain in time that permits the development of alternatives. It also allows for more thorough analysis of innovative approaches and permits the use of more powerful tools by specialists.

COMPUTERS, MANAGEMENT, AND CHANGE

Another interesting facet of the organizational changes emerging with computer usage is the part played by various groups (line and support groups and top management) in effecting change. It is important to note that the occupational type, authority level, and influence of groups participating in change can vary considerably. Thus in establishing or extending computer-based information systems, research has indicated a surprisingly heavy influence by middle line managers and staff (systems) personnel.[17]

The implications of computer usage in large, administrative organizations require some reinterpretation in organizations that contain production functions. The need for technical problem solving and system-oriented approaches to planning is constrained by the state of technical development in production. Computers that are an integral part of production processes (numerical control) are increasing and will further affect the locus of decision making, distribution of responsibilities (e.g., engineering design versus floor supervision; plant technical support groups and line management), plant authority structure (number of authority levels), work structure, and manpower programming.

Information-oriented functions that work in *conjunction* with the production process can be expected to incur changes similar to those described for administrative units.[18] However, the development of *comprehensive* information systems, which bring with them massive organizational changes, depends on the stage of maturity of *all* subsystems (petroleum and chemical). Although comprehensive systems appear to offer compelling advantages in operations, top-management philosophy or economic restraints are some of the factors retarding the achievement of advanced designs and thereby pointing to less regimented approaches.

SUMMARY

The point of departure for this chapter's discussions was the rapid growth of computer usage in a diversity of organizational settings, which has established a basis for widespread organizational changes. Change is materializing in managerial processes, functions, areas of conflict, relationships, roles of new occupational specialties, and structure—let alone posing significant manpower issues in displacement or retraining. Given the basic institutional parameters of financial ability, incorporation of computer-based systems turns on a variety of issues, including information volume, depth and scope of the problem-solving load, breadth of the communications network, and time demands for reporting.

It has been found useful to characterize computer change according to three stages that identify various features. Thus stage I–type changes indicate structural shifts that are largely localized in particular functional areas and are often accompanied by worker displacement. Stage II–type changes lead to more widespread changes in terms of the number of people and functions involved, and start to signal a shift in the character and level of decision making. Also, new needs and opportunities are indicated for the architects and specialists who know well the subtleties of computer operation and the realities of organization life. Change beyond this point (stage III) typically signals a drastic redefinition of structure, functions, and organizational activities.

The character of the production function was established as a major factor contributing to or retarding the adaptation of computer-based processes on a broader systems basis. To the extent that a general system update is dependent on the "automation" of all the principal subsystems, technical complexities or a low state of the art in the production function can seriously retard overall computer advances. Thus organizations that are built largely around information processes (e.g., insurance and banking) may express a potential for computer usage considerably longer than that of systems where the production function is prominent but still not fully defined. However, the functional specialists who support information-based procedures and the production functions are quite vulnerable to computer inroads simply because much of their work is information oriented (e.g., problem solving, analysis, programming, and calculations). Yet many areas of strategy or tactical planning lie outside (thus far) of computer-based procedures due to the highly subjective content of much of these areas.

Nevertheless, computer developments, which are now in the offing, promise even more significant changes for organization function and operation.

QUESTIONS

1. What distinctions converge in organizational change when manufacturing and service activities are compared?

2. In organizational situations where there is a lack of computer knowledge, what strategies might be indicated for establishing a basis for change and preparing people and organizations to assume viable roles?

3. Assuming that the thrust of computer-based changes has been surmised correctly in this chapter, to what extent can these changes become the basis for restructuring work, work relationships, and job content?

4. What shifts appear to be in the offing for the participation of middle-level managers or staff functionaries in decision processes?

5. A classical issue pertaining to computer-based change is its impact on the locus of decision making. What structural and technological factors are likely to encourage (a) centralization and (b) decentralization?

6. What areas of the following types of organizations are likely to (1) encourage computer-based adaptations and (2) resist the ready extension of computer-based procedudes: (a) airlines? (b) department stores? (c) retail food chains? (d) electric (utility) companies?

DISCUSSION CASES

1. In many companies, computer equipment is initially installed in the data processing section of the finance or accounting departments. However, in considering the direction of future computer applications, a much wider circle of departments and personnel is eventually involved. A typical second major project is a manufacturing cost control system (MCCS), requiring a wide variety of reporting (cost, labor hours, scrap, etc.) within a time framework and in a manner quite different from that of the past. Often thought is given to the possible reorganization of skills, training, people, functions, or the departments necessary to support an MCCS. In the past, the manufacturing divisions and personnel had operated autonomously and regarded themselves as self-contained. MCCS, a comprehensive system, becomes operational with the stated purposes of strengthening cost controls and introducing the use of standard costs for managerial cost and budget planning.

   What needs to be reorganized? What are the consequences of overlooking possibilities for reorganization? What are the advantages MCCS offers the firm? What problems might be anticipated? What plan might build in appropriate coping mechanisms?

2. Recall from Chapter 2 that Paul Lawrence and Jay Lorsch have raised some questions concerning the inherent conflict between the differentiation of organizational function for improved performance and the necessity to integrate activities—that is, where and how internal functions fit external demands. These problems must be jointly resolved. Regardless of the situation, the design of the organization structure should reflect a conscious strategy on the part of management. Research undertaken by Pugh and others suggests that this deliberate design effort must include such variables as structural complexity, unit size, the marketing system, and techniques of distribution.

   What are the asks of coordination and control for highly differentiated organizational units (e.g., research, accounting, and sales management)? What offices should be developed for undertaking these tasks?

NOTES

1. Numerical control is the use of computer-derived tapes to guide machine tools through complex procedures; this permits automation.

2. Elmer H. Burack, "Organizational Aspects of Operations Research Groups—Growth and Decline," *Business Perspectives,* 5, no. 2 (Fall 1969); Elmer H. Burack, and Robert R. D. Battlavala, "Emerging Organizational Changes and Functions of Operations Research Groups in Organizations," *Business Perspectives,* 8, no. 3 (Winter 1972); Bernard H. Baum and Elmer H. Burack, "Information Technology, Manpower Development, and Organizational Performance," *Academy of Management Journal,* 12, no. 3 (September 1969): 277–291; and Peter Sorensen and Elmer H. Burack, "Organizational Manpower Planning Responses to Computer Based Change," *forthcoming.*

3. Developed in detail in Ida R. Hoos, "The Sociological Impact of Automation in the Office," *Management Technology,* 1, no. 2 (1961): 10–19.

4. Based on Baum and Burack, "Information and Technology," and Walter Buckingham, "The Human Side of Automation," in Keith Davis and William G. Scott (eds.), *Readings in Human Relations* (2d ed.; New York: McGraw-Hill, 1966), pp. 395–407.

5. Some of these questions are suggested by Richard F. Powers and Gary W. Dickson, "MIS Project Management: Myths, Opinions and Reality," *California Management Review,* 15, no. 3 (Spring 1973): 147–156; Thomas Whisler, *The Impact of Computers on Organizations* (New York: Praeger, 1970); and Burack and Battlavala, "Emerging Organizational Changes."

6. "If You've Time to Spare, Go by Air," *Engineering Opportunities,* 7, no. 10 (October 1969): 8–15.

7. Discussed more extensively in Chapter 10.

8. John Deardon, "Myth of Real-Time Management Information," *Harvard Business Review* (May–June 1966): 123–132.

9. An expansive treatment of this point is provided by Herbert Simon, *The New Science of Management Decision Making* (New York: John Wiley & Sons, 1960).

10. In-house study.

11. Elmer H. Burack and Thomas J. McNichols, *Human Resource Planning: Technology, Policy, Change* (Kent, O.: Kent State University Bureau of Business and Economics Research, 1973).

12. See Elmer H. Burack, "The Impact of the Computer on Business Management," *Business Quarterly,* 30, no. 1 (Spring 1966).

13. F. Mann and L. K. Williams, "Observations on the Dynamics of Change to Electronic Data Processing Equipment," *Administrative Science Quarterly,* 5, no. 1 (June 1960): 217–256.

14. J. A. Vaughan and A. M. Perat, "Managerial Reactions to Computers," *Banking* (April 1967), "How Management Views Computer Operations," *Banking* (June 1967), "Management Views on the Importance of Computers to Staff Promotions," *Banking* (July 1967).

15. Elmer H. Burack, "Impact of Technological Change on Operational Support Functions," *Journal of Purchasing,* 4, no. 1 (August 1969); Baum and Burack, "Information Technology," pp. 279–291; Burack, "Impact of the Computer on Business Management"; Neal Dean, "Computer Comes of Age," *Harvard Business Review,* 16, no. 1 (January–February 1969).

16. Includes T. Whisler and H. Meyer's study of nineteen life insurance companies for the Life Office Management Association (1967) and Rodney H. Brady's study of twelve large manufacturing firms, "Computers in Top-Level Decision Making," *Harvard Business Review,* 45, no. 4 (July–August 1967).

17. Dennis Hackl, "Top Management and the Launching of Change," I.I.T. thesis (1969); Baum and Burack, "Information Technology."

18. Sorensen and Burack, "Organizational Manpower Planning Responses." More on this subject can be found in Sorenson's Ph.D. thesis, "Impact of Computer Automation in Management Development Approaches," Illinois Institute of Technology (1971).

REFERENCES

Baum, Bernard, and Elmer H. Burack. "Information Technology, Manpower Development and Organizational Performance." *Academy of Management Journal,* 12, no. 2 (September 1969): 274–291.

Bunk, V. Z. *Computers and Management: The Executive Viewpoint.* Englewood Cliffs, N.J.: Prentice-Hall, 1971.

Burack, Elmer H. "Computers and Organizational Change." Working paper at the spring conference of the Institute of Management Sciences, 1971.

Dearden, John. "MIS Is a Mirage." *Harvard Business Review,* 50, no. 1 (January–February 1972): 90–99.

Delehanty, George E. "Office Automation and the Occupation Structure: A Case Study of Five Insurance Companies." *Industrial Management Review,* 7, no. 2 (1966): 99–109.

Diebold, J. *Beyond Automation.* New York: McGraw-Hill, 1964.

Garrity, John T. "Top Management and Computer Profits." *Harvard Business Review,* 41, no. 4 (July–August 1963): 172–174.

Goshay, Robert C. *Information Technology in the Insurance Industry.* Homewood, Ill.: Richard D. Irwin, 1964.

Hadler, E. W., and P. Nador. "MIS: How to Get Going." *Business Quarterly,* 36, no. 3 (Autumn 1971): 52–57.

Helfgott, R. B. "EDP and the Office Work Force." *Industrial and Labor Relations Review,* 19, no. 3 (July 1966): 503–516.

Hill, Walter A. "The Impact of EDP Systems on Office Employes: Some Empirical Conclusions." *Academy of Management Journal,* 9, no. 1 (March 1966): 9–19.

Hoos, Ida. *Automation in the Office.* Washington, D.C.: Public Affairs Press, 1961.

Hunt, R. E., and R. Newell. "Management in the 1980s: Revisited." *Personnel Journal,* vol. 50 (1971).

Leavitt, Harold J., and Whisler, Thomas L. "Management in the 1980s." *Harvard Business Review,* 36, no. 6 (November–December 1958): 41–48.

Lee, H. C. "Do Workers Really Want Flexibility on the Job?" *Personnel Journal,* 44, no. 7 (July–August 1965): 365–370.

———. "The Computer vs. Middle Management." *Personnel,* 43, no. 1 (January–February 1966): 4–7.

Mann, Floyd D., and L. K. Williams. "Observations of the Dynamics of a Change to Electronic Data Processing Equipment." *Administrative Science Quarterly,* 5, no. 1 (June 1960): 217–256.

Moan, Floyd E. "Does Management Practice Lag behind Theory in the Computer Environment?" *Academy of Management Journal,* 16, no. 1 (March 1973): 7–24.

Mumford, E., and B. Olive. *The Computer and the Clerk.* London: Routledge & Kegan Paul, 1967.

Myers, C. A. (ed.). *The Impact of Computers on Management.* Cambridge, Mass.: M.I.T. Press, 1967.

Powers, Richard F., and Gary W. Dickson. "MIS Project Management—Myths, Opinions and Reality." *California Management Review,* 19, no. 3 (Spring 1973): 147–196.

Reif, William E. *Computer Technology and Management Organization.* Iowa City: University of Iowa Bureau of Business and Economic Research, 1968.

Rhee, H. A. *Office Automation in Social Perspective.* Oxford: Basil Blackwell, 1968.

Shaul, D. R. "What's Really Ahead for Middle Management?" *Personnel,* 41, 6 (November–December 1964): 8–16.

Simon, H. A. *The Shape of Automation for Men and Management.* New York: Harper & Row, 1965.

Whisler, Thomas L. *The Impact of Computers and Organizations.* New York: Praeger, 1970.

——— and H. Meyer. *The Impact of EDP on Life Company Organization.* New York: Life Office Management Association, 1967.

Part *II*
BEHAVIORAL SYSTEMS

In successive order, the topics of motivation, leadership, social bases for work systems, and decision making are developed in Part II. The behavioral perspectives for organizational analysis in these chapters complement the structural and technological approaches of Part I. In fact the roles assumed by personnel in organizations, individual participation and functioning in decision making, motivational opportunities, and the situational demands imposed on leadership logically emerge from the systems and structures already described. Thus a major point of departure has been established for analyzing "behavioral systems," the focus of Part II.

From the viewpoint of organization analysis, the discussions and approaches of Part I were equivalent to varying impersonal structural and systems elements while largely holding the human inputs constant. In Part II, we increasingly relieve this type of artificial assumption and more realistically confront complex organizational environments.

Learning Objectives

Perspective on Motivation
Feasibility and Need for Motivational Approaches
General Model for Relating Situational and Motivational
    Considerations
Key Ideas in "Needs Theory" Formulations
    Maslow, Shortcomings, and a Revised Model
Herzberg's Model
    Its Relation to Maslow's "Need" Model
Contingency Approaches in Motivation
Role of Money in Motivation
Vroom's Choice Model and Path-Goal Designs
Comprehensive Motivation Model and Approach
    Role of Learning and Change

Chapter 8

MOTIVATION TO WORK

OVERVIEW

   Motivation involves a complex combination of individual needs or drives, desire to do, strength of desire, and goals toward which desire or action is directed. This goal-directed activity may reflect individual awareness or it may be a subconscious effort. Thus it will not surprise the reader to point out that the full thrust of this chapter's development on motivation won't be clear until the successive chapters of leadership and social and work roles have been presented. The perspective in this chapter is that of motivation, but largely from the individual viewpoint. However, fuller understanding of individual attitudes, desire to do, opportunity to do, "felt" pressures, and interaction opportunities must be deferred until the context of individual activity in the organization is explored. Supervisory influences, work demands, and interactions with work associates, friends, or group members are some of the contextual matters to be developed subsequently.

   In this chapter, a selection of major theories and approaches dealing with motivation is described. This structure of motivational notions is initiated with a broad overview of area developments that references key theories and seeks to establish a perspective for viewing them jointly. This is followed (mainly) by descriptions of Abraham Maslow's "needs hierarchy," Frederick Herzberg's "two-factor" theory, and Victor Vroom's "expectancy" theory. This discussion concludes with the description of a comprehensive framework for "putting it together" so that the theories can be viewed in an interrelated manner.

   Then, returning to a basic theme of organization analysis, some organization strategies and a case application are presented that respond to such questions as "Now, what can we do with it?"

   A final note on this chapter's development. Our posture throughout this book is one of "contingency," which supports the selection of approaches best suited to understanding or application in particular circumstances where key conditions are specified. It will be clear shortly that the Maslow, Herzberg, and even more advanced (and recent) statements of expectancy evidence a variety of shortcomings. At times more comprehensive or advanced statements do little to advance understanding, and research may demonstrate (as in some of the recent expectancy pronouncements) that simple formulations may have equal power. Perhaps more importantly, our research and consulting experiences in many different organizational contexts suggest that, *in application,* particular theories or statements may appear to best approximate specific conditions or symptoms and prove helpful in problem resolution.

In short, though one theory may be made to subsume another, we have a great deal to learn in this area. Even a theory such as Herzberg's, which contains basic problems of research methodology, reflects basic truths in organizational matters that can't be dismissed. Truly, a flexible posture is indicated for the student or analyst.

Background

Many approaches to work motivation rest on the assumption that desired behavior patterns can best be produced when the needs, factors, or forces to which people are responsive are determined first, and *then* a strategy is selected that will guide the individual toward a desired behavioral pattern.[1] In the formulation of Abraham Maslow, a particular personal need that is unsatisfied and highest in the order of importance is selected from a *hierarchy* of such needs. When that need is identified, managerial actions or programs are sought that motivate by attempting to satisfy this need.[2]

Some people in organizations are natural "achievers"—self-starters who attempt to move ahead regardless of problems or encouragement. David McClelland[3] has studied achievers extensively and found that they are frequently identified with specific behavioral patterns:

1. *Optimization of risk.* The individual feels himself capable of controlling his environment and is confident that events can be influenced by his own actions.

2. *Need for feedback.* The individual wants evidence of results to ascertain progress toward his objectives and needs, providing a basis for self-correction as needed.

3. *Involvement.* The individual wants a high level of interaction so that he can exercise sufficient control; that is, the outcome is "his."

There is implied here both a goal and a prescription for undertaking motivational programming: to (a) ascertain the needs or deficiencies of personnel and (b) synthesize job conditions, behavioral approaches, and relationships to approximate the "achiever" model.

For the individual as well as the organization, the real and psychological costs of underachievement can be substantial. From the viewpoint of the organization, penalties include lack of individual contribution, coordinated effort, creative ideas, or problem solving; channeling individual effort outside the organization; poor work quality; high turnover and absenteeism; and lackluster behavior, all of which lead to higher operating costs and adverse effects on profit. The individual is penalized through lack of fulfillment in the job environment, dissipation of energy outside his area of primary time commitment, untapped ability, and stagnation of interests and ideas, leading to frustration and indecisiveness, aggressive, often contrary behavior, and sometimes a decision to leave the organization.[4]

This is not to say that *all* people duplicate the "achiever" model when given the opportunity, but it suggests that talent is widely distributed, regardless of degree, and that it is often latent rather than manifest. When this point is considered, along with the changing character of work and a society that emphasizes brain power rather than muscle power, the urgency of the need for effective management approaches to motivation is underscored.

Unfortunately, companies may concentrate on the performance side of organization life instead of on its enrichment. Motivation reinforcement from the company may be entirely in the form of monetary rewards and working conditions. "Motivators," or environmental cues that encourage a high level of accomplishment, are absent.

Chris Argyris [5] would undoubtedly propose that management is exhibiting "low interpersonal competence" in its failure to draw people out, provide leadership, and supply the necessary feedback for corrective action (individual improvement). When management behaves in a manner suggesting goal-oriented, rational programming with a sanction-reward ("carrot-stick") system to control individual action, dysfunction is a likely result.

Some balance is accomplished through the broader approaches to motivation set forth by Rensis Likert.[6] The Likert model builds on a comparatively simple, three-component set containing financial results, individual attitudes, and personal behavior, all of which are viewed dynamically over time. The heart of this motivational model depicts current financial outcomes (economic measures of business performance) as critically dependent on individual behavior patterns derived from past and prevailing attitudes during periods of activity. Use of money rewards, close supervisory control, and the threat of sanctions for poor performance has often been effective for achieving high productivity in the *short run*. However, prolonged exposure to this approach changes individual attitudes, and the modified behavior patterns over a longer time span adversely affect both behavior and financial performance. Note that reversing this process by creating favorable attitudes that enhance individual performance (and financial outcomes) is not easily accomplished.

ARE MOTIVATIONAL APPROACHES FEASIBLE? [7]

Many manufacturing and service industries have been built on rational structures of authority, control, and communication systems (see Part I) that are not easily modified. Additionally, objective decision making and the assumptions concerning people to make a bureaucracy function (orderliness, accuracy, predictability, etc.) are deeply embedded in many institutional environments, and the rate of introduction of new ideas can be very slow. Thus

1. How much personal freedom or potential for self-realization is possible in a bureaucratic hierarchy of well-defined role expectations?

2. Are proposed motivational approaches (e.g., job enrichment, participative decision making) realistic from a behavioral viewpoint? Are they managerially possible? [8]

Research in a wide variety of production and work systems[9] suggests that a significant degree of flexibility exists for bringing about economically acceptable work modifications, even within highly systematic procedures. So-called mass production systems pose a major challenge in this regard, but, even here, some smaller-scale systems (e.g., appliances and auto parts) have undergone successful conversions to more imaginative individual tasks. Secondly, work with several large concerns employing job enrichment techniques[10] indicates considerable potential for performance and individual benefits through restructuring work. However, these programs have been in operation for only a short time, and considerably more data are required.

In short, the outlook is optimistic concerning the ability to successfully rearrange work both to meet economic criteria and assume a more imaginative view of human resources.

PERSPECTIVE FOR MOTIVATION ANALYSES

Undertaking the organizational analyses of motivation issues is assisted by two general approaches. First, it has proved quite helpful to view these behavioral matters within the framework of a general model—the model provides both perspective and a convenient means of organizing ideas and relationships. Second, the utilization of specific motivational theories in conjunction with the general behavioral orientation (expressed in the model) provides the "why's" or the predictability vitally needed for analysis and research.

General Behavioral Orientation and a Model

At the outset, and before proceeding too far, we wish to point out that the general behavioral approach and model incorporate terms that involve a vast area of behavioral literature. We have, as it were, plucked some key ideas for our approaches, and these will be briefly defined and explained. Notions that constitute recurring themes in this book will of course receive greater attention. The basic form and key features of the approach and model are derived from both psychological and systems ideas.

The model, depicted in Exhibit 8–1, displays three main elements, which are *input*, *target group* (individual), and *output* (performance or response). Individual activity is goal oriented—current actions or responses build toward goals of which the individual may be only incompletely aware. Motivation also involves choice among alternative forms of activity. The provision of feedback imparts a learning capability based on past actions that provide important guides to future directions and movement toward valued goals (the feedback idea was discussed in considerable detail in Chapter 6, "Communications").

The point of view assumed in analyses largely determines the specifics of interest in model usage. For example, a company may be considering a monetary incentive program (input) for an office clerical group (target) in order to bolster its performance (output).

Company officials might initially raise some questions, asking "How are they likely to view the company's new incentive program?" The "inner feelings" or affective response distinguishes the under-the-skin feeling from the visual response or output. The immediate result of the incentives may seemingly be increased output, but there also may be growing disenchantment

EXHIBIT 8–1. A General Behavioral Model

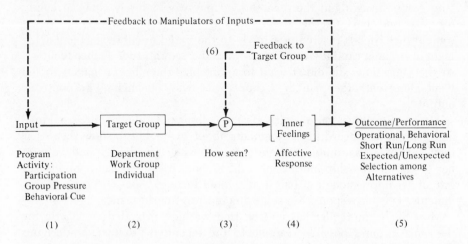

Based on a concept in V. H. Vroom, *Work and Motivation* (New York: Wiley, 1964), p. 6. For a discussion of feedback see, R. L. Kahn and D. Katz, *The Social Psychology of Organizations* (New York: Wiley, 1966), chap. 13.

with the company (inner feelings) that perhaps the clerks are being manipu-
lated. This could bring about severe dysfunction in the longer run.

In this situation, feedback to the individual or group (getting paid more
money as effort is increased) may signal that they can in fact make more
money, but attitudes of resentment may be building because further evidence
of organizational manipulation has been provided. Of course, the company
too derives feedback, and the immediate response of the office to the incentive program may appear favorable—but all the votes are not yet in.

A second example of model usage assumes a somewhat different perspective. Let's examine more closely how one of the individual office members
might have responded to the incentive program. Here differing emphasis
will be placed on other components of the model and the examination will
build on another behavioral explanation of motivation or response.

Delight is a *member* of the official clerical group ("one of the girls") and
cherishes this membership. This group affiliation means a chance for her
to exchange pleasantries, domestic problems, news, views, and general gos-
sip. Also, in the past, support of the group and group solidarity helped put
the office manager in his place when he got too demanding. Clearly, membership is to be cherished.

Past "inputs" of sociability and group achievements have been perceived
by Delight as demonstrating both the power and value of group membership. When Delight saw her own actions as congenial with those of the
group (feedback), she was rewarded with both more group friendliness and
the concessions from office management (learning and solidifying her attitude concerning group values).

Delight is now confronted with the incentive plan. Though the plan promises more pay (one outcome) for some added effort, she is not sure how
"the group" feels about the plan. Added pay would surely come in handy
for gifts (one goal). On the other hand, she values group membership. When
some of her friends reacted negatively to the initial orientation (feedback),
Delight became cautious and took a "wait and see" attitude (inner feeling).
At the same time, she didn't want to antagonize the office manager, so she
went along with the plan in a cooperative way (behavioral response or
output).

After a short time, various girls started complaining about the "speed up,"
and Delight also heard some comments about "we ought to show them that
they can't push us around." Delight got the message (feedback) and, valuing
her group membership more than "a little more bread," became more reso-
lute in her impression of a "bad deal" (inner feeling). She started to display
difficulty (visible response) in achieving incentive performance.

Most likely the reader has noticed that we have provided a scenario for
the office group's possible reaction to the incentive program. Underlying
these possibilities is a welter of motivational theories.

Another possible use in modeling approaches is that of raising questions
regarding logic or consistency. Systematically modeling or arranging key

aspects of a situation or theory should permit the examination of implied relationships, or connection of input to output, raise questions regarding underlying assumptions, and permit side-by-side comparisons with other situations or approaches, which, when fitted to particular organizational circumstances, could suggest some possible or even likely outcomes. Thus it is both the general behavioral model *and* motivational theory that provide the needed power for organizational analyses.

The Maslow theory, for example, suggests that the individual perceives ("how seen?") various possible inputs (money, time off, type of supervision) in the light of his need hierarchy. Where the incentive, "deal," situation, or opportunity offered engages a largely unfulfilled need of the individual, that person is motivated ("turned on") for higher performance (output) levels. Additionally, Maslow provides various stipulations and insights into possible outcomes. Without going into more detail, this example should point up the critical coupling of the modeling approach for organizing important situational items with theory for further explanation and prediction. The question of which theory to use is appropriately asked but difficult to answer. Knowledge of the theories and application experience helps, especially in an area such as motivation where no single theory reigns. Some have proved very helpful in raising important questions and research issues, while at the same time appearing suitable only for specific situations. Some of these important and useful theories will be developed in this chapter.

NEEDS THEORY

Certainly the intellectual and physiological features of individuals help determine their attitudes on issues, their perceptions of their own abilities, their chances to succeed, and their vocational goals, but it must also be acknowledged that important drives emerge from an individual's psychological makeup. That is, given some combination of talents, an individual's responses to particular situations reflect his need structure, as shown in Exhibit 8–2.

This model proposes a stimulus-response situation wherein the individual perceives a situation (2) (e.g., the reward climate of the organization, opportunities inherent in his job, or signs of reprimand or recognition) that leads to some level of response, performance, or behavior (4). However, the characteristics of the response pattern are moderated by the individual's need structure (3) in conjunction with the psychological and physical makeup of the person. The X factor in the model hints at a far more complex structure of relationships than can be depicted here; model simplicity has been sought so as to permit concentration on the juxtaposition of needs with abilities and makeup.

The Maslow model arranges individual needs in a hierarchy of "potency." As a lower-order need is largely satisfied, the next higher need motivates behavior. (An important corollary for management is that a satisfied need is not a motivator.) Primary in the hierarchy are needs associated with maintaining life (physiological and safety), which moves up through a need to feel a part of human groups (belonging) to needs that reflect the fuller realization of individual capabilities—ego (self-esteem and recognition) and self-actualization.

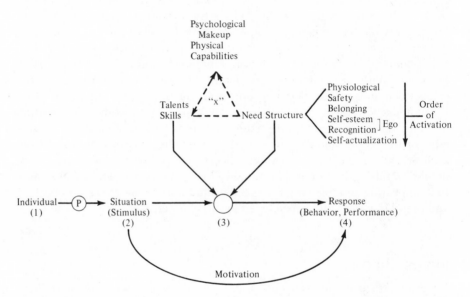

P = Perception

The concept of need hierarchy is developed in A. H. Maslow, *Motivation and Personality* (New York: Harper, 1954).

A second need scheme deals with search, reward, and satisfaction[11]—people are assumed to be always seeking the satisfaction of wants or needs. Their search (1) for alternatives (2) to meet these felt needs is guided by the expected value of achievement. The particular course of action chosen (3) is viewed positively (+) for value of achievement by the individual. Yet (4) in the very process of achievement or attaining goals, (5) an individual's level of aspiration, rather than being satiated, changes and (6) relative satisfaction decreases.

Interpreted from a needs perspective, the scheme means that active needs dictate the individual's efforts to better his or her lot. The alternative interpreted as meeting the active need is attractive, and thus becomes the selected course of action. Yet with the performance that provides a favorable outcome, the satisfaction of the active need leads to activation of the next unfulfilled need in the hierarchy.

Maslow in the Perspective of the General Behavior Model

In this approach, perception or outlook is shaped by the need hierarchy, and specifically by need deprivation or largely unfulfilled needs. Thus the "inputs" of greatest interest for motivational purposes are those that are seen by the individual as responsive to unfulfilled needs. He would be affected especially by those input actions, work opportunities, or the like that touch that specific need "next up" in the hierarchy. If, for example, social needs were largely satisfied, it would be assumed that basic safety and security needs were largely met, and inputs that one views as meeting ego/self-esteem requirements would be favorable. Inwardly, one might welcome the new opportunity or challenge, or experience a sense of rising expectancy for new personal growth opportunity. Not surprisingly, growing enthusiasm with one's job and heightened outputs (performance) could be realized. To the extent that one's initial expectations were realized (feedback), he (or she) would be inclined to more favorably view similar opportunities, to the extent that the ego/self-esteem need remains largely unfulfilled.

Modified Perspective on the Need Hierarchy

The Maslow need model presents a somewhat static picture of individual need structures, which requires examination in the light of subsequent research. One idea (discussed later) is based on the relative intensity of a need that may govern individual activity or behavior (Herzberg et al., 1959). Another approach (also discussed later) interprets the behavior of industrial groups within the framework of the need model (Clark, 1960–61). A third perspective is a longitudinal view of needs—that is, the character of changes in needs over time.

If we view the need hierarchy over time, it becomes clear that changes within the individual in the priority of needs may take place, especially as they relate to his life pattern (see Exhibit 8–3A). A particular need may not be satisfied before the next need in the hierarchy is activated. And although a need may be "satisfied" at a given point in time, it may well become reactivated at some future point in the individual's career pattern—a notion already suggested in the search model of Exhibit 8–2.

There is a familiar story about a man who received a rapid succession of promotions and found his new executive salary inadequate to meet the *felt* needs of his advanced position. Yet a considerably smaller salary had sufficed when he was a middle manager. Clearly, his expected standard of living had changed, and he found his new security need an overriding consideration. That is, he saw maids, club memberships, and multi-car ownership as part of his new life style. Also, needs have an underlying utility (Exhibit 8–3B) that suggests *widely different degrees of satisfaction* (and motiva-

EXHIBIT 8–3. Dynamic Character of the Hierarchy of Needs

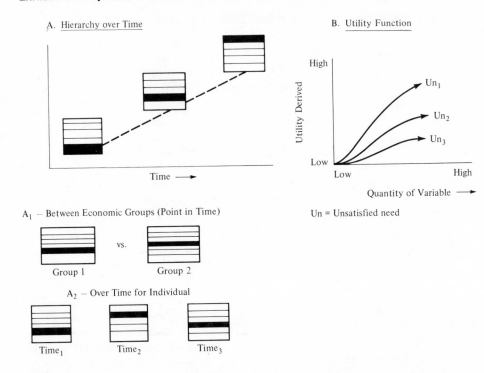

A. Hierarchy over Time

Time →

A_1 – Between Economic Groups (Point in Time)

Group 1   vs.   Group 2

A_2 – Over Time for Individual

$Time_1$ $Time_2$ $Time_3$

B. Utility Function

Utility Derived

High

Un_1

Un_2

Un_3

Low

Low   High

Quantity of Variable →

Un = Unsatisfied need

tion), based on the type and relative amount of a particular need satisfaction that is secured (money, title, office furniture, company car, company-paid insurance, etc.). This also recognizes that many needs may be active simultaneously. Utility is an economic notion, based on diminishing marginal return; that is, some point is reached where more of a desired item brings diminishing gratification.

Closely related to this point is the idea that the needs structure changes over time in response to career growth and success.[12] As one grows older and gains experience, his career flourishes and increasing milestones of success are approximated. One's need for achievement and esteem comes to the fore and increasingly influences one's behavior. The managers and professionals who meet high performance standards increasingly "know" that their efforts will be rewarded—that successful achievements beget more responsibility.[13]

Changes in need structure also accompany the progress of an advanced society, as lower-order needs are provided for and more attention can be focused on higher-level needs.[14]

In our contemporary culture, most physical and safety needs may be largely met. Social or belonging needs have likely achieved some intermediate level of satisfaction, ego needs less, and self-fulfillment needs are likely to go largely unsatisfied. Thus Maslow's concerns and focus on higher-order needs emerge naturally from this perspective. Yet our daily experiences tell us (as portrayed in Exhibit 8–3A) that even now, as of this point in time, wide differences exist between economic groups.

The Maslow Model—Some Shortcomings

It is well worth noting that the initial Maslow formulation emerged as a theoretical statement rather than an abstraction from field research—which may pose considerable difficulties for the researcher when the time comes to operationalize the concepts and test the model or theory. The model is difficult to test, and this situation has likely contributed to the many considerations seemingly not accounted for in the theory or those that appear to be at variance with the model.[15] In research, we would expect to find that individuals are motivated by opportunities to achieve the satisfaction of needs that currently are largely unsatisfied, and in a particular sequence. Although various needs instruments have been developed for field diagnosis, little has been reported to bolster the theory.

One area of research seeking to work with Maslow's notions has included studies by Lyman Porter and/or his associates. In one study,[16] Porter utilized several different instruments to try to get at critical needs factors: a thirteen-item questionnaire focused on need fulfillment in terms of the individual's perceptions of (a) degree of the factor present in the manager's job, (b) how much should have been present, and (c) its relative importance to the job holder. Also, a scale on job attitude (semantic differential) was employed, along with a satisfaction/deficiency measurement. Generally, it was inferred that higher-order needs were described more favorably than lower-order ones.

The earlier discussion of the Maslow formation served to point up some notable shortcomings in this approach. The utility notion described the vast differences that can and do exist between people in terms of preference (need), schedules, and ordering. Additionally, changes over time are a matter to be reckoned with.

Also, the theory hardly reckons with a whole host of factors affecting individual need structure—race, position in authority structure, and culture, for example. Few (if any) data support the idea that all people are capable of activating all levels of the need structure.[17]

HERZBERG'S MOTIVATION–HYGIENE THEORY

Although Frederick Herzberg's two-factor theory ("motivational" versus "hygiene" factors) has borne the brunt of a number of recent criticisms,[18]

its central position in the controversy suggests the importance of these pronouncements. Alternatively, recognizing the widespread use in industry of
programs based on the theory and the great impetus it has provided to
motivation research would command attention for this development.

The initial thrust of the Herzberg research study focused on enlarging the
behavioral scientist's understanding of job attitude.[19] It was hoped that,
with this understanding, improved performance, better human relationships,
and decreased tardiness or absenteeism might be more readily achieved.
Two hundred accountants and engineers were interviewed extensively and
asked about job-related matters that made them unhappy or dissatisfied and
those that made them happy or satisfied. Sifting through the interview data,
the researchers concluded that these people evidenced two dissimilar
(mostly independent) areas of need that affected behavior differently.

1. When people were dissatisfied with their job, their concerns were
   involved with the environment about the job, rather than the job
   itself. These factors (also called "hygiene") were used essentially
   to maintain people in the organization and included

Company policy	Job security and work conditions
Salary	Status
Supervision	
Relations with supervisors, subordinates, or peers	

2. When people were satisfied with their job, the opportunity was
   present to build high "motivation." These factors (the "motivators" were to be found in the job and included

Achievement	Responsibility
Advancement	Opportunity for personal growth
Recognition	Work itself

Joining these points together, Herzberg concluded that "hygiene" factors
are necessary to maintain some level of satisfaction; that they must be regularly replenished; that their absence could result in considerable dissatisfaction; and that their presence didn't build strong motivation to perform.
The "motivators," it was indicated, can lead to strong motivation when
present, and bring about less dissatisfaction when absent. Hygiene factors
and motivators were considered mostly as two distinct concepts representing two different continua, rather than opposite ends of a single continuum.

In the traditional Herzberg view, work is considered a distasteful requirement or means to an end; thus the approach is to entice, threaten,
coerce, or reward individuals in order to secure their contribution to organizational performance. Some type of "pressure" is inherent in work design
and motivational approaches. Little opportunity exists in work structures

for high levels of individual satisfaction and growth, and in many cases these limitations have persisted.

From this description of traditional organization approaches one would rightly infer a management preoccupation in the past with the environment of work rather than work itself. This focus on environment, dubbed "hygiene" by Herzberg because of its overtones of "preventive maintenance," has led to emphasis on such things as work conditions, labor-management relations, pay, and fringe benefits. In Herzberg's view, achievement, recognition and advancement contribute to positive work motivation, while company policy, job security, and work conditions merely alleviate the level of dissatisfaction. Some factors, such as salary and interpersonal relationships, assume a dual role.

Hygiene factors are seen by Herzberg as preventive measures that remove sources of *dissatisfaction* from the environment. Displeasure is likely to be expressed by employees if these factors are deficient, but their restoration is unlikely to bring about anything more than average performance, and they require continuous renewal because of their transient nature.

The key characteristic of the Herzberg theory is its "two-factor" nature. Satisfaction and dissatisfaction are *not* viewed as symmetrical items on a single scale; rather, they are viewed as attributes of different scales. This implies that lessening dissatisfaction leads to the elimination of a "deficiency," but would bring little positive gain. *Different* approaches are required to induce satisfaction.

In the Herzberg perspective, the work activity holds the key to consistently high levels of accomplishment for the organization, while at the same time leading to sustained satisfaction for the individual. Accomplishment, growth, and recognition are the concomitants of performance that permit one to bring to the job the highest levels of creativity. In an era of growing technological advances, the emphasis is clearly shifting to intellectual power in order to maintain, solve problems, and manage advanced information and work units. Consequently, Herzberg's focus on satisfaction in the experience of work itself is timely.

Herzberg in the Perspective of the General Behavioral Model

Moving off from Herzberg's perspective, we see that "inputs" for the general behavioral model would be of two classes—"motivator" and "hygiene" factors. Items generally associated with the hygiene group, such as type of supervision and job conditions, would be seen as important and constantly in need of replenishment because of their relatively short-term effect. To the extent that the individual sees supervisory style as supportive of his work efforts and the physical climate of work acceptable, he is likely to feel that "they" (the organization) are trying—this might bolster his sense of loyalty or confidence in "their" efforts. The outcome would likely be one of decreasing his job *dis*satisfaction with supervisory and job condition matters, and possibly some bettering of output performance, so long as the input dosages continued to be applied. For this example, feedback (realization) might well build his association of organizational input and decreased satisfaction. It also might raise his expectation that this is what the organization ought to have all the time. If the expectation continues to be strengthened for these hygienes, dissatisfaction could be greatly intensified if they were withdrawn.

A similar scenario could be provided for the "motivators," with potentially favorable outcomes for job satisfaction and performance.

Side-by-side comparison of the two models, one employing hygiene inputs, the other motivators, sharpens the reader's detection of a number of research questions that have arisen in connection with Herzberg's approach. For example, we might inquire why these inputs should bring about such widely different outcomes. What happens if only some of the motivators and some of the hygiene are provided? How about the individual himself and the different priorities he might assign due to his own personality and background, let alone economic class and occupational group? Are there related or more basic theories that support the behavioral relationships depicted in these models?

Attempts have been made to answer some of these questions; for example, the Herzberg model has been applied to a wide variety of occupational groupings. The results from these studies indicate occupational variations (and perhaps individual ones, too) that signal further inquiry. No attempt is made here to exhaust the questions or speculations emerging from the use of the behavioral modeling approach suggested here. Rather, we have attempted to point out another area of utility to be derived through modeling, where important questions can be sharpened.

Job Enrichment

The idea suggested by the term *job enrichment* reflects a logical outgrowth of the Herzberg constructs and a direct response to "How do we motivate our people?" Rather than simply trying to *enlarge* a specialized job by adding more duties or activities,[20] the work itself must be enriched so that work challenge and responsibility are improved. In the Herzberg view, recent attempts at improving jobs by increasing the number of operations ("job enlargement") hold little promise for significantly meeting the motivator requirements he had identified.

The extension of Herzberg's research to a wide variety of other occupational groups, including lower-level supervisors, female professionals, and technicians appeared to confirm the Herzberg findings.[21] However, there is some controversy about the validity of the research methods used to confirm Herzberg's theory, which will be discussed shortly.

Relation to Maslow "Need" Framework

The Maslow need structure provides a viewpoint closely linked to the work of Herzberg: that in our society today, lower-order needs have been largely met. Thus additionally fulfilling lower-level needs can lead to little job satisfaction since they are largely taken care of in today's society. Job satisfaction, if it is to be achieved, turns mostly on the attainment of higher-order needs, such as Maslow's "self-actualization." However, it should be pointed out that Maslow viewed any unfulfilled need as a motivator so long as the individual perceived it this way. Herzberg's emphasis was clearly on the higher-order needs for motivation. And as a final point contrasting the approaches, Herzberg's view permitted unfulfilled needs in both the motivator and hygiene categories, whereas the Maslow construction implies a hierarchical (sequential) arrangement with greater force from the unfulfilled needs and movement through the hierarchy in an ordered or "cascade" fashion.

The Theory Viewed Critically

A crucial area of the controversy surrounding Herzberg's model relates to the research methodology of this approach. First, the original study was confined to two occupational groups. Subsequent studies have dealt with many other groups, but the results suggest that the separation of the two-factor categories is not precise.[22] Second, the open-ended procedure used in interviewing is biased toward the recall of recent, as opposed to past, events. Victor Vroom has suggested that the separation of factors between those contributing to a satisfaction or dissatisfaction may emerge from the research employed in developing information.[23] Clearly at issue here is whether important qualitative differences exist between motivator (satisfier) and hygiene (dissatisfier) factors. Dunnette, Campbell, and Hakel have maintained that both "satisfaction and dissatisfaction can reside in the job context." Additionally, such factors as achievement, responsibility, and recognition may be of more importance for both satisfaction *and* dissatisfaction than job dimensions such as work conditions and security.[24] Further, it is possible that motivators may not be any more associated with high performance than are hygienes.[25]

One- and Two-Factor Theories of Motivation

Cummings and Elsalmi have clarified some of the issues of the controversy and offered some useful concepts.[26] They suggest that the organization environment is a crucial variable, relating the Herzberg need categories to one another and thus to overall job satisfaction or dissatisfaction. The research has bolstered the argument for two sets of need categories, motivators and hygiene factors, but found them to be bipolar (at opposite ends of the *same* scale) rather than multidimensional (orthogonal), as Herzberg has contended. Such being the case, motivators and hygiene factors would both be related to satisfaction and dissatisfaction. Under these conditions, it is maintained that the organization climate will affect the types of needs (motivators or hygiene) that will prevail under given conditions.

The crux of the argument is that in an environment where a diversity of needs is satisfied, a motivator, such as the job itself (achievement, recognition, and possibility for growth), is a more important source of overall job satisfaction than hygiene factors, such as interpersonal relationships with peers and subordinates. Conversely, in an environment where many basic needs are *not* being satisfied, hygiene factors are a more important source of satisfaction than motivators. Finally, in an environment where all needs are modestly provided for, motivators and hygiene factors are equally related to overall job satisfaction.

Schwab and Cummings conclude "that to predict whether additional specialization or enlargement (or enrichment) is likely to result in increased productivity depends on a complex interaction between the individual employee and the task environment." [27] They feel that these motivational issues can be meaningfully interpreted within the context of expectancy theory—which follows.

MOTIVATION—A CONTINGENCY APPROACH ILLUSTRATED

In the contingency approach, the identification of key features of a problem or environmental situation establishes the basis for behavioral strategies or innovative organizational designs. Often it will be important, and even necessary, to utilize multiple perspectives or models together (rather than singly) in probing organizational situations. Work undertaken by James V. Clark, which is based on the Maslow model, provides a vehicle to illustrate several approaches to bettering organizational design in this complex area of motivation.[28]

For the moment at least, let's set aside some of the research-related difficulties previously identified with the Maslow formulation and consider the Clark approach as a flexible one with which to handle a cross section of important behaviorally related problems.

Key Elements for Design

The basic structure of the design approach centers on the Maslow need hierarchy, need activation, and the individual motivation and performance described in the section on the Maslow model. The notion of *design* is employed here to emphasize the deliberate actions that the organization or supervisor may elect once the key needs have been identified in an individual or group. The design approach flows as follows.

a. The active or dominant (unfulfilled) need of the individual sets the psychological (need deprivation) stage for organizational inputs, which may prove responsive to this perceived need.

b. Six main areas of organizational variables (and thereby possible strategies) are considered that can prove responsive to unfulfilled needs once the area of needs has been established. Strategies consider their usage both singly and collectively. These are as follows.

1. *Safety needs* (level 2)—plans and programs that prove responsive to employment security, which includes retirement benefits, hospitalization, employment contracts, guaranteed work period, provision of steady work (a problem in the construction trades, for example), and the like. (Level 1 [physical] needs are set aside in this description.)

2. *Membership or social needs* (level 3)—here, three areas of opportunity (many others are possible) are considered that involve interaction opportunity for work group members, status congruence (how well do group members fit together in status?), and type of leadership, which may tend to be oriented to the group needs, or accommodation, or largely production oriented.

3. *Status, ego, or prestige* (level 4)—in this category the strategy receiving attention is that of the individual's perception of participation, the feeling that he is contributing and thereby sharing in the fortunes of the group or organization. At the same time, of course, his being allowed to participate (feedback) and contribute builds his self-concept of importance and worth. Various measures of performance (productivity, absenteeism) should increasingly and favorably reflect the participation opportunities.

4. *Self-actualization* (level 5)—to attain the highest reaches of the Maslow structure, the individual must sense that his other needs have been largely met. The design strategy viewed here builds on the notion of company climate (supportive or nonsupportive); a supportive climate, once other need areas have been met, should serve to meet high levels of both organizational and personal realization.

    c. The potential impact on output performance is suggested once a particular strategy has been undertaken.

    d. Organization officials or decision makers may opt to try various alternative strategies, gain feedback from these in terms of their relative success (based on performance criteria and/or in proving responsive to problems), and thereby assist in guiding subsequent actions.

From the vantage point of organizational design, the areas of strategy suggested here emerge from diverse research findings. Research may provide general guidelines to the relative effectiveness of one technique as opposed to another; the contingency approach in organizational design or problem solving would utilize the research findings as a point of departure in tailoring an approach to the specifics of a given situation. Thus the scenarios that follow may be thought of as different strategies in design to be assumed once the specific needs and opportunities of a given situation have been identified. In the framework of the general behavioral model, inputs are the strategies; strategies are based on the individual's or group's perception of need; and the performance outputs are those suggested in the exhibit that accompanies th discussion.

In Exhibit 8–4, features of the work environment, opportunity to contribute to the organization, leadership style, status congruence, opportunity to develop greater interaction under the influence of various work systems (or group or authority structures) that affect the formation of social structures and groups, and felt employment security are juxtaposed with varying need levels.

Seven common situations, which constitute combinations of environmental factors, are viewed in terms of their potential impact on the Maslow need structure. Objective performance measures such as productivity and turnover are integrated with ideas expressed by this model to present a fairly comprehensive framework for viewing organizational performance. Note the extreme left of the exhibit, where environmental (work group) conditions are depicted. These consist of five important dimensions, including employment security, interaction opportunity, status congruence, contribution opportunity, leadership posture, and company support. They represent the conditions (parameters) under which the need is examined. Features of the Maslow need model are presented in the center panel; physiological, safety, belonging, self-esteem, and self-actualization are at the top of the hierarchy. The bottom strip represents objective performance measures.

The work group condition of column 1 could represent significant unemployment, one in which employment security is at a low point. If the "active" need at this point is the basic one of safety, or meeting the basic necessities of life, performance can be expected to be proportionately high and turnover at a low point. As an alternate interpretation, if low employment security reflects an individual's lack of confidence (perception) in his own abilities or a rejection of the work ethic, a self-fulfilling cycle may emerge that leads to low productivity and high turnover.

In column 2, a mass production type of situation is portrayed. A typical instance would be the automotive assembly line. The work system is such that the mechanical pacing or the rhythm of the line forces levels of productivity (Chapters 3 and 4) regardless of the lack of opportunity for interaction. The outcome here could be high production, but the opportunity to absent oneself would bring characteristically high levels of absenteeism or turnover. However, productivity could be adversely affected if appropriate impersonal controls or supervisory surveillance were not in evidence to ensure the maintenance of line performance. Elaborate management controls represent one managerial response to ensure performance.

In column 3 the interaction opportunities are high, permitting group formation, and security is high but status congruence is low. That is, felt economic needs may be minimal (low priority) and the individual may feel part of the group, but inconsistencies in status may exist because of wide individual differences in skill or background among group members. The membership needs of the individuals in the groups are examined here. In column 4, status congruence is high but individuals may be confronted with a "production centered" supervisor who is typically authoritarian or task centered. The need for group membership may be strong, but unless the technology has features that maintain production, productivity may sag.

It is interesting that other research tends to suggest that productivity may not be low in some of these situations.[29] (Portions of this research were described in Chapter 6.) For the situation described in column 4, the Thurley-Hamblin research demonstrated that the task-oriented supervisor was able to bring about higher levels of performance (as measured by quality rejects) than some of his laissez-faire colleagues.

In column 5 it is assumed that the activated need is higher in the need structure; here the need is self-esteem or belonging. Furthermore, the leadership style is accommodative in the sense that it is laissez-faire, yet the opportunities for the individual to contribute may be few. On the other hand, in column 6, if all the variables are positive (security, opportunity for interaction, status congruence, accommodative leadership, and opportunities for individual contributions), high levels of productivity and low levels of absenteeism are expected to result. At least these would be consistent within the framework of this need model.

In Clark's view, however, the first six types of situations characterize "frozen groups," in the terminology of Abraham Zaleznik. That is, such individuals or groups have yet to realize a high point in their potential. In column 7, a highly supportive situation is seen, with group leadership providing high contribution opportunities for the individual, and the individual *perceives* company reinforcement of his position. We also note that the technological environment must be sufficiently flexible to permit this group adap-

EXHIBIT 8-4. Environment, Needs, and Measures of Performance Work Group Conditions

Character of environment	1	2	3	4	5	6	7
Perception of company environment							Seen as supportive
Contribution opportunity		(e.g., man on assembly line)	Social status differences too great		Low	High	
Type of leadership				Production centered (authoritarian, task oriented)	Accommodative (laissez-faire)	Accommodative (laissez-faire)	Group centered
Status congruence			High	High			
Interaction opportunity		Low	High				High
Employment security	Low	High					High

Needs	1	2	3	4	5	6	7
							"Frozen groups"—Environmental features inhibit development of group and social structure
Self-actualization							xxxx
Self-esteem					xxxx	xxxx	
Belonging					xxxx		
Safety		xxxx	xxx	xxxx			
Physiological	xxxx						
Productivity	High	Low (?)	Low	Low	Minimum	High	High
Absenteeism/turnover	Low	High	High	?	Average	Low	Low

Source: Based on James V. Clark, "Motivation in Work Groups: A Tentative View," *Human Organization*, 19, no. 4 (Winter 1960/61): 199–208.

tation. In this way the individual has the opportunity to achieve his highest level of aspiration: self-actualization.

MONEY AND MOTIVATION

An important area of application for motivational models is examination of organizational approaches to money as a motivator. Edward Lawler suggests that people work for salaries as well as less tangible returns.[30] Lawler maintains that a transition has historically taken place from economic motives to those based largely on psychological or sociological needs. Thus pay has decreased in relative importance as the individual has received more money, and the returns of this utility function have diminished. However, in Lawler's view, pay represents a unique incentive that satisfies both lower- and higher-order needs; thus money has a dual role. For lower-level needs, it contributes directly; for higher-order needs, it provides a mark of achievement and thereby status.

Achievement for a manager is often more difficult to discern than for a professional. The diffusion of managerial talent tends to limit business achievement to the confines of a single company or work system. In industrial work systems, Lawler questions the role of technology as a determinant of the work pace. He proposes that behavior that appears to lead to a reward (pay) tends to be repeated—that pay reinforces behavior.

VROOM'S CHOICE MODEL

Syntheses undertaken by Victor Vroom[31] have contributed substantially to identifying areas of both knowledge and ignorance in motivation theory. Through the introduction of concepts that help to rationalize an individual's development of and selection from alternatives, fruitful areas for motivational research have emerged. Obviously, some of these points are controversial, but ideas such as an individual's subjective valuation of possible outcomes, the "instrumentality" of a choice from among alternatives for securing personal goals and valued objectives, and gauging the likelihood (probability) of a particular outcome permit more concise detailing of motivational approaches.

In short, the individual is attracted to those courses of actions that appear to further valued, personal objectives, and he will continue to seek these out so long as the returns support his expectancies. If the realizations are something less than initial expectancy, redirection may be indicated.

Much contemporary research and theorizing in motivational areas has centered on the basic work of Vroom described under various names, with "goal-path theory" and "expectancy theory" representing two common characterizations. Although various models have been proposed to describe basic constructs of this formulation, the model depicted in Exhibit 8–5, which is based on the work of Galbraith and Cummings, plus John P. Campbell et al.,[32] is grasped fairly easily.

The bracketed steps in the model in Exhibit 8–5 suggest a complex combination of individual judgments concerning the accomplishment of job goals (2) and the immediate rewards or outcomes (3) and (4) gained from these job goal accomplishments. Yet the real key in the individual's formulation of a strategy or line of action is the correction of job goals and outcomes with the achieving of personally valued goals (5). If the job or job accomplishments are not instrumental in fulfilling individually felt needs (or perhaps even worsen his current situation), an alternative line of action is indicated. Where the outcomes are unattractive, or prove to be something less than expected (8), the individual "learns" (9) to seek out other approaches (e.g., seeks other jobs or a new employer) or assumes a different work posture (e.g., apathy).

EXHIBIT 8–5. A Basic Expectancy Model

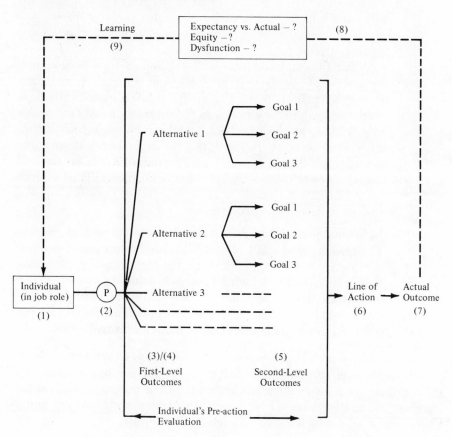

Some Organizational Hypotheses Based on Expectancy Approaches

At times one can gain a fuller appreciation for the power of expectancy theory in motivational analyses, research, and explanations by considering some research hypotheses based on this approach. At the same time, the hypotheses assist in clarifying the basic structure of these approaches. Some key ideas follow.[33]

1. The level of employee performance is significantly correlated with the expectancy of reward.

   Here the employee notes (feedback) that in the past his efforts or those of his colleagues (inputs) have been rewarded (output). Rewards may have been in terms of salary increases, bonuses, incentive programs, or promotion. Also, the rewards may have involved intrinsic matters such as self-esteem, which the individual may have felt personally in connection with achieving high performance.

2. People with high expectation that their efforts result in need fulfillment are likely to be significantly higher in the gratification of needs and job satisfaction than employees with low expectation in these matters.

   Where the employee sees his efforts (inputs) providing a growing sense of satisfaction or fulfillment through performance accomplishment, important learning has taken place for the individual and a basis is established for future personal accomplishments. Thus the reward value is high for fulfillment gains through one's own efforts. To the extent that the supervisor or organization provides the climate or initial learning opportunities for the individual, a powerful force for individual and organizational achievement can be set in motion. Here expectation, gratification, and reward have all been tied together.

3. Individual performance is tied closely to the strength of his need. The greater the strength of individual need as compared to others who have a weak need in the area, the higher one's performance. If an employee has a high felt need to achieve (as compared to another's felt need to achieve), he should (a) perform higher, given equal expectancy of realization in this area, and (b) perform still higher with greater expectation for his realization.

These initial research hypotheses set out a few facets of expectancy theory and also some interesting questions that might be pursued by the researcher. It has probably not escaped the reader that the basic notions of Maslow and Herzberg are related to these hypotheses. The Maslow and Herzberg formulations can be subsumed within an expectancy framework.

Selection among Alternatives

A key problem that motivational theory addresses is the explanation of why a person selects one alternative over another. A priori, we might suggest that it's the one that will further pleasure and/or diminish or avoid pain.[34] In general, the notion is that of a deliberate *or* unconscious selection of a particular course of action from all of those that are physically and intellectually possible. From the viewpoint of organization analysis, it is important that we recognize the influence of the organization in these choices. The classic mass production situation (Chapters 3 and 4) permits few behavioral alternatives, whereas other production systems permit wider latitude of individual discretion in the decision to produce. Choice in other organizational situations is affected by rules, regulations, and procedures. Though it is a digression at this point, the reader might wish to speculate further on the effect of the number, quality, and visibility of alternatives on motivation.

The Vroom model assists in predicting outcomes (pain or pleasure) and links these to observable events. An approach taken by Galbraith and Cummings[35] assists considerably in clearly visualizing how predictability is strengthened. The key notion introduced is that of "second-level outcomes."

Put simply, it is expected that first-level outcomes (e.g., achieving job goals and thus the payoff from these) will in turn lead to particular second-level outcomes (e.g., valued personal goals). Thus one alternative (say no. 1), which is a first-level outcome, can be expected to result in several possible second-level outcomes (see Exhibit 8–5). Another alternative (say no. 2), which also is a first-level outcome, may lead to still other second-level outcomes. Clearly, here we must know which alternative is preferred—and this will depend on the expected relationships between the alternatives (first-level outcomes) and the second-level outcomes.

Choice among alternatives, and thus the expected relationship between outcomes, depends on the strength of one's preference ("valence") and the visibility to one of the connections between first-level outcome and second-level outcome ("instrumentality"). Consequently, choice among alternatives will turn on the strength of individual desire for an outcome (its relative importance or value to the individual) and his ability to "see" the connection between the first-level outcome and the second-level outcomes. Justifiably, Galbraith and Cummings point out that all outcomes are not means to other ends. An outcome may be an end in itself—doing well may be its own reward.[36]

Expectancy: Rewards as Outcomes

In expectancy approaches, first-level (expected) outcomes are associated with various alternatives. In a production situation, the alternatives might simply be the amount of task-related effort. The usual organization measurement for the first-level outcome would be in quantity (units per hour) and quality dimensions. To the extent that output can be varied, these outcomes hold potentially differing levels of attractiveness (valence) for the worker. As Galbraith and Cummings note,

> *The first-level outcome acquires a valence by its expected relationship to the second-level outcomes over which the worker has preferences.* The second-level outcomes are *rewards* and *penalties* that are given on the basis of performance. . . .
>
> The variations in valences, with which the variations in productivity are hypothesized to be correlated, are to result from differences in the worker's preferences for second-level outcomes and differences in the cognized instrumentality of performance outcomes for the attainment of the second-level outcomes. *The second-level outcomes associated with performance can be conceived as rewards and penalties deriving from those groups with whom the worker is interdependent.* In other words, individuals can *attain few of their goals* solely by *their own efforts*—hence they become dependent on others. In similar fashion, the worker, in the performance of his work, can *affect the goals desired by others thereby creating a situation of interdependence.* . . .
>
> The *Vroom model would interpret variation* in the valence of the performance outcomes in terms of the individual's preference for the rewards and the group's success in communicating the instrumentality of performance for the attainment of the rewards. For the operative worker, *those who would have an interest in his performance and ability to supply rewards* would be the organization, his immediate supervisor, and his peers (extrinsic rewards). . . .
>
> Each of the (role) variables can be cast into the model presented earlier. For each group a reward can be specified which carries a valence and will have a perceived instrumentality. For the organization, the usual rewards are wages, fringe benefits, and promotions. Performance will vary directly with the product of the valence of the reward and the perceived instrumentality of performance for the attainment of the reward. Variations in individual productivity should be explainable in terms of variations in instrumentality and/or valence.[37]

Another useful interpretation of motivational response can be made in terms of the individual's *perceived equity* of his situation, relative to his "investments," his returns, and the returns to co-workers. Thus what is important in this view is, for example, not just the *level* of wage received but also education, experience, and the wages and investments of co-workers.[38]

Another concept in the Vroom perspective concerning performance and satisfaction was proposed by Edward Lawler and Lyman Porter.[39] The extrinsic rewards of the "hygiene" approach, as described by Herzberg, are controlled by the organization. These combine with "intrinsic rewards" (satisfactions), which the individual "gives to himself," and with the individual's perception of equity, that is, the rewards he feels he *should* receive vis-à-vis what he actually receives. In this formulation the "equity" notion and the idea of "intrinsic" rewards (much of which may be derived from the job itself, according to Herzberg) go beyond the motivational model that emphasizes the importance of job content.

When all these notions are assembled, they suggest that the motivational force of an individual's act in response to some cue (plan, program, or reward) reflects a dynamic, complex combination of

a. *Perception,* the individual's interpretation of what he sees, which is affected by past experiences, attitudes, and personality factors

b. *Factor synthesis,* an individual, subjective process that brings together

   1. *Job factors* (the "intrinsic" rewards of the Herzberg model), which are embedded in the job activity, with their importance related to need structure (Maslow)

   2. *Environmental factors* ("extrinsic" rewards), which are controlled by the organization and comprise Herzberg's hygiene factors, and

   3. *Equity,* which reconciles an individual's "investment" in prior experiences and education relative to what he expects to realize

c. *Motivational force,* which reflects a joint resolution of

   1. Likelihood of realizing a particular outcome

   2. Desirability of the outcome (in terms of need structure or "intrinsic" rewards), expressing some level of immediacy for fulfillment, and

   3. Reward value or payoff in goal accomplishment

PUTTING IT ALL TOGETHER

Clearly, the elements comprising the motivational picture are many and varied. The fruits of early work by such people as Maslow, Herzberg, and McGregor are still discernible, but a vast new richness and complexity have been added to the picture. Undoubtedly, key elements in an up-to-date synthesis and model for organizational analysis would include

Learning concepts

The many actors in role structure and its intermingling with environmental elements

Essence of goal-path theory (goal-seeking behavior defines an individual line of action)

Dynamic view of Maslow's need hierarchy, permitting simultaneous functioning of all needs and distinguishing between those likely to be hygiene oriented and those representing higher levels of gratification, including the special category of achievers

A COMPREHENSIVE MODEL

Perhaps it is easier, in developing a comprehensive model, to start with the end product of the motivation—say new or renewed learning within an existing job. Here a miniature, self-supporting system can emerge (no. 1 in Exhibit 8–6) as learning facilitates job performance, bolstering individual confidence and morale. However, at an earlier point in time, as suggested by (1), when the individual initially engages in these learning activities, lack of skill, confidence, or active desire would contribute to low morale and lackluster performance. Thus a key question here is how to get the process going. Number (2) highlights the important antecedent conditions for change, including

a. Awareness of a need to learn or change

b. Knowing how to and being capable of change

c. A desire to change

The part played by factors such as climate, training, supervisory facilitation, and the job itself in meeting conditions for change (2), and which emerge from the role system and organization suggested in (3), is clearly discernible. Yet the key is that the individual be able to perceive (4) an action such as training or supervisory support as a means to secure the purposes he values. Also, the relative importance of these acts to the individual (and very importantly to the organization) must accommodate (a) the likelihood of these acts reaching individually valued ends and (b) the amount they would contribute. Thus individual perception is a key element in this portion of the model—a communication challenge to organization officials, managers, and supervisors is evident. It is what the person thinks to be the case, rather than what institutional personnel read into the situation, that counts.

Underlying the individual's perceptions of the situation (its meaning or

EXHIBIT 8–6. A Comprehensive Motivational Model

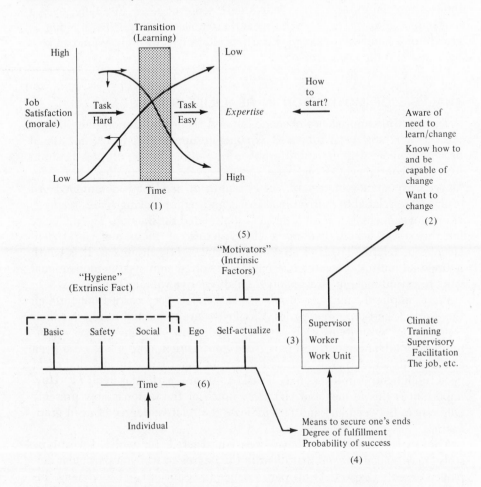

importance) is a set of needs that are simultaneously engaged (5). Yet the profile of relative fulfillment at any particular time is very much an individual matter—each person "sees" multiple requirements, but at vastly different levels. For some people at a particular point in time, lower-order or hygiene-type needs may dominate. For others, higher-order needs may guide individual action or response. For still others, both lower- and higher-order needs may be equally important, and may operate simultaneously. Some of these needs (motivators) prove especially responsive to the job itself, and constitute intrinsic elements. Other needs may prove more responsive to the environment and conditions surrounding the job (extrinsic factors). The extent to which these factors contribute to motivation and their staying power (as a continuing influence) vary widely.

Yet, over time (6) both short- and long-run effects are in the need set

(5). Day-to-day shifts in company relationships or personal requirements for funds appreciably modify the individual's sense of need. Secondly, over a longer time interval, as life patterns and circumstances shift (with aging or growth of a family, for example), further alterations take place (most likely basic shifts in the need profile).

ANALYSIS OF MOTIVATION IN REAL-LIFE SITUATIONS

The multiple approaches of modeling and theory utilization described in this chapter have been proposed as concrete approaches to organizational design, problem definition, and problem resolution. Yet an oft-heard refrain has been contingency—"once the specific needs of a situation," the "employee's expectancy of reward," or "strength of need," are determined. All of these are related to motivational issues and require taking some "reading" of employee feelings, needs, or level of job-related satisfaction. The difficulty for the researcher in gaining a clear picture of these behavioral deficiencies or relative levels of attainment is not lightly dismissed. It is worth noting that multiple research instruments are often employed in motivational work to permit making assessments from alternative vantage points.

For example, the measure of *job satisfaction* has been carried out through the use of Likert-type item scales. Employees are requested to register their "satisfaction" with items such as work conditions, company policy, opportunities for advancement, and pay. *Need gratification* indices have also been constructed, which permit the assessment of need strength and degree of need fulfillment. Employees may be asked, for any particular item: (a) How important is this to me? and (b) How much of the factor is now present? Differences between (a) and (b) indicate the relative degree of need gratification.

Also, *expectation indices* have been constructed, for which Likert-type scales may be constructed that identify the degree to which a particular employee expects (expected) his performance to result in need fulfillment. Finally, the measure of *performance* has been approached by utilizing both objective and subjective (or impressionistic) measures. Level of output, absenteeism, lateness, quality level, and number of new ideas are among the many objective measurements that can be secured. Performance rating by supervisors on quantity, quality, and effort items is an additional or alternate approach in research studies.[40] The descriptions in this section are only suggestive of some of the real-life approaches the student or practitioner may undertake (in conjunction with modeling and a theory base) for design and problem resolution.

ORGANIZATIONAL STRATEGY

The research and theories set forth in this chapter cover a variety of approaches to motivating "man in the organization," yet for the manager or executive interested in applications, several basic themes are of special interest. Viewing the totality of man in his environment, rather than simply as an individual coming into a particular organization, who brings with him certain "fixed" factors such as age, sex, physical features, and ethnic background, Exhibit 8–7 places these factors within the framework of the organization. A preliminary mental set is formed, as the individual makes the employment decision relative to the factors of the environment he sees as essentially fixed. Thus, to some extent, the individual's "variable" factors are tempered by these expectancies and by a reservoir of accumulated experiences, but the "fixed" factors always color his outlook.

From the company's viewpoint, a basic motivational strategy may be an attempt either to *change* behavior, dealing with deep-seated feelings and attitudes (the semivariable factors), or to *manage* behavior, in the sense of working with the individual ("as is") and seeking slow change over time. From the company's viewpoint, a large group of "controllable factors" is at

EXHIBIT 8–7. Formulating Motivational Strategies

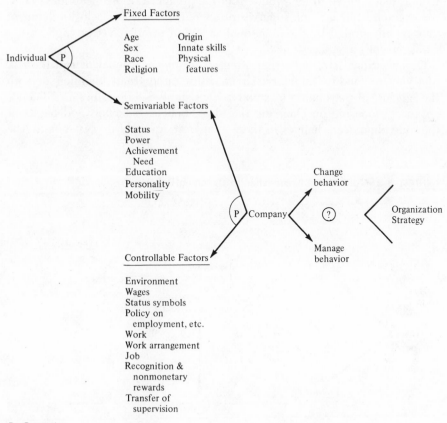

P = Perception

its disposal, and many of them may serve to meet affiliation requirements or high levels of individual performance. Research suggests that these "controllable factors" may have a multitude of effects on individual behavior; thus selectivity is emphasized. "Intrinsic" job factors assume greater importance where work or technology does not itself assure performance. Thus in support groups, research and development units, and service centers, managers must seek nontechnological approaches to ensure high levels of performance. But is it realistic to suppose that individual work satisfaction or self-fulfillment can be set aside in any of these situations? In most areas of our society today, the answer is no, even where satisfactory levels of production may be attainable.

It is clear that motivational approaches must be geared to the specifics of particular organizations and their human resources, current and future. Organizations differ widely in their relative attractiveness to people, despite the fact that they may provide like products or services. It would be more systematic to approach behavioral studies by weighting the importance of factors as they relate to individual preferences and then juxtaposing them against organization needs. Individual outlook and interpretation of environmental "cues" often differ widely from the organization's conceptions. Thus, for example, the lack of supervisory encouragement for self-development may be interpreted by the individual as low in priority, yet be high on top management's agenda.

Organizational strategies that attempt to influence behavior run the risk of trying to modify singular characteristics rather than blending in with the "givens" of personality (Exhibit 8–7). Exhibit 8–8 describes an influence approach, focusing on changing the ideas, beliefs, behavior, and habits of the individual. Yet changes in these areas rest squarely on two points: the

EXHIBIT 8–8. Motivational Approaches to Changing Behavior

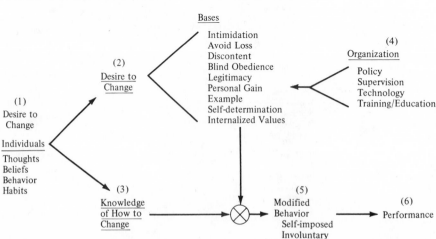

individual must have the desire (motivation) to modify his behavior (2) *and* he must know how to modify behavior through understanding and learning (3).

The key to understanding the desire to change resides in a variety of psychological and sociological approaches, ranging from sanctions (threats) and legitimacy (authority) to position rewards, from intimidation to self-determination. Performance will likely be adversely affected if coercive approaches are used. Organization strategies may include education/training, change of policy, or supervisory surveillance (4). A modified pattern (5) may be self-imposed, involuntary, or coerced. Thus we would expect the performance levels of individuals to vary widely, depending on the interaction of their needs and the approaches selected for influence (6).

CASE STUDY—HOW DO WE MOTIVATE OUR SALESMEN?

A substantial gap often exists between theory and application. The ability to focus perspectives on a particular management problem is a major test of the manager's powers of synthesis, analysis, and problem solving.

A case in point is the problem confronting the divisional sales manager of a large manufacturer and distributor of pharmaceutical drugs, where the level of turnover among younger salesmen who had college degrees approximated 35 percent, which was almost half again higher than the industry average. Also, performance was lackluster among older salesmen. Sales supervisors, all of whom had college degrees, were unable to cope with the situation, and in several cases the sales manager suspected that supervisors' attempts to cope were further compounding the problem. With these developments in mind, the sales manager called a special weekend meeting with all of his sales supervisors (eighteen) and staff personnel (five).

An outside consultant was engaged to attend the meeting. His role was to (a) review the background of turnover with participants; (b) crystallize apparent problem areas; (c) provide different perspectives for the managers and staff; and (d) assist participants in seeking to identify corrective approaches to particular problems.

The consultant proposed models, as illustrated in Exhibit 8–9, that included

a. The Maslow need model (3) over time, along with a renewal model (1)—the former to suggest the transience of various motivational cues based on the Herzberg formulation

b. The utility model (2), to suggest the *different* ways in which salesmen might be viewing the same sales programs

c. A perception feedback model (4), to identify possible changes in levels of aspiration over time, as well as conformity of rewards and situational demands to desired outcomes

EXHIBIT 8–9. How Do We Motivate Our Salesmen?

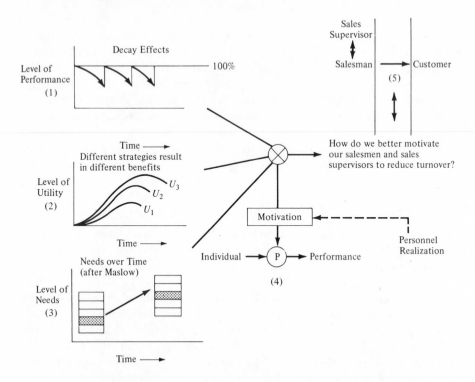

d. A conceptualization of the multiple environments and relationships characterizing the sales situation

Points for Discussion

1. What set of models would you have prepared to probe this situation?

2. How would you synthesize your perspectives (or those proposed)
in developing approaches to (a) the turnover problem among
younger personnel and (b) the performance problem among the
older salesmen?

SUMMARY

Although frequently unstated, motivational approaches are assumed to
be feasible within a variety of institutional arrangements and additionally
productive by way of meeting individual needs. As more research results

come to light, it seems clear that motivational strategies can't be generalized —organizational analyses will take account of psychological, specified sociological, and various situational circumstances.

The need deprivation approach of Maslow, modified to account for highly variable sets of jointly existing needs, plus (possibly) a needs fulfillment model patterned after Herzberg's work, appears to present logical points of departure for defining the psychological makeup of the individual. The achievement models (McClelland) and Adam's equity formulation may act as useful modifications of these basic models.

Vroom's work on goal-path approaches, combined with notions of learning/change, relates logically to the previous descriptions by providing a dynamic basis for anticipating individual actions or response to particular circumstances.

Incorporating these perspectives in organization analyses permits the consideration of important questions, such as the role of money, motivation under particular technological circumstances, and formulating motivational strategies for successfully incorporating minority personnel.

QUESTIONS

1. The text suggests that awareness of a need to change, desire to change, and knowledge of how to change are necessary for enlightened approaches to performance improvement. How do the various approaches for securing a desire to change affect performance?

2. Explore the technique of management by objectives (joint superior-subordinate agreement on goals) as a motivational strategy.

3. Compare and contrast the more popular (e.g., Herzberg) and more recent approaches to motivation.

4. What types of deep-seated motivational problems emerge in seeking to incorporate and develop economically disadvantaged workers in a business or institutional framework?

5. Compare and contrast the one- and two-factor theories of motivation.

6. Compare and contrast *job enrichment* and *job rotation* (taking on different jobs) or *job enlargement* (adding responsibilities) as motivational strategies.

7. What approaches to motivation might be undertaken in small companies evidencing limited job and promotional possibilities—if funds are also limited?

8. Critically analyze the satisfaction-reward-search model in Exhibit 8–2.

9. To what extent must the past experiences and attitudes of the employee be viewed as frozen, or subject to little change, and thereby tending to severely restrict motivational strategies for bettering performance?

10. In seeking to motivate people to higher levels of performance, assignments that stretch needed abilities and enlarge participation in decision making have been approached as specific, corrective approaches. Analyze them critically.

11. Name some jobs (two or three of differing types) in an organization you are familiar with that, based on Herzberg's ideas, are difficult to motivate. Discuss these jobs and suggest possible approaches to building them into a more motivating experience. In the absence of any constructive approach, what would you do?

12. Herzberg maintains that the only effect of improving a hygiene factor (e.g., a wage increase or recreation facilities) is a temporary decrease in *dissatisfaction,* rather than a long-term increase in motivation. In your experience is this true? Discuss.

13. According to Herzberg, some people learn to become "hygiene seekers"; that is, they are chiefly interested in the various "hygiene" rewards they can derive from the job. Do you know such people? Could their jobs be made sufficiently challenging and responsible so that they would be motivated to work harder and place less emphasis on the hygiene factors? Explain.

EXERCISES

1. Behavioral scientists maintain that an important degree of understanding of motivational problems emerges from the recognition of the *differing* ways workers (employees or subordinates) view their environment, as compared to the outlook (perceptions) of management. Develop a model for this assertion and then rationalize your development.

2. Develop a propositional model (set of related propositions) dealing with money, that is, money as a wage, monetary incentive, or salary payment. Utilize these propositions to analyze a situation you are familiar with, making whatever assumptions are necessary.

3. Develop a model portraying the more traditional view of how management might achieve high performance through "hygiene" approaches. Include money as a means of motivating performance.

    In the model, represent dysfunctional processes that may arise from such things as group pressures, individuals seeking to conform to self-image, etc.

OPINION SURVEY 1*

What is your opinion on these statements?

	Agree	Unde- cided	Dis- agree
1. Monetary incentive schemes in plant production operations materially improve profit and performance.	—	—	—
2. Extending monetary incentive schemes to indirect or administrative groups such as clerical, order filling, or maintenance personnel can improve output.	—	—	—
3. Personality and attitude are of little consequence as long as the worker gets the job done.	—	—	—
4. Engineers and professional groups work best when projects are carefully detailed and spelled out, and they are told exactly what is wanted.	—	—	—
5. Pay raises have only a short-term effect; soon, people are looking for more.	—	—	—
6. Job rotation is desirable because it widens individual experience and helps maintain job interest.	—	—	—
7. It is possible to change the behavior of individuals.	—	—	—

OPINION SURVEY 2

What is your opinion on these statements?

	Agree	Unde- cided	Dis- agree
1. Motivational approaches that depend on an explanation or understanding of the problem are more effective than direction.	—	—	—
2. Establishing profit centers for gauging managerial performance is the best way of motivating individual effort, and the only fair way of determining individual capability.	—	—	—

* Developed initially in Robert Tannenbaum and Sheldon A. Davis, "Values, Man, and Organizations," *Industrial Management Review*, 10, no. 2 (Winter 1969): 67–86.

3. Improving working conditions or relationships with management may temporarily decrease *dis*-satisfaction, but does not lead to a long-term increase in motivation.   ___ ___ ___

4. There is little opportunity to change in my organization.   ___ ___ ___

5. All in all, money talks.   ___ ___ ___

OPINION SURVEY 3

What is your opinion on these statements?

	Agree	Unde-cided	Dis-agree
1. People can gain new knowledge, acquire additional skills, and even, at times, change their interests, but it is rare that people really change.	___	___	___
2. It is a company responsibility to foster individual growth.	___	___	___
3. If we were really honest with ourselves, we would admit that the most important motivator, the one that really gets the performance, is money.	___	___	___
4. Beliefs about people—for example, "they can't be trusted" or "they are basically lazy"—can become self-confirming.	___	___	___
5. In order to get people to do things, the outside–in approach of "shoulds," "oughts," or "musts" is more effective than the *inside–out* approach, which seeks individual performance on the basis of something's making sense.	___	___	___
6. If the boss levels with his subordinates, it typically does more harm than good.	___	___	___

NOTES

1. Saul Gellerman has provided an excellent summary of the body of theories we shall use in this discussion in the Gellerman Motivation and Productivity Series:

Motivation in Perspective (Rockville, Md.: BNA Films), *Motivation and Productivity* (New York American Management Association, 1963), and *Management by Motivation* (New York: American Management Association, 1968).

2. Abraham Maslow, *Motivation and Productivity* (New York: Harper & Row, 1954).

3. David McClelland, *The Achieving Society* (New York: Van Nostrand, 1961).

4. Frederick Herzberg, B. Mausner, and B. Synderman, *The Motivation to Work* (2d ed.; New York: John Wiley & Sons, 1959), and *The Nature of Man* (New York: World, 1966).

5. Chris Argyris, *Integrating the Individual and the Organization* (New York: John Wiley & Sons, 1964).

6. Rensis Likert, *New Patterns of Management* (New York: McGraw-Hill, 1961) and, more recently, *The Human Organization: Its Management and Value* (New York: McGraw-Hill, 1967).

7. A strong argument countering many motivational approaches is described by Thomas H. Fitzgerald in "Why Motivation Theory Doesn't Work," *Harvard Business Review,* 49, no. 7 (July–August 1971): 37–44.

8. Ibid., p. 40.

9. This research emerges from various telephone operations, light assembly lines, and miscellaneous manufacturing operations.

10. These techniques incorporate job factors that increase individual opportunities for decision making or expand responsibilities.

11. James March and Herbert Simon, *Organizations* (New York: John Wiley & Sons, 1958).

12. Douglas T. Hall and K. E. Nougaim, "An Examination of Maslow's Need Hierarchy in an Organizational Setting," *Organizational Behavior and Human Performance,* 5, no. 1 (February 1968): 12–35.

13. For a good discussion on this and related motivational research and issues, see Alan Filey and Robert House, *Management Process and Organizational Behavior* (Glenview, Ill.: Scott, Foresman, 1969), pp. 360–387.

14. Altimus, C., *Quarterly Journal of Management Development,* 2, no. 2 (June 1971).

15. For a summary of some of these key points, see Mahmond A. Wahba, "Maslow Reconsidered: A Review of Empirical Evidence of the Need Hierarchy Theory," a paper delivered at the 33d annual meeting of the Academy of Management, Boston, August 1973.

16. For example, Lyman Porter and M. M. Henry, "Job Attitudes in Management: Perceptions of the Importance of Certain Personality Traits as a Function of Job Level," *Journal of Applied Psychology,* 48 (1964): 31–36.

17. Edward E. Lawler III and J. L. Suttle, "A Causal Correlational Test of the Need Hierarchy Concept," *Organizational Behavior and Human Performance,* 7, no. 4 (November 1972): 265–287.

18. For example, see M. M. Schwartz, "Motivational Factors among Supervisors in the Utility Industry," *Personnel Psychology* (Spring 1973).

19. Herzberg et al., *The Motivation to Work.*

20. Charles L. Hulin and M. R. Blood, "Job Enlargement, Included Differences and Worker Responses," *Psychological Bulletin,* 69 (1968): 41–55.

21. For example, Marvin Dunnette, J. Campbell, and M. Hakel, "Factors Contributing to Job Dis-satisfaction in Six Occupational Groups," *Organizational Behavior and Human Performance,* 2, no. 2 (May 1967): 143–174; Robert J. House and L. A. Wigdor, "Herzberg's Dual-Factor Theory of Job Satisfaction and Motivation: A Review of the Evidence and a Criticism," *Personnel Psychology,* 20, no. 4 (Winter 1967): 369–389; V. M. Bockman, "The Herzberg Controversy," *Personnel Psychology,* 24, no. 2 (1971): 155–189; and Donald P. Schwab, H. W. DeVitt, and Larry L. Cummings, "A Test of the Two Factor Theory as a Predictor of Self-Report Performance Effects," *Personnel Psychology,* 24 (1971): 293–303.

22. For example, Dunnette et al., "Factors Contributing to Job Dis-satisfaction," p. 147.

23. Victor H. Vroom, *Work and Motivation* (New York: John Wiley & Sons, 1964), p. 12.

24. Dunnette et al., "Factors Contributing to Job Dis-satisfaction," p. 143.

25. Schwab, DeVitt, and Cummings, "Test of the Two Factor Theory."

26. Larry L. Cummings and Aly M. Elsalmi, "Empirical Research on the Bases and Correlates of Managerial Motivation: A Review of the Literature," *Psychological Bulletin,* 70: 127–144.

27. Donald P. Schwab and Larry L. Cummings, "Impact of Task Scope on Employee Productivity: An Evaluation Using Expectancy Theory," University of Wisconsin working papers (August 1973).

28. James V. Clark, "Motivation in Work Groups: A Tentative View," *Human Organization,* 19, no. 4 (Winter 1960–61): 199–206.

29. K. E. Thurley and A. C. Hamblin, *The Supervisor and His Job* (London: H.M. Stationery Office, 1963).

30. Background for this approach is described in "A Correlation-Causal Analysis of the Relationship between Expectancy Attitudes and Job Performance," *Journal of Applied Psychology,* 52 (1968): 462–468.

31. In Vroom, *Work and Motivation.*

32. This approach and a representation of the expectancy model were suggested in Jay Galbraith and Larry L. Cummings, "An Empirical Investigation of the Motivational Determinants of Task Performance: Interactive Effects between Instrumentality–Valence and Motivation–Ability," *Organizational Behavior and Human Performance,* 2 (1967): 237–257, and John P. Campbell et al., *Management Behavior, Performance and Effectiveness* (New York: McGraw-Hill, 1970).

33. J. C. Wofford, "The Motivational Bases of Job Satisfaction and Job Performance," *Personnel Psychology,* 24, no. 3 (Autumn 1971): esp. 504–506.

34. An approach proposed by Galbraith and Cummings in "An Empirical Investigation."

35. Ibid., pp. 238–240.

36. Ibid., pp. 242–244.

37. Ibid., pp. 247–248.

38. Paul S. Goodman and Abraham Friedman, "An Examination of Adams' Theory of Inequity," *Administrative Science Quarterly,* 16, no. 3 (September 1971): 271–288; Charles S. Telly, Wendell L. French, and William G. Scott, "The Relationship of Inequity to Turnover among Hourly Workers," *Administrative Science Quarterly,* 16, no. 2 (June 1971): 164–172.

39. Edward F. Lawler III and Lyman Porter, "Effects of Performance on Satisfaction," *Industrial Relations,* 7, no. 1 (October 1967): 20–29.

40. For a single research approach combining all of the above-mentioned analyses, see Wofford, "Motivational Bases."

Learning Objectives

Understanding the Situational Basis for Leadership
   Propositions
   "Acceptance" Approach
Some Contributions and Shortcomings of the Michigan
   and Ohio State Leadership Research Studies
Fiedler Model
   Key Assumptions, Approaches, and Shortcomings
Contingency Approaches as a More Flexible, Responsive
      Approach
   Propositions Based on Contingency Approaches
Interrelationships of Leadership and Motivation
Bases for Bringing Contingency Approaches Together

Chapter **9**

LEADERSHIP

OVERVIEW

After a long period of comparatively modest advances, the 1970s witnessed an intensification of theory development and research. This effort dealt with various aspects of leadership, including their links to other areas of behavioral analyses, and including motivation, role, and group processes. The comparatively large number of footnotes in this chapter reflects the intensity of recent efforts.

First, a few words concerning the general orientation of the chapter. In selective fashion, this chapter identifies several streams of key developments of the 1950s and 1960s that provided critical concepts and viewpoints for the rather rapid advances of the 1970s. This base of important leadership notions furnishes the needed understandings for the central chapter discussions concerning "contingency" or situational approaches. Briefly, the analyses of Chapter 9 emerge in the following manner.

As an initial point of departure, leader requirements are viewed in terms of job responsibilities, and some of the shortcomings of this approach are identified. A few leadership propositions are then provided that are suggestive of concurrent areas of recent leadership study and the complexity characterizing these recent approaches. Also, this discussion helps to establish various topics and questions that become the basis for subsequent discussions.

This is followed by a brief historical portrayal of leadership research, further facilitating the joint view of various topics comprising leadership approaches. Three major core areas of leadership approaches are described, starting with the University of Michigan group, then the Ohio State group, and ending with the studies undertaken at the University of Illinois, which are largely identified with Fred E. Fiedler. The Fiedler studies provide a key bridge to the central chapter discussions of contingency approaches.

In order to crystallize some of the important developments in contingency approaches, a number of leadership notions or propositions are provided. These notions identify situational factors that have a moderating influence on leadership approaches and various performance measures. Also, attention is directed to connecting leadership analyses with some of the notions of motivation discussed in Chapter 8, technology notions expressed in Chapters 3 and 4, structure in Chapter 2, and role/group (to be developed in Chapter 11). In the final discussion of the chapter, some integrative models are set forth that suggest, at least conceptually, some possible directions of future leadership study.

The large number of moderating variables emerging under contingency approaches pose major theoretical problems, let alone challenges in measurement and practical difficulties in seeking to cope with these multiple situational considerations.[1] Yet it is out of these contemporary advances that a rich base has been established for future developments. Clearly, a flexible posture in organizational analyses is indicated for the student of leadership as newer notions or refinements continue to emerge.

INTRODUCTION

Important variables in leadership are aspects of the situation (e.g., work technology, leader-member relationships, leader influence), personality traits, level of formal authority, and style.[2] Traditional approaches stressed either the formal authority accorded the position or personal traits.[3] Newer approaches suggest that leadership is more functional: that it depends upon the situation;[4] is affected by the dynamics of the group; and is responsive to technological or economic considerations.

> Leadership is a *function* in the organization, rather than the trait of an individual. *It is distributed among the members of a group* or organization, and is not automatically vested in the chairman or the person with the formal authority.[5]

> Leadership consists of such action by group members as those which aid in setting group goals, moving the group toward its goals, improving the quality of the interaction among its members, building the cohesiveness of the group, on making resources available to the group. In principle, leadership may be performed by one or many members of the group.[6]

When the notion of leadership is approached from the restricted perspective of position or formal responsibility assignment, bases for intercomparison are provided but various shortcomings become evident.

POSITION RESPONSIBILITY AND LEADERSHIP NEED

Aside from the particular abilities brought to the job by a leader or subordinate, work responsibilities dictate some combination of technical, human relations, and administrative skills.[7] Technical skills are the ability to use relevant knowledge, techniques, and equipment, and the need for them increases as specialization or differentiation of tasks takes place. The ability to work effectively with people ("human relations skills") assumes added importance where one works with large numbers of people or where human relations are important to success. Actions that reflect an understanding of overall objectives and sensitivity to system function ("administrative skills") take on added importance where planning, programming, and organizing are highly valued as aspects of the decision process. Thus the individual who possesses these qualities in a given situation becomes a "leadership candidate." The distribution of responsibilities in the organization structure suggests that the balance of administrative–technical–human relations skills indicates both level and position in the structure. For example, administrative emphasis is at the top of the hierarchy, and technical or human relations emphasis is at the bottom.[8]

The skill typology discussed here provides a general basis for comparing job responsibility assignments. These descriptors of skill are developed independently of role occupant, work group members, and shifts in situation over time. This, though providing an initial basis for position specification or formal requirements, requires considerable additional information for describing behaviorality, the leadership role of a position. The following propositions suggest some of these needs.

SOME GENERAL PROPOSITIONS

The following general propositions highlight four areas of interest, including technology, leadership power and influence, social group position/power, and character of the situation.

1. *Technology:* The level of technological advancement influences the amount of needed supervisory direction, so that, in general, the more advanced the system and the greater the reliance on process controls, the less the needed supervisory direction.[9]

2. *Supervisory power:* The greater the supervisor's ability to secure outcomes valued by his group, the greater his influence with the group.[10]

3. *Group position:* The greater the supervisor's (leader's) ability to facilitate the structuring of social relationships among group members, the greater his acceptance by (influence with) the group.[11]

4. *Task situation:* The greater the time pressure imposed upon a group from external sources, the greater the acceptability of supervisory structuring of task activities.[12]

Some research efforts have been directed to exploring the impact of a particular area of variables (such as supervisory influence or elements of the task situation) on leadership approaches and various possible outcomes involving both operational performance and behavioral results (e.g., morale, satisfaction, and felt tension). However, considerable theorizing and research have been more recently directed toward attempting to involve, simultaneously, several areas of moderating variables in contingency approaches. More on this later. Though the efforts of this leadership theory building and research have a prescriptive thrust ("what organizations or leaders ought to be doing"), the willingness and ability of people and organizations to make the indicated changes is a practical area of considerations (assumptions) warranting attention.

Leadership Viewed Conceptually

In Exhibit 9–1, conventional subordinate-leader relationships are displayed in the framework of both organizational (7) and situational (5) influences, where technology (the work system, 6) constitutes a special case. The supervisor-leader role is affected by the interpersonal influences of the subordinates' reference group (2), by the traits, personality, and education brought to the job by the subordinate (7) and the supervisor (1), and by the interaction and influence of the leader's boss and support groups (3). The broken arrows in the boss-leader-support relationship (3) suggest variable personal needs of the leader, depending on location in the authority hierarchy. Measures of the effectiveness of interpersonal relationships such as morale and satisfaction have a bearing on performance (4); the character of this relationship requires careful specification.

An Acceptance Theory Interpretation

The leader-subordinate relationship in Exhibit 9–1 can be probed usefully in the light of "acceptance theory" based on early work of Chester Barnard and Herbert Simon. This formulation focuses on the ability of the leader to influence developments in the environment and on subordinates' willingness to accord authority to the leader.[13] Thus the "authority" of the relationship is conferred by followers' acceptance, usually based on the power of the leader to secure the followers' objectives, including those conferred by the organization and by group members. The leader's latitude of response to group/situational need will be affected by his boss's style and expectations.

This characterization suggests an earlier theme (in Chapter 2)—the *dysfunctions* of actions destined to secure particular goals. For instance, a leader's attempt to enforce conformity through close direction could lead to the immediate desired outcome, but could deter creative approaches in later

EXHIBIT 9–1. Leadership Variables and Performance

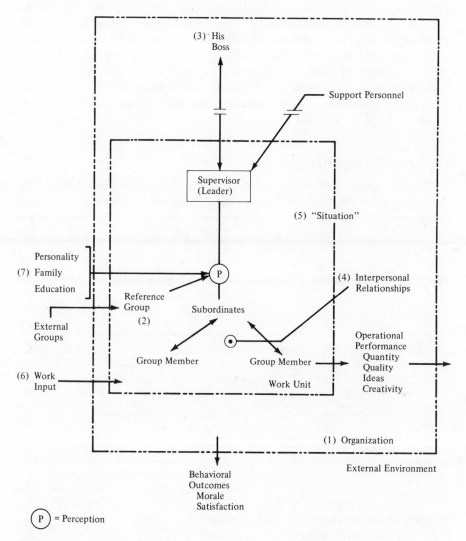

situations. Another example is delegation of responsibility to subordinates—they may lack the information or self-organizing ability to arrive at appropriate and timely decisions.

A final point here regarding "acceptance" approaches concerns the influence of past events and changes over time. The quality of interpersonal relationships, for example, changes over time with shifting organizational circumstances and with the knowledge, understanding, or misunderstanding accompanying these relationships. At one point in time, the formal leader of a newly organized group may have little basis for establishing follower "acceptance" other than his formal authority. Over time, and to the extent that he is able to demonstrate his influence in organizational matters or expertise in technical or interpersonal matters to group members, the formal leader's role may be strengthened. This growing strength will reflect the growing "acceptance" and more wholehearted support of his group members.

Of course, the character of the evolving "leader"-member relationship may worsen with potentially adverse effects. The level of operational performance may be such as to be enough to "get by"; but tension or anxiety may build among group members, and satisfaction may slide considerably.

LEADERSHIP RESEARCH

Exhibit 9–2 summarizes some of the important developments in leadership theorizing and research and reflects new, promising directions for subsequent work. New explorations in contingency approaches, the incorporation of motivational constructs such as the "goal-path" approach, and the leader-

EXHIBIT 9–2. Development of Important Leadership Studies and Events

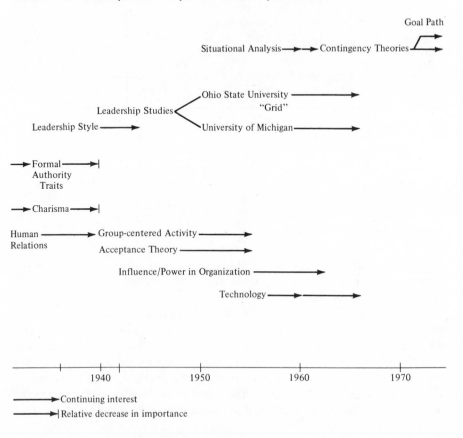

ship conferences at Southern Illinois University (in 1971 and 1973) are suggestive of the renewed interest and progress in this field.

Early leadership research provided the base for more comprehensive research in the 1960s, as well as the formulation of diagnostic and prescriptive models. In the 1970s, leadership analyses included style options, contingency-situational approaches, and group notions. In general, research probes more closely examined aspects of the leader's role, relationships, and influence; features of work task and technology; quality and characteristics of task unit members; and the authority positioning of leader and group members. Exploratory models tended to become more complex as new disclosures and perspectives were introduced.

Changes in our social-economic milieu have also had important implications for leadership concerns. Change is a potent force, shifting the conditions and assumptions underlying research. The social turmoil of the 1960s and 1970s, resulting in part from international military involvement, minority problems, and the growing momentum of technological change, foreshadows significant changes in leadership at national and local levels, and in the far reaches of organizations. The impact of cultural variables and the notion of man's work and meaning in an era of conflict and change are examples of factors redefining the assumptions analysis.

"Employee centered" leadership concentrates on the human aspects of worker problems and seeks to develop effective work groups with high performance goals. In contrast, "job centered" supervision is primarily directed toward productivity.

There is an appearance of similarity between leadership research at Ohio State University[14] and the University of Michigan,[15] although the underlying theoretical constructs are quite different. The Michigan group classified the way subordinates perceive leaders along a scale with "worker centered" at one end and "job centered" at the other. In the Ohio State research, "consideration" and "structuring" are proposed as two styles of leadership. "Consideration" applied to the ability of the leader to establish rapport, two-way communication, and mutual respect ("human relations"). "Initiating structure" is the supervisor's definition of group activity through planning, work organization, and criticizing and initiating ideas. In the Ohio State studies, supervisors described *their own* supervisor's leadership behavior and their impressions of how their superior expected them to lead work groups. Here the variables are orthogonal and may exist in varying combinations (i.e., consideration and structuring) within the same individual.

A particularly promising area of research is that which has taken situational factors into account.[16] Major contributions to this work have been derived from the research of Fred E. Fiedler,[17] which will be described in greater detail later in this chapter. This work casts doubt on the generalizations and association of cordial climate and high performance suggested by the Michigan work, and points to a careful specification of conditions before deducing leadership posture. Furthermore, situational research indicates the importance of the sociometric acceptability of leader to followers as an initial condition for high performance. "Acceptability" is determined through interaction analysis and preference studies, and is aside from the idea of "liking." Finally, the treatment of particular situational variables such as technology, structure, and work environment is closely related to situational studies. For example, the character of the *work environment* (level of technology) has a direct bearing on leadership needs.

MICHIGAN LEADERSHIP STUDIES

As already indicated, the leadership analyses undertaken at the University of Michigan formed one of several principal streams of research that contributed substantially to existing theories. A large number of Michigan research probes were directed toward (a) the benefits of team approaches, (b) cooperation, and (c) a supportive, friendly climate.[18] However, the studies concentrated on employee centered behavior, perhaps at the expense of fully understanding production centered behavior.

In reports by the Michigan researchers in a wide variety of settings, productivity was often shown to be higher in "employee centered" groups, although many of the differences in output were modest—15 percent or less. However, subordinates also expressed less favorable attitudes and less satisfaction with a "production centered" supervisor, rejecting close supervision as an acceptable leadership posture. The Ohio State studies provide a different set of possibilities related to this point.

When variables such as the level of work performance (toward a work standard) and morale (considered in terms of job satisfaction) were viewed jointly, productivity appeared to be generally improved by closer supervision, but morale seemed to rise and then fall. That is, morale appeared to be initially positively responsive to supervisory pressure, then fell off and decreased as added pressure was applied. Yet pressure from *within* the work groups (from colleagues) seemed to be acceptable.

To secure performance and sustain morale in the conduct of work, the following approaches were indicated:

a. Leadership guidance rather than close direction

b. Leadership sensitivity to the behavioral dynamics of socio-technical groups, to a point where a warm, cooperative environment can be fostered

c. Actions that support group formation and maintenance so that performance goals can be realized, permitting individuals to work out social relationships and allowing for acceptable modes of pressuring those who deviate from desired behavior patterns[19]

These prescriptions raise several related questions, which are not readily dealt with in this approach:

a. Are there circumstances under which leader-directed activities may jointly secure both desired performance and behavioral objectives?

b. Must the supervisor be socially *close* to his subordinates in order to work effectively with them? It has been suggested that the supervisor who sides with his subordinates *and* is socially close to them will likely behave in a more helpful fashion, although his effectiveness will be moderated by his influence (power) in the organization.[20]

c. Can one individual shift between alternate postures of "employee" and "production" centered? Do some situations call for combinations of these postures?

OHIO STATE LEADERSHIP STUDIES

Studies undertaken by researchers at Ohio State University led to the identification of "initiating structure" and "consideration." "Initiating structure" was defined as the formalization of work relationships and "consideration" as concern for the human factors in leader-subordinate relationships.[21] These variables are illustrated in Exhibit 9–3.

The desired characteristics of leadership depend on perceptions by (a) the leader's superior, (b) the leader's subordinate, and (c) the leader him-

EXHIBIT 9–3. Leadership and Role Relationships

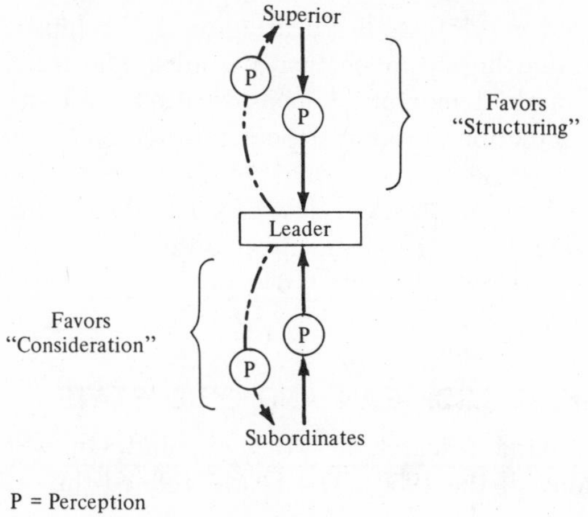

P = Perception

self. Thus the leader is often a "man in the middle." He is subject to pressure from above for performance, so he tends to structure behavior and is encouraged by his superiors to seek results. Conversely, general (versus directive) supervision and participative decision making often elicit favorable responses from subordinates.

"Initiating structure" is viewed in the Ohio State studies as *instrumental* behavior in the sense that it focuses on securing goals, coordinating resources, and establishing time targets, work assignments, and procedures. Dimensions of structuring also include definition and clarification of company policy guidelines and working relationships. Views of the leader *held by superiors* suggest that structuring, a superior's rating of supervising effectiveness, and group productivity are all related. Ratings of effectiveness by the leader's superior encourage a leadership posture of structuring;[22] and results from one study of supervisors indicated that production gain may be realized under highly directive approaches.[23] "Autocratic" supervisors achieved better production and quality than democratic and laissez-faire supervisors. Yet, although *instrumental* behavior may facilitate certain types of goal attainment,[24] analyses described in Chapter 8 suggest some of the dysfunctional consequences of this approach for morale and satisfaction among subordinates. Also, related research has exposed other dimensions of structuring approaches.[25]

"Consideration" is an intuitively appealing idea, most commonly associated with supportive and friendly relationships, and permits employees to play an important role in controlling their task environment. There is evidence that high-productivity departments enjoy supportive leadership. Not surprisingly, patterns have been noted linking consideration to subordinate satisfaction.[26] To say that many subordinates would view support as desirable is confirmed by research.

Some Unanswered Questions

An analysis of some 150 studies bearing on leadership behavior and group response suggested highly inconclusive results. The leadership postures of "authoritarian" and "democratic," "consideration" and "structuring," "direction" and "participation" produced both positive *and* negative correlations. However, the analyses suggest that "patterns of behavior identified as follower oriented, socially distant (low LPC), and structured are most highly related to productivity. The democratic, autocratic and consideration patterns of behavior are not related to group productivity." [27]

LATER WORK AT MICHIGAN AND OHIO STATE

Additional related research at Michigan and Ohio State followed the leadership studies of the 1950s. The results refined the rather coarse definition of variables and pointed toward newer problems. A twenty-seven-company study[28] attempted to gather findings on leadership/productivity and cohesiveness as they pertain to the character of the organization. In general, the findings did not support the hypothesis—which sought to relate consideration, delegation, and productivity—nor did they support the theory that supervisory structuring leads to low productivity, low group feelings, and low satisfaction. The findings suggested that

1. The satisfaction of employees with freedom on the job relates to group influences and enthusiasm (i.e., the effect of the peer group).

2. The satisfaction of employee expectations relates to supervisory behavior (leader-group interaction).

3. Leadership behavior (of supervisors) is not clearly tied in with group productivity.

4. Delegation and group productivity are not related, but delegation affects group drive and enthusiasm.

5. Group output appears to be negatively related to cohesion.

6. There are few instances when organizational generalization relates to leadership. In fact, as the number of organizations in the study grew, the relative proportion where generalizations held decreased.[29]

In an ambitious effort, Bowers and Seashore attempted to integrate results from eight of the Michigan/Ohio State studies, as well as to conceptualize them under a "four factor" theory.[30] Applying the theory to data acquired from an insurance company proved to be inadequate in analyzing leadership and effectiveness, until additional variables were taken into account: (a) work patterns, with time allocations to various activities; (b) personal and motivational factors of subordinates, including drives and level of education; and (c) managerial expertise and level of competitiveness among supervisors.

CLOSER VIEW OF THE OHIO STATE STUDIES

The very large number of studies utilizing the Ohio State leadership instruments warrants closer attention to the results of some of these studies, especially those that crystallize important leadership questions or connect to contemporary research designs.

One research study of interest focused on a question raised at an earlier point in this chapter—the relative influence of the leadership variables "structuring" and "consideration" on organizational performance. In an important research study[31] on this question, two hypotheses were tested:

1. Subordinate satisfaction with role expectations will be positively related to leader consideration.

2. Consideration will have significant moderating effect on the relationship between structure and satisfaction of role expectations.[32]

   a. Under conditions of low consideration, satisfaction will be negatively related to structuring.

   b. Under conditions of high consideration, satisfaction will not be related to structure.

Although recent research studies modify some of the hypotheses that guided this research, the findings of the study provide important insights into some factors favoring newer analysis. At the same time, this study provides a good illustration of, and important link to, the Ohio State analyses previously described.

The first hypothesis follows directly from the Ohio State research, parallels "human relations" notions, and is largely a clarification of other studies. However, the second hypothesis is more subtle, since it asserts that "consideration" can significantly moderate leader-subordinate relationships. Thus in organizations where "structuring" is prominent, and where satisfaction may be low, "consideration" may well be the basis for raising job satisfaction and thereby enhancing motivation. To the extent that the second hypothesis holds, it has powerful implications for prescriptive patterns of leadership. Even where the work system brings with it highly structured activity (e.g., in mass production), it may still be possible to bring about individual satisfaction.

The fact that future technological changes are bringing managerial and support personnel into greater prominence in organizational matters leads to increased interest in the research discussed here since it involved R&D and engineering personnel in an airframe manufacturer and a producer of business machines. Examples of the instruments used by the researchers are as follows.

1. *Satisfaction of employee role expectations.* These analyses were based on employee attitudes toward management (twelve questions) and the firm and job expectations (seven questions). Both questionnaires were built on scales of five degrees, providing the respondent with the opportunity to reflect a position of strong agreement, disagreement, or intermediate feelings about a proposition. Examples:

a. Attitude toward management and firm:
"My pride in working for this company . . ."

Very Poor	Poor	Fair	Good	Very Good

b. Job expectations:
"My chances of getting ahead in this company . . ."

Much poorer than ex- pected	Poorer than ex- pected	Same as expected	Better than expected	Much better than expected

2. *Leadership consideration.* There were fifteen scored questions, each with five possible responses. Descriptions by subordinates of leader behavior were made on the following type of answer: always, often, occasionally, seldom, or never.

3. *Leader's initiating structure.* An additional fifteen questions permitted observations concerning the supervisor's structuring of the work environment. Example:

"He speaks in a manner not to be questioned"

Always	Often	Occasionally	Seldom	Never

Earlier leadership studies often dealt with lower-level personnel. The results derived from engineering and technical personnel in this study confirmed some well-known relationships, but also provided some surprises:

1. *Consideration and satisfaction.* The results indicated a positive relationship that supported previous results, but the magnitude of the correlations varied widely, probably because the effect of leader behavior (consideration) on satisfaction depends on organization climate as well as the capabilities of the leader. For example, the climate of the airframe company was highly structured. In such an environment, the ability and opportunity for leadership to measurably affect satisfaction may have been minimal. When a behavioral factor (leadership) is considered with an environmental factor (impersonal controls or level of technology), what is the *relative influence* of each? Does one dominate?

2. *Initiating structure and satisfaction.* A generally *positive* relationship was found here, strongest in the business machine company and weakest in the airframe manufacturer, probably because additional structuring by leader-

ship is redundant[33] in a highly structured environment. The positive results reported in two other companies might be explained by the character of personnel incorporated in the study: professional-technical groups, as opposed to "blue collar" groups. The researchers proposed that highly trained technical personnel may prefer a "clear definition of role relationships and clear specification or work methodology." [34]

Indeed, it is possible that one trained in engineering, with its emphasis on specification and methodology, may seek structuring in relationships, policies, and "ground rules." But beyond this, freedom of action may be a major issue. The idea that structuring (e.g., along lines of the Weberian model) may help to order the work day and roles of technical and professional personnel, and thereby promote satisfaction, expresses an interesting possibility that runs counter to the often assumed idea that loosely defined roles are to be desired.[35]

Previously, it was proposed that structuring related to the *leader's* exhibiting instrumental, directive, and task-oriented behavior. Reducing role ambiguity for professional personnel supports the research results. However, it is not at all clear that directive or arbitrary behavior *per se* would correlate positively with subordinate satisfaction, especially for professional groups that seek logical rather than arbitrary direction.[36]

As already suggested, a considerable body of research suggests the importance of "consideration" as a moderator between "initiating structure" and criteria such as satisfaction, turnover, work quality, and overall performance. However, contingency approaches suggest careful reexamination of some of the research described above. The inability of "consideration" to exert an important and consistent moderating influence (in this research) on *high-level personnel* was likely the rationale for House's observation (in a later paper) concerning a more careful specification of its effects. House suggested that the level of the group in the authority structure or type of personnel involved must be reckoned with—that "consideration" is a strong moderator of "initiating structure"–satisfaction relationships for *low-level* organizational personnel. Its influence on higher-level personnel is suspect.[37] More observations on the "consideration-structuring" are provided in the subsequent discussions.

Leadership—Satisfaction—Performance

The link between leadership and job performance is highly problematical. Satisfaction or morale is only an indirect indicator of successful leadership. A large body of research indicates that there is no obvious or direct linking of satisfaction and performance, or of leadership, satisfaction, and performance.[38] A comprehensive summary of research studies in leadership[39] supports the notion that employee-oriented supervision ("consideration") is closely linked with job satisfaction and negatively correlated with absence and turnover. Thus if the criteria of successful leadership are to be employee satisfaction or low rates of absenteeism, then leadership behavior based on "consideration" is best.

But if the leadership style is directed toward maximizing productivity, or creativity in the formulation of new products or ideas, it must contend with such variables as social context, motivation, job context, stability of work environment, conditions of employment,[40] personality, and individual differences. In reviewing research on leadership in relation to creativity it seems evident that positive relationships among leadership, morale/satisfaction, and performance may hold, but only under specific conditions that describe the situation, roles, and personalities involved.[41] The numerous qualifications and contingencies noted in conjunction with the "consideration-structuring" constraints provide some of the rationale for reexamining the basic assumptions and thrust of these leadership formulations.

Some Shortcomings of the Ohio State Studies

The leadership studies undertaken at Ohio State since the late 1950s have shown amazing resiliency over time, with literally hundreds of researchers employing the various scales from these analyses. Yet, over the years, some important criticisms have arisen over the use and thrust of these constructs.

More specifically, shortcomings of these leadership studies have concerned the lack of theory concepts and the failure to reckon with situational factors. For example, if one were to extend the implications of the "structure-consideration" constructs, a behavioral theory might emerge in which high values of these two variables (i.e., a "high" situation consideration and structure) would constitute an attractive area of leadership action. And one would suppose that this prescription (high structure and high consideration) could hold across all manner of situations.[42] However, the research already noted and the evidence coming to light indicate that situational variables must be considered. Variables such as the leader's influence in the organization and the subordinates' expectations of leadership behavior must be dealt with if accurate assessments are to be made of needed leadership posture or approaches.[43]

To some extent, the research and leadership constructs identified with Fred Fiedler are a response to these shortcomings (his work is discussed in the following sections). However, we will see that, even here, important gaps exist in this approach.

The concluding analyses of this chapter will expand the discussion of contingency approaches in leadership and highlight possible approaches for the future.

CONTINGENCY APPROACHES IN LEADERSHIP STUDY

As was established in earlier chapters, the introduction of systems theory assisted substantially in the analysis of organizations. The stress of systems theory on the interdependence of organizational subfunctions, the relationship of the parts to the whole, and the influence of organizational environments on organizational functioning helped set the stage for contingency approaches. Increasing the effectiveness of organizational designs or leadership patterns depended on dealing with the broader context of organizational activity, involving both internal and external environments, and adjusting these as circumstances changed. The "best way" was a dynamic rather than static concept.

As we noted at the beginning of the chapter, the situational context[44] of leader-subordinate interactions is a critical factor in defining appropriate leadership styles. More to the point, considering the situational context as a source of moderating variables has provided a significant improvement in systematic approaches to leadership study. Articles, papers, and special reports of Hunt and Hill, the Southern Illinois University Symposia on Leadership, Steven Kerr et al., and Robert J. House (ASQ, 1971) bring together many of the studies contributing to these advancements. The discussions of this section are initiated with a formulation proposed by Robert Tannenbaum and H. Schmidt, based on situational analysis. This is followed by a description of the Fiedler approaches and more general discussions of contingency formulations.

A MODEL BASED ON SITUATIONAL ANALYSIS

Tannenbaum and Schmidt have described an approach similar to Fiedler's formulation of leadership strategies based on situational analysis.[45] They proposed that the choice of a leadership style also take into account the manager (leader), his subordinates, and the situation.

1. *The manager.* The value system of the manager (e.g., "managers ought to manage") and his conviction as to who should assume the burdens of decision making must be considered. Both may be affected by his view of the competence of his subordinates and his confidence in their abilities. Initially, the manager's personality may not be known, and a directive *or* a participative posture may represent a "natural" style. (Note the relation of this point to Fiedler's assignment of leaders to situations that reflect their personality requirements [to be discussed next].)

2. *Subordinates.* As with the leader, the personality factors of others must also be recognized, such as subordinates' need for independence, ability to grapple with unstructured situations, interests, goal orientation, education, knowledge, and expectancies for participation.[46] It would be realistic to expect a shift in the expectancies of workers (and managers) and, especially, new work force entrants as a result of the rapid modification of values and beliefs since the mid-1950s.[47] Also, the individual frequently maintains some type of relationship to a task group (Exhibit 9–1), and the strength of the relationship and the competence of the group must be considered by the leader.

3. *The situation.* The organizational environment, its beliefs, customs, and codes of conduct, can be expected to further condition the approaches of the leader. We have already noted the character of the occupational situation in terms of problem frequency and uniqueness and need for expertise, which suggests other appropriate leadership approaches. These situational elements reflect a narrower view of "situation" than that employed in these chapter discussions.

Also, since long-range organizational objectives are set for multiple goals such as high output, acceptance of change, and career planning, leadership strategies must take them into account as well.

The Tanenbaum-Schmidt approach describes important elements of contingency approaches and thus is useful for a conceptual view of some of these variables. Yet this model (and contingency approaches generally) poses considerable measurement problems in seeking to operationalize these notions. Additionally, seeking to determine or specify the relative influence of moderating variables in particular situations, or even the most important contextual variables (in terms of leadership influence), poses significant challenges to theoretician and field researcher. Studies undertaken by Fiedler have sought to deal with some of these many challenges.

THE FIEDLER RESEARCH

The work of Fred E. Fiedler probably represents one of the most serious and elaborate studies of situational factors, spanning a number of years and involving dozens of studies under a wide variety of conditions. The question guiding the Fiedler research can be paraphrased as follows: In what kind of situation will a particular style of leadership be most effective? [48] This question, in turn, gives rise to some important questions of management: Can men be trained in a particular leadership style? Will an effective strategy for organizational managers and officials permit the assignment of personnel to areas compatible with their capabilities? Should jobs be engineered (reengineered) to more reasonably suit the talents and limitations of organizational incumbents?

The studies conducted by Fiedler and his associates suggest that three major situational factors determine the appropriate leadership role for high levels of performance: (1) the relationships of leaders to group members, (2) the extent of task structuring (definition), and (3) the amount of power accorded to the leader by virtue of his authority and ability to influence events in the organization. The variables are viewed as attributes (low–high, present–absent) rather than as continuous.[49]

First, the *relationship of leader to members* raises the question of the extent to which the leader is accorded the confidence and loyalty of the group.

Second, the *structuring of the work situation* is concerned with the number of alternatives open to subordinates in undertaking work routines, as well as the number of acceptable situations. Structuring may also suggest the specificity of goals for the task group and the extent to which any particular decision can be scrutinized by higher management levels or staff groups.

Third, the *power of the leader* implies the ability to apply sanctions or reward performance.

These factors, in turn, relate to the individual's formal position of authority, the extent to which other organization functions support his activities, and the ability of the leader to secure for the group the organizational accommodations it seeks.

Exhibit 9–4 includes these variables and other key features of the model, and section A sets out the basic pattern of interaction between the leader

EXHIBIT 9–4. Leader Model (after Fiedler)

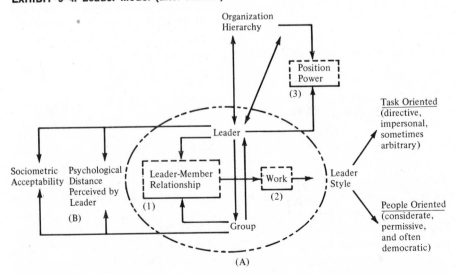

└────┘ – Key situational variables

and his group within the work/task environment. The functionality of the Fiedler model hinges on the sociometric acceptability of the leader (B) and the measurement of the perceived psychological distance (How distant do followers feel they are from leader?) between leaders and followers. An LPC (least preferred co-worker) score provides an important index measurement for these analyses.[50] That is, the predictive capability of the model assumes that the leader will not have been rejected by the group and that the relative closeness ("psychological distance") perceived by the leader provides an index to the best performance under given conditions. (It is important to note that the Fiedler research subsumes a leader-follower relationship that may run counter to casual observation.) Under conditions defined as "psychologically distant," the best levels of group performance were attained.[51]

Once psychological distance is ascertained and the initial condition of acceptability is met, attention shifts to three important situational variables: (1) leader-member relationships, (2) context of work/task, and (3) the position power of the leader. On the basis of this set of three situational variables, two leadership styles are proposed (task centered or person oriented, with the specific set of variables indicating the appropriate style. The prescription may be viewed along the indicated lines,[52] or may be interpreted in terms of appropriate combinations of situational variables, *given* a leadership style. The criterion for either of these possibilities is performance.[53]

The tabulation in Exhibit 9–5 summarizes some of the possibilities of the Fiedler model. In panel A there are several approaches to electing a job strategy, given the leader's shortcomings and strengths. In a situation of change, an important transformation in leader (supervisory) style is indicated. For example, if a leader tends to be directive or task oriented in outlook, the results would suggest job assignments where he is able to develop good relationships with his primary work group.

Another change example involves a period of major technological transition. Initially, the situation is most likely to be unique (unstructured) for all concerned. In this case, with the ability to develop good group relationships, person centered ("considerate") leadership would be the choice. However, as procedures are worked out and the work load becomes more routine, task centered approaches would be appropriate if the leader is able to maintain his relationship to the group. If this is not the case, "consideration" would be the more effective choice.[54]

Panel B of Exhibit 9–5 is based on the same mechanism as panel A, but the focus is on a *set* of situational variables.[55] As changes take place over time (say, for example, in going from a structured to an unstructured task), there will be a modification of conditions, which will indicate different leadership styles. Examples would include (a) the introduction of new technologies and *task* changes from conditions of instability to stability, (b) employee indoctrination and experience reflecting a shift from poor *relationships* to good relationships, and (c) aspects of career management

EXHIBIT 9–5. Two Perspectives of Leadership Situational Variables (after Fiedler)

A. Given: *A Leadership Style**

Leadership style		Task		Leader-follower relationship		Requires
		Structured	*Unstructured*	*Like*	*Dislike*	
People centered	1.	X			X	Considerable finesse
	2.		X	X		Mutual help and cooperation
Task centered	3.	X		X		—
	4.		X		X	Best of poor alternatives; nothing-to-lose stance

Key: X = Moderate level

B. Given: *Situational Variables†*

	Leadership style		*Situational variables*					
	People centered	*Task centered*	*Task*		*Relationships*		*Power*	
			Structured	*Unstructured*	*Like*	*Dislike*	*Strong*	*Weak*
1.		XX	+		+		+	+
2.		XX	+		+			+
3.		X		+	+		+	
4.	XX			+	+			+
5.	X		+			+	+	
6.	X		+			+		+
7.	X			+		+	+	
8.		XX		+		+		+

Key: + = State or condition
  X = Moderate level
  XX = Strong focus

* For a more detailed interpretation, see Joe Kelly, *Organizational Behavior* (Homewood, Ill.: 1969).

† This type of analysis and added interpretation of findings may be found in Fred Fiedler, "Engineer the Job to Fit the Man," *Harvard Business Review*, 43, no. 5 (September–October 1965): 115–123.

involving *relationships* between individual and group as job changes occur. In the last situation, task relationships are subject to constant modification as an individual moves into a new job situation and as relationships begin to solidify—a job move occasions a new cycle. Thus this model assumes a dynamic character, indicating a flexible leadership style.

The notion of specifying the situation reflects a growing body of evidence that dictates careful specification of participants, roles, situations, environment, personal factors, and current as well as past personnel relationships before deducing an appropriate leadership approach. In short, the prescription is that the student of organization or one who is aspiring to lead (influence the behavior of others) recognize and systematically analyze situational requirements, rather than react to events emotionally or according to "natural" style.

Modifications in Fiedler's Formulation

Fiedler introduced further elements of change in a recent paper that indicates further modification in his model and its application.[56] Factoring in time effects of supervisory training and/or experience (for example), this recent formulation admits the possibility for improvement in leader-member relationships or task structure, and thereby the indicated leadership strategy. "Situational favorableness" (e.g., leader control, influence) for the initially untrained supervisor may increase to a point where it matches that of the experienced or trained leader. Fiedler's latest studies appear to support the hypotheses that

1. Tasks would seem unstructured to the *un*trained leader but structured to the trained leader.

2. Training will tend to be dysfunctional for task-motivated leaders with poor leader-member relations.

3. "Low LPC leaders" with good leader-member relations performed no better with training than without it.

His latest research also set forth some expectations regarding task-motivated versus employee-motivated leaders. The application of Fiedler's latest research and findings suggests a possible shift from the 1965 strategy, which was built largely around "engineering the job to fit the man." This more recent formulation suggests a procedure in which the initial determination is one of ascertaining the "where" and "what" of the current organization situation, including the leader's orientation. For these purposes, dimensions of task structure, member relationships, and leader power are plotted on a chart whose axes are "leader LPC score" and "group effectiveness." Then an attempt is made to predict the outcome of leadership training;

that is, "Is there likely to have been an improvement in situation and outcomes as a result of training?" If no improvement is forecast, training should be set aside or consideration should be given to leader reassignment—to a new position where he is likely to be more effective under the *given circumstances.*

Some Methodological and Theoretical Problems in the Fiedler Formulation

As was established in earlier chapters, contingency approaches in research show considerable potential for advancing behavioral science applications. Yet these approaches are more complex than earlier formulations, and reflect both theoretical and operational problems. The research undertaken by Fiedler and his associates over a considerable span of time is a good example of needed and recognized refocusing. Fiedler and his associates sought to characterize important, measurable environmental variables. Those factors that were sought were features of the situation that were thought to exert a strong influence on alternative leader approaches and possible situational outcomes. Fiedler's representation (and necessary simplification) of the work environment involved the three constructs of "task structure," "leader's position-power," and "leader-member relations."

As more research findings have emerged and more effort and time are directed toward a given approach or construct (in replication, validation, or attempted application), a natural process of refinement takes place and reflects apparently important insights into organizational phenomena. At times, of course, major redirection (or termination) may be signaled. At an early point, Fiedler recognized the need for a broader explanation of leadership phenomena anchored on situational variables.

Over time, Fiedler responded to various needs of earlier contingency formulations, and some of these are recognized in his more recent work.[57] In a recent contingency approach, he postulates that group performance "depends on the match between situational favorableness, that is, the leader's control and influence, and leadership motivation as measured by the Least Preferred Co-worker (LPC) scale." [58] This approach points out that leadership training and experience are designed to improve leadership's influence and control, and thereby "situational favorability." The effectiveness of a group or organization is dependent (in the leader's approach) on two key variables, involving (a) the leader's motivational system and (b) the favorableness of the situation—that is, to provide the leader power and influence. The latter reflects (1) leader-member relations, (2) task structure, and (3) position power.

In the earlier Fiedler formulations, the measurement of the "least preferred co-worker" (LPC) was an important situational descriptor in specifying leadership approaches. But more recent research (e.g., George Graen et al.) has disclosed that the LPC measure may be unstable and, even more fundamentally, that a serious question exists as to what it is measuring. Additionally, the notion of a moderating variable such as "situational favorability" is not adequately measured by the three factors proposed by Fiedler, and the construct itself is incomplete. That is, it is incomplete in the sense that it doesn't reckon with relationships among group members and has dealt only with degree of structuring in considering "task." [59] Also, it has been contended that a cultural parameter has to be introduced to bring about theoretical consistency with the Fiedler model.[60]

SOME LEADERSHIP PROPOSITIONS AND NOTIONS BASED ON CONTINGENCY APPROACHES

Several contemporary developments, beyond those already described, have added materially to the state of the art in leadership analysis. In one series of thrusts, past research efforts have provided a valuable base for future extensions. The work of Robert House, utilizing path-goal motivational concepts (Chapter 8), and that of Edwin A. Fleishman, based on the venerable "consideration-structure" constructs, are examples (see the Chapter 9 bibliography). Also, two leadership symposia sponsored by the Department of Administrative Sciences in 1971 and 1973 at Southern Illinois University, with the assistance of Professor J. G. Hunt, have resulted in the development of key publications and a considerable advance in leadership frontiers.

The comparatively rapid changes in leadership formulations, many of which are based on situational considerations, have introduced a large group of variables that moderate relationships between leader and behavior and performance. These variables deal with aspects of structure, task, size, leadership style, and prevailing conditions and relationships, to name a few. A selection of propositions and leadership notions follows that enlarges on those provided early in the chapter. The referencing for these discussions is only suggestive of the body of research and theorizing related to these notions and propositions. More complete discussions of the underlying research will be found in the previously referenced works of Kerr, Schriesheim, Murphy, and Stogdill (1973), House (ASQ, 1971), Fleishman (Symposium, 1971), and the papers/proceedings of the 1971 and 1973 symposia.

1. *Influence of situation stress, threat, and pressure.* Threats to personal safety, time pressure for performance, and operation under high stress conditions pose the need for different leadership strategies. For men going into combat, for example, "high structure" may be viewed as highly desirable to preserve personal well-being and to literally shield the men from personal harm.[61]

Where a task or environment produces stress for the individual or group member, a leader's "consideration" may decrease some of the negative aspects of work-dictated activity by socially supporting the individual.[62]

2. *Degree of nonroutine in task and ambiguity of procedure.* Where tasks are routine, procedures are generally standardized. Yet, as tasks become less routine, and procedures are not supplied for various contingencies, task performance (and opportunity for success) may become increasingly ambiguous. The very nature of these nonroutine undertakings is to create ambiguity. To the extent that individual tolerance for ambiguity is exceeded, high stress can result. However, we also acknowledge the fact that some individuals (e.g., scientists in R&D) may desire substantial levels of ambiguity, to the extent that it permits (and the individual seeks) self-direction. Imposing structure in this latter situation might be expected to decrease both satisfaction and performance. Conversely, to the extent that structuring reduces the ambiguities of stress-producing situations (ill-defined responsibilities, poor procedures), individual satisfaction and performance should benefit.[63]

3. *Interdependence and ambiguity of task.* In a wide variety of organizational situations, task interdependencies exist between individuals, work groups, departments, and even divisions. Common situations encountered in production range from the high task interdependencies of mass assembly to a relatively low level in unit or batch production. In the latter, tasks are carried out in largely autonomous fashion and are generally separated in time and space. Interdependence here is established by mechanical linkage (as in mass production) or procedural sequence.

In department stores, the work of sales personnel is interdependent with credit operations (if a customer's credit must be checked) and other members of the same department (the sales of A may depend on B putting out the stock). Clearly, the character of interdependence varies greatly, and the leader's task, to the extent that it would assist in bridging dependent activities or coordinating them, also varies widely.

If interdependent tasks exist and the knowledge of an individual or group is insufficient to carry out the prescribed tasks, the leader's structuring of tasks may help to clarify relationships and thereby promote coordination, performance and, possibly, satisfaction.[64]

Where technology or procedure provides the needed continuity in interdependent operations, the supervisor's attempts at structuring or close supervision may be seen as redundant, and thereby causing dissatisfaction[65] and poor performance (where performance is not implicit in the technology).

4. *Influence of leader on higher authority figures and ability to secure action.* In the widely diverse situations that arise in organizations it's often the

individual who can "make things happen" or who can secure valued items or actions who is acknowledged as a person with influence. To the extent that this description fits the formally designated leader, he may play a powerful leadership role. This leader's role is additionally strengthened to the extent that subordinates' financial rewards, time off, and other aspects of work-related behavior depend on the prerogatives of (or to some extent are controlled by) the group's leader.[66]

5. *Work group size.* As the size of the work group increases, the simultaneous undertaking of varied and diverse activities can increasingly create frustrations and conflicts for lack of procedure or coordination. Activities that formerly were carried out on an informal basis, and with relative ease, may now cause tension as communications become distorted or strained.

Under these types of coordination, the leader's exercise of structure may be a welcome shift from the ambiguous, often confusing previous conditions.[67]

6. *Technology and leadership.* Robert Dubin has brought together a number of considerations that establish a perspective for jointly viewing technology and leadership:

1. Productivity is influenced by supervisory behavior, *but*

   a. Different types of work setting (production technology) reveal widely different styles of supervisory approaches to securing acceptable performance. These approaches may range from the creation of an atmosphere of autonomy and general supervision in "craft"-type operations to close supervision in highly interdependent systems ("mass production").

   b. Evidence suggests that the effects of supervisory behavior on productivity may be modest.

   c. Technological improvements may outweigh supervisory influences on productivity, but relative effects require considerable study and specification of conditions.

   d. The relationship between supervision and productivity is not a simple one, and even under appropriate conditions, the association is not likely to be linear.

   e. Some relationships between supervision (e.g., direction) and productivity may be inverted "U" functions, so that strengthening a seemingly good approach may actually garner diminishing returns. In other words, too much direction can hurt.

2. The pace of technological change is bringing about increasing concern for the management of systems, so that the management of people is sharing more of the spotlight with the management of technology.

3. Typically, *multiple* organization goals must be satisfied by organization managers, professionals, and officers. Consequently, productivity may be only one item in a complex set of objectives. Thus organizational architects may have to devote more time to carefully balancing multiple objectives.

   As for the task situation,

   a. Unstructured problem-solving situations, which seek a *diversity* of ideas, encourage a loosely structured (organic) supportive approach.

   b. Response to emergencies or high stress, including breakdown, competitive tactics, startup, or change, may dictate either of two possible strategies, depending on cost and available time:

      (1) Unilateral action on the part of the leader when he has the premises for correct action

      (2) The problem-solving stance of (1) when the situation calls for a diversity of ideas

   c. The technological structure of the work environment creates conditions ranging from those that are highly prescribed (diminishing leadership direction needs) to those where the technology provides impersonal direction, to those where managers bridge work routines, to those where technology is a minimal consideration.

These propositional notions assist in clarifying some of the major areas of moderating variables in leadership studies. More are provided in the chapter endnotes. At the conclusion of the following discussion on situational variables related to motivations, contingency notions are drawn together in a general conceptual model.

LEADERSHIP, MOTIVATIONAL PERSPECTIVE

The contingency approaches to leadership expressed in the previous discussions integrate well with the notions of path-goal theories of motivation developed in Chapter 8.[68] Stated briefly, five dimensions of goal-path formulations relating to leadership include (a) magnitude of the rewards for goal accomplishments, (b) connection of rewards to work-goal accomplishment,

(c) probability of employees' achieving work-task goals, (d) opportunity for realizing attractive, intrinsic returns from work-goal achievement, and (e) the personal value and attractiveness of the behavior needed for work-goal accomplishment.

Leadership actions can influence, to varying degrees, the key variables of the path-goal formulation:

1. *Magnitude of the rewards for work-goal accomplishments.* The formally designated supervisor ("formal leader") carries out a variety of responsibilities with direct impact on the financial returns and nonmonetary rewards gained by the individual. Approval of supervisors for wage payment, performance review, authorization of overtime, support in tuition requests, and recommendation for promotion are activities that are regularly carried out. They have substantial impact on both the short-term and longer-run rewards (e.g., through promotion) accruing to the individual.

2. *Clarification of the linkage between work-goal accomplishments and rewards.* The supervisor or formal leader typically retains a continuing contact and relationship with various work group members. He is at the crossroad of the management structure and the employee/work force. His interpretations of qualification for benefits, the workings of monetary incentive programs, and responses to employee questions regarding various rewards are among the many ways in which the leader develops (or can develop) the employee's perceptions of linkages between accomplishments and rewards. Also, to the extent that the supervisor intervenes directly in rewards secured, his consistency and fairness further round out employee understandings, expectancies, and confidence in effort-reward connections.

3. *Likelihood of employee's attaining goals of work task.* The supervisor is able to increase a subordinate's chances of task-goal accomplishments by such things as support in problem solving, cooperative behavior in response to employee requests for assistance, and direct influence on rewards secured.

4. *Opportunity for personal achievement and a sense of realization through work task (intrinsic to job).* Unlocking individual potential for achieving personal needs or realizations turns on the subordinate's opportunity to influence valued aspects of his work task and environment—felt participation in defining task goals (management by objectives is developed in Chapter 12) and ability to exert self-direction and control. The leader's mode of carrying out his responsibilities, his willingness to consult subordinates, his delegation of responsibilities, and his confidence in subordinates are some of the leader

outlooks and actions that influence the opportunity for subordinates' intrinsic realizations.

5. Personal value and attractiveness accorded the behavior needed to achieve work goals. The supervisor or formal leader is in a position to increase the attractiveness of actions needed to secure work goals. Greater attentiveness to members' needs, facilitation through the reduction of "red tape" or improved procedures, and understanding support in high-conflict situations can measurably affect employees' positive perception of the actions needed in work-goal accomplishments.[69]

All of the preceding points regarding leaders' influence on employee expectancies, paths of action, and realization tended to emphasize the potential and largely positive outcomes of these relationships. Yet there is an important degree of symmetry here with actions (or lack of them) bearing on considerable organization dysfunctions. We might well ask: "What happens if the leader is inconsistent in his actions with subordinates?" "What if the leader is too busy with his own 'pyramid climbing' to support the members of his task group?" And what if, for example, evaluation is viewed as a threatening rather than a constructive discussion of goals or feedback (more in Chapters 12 and 13) to guide future actions?

The research literature is quite variable regarding the answers to these questions. To some extent, the literature that has dealt with instances of low "consideration" (Ohio State studies) is responsive to some of these questions.[70] Insofar as lack of orientation or inconsistency of leader behavior creates ambiguity, frustration, or resentment, performance and/or individual behavioral responses (e.g., satisfaction) will likely suffer.[71] Because the supervisor is often a key in preparing (training) subordinates for future promotion opportunities, supervisory training and ability, interest, and willingness to support the subordinate will affect the latter's rewards and promotion prospects.[72]

Leadership Modes and Other Motivational Approaches

If leadership is considered in the light of the Maslow model, for example, a posture involving some level of "consideration" or "structuring" (e.g., high or low) would be interpreted in terms of need fulfillment of subordinates. It would then be appropriate to ask "What level of employee needs (e.g., security, self-fulfillment) are currently being tapped?" and "Given situational demands, what needs do we want to tap?" "What leadership posture is appropriate to situational demands?"

In a similar manner, organizational situations can be viewed in the light of the Herzberg model. In that case, one would seek to clarify the extent to which leader-subordinate interaction patterns merely satisfy "hygiene" needs, as opposed to providing the cues, guidance, and rewards that qualify as "motivators." When motivational models are used with the leadership variables already identified, they help provide an explanation for the relative importance, shortcomings, or dysfunctions of given approaches.

BRINGING CONTINGENCY APPROACHES TOGETHER

The previous discussion of propositions and notions related to contingency approaches is only suggestive of the possibilities in this area. Exhibit 9–6 brings together the contingency items (moderating variables) and the path-goal motivational constructs from previous discussions. It sets out four categories of contingency features, gathered under the general headings *task, personal features, leader,* and *additional factors.* These catagories also include items such as *felt mobility* of the individual and *correspondence* of the leader's and boss's leadership styles. The bibliography provides recourse to some of the studies underlying these contingency factors.

Exhibit 9–6 suggests that the accuracy of the leader's reading or interpretation of a situation will importantly affect the organizational outcomes. To the extent that the leader accurately interprets the situation and is capable of the indicated approach, the negative aspects of a current situation may be diminished (e.g., group members find adversity easier to accept) or positive gains may be realized in performance or behavioral measures. Failure or inability to assume an approach dictated by the situation may lead to highly mixed results: the situation may gradually deteriorate; things may stay static; leader success may have low predictability; or, at times, things may improve but the number of leader failures relative to successes may be high.

Some Practical Application Considerations

The practical requirements of research would dictate that a smaller, more manageable group of contingency factors be considered for a specific project (as opposed to all of those listed in Exhibit 9–6).

In leadership research, where so many moderating variables are potentially operable, the emphasis is typically on that group of variables which seemingly has the greatest power for providing an explanation in a given situation. As in the Fiedler research, a comparatively small but important set may be employed for research purposes.

Also, changes in time, space, or general conditions may dictate quite different leadership styles from those that previously prevailed. For example, in the military example it was suggested that leadership under battlefield conditions may make "structuring" approaches very acceptable for group members. But consider the range of conditions and changes that has emerged

EXHIBIT 9–6. Some Aspects of a Leadership-Contingency Model

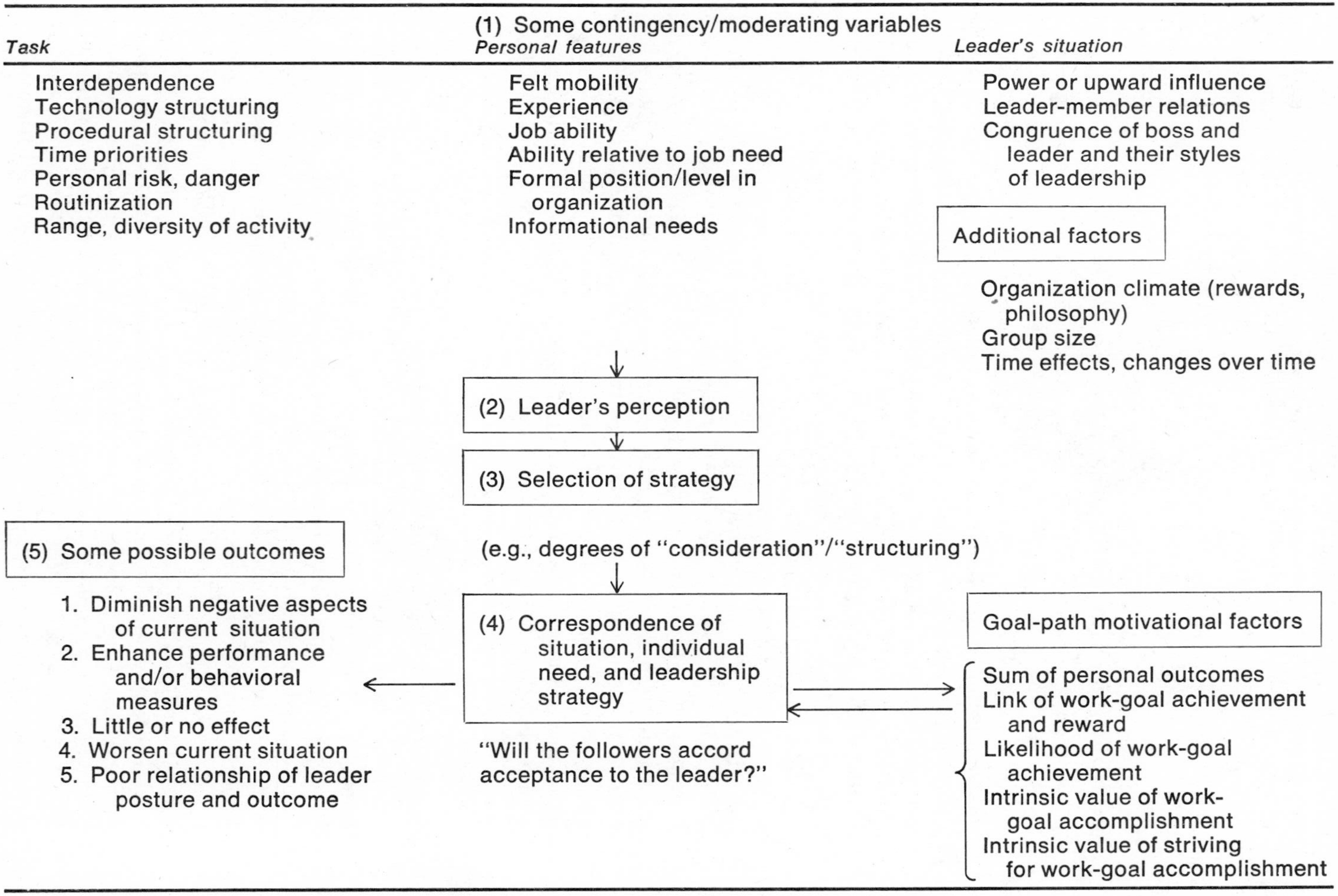

(1) Some contingency/moderating variables

Task

Interdependence
Technology structuring
Procedural structuring
Time priorities
Personal risk, danger
Routinization
Range, diversity of activity

Personal features

Felt mobility
Experience
Job ability
Ability relative to job need
Formal position/level in
  organization
Informational needs

Leader's situation

Power or upward influence
Leader-member relations
Congruence of boss and
  leader and their styles
  of leadership

Additional factors

Organization climate (rewards,
  philosophy)
Group size
Time effects, changes over time

(2) Leader's perception

(3) Selection of strategy

(e.g., degrees of "consideration"/"structuring")

(4) Correspondence of
  situation, individual
  need, and leadership
  strategy

"Will the followers accord
acceptance to the leader?"

Goal-path motivational factors

Sum of personal outcomes
Link of work-goal achievement
  and reward
Likelihood of work-goal
  achievement
Intrinsic value of work-
  goal accomplishment
Intrinsic value of striving
  for work-goal accomplishment

(5) Some possible outcomes

1. Diminish negative aspects
   of current situation
2. Enhance performance
   and/or behavioral
   measures
3. Little or no effect
4. Worsen current situation
5. Poor relationship of leader
   posture and outcome

here: the rebellion of troops against formal authority under battle conditions in Vietnam; differences between stateside and combat duty; and the expectancies of the professional soldier as opposed to the draftee.

Some of the criticisms of even the more recent Fiedler approach have been indicated. Effort is needed in advancing various theoretical aspects of the leadership-formulation characteristics of technology, and the task requires greater translation in terms of reward, structure, and the support features of climate. Other matters may warrant attention and more clarification include the quality of leader-boss and leader-group member relations, the leader's power/influence, reckoning with the personal qualities of the leader, ownership philosophy, and the competence of subordinates. Also warranting closer examination is the relative influence of these situational dimensions under particular conditions.

On balance, contingency approaches in leadership appear quite promising, but extensive work is indicated in both theory building and research. The challenges in operationalizing key variables (problems of measurement) should provide a constant tempering influence on the scope and complexity of the theoretical formulations.

SUMMARY

The leadership theorizing and research described in this chapter should provide organizational and managerial approaches and suggestions for given situations. Yet a cautious, flexible approach is indicated because of the complexity of interrelated or moderating variables. The likelihood of making broad generalizations has been considerably diminished by the disclosures of contingency analyses. Guide points for analysis that emerge from these studies include some of the following.

1. The primary variables underlying leadership strategies include job function, job level, and the characteristics of job tasks and job system.

2. The characteristics of the individuals involved—leader-subordinate relationships, leader-boss expectancies and relationships, and task group characteristics—affect leadership approaches.

3. External forces and groups can modify a leadership mode.

4. Differences in leadership style orientations have arisen from various cultural factors in the past, and they are sustaining important changes.

5. Supportive leadership is a key determinant of social-psychological maintenance under highly structured task conditions.

6. Instrumental (facilitative) leadership is a key factor influencing expectancies (and often realizations) under unstructured conditions.

7. Flexibility in leadership style is highly desirable.[73]

From the standpoint of the individual researcher, it seems clear that a wide variety of perspectives can be assumed in carrying out leadership studies. Yet research approaches must grapple with a broader set of variables than those used to date to fully account for observed leadership behavior or to formulate explanatory models. In organizational development work, where one is concerned with more comprehensive approaches to "climate" improvement or modification, many of the leadership routes indicated in this chapter must be pursued if both consistency and completeness in criteria are to be fulfilled.

Blending the more traditional approaches with recognition of situational variables sets the stage for a leadership strategy. Next, leadership approach, subordinate needs and limitations, and situation must be aligned—a major challenge to organizational managers. The inherent limitations of the leader (e.g., personality), subordinates' requirements, or technological restraints may dictate a revised strategy. Thus, viewing leadership as a strategy rather than as a given type of behavior suggests significant possibilities for individual development and organizational performance.

QUESTIONS

1. Compare and contrast the assumptions and results emerging from the leadership studies at Ohio State University and the University of Michigan.

2. Utilize the model of Exhibit 9–1, which displays leadership and role relationships, to discuss how the approaches taken in the Michigan and Ohio State studies might lead to seemingly contradictory results, depending on the reference role system.

3. What kinds of modification in leader behavior are indicated when subordinates are (1) more colleagues than task groups, or of professional stature, and when (2) group formation opportunities are minimal and relationships tend to form on individual bases?

4. Does the characterization of the leadership approach as employee- *or* task-oriented preclude the joint existence of both in some type of balanced strategy—for example, under conditions of change or where diverse problems are confronted?

5. Identify a leadership situation you are familiar with and then compare and contrast assumptions, underlying models, approaches, and likely recommendations for each of the following:

a) University of Michigan research
b) Ohio State University research
c) Fiedler approach
d) Broader contingency approaches

6. The studies undertaken by Filley, House, and Kerr suggest that rules, regulations, and procedures may be viewed positively (relative to motivation or satisfaction) by certain organization participants. If this characterization of the work situation is viewed as "work centered" or "structuring," develop propositions and models useful in explaining this result.

7. One notion that arises in leadership analysis is the "leader" who sufficiently clarifies relationships and approaches to problem solving and decision making that a high level of stability is perceived.

a) Suggest a few key propositions that tie leadership ideas together.
b) Model these leadership ideas as an aspect of motivation.
c) Use your model to demonstrate possible positive and negative (dysfunctional) outcomes.
d) What type of control is being exercised here?

DISCUSSION ISSUES

1. Consider the views of leadership as three basic types: autocratic, group centered (democratic), and individual. An all-or-nothing view, however, doesn't allow adequate room to explain "styles" which may be best in particular conditions. A situational approach suggests selecting that technique best suited to the situation. The major situational variables include personality (of the group to be managed), task characteristics, task roles (activity of leader and follower), and characteristics of the work group. Yet we must also consider the aptitude of the leader and reckon with such questions as "Must the leader be liked?" (Based on Robert T. Golembiewski, "Three Styles of Leadership and Their Use," *Personnel,* 38 [July–August 1961]: 34–45.)

2. The degree of task structuring is thought to bear directly on role-occupant performance and satisfaction. Yet the research results of House, Filley, and their associates suggest that certain functional groups, such as engineers, may desire structuring to clarify relationships. In what way would one introduce the notions and models of motivation from Chapter 8 (e.g., Herzberg) to shed light on this question?

LEADERSHIP EXERCISES

1. Compare and contrast the leadership approaches for the following situation, based on the research performed at or by (a) the University of Michigan, (b) Ohio State University, (c) general contingency, (d) Fiedler. Indicate any necessary assumptions.

Situation: Manufacturing firm
Facts: Processor of canned and frozen vegetables
Older, mass production-type plant located in California
Low morale and lackluster performance
Plant manager tends to dominate his reporting staff
Focus: 1) The general management group
2) Worker groups

Organization:

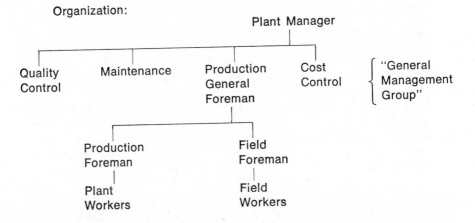

2. Analyze the leadership approaches for the following situation, based on the research on general contingency approaches.
Situation: Manufacturing firm
Facts: Processor of canned and frozen vegetables
Low morale and lackluster performance
Focus: 1) Group A (management)
2) Group B (production organization)

Organization:

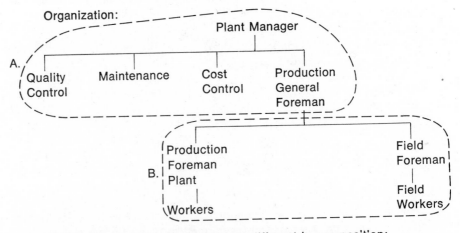

Note that groups A and B are quite different in composition:
A is concerned with overall plant management matters;
B is concerned directly with performance.

NOTES

1. Major problems of measurement and the pacing of theory and measurement developments are proposed by Abraham Korman in "Overview Paper," in J. G. Hunt (ed.), *Proceedings of the Symposium on Contemporary Developments in the Study of Leadership* (Carbondale, Ill.: Department of Management Science, Southern Illinois University, 1973).

2. For some excellent summaries of the current state of the art and new research directions, see J. G. Hunt and J. W. Hill, *Improving Mental Hospital Effectiveness: A Look at Managerial Leadership,* Technical Report 71-4 (Carbondale, Ill.: Department of Administrative Sciences, Southern Illinois University, 1971); proceedings and papers in Hunt, *Symposium on Contemporary Developments in the Study of Leadership* (1971 and 1973); Steven Kerr, Chester A. Schriesheim, Charles J. Murphy, and Ralph M. Stogdill, "Towards a Contingency Theory of Leadership Based on the Consideration and Initiating Structure Literature," College of Administrative Science working papers, Ohio State University (1973); Fred E. Fiedler, "The Effects of Leadership Training and Experience: A Contingency Model Interpretation," *Administrative Science Quarterly,* 17, no. 2 (December 1972): 453–470; and Robert J. House, "A Path Goal Theory of Leader Effectiveness," *Administrative Science Quarterly,* 16, no. 3 (September 1971): 321–338.

3. For a discussion of the relevance and background for trait approaches, see J. Owens, "Use of Leadership Theory," *Michigan Business Review,* 25, no. 1 (January 1973): 13–19. For a good discussion of early research in this area, see Ralph M. Stogdill, "Personal Factors Associated with Leadership," *Journal of Psychology,* 47 (1950): 1–14.

4. Contingency approaches in management received great prominence recently; for example, see Fred Luthans, "Contingency Theory of Management," *Business Horizons,* 16, no. 4 (June 1973): 67–73. However, the attempt of researchers to isolate critical situational factors goes back a number of years; for example, see John K. Hemphill, *Situation Factors in Leadership* (Columbus: Personnel Research Board, Ohio State University, 1949).

5. Edgar H. Schein, *Organizational Psychology* (Englewood Cliffs, N.J.: Prentice-Hall, 1965).

6. Dorwin Cartwright and Alvin Zander, *Group Dynamics* (2d ed.; Evanston, Ill.: Row, Peterson, 1960), p. 492.

7. Floyd Mann, *Toward an Understanding of the Leadership Role in Formal Organizations* (Ann Arbor: Survey Research Center, University of Michigan, 1962).

8. Some of these points are supplied by Robert B. Kahn and David L. Katz in "Leadership Practices in Relation to Productivity and Morale," in Cartwright and Zander, *Group Dynamics,* pp. 602–627.

9. Elmer H. Burack, "Technology and Supervisory Practices: A Preliminary View," *Human Organizations,* 26, no. 4 (Winter 1967): 256–264, and "Technology and Industrial Supervision: A Model Building Approach," *Academy of Management Journal,* 9, no. 1 (March 1966).

10. Fred E. Fiedler, *A Theory of Leadership Effectiveness* (New York: McGraw-Hill, 1967).

11. Ibid.

12. J. A. Dawson, L. A. Messe, and J. L. Phillips, "Effect of Instructor-Leader Behavior on Student Performance," *Journal of Applied Psychology,* 56 (1972): 369–376.

13. In the bureaucratic model of Chapter 2, authority was conceived as downward acting and strictly a structural phenomenon. The "acceptance" concept of authority admits the possibility of either downward- or upward-acting leadership. The "acceptance theory" is commonly attributed to Chester I. Barnard and Herbert A. Simon [and his *Administrative Behavior* (New York: Macmillan, 1957)].

14. Important elements of this work are described by Edwin A. Fleishman in "Twenty Years of Consideration and Structure," S.I.U. Symposium paper (1971). Central features of this approach by Fleishman are described in his much earlier *Leadership Climate and Supervisory Behavior* (Columbus: Personnel Research Board, Ohio State University, 1951).

15. Rensis Likert describes and applies key notions of this research in *The Effective Organization* (New York: McGraw-Hill, 1967) and *New Patterns of Management* (New York: McGraw-Hill, 1961).

16. See Luthans, "Contingency Theory of Management," for a description of recent contingency approaches.

17. Fiedler, "The Effects of Leadership Training and Experience," pp. 453–470.

18. Summarized in Likert, *New Patterns of Management.* These findings have been placed in a more coherent form for application in Likert, *The Effective Organization.*

19. An interesting description of a company application is "When Workers Manage Themselves," *Business Week,* March 20, 1965, pp. 93–94.

20. Aspects of this are pointed up in Fiedler, *A Theory of Leadership Effectiveness* and "Effects of Leadership Training and Experiences."

21. Much of the early work is summarized in Ralph M. Stogdill, *Manual for Job Description and Job Expectation Questionnaire* (Columbus: Bureau of Business Research, Ohio State University, 1960), Ralph M. Stogdill and A. C. Coons, *Leader Behavior: Its Description and Measurement* (Monograph 88) (Columbus: Bureau of Education Research, Ohio State University, 1957), and Ralph M. Stogdill and C. L. Shartle, *Methods in the Study of Administrative Leadership* (Columbus: Bureau of Business Research, Ohio State University, 1955).

22. For an excellent discussion of some of the effects of the posture and approach of higher authority figures on the "leader," see Hunt and Hill, *Improving Mental Hospital Effectiveness.*

23. K. E. Thurley and A. Hamblin, *The Supervisor and His Job* (London: Her Majesty's Stationery Service, 1963).

24. Edwin A. Fleishman and E. F. Harris, "Patterns of Leadership Behavior Related to Employee Grievances and Turnover," *Personnel Psychology,* 15, no. 1 (1962): 43–50.

25. Alan Filley, Steven Kerr, and Robert House, "Satisfaction of R&D Personnel," paper presented at the annual meeting of the Midwest Division of the Academy of Management, Michigan State University, April 1970; and Robert J. House, Alan C. Filley, and Steven Kerr, "Relation of Leader Consideration and Initiating Structure to R&D Subordinates' Satisfaction," *Administrative Science Quarterly,* 16, no. 1 (June 1971): 19–30.

26. Suggestive of these studies is one by Bernard P. Indik, Stanley E. Seashore, and Basil A. Georgopoulos: "Relationship among Criteria of Job Performance," *Jour-*

nal of Applied Psychology, 44, no. 3 (1960): 195–202. For an approach balancing structuring and consideration-type ideas as a team-building strategy, see Robert R. Blake and Jane S. Mouton, *The Managerial Grid* (Houston: Gulf Publishing Co., 1964).

27. R. M. Stogdill, private communication, Spring 1970.

28. Adapted from Stogdill, *Manual.*

29. Ibid. p. 48.

30. D. G. Bowers and Stanley Seashore, "Predicting Organizational Effectiveness with a Four Factor Theory of Leadership," *Administrative Science Quarterly*, 11, no. 2 (March 1966): 238–263.

31. Filley, Kerr, and House, "Satisfaction of R&D Personnel," pp. 7–8.

32. Also supported by J. G. Hunt and J. W. Hill in *Improving Mental Hospital Effectiveness* and R. C. Cummings in "Leader-Member Relations as a Moderator of the Effects of Leader Behavior and Attitude," *Personnel Psychology*, 25 (1972): 655–660.

33. Filley, Kerr, and House, "Satisfaction of R&D Personnel," p. 17.

34. Ibid., p. 17.

35. For example, H. Baumgartel, "Leadership Style as a Variable in Research Administration," *Administrative Science Quarterly*, 2 (1957): 344–360, and Alan C. Filley and A. J. Grimes, "The Basis of Power in Decision Processes," *Annual Proceedings of the Academy of Management*, December 1967.

36. Starting with the early work of Alvin Gouldner ("Cosmopolitans" and "Locals") and proceeding to more recent studies of engineers and scientists in industry. Some of this literature is reviewed in the author's "Managerial Obsolescence," *California Management Review*, 16, no. 2 (Winter 1973).

37. Robert J. House, "Some New Applications and Tests of the Path-Goal Theory of Leadership" (1972), a working paper.

38. For some excellent insights into newer avenues of research considering these variables, see Edwin A. Fleishman, "Twenty Years of Consideration and Structure," in S.I.U. Symposium papers (1971).

39. Victor H. Vroom, *Work and Motivation* (New York: John Wiley & Sons, 1964), pp. 94–174.

40. Ibid.

41. See John R. Hinrichs, "Creativity in Industrial Research," *Industrial Management*, 7, no. 1 (January 1965): 3, and part 2 in 7, no. 2 (February 1965): 11–15. This material appeared originally as part of a management report for the Amercian Management Association.

42. For an excellent discussion relating the "consideration" and "structure" constructs to situational approaches, see Kerr et al., Chester Schriesheim, Charles Murphy, and Ralph M. Stogdill, "Towards a Contingency Theory of Leadership," and Fleishman, "Twenty Years of Consideration."

43. For a consolidation of various contingency discussions, see the 1971 and 1973 S.I.U. Symposium papers.

44. At times, subtle distinctions are implied in the use of terms such as situational analysis vis-à-vis contingency approaches. These terms have been used interchangeably for the purposes of our discussions. For example, the personality of individual participants is considered part of the "situation"—no attempt is made to set psychological variables (for example) outside the impersonal elements of the situation. More advanced treatments may seek to draw distinctions between "situational" and "contingency" along some of these lines.

45. Robert Tannenbaum and W. Schmidt, "How to Choose a Leadership Pattern: Reanalyzed,". *Harvard Business Review,* 51, no. 3 (May 1973): 162–164.

46. Ibid.

47. Shifts in work scene and worker expectation are described in the *Work in America* report, prepared by the Upjohn Institute, for the Department of Health, Education, and Welfare (Cambridge, Mass.: M.I.T. Press, 1973).

48. An excellent discussion of the earlier Fiedler findings and formulation is provided by Joe Kelly in *Organizational Behavior* (Homewood, Ill.: Richard D. Irwin, 1969). For a study providing added support to structural characteristics and situational factors affecting leadership orientation, see Robert D. Rossel, "Required Labor Commitment, Organizational Adaptation and Leadership Orientation," *Administrative Science Quarterly,* 16, no. 3 (September 1971): 316–320.

49. The principal ideas of Fiedler's research and concepts are found in several of his writings: "Theory of Leader Effectiveness" and "Engineer the Job to Fit the Man," *Harvard Business Review,* 47, no. 5 (September–October 1965): 115–123. Also, several writings suggest some newer directions in the Fiedler theoretical formulation, research, and application: "Effects of Leadership Training" (1972), a new publication with Scott, Foresman (1973), and "Leadership," a paper presented at the S.I.U. Symposium (1973). Leadership studies of Fiedler were developed under the Office of Naval Research, contracts 170–106, N6–ORI–07135, and NR177–472, NONR-1834 (Champaign: University of Illinois Press, 1965).

50. Kelly, *Organizational Behavior,* p. 127.

51. Fiedler, "Engineer the Job to Fit the Man."

52. Ibid.

53. Kelly, *Organizational Behavior.*

54. Ibid.

55. Fiedler, "Engineer the Job to Fit the Man."

56. Fiedler, "Leadership Training."

57. Fiedler, "The Effects of Leadership."

58. Ibid., p. 453.

59. George Graen, J. B. Orris, and K. M. Alvares, "Contingency Model of Leadership Effectiveness: Some Experimental Results," *Journal of Applied Psychology,* 55 (1971): 196–201.

60. Terrence R. Mitchell, Anthony Biglun, Gerald R. Oncken, and Fred E. Fiedler, "The Contingency Model: Criticisms and Suggestions," *Academy of Management Journal,* 13 (1970): 253–267.

61. M. Mulder and A. Stemerding, "Threat, Attraction to Group and Need for Strong Leadership: A Laboratory Experiment in a Natural Setting," *Human Relations,* 16 (1963): 317–334, and H. Oaklander and Edwin A. Fleishman, "Patterns of Leadership Related to Organizational Stress in Hospital Settings," *Administrative Science Quarterly,* 8, no. 4 (March 1964): 520–532.

62. Fred E. Fiedler, *A Theory of Leadership Effectiveness.*

63. John R. Rizzo, Robert J. House, and Sidney E. Lertzman, "Role Conflict and Ambiguity in Complex Organizations," *Administrative Science Quarterly,* 15 (1970): 150–153.

64. Fleishman, "Patterns of Leadership," p. 26.

65. Elmer H. Burack, "Technology and Supervisory Practice," *Human Organizations* (1966). This theme is part of the general technology portrayed in Chapters 3 and 4.

66. Fiedler, *A Theory of Leadership Effectiveness.*

67. J. K. Hemphill, "Relations between the Size of the Group and the Behavior of Superior Leaders," *Journal of Abnormal and Social Psychology,* 32 (1950): 11–22.

68. "Path-Goal Theory."

69. Developed more specifically in path-goal terminology in House, "Path-Goal Theory," p. 323.

70. Many propositions related to the Ohio State University constructs of consideration and initiating structure are presented in Fleishman, "Twenty Years of Consideration."

71. Some insights into the impact of role ambiguity are suggested in Rizzo, House, and Lertzman, "Role Conflict and Ambiguity."

72. Elmer H. Burack and Thomas J. Calero, "Effect of the Supervisor on Employee Upward Mobility," in Elmer H. Burack and James W. Walker, *Manpower Planning and Programming* (Boston: Allyn & Bacon, 1972).

73. Recent works incorporating some of these points include Richard Hall, *Organizations: Structure and Process* (Englewood Cliffs, N.J.: Prentice-Hall, 1972), esp. p. 268; T. Von de Embse and George Normen, "Six Propositions for Managerial Leadership," *Business Horizons,* 14, no. 2 (December 1971): 33–43; F. Heller, "Leadership, Decision Making and Contingency Theory," *Industrial Relations,* 12, no. 2 (May 1973): 183–199; Chris Argyris, "CEO's Behavior: Key to Organization Development," *Harvard Business Review,* 51, no. 2 (March 1973): 55–64; and Robert House and Gary Dessler, "The Path-Goal Theory of Leadership: Some Post Hoc and A Priori Tests," in *Proceedings* of the 1973 symposium.

REFERENCES

Beer, M. *Leadership, Employee Needs, and Motivation.* Columbus: Bureau of Business Research, Ohio State University, Monograph 129, 1966.

Babbitt, H. R., et al. *Organizational Behavior: Understanding and Prediction.* Englewood Cliffs, N.J.: Prentice-Hall, 1974.

Blake, Robert R., and Jane S. Mouton. *The Managerial Grid.* Houston: Gulf Publishing Co., 1964.

Blau, P., and R. W. Scott. *Formal Organization.* San Francisco: Chandler Publishing Co., 1962, pp. 140–194.

Bowers, D. G., and S. E. Seashore. "Predicting Organizational Effectiveness with a Four-Factor Theory of Leadership." *Administrative Science Quarterly,* 11, no. 2 (September 1966): 238–263.

Coch, L., and J. R. F. French. "Overcoming Resistance to Change." *Human Relations,* 1, no. 4 (1948): 512–532.

Cummins, R. D. "Leader-Member Relations as a Moderator of Leader Behavior and Attitude." *Personnel Psychology,* 25, no. 4 (1972): 655–660.

Dawson, J. A., L. A. Messe, and J. L. Phillips. "Effect of Instructor-Leader Behavior on Student Performance." *Journal of Applied Psychology,* 56 (1972): 369–376.

Day, Robert C., and Robert L. Hamblin. "Some Effects of Close and Punitive Styles of Supervision." *American Journal of Sociology,* 69, no. 5 (March 1964): 499–510.

Dessler, Gary, and Robert J. House. "A Test of a Path-Goal Motivational Theory of Leadership." *Proceedings of the Annual Meeting of the Academy of Management,* 1972.

Doyle, Wayne J. "Effects of Achieved Status of Leader on Productivity of Groups." *Administrative Science Quarterly,* 16, no. 1 (March 1971): 40–50.

Evans, Martin C. "Leadership and Motivation: A Core Concept." *Academy of Management Journal,* 13, no. 1 (March 1970): 91–102.

Fiedler, Fred. "Engineer the Job to Fit the Man." *Harvard Business Review,* 43, no. 5 (September–October 1965): 115–122.

―――. *A Theory of Leadership Effectiveness.* New York: McGraw-Hill, 1967.

Fleishman, Edwin A. "Twenty Years of Consideration and Structure" in *Symposium on Contemporary Development in the Study of Leadership.* Carbondale, Ill., School of Administrative Science, Southern Illinois University, 1971.

―――― and J. Simmons. "Relationship between Leadership Patterns and Effectiveness Ratings among Israeli Foremen." *Personnel Psychology,* 23, no. 1 (1970): 169–172.

Golembiewski, Robert, and S. B. Carrigan. "Planned Change in Organization Style Based on Laboratory Approach." *Administrative Science Quarterly,* 15, no. 1 (March 1970): 79.

Graen, G., F. Danserau, and T. Minami. "An Empirical Test of the Man-in-the-Middle Hypothesis among Executives in an Hierarchical Organization Employing a Unit-Set Analysis." *Organizational Behavior and Human Performance,* 8 (1972): 262–285.

Grenier, Larry E. "What Managers Think of Participative Leadership." *Harvard Business Review,* 51, no. 2 (March–April 1973): 111–118.

Herold, D. M. "Leader's Hierarchical Influence and Subordinates' Influence as Moderators of Considerate Leadership Style," in John W. Slocum (ed.), *Research in Organizations.* Proceedings of the Ninth Annual Conference of the Eastern Academy of Management, 1972.

Hill, J. W., and J. G. Hunt. "Managerial Level, Leadership and Employee Need Satisfaction," in *Symposium on Contemporary Development in the Study of Leadership.* Carbondale, Ill.: College of Administrative Science, Southern Illinois University, 1971.

House, Robert J. "A Path-Goal Theory of Leader Effectiveness." *Administrative Science Quarterly,* 16, no. 3 (September 1971): 321–340.

———— and Steven Kerr. "Organizational Independence, Leader Behavior, and Managerial Practices: A Replicated Study." *Journal of Applied Psychology* (1973), in process.

House, Robert J., Alan C. Filley, and Steven Kerr. "Relation of Leader Consideration and Initiating Structure to R&D Subordinates' Satisfaction." *Administrative Science Quarterly,* 16, no. 1 (March 1971): 19–30.

————, Alan C. Filley, and D. N. Gujarati. "Leadership Style, Hierarchical Influence, and the Satisfaction of Subordinate Role Expectations: A Test of Likert's Influence Proposition." *Journal of Applied Psychology, 55,* no. 3 (1971): 422–432.

Hunt, Jerry G. "Leadership-Style Effects at Two Managerial Levels in a Simulated Organization." *Administrative Science Quarterly,* 16, no. 4 (December 1971):476–485.

———— (ed.). *Proceedings of the Symposium on Leadership* 1973). Carbondale, Ill.: School of Administrative Sciences, Southern Illinois University, in process.

———— and J. W. Hill. *Improving Mental Hospital Effectiveness: A Look at Managerial Leadership.* Carbondale, Ill.: School of Administrative Science, Southern Illinois University, 1971.

————, and V. K. C. Liebscher. "Leadership Preference, Leadership Behavior, and Employee Satisfaction." *Organizational Behavior and Human Performance,* 9, no. 1 (1973): 59–77.

Jones, Halsey R., and Michael Johnson. "LPC as a Modifier of Leader-Follower Relationship." *Academy of Management Journal,* 15, no. 2 (June 1972): 185–196.

Kavanagh, M. J. "Leadership Behavior as a Function of Subordinate Competence and Task Complexity." *Administrative Science Quarterly,* 17, no. 4 (March 1972).

Kerr, Steven, Chester A. Schriesheim, Charles J. Murphy, and Ralph M. Stogdill. "Toward a Contingency Theory of Leadership Based upon the Consideration and Initiating Structure Literature." Columbus: College of Administrative Science, Ohio State University, 1973 (working papers).

Korman, Abraham. "Consideration, Initiating Structure, and Organizational Criteria— a Review." *Personnel Psychology,* 19, no. 4 (Winter 1966): 349–362.

Lieberson, Stanley, and James O. O'Connor. "Leadership and Organizational Performance: A Study of Large Corporations." *American Sociological Review,* 37, no. 2 (April 1972): 117–130.

Likert, Rensis. *New Patterns in Management.* New York: McGraw-Hill, 1961.

————. *The Human Organization.* New York: McGraw-Hill, 1967.

McGregor, Douglas. *Human Side of Enterprise.* New York: McGraw-Hill, 1960.

Negandhi, Anant R. "Conflict and Power in Complex Organizations." *Quarterly Journal of Management Development,* 3, no. 2 (June 1972): 5–9.

Pelz, D. "Influence: A Key to Effective Leadership in the First-Line Supervisor." *Personnel,* 29, no. 3 (November 1952): 209–217.

Rizzo, John R., Robert J. House, and S. E. Lirtzman. "Role Conflict and Ambiguity in Complex Organizations." *Administrative Science Quarterly,* 15 (1970): 150–163.

Rossel, Robert D. "Instrumental and Expensive Leadership in Complex Organization." *Administrative Science Quarterly,* 15, no. 3 (September 1970): 306–316.

Sales, Stephen M. "Supervisory Style and Productivity: Review and Theory." *Personnel Psychology,* 19, no. 3 (Autumn 1966): 275–286.

Skinner, E. W. "Relationships between Leader Behavior Patterns and Organizational-Situational Variables." *Personnel Psychology,* 22 (1969): 489-494.

Soliman, Hanify, R. I. Hartman, and A. H. Olinger. "Leadership Style under Conditions of High and Low Knowledge." in *Proceedings of the Fifteenth Annual Midwest Division Academy of Management Conference.* South Bend, Ind.: Notre Dame University, 1972.

Steinmetz, Lawrence L., and Charles D. Greenidge. "Realities That Shape Managerial Style." *Business Horizons,* 13, no. 5 (October 1970): 23–32.

Stogdill, Ralph M. *Managers, Employees, Organizations.* Columbus: Ohio State University Bureau of Business Research, 1965.

Strauss, George. "Some Notes on Power-Equalization," in H. Leavitt (ed.), *The Social Science of Organizations: Four Perspectives.* Englewood Cliffs, N.J.: Prentice-Hall, 1963, pp. 41–84.

Symposium on Contemporary Development in the Study of Leadership. Carbondale, Ill.: School of Administrative Science, Southern Illinois University, 1971.

Yukl, G. "Toward a Behavioral Theory of Leadership." *Organizational Behavior and Human Performance,* 6 (1971): 414–440.

Learning Objectives

Meaning and Elaboration of Role Concept Propositions
Social Considerations and Technology in the Taking of Roles
Perspective and Views on Role Performance
Defining Organizational Efficiency Based on Social Performance
Dynamics of Small Groups
Bases for Interrelating Formal and Social System Requirements

Chapter **10**

SOCIAL BASIS OF WORK SYSTEMS

OVERVIEW

The emphasis on systems, begun in Part I, will be continued in this chapter, but the focus will be on the human rather than the technological dimensions of work. The central ideas in this chapter are: How does organizational diversity influence the formation of social systems? To what extent does the principal work activity in the organization affect the character of the personnel system? To what extent does the social system move beyond rules, procedures, and policy and assume its own form?

We will probe the influence of the work activity on the social system in settings that range from the highly structured production technology of manufacturing to the loosely structured hospital unit. The analysis includes task groups with end products ranging from those that are tangible to ideas—with groups *within* a technology (mass production lines), those that *interface* with a technology (production monitoring or quality control), and groups whose work is largely predicated on professional expertise, as in hospitals, research, production control, and industrial engineering.

ROLE

A role consists of one or more recurrent activities out of a total pattern of interdependent activities which in combination produce the organizational output.[1]

This view of role conveys the critical ideas of *systems* (interdependent activities, *function* (one or more activities), and *structure* (recurrent and patterned activities). The concept of "output," as it is used here, in no way restricts consideration of the character of the unit, organization, or institution being studied (manufacturing firm or government agency), although it should be understood that the main concern is with formal organizations.

The concepts of "structure" and "function" as they relate to role warrant some elaboration.[2] Structure implies hierarchy; consequently, roles not only involve work relationships but also regular offices (commonly a set of activities) that make up the structure. Furthermore, the work activities of the offices are logically related, and reflect their level in the hierarchy and their objectives.

The activity sets that comprise organization roles may be described in terms of their members, diversity, and complexity. Single activities may define some functional roles (repetitive, single-element work on a production assembly line, for instance) while others, depending on their location in the system, combine multiple and often diverse elements.

Thus the composition of the activity set discloses the following:

    a. Degree of division of labor. The narrower the span of activities, the greater the fractionation of the work task.

    b. Diversity of work demands. This is reflected in both the number and functional differences of the activity sets.

    c. Level of specialization. Considerable insight can be gained as to the degree of structured knowledge that is encompassed in the role through examination of the activity sets.

    d. Work relationships. The logic of work flow technology (Chapters 3 and 4) is embodied in the activity sets (and roles) comprising a work sequence (as on a production line) or work dependencies (as in an operating room).

Once the activity sets for roles are defined, the basis is established for a wide variety of organizational analyses, such as

    1. Establishing education and training requirements for particular offices/jobs (Part III)

    2. Identifying roles that evidence little in motivationally satisfying elements—roles that are overprescribed, highly routine, or call on few of the role occupant's skills (Chapter 8)

    3. Establishing a basis for communication needs between work-related roles (Chapter 6)

OTHER ROLE DESCRIPTORS AND FEATURES

The relation of organization roles to one another is more fully understood in the light of three notions: cohesion, status, and interaction. *Cohesion* suggests social linkages and reflects the attractiveness of a group (set of roles) for its members. *Status* suggests the esteem with which an individual is viewed by a group (role set), or one group by other groups, or an individual by others in society. *Interaction* defines relationships between role occupants in quantitative terms (e.g., direction of interaction) and qualitative terms (e.g., leader-follower relationships). A "process perspective" flows naturally out of these considerations.

The demands of a work system require the definition of formal roles and primary face-to-face interaction. These lead to secondary relationships with colleagues, specialists, and others who support the primary activities; and physical proximity or work activity leads to informal, social relationships.

Another aspect of the role perspective is the sensitivity of role occupants to changing situational demands. In other words, to what extent does the outlook of role occupants change as their job situation or environmental demands change? There is research describing such attitudinal changes over time,[3] and the results are interesting because they suggest flexibility in human attitudes not clearly understood or actively employed in management strategies for "change management" and "career planning." As noted in Exhibit 10–1, men promoted into supervisory or union steward positions take on the attitudinal sets important for these jobs. With the passage of time, the attitudes appropriate to these positions further solidify, but the attitudes of men who returned to the bargaining table generally reverted to those held at the time 0, before any promotions had taken place.

In the situations described, there is a suggestion that job needs can temper the outlook of role occupants, but one might reasonably wonder about the possibilities for change among higher management levels or other types of occupational groups. Also, to what extent were some of the attitudes (in the union situation) an inherent part of the personality of the men committed to certain career paths, so that a self-fulfilling interest/capability was being realized?

Role performance can be viewed at the margin as that level of activity which is just adequate for carrying out the organization's work mission. This being the case, an important objective of management is to raise organization performance beyond role needs. The topics of leadership (Chapter 9), training and development (Chapter 12), and motivation (Chapter 8) all pertain to structuring a favorable climate for increasing individual contributions to goal achievement. In addition, higher levels of role performance lead to a higher level of individual satisfaction, derived from a sense of greater accomplishment. This is especially true where performance results from a better understanding of one's part in complex organizational functions and a greater expression of individual imagination and creativity.[4]

In order to complete this initial discussion of "role" we need to bring together some of the ideas expressed in the previous discussion in the form of propositions and a conceptual model. The propositions capitalize on the role perspective, and provide a vehicle for reviewing a number of important organizational topics.

EXHIBIT 10-1. Role Requirements and the Outlook of Role Occupants

Time period	Characteristic descriptions*	
	Future foreman	*Future steward*
0	More ambitious and critical More discriminating in loyalty	Same
1 (Promotion)	Develops more favorable attitude toward company as place to work, toward top management, and toward principle of incentive pay	Develops favorable attitudes toward union, toward top union officers, and toward seniority principle (vis-à-vis "ability")
2	Further crystallization of attitudes	
3†		

* Relative to nonpromotables.

† Men who return to bargaining unit assume outlook similar to that of time 0.

This table summarizes research data from S. Lieberman, "The Effects of Changes in Roles on the Attitudes of Role Occupants," *Human Relations*, 9 (1956): 385–402.

1. Motivation and satisfaction

    a. The greater the diversity of activities in a role, the higher the personal (job related) satisfaction—provided that ambiguities are not created and diversity does not overload individual competence.

    b. Values that could be satisfied through surface-level job attention are exceeded by work-derived values (e.g., stimulating socializing on an assembly line compared to work).

    c. The higher the level of activity programming within a role, the less opportunity to develop personal abilities and satisfy personal needs.

2. Social system development

    a. The more the technology of work places role performers near one another, the greater the opportunity for establishing social bonds.

    b. The greater the similarity of role performers in such factors as interests and ideas, the higher the likelihood of establishing enduring social relationships.

3. Structure

    a. The greater the number of activities assigned to each role, or the greater the number of roles taken on by an individual, the less need for coordinative action by "external" agents or specialists.

The discussion and propositions described in this section suggest that carrying out role assignments is more than a simple linear process; rather, it becomes a dynamic elaboration of relationships over time, with the rationalization of secondary relationships and the structuring of a social system (see Exhibit 10–2). Exhibit 10–2 shows that role is dynamic, and amplifies itself beyond its formal structures. At the same time, secondary relationships typically emerge to support the attainment of objectives through the primary work tasks. Finally, the integration of role occupants into the cohesive units of a social system is a natural result of acting out individual work roles.

Friendship and Task-oriented Groups in the Organization[5]

Friendship and interest groups emerge from the formal organization structure and the technological system. In the perspective of the formal organiza-

EXHIBIT 10–2. Role Performance, Work, and Social Systems

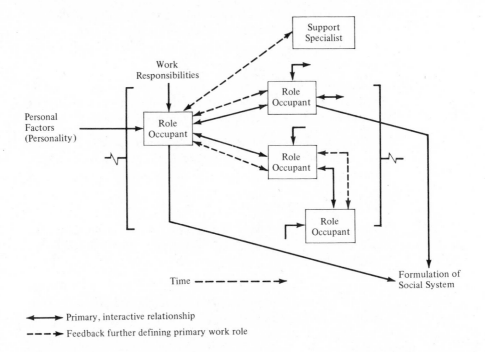

Primary, interactive relationship
Feedback further defining primary work role

tion, groups of superiors and subordinates constitute interlinked blocs for the accomplishment of the formal purposes of the organization. A second important grouping is based on friendships or common interests, which may emerge from similar job experiences in the past or from age, family features, and community activities.

A third and important group is largely defined by the characteristics of the work technology, which include location of process controls and work stations, type of material handling, and pace of work activities.

Several questions emerge here:

1. To what extent may friendship or interest groups influence work methods, performance standards, and productivity?

2. Should work structures be designed to permit the emergence of informal structures and leadership within the technological framework? If so, will these approaches be limited by particular kinds of task/technological structures?

3. Under what conditions may the effects of informal groups run contrary to organization goals?

A MODEL FOR TECHNOLOGICAL-BEHAVIORAL ANALYSIS [6]

The organization can be seen as a patterned system of group activities ("role set") having an "external" system and an "internal" system. The external system of work-related group activity is largely determined by the technological environment, in the sense that work brings about a *necessary conformity* in order to maintain continuity and acceptable levels of performance. On the other hand, the internal system of group activity represents behavior *beyond* that prescribed by the environment (i.e., the work system, policy, rules, etc.) and parallels the social system of the organization—it emerges from the external system. This approach introduces three concepts of individual or group behavior: (a) sentiments (motives, attitudes, feelings), (b) activities (functions dictated by work or environment) and (c) interactions (the action of an individual or group and the response from another). Details of the model are summarized in Exhibit 10–3.

The dynamics of the relationships between the "external" and "internal" systems become more apparent in Exhibit 10–4. The external system of prescribed activity does not alone determine behavior. The interactive character of relationships between key components of the model is a striking feature of this exhibit, which suggests that the internal social system exerts pressure on management (5 to 4). For example, a philosophy of management (2B) that leads to high absenteeism, minimal performance, or unimaginative work might well be subject to review in the face of pressures from the social system. A second example is work systems that have unattractive features. Rising employee expectations and growing employment opportunities force the reconditioning, improvement, or replacement of unacceptable facilities, economic efficiency notwithstanding. Thus the "internal" system (5) has a dual role: (a) fostering its own patterns of relationships and behavior and (b) exerting significant pressure on supervisory, managerial, and professional support personnel.

COMMUNICATION

The communications system assumes a crucial part in role development. It is an indispensable vehicle for transmitting a wide range of formal and informal notions, ideas, values, sanctions, and directions. The transmission of policy, rules, and procedures or supervisory directives utilizes a variety of oral and written media. In the social organization, the communication of friendships, likes, and dislikes is a primary means by which elaboration of the social system takes place.

The part played by communications in role development represents a further elaboration of concepts introduced in Chapter 6 on communications and data-computer ideas in Chapter 7. The range of communication situa-

EXHIBIT 10-3. A Model of Organizational Analysis: Group Behavior I (after Homans)

Perspective	Contextual variables	Key elements		
		Activities	Interactions	Sentiments
External system: technical and physical Group activity based on work	Work technology, equipment and tools Impersonal rules and regulations Hours of work Work conditions Management philosophy, job definition, payment methods, personnel policy Union, comunity groups, and family	Physical motions, line pace Conformity Physical presence Rest periods, movements, distance Volume of work Job content Product movements Safety practices	Team work, progressive manufacturing Participation in meetings Structuring of responsibilities Problem-solving groups Task force study groups Specialization and division of work	Attitudes based on family, community, and friends Early work experience Influence of former associates Habits, drives, and motives derived from culture or related to heredity Notion of value of work, money, etc.
Internal system: adaptive behavior Social systems	Conformity to minimal environmental requirements	Pleasure, security, and fun* Expressing feelings and likings Communications provide key linkage—verbal, signs, motions Frequency, duration, and order	Social relations Friendship groups	Drives, emotions, feelings, and attitudes

* Jointly views activities and interactions.

This table summarizes some of the key points from the analyses of George Homans, *The Human Group* (New York: Harcourt Brace Jovanovich, 1950).

EXHIBIT 10–4. A Model for Organizational Analysis: Group Behavior II (after Homans)

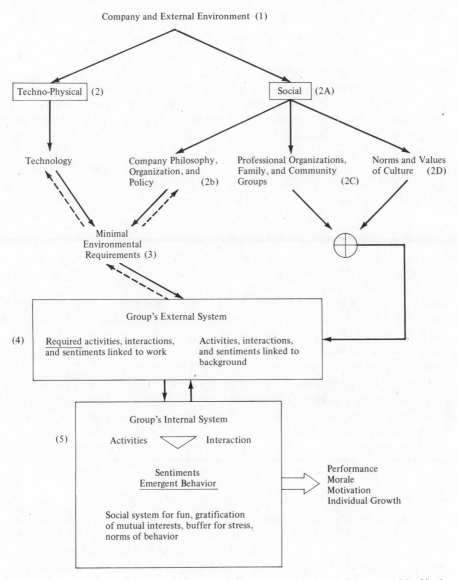

See Homans, *The Human Group* (New York: Harcourt, 1950) and material prepared by North-western University School of Business (Hp 215, 216).

tions extends from face-to-face communications in social and formal groups to systems with mechanistic or electronic modes for transmitting information and data. The interpersonal and impersonal modes of communications shape the roles of organizational participants. Various ideas expressed in Chapters 6, 7, and 10 suggest the factors of participants, situation, and purpose with which design strategies are concerned.

TECHNOLOGICAL CONSTRAINTS ON SOCIAL ORGANIZATION

Technology may be highly permissive or constraining vis-à-vis the social structure. In "unit" (craft level) production systems the small volume of production, the general-purpose equipment, the nonroutine character of work, and the semi-independence of work stations permit movement and personal relationships beyond those possible on a mass assembly line. In more advanced technical systems, the wide dispersion of work stations in continuous production units or the concentration of a small number of personnel in control centers limits interactions. In the absence of necessary work interactions, advanced systems pose a challenge for supervisors in supporting social relationships between isolated positions.

ANALYSIS OF INTERACTION

The structuring of both formal and informal social relationships among managers, supervisors, workers, and groups is reflected in their activities and patterns of interaction. Hand movements, voice tones, body language, and facial expressions can be catalogued, timed, and used as a basis for mapping out work ("sociograms") or social structures. In work situations, knowing the character of the technology and the formal authority/working relationships permits analysis of individual and group performance, which can be used as a basis for planning changes to improve performance.

Traditional industrial engineering practices confined this type of scrutiny to work methods analysis for performance improvement. Modern studies examine a much wider range of variables that link individuals in work-related activities (a representative group of studies is provided at the end of the chapter).

THE SOCIAL SYSTEM: A BEHAVIORAL PERSPECTIVE

In this section we examine the manner in which institutional factors shape the character and needs of the social or "internal" system. In Exhibit 10–5 the character of the institution (1) greatly affects the features of the work activity (2), as well as the extent to which technology and/or professional expertise (3) will influence output features (6).

For example, in advanced process systems the engineering of the production system largely determines performance features of both quantity and quality; in low-level technologies, human effort largely defines output features. Here the social structuring of work-based groups affects quantity and quality. For example, in the growing service sector of the U.S. economy, institutions such as hospitals, insurance companies, and banks exhibit *high* performance when high levels of social efficiency (relationships between

EXHIBIT 10–5. Institutional Performance and Character of the Social System

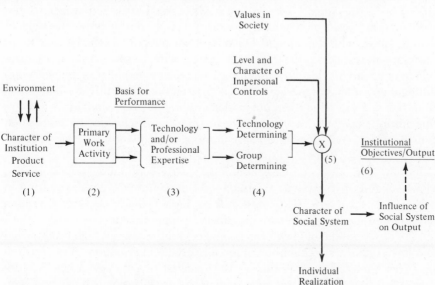

people, individual morale, and motivation, for example) are realized.

Social structures also influence the individual's sense of satisfaction, belonging, and self-actualization (1). Where work function and institutional features require clusters of semiprofessional and professional personnel, social structuring along "collegial lines" would be expected. "Natural lines" of social system development may lead to structures that support *formal* relationships and communicate along hierarchical lines. This formalization minimizes interactions across departmental lines or the penetration of strongly entrenched groups based on formal authority or professional status. The management of an institution might be charged with meddling or manipulation in seeking to modify formal-informal relationships and social ties. Where the work technology brings frustrations and uncertainties for the human participants in the system, bettering the lot of the personnel may be a sound rationale for management's efforts. However, other institutional and work-related situations are not as clear cut.

THE PROFESSIONAL AND ORGANIZATION COMMITMENT

With the growth of our knowledge of "professional," an important occupational classification, it has become clear that such simple descriptive terms really represent complex combinations of notions. For example, men with engineering training and those trained in the natural sciences (chemistry, physics, mathematics) are often lumped together in a category termed "scientist" or "professional." Yet motivational, occupational, and career studies indicate that these roles should be more precisely described in the light of demographic, educational, and behavioral specifics. Thus the classifications "cosmopolitan" and "local," meant to differentiate those with high organization identification (locals) from those with an external professional commitment (cosmopolitans), have been subjected to closer study. Several points from this analysis strengthen our understanding of professional role orientation in organizations, and also relate to previous discussions on motivation ("decision to join," "decision to stay") and a subsequent discussion on manpower planning (Part III), especially employee mobility.

Rather than view "cosmopolitan-local" as a continuum, an alternative view[7] suggests two separate continua—cosmopolitan *and* local, resulting in a simple 2×2 matrix. This view, for example, admits of a cosmopolitan with high professional *and* high organization commitment. The combinations of high organization and low professional commitment or of high professional and low organization commitment are already familiar notions. The research by Mary Sheldon suggests that as the scientist or engineer becomes more successful professionally, the relevancy of the organization is likely to lessen, especially for those with medium-length service. Thus the outside reference group becomes increasingly relevant to the individual professional. The countervailing forces leading to organizational commitment and identification stem from institutional and social "investments," which include such factors as age, length of service, and level of position attained. For example, those with a lesser educational commitment (masters versus doctorates) would have a smaller professional investment and likely a greater organizational commitment. Social involvement within the organization also militates against professional turnover.

Thus, treating the cosmopolitan-local classification as two separate continua (similar to the orthogonal distinction in the Ohio State leadership work) suggests a simple but powerful model for analyzing such things as role relationships, outside role commitments, factors in turnover, and mobility analysis. Social involvement or an expanded, more autonomous role for the professional may assist in retaining the successful, outward-looking organization member. Viewing this issue in a somewhat different light and detecting low organizational identification among various individuals or groups may suggest corrective manpower strategies.

ROLE PERFORMANCE IN PERSPECTIVE

It is now important to sort out means for goal accomplishment—to consider the structuring afforded the human system by technology and institutional framework where human effort, though a dominant force,[8] must be combined with impersonal control systems to secure objectives.

In the environment of a technology-based work system, primary activities and secondary relationships are patterned largely by the mechanisms and work activities of the technology. In such institutional frameworks as a hospital,[9] professionals and nonprofessionals *combine* activities, and there is mutual dependence in carrying out roles. Overall organizational performance necessarily goes beyond formal structures, relationships, and work methods, and to some degree reflects the efficiency (high levels of individual accomplishment with minimal stress and confusion) of the social organization and its human components.

The key question is: Are high levels of combined organization performance, individual satisfaction, and self-realization attainable? One writer asserts that the coordination and cooperation required in a hospital to bring resource capabilities together in a timely, expert fashion depend on the *voluntary* adjustments of organization members and the extent to which they "mutually facilitate their role performances in their daily work." [10]

Exhibit 10–6 notes the needed balancing of formal and informal system and role performers in such an institutional setting. Institutional objectives (1) influence the characteristics of the socio-work system (2) and the extent of mutual dependencies (3). On the one hand, some level of human compliance is dictated by the quality and quantity of services or product (4). These are juxtaposed against human links within and between the subsystems, based on understanding, the outlook of participants, mutual trust, and workable reciprocal relationships. Thus it becomes a major burden for organization management to achieve a balance between human needs and system maintenance.

However, it must be noted that the balance is not static, but dynamic and reciprocal. Improving social performance (a key in contemporary developments in "organization development" or "renewal") permits less formal guides and restraints, and a potential increase in outcomes for both the individual and the organization.

> To the extent that doctors, nurses, and others learn to accept their interdependence and function both according to the demands of their respective roles and according to each other's work problems and needs . . . organizational regimentation and administratively imposed requirements could be further reduced.[11]

Consequently, the result of formal administrative approaches is to channel relationships and communications, often in less productive or individually satisfying ways, as tasks become fragmented (division of labor) and impersonal (5). Thus balancing is needed among primary and secondary relationships, and in such a manner as to take account of the development and growth needs of individuals and the mission of the organization (6). Here the very act of seeking to channel human effort or to emphasize administra-

EXHIBIT 10-6. Role Performance: Interfacing Formal and Informal

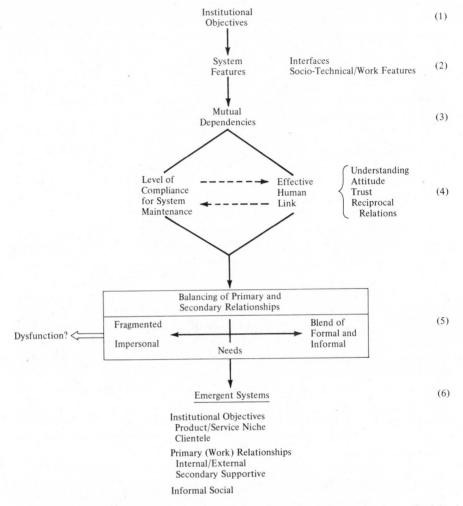

Builds on ideas of B. Georgopoulos in "Today's General Hospital Organization, from a Social–Psychological Viewpoint," Second Annual Conference on Complex Organizations, Kent State University, April, 1969.

tive or professional differences may, even inadvertently, reduce the contributions of important role participants.

In a hospital, the primary institutional objectives are individual assistance and professional services for those requesting them or evidencing need.[12] A hospital is also frequently charged with the responsibility of undertaking research and training and with providing "high quality service to the community." [13] All of these primary objectives have a strong social flavor, and depend on human effort. Responsibility for attaining these objectives rests squarely on the human participants and the major role groups of the organization.

This point is extremely important because it crystallizes a major difference in emphasis (not kind) between organizational situations in which the behavioral model applies and those in which the technological model applies. A hospital's mission places important value on the interfacing of institutional personnel and clientele, which is much more restricted in many organizations and, perhaps, is only approximated in such sub-areas as marketing or sales, where personnel are deeply involved with the clientele. The institutional mission of a hospital or marketing department—the very essence of its activity—hinges on successful performance at the organizational-clientele interface.

In a hospital, the outcome of blending professional competence, coordination, and cooperation among principal task groups (along with medical technology) is concentrated at the staff-patient interface. Anything less than high performance at this point detracts from a fundamental purpose of the institution. Medical technology is not enough. Professional competence is not enough. Timing, rapid response to an emergency, speedy recovery, innovations in service, dedication, and concern in professional service are all contributions of social efficiency that are beyond technology and formally prescribed tasks and responsibilities.

ORGANIZATIONAL EFFICIENCY

A hospital is not an organization that makes unusual demands on social efficiency. This institutional model merely serves to emphasize the needs that are characteristic of most organizations:

1. Efficient resource allocation, which considers both economic and behavioral rationales for high performance and individual self-realization

2. Coordination, control, and integration of diverse but related roles within subsystems

3. Management of internal affairs and human resources that takes into account organization objectives, along with personal and professional needs, and minimizes conflicts

4. Successful blending of behavioral and work systems that takes into account the mutual dependencies of system members and functions in order to realize a potential beyond that of either system viewed independently

5. Adaptability to change and effective management in anticipation of change

SYSTEMS, ROLES, AND MOTIVATION

Systems, roles, and group concepts establish a base for understanding the complex factors surrounding highly motivated performance. This diverse group of factors has been brought together to rationalize a motivational system.[14] Exhibit 10–7 depicts the interlocking of primary roles, where the "primary" individual relates to colleagues, superiors, subordinates, and support personnel.

The actions of role performers are initially directed by individual needs and job objectives.[15] These result in evoked sets of ideas that permit the formulation of alternatives, the consequences of the alternatives, and the likelihood of realization. Motivated behavior is a search for the objectives valued by the individual and the organization, and also may be interpreted as an input to another role performer in a primary role relationship. (If secondary relationships were incorporated in Exhibit 10–7, it would become too cluttered.)

Since the individual's goals and needs are largely interpersonal relations with fellow workers, there is need for an organizational agent to guide and coordinate the individual toward fulfillment of corporate objectives. This is accomplished, for example, by role definition and by leadership, in that a supervisor influences both stimuli and evoked sets of alternatives. This is his means of motivating the behavior of his subordinates. It is the intention of the organization that various stimuli will generate action toward the fulfillment of corporate goals. However, only if personal needs and goals are fulfilled, at least minimally, will the actions of the individual be consistently directed toward the goals held by the company.

Liaison (staff) personnel facilitate coordination. Without concern for the motivation of various role performers, however, the influence of support personnel may be severely limited. Additionally, they may be subject to their own stimulus-motivation pressures toward personal goals and needs.

Both the reward system and the modes of resolving conflicts have a profound effect upon the objective of coordinating individuals toward corporate goals. Division of labor, specialization, and the role system are outgrowths of complex operations that place great strain upon coordination.

Finally, there are certain additional variables, such as size and character of the institution, that influence the model. For example, size of plant, departments, and especially reference groups affects the nature of interpersonal relations and, consequently, the motivation to secure company goals.

In analyzing or designing organizations, one must contend not only with differentiating functions and the effect of this upon motivating individuals but also with the integration of individual motivation and organizational objectives. Both aspects are indispensable. An analogy can be drawn from mathematics—the operations and concepts of differentiation and integration

EXHIBIT 10-7. Role System and Motivating Performance

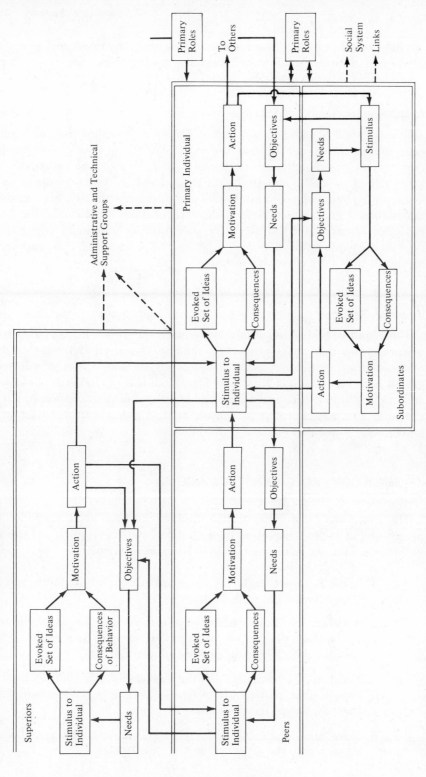

For an elaborate discussion of this type of approach, see Joseph A. Litterer, *Analysis of Organizations* (New York: Wiley, 1965).

are indispensable to, and the essence of, calculus. Organizational planners also need both differentiable and integrative perspectives.

A NOTE ON SMALL GROUPS

Groups tend to develop situational features, including internal communication systems and "pecking orders." [16] The group tries to stabilize its environment, or even attempts to control it. Data on informal leaders can be sifted out of a small-group study and considered in selecting supervisors. This approach provides for both formal and informal authority. Recognizing that informal groups may view leadership functions (facilitating the performance of tasks and the needs for sociability or individual power and prominence) differently than line supervisors provides a specific approach for developing more effective leadership.

Informal Groups[17]

There are two basic types of informal groups: the weekly bridge group and a work group that limits production quotas. The major difference is the relationship to a formal organization. Fostering the formulation of informal groups may provide an environment for encouraging individual innovation and originality in getting tasks done at a high level of performance. A major challenge to management is to convert apathetic or erratic behavior into higher, more consistent levels of performance.

TECHNOLOGY, ROLE PERFORMANCE, LEADERSHIP, AND PRODUCTIVITY

The contributions of leadership to productivity have not been fully explored—reflecting to some extent the incomplete state of research and theory in this area—but the following questions have been raised.[18]

1. What is the character of empirical results that describe supervisory impact on productivity?

2. To what extent can variants in human productivity be attributed to human effort? And to what extent can such variants be accounted for by the supervisory effort itself?

3. What is the character of the leadership role in the formal organization, particularly in terms of requisite skills, considering the influence of the environment?

4. What are the possibilities for viewing the supervisor as a change agent within the organization?

The conclusion is that the impact of the supervisor upon productivity is generally small compared with the impact of the technology, and especially in technically based units. Historically, the supervisory role is seen as one that has been transformed from great power and autonomy to one considerably reduced in its ability to influence performance, as compared with labor relations and technological change. The impact of technological forces on organizational structure has modified the relationship of supervisor to subordinate. It is under these conditions that new skill levels or different types of skill become necessary. Such skills are described as "administrative competence," "human relations competence," and "technical competence." [19]

As a plant achieves greater technical efficiency in "automation," added emphasis is placed on supervisors' technical and human relations skills in dealing with subordinates. On the other hand, higher management may tend increasingly to emphasize supervisors' administrative skills. (Note the different role expectations of supervisor and subordinate.) In short, just as different leadership approaches may be dictated by different situations, different combinations of skill are required under varying technologies, depending on the perception of role relationships and the viewpoint that is assumed.

Role Performance and Change

When the structure of the socio-technical system is modified by change, the role of the supervisor also changes. What it changes to depends on the circumstances. It may become looser or tighter, depending on how high the cost of disruption is—among other things. With the wide variety of technological changes in a complex organizational environment, no single supervisory style will be appropriate at all times.

Changes in organizational structure and technological system also substantially modify work-related behavioral patterns, both individual and collective. In a more automated socio-technical system, supervisors may be expected to supervise technical processes and machines to a greater extent. In many cases workers may even be "adjuncts" to machines and operations.

On the other hand, the supervisor represents an important link between the worker, the small work group, and other aspects of the organization. Thus the supervisor assumes a more important role in terms of behavioral variables, including satisfaction and turnover, as compared with his influence on the production process, now largely governed by technology. Supervision may have to go far beyond seeking to gain the simple satisfaction of work-related needs. In short, the role of supervisor may have very little to do with work activity itself, but the supervisor may assume a more important role in other areas of organization life, particularly human relations.

Analysis of supervisory role requirements is exceedingly complex, and does not readily lend itself to the traditional tools of analysis, but the concepts that have been introduced in these discussions are helpful.

Supervisory Role and Type of Technology

We might first consider two basic types of work systems, one in which the technology is built around information and in the other around manufacturing. In the information system, the supervisor relates to the worker in the preparation of information inputs. In the manufacturing system, support groups such as maintenance, engineering, quality control, and production control vastly complicate role performance, and play an important part in determining needed skills and the locus of responsibilities. The thesis developed in Chapters 3, 4, and 7 suggests that technology is a determinant of overall role requirements, or sets boundaries within which these role requirements are acted out.

The degree of influence is established by the character of the technological system. At low levels of technology, where the system itself does not structure the work, production outputs and administrative performance are governed by the behavior of the supervisor and the capabilities of the worker group. At intermediate levels (mass production systems), the quantity of output is governed by the work system, but quality can be influenced by role performers.

Similarly, in intermediate-level information systems the ultimate limit on quantity is the computational power and speed of the computer, but input and the efficiency of the information network depend on human effort.

In advanced systems, technology governs both quantity and quality—but human effort provides general system support, and not satisfying individual needs may blunt ingenuity and encourage absenteeism and turnover.

ROLE PERFORMANCE AND SYSTEM STABILITY

Two additional characteristics of work systems influence role requirements: (1) unstable or changing situations and (2) system maturity. If a work system is characterized by a high level of instability—the result, say, of an unproved technology or widely varying customer orders—supervisor and worker performance bears on the dispatch with which system changes can meet new production requirements. On the other hand, the more stable the system and the greater the volume of activity, the less frequent the changeovers will be, and the system will depend less on human performance.

In older systems the level of stability is usually such that technical problems are no longer an important consideration. A transition often takes place, indicating (1) role needs for more challenging, creative work or (2) maturing interpersonal relationships demanding greater emphasis on human relations skills. Analysis of stable and unstable work situations suggests an organization/plant-life cycle.[20] Thus the degree of administrative, technical, and human relations skills required in supervisory role performance depends on the maturity of the technology.

In conclusion, it seems clear that, in light of the general range of technological situations, workers could not, in most cases, double their output by greater effort. Furthermore, the relative increase or "potential" is small in comparison with the long-term increases brought about by investment in new methods, machinery, and sources of power.[21]

SUMMARY

The social system is inexorably bound to the work systems of a wide assortment of institutions. From the professionally oriented hospital to the technologically oriented manufacturing, information, or service unit, the effectiveness of the social organization tempers organizational performance. Thus, from the viewpoint of performance, the only real question is the *degree* of influence. The character of the institution provides a basis for gauging this degree. Neither technology, structure, nor impersonal controls alone fully accounts for performance. Yet performance is only one theme of this discussion; the other is the objectives of individuals in the organizational system.

For the realization of individual needs and goals it is necessary to look behind the primary role system and seek the secondary relationships and outlines of the social system. Out of the framework of formal relationships dictated by the purposes of the organization, social systems and structures emerge that may actively support individual realization or merely suit superficial social purposes. Higher-level individual needs are not realized automatically; they require constant attention and enlightened leadership. Tracing primary and secondary role systems establishes a point of entry for determining the necessary human links. Incorporating the environment factor and the characteristics of role occupants aids in a clearer definition of the challenges for designing a viable human system and setting out the guidelines for enlightened management.

QUESTIONS

1. Consider the organization structure in the exercise section of Chapter 6 on communication. Propose an approach to developing a "picture" of this organization based on the approach suggested by Homans.

2. Contrast the model of role relationships for hospitals developed by Georgopoulos with that of the role system in (a) a mass-production plant

and (b) an insurance office. Make any necessary assumptions and state them.

3. What opportunities do you visualize for emergent behavior of the "internal" system to modify key components or processes of the "external" system? For purposes of your response, consider such specifics as (a) young college graduates, (b) more women in responsible positions, and (c) incorporation of minority members in the work force.

4. Develop a general functional statement (Status $= f \ldots$) for *status* in an organization. How do the factors differ when considering
   a) Various supervisory heads?
   b) Different institutional settings?
   c) Various social settings, that is, street-corner society or the country club?

5. What strategies might an organization consider to loosen social structures that tend to support formal relationships among collegial groups, thereby minimizing interdepartmental interactions?

6. In what ways does the organization chart create status considerations in role conflict for office holders? Are there any current or contemplated elements of community activity, dress, mannerism, and the like that will probably further modify the perceived status or roles of various office holders? (Hint: Consider the status of editorial staff members of popular magazines such as *Esquire* and *Playboy*.)

7. What factors are likely to influence the relative future importance of a factor such as seniority? Salary? In general, what factors establish the status of various institutions under emergent social and economic developments?

8. Express and justify your opinion of the following statement: "Opportunities for socialization on the job are likely to result in performance increases."

9. The results of some of the studies undertaken by the well-known Tavistock group in England suggest that engineering design goals should include relatively autonomous tasks for work groups and the emergence of internal leadership.
   a) What restraints are imposed by various technologies?
   b) Can you put these ideas to work in an organization you are familiar with?

10. What types of role expectations are emerging for teachers? Students? Owners (executives) of large companies? Men who "rise through the ranks"?

11. Discuss the interrelationships of such variables as productivity, competition, cooperation, and social cohesion with fellow workers.

12. Do you feel it is practical to enlarge the role of rank-and-file workers to include decision-making areas previously belonging to supervisors?

NOTES

This chapter draws on the writer's paper at the Second Annual Conference on Complex Organizations, "Introduction: A Commentary and Critique of Four Organizational Behavioral Models," in Anant R. Negandhi and Joseph P. Schwitter (eds.), *Organization Behavior Models* (Kent, O., Division of Business Research, Kent State University, 1969). This section was further influenced by a paper by Basil Georgopoulos, "An Open System Theory Model for Organizational Reseach," also reprinted in *Organization Behavior Models.*

1. Daniel Katz and Robert L. Kahn, *The Social Psychology of Organizations* (New York: John Wiley & Sons, 1966), p. 179.

2. Based on ideas in ibid., pp. 179–197.

3. For other aspects of this role orientation, see Mary E. Sheldon, "Investments and Involvements as Mechanisms Producing Commitment to the Organization," *Administrative Science Quarterly,* 16, no. 2 (June 1971): 143–150. Closely related to this research—another paper in the same issue of *ASQ*—is George A. Miller and L. Wesley Wager, "Adult Socialization, Organizational Structure, and Role Orientations," pp. 151–163. Also see Sang M. Lee, "An Empirical Analysis of Organizational Identification," *Academy of Management Journal,* 14, no. 2 (June 1971): 213–226.

4. For emergent areas of role need, see Daniel S. Katz and Basil Georgopoulos, "Organizations in a Changing World," in Frank Baker (ed.), *Organizational Systems: General Systems Approaches to Complex Organizations* (Homewood, Ill.: Richard D. Irwin, 1973); also Katz and Kahn, *Social Psychology of Organizations,* p. 18.

5. Several different dimensions of group-individual orientation can be derived from Linda E. Rich and Terence R. Mitchell, "Structural Determinants of Individual Behavior in Organizations," *Administrative Science Quarterly,* 18, no. 1 (March 1973): 56–71, and Frank Harrison, "Organizational Correlates of Perceived Role Performance at the University and College Level," *Academy of Management Journal,* 16, no. 2 (June 1973): 227–239.

6. Based on George Homans, *The Human Group* (New York: Harcourt Brace Jovanovich, 1950), and special material prepared by the Northwestern School of Business titled "Group Behavior I (HP 215) and II (HP 216)."

7. More on the orientation of professional/nonprofessional personnel may be found in P. K. Berger and Andrew J. Grimes, "Cosmopolitan–Local: A Factor Analysis of the Construct," *Administrative Science Quarterly,* 18, no. 2 (June 1973): 223–236.

8. See, for example, Lawrence B. Mohr, "Organization Technology and Organizational Structure, *Administrative Science Quarterly,* 16, no. 4 (December 1971): 444–459.

9. This section is based on the previously cited "Open System Theory" by Georgopoulos and "Commentary and Critique" by Burack.

10. Burack, "Commentary and Critique."

11. Georgopoulos, "Open System Theory," p. 17.

12. Ibid., p. 3.

13. Ibid.

14. Joseph L. Litterer, *Analysis of Organizations* (New York: John Wiley & Sons, 1966), pp. 25, 186, 345.

15. James G. March and Herbert A. Simon, *Organizations* (New York: John Wiley & Sons, 1958), esp. chap. 1.

16. First note is based on Robert G. Golembiewski and Frank Gibson, *Managerial Behavior and Organization Demands* (Chicago: Rand McNally, 1967), pp. 174–186.

17. Based on Robert Dubin, *Human Relations in Administration* (3d ed., rev.; Englewood Cliffs, N.J.: Prentice-Hall, 1968), pp. 104–126.

18. Robert Dubin, George C. Homans, Floyd C. Mann, and Delbert C. Miller, *Leadership and Productivity* (San Francisco: Chandler Publishing Co., 1967).

19. Ibid.; detail provided in Mann's paper (see n. 20).

20. Some of these points are considered by Floyd Mann in Dubin et al., *Leadership and Productivity.*

21. Dubin et al., *Leadership and Productivity.*

REFERENCES

A. Social Basis of Work Systems (Role)

Berger, P. K., and A. J. Grimes. "Cosmopolitan–Local: A Factor Analysis of the Construct." *Administrative Science Quarterly,* 18, no. 2 (June 1973): 223–236.

Burack, Elmer H. "Papers by Hickson et al. and Darkenwald, Organization Power and Conflict." *Quarterly Journal of Management Development,* 3, no. 2 (1973): 77-85.

Butler, Arthur G., Jr. "Project Management: A Study in Organizational Conflict." *Academy of Management Journal,* 16, no. 1 (March 1973): 84–102.

Davis, K. "The Role of Project Management in Scientific Manufacturing." *IEEE Transactions on Engineering Management,* EM-9, no. 3 (September 1962): 109–113.

Frank, Andrew G. "Administrative Role Definition and Social Change." *Human Organization,* 22, no. 4 (Winter 1963/64): 238–242.

Gibson, Cyrus F., and Richard L. Nolan. "Managing the Four Stages of EDP Growth." *Harvard Business Review,* 52, no. 1 (January–February 1974): 76–88.

Gouldner, A. "Cosmopolitans and Locals." *Administrative Science Quarterly,* 1, no. 3 (December 1957): 282–292.

Graen, George, Fred Dansereau Jr., Takao Minami, and James Cashmar. "Leadership Behaviors as Cues to Performance Evaluation." *Academy of Management Journal,* 16, no. 4 (December 1973): 611–624.

Haire, M., E. Ghiselli, and P. Porter. "Cultural Patterns in the Role of the Manager." *Industrial Relations,* 2, no. 2 (February 1963): 95–118.

Hall, Douglas T., and Edward E. Lawler Jr. "Job Characteristics and Pressures and the Organizational Integration of Professionals." *Administrative Science Quarterly,* 15, no. 3 (September 1970): 271–281.

Harrison, Frank. "Organizational Correlates of Perceived Role Performance at the University and College Level." *Academy of Management Journal,* 16, no. 2 (June 1973): 227–239.

Hickson, D. J., C. R. Hinnings, C. A. Lee, and R. I. Schenk. "A Strategic Contingencies Theory of Intraorganizational Power." *Administrative Science Quarterly,* 16, no. 2 (June 1971): 216–229.

Homans, G. *The Human Group.* New York: Harcourt Brace Jovanovich, 1961.

House, Robert J. "Role Conflict and Multiple Authority in Complex Organizations." *California Management Review,* 12, no. 4 (Summer 1970): 53–60.

Kahn, R., D. Wolfe, R. Quinn, J. D. Snoek, and R. Rosenthal. *Organizational Stress.* New York: John Wiley & Sons, 1964.

Katz, Daniel S., and Basil S. Georgopoulos. "Organizations in a Changing World." *Journal of Applied Behavioral Sciences,* 7 (1971): 342–370. Reprinted in Frank Baker (ed.). *Organizational Systems: General Systems Approaches to Complex Organizations.* Homewood, Ill.: Richard D. Irwin, 1973, pp. 120–190.

Mulder, Mauk. "Power Equalization through Participation." *Administrative Science Quarterly,* 16, no. 1 (March 1971): 31–38.

Payne, Roy L., and Roger Mansfield. "Relationships of Organizational Climate to Organization Structure, Context and Hierarchical Position." *Administrative Science Quarterly,* 18, no. 4 (December 1973): 515–526.

Rice, A. K. *Productivity and Social Organization: The Ahmedabad Experiment.* London: Tavistock Publications, 1958.

Rice, Linda E., and Terence R. Mitchell. "Structural Determinants of Individual Behavior in Organizations." *Administrative Science Quarterly,* 18, no. 1 (March 1973): 56–71.

Rizzo, John R., Robert J. House, and Sidney L. Lirtzman. "Role Conflict and Ambiguity in Complex Organizations." *Administrative Science Quarterly,* 15, no. 2 (June 1970): 150–163.

Roethlisberger, F. "The Foreman: Master and Victim of Double Talk." *Harvard Business Review,* 23, no. 3 (Spring, 1945): 283–298.

Rosen, Hudson R. A. "Foreman Role Conflict: An Expression of Contradictions in Organizational Goals." *Industrial and Labor Relations Review,* 23, no. 4 (July 1970): 541–552.

Roy, D. "Banana Time–Job Satisfaction and Informal Interaction." *Human Organization,* 18, no. 4 (Winter 1959/60): 158–168.

Seashore, S. *Group Cohesiveness in the Industrial Work Group.* Ann Arbor: Survey Research Center, University of Michigan, 1954.

Schein, E., and W. Bennis. *Personal and Organizational Change through Group Methods.* New York: John Wiley & Sons, 1965.

Slusher, Allen, James Van Dyke, and Gerard Rose. "Technical Competence of Group Leaders, Managerial Role, and Productivity in Engineering Design Groups." *Academy of Management Journal,* 15, no. 2 (June 1972): 197–204.

Tosi, Henry. "Organizational Stress as a Moderator of the Relationship Influence and Role Response." *Academy of Management Journal,* 14, no. 1 (March 1971): 7–22.

Tyler, William B. "Measuring Organizational Specialization: The Concept of Role Variety." *Administrative Science Quarterly,* 18, no. 3 (September 1973): 383–393.

White, J. Kenneth, and Robert A. Ruh. "Effects of Personal Values on the Relationship between Participation and Job Attituds." *Administrative Science Quarterly,* 18, no. 4 (December 1973): 506–514.

B. Analytical Approaches in Activity-Interaction Analysis

Arensberg, Conrad M., "Behavior and Organization: Industrial Studies," in John H. Rohrer and Muzafer Sherif (eds.), *Social Psychology at the Crossroads.* New York: Harper & Row, 1951.

Bales, R. F. *Interaction Process Analysis.* Cambridge, Mass.: Addison-Wesley, 1950.

Chapple, Eliot D., and Carleton Coon. *Principles of Anthropology.* New York: Holt, Rinehart and Winston, Inc., 1942.

————, and Leonard R. Sayles. *The Measure of Management.* New York: Macmillan, 1961.

Guest, Robert H. "Of Time and the Foreman." *Personnel,* 32, no. 6 (May 1956): 478.

————. *Organization Change: The Effect of Successful Leadership.* Homewood, Ill.: Dorsey Press, 1962.

Homans, George C. *The Human Group.* New York: Harcourt Brace Jovanovich, 1950.

Richardson, Frederick L. W., and Charles R. Walker. *Human Relations in an Expanding Company,* New Haven, Conn.: Labor and Management Center, Yale University, 1948.

————. *Talk; Work; and Action.* Monograph 3. Society for Applied Anthropology, Cornell University, Ithaca, N.Y., 1961.

Whyte, William F. "Framework for the Analysis of Industrial Relations." *Industrial and Labor Relations Review,* 3, no. 3 (April 1950): 393–401.

Learning Objectives

Concept of "Bounded Rationality"
Centralization versus Decentralization
  Propositions for Rationalizing Decision-making Approaches
Decision-making Systems for Dealing with "Certainty," "Risk,"
    and "Uncertainty"
Differentiating Programmed and Non-programmed Approaches
Middle-management Controversy
Participation of Work Group Members in Decision Making:
    Performance and Behavioral Implications
Locus of Decision Making: Relation to Authority Level, Process,
    and Management Function

Chapter 11

DECISION MAKING: A BEHAVIORAL PERSPECTIVE

OVERVIEW ON DEVELOPMENT

This chapter completes the presentation of behavioral perspectives, theories, and system design approaches of Part II. The approaches to decision making described below pick up many of the themes introduced in Part I and Part II. Aspects of organization structure (Chapter 2) and technological systems (Chapters 3 and 4) constitute the framework and processes about which decision-making approaches are described. Additionally, key models, introduced at various points in previous discussions, are categorized in regard to their relation to decision-making activities.

This chapter also devotes some attention to the impact of change, especially technological, on the decision processes and the locus of decision making. Described as the "middle-management controversy," this discussion on the thrust of change for decision making forms part of a change theme found throughout book, and which is given prominence in Part III (especially Chapter 13, "Change Management").

The concluding discussion of this chapter takes up some selected, contemporary areas of decision issues. Matters such as the role of leadership (Chapter 9), employee participation in decision making, and redefinition of decision roles and activity are described.

TRANSITION FROM BUREAUCRACY

Two mainstreams of organizational theory provide much of the underpinning for decision theory, as well as for many of the research investigations cited in this chapter.[1] In one approach, Max Weber[2] formulated the concept of bureaucracy, which strongly emphasizes the skeletal structure of offices rather than people, providing (a) the allocation of decision-making responsibilities, (b) the natural ordering of channels of communication for information and decision making, and (c) the specialization of functions for decision-making purposes. In the light of current research, and in contrast to the material of Chapter 2 with that of Chapters 8, 9, and 10, bureaucratic theory disregards the behavioral interactions among subordinates, supervisors, and staff functionaries that form an indispensable dimension of decision making.

With equal stress, but perhaps somewhat in the opposite direction, Herbert Simon's approach[3] to modeling decision processes probed the behavioral features of decision processes but failed to integrate the structural influences. However, in the collaboration of Simon with James March[4] a number of broader conceptualizations were proposed, although even they do not constitute comprehensive models. Thus the concepts of bureaucracy are of historical importance in defining decision structure, relationships, and channels of interaction, but they fall far short of explaining the mental processes and nonformal patterns of decision making of the organization.

Structural approaches also fail to take into account both the conscious direction of human activities toward agreed-on goals and their motivational implications. Finally, a purely structural approach to organization decision making does not take into account the lack of predictability and the "bounded" perspective ("bounded rationality") of events influencing problem selection, choice, or solution. And any view into the future must contend with uncertainty in the course of emerging and anticipated development. Thus we must consider structural and systemic as well as behavioral approaches in rationalizing decision-making procedures. Any prescribed conceptual perspective will necessarily involve these elements.

"Bounded Rationality"

The concept of "bounded rationality" receives considerable attention from March and Simon and warrants some elaboration at this point. Decision situations and problems requiring resolution encompass a range of possibilities in terms of our ability to identify, evaluate, and deal with the relevant variables. To the extent that we can influence or determine the variables affecting the decision, identify feasible alternatives, and evaluate each of these possibilities, decision procedure can become more precise and "rational". Yet the facts of organizational life are such that gaps exist in available information, and acquiring more information costs money; outside forces may influence variables we are aware of, and other forces that we are not as yet unaware of may bear on the decision situation. Of course the decision maker may simply choose to ignore some factors that he can't evaluate or "won't be troubled with."

In short, decision makers face a variety of problems and situations where the relevant variables are "masked" and where there are significant limitations in rationalizing the situation. Other factors contributing to "bounded rationality" and decision approaches in dealing with them will be brought out in subsequent discussions.

STRUCTURE AND DECISION MAKING

In a broad sense, the organization structure establishes the locus of decision making. The lengthening of communication lines found in geographically dispersed units or "tall" authority structures (see Chapters 2 and 6) stretches decision systems, and may lead to delegation of responsibilities to maintain the effectiveness of decision performance. However, multiple review of decisions at various levels may be advantageous. Computer-based information systems (Chapter 7) permit the capture of information from widely scattered areas of the organization and funnel intelligence to higher management and support groups. In this way the otherwise excessive length of communication routes and processing time in tall structures is effectively shortened. Consequently, choices between tall and "flat" structures in organization design relate to (a) decision structures based on communication and span-of-control variables and (b) behavioral considerations involving decision participants (Chapters 8, 9, and 10).

Thus a structural approach to decision making must take into account diverse organization parameters, including tall or flat structure, physical centralization or decentralization, communication, span of control, behavioral considerations such as motivation, and the impact of technological or manpower changes (more in Chapters 12 and 13) that unbalance existing relationships or modify variables in decision networks.

THE STRUCTURE CONTROVERSY

From research carried out some years ago in the retail merchandising field [5] emerged the idea that "flat" structures permit a high level of individual development through direct exposure to decision making. Whereas "tall" structures may pose substantial communication problems,[6] reduce top-level influence, and delay the diffusion of change, the flat structure shortens communication time and permits greater flexibility in the introduction of change —or so goes the argument.[7] However, a tall structure tends to narrow the span of control, permitting a higher level of interaction between superior and subordinate, and greater surveillance when needed.

The structural view of decision making must also recognize other organizational attributes that are very much a part of decision processes.[8] For example, the position occupied by the decision maker in the authority structure will affect the initiative and independence with which decisions are made on promotions, capital expenditures, and hiring.[9] Decision makers who occupy high positions in the authority structure typically have great autonomy, but the degree of autonomy is necessarily modified by the extent of physical diversification, etc. For example, as physical diversification takes place, the tendency to decentralize decision making elevates autonomy opportunities for those in the decentralized units. Decision processes further depend upon the relative size or complexity of the organization. Growth in size also leads to the need for hierarchical differentiation, formalization of rules guiding decisions, and a general rationalization of authority processes not witnessed in simple organizations.[10]

Finally, structural analysis must reckon with the nature of the decisions to be made. Rather than be flatly decreed, structure should be molded around the need of the decision task; that is, "groups should organize to emphasize those aspects of structure which increase their ability to solve specific problems."[11] This is especially true for complex decision problems. For example, the specialization of "statistical quality control" emerges from the technical requirements of inspection or quality surveillance.

To more effectively display the links underlying these structural considerations, the following section forms these ideas into a selection of organizational propositions.

PROPOSITIONS AND NOTIONS ON DECISION MAKING

1. The larger the organization, the greater the hierarchical differentiation of authority, use of decision rules (in lieu of centralized authority), decentralization of decision making to middle management, and rationalization of authority[12]—but the greater the reliance on norms and role expectations for integration.

2. Flat structures increase delegation of authority, self-realization, and individual development, and lessen control through direct surveillance.[13] Tall structures extend time for diffusion of change because of a greater number of authority links, and gratify needs for security and social satisfaction, but they may diminish the influence of top officials on lower authority levels, lead to closer control, and create communication problems through distortion and lengthened processing time.

3. The stability of the environment influences the formality and permanency of mechanisms for differentiation and integration. At one extreme, *no* need for change suggests ad hoc informality; at the other, frequent, pervasive changes necessitate flexibility and often require long-run (semipermanent) structural adjustments or modifications of decision structures and processes (e.g., procedures, new departments, or permanent groups).[14]

4. Upper-level managers exhibit greater decision freedom but rely more heavily on subordinates for counsel and information gathering. Lower-level managers find that decisions are typically initiated for them; consultation with their superiors is indicated, but they typically *do not* involve their subordinates in decision behavior.

DECISION MAKING AS A PROCESS

There will be frequent occasions in this chapter to describe decision making as a *process* or system of interrelated activities. Thus its discussions and analyses will reach far beyond the mental processes of the individual decision makers and deal with various steps in decision procedures. A common enumeration of decision stages includes:

a. Problem identification

b. Developing information relative to the problem(s)

c. Identifying alternatives

d. Evaluating alternatives

e. Choosing among alternatives

f. Implementation

g. Feedback for correction or redirection.

This step-wise view of decision making serves a variety of needs important to organization analysis. First, it recognizes that different people, departments, factors, or approaches may be indicated at each step. Complex mathematical models or simulation routines may assist in problem identification, but they provide little by way of identifying alternatives or making choices. Market research may be in a splendid position, because of customer and competitive contacts, to develop information on new needs or competitive threats, but in a poor position to evaluate the thrust of these disclosures against other pressures confronting decision makers.

To furher understand decision process distinctions, consider implementation versus evaluation. "Engineering" may assume key responsibilities for the installation of a new production process, but the accumulation of cost data for evaluative purposes may be more readily (and desirably) handled by "cost accounting."

Further elaboration on decision making as a process and its ramifications are reserved for subsequent discussions, including one on the locus of decision making.

This brief discussion of decision making as a process will bear on the approaches dealing with decision systems.

SYSTEMS PERSPECTIVE ON DECISION PROCESSES

The general observations set forth so far are brought together in Exhibits 11–1A, –B, and –C, which portray (1) the decision maker's environment and the resolution of decision situations into programmable and nonprogrammable approaches, (2) the development of decision processes along programmable lines, and (3) the development of decision processes along nonprogrammable lines.

In Exhibit 11–1A the content of the two major decision environments determines the extent to which objective approaches are feasible. However, the content must be related to quantitative considerations. In other words, it is not just the *number* of items from the external or internal environment that must be considered, but also their relative impact on the decision situation. Thus a given decision may consider matters that are largely internal to the firm's operations, but a single external factor (e.g., cost of capital-market interest rates) may outweigh all other considerations. The relative balancing of decision factors derived from the internal and external environments suggests that the greater the content of decision factors derived from the in-

EXHIBIT 11–1A. Routine–Nonroutine Decision Making

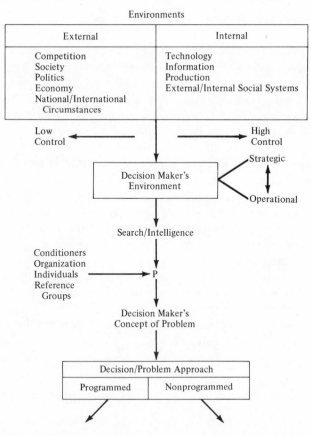

P = Perception

ternal environment (e.g., production scheduling decisions or resolutions of a design problem using known engineering principles on a design), the greater the influence of organizational controls and the more certain the outcome.

APPROACHES TO DECISION SYSTEMS

Decision situations occupy a spectrum (for added detail see Chapter 13) ranging from the certain to the risky (reasonable probabilities of assurance can be assigned) to the uncertain (little structural knowledge and/or high likelihood of unknown forces intervening). In cases of *certainty*, the classical model presumably applies—where it is possible to view all the alternatives and all the consequences, and alternatives can often be translated into quantitative measures as a basis for decision making. In situations involving *risk*, not all of the critical factors are known, and elements of uncertainty are part of the socio-technical or competitive environment; however, probabilities of outcome may be assigned, based on past history or available information. Where *uncertainty* prevails, substantial gaps in knowledge exist, and the common course of action is to introduce a high level of subjective content or value judgment.

In short, the character of the decision situation confronting the job incumbent spans a wide range of variables and affects the knowledge that can be used in analyzing a particular situation. Thus a degree of "bounded rationality," or limited insight into all of the relevant decision factors, characterizes the outlook of the decision maker.

Sometimes the level of bounded rationality is viewed in relation to authority level; that is, the types of decisions made at higher authority levels reflect greater limitations on precisely describing the critical variables for decisions. Access to information, the cost of developing information, individual creativity and imagination, and the length of the decision or planning period are among the critical variables.[15] For example, a corollary of this point is that the longer the planning period, the greater the uncertainty. The challenge to oganizational decision makers is to reduce uncertainty through intelligence-gathering efforts (e.g., market research) consistent with economic and time restraints.

Some decision situations are relatively routine and systematic.[16] Little latitude is provided or sought, and participants in the decision process move along prescribed lines. For example, office processing of sales correspondence is often prescribed for a wide variety of credit and order situations. When exceptions occur, they are brought to the supervisor or office manager for special handling.

In problem-solving decision situations, on the other hand, an individual may be forced to make a decision without being able to fully identify all of the decision elements. For example, it may not be feasible to allow enough time to make a complete search, or a complete search may be too expensive. (An illustration is consumer surveys for new products: enlarging a sampling population is costly, and runs the risk of premature disclosure to competitors.) It also may not be possible to objectively evaluate all the alternatives, or attain general agreement among decision participants. Conversely, some situations (e.g., optimum fuel blend) may lend themselves to optimizing approaches, where it is possible to identify all the relevant variables and to quantify them so that a single (best) solution can be achieved.

A final point in considering decision processes is that top management's desire for established decision rules and controls may violate individual needs. Job routinization to increase "certainty" may eliminate the more imaginative portion of a job, in an attempt to gain conformity through control systems (Chapter 5). It is not surprising that sagging morale or marginal performance may result.

It is not always possible to neatly package decision variables even if all the decision points emerge from inside the organization. Some variables, such as human participants, are difficult to quantify. However, important distinctions exist between internal and external factor sources; and high levels of premise content inside the organization permit greater rationalization of procedures. Distinctions are also made in decision content by level of authority: *strategic* policymaking activity by top management and *operational* decisions and *planning* functions at the middle and lower levels of the organization.[17]

Exhibit 11–1A emphasizes the part played by psychological processes (perception, background, personality, etc.) in formulating the character of decision problems. Interpretation of the problem is a key factor in selecting problem-solving methods. To the extent that a situation is correctly identified as lending itself to a particular line of action, the greater the time economy and the higher the quality of the solution. Thus the conceptualization of the situation/problem is a highly important decision stage.

Undoubtedly the reader has already detected the resemblance of the decision-making portrayal under certainty to the bureaucratic model described in Chapter 2. The presumed ability of the decision makers within the bureaucratic model to identify all feasible alternatives and arrive at the most economic decision was a feature of this approach. Of course, at the same time it was pointed out that high rationality and programmed approaches in decision making often fail to contend with human variability (and potential dysfunction). We also point out that although programmed, routine approaches may be indicated, human performance and personal realization are not lightly dismissed.

Several other features of Exhibit 11–1A are worthy of note and discussion. First, this exhibit emphasizes the differences in decision content for decision makers dealing with strategic as opposed to operational decision making. Strategic decision making is almost completely intertwined with future circumstances, and thus confronts the decision maker with varying levels of uncertainty and complexity and unstable or turbulent conditions. Organization leadership, under these conditions, may well build on the "track record" of decision makers who are able to display consistently good perception of future developments and then discern their impact upon the organization's structure, outputs (products/services), processes, and individual members.

In this initial conceptualization of decision making a continuing scrutiny (search) of the external and internal environments takes place in order to secure intelligence on emerging developments. Yet, at the same time, the decision maker's perception of emergent need/opportunity and thrust for the organization is colored by one's reference group (Chapter 10) and the influence of various role participants. The final conceptualization of problems depicted here is an attempted strategy where (a) past approaches may prove valuable ("programmed") or (b) a problem requires rather unique approaches (nonprogrammed).

Programmed Decisions

Programmed decisions are often considered relatively straightforward, as if one is operating under conditions of certainty (see Exhibit 11–1B). If it

EXHIBIT 11–1B. Routine Decision Making

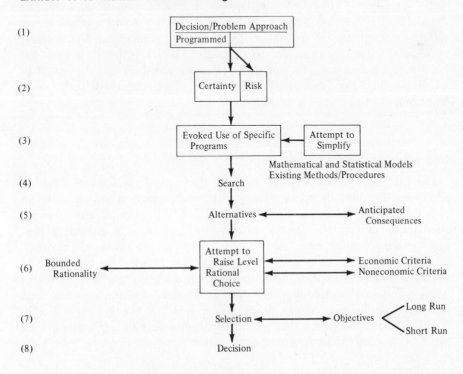

appears that uncertainties exist, an attempt is made to rationalize or reduce the problem to "manageable" proportions, so that specific programs or approaches can be sought. Note that programmed solutions may be applied to a range of problems—to those displaying some degree of variation or uncertainty—so that simplifying assumptions must be made. Consider, for example, the linearity assumption in the linear programming model or the "equal interval scale" in a behavioral study.

Exhibiting models often assist in search routines to generate choice alternatives. As noted in Exhibit 11–1B, the ability to anticipate consequences is a necessary condition for selection among alternatives. Though choice may turn on economic criteria, not all of the decision variables required for "certainty" may be readily apparent (bounded rationality). Choice is also constrained by personal influences, relative weighting of the importance of short- and long-range factors, and the balancing of objective and subjective values.

The discussions of Chapter 8 (on motivation) can provide some added insights into the decision maker's choice situation. If we assume the path-goal posture, we might well establish a pattern of choice among alternatives that the decision maker views as best (likelihood of achievement, goal connection, and relative payoff) for attaining longer-run organizational goals. The objectivity employed in this research, plus the variations between decision makers, has been studied to some extent. Not surprisingly, considerable variations have been found within organizations and between decision makers.[18] However, just the opportunity to compare and contrast decision patterns and criteria can be beneficial in the resolution of seemingly different viewpoints or approaches. A final point, concerning the decision maker's selection among alternatives (Exhibit 11–1B), is that little work has been done to determine the influence of personal values and the extent to which personal goals influence decision-maker choice criteria. Clearly, much work remains to be done in this area.

Nonprogrammed Decisions

Exhibit 11–1C conceptualizes some of the typical elements of decision situations that initially contain many unknowns, which are often found in policy-level and planning decisions involving the external environment. Availability of capital, competitive response, success of a marketing program, unemployment rates, and buying intentions are commonly difficult-to-predict elements in nonroutine decision situations. The reduction of uncertainty, a commonplace decision strategy, is made feasible through intelligence efforts and simplifying assumptions. Models, decision matrices, and simulation studies may be part of solution approaches, but they are typically coupled with assumptions that permit a finite number of alternatives, with satisfactory rather than maximizing outcomes.

EXHIBIT 11–1C. Nonroutine Decision Making

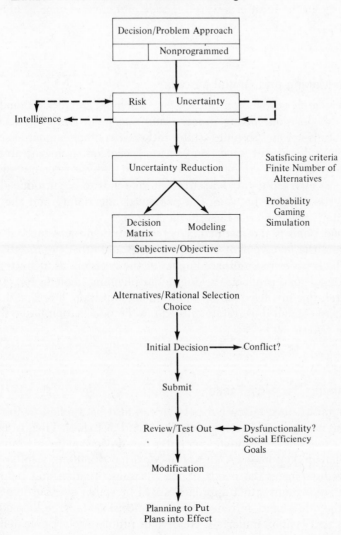

Human coping mechanisms operate in similar fashion to reduce problem complexity. Mental overload is avoided through adaptive processes that keep situational elements to manageable proportions. These mechanisms are necessary for mental well-being. Thus the major task of decision makers is clarifying decision roles, ground rules, assumptions, and limitations. Minimizing conflict among decision participants depends upon the success of such organizational housekeeping.

There is little reason to believe that an initial decision will weather subsequent use without modification or refinement. Dysfunctions become more apparent as a particular decision is tested; for example, social efficiency may be lessened in the pursuit of economic efficiency. That is, behavioral stresses may emerge in the form of lowered morale and creativity, or lackluster performance.

Decision Making and Global Models

Field research on decision making has disclosed some additional dimensions of the decision-making process, and one point concerns uncertainty. Uncertainty is not an "absolute" state; rather, it contains numerous elements with varying degrees of uncertainty. Also, recent research indicates that as the perception of uncertainty in the decision process becomes more pronounced, an increasingly wider set of criteria tends to be introduced, until a balancing takes place between the perceived uncertainty and the number and qualitative character of the criteria utilized.[19]

A second point is the distinction between strategic and tactical decision making and the involvement of support staffs and other organization members.[20] The broader the ultimate impact of the decision, as in strategic decision making (goal, product, or long-range planning choices, for example), the greater the involvement of multiple organization levels and support specialists to combat uncertainty and add to the information base (thus widening the criteria set).

Programming Decision Tasks

The certainty-uncertainty perspective can also be applied to the *type* of decision to be made. This viewpoint, illustrated in Exhibit 11–2, is important because it seeks to differentiate computer-based decision areas from individual or behavioral approaches. In routine decision situations, standard repetitive procedures meet the needs of the decision situation and help assure, with relative certainty, that approaches will be stable over substantial periods. On the other hand, infrequently made decisions may be linked to those situations that contain important creative or problem-solving elements, as in planning or research.[21]

Identifiable situations that readily lend themselves to computerized routines underlie Exhibit 11–2. The areas of computer application suggested by this exhibit have been extended with the greater use of such techniques as gaming and simulation as our knowledge of decision variables has grown. Thus we would expect to see a merging and extension in the areas of computer usage as bounded rationality is pushed back.

Authority level and *organization function* are other features of Exhibit 11–2. The stipulation of parameters influences the analysis of particular decision situations. To understand this point, consider how the characterization would change as we consider (a) general management officials (more cre-

EXHIBIT 11–2. Decision Routines: Basis for Programming

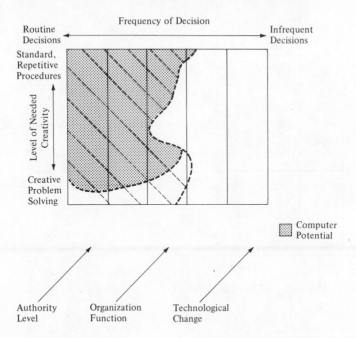

ative and less routine) versus first-line supervisors (more routine and less creative) and (b) line officials versus problem-solving groups (highly nonroutine and/or creative). Thus the computer potential (Chapter 7) of programmable decision areas shifts dramatically as the various groups are considered. Given current technological developments, how will the areas of computer potential displayed in this exhibit be shifted?

THE MIDDLE-MANAGEMENT CONTROVERSY

The decision areas illustrated by Exhibit 11–2 can be further extended so as to illustrate the broader implications for the decision system, as shown in Exhibit 11–3. The increasing use of the computer and management science techniques in decision processes is the focus here, at least to the extent that both behavioral and structural effects are involved.

Exhibit 11–3 provides several important elaborations of points that were touched on in the discussion of Exhibit 11–2. In this representation the use of management science (operations research) models in conjunction with the computer is seen as a powerful means of dealing with various decision situations.[22] For example, these computer and management technologies assist in the routine handling of various repetitive tasks. Yet computer and management science approaches promise important resolutions of complex

EXHIBIT 11-3. New Problem Areas in the Management Decision System

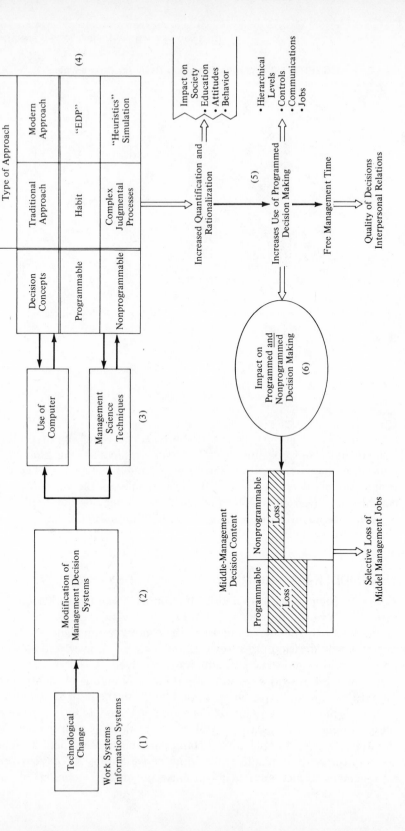

problems, or insight into them, through simulation approaches. Thus trends of increasing attempts to quantify and rationalize heretofore difficult organizational and planning situations are clearly in evidence.

Yet as these models and systematic approaches make inroads into decision making, their impact on various role performers (Chapter 10) and job activities becomes increasingly apparent. The incorporation of the computer and decision models into a decision system can condense (telescope) authority levels, redefine the character of the communication system (type of information, role participants), and permit more elaborate control systems (Chapter 5). Thus Exhibit 11–3, in a sense, moves full circle back to the area of programmable and nonprogrammable decisions (item 6) but emphasizes the influence of growing decision sophistication.

The increasing quantification and rationalization of various decision situations (as in the area of marketing) suggest important changes in the broader reaches of society in terms of educational approaches, management attitudes, and behavior. The increased use of programmable decision situations also has an important intracompany effect on the authority structure, the types of controls that can be employed, the communication possibilities, and the character of jobs. On the one hand, management time may be freed through the use of computer-assisted approaches, improving the quality of decisions and permitting the strengthening of interpersonal decisions. However, middle-management decision areas would be reduced, along with a selective loss of middle-management positions.

The possible shift in the importance of middle management has become the basis for a number of articles offering opposing viewpoints, and at the same time has provided several generations of writers with ample material for discussion. The analyses in this and preceding chapters should make it clear that broad generalizations are of little use. The specification of organizational conditions and the detailing of important variables for decision analysis provide a more fruitful basis for ascertaining the organizational impact of these changes.

DECISION SYSTEMS, POLICY PLANNING, AND INNOVATION

The effectiveness of planning or innovation can be usefully interpreted in terms of the decision structures underlying these processes and the environments from which the inputs for the system emerge—see (1) in Exhibit 11–4A. This exhibit depicts some of the important elements of the decision system (4, 4′) that emphasize goal-oriented approaches in innovative or planning processes. The decision environment—be it internal or external—the technology, and the competitive milieu constitute an important dimension for the types of decisions or problems with which the decision maker is confronted (1). Emerging issues and problems from the environment lead to the involvement of supporting staffs and search (intelligence)

EXHIBIT 11–4A. Aspects of Organization Decision System

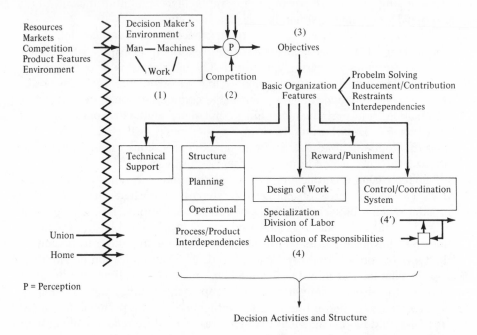

activities, and form a basis for developing alternatives (Exhibit 11–4B [7], [8]). As a decision structure begins to take shape, greater opportunities for improvement become evident. Decision makers will sift through the premises thought to relate to the decisions and will fashion a manageable group from them.

A "simplified" approach suggests that the decision maker frames his concept or view of the problem on the basis of a number of personal factors, the policy framework within the organization, and anticipated needs of the future.

As already noted, we work with a definite set of alternatives or possibilities reflecting bounded rationality and seek to break up a more complex whole into manageable portions (Exhibit 11–4B [5]). Second-level or middle management, plus supporting groups and systems, often heavily reinforce this portion of the decision effort. Attempts may be made to "shake down" information to a point where it can be submitted to top management for choice or for direction in future analysis.

Organization features affect the decision system. They reflect interdependencies, problem-solving capabilities and restraints, awareness of goals, and the importance of work activities directed toward the nonroutine, creative aspects of planning (5). Exhibits 11–4A, –B contrast decision making

EXHIBIT 11–4B. Decision Activities and Structure

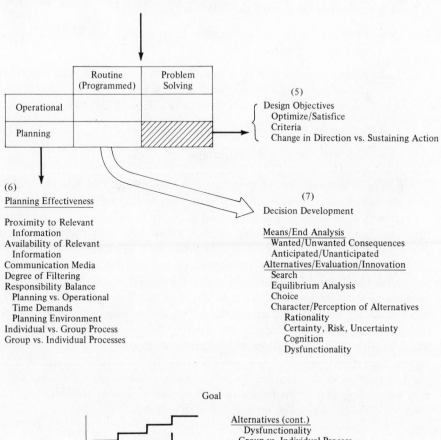

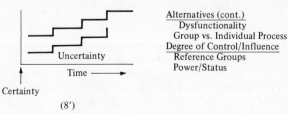

for planning, especially strategic planning, with operational decision making (5) and problem solving that may have a heavy base of routinized decision content.

Planning approaches that touch major dimensions of policy have to do with time horizons that go far beyond current activities. Ideally, we would like to optimize in planning, but, as we have pointed out, "satisfactory" approaches more reasonably characterize the expectations. Naturally, change-of-direction planning may affect the outermost reaches of the organization.

Designing decision structures for situations with new or unique elements (as in planning) contends with the following:

1. Permissiveness of the decision environment latitude to propose new ideas or approaches

2. Extent of routine or operational job content found in the decision maker's areas of responsibility, as opposed to the problem-solving content—this influences his time availability and priorities

3. Individual as opposed to group approaches

4. Role and use of support groups

The formal organization of decision activities would also have to anticipate important behavioral points, including supervisor-subordinate relationships, the susceptibility of the individual or group to environmental or group pressures, rank and status problems that might inhibit participation, and the character of the organization's reward system (Exhibit 11-4B), which takes into account motivation, performance, and standards of achievement.

Exhibit 11–4B proposes that the decision be viewed as a type of means-end analysis (7), displaying a coherent structure of subdecisions and taking into account anticipated as well as unanticipated consequences (which may be thought of as a side-branching of decisions)—described as dysfunctionality. Thus Exhibit 11–4B capitalizes on a variety of decision approaches, noting factors that tend to enhance key aspects of the decision process, and involving (a) sources of decision inputs to (b) organization subsystems for decision processing to (c) attributes of an important class of decisions (planning) to (d) characteristics of goal-oriented activity.

DECISION DEVELOPMENT

Exhibit 11–4B displays some of the important summary points of decision development, with particular emphasis on goal-oriented activity. Characteristically, the decision (planning) horizon is far afield from current events; thus uncertainty (8) and some degree of unpredictability are characteristic of this future time-space. Formulating longer-range goals and the means of securing them necessitates the development of subprograms that reflect careful integration of related (means-end/cause-result) undertakings. At each node of this growing decision structure, contingencies must be anticipated, searches made for better alternatives, and a selection made from the alternatives. The natural limits of cognitive processes (7) in these evaluations lead to analysis and subdecisions that combine both objective and qualitative considerations. The latter reflect the uncertainties of future time-spaces *and* problem/situational elements that are difficult to fully symbolize, such as various aspects of human behavior.

DECISION MODELS FOR ORGANIZATIONAL SYSTEMS

To an important extent, the decision maker, whether a line manager, supervisor, or technical staff member, is frequently called upon to make decisions based on organizational models that materially influence his environment, including his co-workers. The decision environment is replete with diverse pressures, needs, dicta, trends, and groups that importantly guide the character, frequency, and priority of issues.

The exogenous variables of diverse social, economic, political, and ideological trends are an important dimension of decision making. For example, external variables may include the "hard core" unemployed, growing leisure time, and early retirement. In the former, we see society's response to a growing labor shortage, or a concern for social responsibility. Early retirement may reflect technological obsolescence, or simply the desire of the retiree to participate in the "good life" at an earlier point. Both developments concern the decision maker. The employment of labor that is unaccustomed to the discipline of working hours, conditions, and supervision poses substantial personnel problems in training, as well as the necessity for modifying the attitudes of large organizational groups. Early retirement places a new emphasis on manpower planning, anticipation of the attrition of key people, and more careful career planning for those on the way up (Chapter 12).

Economic trends in the external environment, new tax legislation, encouragement of capital expenditures, and/or price increases in the cost of labor may combine to dictate capital-intensive operations (computers for information service or new equipment for manufacturing). This trend has an obvious implication for technological change in the organization and for the need to anticipate the thrust of these developments.

SYSTEMS MODELS FOR DECISION MAKING

In Chapters 3 and 4 a set of models was developed for the analysis of organizational (especially technological) systems. Some of the better-known quantitative models, such as linear programming and PERT/CPM,[23] have demonstrated their utility in systems analysis,[24] and they offer new insights to the decision maker.[25] The Markov model, which has proved to be of increasing value in systems studies of manpower movements and career planning, is discussed in Chapter 12.

One of the important themes expressed by Exhibits 11–1A, –B, and –C pertain to the organization and development of information for uncertainty reduction, problem solving, and decision making. The Bright profile, for characterizing information and production systems, and Woodward's relating of organization structure to a work system (Chapter 4) provide excellent initial points of departure in dealing with complex systems. A number of models serve common purposes, but, additionally, each may serve to illuminate structure, relationships, or change.

The descriptive (qualitative) models aid decision-making processes by assisting in the identification of premises, possibilities, and questions or relationships, and thus form an indispensable part of decision making under complex conditions. The Bright profile permits an examination of existing system characteristics plus the posing of questions based on proposed changes of the system. Woodward's structural model, in its relation to level of technological achievement, poses normative questions in comparing an existing system to the median values derived in her work.

Quantifiable models, such as linear programming and the critical path method (CPM) planning model, also represent bases for dealing with complex systems, though they yield different descriptions or types of "answers." For example, the critical path method focuses on relationships and flows in complex networks and provides important answers for decision making, timing, and feasibility. Linear programming models, to the extent that a host of relations are quantifiable, permit the examination of cost/recourse tradeoffs, insights to economic resource combinations, and conditions for improved performance. Simulation models permit the study of complex systems under a variety of conditions or insights to "what if" questions. Markov models, illustrated in Chapter 12, permit the study of manpower flows between departments, authority levels, and points of entry and exit.

Decision Support Groups: Opportunity and Conflict

From a behavioral viewpoint, the increasing incorporation of these models poses a new set of problems and challengers. The updating of management technologies (model and computer usage) has placed various decision-support groups such as operations research in new positions of power, career opportunity, and potential conflict.[26] The fact that these groups frequently possess a level of technical knowledge and comprehension considerably beyond that of other role holders can readily create tension or even conflict. Supervisors, managers, and officials may be forced to rely on their pronouncements without their own basis of confirmation or denial. Not surprisingly, these decision-support groups may be looked upon with suspicion, which is heightened by the use of technical jargon. Communication problems between the planning/research analyst and line manager are often considerable.

The conflict that has frequently arisen between technical specialist and line manager may be examined with a motivational perspective (Chapter 8).

The decision maker is presented with information inputs involving assumptions and methodologies that are largely unknown to him. As the decision maker possessing the formal authority and trappings of office, his formal leadership role is undercut. (Somebody else is the expert, and he may *have to accept* another's recommendation with little probing or questioning.) Though he may see the recommended course of action as securing important organization objectives (level one) and broader organization goals, this decision path comes with high personal cost. Yet, in the short run (without personal training), he may be unable to identify feasible alternative paths and nevertheless be motivated to try to do so (albeit unhappily) in line with this approach.

In organizations where the technical specialist has been able to gain a cordial reception for his role, new promotional paths and opportunities have often developed. Rather than along the traditional path of the functional activities (production, marketing, and finance), new career routes to the top began to emerge through these specialties.

When decision processes are viewed as multistage, system features are emphasized. Interdependencies are an integral part of this view; consequently, the relationships among organization (structural) functions are emphasized. Second, the chain of activities, carried out over time, emphasizes the increasing uncertainties of fulfillment (e.g., by new competition or new or unexpected legislation and the need for a closely linked control system that will permit redirection as needed. Third, the linked stages (in the manner of "dynamic programming") illustrate the relation and dependency of events in one stage to and on those of the preceding and following stages. In each of these stages the relative successes and the character and scope of problems are affected by developments in the previous stage.

System Dependencies—Participation

Another perspective on decision systems involves interdependencies in work procedures and their effect on joint decision making. For example, where participative efforts are indicated, interaction that is both congenial [27] and constructive adds to the level of existing knowledge and leads to the identification of new alternatives, thus enhancing the quality of the decision.

Exhibit 11–5 makes it evident that decision processes (and systems) necessarily bring together much of what has been said in the preceding chapters about behavior, systems, and structure. Where joint efforts are indicated because of task features (Chapters 3, 4, and 7), analysis must consider

    a. Leadership characteristics (Chapter 9)—the ability to organize and guide task groups, along with the recognition of tasks that lend themselves to individual accomplishment

    b. Situational demands (Chapters 2–4, 7)—task assignments that range from those determined by technology to almost purely intellectual processes (creativity)

EXHIBIT 11–5. Participative Decision Making: Some Design Considerations

	Level and quality of participative decision making			
Character of leadership	Situational need	Communication support	Personal features of participants	Support systems
Understanding	Technology	Use of Technology	Education	Control
Assignment of cooperative effort	Creativity	Needed system features	Experience	Behavioral role
			Sophistication	

Bases for decision responses*

Character of leadership		Communication support	Personal features of participants	Support systems
Formal authority		Manipulation	Expertise	Friendship
Traditional rules		Avoidance	Collegial	Equity exchange
Bureaucratic rules			Professional	
Control of resources				
Responsibility				

* Added details can be found in Allan C. Filley and A. J. Grimes, "The Bases of Power in Decision Processes," *Proceedings of the Annual Meeting of the Academy of Management, 1967*, pp. 133–159.

c. Communications support (Chapter 6)—possibilities to be accounted for in interactions among people and departments. That is, to the extent that channels permit or encourage interaction under attractive conditions, participative processes are enhanced.

d. Personal (psychological) features of the participants—these affect the possibilities in interactive decision making, including the need for alternative approaches and the quality of collaborative efforts

e. Support systems (Chapters 5, 11)—quality/quantity of support personnel, controls, and organization

In designing the decision system for participative decision making, the situational and system features just described establish the basis for a variety of decision responses. Decision interaction may take place on the basis of formal authority or traditional rules, as is often found in bureaucratic approaches. A second collectivity of responses may be established on the basis of expertise or colleague relationships, as in professional organizations (e.g., hospitals). By some, the move to participation in decision making may be seen as manipulative—the establishment of a cordial decision climate will necessitate the development of mutual trust and cooperative work relationships.[28] Power in decision relationships may build on diverse considerations, which may be perceived, desired, or actually utilized by participants. Inability to establish cooperative working relationships, or discrepancies between that perceived as needed versus utilized, form the basis for dysfunction and conflict.[29]

Influence of Situation and Task

The character of the decision task provides a basis for specifying such things as supervisory style, roles, goal processes, and norms in decision behavior.[30] There are three characteristic decision tasks: routine (repetitive and standardized), creative (nonroutine, intellectually challenging), and negotiated. In the latter situation, neither party to the decision process has complete or final authority, and compromise is indicated.

As an example, the prescriptions for *routine decision situations,* featuring centralized coordination, division of labor, and functional specialization, indicate

Structure—specialization and coordination (routine lacks permitting specialization but requires coordination)

Role   —independent effort (emerging from routine but specialized effort)

Style   —high stress, decentralized responsibility, centralized coordination, and general emphasis on quantity and timing

Norms   —level of professionalism exercised

Decision Participation and Leadership

The leader-subordinate relationship is another basis for scrutinizing participation. The posture of leadership can be indicated under three different
levels of participative effort: low, medium, and high. Exhibit 11–6 broadly
correlates the three levels of decision participation with some of the leadership descriptions of Chapter 9 and typical decision situations.

Where decision participation is low, an autocratic-style leadership may
prevail, which may not be far from an authoritarian expectancy found in
some areas of our culture. Motivational strategies turn on reward-punish-
ment, with little solicitation of group-member ideas and mostly one-way communication. Though this low-participation model may appear somewhat
extreme in its mode of people handling, emergency or high stress conditions
(riots, battlefields), plus a leader who has the appropriate information for
decision making, may preclude other decision approaches.

Yet, at the same time, situational analysis may lead to a description of
"emergency" or "high-tension conditions" where a high level of participation
is sought. In air traffic control the controllers work as a tightly knit team,
with various members monitoring ground movement and incoming and de-
parting flights. High-level participation and the involvement of all members
are required to permit servicing large numbers of planes while maintaining
good safety records. Similar analyses could be developed for the participation situations in Exhibit 11–6.

Take, for example, a situation described under high member participation
in decision making. In forecasting new technologies or products, the collective opinions of experts are often sought;[31] also, a key function of the leader
is to seek resolution of apparent problems or differences and gain some
level of convergence on a logical, reasoned estimate. Yet this participative
approach is dependent on both key assumptions and situational parameters.
In this description of forecasting technological developments it is assumed
that various experts could *add* information or perspectives beyond that possessed by a given individual. Also, the situation itself (technological forecasting) is one that commonly crosses state-of-the-art bounds and thus
inclines the decision maker toward participative approaches.

In short, Exhibit 11–6 assists in organizing for analysis some common
areas of decision participation. However, except for some rather pure cases,
the more complex (but insightful) framework of the leader's role (Chapters 9 and 10) must be evoked. We *do* have to contend with such matters
as the decision situation, the leader's power in the organization and his rela-

EXHIBIT 11–6. Leader–Decision Making Model: Participation in Response to Situation

← Level of Decision Participation →

← Task centered   People centered →

	Low		Medium		High
Leader's approach	Sanctions Unilateral decisions	Carrot/Stick Conditional Solicitation of Ideas	Modest interaction and discussion	Active involvement	Decentralize decision making
Designation	Autocratic		Democratic		Laissez-faire
Typical situations	Leader has the premises Severe time restraints Authoritarian expectancy in culture Emergency breakdown Wage incentive systems		Leader guides, but quality of decision and carrying out of decision indicate mutual interaction Policy formulation Setting subordinate job objectives	Group problem solving New product development	Group has the premises Nominal time restraints Desirable cost-benefit relationships: time and costs relative to contribution Highly variable job-shop conditions

Added detail underlying these variables may be found in Keith Davis, *Human Relations at Work: The Dynamics of Organizational Behavior* (4th ed., New York: McGraw-Hill, 1972), pp. 107, 142.

tionship to his superior, limitations/strengths in leader personality, and social acceptance of both leader and decision participants.

Much of the literature on participative decision making or job enrichment subsumes a close connection between participation and such benefits as job satisfaction, work achievement, and individual integration that facilitates the accommodation of change. However, recent research[32] reinforces the need for careful delineation of surrounding conditions. For example, in one research study (of elementary school teachers),[33] those who perceived a lack of decision participation were characterized as young in age and low in seniority, with high role conflict and militant attitudes.[34]

LOCUS OF DECISION MAKING

In the absence of a detailed specification of conditions, an overall characterization of changes in decision making, such as *centralization* or *decentralization,* usually serves no useful purpose. Five factors must be accounted for before descriptions of shifts in decision-making locus can be usefully employed. These include recognizing decision making as a process, authority levels where change takes place, distinguishing the management functions involved, responsibility shifts, and the physical characteristics of the authority structure.

The Process

When decision making is viewed as a process, as described earlier in the chapter, it behooves the analyst to contend with *each* of the major procedures typically ascribed to the process. These range from problem identification to feedback and evaluation.

Trends in the locus of decision making should consider each decision stage. Various stages of the decision process may be particularly vulnerable to the intrusion of management technology—a point that was brought out in Chapter 7, where considerable space was devoted to the *differential* impact of computer-based systems on some of these decision stages. The outcome of that discussion was that problem identification (a) and choice (d) could be expected to reside with top management, whereas other stages, including developing alternatives, evaluation, and implementation, might be assumed by middle-level administrators. In decision making, viewed as a process, the balance between line and staff assignments is important. However, one must also consider the hierarchical level of authority.

Level of Authority

When analyzing shifts in the locus of decision making, one must consider the point in the authority structure where modification is under way. Contemplating changes at the level of first-line supervision poses quite different decision outcomes than considering the middle or upper reaches of the management structure.

Analyses that deal with the locus of decision making may go beyond the authority level consideration and treat the potential telescoping of function and activity, which is a typical concomitant of changes currently under way in organizations. The major impact in decision making may be one of compacting job functions, or even creating new ones ("management services"), rather than simply a shift in the level at which certain responsibilities are to be exercised.

Management Functions

An important dimension of the discussion in Chapter 2 was the allocation of such management functions as planning, control, direction, coordination, and administration, which differ widely in content and assignment across the hierarchy. Consequently, one would distinguish among possible modifications in both qualitative and quantitative content for these various functions. Thus the introduction of a new product could easily shift coordination-control responsibilities and decisions to a new-products manager in marketing, at least until the product displays stable sales patterns.

Another illustration of analyzing decision making from the functional view is one that accounts for shifts in responsibility from tactical to strategic planning. Various support groups have been in the midst of these shifts, and have often become the recipients of increased planning responsibility. On the other hand, strategic planning often includes an appreciable subjective content, reflecting the necessity to deal with trends in the environment. Here, decision processes are more difficult to penetrate with routine or systematic approaches, and consequently upper management echelons may find a high level of subjective content in them.

Transfer of Responsibility

Another complication of analysis is the potential transfer of decision responsibilities *within,* as opposed to *between,* organization subfunctions or subsystems. Thus a shift of decision responsibility may be within the line or the staff organization. It also may be from production to marketing, and of course it may encompass trends within these departments. For example, manpower development responsibilities may now be undertaken by a production manager, as compared with a first-level foreman, or by a marketing manager as compared with a sales supervisor.

Structural Logistics

Chapter 2 suggested substantial differences in the structural configuration of organizational life. This was based on the distinctions between physically centralized and widely dispersed manufacturing plants, field offices, warehouses, administrative units, or sales/service centers. A centralized unit in one physical location suggests different decision approaches than in a corporate unit with fifteen sales centers, each of which has widely differing local markets.

In summary, describing the locus of decision making or potential changes in it requires the specification of function, process, hierarchical level, and the physical characteristics of structure in order to prove of use to oganizational analysts. What underlying factors must be recognized in anticipating shifts in the locus of decision making? The material of earlier chapters suggests that newer achievements in management technology, the diversity and rate of change in competitive markets, and institutional features that may be affected by political or legal considerations will affect the locus of decision making.

Example

Technological changes in basic steel making processes have led to a wide spectrum of changes in domestic steel plants, involving new high-speed rolling facilities, continuous casting, high-speed steel making, advanced controls, and computer applications. Growing areas of interdependency in production operations have demanded the tightening of internal operations. Increased competition from Japan and Germany have necessitated better facilities and product planning, and have pressured managements for substantial organizational and operational improvements.

As a result, staff support specialists at the plant level have assumed heightened responsibilities for production planning and coordination relative to the line-production organization. And the firmer establishment of computer capabilities has reinforced this shift of control responsibilities to staff support functions.

Price competition and the need for accelerating the pace of change among steel companies has resulted, in some cases, in the establishment of R&D functions where they did not exist before. These functions are beginning to assume leadership in the formulation of new products or process ideas, responsibilities that formerly (and informally) resided in many different areas of the organization.

These examples, drawn from the steel industry, amplify our understanding of the process by which the loci for decision making may shift for organizational functions in response to complex internal developments and environmental forces.

The Mission Federal Savings and Loan case situation, at the end of this chapter, provides an opportunity to put to work much of the material of Part II. It shifts the application focus from manufacturing to service in order to extend the scope of these discussions.

SUMMARY

This chapter sets forth a view of decision making in structural, systems, and behavioral dimensions. The early view of decision activities, elaborated around structural considerations, was heavily modified when system and behavioral notions were introduced. Thus the Weberian model fell short in providing a viable perspective for the analysis of decision situations. However, when it is combined with the Barnard-Simon notions, a number of useful possibilities emerge.

Several central variables suggest the complexity of problems confronting decision makers, and thus point toward prescriptive approaches. Characterizations of the authority structure as "tall" or "flat" must be supplemented with some representation of the degree of physical decentralization. Once the physical aspects of the structure are established, the problems and potentialities of communications between organizational departments, functions, and offices must be reckoned with. Communication potential takes into account the available communication technology and situational requirements.

Advanced information systems may permit redistribution of decision processes and functions, but system detail and some degree of functional specification must be considered. Required timing for making decisions and proximity to needed information further qualify this procedure. Elements of decision function and process display widely varying vulnerability to change, and thus must be treated with care.

Several models that were developed in the chapter provide vehicles for opening up the topics of routine and nonroutine decision content and their potential influence on decision activities. Satisfactory approaches focus on simplifying assumptions, on problem reduction, and on the use of revised solution programs to fit current needs. Research and intelligence efforts greatly facilitate the process of decision development, but with some notable dysfunctional shortcomings.

Decision-making models integrate logically with leadership concepts and (as in the case of leadership) require considerable specification of situation if they are to be useful.

QUESTIONS

1. Develop some propositions for the decision authorities and processes attending the review, selection, and implementation of new product or production technologies from the viewpoint of
   a) Consumers of these developments
   b) R&D (research and development) groups that create them.

2. Use the concept of Exhibit 11–2 to compare and contrast decision approaches and computer usage (or potential) for a general manager, policymaker, and production foreman; for a marketing manager, market researcher, and salesman.

EXERCISE

Develop some propositions based on organizational characteristics and design features such as specialization and division of labor that bear on decision-making features, components, or strategies such as coordination, integration, communications and uncertainty, optimizing and satisficing.

CASE SITUATION

Mission Federal Savings and Loan Association has been faced with a serious problem among its younger supervisors, specialists, and officers. Despite the continuation of generally high levels of unemployment in a number of different industries, turnover in this manpower group continues to run at a high level. In light of the continuing need for rapid expansion of the association's services and activities in response to rapid building and business developments in the community, remedial approaches were desperately needed. In just a ten-year period, MFSL has grown from the twentieth to the third largest association in the state. Yet pyramiding costs, failure to adopt and extend modern information-processing techniques, and high managerial turnover were among the factors threatening serious consequences in what otherwise would have been viewed as a desirable outcome (growth in size).

   The president and founder of the association, Frank Griffin, a living example of the modern-day entrepreneur, started out with borrowed funds and a store-front operation. Although MFSL now occupied a huge modern building in the community's main shopping area, Griffin still made his daily rounds, greeted customers, and maintained a high level of involvement in the affairs of the institution. Most of the senior officers were long-time associates of Griffin, having joined the association shortly after its inception. The president and senior officers were members of the board of trustees, along with a group of "outside" professional people, financial people, and several industrialists.

It was only after considerable urging by the group comprising the outside membership that the president consented to "inviting" in Behavioral Sciences for Management, a group specializing in organizational-behavioral problems.

As a member of the consultant's team, you have been assigned the task of sketching out some preliminary models, propositions, and approaches for clarifying problems and for identifying solutions. You recognize that gaining acceptance of your ideas from the principals in the organization will be no small part of the problem.

NOTES

1. Some of these points are brought together in Marshall W. Meyer's "The Two Authority Structures of Bureaucratic Organization," *Administrative Science Quarterly,* 13, no. 2 (September 1968): 211–228.

2. Max Weber, *The Theory of Social and Economic Organization,* trans. A. M. Henderson and Talcott Parsons (New York: The Free Press, 1964).

3. First formulated in Herbert A. Simon, *Administrative Behavior* (1947), and updated in 2d edition (New York: Macmillan, 1957).

4. Herbert A. Simon and James G. March, *Organizations* (New York: John Wiley & Sons, 1958).

5. For arguments concerning the influence of span of control and authority level on decision processes, see James C. Worthy, "Organizational Structure and Employee Morale," *American Sociological Review,* 15, no. 2 (April 1950): 169–179.

6. Harold J. Leavitt, "Some Effects of Certain Communication Patterns on Group Performance," *Journal of Abnormal Social Psychology,* 46, no. 1 (January 1951): 38–50. The arguments on tall and flat structures are drawn together neatly in Harold Guetzkow and Herbert A. Simon, "The Impact of Certain Communication Nets upon Organization and Performance in Task-oriented Groups," *Management Science,* 1, no. 3–4 (April–July 1955): 233–250.

7. Rocco Carzo Jr. and John N. Yanouzas, "Effects of Flat and Tall Organization Structures," *Administrative Science Quarterly,* 14, no. 2 (June 1969): 178–191.

8. Vaughan Blankenship and Raymond E. Miles, "Organizational Structure and Managerial Decision Behavior," *Administrative Science Quarterly,* 13, no. 1 (June 1968): 106–120.

9. Ibid.

10. Meyer, "The Two Authority Structures," esp. pp. 214–215.

11. Selwyn W. Becker and Nicholas Baloff, "Organization Structure and Complex Problem Solving," *Administrative Science Quarterly,* 14, no. 2 (June 1969): 260–271.

12. Meyer, "The Two Authority Structures."

13. Carzo and Yanouzas, "Flat and Tall Organization Structures."

14. Becker and Baloff, "Organization Structure."

15. Blankenship and Miles, "Organizational Structure."

16. Often associated with selected portions of Chester I. Barnard, *Functions of the Executive* (1938), and Herbert T. Simon, *Administrative Behavior* (1957) and *New Science of Executive Decision Making* (1960). The latter is an important basis for the ideas set forth in this section.

17. Strategic and operational distinctions are made in George Steiner (ed.), *Managerial Long Range Planning* (New York: McGraw-Hill, 1963), esp. pp. 6–79, and Robert J. Litschert, "Some Characteristics of Long Range Planning: An industry Study," *Academy of Management Journal,* 11, no. 3 (September 1968): 315–328.

18. Some aspects of these differences between decision makers dealing with complexity and uncertainty are considered in Robert Duncan, "Characteristics of Organizational Environmental and Perceived Environmental Uncertainty," *Administrative Science Quarterly,* 17, no. 3 (September 1972): 313–327.

19. Ibid.

20. E. Eugene Carter, "The Behavioral Theory of the Firm and Top-Level Corporate Decisions," *Administrative Science Quarterly,* 16, no. 4 (December 1971): 413–428.

21. These points are examined in considerable detail in Manley Howe Jones, *Executive Decision Making* (rev. ed.; Homewood, Ill.: Richard D. Irwin, 1962).

22. For example, see David L. Rados, "Selection and Evaluation of Alternatives in Repetitive Decision Making," *Administrative Science Quarterly,* 17, no. 2 (June 1972): 196–207. Early work on the concepts expressed here includes the classic work of Herbert A. Simon, *New Science of Management Decisions* (New York: Harper & Row, 1960), plus related works such as Melvin Anshen, "The Manager and the Black Boss," *Harvard Business Review,* 38, no. 6 (November–December, 1960): 85–92, and Harold J. Leavitt and Thomas L. Whisler, "Management in the 1980s," *Harvard Business Review* 36, no. 6 (November–December, 1958): pp. 41–48.

23. Program Evaluation and Review Techniques and Critical Path Methods.

24. W. J. Fabrycky and Paul E. Torgerson, *Operations Economy: Industrial Applications of Operations Research* (Englewood Cliffs, N.J.: Prentice-Hall, 1966).

25. For a stimulating discussion of the use of quantitative models in the analysis of organizational systems, see Rocco Carzo Jr. and John N. Yanouzas, *Formal Organizations: A Systems Approach* (Homewood, Ill.: Richard D. Irwin, 1972 rev.).

26. Elmer H. Burack and Robert Batlavala, "Emerging Organizational Developments in Operational Research Groups," *Business Perspectives,* 9, no. 2 (Winter 1972); Bernard H. Baum and Elmer H. Burack, "Information Technology, Manpower Development, and Organizational Performance," *Academy of Management Journal,* 12, no. 3 (September 1969): 279–292; also see C. Jackson Grayson, Jr., "Management Science and Business Practice," *Harvard Business Review,* 51, no. 4 (July–August 1973): 41–47.

27. Interesting aspects of conflict are brought out in John M. Dutton, "Analysis of Interdepartmental Decision Making," *Academy of Management Proceedings* (1967),

pp. 85–112; also see Joseph A. Alutto and James A. Belasco, "A Typology for Participation in Organizational Decision Making," *Administrative Science Quarterly,* 17, no. 1 (March 1972): 117–126.

28. For an interesting development of these ideas, see Alan C. Filley and A. J. Grimes, "The Bases of Power in Decision Processes," *Academy of Management Proceedings* (1967), pp. 133–159.

29. The *technique* for developing information in groups may also be greatly affected by the decision maker's approach. For an interesting discussion on nominal groups in *decision making,* see Andrew Van deVen and Andre L. Delbecq, "Nominal versus Interacting Group Processes for Committee Decision-Making Effectiveness," *Academy of Management Journal,* 14, no. 2 (June 1971): 203–212.

30. Andre L. Delbecq, "The Management of Decision-Making within the Firm—Three Strategies for Three Types of Decision Making," *Academy of Management Journal,* 10, no. 4 (December 1967): 329–393.

31. Some of these relationships are developed in Keith Davis, *Human Relations of Work: The Dynamics of Organizational Behavior* (New York: McGraw-Hill, 1967), p. 132, and in an earlier book by Manley Howe Jones, *Executive Decision Making* (Homewood, Ill.: Richard D. Irwin, 1962).

32. Alutto and Belasco, "A Typology for Participation," 17–125.

33. Ibid., p. 123.

34. Another aspect of participative decision making is job enrichment. Although the job enrichment literature indicates both desirable behavioral and performance outcomes, at least one recent study (of state highway employees) denies the productivity result but lends some support to the behavioral (morale) improvement. See Reed M. Powell and John L. Schlacter, "Participative Management—A Panacea?" *Academy of Management Journal,* 14, no. 2 (June 1971); 165–174.

REFERENCES

Alutto, Joseph A. "A Typology for Participation in Organizational Decision Making." *Administrative Science Quarterly,* 17, no. 1 (March 1972): 117–125.

Blumberg, Arthur, Stokes B. Carrigan, Robert T. Golembiewski, Walter R. Mead and Robert Munzenrider. "Changing Climate in a Complex Organization: Interactions between a Learning Decision and an Environment." *Administrative Science Quarterly,* 14, no. 4 (December 1971): 465–481.

Burack, Elmer H. "Organizational and Administrative Problems in Formulating Health Care Systems." *Proceedings of the Fourth Annual Meeting of the American Institute of Decision Sciences,* New Orleans, November 1972.
———. *Structural Strategies.* Glenview, Ill.: Scott, Foresman, in process.

Carter, E. Eugene. "The Behavioral Theory of the Firm and Top-Level Corporate Decisions." *Administrative Science Quarterly,* 16, no. 4 (December 1971): 413–428.

Duncan, Robert B. "Characteristics of Organizational Environments and Perceived Uncertainty." *Administrative Science Quarterly,* 17, no. 3 (September 1972): 313–327.

Hickson, D. J., C. R. Hinnings, C. A. Lee, R. E. Schneck, and J. M Pennings. "A Strategic Contingencies Theory of Intraorganizational Power." *Administrative Science Quarterly,* 16, no. 2 (June 171): 216–292.

Holder, Jack J. "Decision Making by Consensus." *Business Horizons,* 15, no. 2 (April 1972): 47–54.

Holloman, Charles R., and Hal W. Hendrick. "Adequacy of Group Decisions as a Function of the Decision-making Process." *Academy of Management Journal* 15, no. 2 (June 1972): 175–184.

Magee, John F. "Decision Trees for Decision Making." *Harvard Business Review,* 42, no. 4 (July–August 1964): 126–138.

Marks, Barry A. "Decision under Uncertainty: A Poet's View." *Business Horizons,* 14, no. 1 (February 1971): 57–64.

Pollay, Richard W. "The Structure of Executive Decisions and Decision Times." *Administrative Science Quarterly,* 15, no. 4 (December 1970): 459–471.

Rados, David L. "Selection and Evaluation of Alternatives in Repetitive Decision Making." *Administrative Science Quarterly,* 17, no. 2 (June 1972): 196–206.

Zand, Dale E. "Trust and Managerial Problem Solving." *Administrative Science Quarterly,* 17, no. 2 (June 1972): 229–239.

Part *III*
APPLICATION

Part III moves the thrust of the analysis into significant *applied* areas of application.

For a number of years now, there has been a major need for conceptualizing and theory building (Parts I and II) but little effort has been directed to putting these notions into resolving important organizational problems. The student of management has often been left with the uncomfortable feeling that "theorizing and model building is of importance, but how do I put them to work in meaningful fashion?"

This section gives the student of organization the opportunity to think-through the bases for *applying* structural, systems, and behavioral perspectives to (a) organization planning, with particular emphasis on individual and group development (Chapter 12), and (b) the management of change (Chapter 13). The latter is undoubtedly the most crucial task facing managers and professionals in an era of growing complexity, turbulence, and uncertainty.

Chapter 14 provides a comprehensive application case based on various notions introduced in Parts I and II. Chapter 15 sets forth some speculations on the trajectory of emergent trends in organizational and behavioral matters, plus some developments that appear likely.

Learning Objectives

Role of Environmental Change in the Emergence of Needs for
      Organization and Human Resource Development
Bases for Managerial-Manpower Development and Change
Models for Organization Development and Role of Change Agents
      Sequence and Approaches
Management by Objectives: Assumptions, Approaches, Limitations
Quantitative Model for Career Planning and Change
      Important Organizational Problems and Issues

DEVELOPMENT OF ORGANIZATIONS AND HUMAN RESOURCES: A MANPOWER PLANNING PERSPECTIVE

OVERVIEW

The discussions in this chapter are initiated with a brief historical portrayal of the manner in which the concerns for human resources are being redefined by all manner of institutions. Social trends and legislative enactment are some of the important imperatives touched on in this analysis, which establishes a basis for viewing the management of manpower for improving performance and furthering opportunities for individual realization.

With the background established for needed shifts in an organization's concerns regarding human resources, some educational and training strategies are reviewed for improving individual and group performance and achievement. Individual, group, and system undertakings are related to various performance objectives, behavioral issues, and behavioral problems. Programs such as "management by objectives" and "organization development" are described in these discussions. Also, an "organization development" example is provided, based on research and studies we have undertaken.

The final portrayal in this chapter centers on systematic planning approaches for gauging the future manpower needs of an organization. Because of its increasing prominence in these undertakings, a discussion is devoted to a Markov-type model for carrying out planning analyses.

Chapter Orientation: "Development"

The approach in this chapter anticipates major organizational developments of the 1970s leading to a broad approach to increasing human work performances and individual or personal realizations. Consequently, the discussions take up organizational planning designs, group processes for performance and work achievement, and the strengthening of individual realizations for the organization and one's self. This approach involves the planning of undertakings, possible structural realignments, shifts in individual or group job roles and relationships, new roles for leadership within groups and for linking groups, and diverse behavioral issues, including a number of motivational matters.

The term and concepts describing "organization development" remain in a rather unsettled state. For some outside change agents, personnel officials, and academics, human resource development has recently come to mean "organization development" (OD). Also, OD has been viewed as a larger whole comprising such undertakings as job enrichment, sensitivity training, team building, and "management by objectives" (MBO). These viewpoints notwithstanding, the OD focus in this chapter considers mostly group processes—related to the fashioning of effective work teams and integrating them into related systems of work groups. MBO is taken up as a separate section in this chapter.

"Job enrichment," because of its relationship to the work of Frederick Herzberg, was discussed in Chapter 8. Other techniques or aspects of individual development, such as feedback and counseling, are touched on in Chapter 6 ("Communications"), Chapter 8 ("Motivation"), and Chapter 13 ("Management of Change").

The discussions in this chapter move beyond a focus restricted to people development and seek to cast them in a broader human resource planning approach.[1]

BACKGROUND

The leading edge of change in the future will include the new technologies of information, production, and management, interlaced with considerable social dislocation and shifts in manpower inputs. These developments are without precedent in our industrial history.

Technological and social changes have created a need for more education,[2] training, and skill at all managerial and support levels.[3] The lowering of barriers to employment based on sex and race introduces new kinds of manpower problems for management officials.[4] Seniority is coming to mean relatively less in relation to the comprehension of problems, processes, and approaches. The newer manpower elements and work technologies have shifted institutional arrangements: the locus of decision making is altered, role relationships among workers and supervisors are changed (often becoming more collegial), and the need to respond to changing routines has become commonplace. The shift in various facets of decision making reflects a defensive management strategy in response to more finely tuned operations, higher costs of disruption, and increasing complexity and the pace of change, resulting in the growing importance of technical support groups that bolster both corporate and plant operations. Along with the added decision and intelligence responsibilities of support staffs has come realignment of reporting relationships and decision centers. Responsibilities for planning, control, and coordination have shifted upward from department to plant, or from plant to headquarters.

These shifts have been supported by more demanding customer requirements, increasing governmental surveillance (from product quality to anti-pollution measures), and more widespread use of computers, shifting power bases to the holders of specialized knowledge skills. In a similar manner, the spiraling growth of service or administrative units has made "bureaucracy" a fair characterization for a diverse group of businesses and institutions (e.g., hospitals and government agencies). The rapid diffusion of computer use, a defensive management strategy for handling burgeoning paper work and business transactions, has also enlarged the scope of responsibilities and decision activities for support groups (planning, systems), as well as created new offices (manager of information).[5]

Manpower Developments

The technological and organizational shifts described above lead to a redefinition of promotion criteria and career paths. New areas of structured knowledge are required, and necessitate futher education of incumbents, along with *new* talent (skills) that are increasingly difficult to obtain from internal sources. In many firms, organizational shifts and changing skill requirements are pronounced, especially in those firms increasingly successful in rationalizing the production functions.

For instance, some food processing firms require technical talent to support the increased use of automated equipment and to direct and maintain new processes such as quick freezing, dehydration, and new methods of packaging. Greater numbers of graduate industrial engineers have been hired by steel firms for equipment analysis and operational reseach studies. Electronic specialists in engineering and maintenance have been developed, as "wet" chemistry has been displaced in refineries and chemical plants. The number of maintenance personnel in more advanced and stabilized processes has been reduced, but there has been a sharp increase in knowledge and skill requirements for sophisticated planning, control, and study techniques involving network approaches (PERT), linear programming, computer analysis, and computer monitoring devices.

Although some of these technological changes and attendant organizational adjustments are rather visible, they are no more dramatic or important than the need for organizational accommodation to social change. The introduction of large numbers of minority manpower to organizations in the 1960s and increased numbers of women into professional and supervisory posts in the early 1970s has also necessitated the redefinition of promotion criteria and career paths. Are large numbers of minority manpower (and woman power!) to languish at the bottom rungs of the organization, or are career ladders to be erected and training/developmental experiences provided for supporting personal accomplishment and bolstering performance? Integrating racial minorities or women into high-performing work teams poses added behavioral challenges and dimensions, beyond the more immediate considerations of meshing personalities and work routines and formulating objectives. Long-standing biases toward race or sex have led to friction, unresponsive work associations, and at times conflict. The fashioning of cooperative work relationships poses considerable motivational challenges to affect attitudinal shifts and draw individuals into workable bases for performance and personal realization.

As a result of such developments, greater stress has been placed on formal training and less on on-the-job experience. In some cases, in-house training suffices to meet new needs, but more comprehensive programs must often be undertaken, including extended specialized training or self-development in institutions of higher learning.

The threat of obsolescence reflects a devaluing of job-related knowledge, as well as intellectual, situational, or motivational limitations to acquiring new knowledge or skill. (Obsolescence is treated more fully in Chapter 13, "Management of Organization Change.")

Over time, as depicted in Exhibit 12–1, management's approach to preparing personnel for their jobs and anticipating needs for future jobs has shifted dramatically.[6] The emphasis of on-the-job training and promotion from within (1) rested on a seniority base (2), and often on the whim and fancy of the immediate supervisor (2). Orientation and skill training frequently depended on his skill and ability. The success of this task (4) reflected wide ranges of ability and communication skills and the need for insight into current and anticipated (after promotion) job requirements. The idea that today's decisions (e.g., in selection) or training determine tomorrow's possibilities or problems is expressed but not often operational. However, change, expansion, legislative trends, and shifts in population (5) force the more effective use of manpower through reducing developmental time and capitalizing on education, in order to heighten chances for success (6). In no small measure, shifting expectations (6') on the part of both incumbents and new entrants to manpower ranks (7) affect the motivational considerations in manpower development programs.

Aligning Individual "Felt" Need and Development Design

From a motivational viewpoint, it appears that important changes have taken place in worker expectations regarding the quality of work life and opportunity for personal growth.[7] If, as suggested by Maslow (Chapter 8), our advancing culture has led to a situation where basic needs are largely satisfied, growing personal expectations for bettering one's realizations in the

EXHIBIT 12–1. Historical Approaches and Emerging Needs

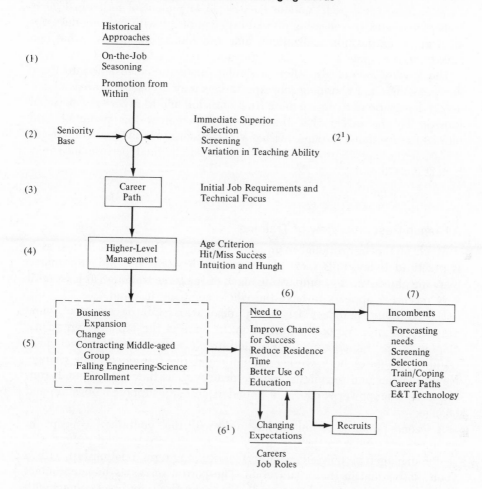

world of work would logically follow. Although the change in expectations appears to be a pronounced trend among the younger people coming into organizational life, exposure of current work force members to multimedia can also be expected to bring about some higher level of these same felt needs.[8]

If these changing expectations are in fact emerging, as appears to be the case, individual decisions to (a) join organizations and (b) produce at good levels of performance may increasingly depend on the opportunity to convert personal expectations to realization. To the extent that an individual perceives the organization as providing job opportunities and development experiences that facilitate the achievement of his or her longer-term, valued objectives, employment may be attractive. Similarly for the job incumbent: if job shifts and developmental experiences enrich current job performances and are seen as instrumental to promotion and attaining valued goals, high levels of individual performance and personal realization may emerge. Clearly, these "goal-path" notions suggest an alignment of individual goals (which may now be reflecting revised expectations?) with training-development opportunities, job realizations, and individual perceptions (what one feels to be the "facts").

The Maslow model also offers a similar, motivational insight into these developments; and changing job expectations may arouse new areas of felt need (deprivation) to derive more from one's job and to experience personal growth. To the extent that the individual perceives this potential, and ultimate realization, through his work performance, individual training or the strengthening of group relationships and individual performance may benefit considerably.

A Human Resource View of Training

Much of the institutional manpower training in the United States, as it is practiced today, falls short of desirable behavioral and human-resource planning objectives. By comparison, much of Japanese training (at least until very recently) appears to have the whole company in mind.[9]

U.S. training practices frequently deal with skill development, new practices, or preparation for promotion. In some of the Japanese programs, employees are trained continuously, and for *all* positions at their level. Such training facilitates both worker mobility and the introduction of change. New problems and techniques can be dealt with as they emerge, and, consequently, manpower is educated to understand and support innovation and change.

A second Japanese technique has to do with the "godfather" concept. In an approach similar to the use of coaches in minority training programs, a senior manager or official assumes a close, long-term relationship with a young individual in the organization. The patron serves as human contact counselor, sounding board, and guide. He or she also is in direct contact with top management and can exert a high level of influence in such matters as promotion, disputes, and the resolution of problems that relate to the protégé.

SYSTEMATIC TREATMENT OF ORGANIZATIONAL MANPOWER VARIABLES

Exhibit 12–2 depicts the consolidation of concepts underlying manpower planning, plus interconnections to other important organizational procedures. Given the manpower perspective, the scheme of Exhibit 12–2 is focused on the paths and end points connecting the longer-range objectives of the firm with the realities of today's organization. Thus attention is drawn to fore-

**EXHIBIT 12–2. Organizational Analysis: Bases for Formulating Manpower Planning
Needs**

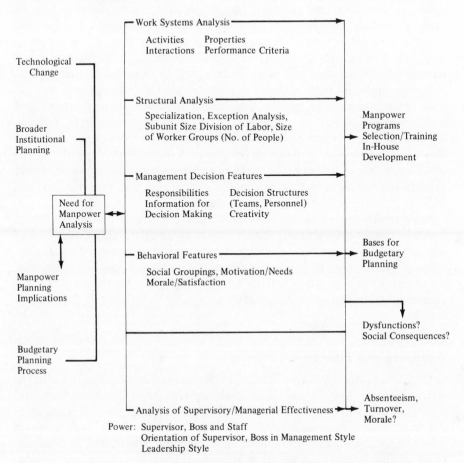

Work Systems Analysis

Activities   Properties
Interactions   Performance Criteria

Technological
Change

Structural Analysis

Specialization, Exception Analysis,
Subunit Size Division of Labor, Size
of Worker Groups (No. of People)

Broader
Institutional
Planning

Manpower
Programs
Selection/Training
In-House
Development

Management Decision Features

Responsibilities   Decision Structures
Information for   (Teams, Personnel)
Decision Making   Creativity

Need for
Manpower
Analysis

Bases for
Budgetary
Planning

Behavioral Features

Social Groupings, Motivation/Needs
Morale/Satisfaction

Manpower
Planning
Implications

Dysfunctions?
Social Consequences?

Budgetary
Planning
Process

Absenteeism,
Turnover,
Morale?

Analysis of Supervisory/Managerial Effectiveness

Power: Supervisor, Boss and Staff
Orientation of Supervisor, Boss in Management Style
Leadership Style

Specialization, Exception Analysis, Subunit Size
Division of Labor, Size of Worker Groups (No. of People)

casting the character of the future environment and tackling such questions
as *how* work systems will change, what *new* organizational groupings may
exist, and what *kinds* of manpower will be needed or sought out both to
design and operate the firm of the future.

From the standpoint of dysfunction, some of tomorrow's forecasted situations will not materialize, and people who have been groomed for important
positions will leave. Furthermore, programs meant to be especially attractive to selected personnel may not be interpreted thus.

Exhibit 12–2 displays the manner of multilevel approach that is often
deemed necessary in preparing the way for thoughtful manpower planning
designs and for strengthening organizational performance. The growing

complexity of organizational procedures and environmental interactions creates work systems with widespread interdependencies. Improving individual performance and planning individual career path depends increasingly on matters beyond training and development technology. Exhibit 12–2 suggests structural, systems, *and* behavioral analyses that may have to be undertaken to increase the assurance that a sequence of individual work and educational experiences will meet expectations in some future time period.

For example, an organization's manpower planning design may encompass the preparation of various department members for supervisory and managerial positions. This individual preparation may necessitate broadening experiences in various work-related departments through job transfers. But the effectiveness of these developmental procedures depends on the teaching ability of encumbents, support and acceptance by peers or various department members with considerable experience, and the visibility and logic of procedures and decision processes.

Additionally, more and more work procedures center on group procedures, and thus the behavioral fit of people (with work associates and group leader/ supervisor) being groomed for higher-level positions is a growing reality, reflecting all manner of group considerations (status, values, and cohesion, for example). These group activities form a key basis for the chapter's discussion on organization development.

Budgeting and Manpower Planning

Budgeting constitutes a vehicle for both planning and control since, in the course of budgeting, longer-range goals are translated into time, cost, and functional objectives (see Exhibit 12–3).[10] Formulating the cost of manpower targets, along with review procedures (*1*), reflects a dynamic in which targets and accomplishments are regularly scrutinized and adjustments are made or actions are taken as needed. There is a continuing reevaluation of performance standards or ratios of workers to supervisory personnel (*2*) as modifications take place in the balance and composition of the organizational and work system (*3*). For example, programs of continuing technological improvement necessitate a regular reexamination of labor productivity, ratios of subordinates to supervisor, and measures of performance (output/man-hours, for example).

In the translation of plans and programs into manpower requirements (*4*), organizational needs and human necessities must be reconciled (*7*) to wage/benefit policies, manpower processing procedures, education, training, and role performance. At the same time, this reconcilement must account for the forces in the external environment affecting key features of the labor supply (*8*), including salary levels, proximity, numbers, and composition (education, skills, and sex, for example).

From Exhibit 12–3 it is evident that manpower forecasting (*A*) constitutes a basic input for budgets. Monitoring important trends in the external

EXHIBIT 12-3. Manpower Planning and the Budgetary Process

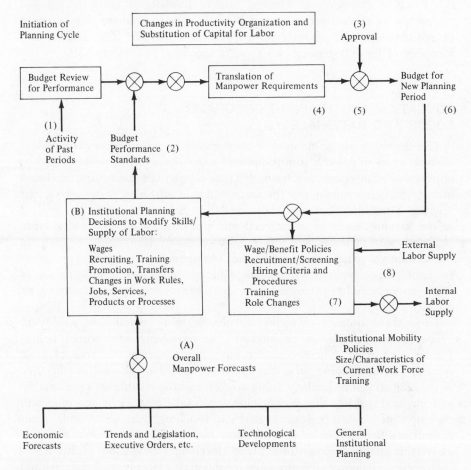

This model benefits from a development by Frank H. Cassell of Northwestern University (July 1968).

environment and translating them into manpower components is a basic task of manpower planning. From manpower forecasting (A) emerge the more detailed manpower planning decisions (*b*), which must be made in order to launch planning programs (2) and certify the validity of the broader budget design (*1*) and conformance to institutional objectives. Thus the ability to establish consistent, meaningful manpower programs may require the tempering of rules, jobs, services, and procedures if the budget is to be successful.

If we step back and view Exhibit 12–3 as an overall development, the key elements are (1) the interconnection of manpower systems to other organizational systems—in this case, budgetary processes; (2) the dynamic character of these systems in response to both internal and external changes, which continually modify inputs and thus the outputs of these activities; and (3) the dynamic character of change, which necessitates both the careful integration of related activities and a mechanism to accommodate a major or sudden shift. Coping mechanisms become critical in the effective performance of these systems. (This topic is expanded in Chapter 13.)

EDUCATION AND TRAINING PROGRAMS: FOCUS AND RATIONALE

The development of manpower resources is a major concern for policy-makers, so as to smooth transitions and support the attainment of change objectives.[11] Education and training (E&T) programs for professional and managerial personnel include the modification of attitudes, perspectives, and abilities. These three outcomes are detailed in Exhibit 12–4, and are applied to the varying needs of managerial and professional groups.[12] Modifying *skills* is typical of lower-level supervisory programs. Conversely, developing or expanding a perspective (seeing the "big picture") is central to programs for middle managers and top officials. Changes in outlook or attitude are of major importance in developing individuals for moving up to managerial or executive ranks.

These three training objectives involve learning experiences, ability to conceptualize (change in perspective), or modifying deep-seated beliefs (attitude change). These considerations imply varying degrees of time commitment to training programs and raise questions about the efficiency of the educational technology being applied and the attributes of personality and physical makeup that permit changes to take place. For example, skill development is often built on instruction, coaching, simulation, and/or on-the-job practices. Much of this we know how to do. Also, approaches such as systems analysis aid considerably in developing conceptual abilities.

However, changing attitudes calls for modifying deeply rooted individual ideas, and may take a long time—and still not be successful. The complexity of attitudinal change has led many to elect alternative strategies, such as "management by objectives,"[13] which is oriented toward *goal attainment* (performance objectives) and sets aside the uncertain past successes of education and training.

Changing attitudes, perspective, or abilities is also contingent on certain behavioral considerations, such as individual desire or motivation to change and knowledge of how to change. Motivation to participate and/or learn is a complex matter, influenced by policy climate, work climate (supervisor, colleagues, and work group), the organizational social system (what's permissible? desirable? acceptable?), and individual makeup (intelligence, desire to achieve, age, etc.).

Second, knowing how to change hinges on learning technology, effectiveness of communication, physical conditions, contact time, number of partici-

EXHIBIT 12–4. Conceptualizing Thrust of E&T Programs

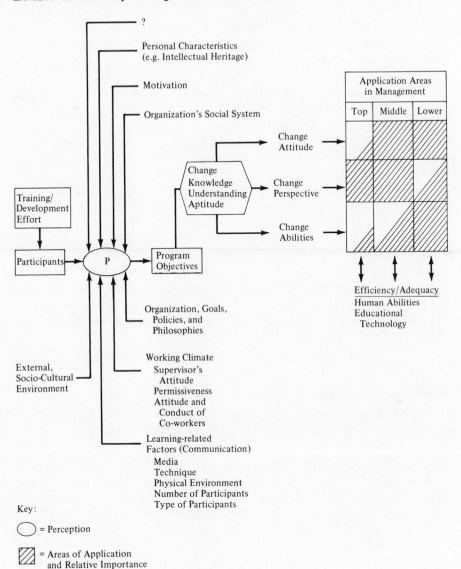

Key:

◯ = Perception

▨ = Areas of Application
    and Relative Importance

Suggested in part by R. J. House, "Management Development: A Conceptual Framework and Some Propositions," Baruch School Paper (New York, 1965).

pants, appropriateness relative to desired accomplishments, and so forth.

In short, E&T programming necessitates a wide assortment of structural, technological, and behavioral matters in order to prescribe design directions and to assist in the rigorous analysis of ongoing programs.[14]

Educational Strategies and Effectiveness

Results from one research study [15] make it clear that widely different views are held by manpower officials and practitioners on the effectiveness of various E&T approaches. Although developmental needs are summarized above under three broad categories (attitude, perspective, and skill), the research project examined a more detailed agenda of strategies (nine) and needs (seven). When these needs and strategies are examined in terms of effectiveness, considering (a) expert opinion and (b) a summary of relevant literature, a most interesting two-way comparison emerges. Highlights are summarized in Exhibit 12–5.

It is immediately apparent that (1) substantial differences exist among the experts and the literature concerning relative importance, and (2) there are other, major differences between the consensus of what these experts see as relatively important and the literature concerning the same methods.

These differences between expert opinion and research results crystallize several striking problems. To begin with, if the literature is reasonably correct in its assertions on various strategies, many firms have failed to devise an appropriate need and educational strategy. Dysfunctional behavioral consequences, dissipation of needed energies, and loss of efficiency crop up as important outgrowths of these mistakes.

Role Expectations and Conflict

Another point in Exhibit 12–5 concerns the influence of colleagues, boss, and members of the social system on possible outcomes of developmental programming. Note (in Exhibit 12–6) that personnel who have been processed through some form of E&T experience a change in expectations [16] regarding organizational outlooks (e.g., innovation, creativity, teamwork, and cooperation), system support (e.g., help from support groups, bosses backing up subordinates), and career opportunities (e.g., promotion, review, and wage and salary matters). In other words, they have new ideas about what should be. For example, individual competitive drive may be lower in favor of more participative, group-oriented activity.[17] At the same time, growing hostility to authority, or even assumption of the managerial role, may occur.

Exhibit 12–6 clarifies some of these points [18] and notes the opportunity for tension/conflict to emerge where the cues from the environment differ substantially from (lack of congruence with) those of the individual, which are often newly formed. Supervisory programs frequently emphasize more systematic approaches to problem solving, and require increased reliance on the boss, colleague, and professional support groups. These systematic approaches assume a reasonably "congenial" climate where predictability is enhanced through better control and coordination of activities.

EXHIBIT 12–5. Training Methods and Effectiveness: Highest and Lowest Ranking*

Strategy/method	Objective of method				
	Knowledge gain	Change attitude	Problem-solving skill	Inter-personal skill	Acceptance
Case study	2		1		2*
Conference method	3	3*	9	3	1
Lecture	9*	8		8	8
Business games			2		3
Films			7		
Programmed instruction	1	7		7	7
Role play	7	2	3	2	
Sensitivity training	8	1		1*	
Television lecture		9	8	9	9*

* Reflected rather low order of agreement in mean value and ranking.

Based on a presentation of Stephen Carroll Jr., Frank T. Payne, and John J. Ivancevich of the 12th annual meeting of the Midwestern Division of the Academy of Management, Michigan State University, April 1970.

EXHIBIT 12–6. Training, Role Expectations, and Conflict

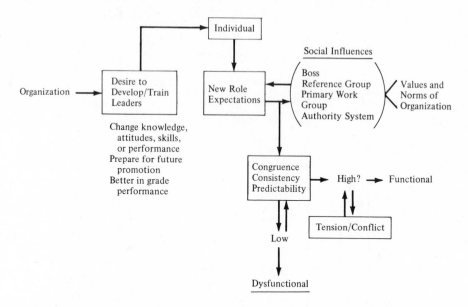

Unfortunately, the expected outcomes are too often only partially forthcoming or do not materialize at all. Thus, even for the most loyal supervisors or trainees, frustration rises rapidly and tension or conflict may set in. It is because of these types of experience that the focus of contemporary developmental programs has frequently shifted toward (a) involving superiors, supportive groups, and colleagues in joint efforts, (b) building effective working relationships, and (c) strengthening team and project efforts for joint undertakings.[19]

Consequently, developmental programming may literally pit the trainee against long-standing modes and standards of organization behavior—a posture of "business as usual" and a reluctance to change, or lethargic adjustments that simply do not reflect the urgency of emergent situations. At this point, it would be appropriate to consider such E&T approaches as organization development that seek to reckon with some of the difficulties or partial remedies that do not fully consider the interdependencies of human activity in organizations.

ORGANIZATION DEVELOPMENT (OD)

Beyond individual training and development, one must look to processes that deal with interpersonal interactions or group processes and the linking of groups into effective work systems featuring cooperation and good working relationships. *Organization development* is a relatively new concept of planned intervention into organization climate or interpersonal interactions, utilizing behavioral science hypotheses and findings. Confrontation, choice, and collaboration are stressed, to assist organization members in removing barriers to achieving organization potential. Goal specifics might include developing an open problem-solving climate, extending individual competence to diminish the use of authority, and the formulation of reward systems to acknowledge both individual and institutional goals.[20]

The very newness of organization development as a field of applied behavioral science approaches has led to some confusion in both definition and methodology. For example, techniques such as sensitivity training, lab training, and counseling have been subsumed within OD. However, job enrichment and "management by objectives" techniques have also been tied into OD efforts. Also, OD has been viewed as essentially a strategy for change, and thus could qualify for inclusion in the change management chapter (13). In the light of the scope of these developments, we have confined this chapter's discussions largely to group-related processes for developing individual and group participants, and for facilitating change processes. The analyses are cast within the manpower planning perspective described in the initial discussions in this chapter.

OD—In a Systems Perspective

These approaches build importantly on the work of Abraham Maslow and Douglas McGregor (theory X as opposed to theory Y). The Maslow model (Chapter 8) establishes a perspective on individual need and opportunities for need fulfillment through individual (participative) realizations within task groups, leadership influences, peer support, social acceptance, goal-oriented activity, and training and control through group member and organizational feedback. The McGregor theory (Y) sees man, in contrast to the "machine model," as possessing feelings—evidencing the ability to think and contribute to organizational performance. Although approaches to "organization development" have been highly particularized to specific organizational circumstances, some general elements and sequences are frequently subsumed.[21]

Exhibit 12–7 provides a system-type representation of these organization development approaches. First, it highlights key steps in OD procedure and process:

1. *Problem identification.* The measures of operational and behavioral performance serve as signals of potentially serious, organizational problems. Typical operation performance measures include handling costs, costs of order creation, costs of manufacturing and productivity, and—more directly associated with human effort—turnover, absenteeism, tardiness, and difficulty in hiring or retaining desired people. From a behavioral viewpoint, morale or satisfaction, loyalty, and high tension or conflict would be matters of concern.

EXHIBIT 12–7. General Model in Organization Development Approaches

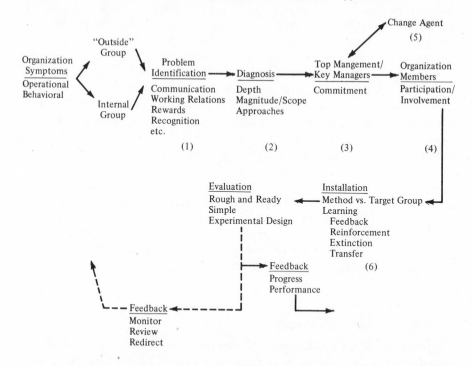

2. *Diagnosis.* Here an attempt is made to detail both the depth and the magnitude of existing problems, along with a tentative identification of an appropriate OD approach. "Depth of problems" considers the number and variety of behaviorally related issues that seem to relate to the previously identified symptoms. Poor communications (upward, downward, laterally, within or between groups), poor working relationships (within and between groups or as they involve support activities), lackluster leadership (unresponsive to situational needs considered within group—situational restraints), and lack of motivation (acceptance/belonging, participation, sense of recognition or achievement) are among the common problem areas in OD approaches. The specifics of the OD method would be appropriately designed for the problem area.

Diagnosis also has a scope dimension: How extensive is the OD intervention in terms of number of people, functional groups, or structural units?

3. *Commitment.* Acceptance and visible, active support by top management and key middle-level managers are usually indispensable to success. The time, energies, and money put into a broad-front, OD approach can be substantial. The fact that "results" may not be discernible for months, or even years, necessitates high commitment by these key people.

4. *Manpower participation.* Moving beyond commitment, "participation" raises the matter of the involvement of various organizational levels, *includ-*

ing task group members. To the extent that work procedures or relationships may be rearranged, the inputs from those directly involved may provide good, workable approaches and gain commitment to the program. Needless to say, securing the wholehearted commitment and support of involved supervision can be expected to directly affect results.

5. *Change agents.* The relative effectiveness of an external versus an internal change agent (the individual coordinating the change designs and processes) is a moot point. Specific organizational circumstances will frequently dictate preference for one over the other. Yet, regardless of choice, the role requires filling to assure the needed coordination, follow through, and longer-run continuity.

6. *Learning.* OD frequently involves intensive and varied learning experiences that may seek to bolster the preparation of individual members, the interworking of group members, and the shifting of formal leader roles from direction to support, thereby incorporating support-group capabilities and fashioning cooperative working relationships between groups. Here, learning requires a careful separation of method from target groups, which were referenced under "diagnosis." The learning referred to here involves "methods" or approaches of learning theories (reinforcement, feedback, extinction, and transferability) and techniques (role play, gaming, and lab exercises).

Methods are not at all similar in their response to particular problems. For example, role play is quite effective in interpersonal skills or changing attitudes; the case method can prove effective in problem solving and securing knowledge; lecturing may assist in furthering general understanding or perspective. (A number of techniques are referenced and compared in Exhibit 12–7.)

7. *Evaluation.* Both operational and behavioral measures may be employed in problem diagnosis and assessing the results of OD interventions. Assessment may range from rough and ready pre- and/or post-test designs to simple pre-test–post-test to pre-test–post-test–central group designs. Broad, comprehensive, evaluative approaches are desired objectives, but a fast change or organizational circumstances will frequently dictate a lesser achievement.

In the "learning" step it was noted that method and target group be separated. This same distinction should apply in evaluation procedures on the impact of the program on the target groups and the relative effectiveness of the methods employed—to serve as both feedback and guides for subsequent undertakings.

8. *Feedback, redirection.* These terms relate directly to the evaluative component just described. In the manner of gaining closure and securing control (Chapter 5), OD is no less a procedure or undertaking than various work-related procedures—and is often greater. Consequently, it requires its own administrative, control, and evaluative components.

Information and data are conveyed through multiple channels and serve diverse purposes. Group members need feedback to gauge progress and identify new problems requiring resolution. Supervision (formal leadership) requires feedback to judge the success of intra- and intergroups, which would permit systematic review and equitable participation in benefit and promotion opportunities.

In addition, areas of individual, group, and support responsibility are delineated; performance criteria are proposed that, after extensive review at all organizational levels and top-management scrutiny, appear to be both acceptable and useful.

OD Application—Illustrated

For a recent organizational study involving a large architectural-engineering firm, a university-based research team was requested to meet with the ownership of the firm, review events that had transpired in the recent past, and propose an approach to problem resolution. The highlights of this initial study, its eventual installation, and subsequent developments, which took place over a one and one-half year period, are presented below. This summary discussion parallels the key points just described.

A. *Problem identification.* Growing turnover among newer (and young) organization members, the threat of unionization of paraprofessional and professional groups, employee complaints concerning pay, and high internal tension (at times conflict) combined to bring management to the point of wishing to resolve these pressing issues.

For this organization of some 300 professionals, some 75 were interviewed, including owners, managers, supervisors, and work group members. Interviewing and questionnaire designs recognized both work flow communications and formal authority relationships. For example, work-related groups necessitating cooperation were included. Questionnaires were also submitted to these individuals. In addition, records were scrutinized and (for example) measures of promotion, turnover, pay range, and time-in-grade/promotion/performance were developed. In typical fashion, few internal control figures of real consequence existed. However, a budgetary and project framework provided some of the figures needed subsequently for evaluating group performance.

The results of these problem identification efforts indicated multifold problems for (a) individuals, (b) supervision, (c) working groups, and (d) the organization:

a. *Individuals.* Lack of sense of accomplishment or meaningful participation in organizational processes. Poor communication of "where I stand" and "how am I doing?" Poor visibility regarding whom to turn to for problem solving or personnel matters. Vague criteria for pay, benefits, and promotion. Supervisors were not viewed as effective in work accomplishments, support, or responding to personal needs. Lack of systematic bases for judging performance.

b. *Supervision.* Sense of being bypassed, holding an empty title. Lack of rapport with managers; lack of communication, or contact, with owners. Lack of general criteria to gauge group or personal performance. Lack of systematic bases to judge grounds for performance, pay, and promotability.

c. *Groups.* Working relationships frequently compromised by blurred understandings of responsibility, status designations ("junior" vs. "senior," architect vs. engineer, designer vs. architect, etc.), and uneven, resident capabilities among task groups as well as support groups.

d. *Organization.* Lack of personnel policies, rules, procedures covering such matters as pay, promotion, organizational goals, grievance handling, and administrative support. Lack of offices to support personnel procedures, maintain communication and action channels, and foster continuing personal examination to facilitate organizational development; and lack of innovation and renewal of ideas and purposes.

B. *Diagnosis.* From the problems previously described, it is not difficult to deduce that problems touched virtually every department and level ("scope") in the organization—from top management to work group member plus technical and administrative support areas. All organizational levels, and especially top management, participated in diagnosis and proposed approaches. In terms of depth, a wide range of individual, group, and organizational issues was described, involving participation, achievement, communications, clarity of goals and objectives, cooperative working relationships, interpersonal competence, and leadership. Preliminary diagnoses and prescriptions were discussed with review or "sounding board" committees at the employee, supervisory, and managerial levels. The prescriptions indicated for dealing with these problems involved structural, process-procedure, and individual/group approaches spanning a period of more than a year. Key points included:

Structure; that is, formalization of a personnel function ("personnel development") or formation of task groups to carry out principal operations, containing well-balanced resident talents, including both architectural and engineering. A final point in structural rearrangement called for a physical redeployment of facilities to permit the bringing together of task groups.

Process/procedure; that is, policies and procedures were proposed touching on the matters outlined under "problem identification." In addition, a new salary-benefit system was proposed.

a. *A structure of committees* was also proposed, which was to assist in longer-range technical problem solving, in procedural and work flow review, and to provide counsel to top management and review salary-benefit matters.

b. *Group-individual.* The proposed redefinition of supervisory performance and erection of a standing matrix-type structure of work groups, juxtaposed to support groups, indicated an extensive redefinition of roles for supervisor and participants. Group members were carefully reviewed and assigned, based on diverse formal (technical performance, seniority) and behavioral considerations (compatibility, formal/informal relationships, "ability to work together"). With the eventual installation of the plan, choices and assignments were carefully reviewed with the people involved. (To the extent possible, differences of opinion were resolved prior to formalizing moves.)

c. *Commitment.* Efforts at securing commitment of top management and key managers by the outside consulting/research group were undertaken from the time of the project's initiation. Extensive involvement of all organizational levels in problem identification, diagnosis, and possible approaches assisted in gaining interest, identification, and ultimate commitment. When top management was openly prepared to accept its role in contributing to existing problems and enthusiastically entered into creative approaches to problem solution, the commitment of the other key organizational areas came fairly easily.

d. *Manpower participation.* As already noted, a high level of organizational involvement was sought from the very initiation of the study. Involvement of some one-quarter of the professional organization in questioning and interviews, plus the later use of multiple committees to assist in diagnosis and review, eventually touched all key areas of the organization. Such administrative functionaries as "secretaries" were also involved in the study, and proved to be particularly helpful in gaining understanding of the issues.

e. *Change agents.* At the outset of the study it was agreed that the outside (university) participants would play only a counseling or advisory role. The highly technical activity of the firm suggested that a firm member who had the technical credentials, intellect, and personality features could likely gain needed legitimacy and acceptance.

When the decision was made to proceed with the study and installation, an organizational member was identified who possessed the necessary qualifications and was desirous of assuming the role of "personnel development" (and internal change agent). His subsequent success in assuming the developmental perspective, acquisition of personnel techniques, acceptance by the organization, and the monitoring-coordinative role amply demonstrated the appropriateness of his selection.

f. *Learning.* The central target groups of the developmental ("learning") procedures were the task groups. Clarification of work environment in terms of policy, work procedure, communication channels, and recourse for personal matters considerably reduced the tensions and ambiguities in these areas. This learning was met through "cascade" orientation approaches (from top to first-level management, first-level management to second-level management, etc.), which served to legitimize leadership roles and convey information to the whole organization. Also, an agenda of typical questions was prepared and was discussed in question-answer sessions. Higher-level authority figures attended these sessions to further support formal leaders and respond to broader questions. Great care was taken not to undermine the role of the task-group leader.

Intragroup working procedures grew as natural extensions of the high-level professional approach of *colleagues*. Job titles reflecting major status distinctions were reduced and greater professional detachment was encouraged in reviewing suggestions or soliciting ideas. Training sessions, conducted among task-group heads, encouraged participative sessions through role play and simulated question-answer-idea sessions. Colleagues provided feedback of the response or strategy elected by their member in dealing with the situation. Periodically, top management was invited to these sessions and served to reinforce policy concepts or matters of working procedures previously reviewed with them ("personnel development").

g. *Evaluation, feedback, redirection.* Before the university group agreed to participate in the project, agreement was reached on various evaluative and post-installation procedures. First, since virtually the entire professional organization was to participate in the OD program, a general pre-test and post-test approach was to be taken. One year from the date of the initial installation, an interview-questionnaire approach was again to be carried out and the results compared with the initial findings and interpretations. In addition, various "hard" figures, reflecting behavioral performance (turnover, alignment of individual evaluation-seniority-salary), were to be developed. Also, interviews were to be held at the key schools furnishing graduate students, and also with former employees, to establish new performance criteria and gain insights into organizational progress.

It was further agreed that, some six months after installation, a member of the university's installation team would meet in extended session with "personel development," key managers, and top management to review progress and provide counsel or feedback as indicated. This meeting, and the feedback session disclosed that almost two-thirds of the major program undertakings were on target and starting to achieve the anticipated results. However, the pressure of new business delayed the undertaking of some of the initial design plans pertaining to the personnel development of selected organization members (formal education, tutorials, and overseas visits).

The twelve-month check actually took place some fifteen months after the initial installation. The preparation, orientation, and introduction of new policy, procedures, descriptions, and working relationships was truly impressive. The ability of the "personnel development" member to gain acceptance and secure the assistance of organizational members in personnel-related undertakings, plus his own gain in behavioral understanding, were obvious factors in the success of the fifteen-month achievements.

On the other hand, discussions with key people and the turnover among selected professional groups indicated that some deep-seated attitudinal issues and policy matters had not been resolved. It appeared that important status distinctions still existed in some groups, which led to a blockage of full individual participation and a sense of contribution. Other perceived inequities still existed among young, well-educated people, who viewed more senior people, with higher pay as "inferior" in educational preparation "and contribution"! Though a program of individual development was to have taken place on a selective basis, it was only a partial success due to the continuing pressure of new business.

Another OD Model: The Management Grid

The leadership studies at Ohio State (Chapter 9) established an essentially orthogonal relationship of alternate supervisory approaches, described as "consideration" and "structuring." Robert Blake and Jane Mouton formulated a systematic program and approach to organization development not unrelated to this body of behavioral theory. They crystallized important leadership strategies for strengthening interpersonal and team relationships to attain goals and better manage change.[22]

A key idea is that varying *combinations* of task and people orientations are possible, depending on situational needs. Exhibit 12–8 describes some typical leader orientations and their implications for organizational personnel. The implementation of a team-building program for (a) recasting orientation, activities, and relationships to develop strong working teams and (b) developing appropriate leadership practices within these teams is easily a multiyear project.[23] Some of the proposed steps include orientation of boss and subordinates to behavioral concepts, team training, strengthening, on-site working relationships, and goal establishment, plus facilitative procedures to help ensure success for organization changes.[24]

Managers must also be provided with a basis on which to gauge the effectiveness of new relationships that they have assumed, as well as the functioning of systems or subsystems involving multiple task groups. Officials or top management and change agents need measures of cost and time commitments, results, or bases to judge benefits and the opportunity to exercise options for redirection.

It should be evident from this description of highlights in Exhibit 12–8 that, depending on depth and scope, OD intervention can be a very comprehensive and demanding organizational effort.

EXHIBIT 12–8. Alternate Leadership Approaches

	Supervisor's "structuring" of work activities		
	Low	*Medium*	*High*
Supervisor's level of people-centered behavior — Low	Marginal performance—neither satisfying people's needs nor job-related requirements	Intermediate achievement	Concentration on work/technology; minimum concern for people
Medium	Intermediate achievement	Modestly balanced approach, achieving a threshold level of human needs	Intermediate achievement
High	Highly supportive climate for people (needs, etc.)	Intermediate achievement	Designed to achieve an excellent work relationship, satisfying both people and task needs; team achievement

MANAGEMENT BY OBJECTIVES

No discussion of training or organization development would be complete without considering management by objectives (MBO). This fast-growing area of programmatic activity in private and public sector organizations seeks to involve superior and subordinate in goal determination for the subordinate. Importantly, the jointly determined goal for the subordinate also relates to the goals of the superior, so that a logical structure is fashioned for interrelating various levels of the organizational hierarchy. On the positive side, it can be said that MBO can assist in securing numerous organizational benefits: clarification of responsibilities, strengthening planning and control, bettering the relationship of supervisor and group member, and facilitating the development of objective criteria for judging individual performance.[25]

In one type of MBO approach the manager of a department, for example, may sit down with one of his supervisors both to review past developments related to the supervisor and jointly plan the supervisor's undertakings for the forthcoming period (typically one year). Within the framework of departmental objectives for which the manager will be held accountable (and, hopefully, participated in determining), the supervisor's target objectives start to take shape. "What have you been able to do in the past?" "What problems have you encountered?" "What possibilities do you [the supervisor] foresee for this coming year?" "Will you be able to get needed assistance?" These questions suggest some of the diverse issues discussed in these interactions. Clearly, considerable experience, information/data availability, and sound judgments must be combined to obtain answers for them.

Dealing with uncertainty (for added detail see Chapters 7, 11, 14) and complexity will have a considerable influence on these discussions, regardless of sincerity or intent. The outgrowth of this interactive process should be some individual target objectives, within the framework of department objectives, that are viewed as acceptable and desired by the organization (represented by the manager) and attainable by the supervisor. Further, if all has gone well, the end product of this process will include some clear bases for judging supervisory performance and commitment, and positive motivation by the supervisor to secure them, as well as a game plan for undertaking the program in the forthcoming year.

These descriptions have been couched in speculative terminology because it's not always clear that intent and realization will coincide. Surprisingly, little research has been undertaken in evaluating MBO performance, but two recently reported analyses, by John Ivancevich[26] and Henry Tosi and Stephen Carroll Jr.,[27] raise some important managerial and behavioral issues that will likely receive more attention in the future:

1. Deterioration of the motivational aspects over time, reflecting lack of full group member participation, paper work burden,

overemphasis on quantitative measures, and increasing the administrative burden of managers

2. Are there more effective ways for integrating MBO into organizational processes? For example, should change agents or a personnel department be utilized?

3. What approaches should be considered to securing top-management commitment?

4. Have realistic objectives been established at lower hierarchical levels?

5. What are the approaches to avoiding the possible extinction of MBO's motivational effects over time? [28]

The answers to some of the questions about MBO are only now starting to trickle in. Individual organizational circumstances, effectiveness of change agents, and numerous environmental factors complicate the researcher's situational interpretations. With these precautions in mind, the research of Ivancevich and Tosi/Carroll seem to suggest that

a. Management's active participation in program design and implementation can positively affect the sense of job satisfaction experienced by managers[29]

b. There must be an actual involvement of manager with group member to establish the reality of the process

c. Top management must demonstrate program commitment through its behavior (e.g., time involvement, budget, etc.) [30]

d. Some form of continuing reinforcement of learning experiences and commitment must be exercised [31]

It also seems evident that the provision of a monitoring capability (by "personnel," for example) will help to assure program redirection, the development of new information, or the strengthening of relationships to make MBO an important and viable manpower development experience—one that can be behaviorally satisfying and personally rewarding.

A MODEL FOR MANPOWER PLANNING AND CHANGE

Markov-type models have received growing attention[32] from manpower/organizational analysts. The concepts of Markov chain analysis and matrix operations are a powerful new set of tools for organizational analysis—where situations conform to the underlying assumptions of the model. Thus a firm grasp of the situations suitable for Markov analysis depends on understanding the objectives and assumptions of this analytical technique.

The model permits a systematic analysis of, and numerical solution to, manpower requirements[33] at various hierarchical levels, or for a given set of offices, where

1. Structural relationships are stable; that is, the number of positions remains the same

2. Alternatives for movement or transfer are stable and can be completely identified

3. Sufficient data exist so that (a) promotion/transfer paths can be mapped out and (b) probabilities can be calculated for the likelihood of an individual's assuming any of the alternative states (stay put, promote, transfer, etc.)

4. Promotional queues are not accommodated; rather, each period introduces a fresh selection process—"the model has no memory."

Sources for other assumptions and implications of the Markov model are in the notes of this section. The list of contingencies or assumptions is impressive, yet highly useful information can be derived, and approximations[34] may sometimes provide adequate answers.

Development of Technique

Briefly, the system works as follows. In period-to-period analysis, the transition probabilities or the likelihood that a particular person will assume a given state in a succeeding time frame depend only on the preceding outcome—the probabilities remain constant. Thus in matrix operations it is possible to operate on a set of initial job assignments that are distinct, and that have a given number of people assigned to them, and to determine the movement of this group among predetermined outcomes (leave, promote, etc.). This procedure can be followed for as many time periods as are desired and feasible, given the underlying model assumptions and the usual intervening variables (unanticipated competitive moves, changes in government policy, etc.) that attend future-planning projections.

It becomes possible within this career planning concept to determine the probability of a trainee, supervisor, or manager remaining in position (or grade) or moving to each of the other possible states by some future time. Here it would be feasible to test alternative ("what if?") promotion strategies that could provide comparisons of manpower needs, implications for manpower needs of various organization configurations, size of support groups and facilities given a particular flow of manpower, length of time individuals may expect to stay in a grade, and the sufficiency of promotion opportunities relative to the type and number of personnel currently assigned to the various positions.

One of the keys in utilizing the Markov model is the ability to define the present state (functional area, authority level, or even age), so that the probability of movement to future states depends solely on factors related to the current state.[35] A further specification, which lessens computational complexity, is one in which "interstate" movement is independent of the time interval, that is, the assumption of stability of the matrix's transition probabilities over time.

Data requirements include demographic information (age, length of service, and education) and job or employment history in the firm, including the jobs held and the dates for both current and *former* employees. From the standpoint of sampling, some combination of current and former employees, with an eye to future needs, is a typical balancing of the data represented in the model.

Three steps are taken in developing the Markov-type planning model:

1. Construct transition matrices of probabilities for each time frame for the period encompassed by the data.

2. Compare the matrices to determine the extent of deviation on a period-to-period basis—aggregate or redevelop data to the extent possible so that a single, representative matrix becomes feasible.

3. Manipulate models, examining (a) the outgrowth of current policy and practice, and (b) existing policy for inconsistencies.

A simplified example illustrates Markov-type analysis for managerial-professional personnel in a functional organization.[36] (We will assume that the underlying model assumptions have been met.) The organization contains the principal functions of engineering, manufacturing, marketing, and services. Each of these, in turn, provides three levels of authority (e.g., in engineering, E_3, E_2, and E_1, the lowest level), with the head of each department or function reporting to a general manager (G). The study is for planning manpower organization in the face of a number of alternative environmental developments or changes.

Although we will deal with only one set of assumptions concerning future conditions of change, it is important to recognize that the same type of analysis may be undertaken under a wide variety of assumptions. Furthermore, it is assumed that sufficient data have been made available or developed in order to map out career ladders (paths) inside the organization, including data for people who have left the organization. Of course, we might also wish to make some assumptions concerning the likelihood of movement on various career paths for specified time intervals and note the impact on the existing (or contemplated) managerial-professional group. In short, powerful analyses are indicated when we compare an assortment of likely "what if?" questions to the data or model and then note their impact on the outcomes.

The initial assignment of managers and probabilities of moves are shown in Exhibit 12–9.

1975–76 SHIFTS

Turnover for the period 1975–76 (initial size of managerial-professional group is 2,914) indicates that 221 (7.6 percent) of the managers and professionals departed in this period. However, there was considerable variability between functional groups. For example, of the 386 managers and professionals in service activities in 1975, 358 were expected to remain in 1976, given the career patterns (including losses) of past years or those anticipated for the future. This amounted to an overall attrition of 7.3 percent (28/386), with some 21 of the 1975 service group ("exit" percentages times 1975 group size) actually leaving.

The exit statistics of Exhibit 12–9 are also noteworthy, for a number of variables underlie these figures, ranging from labor market conditions to degree of leadership expertise and organizational support (supportive climate). For example, the statistics indicate that the various managerial positions in the service groups have a turnover ranging from 5 percent at the supervisory level to 13 percent at the senior managerial level. When compared with the range of turnover for other functional areas, this is a matter commanding the attention of the manpower analyst.

What is an acceptable figure and/or that should be expected? Is turnover too high? Is it high enough in some areas? Are sufficient career possibilities visible to job incumbents? What interconnections might be implied between morale-motivation-performance?

Promotion and *demotion* patterns are also depicted by the table of transition probabilities in Exhibit 12–9. The intersections of row and column figures, which represent managerial personnel who stay in grade, indicate that most of the senior managerial positions (e.g., Mf_3 and Mk_3, except S_3) exhibit the highest stability (no change) in their respective functional areas. On the other hand, intradepartment movement (promotion) was considerable in some cases, for example, 11 percent (S_1 to S_2) and 7 percent (Mf_1 to Mf_2). Yet only 3 percent (Mf_2 to Mf_3) and 2 percent (S_2 to S_3) were moves into higher managerial levels.

Career paths that permitted cross-departmental movements (say for managerial development of project work) were typically low, although the shift (mobility) of senior managers from marketing (Mk_3) to engineering (E_3) was 3 percent, and also 3 percent for service (S_3) to engineering (E_3).

EXHIBIT 12-9. Transition Probabilities for Managerial Moves, 1975-76

Distribution of managers 1975		E_1	E_2	E_3	Mf_1	Mf_2	Mf_3	Mk_1	Mk_2	Mk_3	S_1	S_2	S_3	G	Exit
321	E_1	.79	.07	0	.01	0	0	.01	.01	0	.02	.01	0	0	.08
386	E_2	0	.84	.05	0	.01	0	0	.02	0	0	0*	0	0	.08
206	E_3	0	.01	.90	0	0	0*	0	0	.02	0	0	.01	.01	.06
492	Mf_1	.01	.03	0	.86	.07	0*	0	0	0	0	0	0	0	.05
286	Mf_2	0	0	.02	.02	.83	.03	0	0	0	0	0*	0	0	.09
84	Mf_3	0	.02	0	0	.02	.86	0	0	.02	0	.01	0	0	.07
288	Mk_1	.02	.01	0	.01	0	0	.79	.06	0	0*	0	0	0	.10
293	Mk_2	0	0	.03	0	.01	0	0	.84	.06	0*	.01	.01	0	.06
160	Mk_3	0	.01	0	0	0	.01	.01	.02	.86	0	0	.01	0	.07
136	S_1	.01	.01	0	0	0	0	0	0	0	.81	.11	0	0	.05
149	S_2	0	0	0	0	0	0	0	.01	.01	0	.84	.02	0	.11
101	S_3	0	0	.03	0	0	.01	0	0	.01	0	.02	.80	0	.13
12	G	0	0	0	0	0	0	0	0	.08	0	0	.08	.76	.08
	Exit	0	0	0	0	0	0	0	0	0	0	0	0	0	1.00
Distribution of 1975 group in 1976		267	368	214	436	286	82	233	276	163	119	150	89	10	221

* There was a single individual in this cell, but the transition probability was zero when rounded to two significant digits.

Data reproduced with permission of Victor H. Vroom and Kenneth R. MacCrimmon, "Towards a Stochastic Model of Managerial Careers," *Administrative Science Quarterly*, 13, no. 1 (June 1969): 34.

LONGER-RANGE MANPOWER AND CAREER PLANNING, 1975–80

If the probabilities of movements among positions/alternatives in Exhibit 12–9 are stable over the interval of the planning period (in itself representing the testing out of a "what if?" question), such that (a) organizational policy guiding these moves does not change and (b) decisions for current moves relate to current developments (independent of past events), additionally interesting analyses become possible. The outcome of these assumptions makes it feasible to undertake matrix operations (to take higher powers of the original probability matrix).

In this example the matrix is raised to the fifth power, corresponding to a five-year interval, and produces the matrix depicted in Exhibit 12–10, which shows the expected proportion of 1975 managers in each alternative state for the five-year period 1975–80. Several powerful lines of analysis become possible here.

In one analysis, incumbents or new recruits (1975) could be told their chances of staying in grade or moving to positions of substantial responsibility. This ignores the motivational implications of undue periods of residence in a position without transfer or promotion. For example, E_1 to E_1 is a 32 percent chance, or Mf_1 to Mf_1 is a 49 percent chance. Also, exit figures are noteworthy, indicating a loss of some 35 percent of the supervisors in engineering (E_1) and about 40 percent in marketing (Mk_1). The relatively high attrition of senior managers in service is 43 percent (S_2) and 48 percent (S_3).

Another interesting type of analysis that can be undertaken with the data of Exhibit 12–10 is to note the number of personnel who will have to be secured (recruited) over the 1970–75 period. This has clear numerical implications, but—more importantly—indicates a major internal challenge to company leadership in cultivating or supporting these trainees. Also, the magnitude of screening and carefully introducing these new institutional members to organization society is not small.

LONGER-RANGE MANPOWER PLANNING AND RECRUITING REQUIREMENTS, 1975–80

The projected recruiting load suggested by the analysis of Exhibit 12–10 over the five-year span can be viewed in greater detail on a year-to-year basis (Exhibit 12–11). For purposes of illustration, an annual 2 percent additional requirement of manpower is assumed, along with the Markov assumptions of the earlier discussion. The sources of manpower for a position in any particular year constitute the manpower group of the initial period of analysis (1975), plus those still in the organization from this initial group, plus the residual group of those recruited in each of the subsequent years. Thus Exhibit 12–11 presents a year-by-year summary analysis of recruiting

EXHIBIT 12-10. Estimated Transition Probabilities for Managerial Manpower, 1975-80

1975	1980													
	E_1	E_2	E_3	Mf_1	Mf_2	Mf_3	Mk_1	Mk_2	Mk_3	S_1	S_2	S_3	G	Exit
E_1	.32	.16	.02	.02	.01	0	.02	.02	0	.04	.03	0	0	.35
E_2	0	.43	.14	0	.02	0	0	.04	.01	0	.01	0	0	.34
E_3	0	0	.59	0	0	.02	0	0	.06	0	0	.03	.01	.28
Mf_1	.02	.02	0	.49	.19	.01	0	0	0	0	0	0	0	.25
Mf_2	0	.07	.01	.05	.42	.07	0	0	0	0	.01	0	0	.36
Mf_3	0	0	.07	0	.06	.44	0	0	.07	0	.03	0	0	.31
Mk_1	.04	.05	.01	.03	.01	0	.31	.13	.02	.01	.01	.01	0	.38
Mk_2	0	.04	.02	0	.04	0	0	.43	.15	.01	.03	.02	0	.27
Mk_3	0	0	.10	0	0	.02	.02	.07	.49	0	0	.01	0	.30
S_1	.03	.03	0	0	.01	0	0	.01	0	.35	.26	.01	0	.28
S_2	0	.02	.01	0	.04	0	0	.03	0	0	.42	.05	0	.43
S_3	0	0	.08	0	0	.02	0	0	.03	0	.05	.34	0	.48
G	0	0	.03	0	0	.01	0	.01	.18	0	.01	.16	.24	.37
Exit	0	0	0	0	0	0	0	0	0	0	0	0	0	1.00
Expected distribution of 1975 group in 1980	129	281	227	270	251	75	101	205	161	68	132	59	6	948

Data reproduced with permission of Vroom and MacCrimmon, "Towards a Stochastic Model of Managerial Careers."

EXHIBIT 12-11. Estimated Recruiting Requirements, 1975-80

Estimated supply and requirements						Positions						
	E_1	E_2	E_3	Mf_1	Mf_2	Mf_3	Mk_1	Mk_2	Mk_3	S_1	S_2	S_3	G
1975 distribution	321	386	206	492	286	84	288	293	160	136	149	101	12
1976 internal supply	267	368	214	436	286	82	233	276	163	119	150	89	10
Input needed '75–'76 = 274	55	44	5	60	15	1	56	13	6	16	5	2	1
1976 distribution	322	412	219	496	301	83	289	289	169	135	155	91	11
1977 required	328	420	223	506	307	85	295	295	172	138	158	93	11
1977 internal supply	268	390	277	440	299	82	234	273	171	118	155	81	9
Input needed '76–'77 = 288	60	30	—	66	8	3	61	22	1	20	3	12	2
1978 required	335	429	228	516	313	86	201	301	176	140	161	95	11
1978 internal supply	272	393	235	451	305	83	238	276	174	120	158	83	10
Input needed '77–'78 = 301	63	36	—	65	8	3	63	25	2	20	3	12	1
1979 required	342	437	233	526	320	88	307	307	179	143	165	97	12
1979 internal supply	278	408	242	458	311	85	243	287	178	123	161	84	10
Input needed '78–'79 = 297	64	29	—	68	9	3	64	20	1	20	4	13	2
1980 required	349	446	237	537	326	90	313	313	183	146	168	99	12
1980 internal supply	282	414	250	467	317	86	249	291	181	125	164	86	10
Input needed '79–'80 = 310	67	32	—	70	9	4	64	22	2	21	4	13	2

Data reproduced with permission of Vroom and MacCrimmon, "Towards a Stochastic Model of Managerial Careers," p. 39.

needs. Not surprisingly, the lower-level supervisory jobs will require a heavy influx of new candidates. In one case (E_3), however, the supply of lower-level managers exceeds the ability of the organization to absorb them.

SUMMARY

Change is the shifting substance upon which manpower officials and policymakers must use relevant structural, systems, and behavioral notions for planning organization manpower strategies. Shortages of managerial and professional talent, bettering the performance of existing employees, compelling individual needs, and the pace of change all require a good job of anticipating the shape of future needs and developing manpower resources. Systematic approaches to analyzing organization areas provide a sound base for ascertaining manpower issues.

The discussion of manpower and organization development centers around several conceptual models, including programs that appear to hold promise for improving both individual and group performance, as well as for facilitating change.

The chapter concludes with a review of an important model for manpower planning studies, Markov analysis. Various organizational and behavioral issues are intertwined in this model.

The Peerless Pharmaceuticals case at the end of this chapter permits application of a broad cross-section of these approaches.

EXERCISES

1. *Development program.* A large, regional chain of department stores (some 50) located in the southwestern United States wants to introduce a training program for its new employees, both floor personnel and those who will eventually assume supervising roles.
   a) Prepare some key behavioral propositions that would assist in providing guidelines for this undertaking.
   b) Brieflly outline your approach to designing a program for this chain.
   c) Indicate any necessary assumptions.

2. *Organization development.* Consider a department store you are familiar with.
   a) Briefly describe it—and state the necessary assumptions.
   b) Now assume that analyses of behavioral and operational measures suggest general problems in four key departments (such as men's furnishings, appliances, dresses, and hardware), such as poor stock replenishment, failure to refer customers to other departments, lack of joint advertising promotions, low job satisfaction, and complaints

concerning lack of promotional opportunity. The growth of supermarket competition in your key lines indicates the need for change—to strengthen departmental performance and cooperative activity, and to enhance individual opportunity for growth.

c) Develop a preliminary proposal and description for the store manager on the key departments.

d) Make and state any necessary additional assumptions.

3. *Peerless Pharmaceuticals, Inc.* Peerless is an old-line manufacturer of chemicals and drugs with several manufacturing plants, whose products are sold on an international basis. In recent years, largely through the efforts of the founder and the energetic personnel he had gathered about him, sales approximated $20 million per year. With the retirement of the founder and the passing of leadership to his son, the business began to assume a new look. Several new staff support functions were initiated, including systems, marketing research, and personnel. The personnel department had a particularly urgent problem because of (a) the near retirement of a large group of highly effective managers and officials (few had college degrees); (b) rapid growth, necessitating rapid expansion of the company's sales department; and (c) increasingly high turnover among younger company employees.

Frank Jackson, newly appointed head of personnel, had a good background in personnel practices and business functions, and a generous amount of common sense. These qualities, joined with his formal schooling, provided an effective combination of theory and practice for approaching the manpower problems of the firm.

Part 1: Planning for Supervisory Development

After considerable deliberation, a decision was reached to formulate a program for more systematic indoctrination and development of new company personnel. At the same time, it seemed clear that providing for the needs of *tomorrow's* managerial candidates required better decisions *today* in terms of both selecting people and incorporating them into the company's work force. From these thoughts a tentative program emerged that reflected common agreement that product knowledge was the most important factor for company sales personnel, supervisors, and future managers. The following represents the proposed plan.

1. Men selected for sales force replacements and expansion, along with home office trainees (selected at the rate of one every six months), would spend their first period in the company's Atlanta plant. All these men had college degrees, but no restrictions were placed on the field of concentration.

In the Atlanta plant, men were to learn the manner of processing (milling) ingredients, along with the management of plant facilities. Supervision of the trainees was the responsibility of one of the two assistant plant supervisors. Periodically, the plant manager was to provide oral reports to company headquarters on the progress of managerial trainees, but no similar requirement was indicated for the sales trainees. Furthermore, managerial trainees were in residence for a period of two to three months, while sales trainees spent only two weeks.

At the conclusion of the tour at the Altanta plant, the managerial trainee was required to prepare an evaluation report of his training, but no such requirement existed for the sales trainees.

2. The second phase of the training program centered around the Cleveland complex, which consisted of the company headquarters and two important plants. The summary for the program in the Cleveland area was as shown in Exhibit A.

EXHIBIT A

	Sales trainees	Management trainees
Plant A (chemical processing)	yes	yes
Plant B (milling)	yes	yes
Time	2 weeks/ plant	2 months/ plant
Focus:		
Machine operation		
Order scheduling	1 day	1 week
Order receipt and process		
Responsibility (on job)	foreman of operator	foreman of operator
Report: Nomenclature, machine operation, and product preparation	no	no
Text : On same	no	yes
Supervisor's reports	yes	yes
Personnel manager's feedback session	—	yes
Sales supervisor review	yes	—

a) Make and state the necessary assumptions.
b) Analyze the proposed program from the viewpoint of concepts introduced in phase 2.
c) Set out a tentative agenda for improving the indicated program. What assumptions and possible dysfunctions underlie your proposal?

With the conclusion of the plant and home office program, each management trainee was interviewed by the personnel manager and the analyses of the supervisory reports and tests and his trainee reports were discussed openly with the candidate. The candidate was requested to provide an honest evaluation of his training experiences. If the supervisory reports were largely adverse, the candidate was released. If the candidate was to be retained, it was assumed that the breadth of exposure to company activities would permit a managerial trainee to designate his choice of assignment. A choice of jobs by the managerial trainee was to be satisfied by assigning him to a regular salesman for a short period (one or two rounds of customer contacts). After this he would receive a territorial assignment. Regular sales trainees followed a similar procedure after their formal training, that is, assignment to a regular salesman and then to working his own territory.

Part 2: A Recruit's Experience

Bob Jensen, with a degree in liberal arts, was selected as a managerial trainee because of his good performance in interviewing, solid recommendations, and average class performance. Furthermore, he scored well on the intelligence and aptitude tests, indicating general interest in business, selling, and production. The following incidents summarize some of the highlights of his field experience in the plants of the drug manufacturer.

In Atlanta he was told to walk through the plant, ask questions, and report two times per week to the plant manager. The assistant plant supervisor, Jim Doyle, had but one year of college and then had been forced to drop out because of financial problems. He was very competent, and mechanically inclined, and he assumed responsibility for plant maintenance functions, which kept him very busy.

Doyle was most unhappy when he learned of his "baby sitting" assignment, and didn't hesitate to apprise the production superintendent and Bob Jensen himself. Nevertheless, Doyle accommodated Jensen as best he could, and thought he did a good job with him. Consequently, Doyle was shocked when, after a week, Jensen complained that he wasn't learning anything and was wasting his time.

In the two Cleveland plants, Jensen moved from department to department, taking on actual machine assignments.

At the conclusion of the training period Jensen discussed the entire program with the personnel manager. He felt very strongly that the program was far too long and that a two-week tour of the plants would be more than adequate. In turn, Jensen was told that his performance had been no more than average, that he lacked initiative, and that he wasn't putting his all into the job.

a) Propose a model (or models) for analyzing this organizational situation.
b) How would you approach this program as a motivational-learning experience?
c) What complications in training are posed by the character of the technology?

NOTES

1. Various discussions of technological change (computer and manufacturing), as they relate to development, draw from Elmer H. Burack and Thomas J. McNichols, *Human Resource Planning: Technology, Policy, Change* (Kent, O.: Bureau of

Business and Economics Research, Kent State University, 1973). Core research reported in this publication draws from a study supported by the Manpower Administration, U.S. Department of Labor. Additional research and discussions of change and manpower development, including minority manpower and assessment centers, may be found in Elmer H. Burack, *Strategies for Manpower Planning and Programming* (Morristown, N.J.: General Learning Press, 1972), and Elmer H. Burack and James Walker, *Manpower Planning and Programming* (Boston: Allyn & Bacon, 1972).

2. For various aspects of educational need, see, for example, Elmer H. Burack and Peter F. Sorensen Jr., "Manpower Development and Technological Change: Some Considerations for Revised Strategies," *Journal of Management Studies,* 8, no. 3 (October 1971): 304–315.

3. A sense of the range of these issues can be gained from Burack and Walker, *Manpower Planning and Programming.*

4. For issues in the area of minority manpower, see Elmer H. Burack, F. James Staszak, and Gopal Pati, "An Organizational Analysis of Manpower Issues in Employing the Disadvantaged," *Academy of Management Journal,* 15, no. 3 (Fall, 1973): 255–272. For another manpower dimension of change, contrasting size of firm, challenge, and reward, see John A. DePasquale and Richard A. Lange, "Job Hopping and the MBA," *Harvard Business Review,* 49, no. 6 (November–December 1971).

5. See Bernard H. Baum and Elmer H. Burack, "Information Technology, Manpower Development, and Organization Performance," *Academy of Management Journal,* 12, no. 3 (September 1969): 279–292.

6. This section utilizes some of the notions expressed in Lawrence F. Ferguson, "Better Management of Managers' Careers," *Harvard Business Review,* 44, no. 2 (March–April 1966), esp. p. 139.

7. The rather controversial report prepared in conjunction with the Upjohn Institute and under sponsorship of the Department of Health, Education, and Welfare is a good compilation of some of these new "felt" needs; see *Work in America* (Cambridge, Mass.: M.I.T. Press, 1972).

8. Developed in Elmer H. Burack, "The Growing Controversy Concerning Quality of Work Life," *Technology and Human Affairs,* 5, no. 2 (Summer 1973): 4–7.

9. Peter F. Drucker, "What We Can Learn from Japanese Management," *Harvard Business Review,* 49, no. 2 (March–April 1971): 110–122. It is worth noting, according to my contacts with a Japanese consultant, that a major redirection of practices may be under way, with major import for the practices described in this section.

10. Frank H. Cassell of Northwestern University has utilized the budgetary perspective with good results in his manpower planning studies; this section benefits from some of this work.

11. For some approaches to organization for change and to gaining employee commitment, see Douglas S. Sherwin, "Strategy for Winning Employee Commitment," *Harvard Business Review,* 50, no. 3 (May–June 1972): 37–47.

12. Some of these basic points may be found in Robert J. House, "Management Development: A Conceptual Framework and Some Proportions," Baruch School working papers (New York, 1967). For additional perspectives, see John J. Morse, "A

Contingency Look at Job Design," *California Management Review,* 16, no. 1 (Fall 1973): 67–76.

13. As in an earlier discussion of participative decision making (Chapter 11), important behavioral and performance benefits may be ascribed to a management program with a full validation of its underlying assumptions; this is the situation with MBO, where research results continue to indicate mixed effects. The claimed advantages of planning, controlling, and motivating, for example, have been examined by John M. Ivancevich in longitudinal fashion, and they suggest considerable extinction of short-run benefits unless there is a clear demonstration of continuing management commitment and support of early training efforts. See John M. Ivancevich, "A Longitudinal Assessment of Management by Objectives," *Administrative Science Quarterly,* 17, no. 1 (March 1972): 126–138.

    One recent approach to improving the gauging of manpower potential is embodied in the career/assessment center; see Saul Gellerman, *Management by Motivation* (New York: American Management Association, 1969).

14. A matter tangential to these discussions yet of major importance in applications of organization analysis concerns the introduction and update of minorities in organization. Issues here are replete with a wide variety of behavioral issues and challenge-change competency. For example, see Israel Unterman, "Some Aspects of the Project on Education in Business Administration for Negroes," *Academy of Management Journal,* 13, no. 2 (June 1970): 165–178; Theodore V. Purcell, "Case of the Borderline Black," *Harvard Business Review,* 49, no. 6 (November–December 1971). Also see Timothy B. Blodgett, "Borderline Black Revisited," *Harvard Business Review,* 50, no. 2 (March–April 1972).

15. This draws on research reported by Steven Carroll Jr., Frank T. Paine, and John J. Ivancevich: "The Relative Training Effectiveness of Alternative Training Methods for Various Training Objectives," paper delivered at 12th annual meeting of Midwestern Division of Academy of Management, Michigan State University, East Lansing (April 1970).

16. Exhibit 12–7 is based on research described by Robert J. House in "Leadership Training: Some Dysfunctional Consequences," *Administrative Science Quarterly,* 12, no. 4 (March 1968): 556–571. For related work, see A. J. Sykes, "The Effects of a Supervisory Training Course in Changing Supervisor's Perceptions and Expectations of the Role of Management," *Human Relations,* 15 (1967): 227–243.

17. John B. Miner, "Changes in Student Attitudes toward Bureaucratic Role Prescription during the 1960s," *Administrative Science Quarterly,* 16, no. 3 (September 1971): 351–369.

18. Robert J. House has called attention to a number of these points in "Leadership Training," pp. 556–571.

19. A rash of new materials is emerging in this area. Several that are suggestive of the possibilties and issues to be resolved include Wendell French et al., "Organization Development—Objectives, Assumptions, and Strategies," *California Management Review,* 12, no. 2 (Winter 1969): 23–34, Charles P. Bowen, Jr., "Let's Put Realism into Management Development," *Harvard Business Review,* 51, no. 4 (July–August 1973): 80–88, and Robert R. Blake and Jane S. Mouton, *The Managerial Grid* (Houston: Gulf Publishing Co., 1964). The latter is among the first of these more complex, innovative designs.

20. Daniel Kegan, "Organization Development: Description, Issues, and Some Research Results," *Academy of Management Journal,* 14, no. 4 (December 1971):

453–464. For a somewhat different viewpoint, see a review of the Addison-Wesley Series on Organization Development in *Administrative Science Quarterly,* 16, no. 1 (March 1971): 133–137.

21. For another description of OD approaches and an application example, see John P. Gibson, John M. Ivancevich, and F. Donnelly, *Organizations: Structure, Processes, Behavior* (Dallas: Business Publications, 1973), chaps. 13 and 14.

22. Blake and Mouton, *The Managerial Grid.* Also see Robert R. Blake, Jane S. Mouton, Louis B. Barnes, and Larry E. Greiner, "Breakthrough in Organization Development," *Harvard Business Review,* 42, no. 6 (November–December 1964): 133–155.

23. Based in part on Blake et al., "Breakthrough," p. 136.

24. Blake et al., *Organization Development.*

25. Numerous works exist in the MBO area; however, a basic list would include Peter F. Drucker, *The Practice of Management* (New York: Harper & Row, 1954; Douglas McGregor, "An Uneasy Look at Performance Appraisal," *Harvard Business Review,* 35, no. 3 (May–June 1957): 89–94; and George S. Odiorne, *Management by Objectives—A System of Managerial Leadership* (New York: Pitman, 1965) and *Administration by Objectives* (Homewood, Ill.: Richard D. Irwin, 1971). Its growing institutional diffusion is suggested by Rodney H. Brady, "MBO Goes to Work in the Public Sector," *Harvard Business Review,* 51, no. 2 (March–April 1973): 65–75.

26. Ivancevich, "A Longitudinal Assessment," pp. 126–138.

27. Henry Tosi and Stephen J. Carroll Jr., "Improving Management by Objectives: A Diagnostic Change Program," *California Management Review,* 16, no. 1 (Fall 1973): 57–67.

28. Ivancevich, "A Longitudinal Assessment," p. 127.

29. Ibid., p. 135.

30. Tosi and Carroll, "Improving Management," p. 66.

31. Ivancevich, "A Longitudinal Assessment," p. 123.

32. Vroom and MacCrimmon, "Towards a Stochastic Model," p. 27.

33. This model is taken up in additional detail by Burack in *Strategies for Manpower Planning and Programming,* and in Burack and Walker, *Manpower Planning and Programming.*

34. Also in Ronald G. Benson and Charles R. Klasson, "A Computer Simulation Model for High Talent Personnel" (in Burack and Walker, *Manpower Planning and Programming*), some alternate approaches are proposed for generating probability figures in lieu of adequate historical data or in contemplating new organizational units. The approaches described simulate interaction between individual and environment, including a mathematically weighted expression for well-known employee attributes (achievement potential, education, age, and years of experience).

35. Vroom and MacCrimmon, "Towards a Stochastic Model," p. 29.

36. Ibid., esp. pp. 34–41. With the permission of the authors and the publisher of *Administrative Science Quarterly* (13, no. 1 [June 1968]: 26–47).

REFERENCES

Manpower Planning

Argyris, Chris. "The CEO's Behavior: Key to Organizational Development." *Harvard Business Review,* 51, no. 2 (March–April 1973): 55–65.

Baum, Bernard, and Elmer H. Burack. "Information Technology, Manpower Development, and Organization Performance." *Academy of Management Journal,* 12, no. 3 (September 1969): 279–292.

Belbin, R. M. "The Discovery Method." *Training,* 10, no. 11 (November 1973): 38–44.

Burack, Elmer H., and James W. Walker. *Manpower Planning and Programming.* Boston: Allyn & Bacon, 1972.

———. *Strategies for Manpower Planning and Programming.* Morristown, N.J.: General Learning, 1972.

Cassell, Frank H. "Manpower Administration: A New Role in Corporate Management." *Personnel Administration,* 34, no. 6 (November–December 1971): 33–37.

Gibson, Charles H. "Volvo Increases Productivity through Job Enrichment." *California Management Review,* 15, no. 4 (Summer 1973): 64–67.

Goodman, Paul S. "Hiring, Training and Retraining the Hard Core." *Industrial Relations,* 9, no. 1 (October 1969): 54–66.

Haire, Mason. "Managing Management Manpower (Model for Human Resource Development)." *Business Horizons,* 10, no. 4 (Winter 1967): 23–28.

Luthans, Fred, and D. D. White. "Behavior Modification: Application to Manpower Management." *Personnel Administration,* 34, no. 3 (July 1971): 41–47.

Maki, Dannis. "A Programming Approach to Manpower Planning." *Industrial and Labor Relations Review,* 23, no. 3 (April 1970): 397.

Monet, David, and Dalmar Fisher. "Managerial Career Development and the Generational Confrontation." *California Management Review,* 15, no. 3 (Spring 1973): 46–56.

Orth, Charles D., and Frederic Jacobs. "Women in Management: Pattern for Change." *Harvard Business Review,* 49, no. 4 (July–August 1971): 139.

Rowland, K. M., and M. G. Sovereign. "Markow-Chain Analysis of Internal Manpower Supply." *Industrial Relations,* 9, no. 1 (October 1969): 88–99.

Solie, Richard J. "Employment Effects of Retraining the Unemployed." *Industrial and Labor Relations Review,* 21, no. 2 (January 1968): 210–225.

Vancil, Richard F. "Better Management of Corporate Development." *Harvard Business Review,* 50, no. 5 (September–October 1972): 53–62.

Vroom, Victor H., and K. R. MacCrimmon, "Towards a Stochastic Model of Managerial Careers." *Administrative Science Quarterly,* 13, no. 1 (June 1968): 26–46.

Wohlking, Wallace. "Attitude Change, Behavior Change—The Role of the Training Department." *California Management Review,* 13, no. 2 (Winter 1970): 45–49.

Organization Development

Beer, Michael, and Edgar F. Huse. "A Systems Approach to Organization Development." *Journal of Applied Psychology,* 8 (1972): 79–101.

Buchanan, Paul C. "Laboratory Training and Organization Development." *Administrative Science Quarterly,* 14, no. 3 (December 1969): 466–480.

Carroll, Stephen J., and Henry L. Tosi. "Goal Characteristics and Personality Factors in a Management by Objectives Program." *Administrative Science Quarterly,* 15, no. 3 (September 1970): 295–305.

French, Wendell L. "Organization Development Objectives, Assumptions and Strategies." *California Management Review,* 12, no. 2 (Winter 1969): 23–34.

———— and Cecil H. Bell. "A Definition and History of Organization Development." Academy of Management, 31st Annual Meeting, August 15–18, 1971. *Proceedings,* pp. 146–152.

Friedlander, Frank, and Stuart Greenberg. "Effect of Job Attitudes, Training and Organization Climate on Performance of the Hard-Core Unemployed." *Journal of Applied Psychology,* 55, no. 4 (August 1971): 287–295.

Gibson, Charles H., John M. Ivancevich, and F. Donnelly. *Organizations: Structure, Processes, Behavior.* Dallas: Business Publications, 1973, esp. chaps. 13 and 14.

Greiner, Larry E. "Evolution and Revolution as Organizations Grow." *Harvard Business Review,* 50, no. 4 (July–August 1972): 37–46.

————. "Red Flags in Organization Development—Six Trends Obstructing Change." *Business Horizons,* 15, no. 3 (June 1972): 17–24.

Hall, Douglas T., and Edward E. Lawler II. "Job Characteristics and Pressures and the Organizational Integration of Professionals." *Administrative Science Quarterly,* 15, no. 3 (September 1970): 271–281.

Harrison, Roger. "Understanding of Our Organization's Character." *Harvard Business Review,* 50, no. 3 (May–June 1972): 119–128.

House, Robert J. "T-Group Education and Leadership Effectiveness: A Review of the Empiric Literature and a Critical Evaluation." *Personnel Psychology,* 20, no. 1 (Spring 1967): 1–32.

Kegan, Daniel L. "Organizational Development: Description, Issues, and Some Research Results." *Academy of Management Journal,* 14, no. 4 (December 1971): 453.

Lundberg, Craig C. "Planning the Executive Development Program." *California Management Review,* 15, no. 1 (Fall 1972): 10–15.

Miller, Andrew, Charles Tillinghart, and J. Garrison. "Boise Cascade's Organizational Renewal Project." Academy of Management, 31st Annual Meeting, August 15–18, 1971. *Proceedings,* pp. 185–194.

Nord, Walter R. "Beyond the Teaching Machine: The Neglected Area of Operant Conditioning in the Theory and Practice of Management." *Organizational Behavior and Human Performance,* 4 (1969): 352–377.

Raia, Anthony P. "Organizational Development: Some Issues and Challenges." *California Management Review,* 14, no. 4 (Summer 1972): 13–20.

Randall, Lyman K. "Common Questions and Tentative Answers Regarding Organization Development." *California Management Review,* 13, no. 3 (Spring 1971): 45–52.

Seashore, Stanley E., and David G. Bowers. "Durability of Organization Change." *American Psychologist,* 25 (1970): 227–334.

Tannenbaum, Robert, and Sheldon A. Davis. "Values, Man, and Organizations." *Industrial Management Review,* 10, no. 2 (Winter 1969): 67–86.

Learning Objectives

Establishing Parameters for Understanding Organizational
    Change
External versus Internal Bases for Change
Bases for Undertaking Individual and Group Change
  Approaches to Behavioral Change
   Role of Change Agents
Managing Change to Cope with Individual Relevance and
    Threatened Obsolescence
Individual Response to Various Forms of Change
Information Requirements to Support Change Management

Chapter **13**

MANAGEMENT OF ORGANIZATION CHANGE

CHAPTER DEVELOPMENT

This chapter is developed in three major sections. In the first section a general orientation to the management of change is presented. Major forces for change that are challenging organizational decision makers, including technological and social trends, are described.

In the second part, the management of change is described from two important perspectives: one deals with general environmental forces that shape organization structure, process, and relationships ("level one"); the other deals with the management of human factors and behavioral issues in change ("level two").

The third section deals with some contemporary issues that are assuming increasing importance in the management of change—human resource obsolescence and formulating individual career designs are briefly described in this section.

Part 1: Introduction

From a rather unlikely source has come an insightful, historical description of the gathering energies of change and their explosion in the last half of the twentieth century. In his book *Future Shock*,[1] Alvin Toffler describes in dramatic fashion the compression of time that is characteristic of accelerating change: of the 800 life times of human existence (50,000 years), some 650 are accounted for by the cave era, seventy more in achieving writing, six for printing, four for time measures, two for electric power, and one life time for the achievement of current goods. The gathering pace of technological accomplishment is also reflected in a growing speed-travel capability: progression from 100 miles per hour in the locomotive to 400 miles per hour in propeller craft, to 4,000 miles per hour in a jet, to 18,000 miles per hour in a space rocket.[2]

Studies carried out for the U.S. Department of Labor and at Stanford Research Institute provide additional descriptors of the pace of change:

the labor studies reveal a dramatic decrease in the time taken for technological accomplishments, ranging from sixty-five years for the electric motor (in the 1800s), thirty-four years for accomplishing full-scale production of such items as vacuum cleaners and refrigerators (before 1920), and eight years for similar items in the 1939 to 1959 period.

Change has become a way of life, and the notion of "transience," proposed by Toffler, fairly describes organizational life. Aspects of transience that are especially interesting include

    a. Impermanence in knowledge, valued behavior, national objectives, desired career paths, and the good life
    b. Impermanence in ties with people, found in transient friendships and job mobility
    c. Temporary organizational arrangements, such as project and task force groups, and simulated organizational environments used to develop specific areas of experience
    d. New, transitional structures, such as "halfway" houses, to ease personal dislocations caused by the movement of personnel in and out of different occupational situations, or from occupational life to leisure-time activities [3]

STATE-OF-THE-ART BOUNDARIES

Generally, improvements in an existing state of the art usually have a different impact on manpower and organization than change which involves moving to a new technology or state of the art. Abrupt, one-step changes to a new state of the art (e.g., hand calculation to computers, or introducing minority people for the first time into an organization) are usually highly visible—the organization is put on notice that major developments are in the offing. And one-step changes typically put managers or workers under heavy pressure during a short time interval; the individual may have to reconcile his or her knowledge and practices with new situational demands. On the other hand, the process of change within a state of the art, "accretion," is sometimes almost imperceptibly slow, and its significance lies in the cumulative effects of such change over an extended period. Indeed, the cumulative effect of accretion may rival the impact of one-step change.

The actions of organization decision makers serve to set the internal forces for change in motion, and one organizational/policy issue involving change concerns strategies for new-product introduction.[4] Where products are to be introduced at a relatively rapid pace and where they represent major departures from existing material, product, or production technologies, research and development is a central activity. Sophisticated operational programs and appropriate administrative and staff support groups may be required. However, where production and service policies are built around stable product offerings, a more conventional marketing orientation usually exists. These observations generally hold for both small and large firms, to the extent that institutionalizing change in product strategies indicates sophisticated planning and programming.[5]

LINKING THE ORGANIZATION TO CHANGE [6]

In another area of institutionalized change the architects of reorganization must provide support systems to ease transition pains, as well as restructure functional units and relationships. Success hinges upon providing intermediaries who can unite policy requirements and institutional objectives [7] under various change conditions: (a) change that is not desired, (b) temporary and infrequent change, (c) frequent but specific change, and (d) continuing change.[8]

Where change is not desired, stable organizational relationships remain, and the mere presence of the innovator or innovating unit helps the system adapt. Informality often characterizes this situation—where an unofficial arrangement couples the innovator and the "linker" to the organization, or the innovator interacts with the organization through the linker.

Where change is relatively short in duration and infrequent, project or task force groups, ad hoc meetings, and outside specialists or consultants provide the necessary intelligence, coordination, and linkage. Activities can be carried out directly among officials and innovators, or indirectly by using a linker as an intermediary.

Where the pace of change quickens but still falls within specific bounds, the linking subsystems are more formal [9] and the cost increases.

A policy of continuing change calls for formal functional units for launching change (e.g., research and development) and interpreting it (e.g., engineering). Problem solving, innovation, and conflict resolution are important attributes of the organization that is geared up for institutionalized, continuous change.

LAUNCHING AND DIFFUSING CHANGE

A policy of planning for change involves strategies for gauging its point of entry and scope in order to predict its effect on various levels and functions of the organization. To the extent that the shape and rate of change, and the areas affected by it, can be anticipated, orderly rather than chaotic outcomes become a realistic possibility.

Trends in the external environment (which we will characterize as a part of "level one" changes), including competitive shifts, consumer tastes, and economic and social phenomena, are important determinants of change. Some of them call for major policy adaptations. The transformations of scientific innovation to technological applications for process, product, or material often lead to capital investment decisions by top management.

A recent pilot study by a government agency of leaders in scientific innovation and technological change indicated that such firms are often not sales leaders. However, it is likely that an innovation introduced by one firm today will be considered by other industry members next month or next year. The exchange of information among professionals or industry members has made this a practical reality. Consequently, the action of *industry* innovators has great import for top management in its policy of managing change. This policy formulation generates the need for "translating" change by key groups in the organization, such as engineers, programmers, and project study groups.

The translation and interpretation of change may lead to (a) modification of organizational procedures, such as decision making, (b) changes in the bases for problem identification or problem solving, as in the case of the introduction of computer technology, or (c) the "who" or "how" of evaluating alternatives. Also, many times the launching of change indicates a modification of abilities, education, and even personalty characteristics so as to be compatible with the demands of emergent management systems.[10]

MANAGEMENT OPTIONS IN CHANGE [11]

We have already seen the manner in which technological change shapes work requirements.[12] But top-management philosophy and the availability and choice of financial resources also are meaningful variables in achieving change objectives. However, behavioral responses are intertwined with some organizational modifications, which then become "observed change."[13]

In short, the change-management viewpoint traces through the logical outgrowth of contemplated changes and translates them into system, structural, and behavioral specifics. However, this viewpoint also accommodates interactive considerations: anticipated behavioral effects may dictate *re*planning various options, such as the balancing of line-support responsibilities or the modification of system components.

Part 2: Perspectives for Managing Change

An approach to analyzing and managing problems of change requires a perspective that encompasses both the institution and the individual. As noted in Exhibit 13–1, changes that shape the basic character and thrust of the organization often arise from the external environment. New legislation, social unrest, developments in international trade (e.g., sources of oil), and scientific invention are examples of external environmental factors that bring a thrust for institutional change. These trends and shifts are largely outside the control of decision makers, though at times coopting, or merging with the

EXHIBIT 13-1. Perspective for Viewing Change Forces

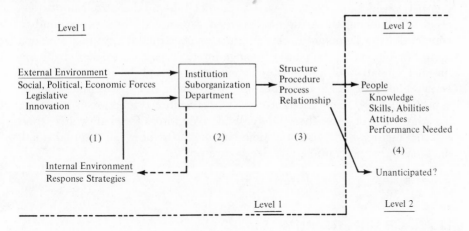

competition, or even lobbying have been known to influence some of these factors.

The second level of change depicted in Exhibit 13-1 concerns the needed shifts in individual knowledge, approaches, and performance within the changing internal environment of structure, procedure, and relationships. "Level one"–type changes deal with the broader, impersonal forces shaping institutional response, while "level two"–type changes are concerned with interpersonal processes. Level two–type changes, as we will develop them in this chapter, will involve *methods* (information, skill training, and the like) and *targets* (attitude, role structure, and relationships, for example).[14]

LEVEL 1 CHANGES—EXTERNALLY BASED

Typically, the external environmental forces pressure organizational decisions for responsive or coping strategies. External changes, such as the growth of leisure time, provide *opportunity* in various areas of recreation equipment but may *threaten* makers of traditional lines. Externally based change, to the extent it is largely uncontrolled or unpredictable, creates instability and uncertainty in organizational affairs. New technologies threaten old technologies; and institutional attempts at legal compliance, as in hiring minorities, necessitate vast adjustments in organization, procedure, and relationships. In general, then, externally based change, to the extent that it touches the fabric of institutional activity, output, or operation, will affect organization structure (see Chapter 2), procedure, work activity, and/or relationship.

Exhibit 13-1 also suggests that important change forces shaping the

institution may be self-directed or internally derived, and it goes without say-
ing that considerably greater levels of predictability and control can be exercised in launching these forces. Top management's decision to respond to
competition by launchng a new product or constructng new facilities is a
highly visible (and predictable) change force. Of course, a major change in
internal climate—for example, when a management becomes more concerned about the quality of work life or a greater community role—can be
expected to affect major modifications in organizational function or structure.
To a large extent, even these internally derived forces for change arise from
external factors, but substantial time lags may exist between external trend,
decision maker perception, and decision response.

LEVEL OF UNCERTAINTY

It should be noted that several different levels of uncertainty have been
indicated here. In one form, we are able to discern the forces of change at
work over a time interval. To the extent that we are able to identify the
factor and trace its trajectory and impact, it is possible to plan organizational
response by carrying out orderly procedures and programs. Alternatives can
be identified and acted upon (see Chapter 11). On the other hand, where
the change forces come unexpectedly, as in an international incident or
through poor monitoring on our own part, the forces may prove quite
disruptive. Clearly, the preciseness with which change areas can be predicted
will greatly affect the smoothness of change and the dislocation of personnel
and organization.

The level of uncertainty that confronts organizational decision makers in a
change situation will affect planning designs, potential description, and coping ability. Yet the environmental circumstances (economic, political, etc.)
surrounding organizations vary widely, as do organizational specifics such
as size. Thus a contingency approach would indicate the examination of
factors external and internal to the organization in order to better discern
uncertainty challenges and the needed organizational response. Exhibit 13–2
summarizes four classes of factors that mediate or influence organizational
vulnerability to the vagaries of change:

1. State of organizational development. As suggested in Exhibit 13–2, the
age of the organization is a factor to the extent that age permits it to stabilize
operations and develop the support groups, procedures, and repertoire of
experiences that permit handling change in a somewhat routine fashion.
Also, the business form and its dependence on innovation or technology vitally affect the pace of change and the uncertainties confronting the organization. Research and development or engineering units have been confronted with a high level of change, which at times has placed officials and
functional heads under great stress. Various service units, such as banks and

EXHIBIT 13–2. Environmental and Institutional Forces in Change

---

$$Certainty \leftarrow ??? \rightarrow Uncertainty$$
"How Precisely Can We
Anticipate Change Areas?"

1. State of Organizational Development
   - Age
   - Stability
   - Business Form
   - Maturity of Functions
2. Character of Technology
   - Managerial Technology
     - Computers in Decision Making
     - Mathematical Methods
     - Problem Solving
   - Computer Technology
     - Breadth/Depth of Use: State of Art
     - Commonsense Applications
   - Manufacturing Technology
     - Advanced Controls vs. Manual
     - Automatic Equipment
     - Time since Major Changes
     - Level of Material Handling/Packaging Equipment
     - Level of Required Worker Involvement
     - Evenness of Production Cycle
3. Management Philosophy and Style
   - Risk Taking
   - Innovation
   - Age
   - Education
   - Style of Decision Making
4. Organization's Market Influence
   - Economic Size/Power
     - Sales Channels
     - Sales Leadership or Control of Market
     - Ability to Vary Service/Output and Influence Market
   - Variability of Raw Material/Final Product
     - Natural vs. Processed
     - Seasonality
     - Quality

---

insurance companies, assumed a rather placid internal environment until the advent of the computer.

2. *Character of technology.* From one vantage point, the quality and capability of the available management technology affect coping ability. Capability in statistical forecasting and computer models, for example, may vastly bolster a firm's ability to anticipate and deal with change and attendant uncertainties.

A firm's dependence on *manufacturing* technology poses a different set of problems, compared to service units. Manufacturing systems embody technologies that are subject to wide degrees of change, depending on their capacity, operating principles, and age. In some areas the advent of new control concepts has resulted in vast changes in operating systems. In the electronics industry, the rapid pace of change has obsolesced whole systems and the level of organizational readjustment has been considerable.[15]

3. Management philosophy and style. Management's outlook on risk or risk taking, or its desire to avoid risk, influences the potential for disruption. The decision maker's willingness to deal with risk—his confidence in dealing with uncertainty—affects the plans and programs a company launches and the exposure to disruption from this risk taking.[16] The degree of certainty that can be described in forecasting change may prove to be beyond management's intentions or planned programs.

4. Organization's market influence. Economic size and power can bear directly on the institution's influence over external change forces. Cooptation and lobbying are two tactics that affect the impact of change. Where one firm has product or service leadership, it also has the power and control for launching change and thereby significantly reducing its uncertainty, but thereby increasing that of its competitors or industry members.

Another consideration in uncertainty is the stability of input materials. For example, firms that utilize livestock or farm produce (meat packers, canners, food wholesalers, supermarkets) are frequently subject to wide-ranging changes in price, availability of supply, and demand. For some, uncertainty may mean simply passing along a price change, but for others (departments or firms), more procedures or tools of analysis may have to be developed. For example, the inability of firms to obtain various metals, such as brass or aluminum, at competitive prices forced a change to plastics, and thereby the development of new engineering and operational capabilities.

CHANGE PARAMETERS

For purposes of organization analysis it is well to recognize that change has often assumed some characteristic forms. To the extent that these can be predicted, organizational shifts can be anticipated and potential disarray lessened. Some change representations, such as the "product-life cycle" (initiation, growth, maturity, and decline), decay functions in depicting the relevance of engineering knowledge,[17] and the predictable decline of average time for scientific innovation or developments, are suggestive of areas involving considerable analysis of change forces. Our studies of the launching and diffusion of computer technology in organizations[18] further support the notion of treating change forces in a more systematic manner.

The launching of computer-based technologies provides a vehicle for describing some important parameters of change. In Exhibit 13–3, four characteristic forms of information-related change are depicted, and each implies

EXHIBIT 13–3. Parameters of Computer-related Change

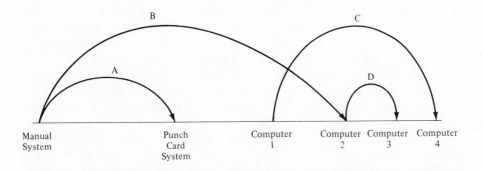

some latitude of modification of organization structure, procedure role activity, and role relationships. Each, also, has served to change the amount, type, and level of knowledge and experience requirements for a subsection and its role participants.

Magnitude of Change

In general, the greater the *magnitude of change* from the prevailing organization, activities, and conditions, the greater the necessary accommodation in organizational structure, approaches, and job roles. In Exhibit 13–3, change patterns A and B illustrate some of the issues associated with magnitude of change. Change pattern B depicts a transition from essentially manual office procedures to second-generation office equipment (a common type of change in the late 1960s). In this type of change, office procedures changed completely and new organizational units were created to design, plan, and guide the new technology in operation. Considerable numbers of low-skilled and older workers were eliminated in this type of transition.[19] On the other hand, change pattern A depicts a more modest update of facilities and procedures. With the institution of more modern procedures, some jobs were eliminated, others required retraining in new methods, and some work was routinized. Yet in comparing the overall magnitude of change (B versus A) from the point of departure for the then-existing system, B implied many more organizational accommodations.

Point of Departure for Change

Closely related to "magnitude" is the level of sophistication already achieved in the organization. If, as in change D (Exhibit 13–3), the structure, organization, and job roles already exist for computer operations, the installation of next-generation equipment is frequently a refinement of the then-existing system. No new technology bounds are crossed. Yet the crossing of technology bounds is precisely the situation in *B*, where (with the added complication of "magnitude") major adjustments were signaled. However, it is well to point out that within state-of-the-art technology, changes can be very significant. These could approximate the changes involved in crossing technology boundaries, if major refinements have been introduced.

Change form *C* suggests a major transformation within a state-of-the-art technology in the transition from generation 1 to generation 4 equipment. Although both are based on computer capabilities, there is little resemblance in power or capability. Underlying this change is a major transition in the mode of organization-system function and operation. This type of move has generally signaled the adaptation of integrated-type management systems, where functional areas become more interdependent and new problems emerge in internal control, coordination, and planning.

The Pace of Change

The final point to be brought out concerns the rate of change, or the time made available to organizational units and personnel for adjustment to new or modified conditions. The cumulative effect of a series of changes contributes to instability if too little time is provided to adjust—to work out problem-solving patterns or establish working relationships—before a new change is "sprung" upon personnel or a unit. When one recognizes that effective cooperation, communications, and working relationships may be the products of lengthy periods of joint work, one's appreciation grows for the influence of *pace* of change and its potential for disruption.

Social-based Change

The analysis of socially oriented change can usefully draw on the parameters of change previously described. This approach involves magnitude, pace, and point of departure. For example, the introduction of minority groups (blacks and Latins) into otherwise white organizations has involved a wide variety of organizational accommodations. Where organizations were largely all white previously, initial introductions of minority training programs (large magnitude of change) have led to tension, and even conflict. Similar outcomes resulted where these changes were made rapidly (as in legal compliance) and without preliminary planning and reorientation of key personnel in positions of formal and informal authority. On the other hand, problems of readjustment were lessened appreciably when the point of departure for company programs was characterized by an established work employment history for minorities, so that new employee additions were hardly discernible. The supportive relationships, good communications, and previous experience reduced the threat and eased the transition.[20]

In summary, the change parameters dealing with magnitude, point of departure, and rate imply varying degrees of organizational adjustment and accommodation. As illustrated in Exhibit 13–1, organization structure, procedure, relationship, and job role may be touched. Change also touches the individual job holder and affects the very existence of the job itself, let alone the formal knowledge and experience needed in modified job roles. In general, organizational adjustment is confounded where the magnitude of change is considerable, state-of-the-art bounds are crossed (involving point of departure), and the change is fast paced. In all cases, however, the specific organizational and personnel adjustments will be contingent on the particulars of the situation.[21] Technological change was used as an important vehicle for these discussions in order to ease into the complex area of change. The behavioral dimensions complicate the issues.

TYPE 2 CHANGE—BEHAVIORAL ISSUES

We will use the parameters of change discussed in the preceding section because they will help us discern the feasibility and degree of individual accommodation. However, additional perspectives must be introduced here to open up some of the complex behavioral issues underlying individual or group change. We will also be concerned with *how* to bring about change involving organizational members, and here the analyses of Robert L. Kahn and Daniel Katz have proved especially helpful.[22] Further, it is well to recognize that where individual or group change is feasible, so that needed skills or aptitudes are present, the *methods of change*, involving training or development technology, must be distinguished from the *targets of change*, involving deep-seated motivational (Chapter 8) and leadership (Chapter 9) matters.

Methods of Change

In considering the methods of change, a variety of phenomena comes into view. For the purposes of our discussion, these will not be extensively analyzed, for they constitute topics in their own right, but they include:

a. Information—type, quality, and availability

b. Skill training—imparting needed manual skills, attitudes, or conceptual perspectives

c. Counseling—interpersonnel, one-to-one or one-to-group processes

d. Peer group influence—utilizing group norms or values, plus feedback, to (re)align the behavior of individual group member

e. Organization development techniques—attempts at solidifying task-related groups and then interlinking them to parallel work and communication lines and thus enhance both work and behavioral performance

f. Feedback—a powerful tool for conveying group sanctions or rewards to redirect individual member behavior (Chapter 10); for providing information (Chapter 6) from past performance as a basis for redirection, as in "management by objectives" programs; and for providing information to the individual to confirm reward expectancies (Chapter 8), redirect individual activity, or facilitate learning

g. Structural alteration—redefining task group or formal organizational functions so that new capabilities are incorporated, missions expanded or redefined, or activities curtailed

The contingency outlook would suggest that these methods can't be uniformly effective but, rather, will "depend on the situation." Kahn and Katz summarize some of the likely results of these strategies for behavioral change, and other research and analysis has addressed itself to these same matters.[23] Exhibit 13–4 summarizes some key behavioral change strategies, their focus, and possible results. The strategy items and focus have already been discussed and need not be reintroduced, but the impact areas require elaboration.

At the outset, we should turn to some assumptions regarding individual change if the indicated impacts in Exhibit 13–4 are to take place. The number of assumptions is a sobering factor in considering the difficulty of bringing about individual or group changes (other factors will be considered shortly). Let us simply note that we are assuming we will be able to provide new insights or knowledge for the target group, alter motivational patterns, and influence other job holders to work with the target group and still retain their new behavior in the climate of the actual job.

The effectiveness of providing new or additional information will depend directly on the ambiguity of the existing situation—the misunderstanding or lack of understanding due to lack of information. Of course, where information for understanding has been lacking, there is no assurance that its provision will bring people to a proper understanding or will change adverse impressions.

Individually directed methods, such as counseling, may prove responsive to the problems or blockages visualized by the individual. And to the extent that the approach is particularized, and carried on outside a job role, good results may emerge. Individual questions can be answered and added insights provided as needed. Of course, a basic change problem may be embedded in the delivery technique. To the extent that an individual problem is affected by *other* attitudes or relationships, only "half" of the problem may be solved, or perhaps not at all.

EXHIBIT 13–4. Methods of Behavioral Change, Focus, and Effect

Strategy	Focus	Likely impact
Information supplied	Provide rationale for program, new expectancies	Effective if lack of information has existed or situation is ambiguous; otherwise little power in absence of other approaches
Counsel/therapy (individual)	Change attitude, even personality, by providing insight into own motivation—thereby role re-structure and changed relationships	Tenuous, and often unpredictable, if individual is removed from social milieu reinforcing current outlook, is provided with new insights, and system changes are brought about, may prove effective
Peer group influence	Shift attitude/behavior of associates, often of similar status; seek to better intragroup relations or team function; in temporary groups use as instrument of change	Conditional; significance and relevance of decisions for individuals involved are critical; also, latitude of decision-making power important in establishing significance of group discussion; may often require legitimizing of change by organization and possible structural change
Sensitivity training	Exploration of leadership and group processes, as with peers and those unassociated with particular organization roles; restructure people values; gain insight into own behavior; improve interpersonal processes	Conditional; must reckon with degree of individual's role changes; is dependent on corresponding organization and system changes
Groups (system related) Without or with feedback Without or with acceptance and change Legitimation of top management	Systematic involvement of group processes at all organization levels; improve understanding of organizational processes, relationships, and individual approaches; clarify managerial philosophy and operational procedure	Mixed to good in clarification of philosophy, procedure, authority and responsibility, and relationships; good in dealing with misunderstanding; useful in bettering intragroup relationships and supporting system procedure, need, and cooperative working relationships. Deep-seated problems related to conflicts of group interest (owner vs. non-owner); status differences may persist. Full development of institutional system takes extended time, often years. The more comprehensive the effort and legitimation of change, the greater likelihood for success.

Based in part on Daniel Katz and Robert L. Kahn, *The Social Psychology of Organizations* (New York: John Wiley & Sons, 1966), esp. chap. 13.

The influence of one's peer group can be a powerful factor in bringing about individual change, especially where group membership is highly valued and the threat of sanctions is respected. The influence of the group on the individual may be worked out through pressures, but the opportunity for one to participate in group processes may provide the needed proof (see Chapter 10) or conviction for change. Internationalization of behavior, discovery based on one's own experiences, and the potential to raise one's level of aspiration through concrete achievements are key facets of participation.[24] Thus if the group is flexible to the point that open, free-flowing interactions can prevail, and the group's activities and results are legitimized by the organization, this approach could be a powerful factor in change.

The problems and opportunities in sensitivity training touch on matters already identified in the previous approaches. To the extent that individual behavioral changes take place outside the work climate, the usual "reentry" problems must be dealt with upon return to one's work role. If other work-role holders are undergoing similar training, the opportunity for successful changes is improved considerably.

Various group processes may deal successfully with matters of philosophy, procedure, relationships, and misunderstandings. To the extent that groups gain added insights to the workings of other groups, cooperative working relationships may be bettered. Also, as noted, group techniques may considerably facilitate the working out of individual problems. However, it is well to point out that deep-seated attitudes or problems may resist these approaches for some time, or may never be really resolved. The more complex the system of group relationships, the longer the time for resolution. Months can easily stretch into years.

A final point has to do with the climate for change and reinforcement of change patterns.[25] Clearly, "business as usual" won't do—alteration of the organizational climate to meet the needs and revised expectations of the target group is crucial to successful change. Newly grafted-on skills, attitudes, or approaches can prove extremely fragile for lack of climate support. In addition, support is not a mere acknowledgment or one-time event—periodic doses will be required to reinforce a new pattern (more on this shortly), perhaps for an extended period. Feedback will be required for a group, department head, official, or individual to gauge the effectiveness of new behavior, changing situations, and the (possible) need to develop new change strategies.

BEHAVIORAL CHANGE—THE TARGET GROUP

It will be well to reiterate some questions that have already been implied or raised concerning the change of the individual or group. Is he or she (or it) aware that change (level 1) has taken place? To the extent that level 1 changes affect a role holder, is he aware of his need to change? Does he have the needed aptitudes, skills, or abilities to change? Does he know how to change to a modified job, role relationship, or whatever? Does he want to change? Although the questions are briefly phrased, it should be clear that a greatly diverse area of problems and issues has been raised here.

It doesn't always follow that an individual is aware of level 1–type changes and, more particularly, the extent to which they may affect him. At times change may take place through a form of accretion, with the magnitude of change comparatively small but recurring in a regular fashion. Supervisors and managers whom we have dealt with were often unaware of the cumulative thrust of these changes on the work environment, including the modification of role demands on their own jobs.

Where change carries over to a new technological form, diverse implications are possible for job holders. Emergent job roles may require new areas of knowledge or skill, or may largely de-skill existing jobs. Obviously, training can prove responsive to some of these modifications, but only to the extent that the individual is able to physically and mentally (or intellectually) accommodate these needed modifications, and is willing to make the transition. In one of the basic steel producer cases in our research, men chose early retirement rather than the extensive and prolonged training required to operate in a new technology.

Even where an individual is fitted out with new skills, he may not know how to cope with or play out his role in modified circumstances. The need for new work relationships and interactions will go beyond simple skill training and will involve new behavioral patterns.

Whether the individual *wants* to change raises the whole span of issues developed in the chapters on motivation (Chapter 8) and the closely allied matters of leadership (Chapter 9). Utilizing the Maslow perspective raises the question of the extent to which new skills, outlooks, or desired behavior meet the "activated" needs of the individual. Where new demands appear redundant or seem to require more personal effort, individual tension is increased and conflict or sullen compliance may result. Where it can be demonstrated that new performance patterns can perhaps enhance performance or extend personal realizations, individual change may be greatly facilitated. For example, social needs may be furthered through participation within group processes or by achievements that raise the ego.

If one assumes an expectancy posture, the interconnection of training strategy, target of the training effort, and personal goals is important. The strategy for behavioral change (e.g., information, peer group influence) must lead to first-level outcomes (new skills, aptitudes, or perspectives, for example) that can be visualized by the individual as securing valued second-level outcomes (goals) for him. Furthermore, the path or change strategy must be seen as superior in degree and likelihood of achievement to alternative behaviors. If the job holder sees that the organization isn't serious about his changing, little change can be expected and it will be business as usual (potentially, a more attractive alternative than going through the work of learning something new). Another situation might involve the individual's identification of attractive outside job opportunities, which may appear much more inviting than making the required personal changes.

Thus the expectancy approach to the question "Does the individual want to change?" raises a number of important questions for the organization analyst:

1. What personal outcomes (level 2) are valued by the individual?

2. Can the individual see a linkage between the outcomes of the training strategies (level 1) and the goals he values?

3. Has he been fitted with the needed abilities to meet first-level requirements?

4. Will the environment support first-level requirements?

5. What alternative behaviors may present themselves to the individual? Have we demonstrated the attractiveness of the training strategy for the goals he desires and in consideration of alternative actions he may visualize?

6. Will appropriate feedback be provided to build individual confidence in developing new skills, support modified behavior patterns, and bolster personal realizations in new achievements?

These questions suggest some of the key matters to be considered by the student of organization or the analyst who seeks to use the broad theories and perspectives of earlier chapter discussions. For this particular example, it should be clear that the expectancy approach could be most fruitful for dealing with individual "desire to change."

Change Approach

Before we conclude this section on behavioral change a few comments on orientation to change approaches may prove helpful. Most of the specifics have already been described, but a breakdown of the process of individual change into discrete stages can provide the needed perspective for tying change approaches together. Kurt Lewin has characterized major change stages as "unfreezing" past behaviors, establishing new patterns, and then "refreezing" or establishing them so that they can become self-directed activity.[26]

For organization members, the impact of level 1 changes (described earlier in this chapter) brings new procedures, relationships, and the need for modified role performances. For role occupants, the habits and relationships that were needed in the past for success must be "unfrozen"—the individual must be prepared to let loose of them or to assume a mental set that permits remolding them to new needs. Yet we all realize that sameness is often cherished and the leaving behind of the "proven" or "familiar" creates considerable tensions and anxieties. Thus a key task of supervision in change (Chapter 9) is to assist the loosening of old work patterns and ways—and shifting work partners, patterns, and procedures may represent tangible approaches to such accomplishments.

The chance to talk things out with other group members may ease tensions and provide some of the needed interest for the impending change. Leaders will also have to supply some of the initial rationale for the change (supporting individual motivation to change) and anticipate the tensions likely to accompany this process. Where change has been very rapid, the magnitude great, or technological or social bounds have been crossed, individual apprehensions will prove to be very real. The individual has moved far beyond touch with the familiar or proven.

As training strategies for behavioral change are introduced, an attempt is made to establish new work patterns and performances. Close support, encouragement, and correction will be needed by supervisor and co-worker alike. Learning at this stage, as depicted in the comprehensive model of Chapter 8, is exceedingly difficult, progress is slow, and at times there may seem to be little to show for one's efforts. However, as newly learned patterns or approaches start to take hold, feedback to oneself ("I can do it" or "This change really was necessary") provides self-reinforcement. At the same time, further encouragement by leadership and one's peers can enhance individual adoption of these new patterns.

When an individual's awareness of "newness" starts to recede, periodic feedback and supervisory support should assist in solidifying the work performance. The organization's monitoring of these performances, periodic feedback, and occasional correction will likely characterize the firming-up of the newly established patterns of individual activity.

Starting Things Off—Loosening Old Performance Patterns

Lewin's work, along with describing some discrete stages in individual change processes, also suggests an orientation for setting the processes of change in motion. Utilizing a simple notion described as "force/field analysis," the strategy for change suggests an approach where the driving forces for change, as perceived by the individual, exceed the restraining forces. The idea that the old and familiar is attractive and not lightly given up would constitute a restraining force in change. Also, poor procedures, the perception of instability, and lack of understanding (need for information) could constitute additional restraining forces. Thus old relationships, work patterns, modes of work conduct, and problem-solving approaches would be major restraining forces to overcome. And the greater the required departure from these, the greater the restraining forces to be confronted or overcome.

The "driving forces" for change may simply seek to outweigh the restraining forces or to identify a path where less resistance will be encountered. Being able to discern the magnitude and composition of restraining forces versus the forces at the command of the organization is vital to a successful change accomplishment. The time available to effect a strategy or an alternate undertaking, given the pace of change, may either permit considerable latitude in approaches or restrict alternate actions.

In considering the driving forces, the positive forces that can be employed for change, a number of the motivational issues previously described come to the fore—and won't be repeated—but it is well to consider such matters as the individual's assignment of priorities to his goals, types of organizational controls used, alternative change processes, and the options the organization may exercise. The organization may modify its sanctions or rewards, redefine roles, change expectations, or present varying combinations of these. It may also be able to provide new opportunities for self-accomplishment, achievement, recognition, or social acceptance, which may further encourage the individual's dropping of old ways and assuming a mental set conducive to change.

Research indicates that various antecedents to change exist—some degree of internal tension and the authority-prestige of the supervisor or influential agent.[27] Tension and a felt need for change lead to seeking out new arrangements to relieve existing pressures. The strength and legitimacy of the supervisor or influential agent promote acceptance of change by organizational personnel and permit the processes to be set in motion.

The conditions and subprocesses through which change takes place move from general antecedent conditions and narrow down to identifiable transformations. For example, general objectives or targets are translated into specific subgoals that provide a step-wise movement toward general objectives. Secondly, "unfreezing" the older social links to informal groupings occurs, and new roles and social relationships are assumed. Next, the feelings of tension, or sometimes inadequacy, experienced by organizational personnel who are caught up in change eventually give way to a rebuilding of self-esteem as confidence is restored. The final subprocess of change is an internalization of the rationale for change. At this level the individual is able to intellectualize the ideas and prescribed behavior for change, and he is able to successfully fend off the tensions that were part of the pre-change conditions.

Implied in these analyses are bases for overcoming resistance to change (without dysfunctional consequences) and for the use of "influence agents" to catalyze movement toward new areas.

In summary, these change approaches go to the heart of setting individual behavioral change in motion. They consider a step-wise process of change with each stage requiring different strategies, so that the items of Exhibit

13–3 should be viewed as possible strategy sets rather than unitary approaches. The approach described here has also referenced subconsiderations as the "controllability" of the desired behavioral changes and organizational options as "driving forces." The final discussion of Part 2 concerns the use of "change agents" as facilitators of behavioral change processes.

Change Agents[28]

Change agents may be part of a high-prestige "inside" support group or they may be "outside" consultants. Internal group members who have appropriate knowledge and are recognized for their ability to perform can play a strategic role in change programs. Change agents and organizational members must demonstrate their ability to work together in a decision and analysis environment that supports interaction and mutual goal determination, bolsters the spirit of inquiry, and permits mutual opportunity of influence (see Exhibit 13–5).

We have already noted that the character of variables that must be dealt with in terms of their relative uncertainty and controllability will bear on the specificity of change programs and the need to provide for contingencies. Exhibit 13–5, based on the work of Warren Bennis, also suggests that change agents, organizational participants, and officials will have to consider the communicability of various new procedures or proposed solutions. Another point the exhibit emphasizes is considerable early discussion. The level of uncertainty of change variables ties directly into the validity with which knowledge of them can be applied. The greater the uncertainty, due (for example) to imprecise knowledge or understanding of underlying relationships, the less valid the applied knowledge.

Exhibit 13–5 also shows that severe organization restraints may inhibit or even block the work of change agents. Wielders of influence or power may challenge or seek to preempt the contributions of knowledge holders in change processes, especially if power bases (see Chapter 10) are weakened or undermined. For example, the forecast of emergent markets might suggest the dropping of existing product lines and the introduction of new items. A sales manager whose influence has been largely based on extensive experience with an older line would be understandably reluctant to support the new line, or perhaps a new sales manager.

The exhibit's programs for changing behavior have been largely dealt with in previous discussions; however, the exhibit brings out a few additional dimensions: changing behavior may emphasize the need for elite groups or widely acknowledged leaders in an organization either to take the lead in convincing members of the need for change or directly intervene with key organization members to facilitate the process of change.

EXHIBIT 13–5. Utilizing Change Agents in the Change Process

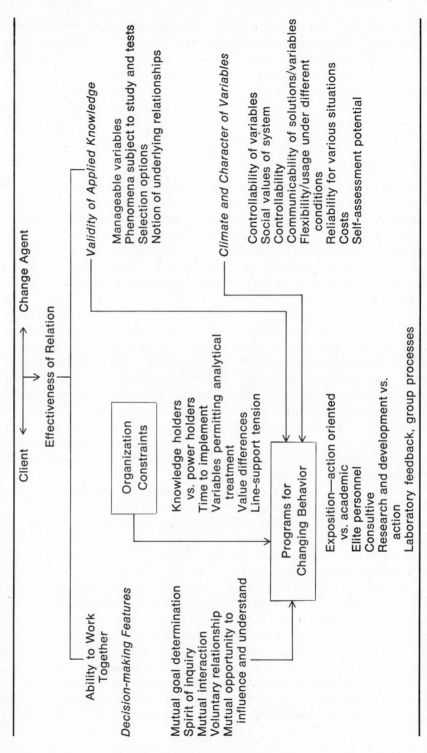

A number of these points are developed at considerable length in Warren Bennis, *Changing Organizations* (New York: McGraw-Hill, 1966).

Part 3: Change-Management Applications

OBSOLESCENCE

Successful change management calls for understanding the principal features of obsolescence, the factors bringing it about, and the manner in which they impinge upon individuals and jobs in the organization.[29] The rapid advances of computer-based systems (Chapter 7), along with major advances in the technologies of production (Chapters 3 and 4) and management methods, have outrun expertise based upon experience. This problem is even more critical in the light of anticipated shortages of key managerial and professional personnel: change in technological areas increases obsolescence by modifying work or situational requirements.

Skill obsolescence results from

    a. Extension of computer usage, complicating decision making by lessening the importance of value judgments and experience, and increasing the importance of formal education and system functions

    b. Faster-paced, more delicately balanced operations with high costs of disruption, necessitating better understanding of production economies and watchful alertness

Job obsolescence results from

    a. Increasing use of operations-research techniques and advanced study techniques that modify the job content of (often lower level) jobs, permitting the use of less-skilled personnel

    b. Consolidation of jobs through computer usage and greater reliance on support groups

Three perspectives assist in rationalizing the dynamics of obsolescence:

1. A corporate policy environment that tempers the character of change and coping responses

2. Dimensions, breadth, incidence, and scope of change (magnitude, point of departure, and rate)

3. Personal features of the individual that moderate or accentuate obsolescence vulnerability (e.g., desire and willingness to learn). A number of these have been brought out in Chapter 8 on motivation, plus the discussions in Part 2 of this chapter.

These points are summarized briefly in the following section; since they have been touched on in Parts 1 and 2 of this chapter, obsolescence dimensions are emphasized.

Policy Environment and Obsolescence

Policymakers play a dual role in both launching and ameliorating the threats of change. They initiate change through policy, creating the factors instrumental in making individuals "obsolete"; they also, on the one hand, determine the climate that may encourage continuing self-appraisal and development, or, through neglect, fail to provide necessary adjustments of work conditions or supportive programming. We have termed this failure to plan "response management" rather than "planned management."

The specifics of change initiated by policymakers are fashioned by technical agents of change, including programmers, engineers, and product development groups, plus the consultants and internal elite groups described previously. Typically, the deliberations of policymakers and technical change agents are dominated by economic criteria or impersonal considerations; manpower agents, or "translators" of change, often assume a secondary role.

A prescription for comprehensive manpower planning would dictate (a) timely translation of external developments to internal manpower needs, (b) developing skill inventories, (c) detailed forward planning of business and change, (d) strengthening personnel resources, and (e) building supportive data. Inability to generate such information-gathering efforts on a timely basis and to communicate needs to appropriate functionaries, as well as to the individual, contributes to the deterioration of human capabilities.

The main interconnection between emergent change and the form and degree of its effect upon the individual is centered in job and organizational shifts that influence the needed qualities of the individual. The rearrangement of jobs, tasks, and relationships as a consequence of the introduction of new product lines or a computer-based information system necessitates the realignment of people and work tasks. At the very least, new education and training routines are indicated. Yet some demands may go considerably beyond those areas responsive to training efforts. Formalized programs of education may be indicated wherever new bodies of knowledge, concepts, or approaches are indicated. In other cases, new requirements may go beyond intellectual or physical requirements. In the latter two cases, the end result may be the same, especially if the individual can't or won't meet emergent needs.

The decision structure is another instance where the implementation of policy programs establishes a threshold of needed managerial competency and adaptability. As previously noted, the introduction of new management technologies (including analytical and numerical methods related to inventory, finance, marketing, and production) places high stress on individual supervisors and managers, even those who graduated from college as recently as the mid-1960s. Of course the pressures on individuals are highly uneven, since it is necessary to take into account the manner of dividing responsibilities between authority levels and functional groups.[30]

Change Parameters

Two change characteristics discussed earlier in the chapter are magnitude and rate.[31] In accretion-type change, the gradual modification of work systems, jobs, and procedures often presents detection problems. Not surprisingly, the response of some individuals in such situations is "business as usual"; for others there may be a slow growth in tensions or anxieties, but this may not be attributed to the growing discrepancy between expertise and job needs. Although there could be adequate time to introduce needed programs of formal education, training, or directed experiences, individual unawareness or unwillingness to cope and management's lack of problem recognition or reluctance to act combine to forestall remedial approaches. To the extent that programs are enacted, they are typically defensive in character—"crash" programs.

One-step changes (crossing boundaries of the state of the art) are usually highly visible and signaled by the construction/installation of *new* plants, production lines, system controls, or information systems. Although manpower officials are likely to be aware of impending changes, they are frequently left out of planning stages where manpower considerations enter in, or they may enter into deliberations in a cursory manner. The traditional focus of planning is on the economies and physical aspects of change, reflecting insensitivity to manpower issues or the activities of "initiators" and "agents" of change.

As noted earlier in the chapter, individual adaptation to change may be made difficult by the degree of departure from the existing system and the *rate* at which change emerges. For example, movement from a first- to a fourth-generation system poses greater problems than third- to fourth-generation changes. Also, adapting to a major change in, say, one month is more difficult than a "rolling" adjustment over an extended time.

The Individual

The response of the individual to change involves both his desire to change and his ability to relate knowledge to need. Here we consider the following factors:

1. Detection ability (sensitivity and awareness)

2. Motivation

3. Career development path, including degree of professionalism

4. Use and adaptability of the knowledge base that one has acquired from education and work experiences

The ability of an individual to detect change is influenced by proximity to strategic information channels, formal company procedures and systems of communication, level of formal education, and exposure to change. To the extent that accretion characterizes emergent change, detection is more difficult. However, access to strategic information through formal or informal information channels may alert individuals to impending developments and their effect. Clearly, if company or manpower officials provide programs for apprising individuals of change, or provide suitable programs anticipating the emergence of change, the detection needs of the individual are reduced. Finally, educational background or exposure to change can lead an individual to seek out the signs of change before the change fully materializes.

Motivation (treated at length in Chapter 8), along with temperament and other personality traits, bears directly on individual response to obsolescence. Change shifts individual requirements to meet work needs, and people react differently to pressure, to demands for more rapid response time, and to faster-paced, more complex activities. For those older than thirty-five or forty, energy demands can significantly surpass capacity. Also, age may work against adaptability because of family requirements and community commitment.

Change may be resisted where the prevailing posture is "don't rock the boat." Threats to customs or habit, fear of the unknown, the security of the familiar, and displacement of human skills by technological advances [32] are all considerations favoring the status quo.

Job accomplishments and needs are affected by the motivation and career objectives of the individual. Where policy programs and boss-subordinate relationships encourage the maintenance of individual relevance, alertness to new conditions and self-improvement are likely outcomes. The greater the obscurity of these linkages, the more uncertain the motivation to respond in a positive manner—although some individuals have a strong desire to achieve [33] and thus may be sufficiently self-directed to stay abreast of work-related needs. Unfortunately, such achievers are rare.

Finally, group pressures for conformity, competition from colleagues or friends, and an organizational climate of support for individual development all bolster the motivation of individuals to "keep up."

CAREER PATH

Technological advances have made the notion of a "half life" for early career education a convenient concept,[34] and the key ideas of the half life are integrated with the career-path model in Exhibit 13–6. The upper portion of the exhibit suggests an individual's gain in "store of knowledge," with his accumulation of job experiences, contacts with colleagues, and formal educational experiences. Initially, knowledge gain is rapid, reflecting the structured learning of college or university life, though this gain is largely devoid of organizational experience. In the world of work, the source of knowledge gain is largely reversed, with inputs mostly from organization-related experiences.

The broken line in this characterization depicts occupational demand. Through a process of accretion or one-step change, occupational requirements increase and may start to overtake the acquisition of relevant knowledge by a role holder.

The pace of knowledge change vis-à-vis occupational demand relates to the level 1 changes described in Part 2 of this chapter. Individual gains of relevant knowledge depend on personal factors previously identified (motivation, for example, or proximity to relevant knowledge, or physical energy). The "difference" between occupational demand and an individual's gain in revelant knowledge is crucial in career development and individual achievement. In the lower panel of Exhibit 13–6 a half-life representation is depicted for knowledge decay. The relevant point is the characteristic profile of knowledge decay, which in turn relates to changes in state of the art. The

EXHIBIT 13–6. Career-path Model

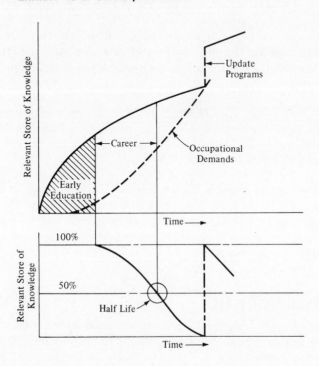

increasing pace of change described in Part 1 of this chapter has resulted in more steeply inclined decay curves for a variety of engineering specialties, as well as various management areas. By the early 1960s the half life for some engineering areas (e.g., electronics) was around six years, whereas it was some eleven years a decade previously.

Another point to be brought out from the career-path model is the result of updating, retraining, or continuing development programs. These undertakings can help the individual stay comfortably ahead of occupational requirement and maintain a sense of personal confidence and achievement.

The lag in an individual's stock of knowledge relative to occupational demand may turn on important behavioral matters; for example, the waning of knowledge may reflect loss of interest in an occupation, lack of promotion, or growing outside demands. To the extent that career counseling can achieve greater correspondence of individually valued goals and job paths with organizational requirements, a high level of personal energy can be harnessed for personal and organizational gain. Also, the degree of professionalization may play a major role, in the sense that higher levels of accomplishment suggest greater dedication to education and to maintaining relevance.[35]

We see, therefore, that considerable insight into obsolescence is provided by analysis of policy environment, the characteristics of change, and the personal features of the individual.

The task of change management is clear: building an understanding of organizational life, structure, and process to fashion mechanisms for coping with the diversity of emerging change. Coping responses in organizations build on the preserving of human dignity and usefulness while simultaneously seeking to better the opportunities for attaining institutional objectives. Toffler states well the central core of concern for the organization's agents of change:

> To survive the superindustrial revolution, we must take a fresh look at all our personal and social coping mechanisms. We must build future-shock absorbers into our lives and into the emerging institutions of tomorrow's society.[36]

One of the keys to a viable coping response is developing an operational *detection system*. At an early point, this system should permit those charged with change responsibilities to anticipate change, both internal and external, and to formulate coping responses.[37] An underlying base of information is indispensable to a coping system.

INFORMATION SYSTEMS

The discussions of Chapter 7 on computer-based information systems outlined the utilization of an information capability for obtaining change detection data. In Exhibit 13–7, stress is placed on capturing behavioral information, preceded by research and followed by the collection of more conventional statistics. Relevant behavioral data (3) must go far beyond the typically collected demographic type of information and seek to bring into play a variety of behavioral tools for better assessment and career development in response to change. Manpower administrators (5), who are at the heart of the operational system for coping with personnel-related change, build on behavioral models of the type described in Chapters 8–11. Coping programs that emerge for the manpower resources of the firm affect manpower resources (8) per se and organization structure and function (7).

EXHIBIT 13–7. Manpower Information System

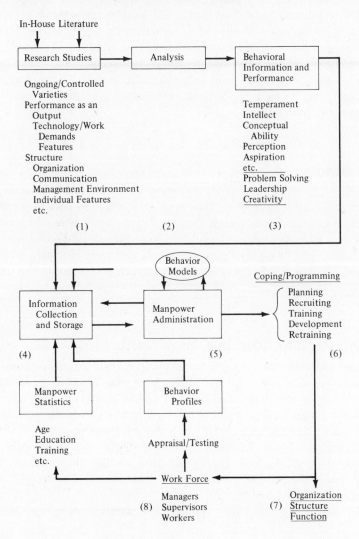

It is important to note that Exhibit 13–7 identifies information inputs and subsystem elements that are largely absent from present-day organizations. Of the several hundred companies covered in our various manpower studies, a considerable number still reflect cursory treatment of personnel records, often going little beyond the recording of legally required reporting information. A few large companies, such as Exxon (Standard Oil of New Jersey) and Sears, encode varying amounts of behavioral data, but they are the exceptions rather than the rule. Comprehensive approaches to obsolescence avoidance and the development of thoughtful career plans call for a level of information planning, interaction with individual organization members, and the cooperation of various managers and officials that is not even approximated in existing organizations.

Information capability easily leads to detection audits for spotting mismatches of job and individual that could lead to turnover or obsolescence. Detecting weaknesses of the work structure in the course of systematic monitoring argues for new capabilities, in that it becomes possible to forecast emergent job trends through, say, Markov chain analysis. Computer-based job matching or the joint surveillance of man, job, and change trends are rapidly assuming a sophistication warranting serious attention by the managers of change.[38]

Forecasting

Another direction that needs attention and that depends upon a solid information base is forecasting. The opinion of planners notwithstanding, the projection of activities or trends cannot move beyond detailed knowledge of people and jobs. Assembling trend data from the external environment of an organization and its internal manpower, job, and technological variables permits anticipation of areas of need. This approach is superior to the "response" management of past years.

INDIVIDUAL AND COMPANY VIEWPOINTS IN CHANGE

Where individuals are caught up in change, their interest is aroused. It is increasingly necessary to allocate time at regular intervals to introspection and to gauging the depth and breadth of life changes.[39] This approach to self-analysis leads to a program of *attempting* to regulate the pace of change to the extent that the individual can influence these processes. Delaying or simplifying change to lessen its negative effects represents one type of effective strategy. Coping approaches that modify the pace or shape of change lower the level of environmental stimulation of the cognitive mechanisms of the individual.[40]

Individual coping responses, among other factors, are a function of education and training, length of service, and authority level. The penalties for failure are easily seen: displacement, obsolescence or marginal performance, tension, frustration, or conflict.

Bringing the individual to a point where he is prepared to cope and move toward some positive program of development is a central motivational challenge.[41]

The Institutional Viewpoint

A company's coping responses emerge from a realistic estimate of need. Future and current manpower needs are often interpreted in terms of general educational criteria—a gross measure—for lack of more precise criteria. Also, recognizing the longer-term deficit of specialized managerial and professional personnel, along with greater acknowledgment of the need for bettering the lot of the individual in organization life, indicates good detection capabilities of manpower officials for leadership potential and promotion.

NEW SUPERVISORY ROLE

Both the pace of change and the rotation of supervisory personnel for developmental purposes mean more transitory relationships between supervisor (leader) and subordinate. Consequently, other situational or climate factors may assume greater importance for motivation, and preliminary results from the study of a major retail chain support this idea.[42] In particular, such things as "concern" for employees, cordial relationships, and good communications may assume an increasingly greater burden for motivating employees, compared to the traditionally important relationship of supervisor and subordinate.[43] Thus, to the extent that a supervisor spends less time in a particular position, role relationships are temporary, and individual organization members tend to look to the "greater" organization for important motivational cues and support. One research experience in a large, metropolitan bank indicated a suprisingly strong worker orientation toward general institutional management rather than department supervision.

In short, the era of the "mobile manager" is here, and regardless of whether movement is intra- or interorganizational, even greater emphasis is placed on creating a sound climate for individual performance and realization.

NOVEL ORGANIZATION APPROACHES

The managers of change are increasingly led to seek novel organizational contrasts and approaches for bettering performance. Toffler has discussed several interesting possibilities, which start with ways of thinking about change and ways of classifying people relative to "changeability." [44] The various job positions occupied by the individual constitute transitional states or plateaus between changes of state. In one prescriptive approach, the creation of temporary organizations, which permits assembling similar situational groups, facilitates the exchange of experiences and a working out of short- and long-range strategies, while preserving identity and self-esteem. [45]

However, organizational constructs for people *actively* engaged in organizational affairs are no more important than transitional units that permit (a) a gradual phasing out of individuals or (b) slowing change down so that people can be eased into different positions. Recognizing the behavioral needs of individuals in these situations helps preserve individual dignity and a feeling of worth. Toffler also proposes "frozen centers," where the environment would be tension free, with personnel largely shielded from the effects of rapid change. [46]

The ability of management to cope turns on its mapping the ramifications of change for manpower resources and then developing the required climate, procedures, organization, and technology. The close interplay of initiators of change with agents and translators of change establishes the necessary organizational interaction patterns for adapting to change. Managing change points to establishing a supportive climate sufficiently flexible in work hours, teaching programs, persuasion, and demonstration that individual participation is seen as a strategy satisfying both the individual and the organizational objectives. Intellectualizing change calls for an interpretation of technology. This means that the variables of age, education, developmental programming, career planning, and the like must be balanced against allocation of responsibilities, span of command, and technology.

CHANGE MANAGEMENT IN EDUCATION

Among educators, the problems of ghetto areas and the lack of innovation in education have led to an almost complete collapse of traditional programs. The need to introduce enlightened changes is manifest, and rests on the insights and beliefs of the educators who administer and manage a school. [47] One example in this area describes a particular program in change that was built around some forty hours of small-group discussion among school administrators and was aimed at exposing new alternatives and extending two-way communication sensitivity for better understanding of colleague behavior.

SUMMARY AND EXAMPLES OF CHANGE

To crystallize all the management-of-change notions into a single, compact thought would probably be to say something like this: "Viable change management hinges on a mode of thinking, a philosophy of management, that leads to active support and encouragement of manpower development efforts on an organization-wide basis." In this chapter two perspectives on change management have been advanced: "level 1," which considers change at the institutional level and deals with the forces shaping organization processes and activities, and "level 2," which takes up the methods and targets of behavioral change.

Part 3 of this chapter has been devoted to a brief discussion and development of people-related issues in the management of change. Forestalling individual obsolescence and dealing with career-path approaches are undertakings replete with behavioral challenges. Institutional policy, structure, motivation, leadership, job roles, and job systems—plus a host of personal factors—are some of the many matters to be dealt with in these applications of change-management notions.

The following sections summarize some important instances of change that have led to fruitful group discussion and analysis.

Technological Change

Research by Hoos treats the sociological implications of office automation, and some of his results indicate a blurring of lines of demarcation between office and plant forces. Also, the decline of the clerical function is noted, and this raises some important problems of career opportunities and mobility for the large number of people who have made major career commitments to office activities. These are serious problems in situations ranging from government bureaus to mail order houses.

An English study by Emery and Marek, conducted in a power plant, suggests that the factors that contribute to the ease of change include the long-term stability of the economic environment, the stability of the internal environment (particularly the labor force), and confidence in management's ability to cope with technological change. The character of the change itself is suggested by noting that the number of critical points in power plant operations increased substantially.

For example, the number of malfunctions requiring less than five minutes to remedy increased from two in the old system to approximately nine in the new system; those requiring more than five minutes numbered three in the old system and were not encountered in the new system.

Emery and Marek suspected that, below a certain level of technical knowledge, it was unlikely one could develop and sustain a map of the complex process when one was continually moving about. Additionally, under the new conditions, there was much more to know and yet it was more confined to the mental level. The supervisory role was considerably changed as the operators' job was unified; and the time span for supervisory response was shortened. A new posture is indicated for crisis performance, as the supervisor is often called upon for emergency situations.

Urban Police Force and the City Milieu

In the 1960s Orlando Wilson, then head of the Chicago Police Department, attempted to bring about changes in the department after a long period of turmoil, confusion, and political intervention.

a. Faced with the prospect of massive civil rights demonstrations, Wilson ordered special training for departmental personnel.

b. Looking beyond the troublesome summer, Wilson set up community workshops in twenty of the city's twenty-one police districts.

c. Wilson took steps to increase the number of Puerto Rican officers, noting that Puerto Ricans were an important part of the city's social milieu.

d. The heart of Wilson's approach was his concept of aggressive, resourceful, relentless patrolling by regular-beat officers. This, in turn, was supported by an expanded, modern communications center that blended experienced manpower and sophisticated equipment, involving the use of the computer and scientific planning and methods. To improve the efficiency of patrolling units, many men received advanced training from Northwestern University's Traffic Institute. Wilson assumed that as police became more professional, there would be major changes in the attitudes of the police toward the populace and the populace toward the police.

e. Wilson also recruited better cadets and improved their training to develop a new breed of officers.

Urban Motormen and the Union

Attempts were made to bring about changes in the union structure of the motormen of a large public transportation system. This case exemplifies the challenges of attempting to bring about rapid change when one must deal with the natural resistance to change inherent in hierarchical structures or covenants developed in past years.

A large group of blacks, comparatively new to the motormen's organization, were confronted with a seniority system. In a comparatively short time their numbers rose to almost 50 percent of the total union membership. Nevertheless, they had very little say in the union.

Agreements that involved retired motormen's retaining voting privileges and committee structures that helped reinforce the position power of experienced WASP personnel in this organization are examples of the complications restricting change.

Students and the University

Many colleges in the United States have traditionally maintained a strong hierarchical structure, with policy formulated by the president and board of trustees, and in the case of public institutions by city, county, or state legislative bodies.

At a large private liberal arts college near a metropolitan center, the president dominated all important internal decisions and assumed the major role in fund-raising activities. Decision making was hierarchically oriented, but the locus of power was clearly at the top. Thus the officers had major administrative responsibilities but few budget prerogatives. Major programs, planning, and direction were guided by the president. The academic staff had only modest influence and the students virtually none.

Propose some approaches to introducing change, but be sure to identify the criteria by which the effectiveness of the proposals is to be judged.

Disadvantaged Workers

Federal legislation, reinforced by enactments of state governments and heavy political pressure, has necessitated the serious undertaking of programs for providing jobs for the economically "disadvantaged" in society.

In one large chain food store, contracts covering several hundred disadvantaged were secured from the U.S. Department of Labor, under the Manpower Development and Training Act, for supporting its employees through job subsidies. Because of the variety of store locations serving a number of culturally differentiated neighborhoods, the problems of incorporating trainees into the work force were diverse and substantial. They included punctuality, appearance, manners, and job skills. These problems were further complicated by managers in the store and the home office who were predominantly Caucasian and oriented to traditional American work values.

What structural system and behavioral approaches are indicated for achieving a situation where the disadvantaged become a *permanent* part of the work force?

Technological Change—Organizational and Individual Response

In a number of steel companies the conversion from open hearth to basic oxygen furnaces created problems of individual adjustment to change. For example, instead of a single changeover ("heat") in a six- to eight-hour period for the open hearth, the basic oxygen furnace might call for a heat every hour. Instead of one changeover per shift, there might be twelve per shift.

Given this type of technological transition, what qualities are indicated for successfully transferring from the slower to the faster-paced units? What challenges confront management in helping to modify negative work conditions? What is the effect of the age of the incumbents? What types of bridging technologies and techniques are indicated?

NOTES

1. Alvin Toffler, "Future Shock," *Playboy,* February 1970, p. 97, and March 1970, p. 88.

2. Ibid., February 1970.

3. Ibid., pp. 204–206.

4. For an insightful study, see Tom Burns and G. M. Stalker, *"The Management of Innovation* (London: Tavistock Publications, 1961).

5. Robert J. Litschert, "Some Characteristics of Long-Range Planning: An Industry Study," *Academy of Management Journal,* 11, no. 3 (September 1968): 315–328.

6. Based on notions expressed in Rolf P. Lynton, "Linking an Innovation Subsystem into the System," *Administrative Science Quarterly,* 14, no. 3 (September 1969): 398–417. For closely related ideas, see Paul R. Lawrence and Jay W. Lorsch, *Organization and Environment: Managing Differentiation and Integration* (Boston: School of Business Administration, Harvard University, 1967).

7. For a discussion that combines notions of organization development linkers and teams, see Edgar F. House and Michael Beer, "Electic Approach to Organizational Development," *Harvard Business Review,* 49, no. 5 (September–October 1971): 103–112. It is well to recognize that conscious or deliberate attempts at people-related change, as in training or management development, must incorporate conscious, behavioral change objectives; for example, see George S. Odiorne, *Training by Objectives* (New York: Macmillan, 1970).

8. Lynton, "Linking an Innovation Subsystem into the System."

9. Ibid.

10. These points can be generalized to suggest that preparing people for change must involve a change in individual knowledge, attitude, skills, or performance. See Herbert H. Hand, Max D. Richards, and John W. Slocum Jr., "Organizational Climate and the Effectiveness of a Human Relations Training Program," *Academy of Management Journal,* 16, no. 2 (June 1973): 185–195.

11. Based on Daniel Katz and Robert L. Kahn, *The Social Psychology of Organizations* (New York: Wiley, 1966), chap. 13.

12. For an interesting discussion of philosophy/ideology, coping with change, matrix approach, and organization interests versus people interests, see Roger Harrison,

"Understanding Your Organization's Character," *Harvard Business Review,* 50, no. 3 (May–June 1972): 119–128.

13. An interesting Ph.D. thesis on these various postures is described by Carl Spetzler of Illinois Institute of Technology (1967).

14. A useful distinction developed by Katz and Kahn in *The Social Psychology of Organizations,* esp. chap. 13.

15. For some of the many changes taking place here, see Elmer H. Burack, "Industrial Management in Advanced Production Systems: Some Theoretical Concepts and Preliminary Findings," *Administrative Science Quarterly,* 12, no. 3 (December 1967).

16. Considerable variations exist in decision maker's perceptions of uncertainty. For an interesting study, see Robert Duncan, "Characteristics of Organizational Environments and Perceived Environmental Uncertainty," *Administrative Science Quarterly,* 17, no. 3 (September 1972): 313–328.

17. Stephen Zelikoff, *Training and Development Journal.*

18. See Elmer H. Burack, "Impact of Computers on Business," *Business Quarterly,* 30, no. 2 (Spring 1966): 35–45, and Bernard H. Baum and Elmer H. Burack, "Information Technology, Manpower Development, and Organizational Performance," *Academy of Management Journal,* 12, no. 3 (September 1969): 279–293.

19. Burack, "Impact of Computers on Business."

20. Some of these considerations are developed in Elmer H. Burack, James F. Staszak, and Gopal Pati, "An Organization Analysis of Manpower Issues in Employing the Disadvantaged," *Academy of Management Journal,* 15, no. 3 (September 1972): 255–273.

21. A number of situations under the stress of technological change are examined in Elmer H. Burack and Thomas J. McNichols, *Human Resource Planning: Technology, Change,* (Kent, O.: Bureau of Business and Economic Research, Kent State University, 1973).

22. Katz and Kahn, *Social Psychology of Organizations,* esp. chaps. 13 and 14.

23. For example, Elliot Jacques in *The Changing Culture of a Factory* (London: Tavistock Publications, 1951): F. E. Emery and E. L. Trist, "Socio-Technical Systems," in *Management Sciences Models and Techniques* (London: Pergamon Press, 1960), vol. 2; Katz and Kahn, *Social Psychology of Organizations,* esp. chap. 13; Floyd C. Mann, "Studying and Creating Change: A Means to Understanding Social Organization," *Research in Industrial Human Relations,* no. 17, pp. 146–167; Nancy Morse and E. Reimer, "The Experimental Change of a Major Organization Variable," *Journal of Abnormal and Social Psychology,* no. 52, pp. 120–129; and R. J. Lippitt, J. Watson, and B. Westley, *The Dynamics of Planned Change* (New York: Harcourt Brace Jovanovich, 1958).

24. Katz and Kahn, *Social Psychology of Organizations,* p. 390.

25. See Hand, Richards, and Slocum, "Organizational Climate." Other characteristics of environments in change are developed in Burack and McNichols, *Human Resource Planning,* and Elmer H. Burack and Frank H. Cassell, "Technological Change and Manpower Developments in Advanced Production Systems," *Academy of Management Journal,* 10, no. 3 (September 1967): 293–309.

26. Kurt Lewin, "Group Decisions and Social Change," in T. M. Newcomb and E. L. Hartley (eds.), *Readings in Social Psychology* (New York: Holt, Rinehart and Winston, Inc., 1947).

27. Based largely on ideas proposed in Gene W. Dalton, "Influence and Organizational Change," in Arlyn Melcher and Anant Negandhi (eds.), *Proceedings of Complex Administration Research Institute* (Kent, O.: Bureau of Research, Kent State University, 1969).

28. Dealt with at considerable length in Warren Bennis, *Changing Organizations* (New York: McGraw-Hill, 1966).

29. Some references that provide an overview of obsolescence and the emergent challenge to manpower include Elmer H. Burack, "Meeting the Threat of Managerial Obsolescence," *California Management Review,* 15, no. 2 (Winter 1973); idem and Gopal Pati, "Technological Change and Managerial Obsolescence," *M.S.U. Business Topics* (Fall 1970), pp. 49–56; James J. Rago Jr., "Managerial Obsolescence: Job-Person Interaction, Change, and One's Marketability," Cleveland State University, Department of Management working papers; Wallace R. Brode, "Approaching Ceilings in the Supply of Scientific Manpower," *Science,* 143, no. 3604 (January 24, 1964): p. 313; Lester J. Weigle, "The Growing Problem of Executive Obsolescence," *Dunn's Review and Modern Industry,* 83, no. 43 (April 1964); Donald N. Michael, "Some Long Range Implications of Computer Technology for Human Behavior in Organization," *American Behavioral Scientist,* 9, no. 8 (April 1966): p. 29; and Walter Buckingham, "The Human Side of Automation," in Keith Davis and William G. Scott (eds.), *Readings in Human Relations* (2d. ed.; New York: McGraw-Hill, 1966), which suggests new knowledge for managers and increased importance for planning and control skills.

30. Many of the points are detailed in Burack, "Industrial Management in Advanced Production Systems."

31. Characteristics of change are discussed in greater detail in Burack and Cassell, "Technological Change and Manpower Developments in Advanced Production Systems."

32. See Alvin Zander, "Resistance to Change—Its Analysis and Prevention," in Peter B. Schoderbick, *Management Systems* (New York: John Wiley & Sons, 1967); M. Stewart, "Resistance to Technological Change in Industry," *Human Organizations,* vol. 16 (1957); William F. Whyte, *Men at Work* (Homewood, Ill.: Dorsey, 1961), p. 228; and W. Douglas Seymour, "Retraining for Technological Change," *Personnel Management* (December 1966), p. 183. Also see George Strauss and Leonard R. Sayles, *Personnel: Human Problems of Management* (2d. ed., rev.; Englewood Cliffs, N.J.: Prentice-Hall, 1967), pp. 30–38.

33. For example, see David C. McClelland, "Achievement to Motivation Can Be Developed," *Harvard Business Review,* 43, no. 6 (November–December 1965), and idem, *The Achieving Society* (Princeton, N.J.: Van Nostrand, 1961).

34. Some relevant items include Robert Dubin, *Human Relations in Administration* (3d. ed., rev.; Englewood Cliffs, N.J.: Prentice-Hall, 1968), p. 4—from a discussion by Edwin Mansfield, "Diffusion of Technological Change," *Review of Data on Research and Development,* prepared by the National Science Foundation (1961). See also H. Igor Ansoff and John M. Stewart, "Strategies for a Technology Based Business," *Harvard Business Review,* 47, no. 6 (November–December 1957): 71.

35. One concern reflects blocked mobility (promotion) paths, need for individual autonomy, and adverse behavioral effects, which can emerge from inattention to

these matters. See Robert D. Rossel, "Autonomy in Bureaucracies," *Administrative Science Quarterly,* 16, no. 3 (September 1971): 308–315. Also Alvin Gouldner, *Patterns of Industrial Bureaucracy* (Glencoe, Ill.: Free Press, 1954). For additional dimensions and discussions of these issues, see Richard Ritti, "Work Goals of Scientists and Engineers," *Industrial Relations,* 7, no. 2 (February 1968): 118–132, and Howard S. Becker and James Carper, "The Elements of Identification with an Occupation," *American Sociological Review,* 21 (June 1956): 341–348.

36. Toffler, "Future Shock," March 1970, p. 89.

37. Burack, "Managerial Obsolescence."

38. Described in Elmer H. Burack and James W. Walker, *Manpower Planning and Programming for Planning and Change* (Boston: Allyn & Bacon, 1972); also Elmer H. Burack, *Strategies for Planning and Programming* (Morristown, N.J.: General Learning Press, 1972).

39. Toffler, "Future Shock," March 1970, pp. 89, 90, 96.

40. Ibid.

41. Albert N. B. Nedd, "The Simultaneous Effect of Several Variables on Attitudes toward Change," *Administrative Science Quarterly,* 16, no. 3 (September 1971): 258–269.

42. Frank Smith in a paper delivered at the Conference on Productivity Improvement, sponsored by the U.S. Department of Labor, Midwest Region, Chicago, May 1972.

43. A major theme in Hand, Richards, and Slocum, "Organizational Climate."

44. Toffler, "Future Shock," March 1970, pp. 96, 179.

45. Ibid.

46. Ibid., p. 174.

47. Draws on an article by Hope Justus, "Educators Go Back to School," *Chicago Daily News,* July 30, 1969.

Learning Objectives

Review of Major Themes, Concepts, and Relationships Set Out
    in the Book

Application Case and How to Use the Wide Assortment of Models,
    Perspectives, and Approaches Proposed in the Book

Chapter 14

COMPREHENSIVE APPLICATION

This chapter has two principal purposes: to review and summarize the major themes presented in this book and to provide an application case in which many of the concepts are applied. In keeping with the mode of topical presentation established in past chapters, models and summary discussions will be employed.

THRUST AND THEMES

This book emphasizes a systems approach to organizational analyses, supported by ideas from behavioral research. Its major themes build toward a simultaneous involvement of structure (Chapters 1 and 2), systems (Chapters 3–7), and behavioral notions (Chapters 8–11) for undertaking organizational studies and coping with emergent, related matters. The use of conceptual models was proposed for bringing together a variety of perspectives for a particular need or situation. Key challenges facing managers and organizational analysts are the management of organizational change (Chapters 13 and 15) and improving the work climate, utilization, and personal realizations of human resources (Chapter 12).

One of the important themes advanced the notion of a flexible approach in thinking about and dealing with organizational phenomena. The pace of environmental and organizational change is so rapid that flexible structures and approaches are required for assembling ideas and then organizing them to meet the needs of a particular situation. Conceptual models and approaches, used throughout the book, were proposed to meet these needs. These modeling approaches are an important step beyond classification (taxonomical) techniques and assist in arranging critical variables to amplify relationships, sharpen the identification of factors contributing to problems, and thus facilitate the processes of management and support groups.

Flexibility has also been demonstrated in various situational or contingency approaches, illustrated, for example, by the discussions of technology (Chapters 3 and 4), control (Chapter 5), motivation (Chapter 8), and leadership (Chapter 9). Flexibility also requires that the analyst be prepared to formulate newer models and analysis approaches as added research findings emerge, research directions are reexamined, or circumstances change.

Finally, an opportunity has been provided to assume a flexible, problem-solving approach in the variety of real-life questions and situational problems posed at the conclusion of each chapter.

MANAGEMENT OF ORGANIZATION CHANGE

The particular chapter devoted to this topic (13) and the recurrence of the change theme throughout the book reflect the importance assigned to this area. Many instances of the change theme have been provided: Chandler's notions of strategy and structure and their shifts in form and thrust with changes in environmental opportunity and need (Chapter 2); research on technological change that moves beyond the cross-sectional, point-in-time portrayal of earlier technological studies (Chapter 3); the influence of learning on perception and motivation (Chapter 8); and contingency approaches in leadership and modification in leader strategies as situational factors or relationships shift (Chapter 9).

The discussions of Chapter 12 on individual and organization development portrayed another dimension of the change theme. Management by objectives, for example, can be viewed as a patterned approach to guide (or change) individual actions toward agreed-on goals. The enlargement of individual potentialities and the facilitation of personal realization most often involve changes in individual knowledge, perspectives, or skills. And one need not move very far beyond this point to indicate that the models and procedures of "organization development" are to facilitate change and promote the interworkings of institutional units and task groups and members.

The change theme also acknowledged characteristic forms of change and, at times, the patterned forms assumed by them. Innovation, environmental trends, social change, and technological change interlace the book's discussions. Additionally, the discussions of Chapter 13 sought to establish some characteristic dimensions of change that prove quite valuable in organizational study.

PROBING COMPLEX ENVIRONMENTS

Though one readily acknowledges the complexity of organizational matters touched on in these discussions, an array of concepts and tools has been referenced to meet some of these needs. The notion of a technological scale of sophistication, advanced by Woodward (Chapter 3), facilitates a crude ordering of industrial units for various structural inferences. The profile analyses developed by Bright (Chapter 4) permit systematic characterizations of control or technical sophistication within technological systems. Though still quite crude, environmental analyses utilizing uncertainty and complexity concepts (Chapters 2 and 4) suggest ways of systematically probing these environments for forces or elements shaping organizational structure or process.

Some of the numerical analyses that suggest systematic bases for probing systems were also portrayed. The simulation example in Chapter 11 for analyzing a decision system and the Markov model in Chapter 12 for manpower studies suggest some of the possibilities in this area.

Of course, the model approach, already discussed at great length in this summary, represents a realistic attempt to pierce complex situations and identify relevant variables and relationships.

INTERDEPENDENCE OF ISSUES

It has not gone unnoticed by the reader that organizational situations reflect a complex of variables inextricably woven together, so that a single tool or approach is unlikely to prove rewarding. Although conceptual models, propositions, and the like desirably emerge from a plane of integrated ideas, particular situations suggest the kinds of notions that will dominate. Yet, in arriving at key ideas and models instrumental in solution, a number of topical "boundaries" (e.g., motivation or role) will likely be crossed. As an example, a particular technological system (Chapters 3 and 4) is an initial state determining the general character of a problem. Yet the sociotechnical perspective readily moves us in several possible directions involving other aspects of systems (control, Chapter 5; communications, Chapter 6) or structure (Chapters 1 and 2) or behavioral ideas (Part II). (Hopefully, not too many beyond these!)

However, resolution of the particular situation may turn on specific motivational or control issues. Similarly, an issue may initially seem to involve motivational matters (Chapter 8), which in turn are tied to relations with a group's leader (Chapter 9) and the roles played by leader and group member (Chapter 10). To the extent that computer-based technologies (Chapter 7) may underlie group decision activities (Chapter 11), the introduction of these additional concepts can add to the richness (and complexity!) of the analyses. The following model brings together many of the themes referenced in this discussion of interdependency.

Interdependence Viewed Conceptually

A vertical slice from the organizational milieu reveals at one glance a complex of structures, systems, people, and relationships. Interfaces are

EXHIBIT 14–1. Composite View of Models, Notions, and Approaches

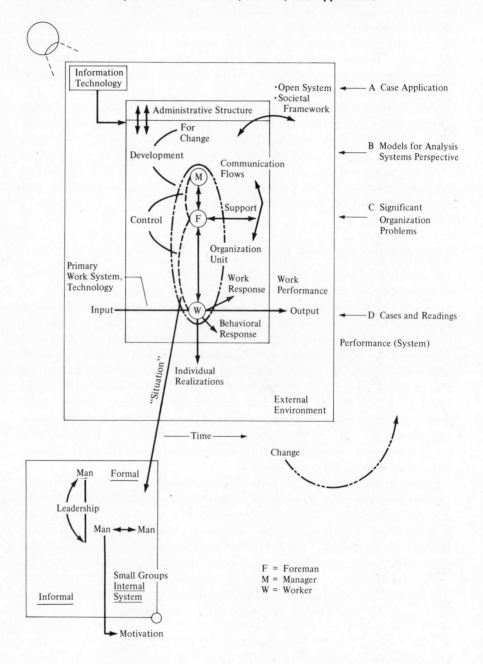

complex and compound—well-trained eyes will be able to pick out the organization structures, the technological and behavioral systems, along with the people and interaction patterns that make up this institution. As noted in Exhibit 14–1, welding Parts I and II of the book together suggests the composite view. Work and communication systems permit the major work missions of these units to be accomplished while providing information flows supportive of work functions. Formal organization structures and arrangements blend into the informal—formal roles are assumed in the furtherance of institutional objectives and become pivotal points in the "internal system" of formal role structures. Motivational considerations pervade the total system of formal and informal roles and are the forces that can "turn people on" and lead to performance outputs beyond "design." Of course, the level of performance jointly depends on the technological and behavioral systems. To the extent that the technological variables dominate, qualitative and behavioral measures tend to turn on the human system. As technological dominance lessens in administrative systems, for example, behavioral variables assume increased importance.

APPLICATION OF CONCEPTS

The viewpoints and approaches undertaken in this book have sought to move beyond the review or recounting of existing theory and research to their application in a variety of organizational situations. Beyond the format provided by end-of-chapter questions, the application situations with examples from the oil, steel, baking, insurance, and public transit industries sought to convey the latitude of application needs and opportunities. Here again, conceptual models were key vehicles for analysis. The development of human resources and organization (Chapter 12), management of organizational change (Chapter 13), the Sweet Products case (the major discussion of this chapter), and the emergent organizational issues treated in Chapter 15 all represent extensions and applications of the notions advanced in Parts I and II of the book.

The concluding discussion of this section, prior to the presentation of the application case, highlights important chapter topics.

REVIEW: SOME IMPORTANT CHAPTER TOPICS AND NOTIONS

Exhibit 14–2 provides a compact, conceptual view of key research ideas and notions from earlier discussions. No attempt is made to capture the full range of previous discussions, but some of these summary highlights should prove useful for review purposes. Review of these points will assist the reader in following the summary case that concludes this chapter's discussions. Each panel provides one or two key sketches for recall, based on

EXHIBIT 14–2. Some Key Chapter Topics and Concepts

Panel	Description	Notes on Key Ideas	Model/Sketch
1	Structure (Ref.: 1, 2)	• Basic design concepts portrayed as specialization and division of labor • Strategy/structure theme advanced for structural growth and rationalization • Weber advances the bureaucracy notion, the "ideal" model—enter dysfunction • Design approaches must resolve the tension between differentiation and integration	(1) Structure
2	Socio-Technical System: Small Groups/Roles (Ref.: 3, 4; 10)	• Notion of technology continuum and technical ordering of industrial units • Level of technology and impact on structure, use, and distribution of various employee groups • Static vs. change dynamics and impact on structure • Portrayal of input-process-output work system • Intermingling of human and work elements within inter-dependent complex • Formal relationships and work system • Emergence of informal groups and social relationships influenced by technical system • Notion of social efficiency and behavioral (vs. output) performance	(2) Socio-Technical System: Small Groups/Roles
3	Communications-Information Systems (Ref.: 6, 7, 11)	• Communications as interpersonal processes • Communications as systems: information flow, encode, decode, distortion, and properties • Communications structures • Possible use and impact of computer-based system on organization, structure, relationships, and decision making	(3) Communications-Information Systems

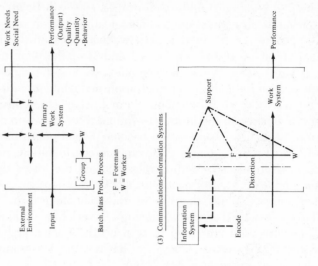

EXHIBIT 14-2. (Continued)

Panel	Description	Notes on Key Ideas	Model/Sketch

Model/Sketch

Panel	Description	Notes on Key Ideas
4	Motivation (Ref.: 8)	• Need structure and deficiencies • "Hygiene" factors/motivators • Goal-path: valued goals, path, possible and probable • Operational performance vs. behavioral performance
5	Leadership (Ref.: 9)	• Contingency approach: strategy shifts over time; nature of work task; character of group; group-leader relationships; leader-boss relationships; leader influence in organization environment
6	Evaluation and Control: Decision Making (Ref.: 5)	• Performance criteria • Interpersonal bases for control • System controls; subsystem controls • Feedback • Control bases: technology, social, colleague, etc.; personal-impersonal; administrative technology (budgets)

(4) Motivation

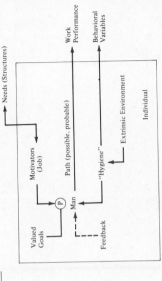

(5) Leadership

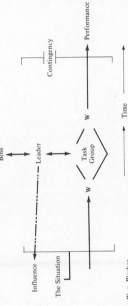

W = Worker

(6) Evaluation and Control: Decision Making

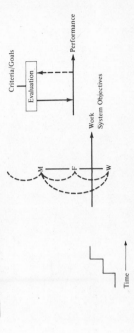

EXHIBIT 14–2. (Continued)

Model/Sketch

Panel	Description	Notes on Key Ideas	Model/Sketch
7	Decision Making (Ref.: 7, 11)	• Goals-means-ends • Certainty-risk-uncertainty; decision horizon • Maximizing vs. satisfying • Bounded rationality • Information technology	(7) Decision Making 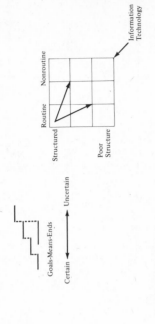
8	Individual-Organization Development (Ref. 12)	• Individual development and change • Group linkages, relationships, and change • Organization development techniques: council, lab, etc. • Use of feedback • Management by objectives (MBO)	(8) Individual-Organization Development 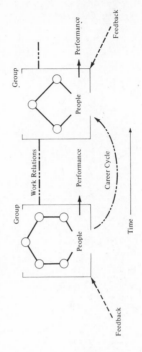
9	Management of Organization Change (Ref.: 13)	• Change: point of departure, magnitude, rate, scope • Change patterns • Management of individual change: unfreeze-set-refreeze, awareness-need-ability-desire • Time effects; cycling, individual accommodation • Feedback	(9) Management of Organization Charge 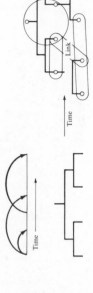

chapter developments. In addition, relevant chapters are referenced and some key notions are summarized.

The following application case, Sweet Products, portrays the progressive buildup of information and insights through the use of conceptual approaches. This demonstration case touches on much that has been presented in Parts I–III.

Sweet Products ("How Do We Improve Our Turnover?")

Introduction

Sweet Products, a forty-year-old company, produces a broad but inexpensive line of candy products for institutional (dispensing machine) and commercial (supermarket) outlets. Reasonable quality, quick shipment in response to short-run demand, and low cost were the principal bases upon which the company had thrived and grown.

In 1970 the family-held company became a public corporation, and a vast modernization program was launched.

Work force. The work force of Sweet Products was built around a stable interracial nucleus of 400 employees with an average twelve years of company experience and relatively good records of attendance and performance. The production people in this group were mostly black women assigned to packaging operations, plus a number of men assigned to heavy manual tasks. In the supervisory force, women were assigned entirely to first-line supervisory positions; men occupied all other supervisory and managerial positions.

Because of the inherently low-cost/low-profit operations of the industry, very few professional people were attracted to a company such as Sweet Products, and management depended on developing managerial talent from the ranks (Chapter 12). With few exceptions, the supervisory group consisted of people with a background emphasizing experience rather than education. Indeed, their detailed knowledge, based on experience, was critical to company success: satisfactory equipment operation, personal control of orders, "secrets" of machine function, and personal knowledge of individual employees. Leadership (Chapter 10) was exerted face to face, but styles varied widely.

Work system. The work system of Sweet Products was based on a large number of mechanized operations, but it operated in a disjointed fashion. Although plant operations displayed a high level of interdependency because of product relationships (e.g., raw material mixing to product forming to packaging), material transport and intraprocess handling were largely manual. The character of the process had permitted functionalization, so that division of labor was embodied in production departments (such as mixing, forming, packaging, and special products). Yet in the period 1955–65 many industry members had updated their processes through mechanization of production equipment, installation of electrical equipment controls, and the integration of process units into unified production systems (Chapters 3 and 4). Although these industry improvements created highly interdependent systems with high breakdown costs, their cost performance was difficult to match.

Developments after 1972

In 1972, when it became clear to the family management of Sweet Products that its growing size (Chapter 2) demanded a broader capital base for current and planned needs, the company "went public" (sold stock). The internal management structure was strengthened and "rounded out" with the addition of several professional managers from the outside (Exhibit 14–3), plus a shift from functional organization to product-line managers (recall the meat processing unit of Chapter 2). The purpose of the product manager concept was to create positions where specialization would presumably ensure on-time, low-cost performance.

In addition, internal controls (Chapter 5) were strengthened through (1) creation of the product-line managers, (2) codification of procedures for quality assurance and rules for employee conduct (impersonal controls), (3) creation of "arm's length" monitoring of quality and performance through reassignment of support groups to the general manager, and (4) addition of some automatic controls to production equipment.

All material handling functions, from warehousing through intraprocess movement, were mechanized and equipped with advanced controls. These improvements created a highly interdependent system (Chapters 3 and 4), approximating advanced mass production, in which operators assumed greater standby functions; material handling help (almost all male) was drastically reduced; more line and fewer individual operations were carried out; and higher rates of performance were realized.

In the late 1960s a number of important developments in the general economy had a bearing on developments at Sweet Products. More stringent government regulations affected purity and product standards (events in the general environment impinging on decision processes of organizational decision makers [Chapters 2 and 11]) and underscored Sweet's management's strengthening of quality control and rationalization of rules. Inflation continued, but the labor shortages of the mid-1960s evaporated.

Manpower Trends at Sweet

The stable nucleus of manpower (Chapter 12), which characterized the early years of Sweet's work force development, changed considerably with the work force expansion of the 1970s. Aside from the group of 400 older employees, almost all newer additions (several hundred) were young "disadvantaged" people in their late teens or early twenties. Turnover among this newer group was extreme—as high as 250 percent. Furthermore, an inordinate amount of confusion among both old and new employees resulted from organizational changes, and Sweet's compensation system was changed in an attempt to attract and retain employees. But company management was dismayed by lackluster performance, sullenness, and growing complaints from the employees.

Introduction of Consultants

A management analyst and a behavioral scientist, called in by Sweet Products to consult on its problems, proposed a framework of conceptual perspectives for analyzing its organizational problems. As a point of departure, it was decided to map out the job structure implications of the modernization program. Second, a series of behavioral analyses was proposed, beginning with roles and then branching out into motivational issues, including the effects of leadership. Finally, the implications for change were to be explicitly considered in terms of management's manpower planning and programming for the future, and possible prescriptions (Chapter 13) for strengthening management's plans were to be offered.

Thus the project tended to divide itself into two main areas: (1) short-run analysis and amelioration of current problems and (2) longer-run studies to avoid making existing problems worse and to permit the implementation of a well-thought-out plan for the future. The order of these analyses was suggested by the circumstances, but using any of them as a point of departure would have led to similar results.

Analysis

1. Technology and job structure. The disjointed aspects of the production system were immediately apparent. The manufacturing system was apportioned into a large number of subsystems paralleling the main functional work activities of producing candy and closely related products—departments for storing, mixing, and packaging. Packaging activities reflected considerable division of labor (Chapter 2), with employees typically carrying out simple and routine but highly fractionalized operations. Many jobs in production departments were on incentive pay. The characteristic mode of manpower assignment reflected individual work, plus two-, three-, and four-person gangs. Simple visual inspecton of work operations indicated that women performed most of the production (packaging) operations whereas male help was assigned to the heavier material handling and trans-

EXHIBIT 14–3. Sweet Products Organization, 1968 and 1972

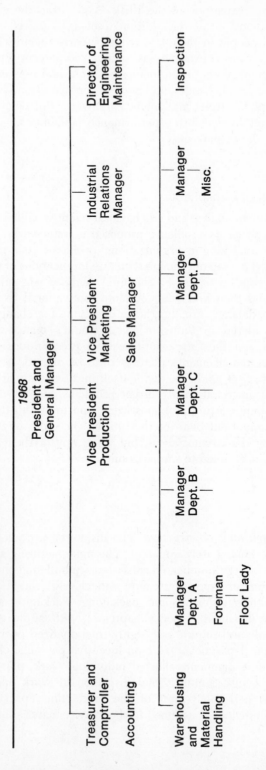

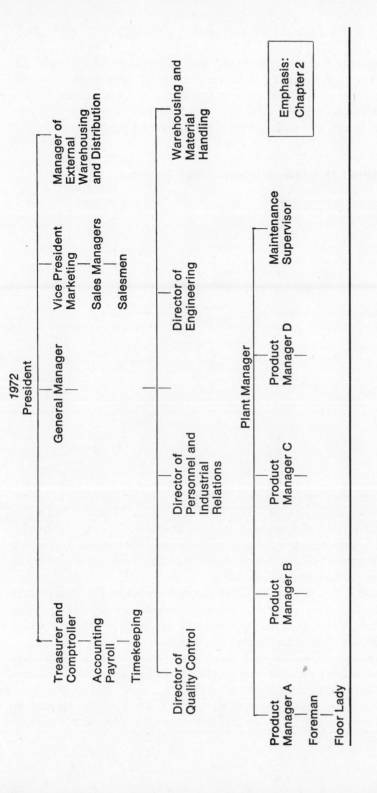

1972
President

General Manager

Treasurer and Comptroller

Accounting
Payroll

Timekeeping

Director of Quality Control

Director of Personnel and Industrial Relations

Vice President Marketing

Sales Managers

Salesmen

Director of Engineering

Manager of External Warehousing and Distribution

Warehousing and Material Handling

Plant Manager

Product Manager A

Foreman

Floor Lady

Product Manager B

Product Manager C

Product Manager D

Maintenance Supervisor

Emphasis: Chapter 2

fer activities, which were carried out under particularly poor work conditions.

The ingredients for conceptualizing the problems would include differences in sex, age, seniority, race, environmental work conditions and, possibly, character of work assignment (crew size and composition). Thus a general systems description (Exhibit 14–4), which depicted management's problem symptoms, was replaced by a more detailed perspective (Exhibit

EXHIBIT 14–4. Systems Overview, Sweet Products

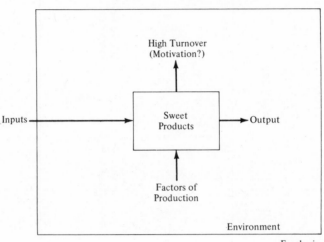

Emphasis:
Chapters 2, 7

14–5) as information was developed. In Exhibit 14–5 the detailing of factors underlying the systems representation of 14–4 provides the particulars necessary for understanding the problems at Sweet Products. For example, Exhibit 14–5 depicts customer changes and contingencies that, when considered jointly with outmoded production facilities, compound *uncertainty* and *variability* in production and control.

Exhibit 14–6 brings out the employee (manpower) side. For example, the male-female distinction is seen as of some importance in distinguishing personal needs. Varying career commitments are also emphasized, which takes into account such factors as sex, age, and race.

And worker controls are brought about in two ways: monetary incentives for those assigned to piecework, and procedures and supervisory surveillance for workers assigned to time-pay jobs.

Career and living needs, viewed alongside features of the technology and control system, suggest the factors determining employment attractiveness at Sweet Products.

EXHIBIT 14–5. Some Implications of Marketing and Technology Variables on Worker Deployment and Work Demands

Variables	Immediate ramification	Leads to	Potential organizational effects
Low profit Strong competition	Outmoded technologies Maintenance	Old equipment Frequent breakdown Work conditions deteriorate	Uncertainty (?) Variability (?) Employee temperament? Earnings stability?
Consumer Demands for widely varying packages, etc.	Flexible, diverse, and often small packaging lines and functions		
Demands for prompt order shipments Need for special deals	Frequent line change Establishing inventory		Uncertainty? Interaction Variability? Opportunities?

Emphasis:
Chapters 2, 4, 7, 8

EXHIBIT 14-6. Manpower Inputs: Some Differentiating Factors—Preliminary Analysis

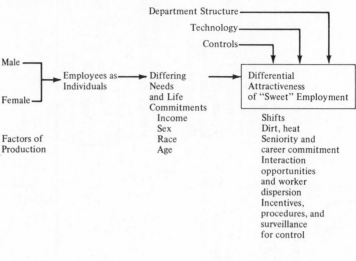

Emphasis:
Chapters 3, 4, 5, 8

2. Turnover analysis. Analysis of turnover statistics revealed that turnover clustered in several different departments that varied in work conditions, income potential, and supervision. Interviews with a randomly selected group of employees from various departments and shifts, and representing both males and females, indicated wide differences in perceived income expectancies, based on an equity comparison with what others might be earning in similar jobs, and an absolute judgment reflecting fairness vis-à-vis their level of energy expenditure and expected standard of living.

The modeling of variables from this phase of the study is presented in Exhibit 14-7; the leadership variable was added. The material of Chapters 9 and 10 would argue for examining leadership posture and situational variables such as technology.

EXHIBIT 14-7. Model Based on Turnover Study

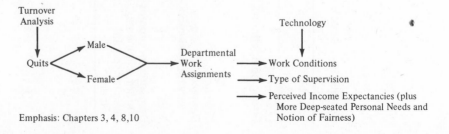

3. Supervisory role analysis. Personal interviews with supervisory and managerial personnel revealed a wide range of attitudes concerning supervisory role in response to perceived situational needs. As noted in Exhibit 14–8, first-line supervisors (floor ladies) and foremen visualized quite different roles for themselves. Most correctly grasped the interdependent character of operations, but important differences existed in their estimation of the felt need for direction, cooperation, and congeniality. Of course, there were legitimate differences between departments in terms of machine breakdown, material variability, and worker experience.

Exhibit 14–8 also distinguishes situationally viewed role needs from individual self-perceptions. A joint view of environmental, managerial, employee, and work variables at Sweet Products leads to a complex model for ascertaining role demands, especially in considering a particular department or job. For example, production departments had more stable work groups than material handling or processing activities, so that, *ceteris paribus,* scheduling workers was less of a problem to the extent that they were more likely to be present. Yet breakdown and disruptions in material flow were frequent in these departments, with a consequent variation in worker incentive earnings, thus creating the need to balance job-pay opportunities

EXHIBIT 14–8. Supervisory Role Perceptions at Sweet Products

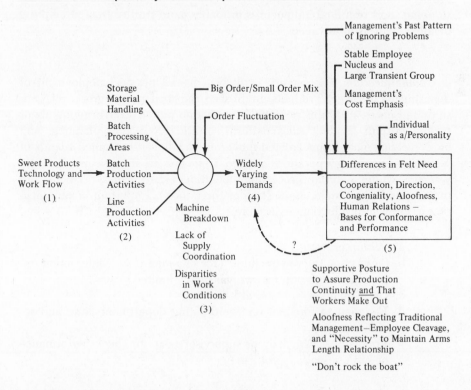

to avoid serious inequities. However, regardless of situational needs, individual supervisors visualized the image they should project and the type of role they should play—sometimes at variance with situational demands but projecting their own idea of the "ideal" supervisory model.

Exhibit 14–9 reflects the consulting team's expectations of the interactive effects of important organizational variables (technology, supervisory style, worker attributes, work conditions, and production flow) on output variables (morale, performance in quantity and quality terms, and turnover):

a. Supervisory style affects morale and the quality dimension of performance.

b. Supervisory style, even if authoritarian, may secure high levels of performance, but at the expense of morale and turnover.

c. Adverse work conditions have a negative effect on turnover, and this condition may be compounded by conditions in technology (frequent breakdown) or erratic production flow.

Where organizational variables move counter to each other, such as supportive supervision versus adverse work functions, the juxtapositioning is clear but a final judgment of their joint resolution must be reserved, pending the accumulation of further data. Discovering where uncertainties exist and stopping short of a final judgment is probably more fruitful than attempting detailed analysis in advance.

4. Communication. The factory work system and physical deployment of departments of Sweet Products established the structure of group relationships and necessary (plus potential) interaction patterns for bringing about factory output. Product sales patterns, erratic production planning, and older technological forms created numerous, small, self-contained islands of workers—packaging operations ranged from one to four people (mostly women) while material processing operations were batch oriented and built around small male crews (two or three men). Important communication patterns in production areas were

a. Within crews

b. Supervisor to crew member (for one-man crews, interaction opportunity with other crews was highly limited)

c. Crew member to material handler

d. Foreman to foreman for coordinating department flows and socializing

e. Foremen to floor lady or supervisor (e.g., to check performance or settle a worker problem)

EXHIBIT 14-9. Supervisory, Personal, and Situational Variables in Role Performance

Depart-ment	Work conditions				Flow of pro-duc-tion	Supervisory style	Worker		Outputs			
	Technology	Dirt	Heat	Physical			Se-nior-ity	Accep-tance of super-vision	Perfor-mance quan-tity	Quality	Job satis-fac-tion	Turnover
A	Stable	Little	None	Light	Steady	Worker centered	High	Yes	OK	OK	Good	OK
B	"	"	"	"	"	Authoritarian	"	"	OK	OK	Fair	OK
C	"	"	"	"	"	Casual support	"	"	OK	Fair	Good	OK
Work Conditions												
H	Stable	High	High	Heavy	Steady	Worker centered	High	Yes	OK	Fair	Good	Marginal
Supervision, work conditions, and technology												
J	Breakdown	High	High	Heavy	Erratic	Authoritarian	Low	Yes	Mar-ginal		Poor	High

Emphasis:
Chapters 3, 4, 8, 9, 10

The patterns of communication and interaction that emerged informally were created by design or were influenced by work flow, and are depicted in Exhibit 14–10. This exhibit mirrors the type of model described in Chapter 6 and thus provides a general point of departure for analysis. Specific observations on Sweet Products communications include the following:

a. Interaction patterns emerging from technology and process flow restricted social interactions in some areas.

b. Supervisory interaction with workers was of two main types: one of close surveillance in those areas representing adverse conditions or where the supervisor considered the "proper" relationship as authoritarian, and one that was *supportive* in the sense of casual observation, response to needs for supplies, and organizing activities in case of the frequent breakdown.

EXHIBIT 14–10. Communication Flow and Personnel Interaction Patterns

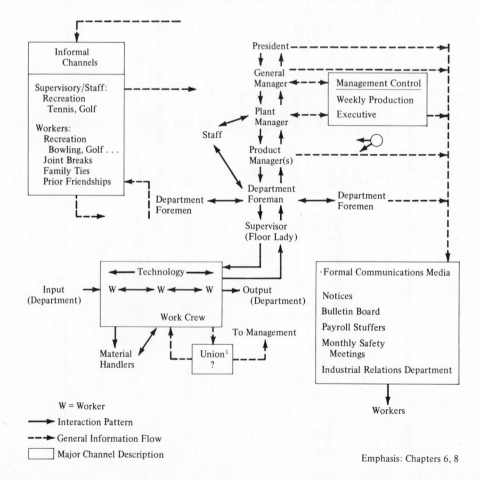

W = Worker

→ Interaction Pattern

--→ General Information Flow

☐ Major Channel Description

Emphasis: Chapters 6, 8

c. Informal interaction patterns among supervisors and staff were poor because of wide disparities in age, education, and experience. Product managers were long on experience but low in educational attainment. A small group of new employees, brought in from the outside, had good experience *and* education. The balance were small splinter groups that were highly ineffective in most of their contacts. Formal channels (safety meetings and the bulletin board) were perfunctory or ritualistic and *conveyed little or no useful information* to employees concerning work adjustments, managerial viewpoints, incentive information, bases for earnings, or management's plans for the future.

d. Formal channels *captured little or no useful information.* The eyes and ears of management, industrial relations, was poorly organized as an intelligence net in that the union was largely ineffective and thus could not coalesce employee ideas, let alone channel them to management. Also, management's awareness of the need to communicate had not been translated into a program. Furthermore, lack of response by management in the past had been interpreted as an "I don't care" attitude, and supervisors had learned to look but not be concerned.

The communication structure at Sweet Products was found to be highly ineffective, at both formal and informal levels, for meeting the social needs of workers and supervisors alike, let alone the requirements for the conduct of business. Information gaps and distortion, along with growing frustration and management's sense of being out of contact with its employees, were natural outgrowths of structural and motivational deficiencies in communication. Under the existing circumstances, there was no functional way for associating a statistic such as turnover with the underlying organizational sources of the problem—appropriate prescriptions could not arise under these circumstances.

5. Reward (motivational) climate. This area of inquiry attempts to emphasize and probe the forces that lead to high levels of individual performance and thereby also secure valued personal objectives. Thus this analysis is concerned with aspects of the organizational environment ("extrinsic rewards") as well as work itself ("intrinsic rewards"), items also identified as "hygiene" and "motivator" factors. Sweet Products provided a typical array of fringe benefits (hospitalization, vacation plan, time off for illness, shift differential, and noncontributory retirement funding). Direct compensation was either standard time-pay or base pay plus incentive bonus. Psychological reward or personal satisfaction (sense of personal achievement or need fulfillment) was a more subtle factor, and suggested a closer examination of work arrangements and work activity.

The reward climate was characterized in terms of monetary benefits, social benefits, and psychological rewards. Exhibit 14–11 seeks to assemble aspects of monetary rewards (*3A* and *10*) with the rewards derived from the influence of socially acceptable peers (*4A*) and inherent features of the job (*2*) to gain an overall approximation of the reward climate. This model suggests that performance (*7*) at Sweet Products, based on effort put forth (*6*), reflects both the value of the reward and an effort-reward expectation (*5*) perceived (*4*) by the individual.

EXHIBIT 14–11. The Reward (Motivational) Climate at Sweet Products

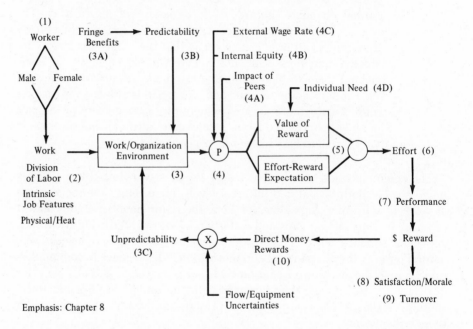

Emphasis: Chapter 8

Yet information gleaned from earlier company analysis suggested that the uncertainties of some production flow or equipment breakdown (*10*) lent an unpredictable dimension to anticipated earning in some areas (*3C*). Further, attributes of work, such as "intrinsic" job features or physical conditions of work, might well adversely affect effort-reward expectations. These effects could be compounded or ameliorated by perceptions of internal equity or fairness (*4B*) relative to co-worker effort-reward and external wage rates (*4C*).

Thus in contemplating the reward climate, numerous points are indicated from which performance (*7*) and satisfaction/morale or turnover (*9*) are likely to be influenced. Individual needs (*4D*) vary widely, as does the manner in which employees perceive their lot in life as part of the Sweet organization. Such organizational parameters as (a) work conditions, (b) supervisory acceptance and style juxtaposed to situational need, (c) sex (differing life needs), (d) external labor conditions and wage levels, along with the internal wage structure (equity and potential job alternatives), and (e) technology and work flow (stability, certainty, and deployment of workers) bear directly on Sweet management's initial point of inquiry—turnover and lackluster performance.

Management Planning for Change

The initial thrust of the planned capital improvement program at Sweet Products was to rationalize the production system. The shift from large batch and intermittent operations to a mass production-type of system pointed to widespread changes in organization and manpower. Planned improvement in warehousing and material processing, along with the use of mechanical and electronic equipment for interstage product movement, promised a system with vastly improved performance potential. But this was not without its implications for both modifying and redirecting the composition, expertise, and energies of management and staff support groups, plus the need for realigning major areas of blue-collar work. Consequently, the problems of turnover and lackluster performance had to be viewed within the longer-run picture of change. Consequently, the analysis considered amelioration of existing problems a separate, distinct area of concern, but only as the first step toward better utilization of manpower, better performance, *and* improved employee benefits.

A "change management" posture dictated a careful, thorough review of Sweet management's product-policy plans for the future, and the identification of characteristics of the technological system that would meet volume, cost, and quality demands. In manpower terms, Sweet's 1964 technology gave way to a system featuring many operator-monitoring functions, rather than direct worker intervention. Worker-governed job cycles were to be "traded off" in favor of more capital-intensive operations requiring a high level of staff support, including engineering, maintenance, quality, and planning groups. Hour-to-hour and day-to-day management response functions would no longer suffice to meet the demands of a highly rationalized system. Advance planning, superior cost/quality control, and new information are all necessary concomitants of an advanced business system.

An existing computer group (lodged in accounting), concerned largely with transaction processing, was soon to have a vastly expanded area of responsibility, and was to play a central role in the new system. All levels of staff support were to assume new prominence, along with the production management group. In light of the numbers and competency of the existing managerial force, a significant degree of obsolescence loomed up as an immediate aftermath of the planned changes and as a direct threat to plans for attaining new performance potential. Consequently, indicated approaches for manpower planning and programming suggested

1. Appraisal of existing manpower to uncover potential for operating and technical positions

2. Appraisal of existing supervisory and staff manpower to gauge potential for redeployment and future growth

3. Close examination of computer and production technology possibilities for providing needed bridges over existing manpower deficiencies

4. Replanning career opportunities and potential in the light of planned objectives and formulating individual manpower programs based on new ideas of needed skills, concepts, and perspectives for all levels of existing and contemplated management. Potential impact on manpower would be limited by the organizations ability to more precisely spell out organizational and system needs in behavioral and skill terms.

The diversity of planning for change is more readily grasped from Exhibit 14–12, which captures the main threads of this discussion. Several alternative directions could be assumed by management that, ideally, would reconcile institutional and personal objectives.

Avoidance of turnover and lackluster performance in the organizational system was tied to top management's ability to seek out longer-run economic solutions that could be reconciled with individual needs and expectancies. New production facilities promised better economic performance, but the latter was restrained by the ability of the human organization to perform effectively. The new facilities, per se, possessed little humanizing quality—thus a socially efficient manpower system called for a "design" beyond mere production engineering. The human equation called for the assembly of a set of assumptions quite different from those underlying Sweet Products at its inception many years ago. Some of these assumptions and their implications for redesign follow.

1. People are not favorably disposed to "being told" what to do. Thus reorientation of supervision is indicated, plus the creation of a reward climate that will lessen dependence on direction or close surveillance (e.g., better worker orientation and training would permit higher performance, yet lessen supervisory needs).

2. Higher levels of self-determination and involvement are indicated (e.g., participation in work assignment and work arrangements that don't seriously compromise performance and organization), as well as the opportunity to voice ideas in areas such as com-

EXHIBIT 14–12. Planning Change

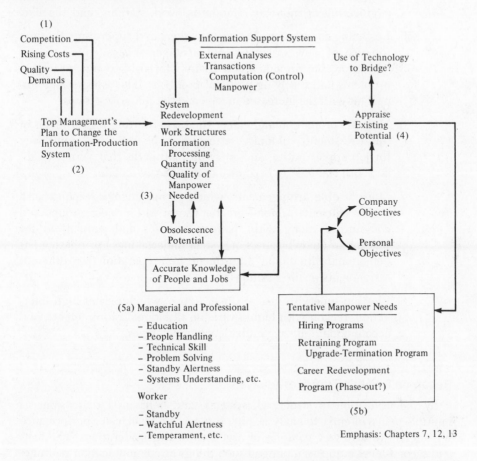

(1)
Competition
Rising Costs
Quality
Demands

Top Management's
Plan to Change the
Information-Production
System
(2)

Information Support System

External Analyses
Transactions
Computation (Control)
Manpower

Use of Technology
to Bridge?

System
Redevelopment

Work Structures
Information
Processing
Quantity and
Quality of
Manpower
(3) Needed

Appraise
Existing
Potential (4)

Obsolescence
Potential

Company
Objectives

Personal
Objectives

Accurate Knowledge
of People and Jobs

(5a) Managerial and Professional

– Education
– People Handling
– Technical Skill
– Problem Solving
– Standby Alertness
– Systems Understanding, etc.

Worker

– Standby
– Watchful Alertness
– Temperament, etc.

Tentative Manpower Needs

Hiring Programs

Retraining Program
 Upgrade-Termination Program

Career Redevelopment

Program (Phase-out?)

(5b)

Emphasis: Chapters 7, 12, 13

munity relations or product features. Worker committees would
be indicated here.

3. Motivational needs are likely to be evidenced within and between
   managerial, professional, and worker groups, indicating a wider
   latitude of choice of compensation among such things as short-
   or long-run payoff and indirect fringe benefits versus direct compensation.

4. Greater attention to stability and predictability of earning patterns indicates a lessening emphasis on monetary incentives and
   greater attention to measured work plans that permit a fair day's
   work, lessen physical effort, reduce supervisory/staff support tensions, and allow contingencies to be reconciled. This calls for
   tightening the performance of the whole management system,
   including better scheduling and inventory policies to provide

adequate materials, efficient performance standards, and human engineering of monetary standards, work stations, and the like.

5. Lessening the tensions between workers and supervisors through the use of new organizational arrangements, such as coach/ counselor, that provide a new channel for airing company-related problems and resolving personal problems. This is especially important with the increased involvement of minority groups.

6. Multiple promotion and career tracks, permitting higher levels of self-assessment, voluntary setting forth of individual candidacy for job opportunities, and entry into job paths that permit qualified "fast runners" to become more upwardly mobile.

7. More flexible arrangements, which permit change response in a highly efficient fashion—greater use of task-project groups and committees, along with "halfway" houses and simulations for phasing in (new business or system undertakings) or phasing out (emotional/situational adjustment in preparation for different assignments or life positions).

8. Flexible supervisory-subordinate ratios, which permit high interaction, reckon with highly variable situational requirements, and accommodate diverse individual competencies.

Recap on Sweet's Turnover Analysis

By the utilization of structural, systems, and behavioral dimensions as multiple points of entry to analysis, high turnover and lackluster performance were found to involve a complex of organizational considerations. The first- and second-level inquiries identified such things as communication malfunctions, deficiencies in reward (motivational) climate, and poor supervisory-subordinate relations. Development of information was heuristic, in that the derivation of data and ideas at one point frequently indicated areas of inquiry for the next stage of analysis. Identifying many of the key issues underlying Sweet's most immediate problems pointed to in-depth probes and corrective measures for the short-run problems, but these approaches could not be dissociated from the longer-run perspective.

Sweet Products—Postscript

In response to the extensive organizational analyses undertaken at Sweet Products, the executive group decided to undertake a multiphase, multiyear program. Before any specific actions could be undertaken, it was decided to deal with and strengthen those areas most readily lending themselves to change (without disruption to people or process). This initial thrust, then, was to deal with strengthening the personnel-manpower function that was to play a central role of liaison and coordination in the subsequent changes. Along with the strengthening of personnel-manpower, phase 1 was to include the clearer establishment of policy guide lines—to reduce wide disparities or confusion (in procedure, evaluation, and provision of information to employees) but not to structure to the point that roadblocks would be thrown in the way of innovative action or stifle organizational practices. Communication procedures also were to be established in order to provide workable channels for handling grievances and information—and procedures that would assure answers.

Finally, as a part of phase 1, wages and benefits were examined for all employees relative to competition and other industrial units, and in consideration of labor market conditions and the announced desire of top management to "attract and retain people who could support the organization's purposes and whom the organization could support in terms of their personal needs and/or career development." Also, management desired to establish compensation guidelines and clear promotional criteria to reduce widespread inequities. Employees were fully apprised of management's intentions, both formally and informally, before these adjustments were made and these procedures established.

Phase 2 was initiated approximately one year after phase 1, and had the announced purpose of dealing with some of the more subtle and difficult aspects of change. In this phase, major efforts were made to strengthen task and work group relationships, link technologically related departments, and activate a promotion program encouraging the participation of interested work force members (without regard to race or sex). In terms of promotional opportunities for work force members, the consolidation and strengthening of the personnel-manpower function greatly facilitated training and self-improvement efforts for interested personnel. With evidence from organization officials of their desire to improve organization activities and with the changing (improving) character of the climate (rewards, communications, increasing trust, support of individual efforts to self-improve), critical measures of behavioral performance also reflected improvements. Reduction in turnover and the willingness and desire of employees to make suggestions or "level" with their supervisors were some of the promising signs of organizational-manpower improvements.

The next activity undertaken as part of phase 2 was to deal more concretely with interpersonal relationships among work group members and to make conscious efforts to forge understanding relationships between task-related groups. In its first phase, the progress of the program was quite rapid. In the second phase, it appeared that several years might be required to meet its stated objectives. Progress appeared to be slow but persistent, and largely in the right direction.

CONCEPTUAL APPROACHES—A FINAL NOTE

This book's emphasis on flexibility, multiple perspectives, and a fund of ideas and insights that can be adjusted in the light of new needs or emergent results mirrors a view of current and anticipated requirements for managing, analyzing, and administering complex organizations. Regardless of institutional circumstances (production or service, private sector or governmental), approaches are called for that transcend conventional boundaries. The more mobile manager and professional man or woman has become a fact of life, which means multiple job experiences and the need to relate one set of experiences to various institutional settings. Maintaining individual relevance is directly connected with a high level of organizational performance. Conceptual approaches should be viewed as one means of satisfying both of these requirements.

In the next (and final) chapter, some speculations are set out regarding emergent problems and possibilities for organization analysis in the future.

Learning Objectives

Institution Niche, and Mission and Impact on Organizational
   Issues
Current and Emergent Trends and What They Portend for
   Organizational Issues and New Structures
Growing Issues in the Quality of Work Life
Organizational Issues Associated with Minority Work Force
   Members

Chapter **15**

TOWARD THE FUTURE

APPROACH

The discussions of this final chapter are initiated with a few brief comments on the posture of organizational analysts as they confront wide-ranging institutional differences in an era of change.

Next, an overview is provided of several important environmental trends affecting the focus and concerns of organization analysts in the 1970s, and which are likely to influence some of the major organizational issues in the 1980s. Work force composition, educational trends, changing age distributions, and obsolescence are among the matters briefly referenced.

Then three areas of organizational concern are developed in some detail: the emergence of new structures and roles and growing "temporariness" in organizations, quality of work life, and minority manpower in the work force. The issues involved in these three discussions draw heavily on the structural, systems, and behavioral concepts and approaches of previous chapters.

ORGANIZATION ANALYSIS: INSTITUTIONAL DIFFERENCES

Managers performing within complex, changing institutional environments must increasingly operate from a flexible base of perspectives, tools, and approaches that are not bound to highly specific information. Yet the institutional mission or objectives, the service or product provided, and the clientele served are examples of dimensions of organizational form leading to wide differences in the specifics of particular units. The set of objectives/service (product) that is offered to a clientele imparts a uniqueness in relationships of people, structures, and processes that tends to encourage particular approaches for organization analysis. A few examples will clarify this point.

A production-oriented firm committed to the manufacture of a product such as automobiles places heavy emphasis on the logistics of material movement, large-batch and mass assembly procedures, and sophisticated planning and control support systems. Thus the behavioral problems of man-machine interaction are extensive—along with the diverse aspects of group relationships, individuals assuming linking-pin or coordinative roles, and inherent conflicts of horizontal (process oriented) and vertical communication.

In service institutions such as insurance companies, information handling and a high level of interaction with the clientele account for extensive field structures and the character and importance of information-communication lines. The behavioral problems relate to complex, decentralized structures, change in the loci of decision making as a consequence of computer operations, and personnel displacement or job elimination resulting from technological change.

Another example of a service institution, yet one giving rise to *additional behavioral concerns,* is the public service firm—for example, the utility. Studies of these institutions indicate that the servicing of multiple publics (*stockholders* and *utility clients)* strongly influences policy processes and decision making. Consequently, behavioral analyses, in addition to dealing with the types of problems already cited (utilities have both far-flung production functions and field service units), *treat other pressures or needs characteristic of these organizations.*

Two additional public service institution forms that are worthy of note are government agencies and health care units. Both are important in our daily life, and both provide services in response to client need. In addition, both are slated to play even more important roles in the future. In hospitals, bringing various role systems (professional, medical, nursing, and administrative) together with medical technology (equipment and procedures) and patients leads to a highly interactive system, replete with communication and behavioral problems. The extension of health care coverage to the neighborhood level and the rise of health medical organizations (HMOs) signal new environmental pressures and conflict (e.g., responsiveness to the local citizenry versus the rigidities of formal organization structure and processes).

Most government agencies display varying degrees of the bureaucratic form—they involve a complex interplay of political systems, stability and change (civil service versus elective offices), impact of regulation, decision making, and even employee displacement or changes due to automation. The need for change, displayed against a backdrop of generally stable, unchanging conditions, augurs many areas of growing importance for organization analysis. The approach described for these analyses would not differ much from those already portrayed, although in each institutional framework certain problem areas or relationships would tend to be highlighted. In brief, *conceptual* approaches to organizational analysis differ little when one is confronting a wide cross section of institutional settings. The organizational priorities in the various settings, however, *do* differ materially, and thereby become the specific concerns of particular studies.

TRENDS SUGGESTING FUTURE CONCERNS IN ANALYSIS

Clearly, important trends already under way in our society will have an important bearing on the future character of organizational problems. For example, *technological change* has cut a wide path through various organizations, and promises to remain a primary force. Such industries as food, metals, communications, and fabrication are examples of highly vulnerable targets for technological change, thereby modifying manpower needs, structure, and behavioral matters. The exponential development of the *computer* in the 1950–70 period will extend far beyond the 1970s. This phase of technological change is even more potent, for it poses potential and problems for people and organizations at many levels and in many types of organization, from schools, to manufacturers, to hospitals, to transportation, to communications.

Rising Educational Level

Substantial increases in levels of educational attainment since the end of World War II, continuing through the current concern with job training for the disadvantaged, is resulting in a better-educated, more articulate job applicant, recruit, and employee. The reduction in the relative number of people willing to settle for work as an end in itself (to meet security needs) and the relative growth of those seeking self-actualization and personal growth from the job will be of increasing importance to organizational analysis.

Growing educational achievements are also likely to affect the character and quality of interpersonal relationships, where educational differences between "superior" and "subordinate" are largely removed, or even reflect those instances where the "worker" is educationally better prepared.

Larger Numbers of Young and Old

The normal progression of people through organizations, predicated on seniority, will have to be significantly adjusted as the relative number of middle-aged people, the reservoir of middle and top management, decreases. These pressures will accelerate the movement of younger people into important managerial positions, and will intensify the types of behavioral problems likely to emerge (communications, authority relationships, tension and conflict, for example).

More Sophisticated Organizational Functions

Growing numbers of professionals in such areas as personnel, organizational analysis, and manpower planning will call for organizational environments attuned to investigation and experimentation. Greater and more widespread use of professionals in these areas will help to assure common bonds with other organizational members, and thereby improve communication and secure support for behavioral study.

Changing Composition of the Work Force

Work force trends, already pronounced, involve greater numbers of minority group members, including women. The successful incorporation of these elements into the work force, and the creation of realistic promotion paths and career opportunities, will be major organizational challenges in forthcoming years. Differences in career expectations and value systems, along with considerable levels of prejudice, promise even greater challenges of accommodation in such areas as social acceptance, leadership, motivation, and social relationships.

Incorporation of minority elements will also place stress on existing power structures, seats of authority, and ways of doing things. These pressures will appear in all manner of organization, from unions to police forces, from medical schools to hospitals, and from petroleum companies to retail store chains. Problems of attitude change, acceptance, motivation, and other behaviorally related matters will achieve added prominence.

Organization Complexity and Size

In spite of court action, government processes, and emotional appeals, many companies or institutions continue to grow and conglomerate. Complex relations between acquired firms pose considerable challenges for structure and group processes (communication and decision making). To an important extent, approaches of the past (more decentralization) are likely to prove unsatisfactory, requiring the formulation of newer modes of organization. Also, the advent of multinational firms takes the behavioral challenges posed by conglomerates and casts them in a grand design with the world as the "state," thereby introducing many new cultural variables that must be considered. Organizational notions such as bureaucracy or decentralization are also likely to fall short of answering many of the organizational problems posed here, thereby intensifying the search for improved organization formats and approaches to analysis.

Obsolescence and Change Management

Translating the impact of change on people in terms of needed knowledge and skills for work performance should now be recognized as a major task.

Also, regulating the processes of change so as to take into account the ability of the organization and its personnel resources is a substantial challenge.

REEXAMINATION OF BEHAVIORAL ASSUMPTIONS

Recent work in motivational theory (to cite only one example) makes it clear that some previously held theories, such as one- and two-factor motivational explanations, are susceptible to additional, critical examination. Also, newer theories must be advanced to account for shortcomings in recent formulations, as well as for newer situations or those recurring with greater regularity. A motivator like money, at one time viewed as part of classical theory but relegated to a more pedestrian role by behaviorists, has been reexamined of late to reveal a multifaceted role. Path-goal extensions of motivational theory have been proposed with good effect in leadership areas.

Another area likely to receive considerable attention is attitude formation and expression as affected by events outside the organization (family relations and early childhood) and within it. The study of attitudes is central to behavioral science, yet the promise of new findings is likely to cause a reexamination of possibilities for influencing and developing organizational personnel. Applied areas such as "personnel" are destined for considerable revitalization, based on the emerging findings of the behavioral and management sciences. Also, new tools and approaches, such as "organization development," largely fashioned by the behavioral scientists, will likely gain more attention in organization behavior approaches.

ORGANIZATIONS IN CHANGE: NEW STRUCTURES AND ROLES

The incessant pace of change, described in earlier chapters (3, 4, 7, 12, 13), seems likely to engender further, far-reaching changes in organization structure, processes, and bases for dealing with organizational members. The social, technical, legislative, and economic components of change (previously described) continue to be reinforced through such developments as the widespread mergers and divestitures of the business community, reorganization in governments, and continuing national and international crises. Organizations are thrust into highly unsettling conditions that are often characterized by uncommon conditions and unexpected events.

Newer structural modes of organization,[1] shifting roles for institutional members, and a growing need to periodically renew vital processes and arrangements[2] of organization are likely outcomes of environmental change, some of which are already in evidence. Though the incidence of environmental change will not be felt uniformly among organizations or encompass all institutional units, major areas of both the private and public sector are involved. At the same time, some change events are of such widespread importance (war, energy crises, pollution, inflation) as to be felt by most of the country's citizenry (as well as the world). Thus the turbulence and uncertainty confronting organizations are reinforced in the daily lives of the human resources manning these units. The inappropriateness of many bureaucratic arrangements is underscored because of their inability to adapt to fast-pace change. The management of change and organizational adaptability signals flexible internal arrangements such as modular units (e.g., project groups) and transient rather than permanent arrangements.

Beyond Bureaucracy

The economic, social, and environmental conditions that gave rise to and supported bureaucratic-type structures in the past continue to recede and signal further internal dysfunctions and changes beyond those described in Chapter 2. In past periods, moderately paced change and workable levels of certainty permitted the erection of more stable, longer-lasting organization structures that were largely hierarchical. Common recurring situations, procedures, and activities encouraged the subdivision of manpower efforts and the routinization of undertakings. Conformity, which was frequently rewarded, reflected a successful institutional strategy in the light of general economic circumstances and considerable individual need.

When lower-level needs centered on economic requirements or personal security, and in light of limited job opportunities, individuals understandably turned toward particular institutions for subsistence, even survival. People subordinated their own interests and were inward directed for rewards. Their future often rested with the organization, and a longevity-loyalty cycle was established and reinforced. A humanistic approach to the management of traditional bureaucratic organization often was unneeded (or disregarded) for achieving economic objectives.[3] Yet, as already noted, structural rigidity in the face of change, rather than flexibility or adaptability, and failure to reckon fully with the human dimension undercut the essence of bureaucratic structures.

This severing of the bureaucratic roots of organization was furthered by changing social mores and patterns (e.g., mobility and life styles) and the formidable base of legislation that emerged after World War II and continued into the '70s. This legislation mandated an organizational concern for human resources, as well as actions for bringing about equitable internal arrangements (sex and race distributions, for example) and procedures (e.g., equity in hiring, pay, and promotional opportunity). The disarray of the bureaucratic arrangement was largely completed through its failure to recognize and tap or harness the individual creativity and talent needed to cope with its complex affairs. Also, we see the failure to support individual innovation and performance in a world with vastly changed ground rules for competition, economic survival, and social action.

Enter: New Roles and New Structural Arrangements

The conceptual approaches to organization analysis described throughout this book lend themselves to capsulizing the preceding discussion on change and to suggest some likely thrusts of these developments on organization structure and member role. Exhibit 15–1 suggests that the environmental changes enfolding international occurrences, innovation, and various trends project an era of increasing organizational turbulence and uncertainty.[4] One component of these shifting conditions is more frequent occurrence of one-time situations and the unexpected. Anticipated changes are also likely to witness the furthering of organizational complexity as interactions and dependence between economic, governmental, and community units and bodies grow and as work embodies more advanced technologies and procedures.[5] Environmental change also incorporates shifts in individuals' roles, reflecting widening job opportunities, greater mobility, more interest in higher-level personal achievements, greater individual importance in organizational matters, and modified expectations regarding opportunity and "one's due."

Three areas of organizational prescription for the future emerge from the events depicted in Exhibit 15–1. The accomplishment of flexible, adaptive structures suggests transient rather than semipermanent arrangements, formation of modular structural units (e.g., project teams) in response to specific situational requirements, senior personnel assuming critical linking-pin roles through coordination and communications, and the erection of matrix-type organizations to deal with complexity and multiple, cross-functional projects. Project-type units and matrix structures, initially associated with the aerospace industry, are gaining prominence in various industrial and governmental pursuits.

A second area of organization, also seen as receiving a great deal of attention, is the use and support of human resources. The changing role of individuals in society and organization life, societal demands, and organizational need indicate a new stance (policy and approaches) vis-à-vis organizational personnel. The complexity of decision situations, the need to maintain the flow of high-cost facilities, and the growing diversity of the perspectives and tools needed for problem solving and innovation indicate higher levels of joint involvement of line managers, staff, support groups, and personnel from various organization levels.[6]

As overall levels of education move upward and advanced education becomes commonplace, "colleague management" approaches will likely gain wider usage. Supplementing or supplanting control by supervisory direction (or procedure) can permit relationships to assume a more professional basis, turning in an inner direction rather than toward outward manipulation.[7] Related to the trend toward colleague management would be the transient nature of internal organizational relationships, imparting a temporariness (and perhaps increasing tension for individuals!) to traditional supervisory-

EXHIBIT 15-1. Change and the Redefinition of Organization Structure and Individual Role

Environmental Change

{
International Developments

Trends
- Social
- Technical
- Economic
- Legislative

Pace of Innovation
}

{
Conditions of Operation
Turbulence
Uncertain/Unexpected
One-Time Situations

Organizational Complexity
Nonroutine Problems

Fluidity of Individual Roles
Mobility
Expectations
}

- Need for Flexible Adaptive Structures → A
- Utilization and Support of Human Resources → B
- Information for Communications and Decision Making → C

A. Flexible, Adaptive Structures
- Modularization
- Temporary Structures
- Matrix, Project Organization
- Executives and Managers as Coordinators and Key Communicators

B. Utilization and Support of Human Resources
- Accommodate Role Shifts
- Participation in Decision Making
- Joint Staff Support–Line Involvement in Decisions
- Colleague Management
- Multiple Authority Level Representation, Participation
- Lower Organizational Level of Decision Making
- Build Human Relations Skills for Collaboration, Contingency Leadership, and to Bridge Temporary Relationships

C. Information for Communications and Decision Making
- Further Diagonal and Lateral versus Vertical Communications
- External Use of Information
- Technology
- Effective Management and Use of Information

Draws on points developed in Alvin Toffler, *Future Shock* (New York: Random House, 1970), chap. 7.

subordinate bonds. Also, colleague-type relationships would be furthered by the sharing of more widespread standards for managerial actions, reinforced by the considerable enrollment in graduate schools of business.[8]

Greatly heightened involvement and use of human resources place a premium on the interpersonal skills of organizational managers, executives, and supervisors.[9] The personal flexibility implied in leadership contingency approaches and the wide range of situations encountered in organizations will place a premium on developing the human skill of key personnel. At the same time, the building of functional groups as effective teams and the linking of groups through functional relationships further rounds out the large-scale, developmental undertakings likely to accompany organizational adaptation to change.[10]

The third area of organizational need arising from environmental developments pertains to information. The amount, type, and frequency of information usage are seen as critical to providing the needed underpinning for more complex decision-making undertakings. Yet information *availability* is no guarantee of adaptability to a specific need unless key managers and specialists know how to employ the information and unless the information processes themselves are well managed. Information features and usage are a subset of the broader problems and issues of communications. Traditional communication lines, which encouraged vertical transmittal of information and prescribed patterns, are increasingly likely to provide an unworkable arrangement for fast-changing situational needs.[11]

These observations concerning the possible direction of organizational adaptions to environmental developments have been described by John Gardner as generally necessary, unavoidable, and a response to the acceleration of change.[12] It is a situation, he suggests, that calls for "self-revival," institutionalized change, and continuing structural accommodations in response to changing needs.

QUALITY OF WORK LIFE

Critical examination of the quality of work life for individual satisfaction and motivation appears slated to receive considerable attention in the near-term future.[13] Various aspects of quality-of-work issues, including motivation, satisfaction, "blue-collar blues," prestige, and alienation, have been receiving widespread attention by the printed media, radio, and television. A report prepared by a task force from the W. E. Upjohn Institute (Washington, D.C.) for the Department of Health, Education, and Welfare, *Work in America*, has become one of the most widely discussed and debated publications dealing with behavioral matters in recent years. Excerpts from the report, expert confirmation, and loud denials have been recorded across the country in the nation's newspapers and magazines.

Bound up with the quality-of-work issue are several key questions:

a. *What is the existing situation?* In the main, are people satisfied with their jobs? Are problems of motivating people for performance largely isolated or are they widespread problems confronting major segments of the population? Do appreciable differences exist in personal satisfaction or realization between various employed categories such as managers, supervisors, professionals, and "blue-collar" workers?

b. *In recent years, have these characterizations (i.e., satisfaction, etc.) changed appreciably, and if so, in what direction?* With the pronounced shift toward the computer and automation of industrial processes, has individual satisfaction or motivation to perform been adversely affected? How has the movement of society toward higher plateaus of education and individual opportunity affected people's expectancies and realizations for work and the work environment?

c. *Are there compelling reasons for confronting these matters on a broad front, or even as a national problem?* Do environmental changes and shifts in the problems confronting institutions indicate that satisfaction and motivation are assuming, or must assume, higher organizational priorities?

These questions are posed at this point to crystallize some of the arguments centering on the HEW report.

Many elements of this controversy rest on dimensions of structure, systems/process, and behavior described in this book. Various elements of production technologies (Chapters 3 and 4) and information technologies (Chapter 7) represent the work core about which much of the controversy has swirled. The focus by institutional officials on organizational performance that is based primarily on traditional operational measures of productivity is increasingly challenged and questioned. Do events and shifts in the environment and changes in the character of organizational activities indicate greater concern for human resources and behavioral outcomes, altruistic motives notwithstanding? The socio-technical theme advanced in Part I, and bolstered by the behavioral discussions and analyses of Part II, assists in sharpening important problems, questions, and assumptions related to this controversy. At the same time, to the extent that these problems and challenges may exist in many organizations, an agenda for future questioning, inquiry, and research is established.

Socio-technical Perspective

The socio-technical theme offers a viewpoint for quality of work-life analysis that has proved useful. One major thrust of socio-technical approaches has been that the output and performance of work systems are often dependent on the joint product of technology and human resources.[14] Thus the technology of work per se can't solely sustain output or meet performance standards over time—any more than unaided human effort can—at least in the systems throughout our advanced society.

A second feature of the socio-technical perspective has been that the intertwined technological and human components are embedded in an environment that has various values, cultures, and practices. High interdependencies exist between organizations and environment as the former draw on the latter for various resources and then exchange the outputs of product or service for funds that facilitate subsequent exchanges. At the same time, the environment imposes various restraints and pressures upon the organizations of a social, political, economic, and ideological nature, which engenders some level of organizational conformity (at times minimal), some mode of activity, and a definite response. Societal forces, pressures, and restraints are major considerations in setting roles for institutions, groups, and people.

Thus these characterizations of socio-technical systems suggest that an important part of technological or organizational system designs involves *social* designs.[15] System designs affect such considerations as work group size, job responsibilities, titles, work diversity, latitude of people in decision making, structuring of activity, authority structures, and spatial positioning of work force members. And with these are found individual opportunities for communications and interaction, a sense of personal participation and contribution, realization of career aspirations, and a sense of personal worth and dignity. To what extent can socio-technical designs be adjusted while meeting operational performance criteria? To what extent *must* adjustments be made in socio-technical designs to the extent these affect the "people components"?

Louis Davis has suggested some answers to these questions that are helpful in expanding the approaches of organizational analysis. Frequently, the gains of productivity or efficiency are viewed as a tradeoff leading to diminishing behavioral outcomes (e.g., sense of personal satisfaction) or quality of work opportunities. Yet Davis suggests, on the basis of various socio-technical studies (perhaps a hundred or so), that considerable adaptability exists in socio-technical systems.[16] Further, he believes that several points require rethinking and evaluation in order to achieve socio-technical designs permitting more imaginative uses of human resources:

1. Productive efficiency and quality of work do not necessarily represent direct trade-offs. Some evidence already exists that both good operational performance *and* quality of work can be jointly secured, even in mass production-type systems.

2. Work systems or technologies are frequently flexible enough to accommodate social system needs.

3. Procedure, instructional controls, direction and regulation of human performance leads naturally to coercion, begets more control, etc.

4. Important improvements in socio-technical systems have taken place after institutional officials, specialists and others have carefully rethought through work designs and, essentially, how their organizations work.

5. Responsible autonomy (plan, regulate, control own world), self-regulation and self-organization can facilitate individual adaptability, variety of experience and sense of participation. Individuals and groups can accept responsibility for their activities. . . . Work redesigns along the indicated lines can bring about enhancement of cooperation, sense of commitment, self-development and satisfaction.[17]

When these points are brought together within the socio-technical framework, a complex series of needs, possibilities, and constraints is indicated in probing "quality-of-work issues." Certain areas of generalizations appear to be indicated:

1. Environmental changes in advanced or high technology areas (e.g., electronics, aerospace, process industries) augur a higher premium on human inputs for innovation, creative problem solving, and sustaining performance and work flow.

2. Legislative enactment (e.g., the fair employment and manpower acts) has erected a base of needed conformance (and enforcement) requiring widespread adjustments in organizational procedures involving human resources.

3. Environmental changes, involving shifts in societal norms and values regarding life style, work ethic, institutional allegiance, felt individual mobility, and personal expectation, signal changes in managing and dealing with human resources.[18] The "encouragement" of institutional efforts along these lines is brought about by hard-nose economic considerations involving absenteeism, turnover, tardiness, lack of dependability, undue delays, poor quality, sabotage, lackluster performance, and minimal compliance for retention.

Yet, beyond these points, what can be said about many of the earlier questions regarding the scope of worker dissatisfaction and the need to provide variety or "responsible autonomy" and the like?

Unfortunately, considerable disagreement still exists on the definition and measurement of dissatisfaction, alienation, and other behavioral descriptors,[19] let alone well-accepted general statistics and historical bases for comparison. At the same time, generalized descriptions (indictments) or prescriptions (e.g., "self-organize," "adaptable," "participative") fall short of accurately portraying the needs and dynamics of particular situations.[20]

The viewpoints and approaches developed throughout this book have centered on the individual organization and the particulars of its situation. It is true that the previous generalizations point to areas of potential concern for organizational analysts, but corrective approaches must ultimately center on particular institutions and contingencies. General observations and descriptors must be replaced eventually by specific questions emerging from the circumstances of a given organization. Blue-collar workers may be generally unhappy (or unhappier than previously), but what's the situation with our office people or factory workers? White-collar workers in general may be more satisfied than blue-collar workers, but are our engineers more satisfied than our managers? Is either group satisfied? Are their attitudes or sense of personal realization affecting performance? Can both operational performance and behavioral outcome be improved? What latitude or flexibility exists in our socio-technical system? Is the sense of impending change such that the performance of various individuals or groups will be adversely affected?

The opportunity for fruitful work is indicated, utilizing tools and approaches of organizational analysis to probe the complex issues related to the quality of work in our organizations.

MINORITY MANPOWER IN THE WORK FORCE

Equal-employment legislation and the manpower acts (beginning in the early 1960s) have changed the complexion of many organizational units and have occasioned a surge of human resource problems new to many. The scope of internal changes has been vast as some organizations have introduced significant numbers of racial minorities for the first time (blacks especially, plus Mexican Americans and other Latins), albeit in unskilled categories. Others have confronted the problems of preparing minority groups for promotional opportunities. And, finally, a small number have sought to deal with the issues connected with racial minorities who have already achieved higher rungs on the promotional ladder. Changes in the internal composition of racial minorities, the greater visibility and participation of minority representations in organizational activities, and their assumption of authority or power positions have been frequently accompanied by high tension and conflict. Differing value systems and norms of conduct and behavior chafe incumbents and new job entrants. Underlying this friction, one frequently finds, are wide differences in expectations regarding acceptable behavior and one's realization from the world of work.

In short, the introduction, effective use, and promotion of racial minorities have posed significant behavioral challenges requiring analysis of underlying organizational structures, systems, and socio-psychological matters. These brief notes seek to identify some of the major issues likely to warrant the attention of organizational analysts. Remarks are organized along the lines suggested by the composite model in Exhibit 14–1.

Racial Minorities as Inputs to the Organization

The introduction of racial minorities to organizations in substantial numbers, where they have been few in number or largely absent in the past, has sharpened issues of differing norms of behavior, learning-training, and motivation. Street jargon, "black talk," low work skills, poor work histories, and criminal records have been part of the pre-employment dialogue with minorities. These activities have challenged long-accepted notions of the work ethic and interpersonal communications and understanding. The "gate keepers" for the organization manpower inputs (personnel) have at times been confronted with the need for traumatic role changes (for themselves and managers) as they have sought to introduce work force members who would have been rejected out of hand by yesteryear's standards. To the extent that the altered posture of these gate keepers has been mandated by law or internal edict, employment processes are additionally strained. Where applicants have been favorably considered for employment, the early picture of organizational life reflected in pre-employment processing may simply have reinforced the notion of "whitey," "white organization," and the "repression" of social minorities.

The lack of basic communication and work skills has imposed problems of internal need and adjustment encountered only infrequently in the past. That which was often taken as "given" (i.e., verbal, reading, writing, and arithmetic skills) has become an important variable affecting the acceptance and success of the new employee. Since more fundamental skill training has been required than what is ordinarily available in many organizations, attempts have been made to devise new strategies to impart such skills. "Vestibule" (pre-job) training, coaching, work simulation, and high support by other minority members have been among the many schemes employed with mixed success.[21] Some of the behavioral matters emerging at this stage of employment processing include the creation of a climate for learning, behavioral acceptance by incumbent workers, and modifying behavioral patterns to make them more congenial with existing systems, while at the same time adjusting established systems (hours, time for training, assistance, etc.) to the needs of new entrants.

Retention, Decision to Produce, Upward Movement

As depicted in Exhibit 14–1, the assumption of a work position by a new work force entrant is the taking of a work role within some type of task group. The work system defines a formal work role and thus imposes various skill needs, cooperative interactions, and work performances for success. Job-related training is challenged to meet important areas of these requirements. At the same time, the new role occupant assumes some level of informal relationship with task group members—organizationally, the task group leader is challenged in his role as a facilitator. A leader is needed who can assist new group entrants work out satisfying relationships that not only support operational performances but meet personal needs and thereby further support operational performance. Yet it must be said that the supervisor himself is often challenged in his own beliefs or predisposition toward a minority member. His behavior may be the determining factor in the success or failure of the minority individual. Thus the task group leader is a central figure in integrating new work entrants into the task group. Formal role needs must be met for task or technical purposes. Also, the informal needs are great that lead to a satisfying social experience in the world of work, and thereby the personal conduct and performance supporting the organization and operational performances.

The task group leader then enters this complex web of relationships, technical activities, and behavioral/operational outcomes at several different levels. The outlook and potential performance of the formal leader warrant initial attention. Will he understand the positional requirements as a facilitator for the new work force entrants? Does he possess the needed outlooks and skills to meet the indicated situational needs for change? Can he make the indicated adjustments (if needed) in his own approaches?

Secondly, the leader, in assuming a contingency posture, must reckon with work task, group, and varying environmental factors in assisting minority members work out their group member (formal and informal) roles.

A third point is that, to the extent the preceding have been successful, facilitating the motivation of group members for successful performance and personal realizations may constitute a significant challenge to the leader. His approaches and attitudes directed to minority members, shape their perception of the broader organization and the attractiveness of this environment.

The formal group leader also influences monetary and psychological returns to group members. His sensitivity to personal needs, pressures, and fears can provide the basis for establishing a solid foundation for encouraging individual performance and personal realization. However, the success of the leader may be influenced (even greatly) by his relationship with his boss, the boss's accord with supervisory actions, the boss's demands for performance, and the boss's understanding of the group situation and individual need. If the group leader's actions are greatly constrained by organizational controls, his boss's expectations for performance, or the (unsettling) incessant demands of environmental change (new services or products, constant influx of new people, need to meet new administrative requirements, external changes of law imparting instability to operation or performance), the leader's success may be greatly compromised.

In brief, retaining a minority member and motivating his performance pose a wide range of behavioral analyses within the contingency perspective. Individual need, interpersonal relationships, leader influence, latitude of action, and communications effectiveness are all part of this complex matrix. To the extent that successes are achieved in facilitating the minority worker's assumption of work and social roles, the ground may well have been laid for his personal development in the future.

Individual career progress will depend importantly on one's having successfully performed in work and social roles and having acquired valued skills and abilities for higher-level responsibilities and more demanding work assignments. The formal leader may directly influence the instilling or substitution of personal goals that view promotional achievements as valued, personal accomplishments. To the extent that the formal leader (again) acts as a facilitator in individual growth, the way may be prepared for significant personal achievements of minority members in the future. Support groups may play a highly important role in helping to identify career opportunities, skills, and the approaches needed for job-related experiences, as well as the way to assure future promotional targets.

A related area is the inherent capabilities or limitations of people. Long-standing notions of skill or capability and their relationships to cultural variables (the "unskilled black"), along with the inclination to test and predict various work skills and abilities, will be receiving considerable attention by organizational analysts. The reexamination or setting aside of many testing procedures because of their cultural bias is evidence of the importance and prevalence of this problem.

TOOLS FOR ORGANIZATION ANALYSIS

The trends described above and elsewhere in this book portend the continued growth of organization complexity. Individual flexibility, coupled with many of the approaches already cited, will comprise a combination particularly well suited to the challenges just presented. In particular, *systems approaches*, which highlight communication flow and feedback, and techniques of simulation modeling using the computer are procedures well suited to complex organizational environments. Thus the need is for enlarged systems modeling that more realistically captures the dynamics of organizational activities and permits the examination of phenomena under a variety of conditions. More importantly, it permits the work of the organizational analyst, at least in part, to be removed from the actual situation, where various economic or physical restraints do not permit manipulation of parameters yet comparison can be made between model and reality.

Emerging trends and organizational issues promise an exciting era of new challenges, problems, and accomplishments for organization member and analyst alike.

NOTES

1. Alvin Toffler, *Future Shock* (New York: Bantam Books, 1970), esp. chap. 7.

2. John Gardner, *Self-Renewal* (Evanston, Ill.: Harper & Row, 1963).

3. Toffler, *Future Shock,* pp. 125–136.

4. For some observations on the connections of size and technology to this theme, see Pradip N. Khandwalla, "Mass Output Organization of Operations Technology and Organizational Structure," Faculty of Management working paper, McGill University (1973).

5. Lawrence Foss, "Managerial Strategy for the Future: Theory 2 Management," *California Management Review,* 15, no. 3 (Spring 1973): 68–81.

6. Elmer H. Burack and Robert D. Batlavala, "Operations Research: Recent Changes and Future Directions in Business Organizations, Business Perspectives," 9, no. 1 (Spring 1972): 15–22.

7. William F. Whyte, "Organizations for the Future," in Gerald G. Somers (ed.), *The Next Twenty-five Years of Industrial Relations* (Madison, Wis.: IRRA, 1973), pp. 129–156.

8. H. Igor Ansoff, "The Next Ten Years in Management Education," paper presented at the 36th annual conference of the Graduate Library School, University of Chicago, April 1973.

9. David Moment and Dalmer Fisher, "Managerial Career Development and the Generational Confrontation," *California Management Review,* 15, no. 3 (Spring 1973): 46–56.

10. For some interesting observations concerning the future, see Marvin J. Cetron and Don H. Overly, "Disagreeing with the Future," *Technology Assessment,* 1, no. 4 (1973): 245–255.

11. Toffler, *Future Shock.*

12. Ibid.

13. Elmer H. Burack, "The Quality of Work Life: A Complex and Controversial Situation," *Technology and Human Affairs,* 5 no. 2 (Summer 1973): 4–7.

14. Louis E. Davis, "Quality of Working Life: National and International Developments," in Gerald G. Somers (ed.), *Proceedings of the Twenty-fifth Anniversary Meeting, Industrial Relations Research Association* (Madison: University of Wisconsin Press, 1973), pp. 121–128.

15. Ibid., p. 123.

16. Ibid., pp. 122–126.

17. Ibid., pp. 126–127.

18. For one dimension of these changes, see Dan Jacobson, "Willingness to Retire in Relation to Job Strain and Type of Work," *Journal of Industrial Gerontology* (Spring 1972).

19. Harold L. Sheppard, "Some Selected Issues Surrounding the Subject of the Quality of Working Life," in Somers, *Proceedings,* pp. 137–153.

20. J. Champagne, "An Organization of People," in Somers, *Proceedings,* pp. 129–136.

21. Elmer H. Burack, James Staszak, and Gopal Pati, "An Organizational Analysis of Manpower Issues in Employing the Disadvantaged," *Academy of Management Journal,* 15, no. 3 (September 1972): 252–272, and Elmer H. Burack and Gopal Pati, "Approaches to Effective Management of Minority Manpower," in *Proceedings of the Conference on Minority Manpower Employment and Utilization* (Washington, D.C.: U.S. Department of Labor, Manpower Administration, 1972).

REFERENCES

Adelson, Marvin. *The Technology of Forecasting and the Forecasting of Technology.* Santa Monica, Calif.: System Development Corp., 1968.

Baier, Kurt, and Nicholas Rescher. *Values and the Future.* New York: The Free Press, 1969.

Baker, Frank. *Organizational Systems: General Systems Approaches to Complex Organizations.* Homewood, Ill. Richard D. Irwin, 1973.

Baram, Michael S. "Law and the Social Control of Corporate Technology." *Technology Assessment,* 1, no. 4 (1973): 225–237.

Bell, Daniel (ed.). *Toward the Year 2000.* Boston: Houghton Mifflin, 1968.

Bennis, Warren G. *Changing Organizations.* New York: McGraw-Hill, 1966.

Boyle, M. Barbara. "Equality Opportunity for Women Is Smart Business." *Harvard Business Review,* 51, no. 3 (May–June 1973): 89–96.

Burack, Elmer H. "Management Strategies for Obsolescence." *California Management Review,* 15, no. 2 (Winter 1972): 83–90.

———— and Robert B. D. Batlevala. "Operations Research: Recent Changes and Future Expectations in Business Organizations." *Business Perspectives,* 9, no. 1 (Spring 1972): 15–22.

Burack, Elmer H., and Thomas J. McNichols. *Human Resource Planning: Technology, Policy, and Change.* Kent, O.: Bureau of Business and Economics Research, Kent State University, 1973.

Burack, Elmer H., and Gopal Pati. "Approaches to Effective Management of Minority Manpower." Forthcoming.

————. "Technology and Management Obsolescence." *Business Topics* (M.S.U.), vol. 18, no. 2 (Spring 1970).

Burack, Elmer H., James Staszak, and Gopal Pati. "An Organizational Analysis of Manpower Issues in Employing the Disadvantaged." *Academy of Management Journal,* 15, no. 3 (September 1972): 252–272.

Davis, Louis E. "Quality of Work Life: National and International Developments," in Gerald G. Somers (ed.), *Proceedings of the Twenty-fifth Annual Meeting, Industrial*

Relations Research Association. Madison: University of Wisconsin Press and IRRA, 1973.

—————— and J. C. Taylor (ed.). *The Design of Jobs.* Baltimore: Penguin Books, 1972.

Diebold, John. *Beyond Automation.* New York: McGraw-Hill, 1964.

Dubin, Robert (ed.). *Handbook of Work, Organizations and Society.* Chicago: Rand McNally, 1973.

Elsner, Henry, Jr. *The Technocrats.* Syracuse, N.Y.: Syracuse University Press, 1967.

Flowers, Vincent S., and Charles L. Hughes. "Why Employees Stay." *Harvard Business Review,* 51, no. 4 (July–August 1973): 49–61.

Foss, Lawrence. "Managerial Strategy for the Future: Theory 2 Management." *California Management Review,* 15, no. 3 (Spring 1973): 68–82.

Gardner, John. *Self-Renewal.* Evanston, Ill.: Harper & Row, 1963.

Gibson, Chares H. "Volvo Increases Productivity through Job Enrichment." *California Management Review,* 15, no. 4 (Summer 1973): 64–67.

Gordon, Theodore J. *The Future.* New York: St Martin's Press, 1965.

Greenberger, Martin (ed.). *Computers and the World of the Future.* Cambridge, Mass.: M.I.T. Press, 1962.

Greiner, Larry E. "What Managers Think of Participative Leadership." *Harvard Business Review,* 51, no. 2 (March–April 1973): 111–118.

Helmer, Olaf. *Social Technology.* New York: Basic Books, 1966.

Jacobson, Dan. "Willingness to Retire in Relation to Job Strain and Type of Work." *Journal of Industrial Gerontology* (Spring 1972).

Jantsch, Erich. *Technological Forecasting in Perspective.* Paris (France): Organization for Economic Cooperation and Development, 1966.

Jones, Edward W. "What It's Like to Be a Black Manager." *Harvard Business Review,* 51, no. 4 (July–August 1973): 108–117.

Kahn, Alfred, Jr. *Theory and Practice of Social Planning.* New York: Russell Sage Foundation, 1969.

Kahn, Herman, and Anthony J. Wiener Jr. *The Year 2000.* New York: Macmillan, 1967.

Kerr, Clark. "Educational Changes: Potential Impacts on Industrial Relations," in Gerald G. Somers (ed.), *The Next Twenty-five Years of Industrial Relations.* Madison: University of Wisconsin Press and IRRA, 1973, pp. 187–197.

Likert, Rensis. *The Human Organization.* New York: McGraw-Hill, 1967.

Lipset, Seymour M., and Reinhard Bendix. *Social Mobility in Industrial Society.* Berkeley: University of California Press, 1964.

Machlup, Fritz. *The Production and Distribution of Knowledge in the United States.* Princeton, N.J.: Princeton University Press, 1962.

Management Education: Implications for Libraries and Library Schools. Papers of the 36th annual conference of the Graduate Library School, University of Chicago, April 1973.

McClelland, David. *The Achieving Society.* New York: The Free Press, 1961.

Mead, Margaret. *Continuities in Cultural Evolution.* New Haven, Conn.: Yale University Press, 1964.

Milliken, J. Gordon, and Edward J. Morrison. "Management Methods from Aerospace." *Harvard Business Review,* 51, no. 2 (March–April 1973): 6–31.

Miner, Jack B. "The Real Crunch in Managerial Manpower." *Harvard Business Review,* 51, no. 6 (November–December 1973): 146–158.

Moment, David, and Dalmer Fisher. "Managerial Career Development and the Generational Confrontation." *California Management Review,* 15, no. 3 (Spring 1973): 46–56.

Morse, John J. "A Contingency Look at Job Design." *California Management Review,* 16, no. 1 (Fall 1973): 67–76.

Nanus, Burt, and Robert E. Coffey. "Future Oriented Business Education." *California Management Review,* 15, no. 4 (Summer 1973): 28–39.

Nolan, Richard L. "Plight of the EDP Manager." *Harvard Business Review,* 51, no. 9 (May–June 1973): 143–153.

Rice, A. K. *The Enterprise and Its Environment.* London: Tavistock Publications, 1963.

Roberts, Karlene H., and Frederick Savage. "Twenty Questions: Utilizing Job Satisfaction Measures." *California Management Review,* 15, no. 3 (Spring 1973): 82–91.

Rodhoretz, Norman. *Making It.* New York: Random House, 1967.

Schon, Donald A. *Technology and Change.* New York: Dell, 1969.

Sheppard, Harold L. "Some Selected Issues Surrounding the Subject of the Quality of Working Life," in Gerald G. Somers (ed.), *Proceedings of the Twenty-fifth Anniversary Meeting, Industrial Relations Research Association.* Madison: University of Wisconsin Press and IRRA, 1973.

———— and Neal Herrick, *Where Have All the Robots Gone?* New York: Free Press–Macmillan, 1972.

Shocker, Allan D., and S. Parkash Sethi. "An Approach to Incorporating Societal Preferences in Developing Corporate Action Strategies." *California Management Review,* 15, no. 4 (Summer 1973): 106–109.

Simon, Herbert A. *The Shape of Automation for Men and Management.* New York: Harper & Row, 1965.

Somers, Gerald (ed.). "The Next Twenty-five Years of Industrial Relations." *Proceedings of the Twenty-fifth Anniversary Meeting, Industrial Relations Research Association.* Madison: University of Wisconsin Press and IRRA, 1973.

————. *Proceedings of the Twenty-fifth Anniversary Meeting, Industrial Relations Research Association.* Madison: University of Wisconsin Press and IRRA, 1973.

Theobald, Robert. *Technology and the American Economy.* Report of the Commission on Technology, Automation and Economic Progress (vol. 1), 1966.

Touraine, Alain, Claude Durand, Daniel Pecant, and Alfred Wilener. *Workers' Attitudes to Technical Change.* Paris: Organization for Economic Cooperation and Development, 1965.

Whyte, William F. "Organizations for the Future," in Somers, *Proceedings.* Madison: University of Wisconsin Press and IRRA, 1973, pp. 129–140.

Work in America. Report prepared by a task force of the Department of Health, Education, and Welfare for the W. E. Upjohn Institute. Cambridge, Mass.: M.I.T. Press, 1973.

INDEX